MEDICAL
LANDMARKS
USA

D0958202

MEDICAL LANDMARKS USA A TRAVEL GUIDE

to Historic Sites,
Architectural Gems,
Remarkable Museums
and Libraries,
and Other Places
of
Health–Related
Interest

MARTIN R. LIPP, M.D.

McGraw-Hill, Inc.
Health Professions Division

New York   St. Louis   San Francisco   Colorado Springs   Auckland   Bogotá
Caracas   Hamburg   Lisbon   London   Madrid   Mexico   Milan   Montreal
New Delhi   Paris   San Juan   São Paulo   Singapore   Sydney   Tokyo   Toronto

MEDICAL LANDMARKS USA

1234567890 D O C D O C 9876543210

ISBN 0-07-037974-2

This book was set in Palatino by Progressive Typographers.
The editors were J. Dereck Jeffers, Gail Gavert, and Mariapaz Ramos-Englis; the production supervisor was Annette Mayeski. The text and cover were designed by José Fonfrias. R. R. Donnelley & Sons was printer and binder.

Library of Congress Cataloging-in-Publication Data

Lipp, Martin R.
  Medical landmarks USA : a travel guide to historic sites, architectural gems, remarkable museums and libraries, and other places of health related interest / Martin R. Lipp.
       p.   cm.
  Includes bibliographical references.
  ISBN 0-07-037974-2
  1. Medicine—United States—History—Guide-books. 2. Medical museums —United States—Guide-books. 3. Medical libraries—United States—Guide-books. I. Title.
  [DNLM: 1. Health Facilities—United States—guidebooks. 2. History of Medicine—United States. 3. Libraries, Medical-United States—guidebooks. 4. Museums—United States—guidebooks.]
  R151.L56   1990
  610'.74'73—dc20
  DNLM/DLC
  for Library of Congress   90-5507
                                                                 CIP

*For
the women in my life:
Natividad, Michelle,
Melissa, and Deborah*

CONTENTS

ABOUT THIS BOOK

THIS BOOK IS REALLY four volumes in one: it is at once a travel guide, a reference work, an anthology of stories, and a history text on health care in the United States.

MEDICAL LANDMARKS USA: THE TRAVEL GUIDE

As a travel guide, this book focuses on sites of interest to health professionals across the country, because their histories are important, or their accomplishments make them stand out, or perhaps because they are just fun, interesting, and attractive to visit. The book tells you where to go, what to see, and what advance arrangements are necessary to make sightseeing possible. There are addresses and ZIP codes to help you find locations, phone numbers so you can make advance arrangements, directions where appropriate, and information regarding hours of operation and admission costs.

The entries under each city are organized as follows: (1) teaching institutions; (2) hospitals and clinics (these first groups are organized more or less in order of founding); and (3) museums, libraries, professional organizations, and miscellaneous landmarks such as birthplaces, historic homes, gravesites, notable plaques, and the like. Some of these are more fun to read about, some are more fun to visit, and some are simply listed because they have had too much regional or national influence to be ignored.

Contrary to popular assumption, our major health care institutions are generally not closed to the public. There are, of course, different levels of accessibility for tourist attractions of all kinds, separate from whether or not they are of health-related interest. Few places welcome visitors 24 hours a day or seven days a week. Some require advance preparations or reservations. All expect that visitors will be respectful and considerate of the people who depend on the facilities for important services. These places tend to fall into one or more of three categories:

1. Open to the General Public. Most of the attractions listed belong to this category. Wander around the grounds during the daytime most days of the week; observe the architecture; inspect plaques, statues, and art work. Walk through both the "public" parts of buildings to look at displays, artwork, and exhibitions in the entryways, waiting rooms, and corridors, and semi-public areas like professional libraries and museums. With rare exceptions, you are not allowed in patient care areas, hospital rooms, laboratories, or operating rooms. When in doubt, ask — and always be sensitive to the privacy of patients and workers.

2. *Open to the General Public with Access Controlled.* Some institutions — to protect patients and employees from an unregulated flow of visitors — restrict freedom of access by the general public, but are happy to show interested people around their grouunds and parts of their buildings in limited numbers as members of guided tours. Arrange such tours in advance. Where such tours exist, I have described how you can make appropriate arrangements.

3. *Open Only to Those with Special Credentials.* For the most part, the only thing needed to see any of the sites listed here is interest, whether it is personal or professional. To be sure, you may need more credentials to examine a 600-year-old-manuscript or to observe an intricate surgical procedure. However, you don't know until you ask, so request access to anything and everything that interests you. Enthusiasm will often open any door.

It's also often worthwhile to look for medical history in places that aren't strictly speaking medical landmarks. Local and regional historical museums, historical theme parks, and science and technology museums often have wonderful health science exhibits. Check local newspapers or guides.

A final caution: Buildings are torn down, phone numbers and visiting hours change, even large institutions close down and/or change their name and locations. Always check on current conditions before you venture forth.

MEDICAL LANDMARKS USA: THE REFERENCE WORK

One of the most enjoyable aspects of writing this book was finding bits of fact that not only expanded my knowledge of the health professions but were also interesting, amusing, or astounding in their own right. For instance, do you know where the first Jewish, Catholic, and Protestant hospitals in America were located? The first schools of optometry, pharmacy, dentistry, nursing, osteopathy, and chiropractic? The answers are here.

This book is the only one to list all the U.S. museums of health care interest, including medical, dental, opthalmologic, urologic, and psychiatric. If you want to see wonderful collection of bones or microscopes or dental tools or eyeglasses, this book will help you find them. If you want to find memorials, tributes, or homes dedicated to great doctors, dentists, or nurses, they are listed here; for example, visit the grave of William Beaumont or Clara Barton or tributes to four different individuals who claimed to have invented anesthesia.

In addition, you will find fascinating facts to contemplate, not only for their conversational value but also for their contribution to the evolution of health care in this country. Which medical school was named after a man who is honored in the Cowboy Hall of Fame? Where and when were surgical greens (as opposed to the old eye-fatiguing white scrubs) first introduced? Which psychiatric hospital was the first in the country to have a farm, a swimming pool, a gymnasium, and a ski jump? What three contemporary medical schools used to be homeopathic institutions? Who is the only woman physician honored in the Statuary Gallery in the U.S. Capitol building in Washington, DC?

The issue of "medical firsts" has been a vexing one for me. It's a rare medical scientist who trains and spends an entire career in only one place. If a doctor makes a landmark contribution or discovery, all the various institutions he or she touched may claim some part of the credit. Often, various institutions claim priority for the same procedures, discoveries, and pieces of equipment. I've sorted these claims out as best I could. Inevitably, I may have slighted some who should have been mentioned and parceled out credit inappropriately.

MEDICAL LANDMARKS USA: THE ANTHOLOGY OF STORIES

Medical Landmarks USA brings alive a great many diverse and remarkable stories from the history of health care in our country. No one could have invented Painless Parker, America's legendary tooth-plumber, or Mother Mary Bickerdyke. AJ Still and DD Palmer founded entirely new schools of therapeutics, winning far more enemies than adherents with their colorful personalities and idiosyncratic styles, but their influence lives with us even now, growing with time.

Some institutions have histories to rival those of the most colorful individuals. New Orleans' Charity Hospital has survived three monarchies, the confederacy, floods, typhoons, and the cumulative mismanagement of hundreds of years—yet somehow it has endured. America's most long-lived nursing home was begun in the ante-bellum South, operated by black nuns, unable to wear their habits in public.

If you like improbability, read about Walter Reed, one of our most esteemed medical heroes, as physician for Cochise, the feared leader of the Chiricahua Apache, in a setting which would eventually become a segregated psychiatric hospital for blacks only. If you like heart-warming stories, few can compete with the family dynasties of the Mayos and the Menningers, group practice pioneers in the Midwest who revolutionized their own particular areas of medical practice and established enduring institutions in the process. What wonderful contributions these people made!

If you are curious about homeopathy or eclectic medicine or the beginning of dentistry or how nuns pioneered medical care on the frontier, the stories are all here.

MEDICAL LANDMARKS USA: THE HISTORY TEXT

As history, *Medical Landmarks USA* is a mosaic. The color and texture are in the individual locations; a pattern emerges only as you put the pieces together, observing replication and flow from one area to another: the hospitals that begin largely as charitable community efforts, funded and operated by volunteers, gradually becoming professionalized and increasingly economic endeavors; the professional schools started by talented, energetic, and sometimes mercenary individuals, gradually gaining institutional sponsorship and scholarly substance; and the research breakthroughs, generations ago accomplished mostly by brilliant iconoclasts, now the result of extraordinary teamwork choreographed by vast bureaucratic organizations.

Still, all history is ultimately about people. Health care institutions in particular are intricate and complex creations, forever dependent on repetitive tasks which must be performed conscientiously and knowledgeably, if the institution is to attain distinction. I have tried to give credit to scientific attainment, but I have had to skimp when it came to recognizing the warm hearts, the caring hands, the loving actions of millions of people on whom our institutions depend. Without all of them working in concert, our health care institutions fall apart. Ultimately, this book is a tribute to what is and has been unique in health care.

Good health is one of life's great blessings — and the pursuit of good health through the auspices of our various health professions has been one of the great public adventures in American history. As you tour our country's health institutions and monuments, you will also come to see American culture from a fascinating and often under-appreciated perspective: a country's boundless and enormously expensive preoccupation with its own physical and emotional well-being. As we see our past more clearly, we will see ourselves anew and perhaps will be more able to plan intelligently for the future.

ACKNOWLEDGMENTS

It is both a pleasure and an obligation in a work of this magnitude to give recognition to the many people who helped make this book a reality. In particular, I would like to thank

Gail and Tremaine Arkley, who gave me support and encouragement from the very beginning of this project;

Gretchen Worden, Jim Edmonson, Greg Higby, Ben Swanson, Jack Gottschalk, and Ray Kondratis, who so generously shared their knowledge of health care museums and history;

the very helpful people at the National Register of Historic Places—including Debbie Kraybill, Laurie Anderson, and John Byrne—without whom my research would have been enormously more time consuming;

and, of course, my wonderful family—Natividad, Michelle, and Melissa—whose patience with my writing isolation and traveling absences made the entire endeavor possible.

So many other people have helped me in the gathering of material for this book that I am compelled to use the impersonal expediency of a collective thank you. Literally hundreds of names could be listed: friends and family, public relations people and librarians, museum folk and historians, college deans and tour guides, administrators and secretaries, in virtually every state of the union. To all of them, I express my gratitude.

MEDICAL LANDMARKS USA

MEDICAL LANDMARKS: A HISTORICAL PERSPECTIVE

NONE OF THE LANDMARKS listed in the following pages stands alone; all are part of a vast panorama that extends across time and geographical and cultural boundaries. This introduction sketches some of the outlines and themes of that panorama to provide the reader with a context in which to place individual landmarks.

HOSPITALS

In the early years of the United States there was little that we would recognize as formalized medical treatment. The first hospitals were hardly more than poorhouses, basically sheds or small buildings, where those without resources could find protection from the elements. The first of these almshouses was founded in 1658 and eventually grew to become Bellevue Hospital in New York City. Other early structures for the sick were the pesthouses, where those who were found to have smallpox, yellow fever, the plague, and other fearsome diseases were sent to die. These were particularly prominent in port cities, where every new ship arriving might include crew members or passengers with some dread contagion. Here and there, small facilities were established to provide some comfort to the sick and needy, such as the early predecessors of Philadelphia General Hospital and Charity Hospital in New Orleans, both established in the 1730s.

America's first true hospital was chartered in 1751 in Philadelphia as a result of a confluence of needy immigrants, a Quaker-inspired social conscience, civic prosperity, and some competent physicians. By 1800 there were really only three true hospitals in the entire country: the Pennsylvania Hospital, Charity Hospital in New Orleans, and the New York Hospital. During the next half century, many of the larger cities in the growing country had added hospitals to care for their own impoverished sick, but by 1850 there were barely 50 such institutions in the entire country. People who could afford to do so, and anyone outside a metropolitan area, simply dealt with sickness by staying at home, sometimes calling a physician and often not.

The Mid-1800s At mid-century several developments started to change this picture. First came the invention of anesthesia in the 1840s, which made operations painless although hardly safe, since it would be another half-century before the widespread use of surgical antisepsis removed infection as the major postoperative killer. Lister first introduced surgical antisepsis with continuous carbolic acid spray in 1865, but acceptance of the breakthrough spread slowly through American hospitals.

Another important factor was the lesson about hospital-based nursing care learned in two important wars, first the Crimean War (1854–1856) and later the American Civil War (1861–1865). In the Crimea, Florence Nightingale—without any understanding of germs but with a practical knowledge of their impact—demonstrated that wound mortality could be dramatically lowered by reducing hospital crowding and by providing patients with fresh air and scrupulously clean surroundings. The Civil War, in which both sides built on these lessons and provided their wounded with well-ventilated temporary hospitals, demonstrated the practical utility of hospital-based nursing care in America. After the war, the doctors who cared for the sick and wounded, the demobilized soldiers who had been patients, and the untrained nurses who helped as best they could, carried the reputation of Civil War hospitals to their hometowns.

Many of these new hospitals were denominational institutions, founded by religious and cultural groups to care for "their own kind" in an atmosphere that respected and nurtured cherished customs. Catholics wanted hospitals in which last rites were readily available; Jews wanted institutions which abided by kosher dietary laws; Germans wanted to be able to talk to hospital personnel in their own language. The first Catholic hospital in this country was founded in 1828, and, when a denominational hospital was established in a given city, the first one almost invariably was a Catholic institution.

Hospital Construction and Design In the middle years of the century, the method of financing hospital construction changed also. The earliest hospitals in the US were generally built with small donations from large numbers of contributors. By the 1850s, America's rapidly expanding economy had created huge fortunes, and wealthy donors were responsible for an increasing number of hospitals: Touro of New Orleans, Roosevelt in New York City, Reese in

Chicago, Wills in Philadelphia, as well as Vanderbilt, Whitney, Rockefeller, Hopkins, and many others. By 1872 there were 178 hospitals in the country, and virtually all of the new ones were built on the "Nightingale plan." This was the pavilion style, in which there was a separate hospital building for each hospital function, each never more than three stories tall, with each bed having access to light and air and sunshine. Hospital wards were all constructed as long rectangles, lined with tall windows, with the nurses' station at the entryway and sanitary facilities at the far end. The various pavilions were then linked by long corridors, which both connected them and allowed the pavilions to be at safe distances from one another. This was the standard hospital design well into the twentieth century, and remnants of this pattern persist wherever nineteenth century hospital buildings have managed to survive.

The finest realization of the pavilion plan in the US — and one that served as a model for many hospitals to follow — was the Johns Hopkins Hospital, erected in 1885. Hopkins boasted central administration and apothecary buildings and a string of seven pavilion wards, all connected by a corridor which was open at intervals to prevent air from one pavilion being conveyed to another. There were also separate buildings for the pathologic laboratory, kitchen, laundry, nurses's home, dispensary, teaching amphitheater, and stables.

Obviously, such hospitals — especially if they were to house many patients — required large plots of land. When land became in short supply, especially in crowded cities, the first changes were to move the pavilions closer together, and then to add additional floors, usually with each additional story set back a bit from the one below it, to create minimal possible interference with air flow and light. After the turn of the century, hospital construction increasingly relied on vertical rather than horizontal expansion. This progression was made possible by such engineering advances as the use of structural steel and the invention of elevators with the power to operate in skyscrapers. Fears about reduced ventilation (which had initially spawned the Nightingale pavilion) were allayed by studies showing that air is less polluted and moves faster at higher altitudes. Other studies demonstrated numerous economies in maintenance and repair with the vertical monoblock. By the 1920s, the monoblock had virtually replaced the pavilion style in all new construction.

Continued Scientific Advances At the same time, other scientific advances added to medicine's reputation and made hospitals seem increasingly attractive to the general public. Widespread adoption of surgical antisepsis had dramatically lowered surgical mortality rates from an average of 70 percent to less than 10 percent. A wider range of operations was available too: amputations, which had previously dominated the operating room, slipped to less than 1 percent of the caseload. The introduction of radiographic (x-ray) techniques and a wide range of laboratory methods turned diagnosis into a far more refined skill.

As a result, paying patients started coming to the hospital in significant numbers, and more hospitals were built. Though there were only 178 hospitals in 1872, by 1910 there were 6000. Increasingly, these hospitals had single and double rooms to accomodate paying patients. There was an increasing range of services too. Hospital social work was introduced, dietitians were added, more complex medical and business record keeping was necessary, and hospital administration became a profession in its own right. Merely processing paperwork became a major hospital function, accountable for a growing percentage of hospital work space.

Post-World War II In the mid-1940s, returning World War II servicemen accustomed to free health care in the military increasingly demanded health care insurance as an employee benefit. Aided by collective bargaining and favorable court decisions, the number of people with some form of group medical insurance doubled from 1945 to 1950, so that for the first time over 50 percent of the population was substantially freed from paying hospital and medical bills.

The depression and the World War II years had effectively precluded hospital-building on any large scale, so by 1946 the nation was severely short on hospital beds. In that year Congress passed the Hospital Survey and Construction Act, popularly known as the Hill-Burton program, which was intended to encourage construction of hospitals in areas where they would otherwise not be built. The government provided up to two-thirds of the total cost of construction and equipment to both private and public health care facilities. Though initially aimed at aiding small rural hospitals, Hill-Burton was soon amended to include urban hospitals and, in 1962, it was further extended to include urban outpatient facilities. By 1950 hospitals had become the fifth largest industry in the United States.

Nearly 7000 Hill-Burton projects were completed around the country, to USPHS standards, which resulted in technically efficient institutions that nonetheless had a sameness about their appearance. Typically, there was a rectangular vertical element, shaped like a matchbox (containing patient wards, surgical areas, etc.), with a horizontal area at its base that contained administrative and ancillary services, such as laboratories, x-ray facilities, and the like.

The architectural style of hospitals in the post-World War II years was likewise altered by rapid technical and social change. The postwar baby boom meant that obstetric departments and nurseries boomed as well. The development of rehabilitation medicine among injured veterans led to hospital departments of physical and occupational therapy. After desegregation, the South had no further need for separate wards and hospitals for both blacks and whites. As house staff came to be paid living wages, the number of hospitals that felt compelled to provide on-site housing for interns and residents decreased. Instead, young doctors could be expected to find their own apartments away from the hospital. As hospital-based nursing schools were phased out in favor of university programs and women's liberation made it possible for young women to live on their own, hospital nurses's residences gradually disappeared.

In their place, hospitals have constructed medical office buildings to cement ties between hospitals and their physician staffs. An increasing number have added ambulatory care centers, as they have sought to compete in the provision of outpatient services. Some have tried to cater to growing feminist consciousness by adding women's health centers. Others have added hotels, motels, and apartment buildings to lure families of inpatients, or to attract out-of-area outpatients.

Medicare and medicaid legislated in 1965 not only extended health care benefits to the elderly and the poor, they were initially a bonanza for medicine and its institutions, which could now expand, confident that they would be reimbursed for a wide range of services. In 1966 President Lyndon Johnson announced that health care was a right, not a privilege, a perspective that led to massive infusions of federal money into what was quickly becoming the health care industry.

MEDICAL SCHOOLS

The first medical school in this country was founded in 1765 when the University of Pennsylvania chartered its medical college. By 1800 there were three more medical colleges in the country, one in New York founded in 1768 (the Medical Department of Kings

College, now Columbia University), one in Boston founded in 1782 (Harvard Medical School), and one in New Hampshire founded in 1797 (Dartmouth).

In the nineteenth century there were three types of medical school: those organized by hospitals, those organized by universities, and those established as proprietary institutions — in which the schools were owned by the faculty, who operated the schools with student fees and pocketed anything left over after expenses were paid. In practice, the vast majority of medical schools, whatever their official sponsorship, were of the proprietary type and run on the profit motive. As a result, there was a strong incentive to keep income up by admitting as many paying students as possible, without regard to admission criteria or performance standards, and to keep expenses low, by keeping courses few and brief and reducing facilities to a bare minimum.

In 1850 there were 38 medical schools in the country, but by the end of the century there were 160. The latter figure, even though it represents a fourfold expansion on the mid-century figure, gives little indication of the 457 schools that had sprung up around the country, many lasting only a few months or a couple of years. There were schools of enormous variety: straight medical (so-called allopathic), homeopathic, osteopathic, chiropractic, botanic, eclectic, and more. There were schools for blacks, women, and every geographic region.

It is true that many of these schools were of marginal quality and some were just diploma mills, but their sheer numbers made medical education available to the masses, not just to children of the wealthy, who heretofore had been the only ones who could afford a true university education. In many states, especially in the early years of the century, it was not even necessary for prospective physicians to go to medical school at all. A brief apprenticeship would often suffice.

By the beginning of the twentieth century, most medical schools in the country remained pretty marginal affairs: run as proprietary institutions, the majority had minimal or absent criteria for admission, instruction was almost entirely confined to the lecture room, laboratory training and patient contact were highly variable, and university affiliation tended to be nominal or absent.

All this changed in 1910. There had been sporadic efforts to improve medical education in the past. Indeed, the AMA was formed in 1846 with educational reform in medicine as one of its principal tenets. In 1907 the AMA began inspecting schools for the quality of education provided, and 82 were judged acceptable, 46 doubtful, and 52 unacceptable. In 1910 the Carnegie Foundation published an "objective" assessment of the nation's medical schools, and the resulting impact was profound. Based on inspections of 155 schools by the Carnegie Foundation's Abraham Flexner, together with an official from the AMA, the resulting document pulled no punches, and many of the conditions exposed were shocking. In the years that followed, 80 schools closed and the rest made significant improvements. The model that Flexner proposed as the ideal medical school remained dominant for the next 60 years and is still the most influential single standard. Flexner's model stressed the importance of science and research, required university affiliation and teaching hospitals over which the medical school had substantial influence if not complete control, and emphasized the importance of high admission standards for students and full-time employment for faculty. These standards were largely cemented into place with the help of previously unprecedented millions of dollars from John D Rockefeller's General Education Board, all targeted to create and support academic medical centers that fit the Flexner model.

PSYCHIATRIC HOSPITALS

Though sometimes regarded as distinct from the rest of the nation's health care system, psychiatric facilities have often accounted for 50 percent and more of the country's hospital beds. Some of the country's first hospitals were in fact psychiatric hospitals, which have evolved since 1773 when the first such institution was established in Williamsburg, Virginia. During the following two centuries, the major changes in style and appearance were occasioned by periodic idealistic efforts at reform, which were then gradually altered in the postreform years when hospital administrators were confronted with the realities of housing large numbers of the mentally ill, which the reform institutions were never designed to serve.

The country's oldest private psychiatric facilities started at the beginning of the nineteenth century and were modeled after the Quaker-built York Retreat in England. The Friends Hospital in Philadelphia remains the longest-lived example of this style, a peaceful and secluded institution with a vast expanse of grounds and buildings of a homey scale.

The next major development was a crusade led by Dorothea Dix, a Boston teacher committed to improving the plight of the impoverished mentally ill. Dix's efforts led to the establishment of some 40 state-supported institutions throughout the United States. These were built from the 1850s onward, most of them following the design of Thomas Kirkbride, superintendent of the Pennsylvania Hospital for the Insane. Kirkbride was confident that insanity could be cured if patients were isolated from the damaging influences of friends and family and were instead put in an asylum that fostered improvement by providing calm and pleasant surroundings, well-ordered activities, fixed schedules to help regulate the mind, and an environment that was itself the quintessence of order and rationality. Kirkbride developed detailed architectural plans for such institutions, and hospitals built on his ideas were erected in almost every state in the union. The Kirkbride plan was for a hospital housing no more than 250 patients. The dominant feature of such hospitals was a prominent central administration building, with wings on either side extending in a linear fashion, each successive wing set back from the one preceding it. The central building housed the superintendent's apartment, and female patients were in wings on one side and male patients on the other, with the most severely disturbed patients being in the rooms most distant from the administrative center. As patients improved, they were moved closer to the center.

The first Kirkbride structure was opened in 1848 in New Jersey and is no longer intact, but wonderful examples of this style can still be found in most sections of this country (the most fully realized example is in Alabama and is now called Bryce Hospital). Some of these structures were extremely imposing and their ornateness and/or grandeur led them to be called "pauper palaces" by critics (see the description of the one in Buffalo, New York).

Kirkbride hospitals continued being built almost to the beginning of the twentieth century. Thereafter structures were added, utilizing whatever utilitarian architectural standards were locally in vogue. By the 1950s, when the number of psychiatric inpatients nationwide hit its peak, most psychiatric hospitals had vast grounds filled with rambling structures usually grafted onto the original buildings, now a maze of interconnected additions. It was during this era that mental illness was labeled "America's number one health problem."

When deinstitutionalization became a fact of psychiatric life in the 1960s, scores of these buildings suddenly became vacant. Because many such institutions were built in rural areas, away from land-hungry urban developers, the buildings frequently escaped destruction. Some either have found other uses or remain vacant shells, mute reminders of former efforts to treat our nation's insane.

As a result, the longest-lived and most historic medical buildings in many states are located at psychiatric facilities.

AFTER THE 1960s — AND BEYOND

Since the 1960s, the dominant health care facility in major metropolitan areas has been the academic health center, composed of a medical school, one or more hospitals, often other health professions schools, sometimes facilities for various specific conditions and diseases, and various research and ambulatory care or outpatient facilities.

One reason for the ascendancy of the academic medical center was that, as the hospital system was being expanded by the Hill-Burton legislation, biomedical research was likewise expanding through the support of the National Institutes of Health. The NIH was actually established in 1930, but its research program remained mostly in-house until the 1950s and 1960s, when there was a vast expansion of NIH "extramural" support for research and training, both in basic science and in various medical and surgical specialties and subspecialties. Much of this effort was prompted by WWII government-sponsored research, which helped lead to such developments as penicillin, cortisone, and gamma globulin.

Another development of the 1970s vastly increased the power and wealth of medical schools. Prior to 1970, a significant amount of postgraduate medical training was carried out in community hospitals that operated their own training programs for interns and residents independent of medical schools. In 1970 the influential Millis report recommended that all advanced training of medical school graduates become the responsibility of academic medical centers. As a result, hospitals that failed to "affiliate" with medical schools tended to lose their house staff programs. Now about 1 percent of the nation's hospitals train about 50 percent of the residents.

Another reason for the rise of academic medical centers was the growing public concern in the 1960s and 1970s about a developing shortage of physicians. The Federal government supported the growth of medical educational facilities in the 1960s with the passage of legislation, especially the Health Professions Assistance Act, which allotted one federal dollar for every local dollar given to develop new facilities in existing schools, and two-dollars-for-one in newly created schools. With these and other funds freely provided, the number of medical schools expanded from 72 4-year and seven 2-year schools to 127 4-year schools, and existing schools mushroomed in size as well. The number of buildings on campus multiplied as Congress enacted various federal programs in the late 1960s, many of a "categorical" nature, promoting the development of specific kinds of health facilities, e.g., for rehabilitation, mental retardation, nutrition, alcoholism, child health, and the like. As a result, academic medical centers started becoming vast enterprises, composed of interrelated institutions with varying proportions of research, patient care, and education.

However, a score of the new medical schools have been community-based schools, for the most part designed to be primary care rather than specialty oriented, and these institutions have tended to differ from the dominant academic health center model. Instead, they consist primarily of a basic science and administrative facility, often built on the campus of an existing university, and all clinical training is conducted in often widely dispersed, preexisting community and regional hospitals.

In the 1980s, as health care began to consume more than 10 percent of the nation's gross national product for the first time (it had been only 5.3 percent in 1960), employers, insurers, and the government became deeply concerned about unbridled increases in expenses. The result was a concerted effort to find ways of putting constraints on health care spending. Managed care organizations proliferated, along with new governmental policies and rules regarding insurance reimbursement. Efforts to keep costs down resulted in transferring many services from an inpatient to an outpatient basis, resulting in a huge oversupply of hospital beds. Competition for patients intensified and marketing efforts kept pace. Hospitals spruced up old buildings and put enormous effort and money into the design of new facilities to make them ever more attractive to the public. Gone were the old Hill-Burton utilitarian, government-regimented boxes. Soft colors, "home-like" atmosphere, natural lighting, artwork, and huge atriums with greenery and flowers flourished. Some hospitals even constructed facilities based on shopping-mall concepts, so that patient-consumers could visit the hospital, have a meal in a stylish restaurant or deli, and do some shopping for various goods and services at the same time. By the end of the decade, hospitals and other health care facilities ranked third among all types of buildings in the dollars spent on construction.

In general, the big tended to get bigger, and the marginal tended to close down. Hospitals were traded like baseball cards by huge health care chains. Individual hospitals merged with others in order to avoid expensive duplication of services and to achieve advantages of scale. Other survival strategies included vigorous marketing to both physicians and patients, developing specialty or boutique services such as cardiac rehabilitation, adolescent chemical dependency units, or women's health care units — as well as implementing vigorous cost-cutting strategies. Nevertheless, record numbers of hospitals closed in the late 1980s, including 81 general and 21 specialty hospitals in 1988 alone. Most hospital administrators blamed shortages of physicians, patients, and/or money, especially inadequate medicaid and medicare payments, saying that the burden of providing increasingly expensive, technologically sophisticated, high-standard care for the nation's poor and elderly without private insurance ultimately closed the hospitals down.

The nation's public hospitals — the city and county hospitals around the country, some of them begun as almshouses up to two centuries ago — suffered grievously under these pressures. In the wake of 1960s activism, rising standards for medical care, and expectations for equal treatment, representatives of impoverished groups lobbied for "mainstreaming" — integrating health care for the poor with that for the middle class. The heavy load of uninsured, medicaid and medicare patients — made worse by the disproportionate numbers of AIDS patients seeking care at public hospitals — added a financial imperative to institutions chronically plagued by inadequate budgets, bureaucratic entanglements, political shenanigans, and persistent shortages of supplies, equipment, and personnel. Beleaguered city councils and county supervisors, strapped for funds and unable to operate such hospitals efficiently, tended to close them or sell them or find universities or private corporations to operate them. In 25 years, the total bed capacity of city and county hospitals in Boston, Baltimore, Chicago, and the District of Columbia dropped by two-thirds. Cities like Newark, Seattle, and Kansas City got out of the hospital business entirely. Even the venerable Philadelphia General Hospital closed its doors and was leveled to the ground.

Simultaneously, the nation's training schools for the health professions were undergoing similar cataclysmic changes. The first professional nursing schools, for example, were established in the 1870s. By 1902 there were 545, and 8 years later there were 1100. For the next half century, the hospital-based 2-year diploma nursing program remained the country's standard. By the 1960s, however, growing professionalism among health professions in general and in nursing in particular led to the new standard of a 4-year college program leading to a baccalaureate degree. Diploma programs closed by the score each year. However, as young women sought out other opportunities from an increasingly diverse array of options, declining applications to nursing schools generally meant that not just the diploma programs suffered: even such prestigious university programs as those at Northwestern and Boston University closed their doors.

The same phenomenon of declining applications and enrollments affected virtually all health professions schools, from pharmacy and podiatry to medicine and such allied health professions as surgical technology. The 1970s and 1980s witnessed the closing of five dental schools, and 1990 is expected to mark the first closure of a medical school in many decades (the Oral Roberts University School of Medicine). Medical school applications hit an all time high of almost 43,000 in 1974, but by 1988, applications had plummeted to 28,000.

There will be more closures in all the health professions. Fewer students, it seems, are willing to make the commitment of time, deferred gratification, and devotion that the health professions require, especially in this time of malpractice litigation and bureaucratic intervention into practice. Many feel there are too many attractive alternatives, offering more material rewards, at the cost of fewer personal sacrifices.

What will the future hold for the nation's health care enterprises? In truth, no one knows. Some demographic trends are clear, however, and these will have a major impact: the population of the US is continuing to grow, and the proportion over 60 will expand more rapidly than the population itself. Illness and human suffering will continue, and the need for skilled and compassionate health care givers will certainly continue to grow. Likewise, we can expect continued evolution of medical knowledge and medical technology and continued pressure on health care providers to be cost-effective and socially responsible in what they do. The result is that while the demand for services will continue to grow, only the most efficient providers will survive, and we can expect continued concentration of health care services in the hands of institutions that are already big and growing, while marginal providers will fall by the wayside. In the meantime, the confident and the hopeful are poised for growth, though embarked on building programs whose watchword is flexibility.

The only certainty is the inevitability of change.

The medical landmarks described here tell a story of what has been our nation's health care history, and what is our nation's health care present. Take some time to savour what exists now. Not everything that is precious will survive. Enjoy what we have, while we have it.

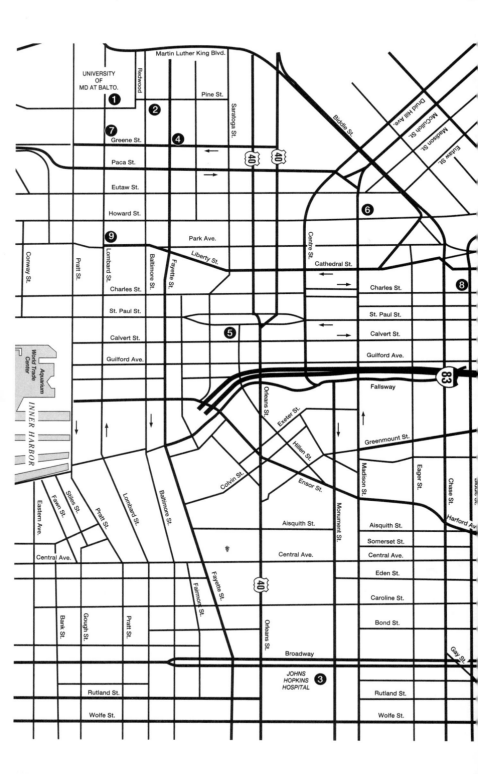

GREAT MEDICAL CITIES

Baltimore

Including Catonsville and Towson

Map Key ───

1. University of Maryland Medical Center
2. Baltimore College of Dental Surgery, Dental School, University of Maryland
3. The Johns Hopkins Medical Center
4. Old Baltimore General Dispensary
5. Mercy Hospital
6. Maryland General Hospital
7. Cole Pharmacy Museum
8. William P Didusch Museum of the American Urological Association
9. Emerson Bromo-Seltzer Tower

These key numbers will be found at appropriate points in the text.

BALTIMORE'S ROLE AS A great medical city is embodied in its two university medical centers, each of which served, in its own way, as prototype for the rest of the nation. A scant few miles separate them; each is proud of its heritage and eager to make the tangible evidence of its contributions available to the interested public. The historically-minded visitor will discover not only good stories here, but also places both welcoming and significant.

The University of Maryland was the first institution in this country to make medical education available to the sons of the middle class. Its medical school was available to anyone who could pay the modest admission fees, and did not require the full university education that was then the prerogative of the wealthy. This school became a dynamic force that helped to mold the pattern of medical education for the next 100 years. Though proprietary institutions would eventually become outmoded and fall into disfavor, the University of Maryland's nineteenth-century achievements made it a dominant institution, a genuine trailblazer. It remains one to this day.

Even in the health professions many people do not know that dentistry, as a distinct profession, is a uniquely American invention. It had its academic birth here in Baltimore, at what is now the University of Maryland. The National Museum of Dentistry will soon be built here, as a tribute to Baltimore's contribution to dentistry.

Baltimore's most famous medical institution, however, is Johns Hopkins. Now 100 years old, Hopkins has been the dominant model institution for most of its century of existence. Since its founding, in 1889, Hopkins has provided the standard for scientifically based medical education in this country. All other US medical schools have struggled to emulate the Hopkins example.

Any visit to Baltimore needs to be structured around the two university medical centers. Each area can be comfortably toured in a few hours. The Hopkins campus is self-contained, an area unto itself. The University of Maryland campus is located on the edge of downtown, and visitors here can easily walk to other landmarks (e.g., the Emerson Bromo-Seltzer Tower, the Old Baltimore General Dispensary and the Cole Pharmacy Museum).

(1) *University of Maryland Medical Center* 737 West Lombard Street 21201. (301) 328-3801. This medical school evolved from a series of lectures on midwifery, anatomy, surgery, and physiology given in 1802 by John Beale Davidge, in his home. By 1807 Davidge had attracted more students and two additional lecturers, and the three doctors decided to found their own medical school. It became the fifth surviving medical school in the country, the first free-standing school separate from a university, and the first proprietary (for-profit) school as well. In the latter respect, it launched a revolution; by the end of the century several hundred imitators had followed the Baltimore pattern.

The medical school had problems from the beginning with public disapproval of anatomic dissection (and the associated grave-robbing); its first anatomic theater (behind Dr. Davidge's home) was demolished by an angry mob. When a substitute building (now known as Davidge Hall) was erected, in 1812, it was built like a fortress, surrounded by walls several feet thick, with anatomic dissection rooms hidden under the portico, and disguised passageways to allow students and faculty to escape from attackers when necessary. (The Old Westminster Burial Grounds, from which cadavers were most commonly "liberated," can be seen two blocks away at the corner of Fayette and Greene Streets.)

In 1823, the Baltimore Infirmary was built opposite Davidge Hall. It was the the first hospital founded by a medical school specifically for the purpose of clinical instruction, and was the first hospital in the United States to employ Catholic Sisters as nurses. Senior students lived in the hospital and helped to care for patients; this was the first intramural residency program in the country. The Baltimore Infirmary was appropriated by the Union Army during the Civil War. The name was changed to University Hospital in 1897.

Other firsts associated with the school include

1848	First school to require anatomic dissection
1853	First to use biopsy techniques and the microscope in the diagnosis of malignancy (Francis Donaldson)
1867	First professorial chair in diseases of women and children
1956	First use of ultrasound techniques to visualize soft tissue structures (Joseph Holmes)
1967	Establishment of the Shock Trauma Center, recognized world-wide as the model for emergency medical treatment

In 1913 the University of Maryland absorbed the Baltimore Medical College (which had been founded in1881); in 1915 it obtained the facilities and personnel of the College of Physicians and Surgeons (which had started classes in 1872).

The School of Pharmacy dates from 1841, making it the fourth oldest in the nation. The School of Nursing began in 1889.

The present medical center in downtown Baltimore comprises 33 acres and includes the modern 747-bed University Hospital, a new VA medical center, the Shock Trauma Center, and numerous other buildings. The Historical and Special Collections of the Health Sciences Library (at 111 South Greene Street) have a particularly fine rare book selection as well as a small museum.

The chief attraction for historically minded visitors, however, remains **Davidge Hall,** the oldest building in the western hemisphere in continuous use for medical education. Most of both the interior and the exterior is original, from the staircase balustrade to many of the doors and fanlights. This remarkable domed building, modeled after the Pantheon in Rome, is still used daily for lectures and administration. Though the structure appears relatively modest in size when viewed from the street, it nonetheless houses two huge amphitheaters. The lower of these two, Chemical Hall, gets its name from the brick kiln-like niches built into its front wall; early students used these for chemical experiments. Eight tiers of chairs provided daily seating for hundreds of students, winter and summer, decades before central heating and electric lighting. Directly above Chemical Hall is Anatomical Hall, a huge theater lighted by a large central skylight and an enormous chandelier. Circling the

Anatomical Hall, Davidge Building, University of Maryland *(Courtesy of the University of Maryland School of Medicine)*

back of the room, on the highest tier, is the original railing, carved with medical students' graffiti dating from the early 1800s. The walls here are lined with antique anatomic drawings, medical diplomas dated as early as 1815, and an exhibit on the history of spectacles. Tucked behind and around Anatomical Hall is a network of secret passages, cubby holes, and the like. These are filled with some museum displays, including antique instruments, dried-out and partly dissected cadaver specimens, and a whiskey barrel. The latter was of the type used for the clandestine transport of cadavers to other medical schools. Baltimore, in the early nineteenth century, was the third largest city in the nation and was blessed with a busy seaport. This resulted in a steady supply of cadavers, which this school sold to others that were less favorably situated.

Tours of Davidge Hall are available only to groups, by prior arrangement with the Alumni Office (328-7454).

② *Baltimore College of Dental Surgery, Dental School, University of Maryland* 666 West Baltimore Street 21201. (301) 328-7101. This institution, founded in 1840, was the first college of dentistry in the world. At the end of the eighteenth century dentistry was not an organized profession. Dental treatment, where it existed at all, was performed by occasional physicians, a few itinerant dentists of no particular training, or adventurous barbers and blacksmiths. In 1805 Maryland became the first state to require that people practicing dentistry submit to an examination to demonstrate their abilities, and in 1810 Horace Hayden became America's first licensed dentist.

The first college-level lectures on dentistry were delivered at the University of Maryland School of Medicine between 1823 and 1825, by Hayden. Later, Hayden and Chapin Harris (who had learned dentistry from his brother, in Bainbridge, OH) resolved to start the first school of dentistry; they received their charter from the Maryland Assembly in 1840. The first course of study lasted from November through February, and the two students who managed to complete the curriculum were granted degrees of Doctor of Dental Surgery (DDS) on March 9, 1841. This program became the prototype for schools around the world.

In the years that followed, a number of competing programs grew up in Baltimore: the Maryland Dental College (1873), the Dental Department of the University of Maryland (1882), and the Dental Department of the Baltimore Medical College (1895). In 1924, they all merged to form the University of Maryland Dental School. The school still retains the name Baltimore College of Dental Surgery because of its historical significance as the first dental college in the world.

Although the school has occupied a number of different buildings during its evolution, it moved to its present home in 1970, the very modern Hayden-Harris Hall. In the basement is a three-room museum of dental history, crammed into rooms that are also being used for other purposes. The collection includes objects from the school's own history, artificial dentures representing various stages in the development of dental prostheses, numerous dental instruments and chairs, examples of office equipment, and memorabilia of the profession's leaders. During my visit, there was also a fine exhibit on oral health through the ages, including breath perfumes, tongue scrapers, mouth washes and mouth sponges, travel toothbrushes, toothpastes and tooth powders, and some wonderful early-nineteenth-century toothpicks made of ivory, horn, and silver. Most of the vast dental history collection is currently in storage, pending a $2 million fundraising effort to establish a **National Museum of Dentistry,** which will run the full length of the building on the fifth floor. Call the curator's office (328-8314) for current information.

③ *Johns Hopkins Medical Center* 500 North Broadway 21205. (301) 955-5000. Johns Hopkins has been the most influential medical center in the twentieth-century evolution of scientific medicine.

Johns Hopkins, early photograph of exterior *(By permission of Alan Mason Chesney Medical Archives; Gudekunst, photographer)*

Hopkins was the first institution that truly integrated teaching, research, and patient care; it established a pattern that has been copied throughout the United States. The early Hopkins faculty was composed of people whose influence dominates the profession even now, a century later; and Hopkins students have spread out across the land, becoming professors and deans, disseminating Hopkins techniques and values, and perpetuating the Hopkins reputation and mystique.

The institution takes its name from a Baltimore merchant named Johns Hopkins, who, in 1867, arranged a $7 million bequest — then the largest philanthropic gift in the country's history — to be split evenly between a hospital and a university, including a medical school which would have no peer in the United States.

The hospital buildings, laid out on Florence Nightingale's pavilion plan, were designed by John Shaw Billings and took 12 years to finish. The hospital, with its 17 buildings, was the first in the country to be equipped with central heating. It also had a revolutionary ventilation system that ensured that no air would be rebreathed or come into contact a second time with any patient.

The hospital opened in 1889; the medical school's opening was delayed by the fact that the benefactor's Baltimore & Ohio Railroad stock, which Mr. Hopkins had assumed would cover operating costs, suddenly stopped paying dividends. A group of women came forward — daughters of Johns Hopkins University trustees — and agreed to raise half a million dollars, on the condition that qualified women students be admitted along with the men. After the arguments gradually died down, the women were given the go-ahead. When they handed over the money they demanded that all entrants to the school be subject to the stiffest of entrance requirements: a college diploma; proficiency in French, German, and Latin; and a strong background in the sciences. These standards were so incomparably high that one professor quipped to another: "We were lucky to get in as professors, for I am sure that neither you nor I would ever get in as students."

The core faculty, forever after known as "the Big Four," was composed of William Welch, aged 34; William Osler, 39; William Halsted, 37; and Howard Kelly, 31. All gifted teachers, they were destined to transform the profession of medicine.

Welch was a fine pathologist concerned with clinical relevance. He discovered the bacillus that causes gas gangrene. He conducted the first clinicopathological conferences in the country, integrating laboratory work with bedside care. He inaugurated, and became editor-in-chief of, the first American basic medical research journal, *The Journal of Experimental Medicine.* His genius, however, was for organization, strategic planning, and spotting people and trends that would thrive in the decades ahead. First as Hopkins' dean, and later as "gray eminence" to Rockefeller's General Education Board (which funded most of the major innovations in medical education during the first third of the twentieth century), president of the AMA, and dominant member of dozens of committees and boards, Welch was the most influential physician of his time. One of his protégés, Abraham Flexner, wrote the influential *Flexner Report,* which called Hopkins the best medical school in the country — the model for all others to follow. Welch hand-picked the people who would lead the profession until well after World War II.

Osler is still revered throughout the world as the giant of the wards, the quintessence of the doctor as renaissance man, humanist, and cultural being. Witty, learned, articulate, always quotable and charismatic, with a firm mastery of classical literature, he, more than any other, turned the Hopkins community — students and faculty — into a "happy band." His book *Principles and Practice of Medicine* was lucid enough and innovative enough to entice John D Rockefeller, Sr., to make his first financial contributions to medical education. Osler's clinical contributions included the delineation of the features of what is now known as subacute bacterial endocarditis (characterized by nodes and skin lesions, and now known by his name), and the description of polycythemia vera. Osler's greatest contribution was in clinical teaching. He got the students out of the lecture room and onto the wards. He established the first residency in internal medicine.

Halsted was the consumate surgeon: meticulous, scholarly, passionate. He is credited with introducing the use of rubber gloves into surgery. He discovered regional nerve-block anesthesia, and devised the radical mastectomy for breast cancer. He revolutionized surgery with his emphasis on anatomic understanding, technique, absolute cleanliness, and careful reconstruction of tissue. He developed new operations for intestinal and stomach surgery, gallstone removal, hernia repair and thyroid problems.

Kelly is "the father of gynecology"; he established the field as a specialty in its own right. Though he made many contributions to his profession, his name is best known to the medical public these days for the surgical clamp he developed, a relatively long handheld tissue clamp with a curved tip. He approached his profession with reverence, in every sense: he assembled a prayer meeting before each operation.

The Big Four, however, formed only the core. The rest of the faculty were outstanding as well, and with their students created an extraordinary record. The medical school opened officially in 1893; it and its associated institutions have been making important contributions from the very beginning:

1893   First successful catheterization of the male ureter (James Brown)

1897   Isolation of adrenalin, the first hormone isolated from any endocrine gland (John Abel)

1901   First monitoring of blood pressure during surgery (Harvey Cushing)

1902   First perineal prostatectomy, removing the prostate without damaging sexual function (Hugh Young)

1907   First description of intestinal lipodystrophy, or Whipple's disease (George Hoyt Whipple)

1907   First successful growth of animal tissue *in vitro* and birth of tissue culture (Ross Harrison)

1909   Discovery of the pituitary as the master endocrine gland (Harvey Cushing)

1911   First "Art as Applied to Medicine" Department

1912   Opening of the Harriet Lane Home, first children's hospital built as a part of an academic medical center

1913   First use of renal dialysis in an experimental animal (John Abel)

1914   Discovery of thalassemia minor (by MM Wintrobe)

1916   Discovery of heparin and its usefulness in preventing blood clotting (Jay McLean and William Howell)

1918   First use of ventriculography and pneumoencephalography for neurologic and neurosurgical diagnosis (Walter Dandy)

1921   Discovery that sunlight prevents rickets (Paul Shipley and Edwards Park)

1929   Development of the hematocrit method for measuring red blood cells

1944	"Blue-baby" operation for Tetralogy of Fallot opens the modern era of heart surgery (Alfred Blalock and Helen Taussig)
1958	First use of cardiopulmonary resuscitation, or CPR (Guy Knickerbocker, William Kouwenhoven, and James Jude)
1971	First total knee replacement (Lee Riley)
1973	First implantable, rechargeable cardiac pacemaker (Robert Fischell)
1975	First successful desensitization treatment for severe allergies to bee stings (Lawrence Lichtenstein)
1978	Nobel Prize awarded to Daniel Nathans and Hamilton Smith for discovery of restriction enzymes in 1968
1984	First use of genetically engineered tPa to stop heart attacks

In the first third of the twentieth century, Hopkins was so much in the vanguard of modern scientific medicine that it really had no peer in this country. In the latter half of the twentieth century it has lost its dominance in the fields of medical education and research. The reason is not so much that Hopkins has faded as that so many other medical centers — by following Hopkin's example and by hiring its graduates — have achieved comparable levels of quality and productivity.

Hopkins' School of Nursing had rougher sledding. Established in 1893 as the Training School for Nurses, it attracted an extraordinary faculty, including Isabel Hampton, Adelaide Nutting, and Lavinia Dock, who together dominated organized nursing in the early years of this century. They were prime movers in the endeavor that launched what is now the American Nursing Association. When Hopkins expanded its nursing training from two years to three, with a six-month probationary period, the new model became a national standard for diploma nursing education. However, a decades-long stuggle to establish a university-based school of nursing with a baccalaureate program to replace the diploma course was in vain, and the hospital school of nursing closed in 1973. It was revivified in 1983 as a full-fledged School of Nursing.

Today, Hopkins remains on the cutting edge. The Hopkins Health System is always one of the top recipients of federal dollars for biomedical research. An $85-million medical research building is under construction, as are various of other projects. Hopkins has recently acquired several other Baltimore hospitals, set up its own HMO, and established a for-profit arm that seeks venture capital to develop and market Hopkins inventions.

There are no formal tours here, but anyone wishing to stroll the campus can pick up a Visitor's Guide at the information desk in the hospital. This is a 44-acre campus with several dozen buildings, so there is a lot to see. Most attractive to my eyes are the three remaining original buildings, dating from 1889: the Billings Administration Building, the Marburg Building, and the Wilmer Building. These are Queen Anne style structures, constructed of pressed brick with generous ornamentation. The Administration Building is crowned with a large dome, topped with a central spire, under which is an octagonal rotunda. The central feature under the glass dome is a large statue of Christ the Consoler. The interior has been beautifully refinished, with most of the original detail left intact, including marble floors, oak woodwork, brass candelabra, and the like. The three upper floors, whose stately balconies rim the vast open rotunda, used to provide sleeping rooms for house staff; now they are used for administrative purposes. The Marburg and Wilmer Buildings, flanking the Administration Building on either side, have both suffered from renovation and the addition of third floors, but their exteriors are otherwise substantially intact. Their interiors have been totally remodeled, and now have the feel of very plush modern buildings. As you stroll through the hospital corridors, keep an eye open for the telltale brick lining the walls, which alerts you that you are walking through part of the tunnel system that connected pavilions now long gone. Many of these above-ground tunnels have been beautifully restored; their large expanses of window look out on numerous gardens.

The Brady Institute is a urologic institute that was founded by Diamond Jim Brady in 1915 and now located in the Marburg Building. Hugh Young (considered the founder of modern urology) operated on Brady's prostate. So pleased was Brady with the operation—and the fact that his sexual function was unimpaired—that he endowed the first such institute in the country. A portrait of the benefactor hangs in the Institute's library.

The Harriet Lane Home no longer exists. Its organizational successor, the Children's Center, occupies an eleven-story building behind and to the left of the administration building.

The William Welch Library, a limestone Renaissance-style building dating from 1929, is located at the corner of East Monument Street and Washington Street. On the second floor of the library, in the West Reading Room, hangs John Singer Sargent's famous group portrait *The Four Doctors,* depicting the assembled Welch, Osler, Halsted, and Kelly. The third floor houses the **Institute of the History of Medicine,** the oldest academic department of its kind in the United States. This floor is also home to one of the country's largest medical rare book collections and a small but choice museum collection. When I visited there were exhibits on Chinese pharmacy and therapeutics, phrenology, and Greco-Roman surgical instruments, among other topics. The Givens Rare Book Room, on this floor, has Florence Nightingale's wheelchair on permanent display.

The old Phipps psychiatric pavilion still stands, just to the left of the main hospital entrance on Wolfe Street. When it was built, in 1912, it represented the first psychiatry department and clinic integrated into a general teaching hospital, and the founders hoped that this would be the beginning of psychiatry's acceptance and integration into medicine generally. Psychiatry now occupies a new (1982) building across McElderry Street, and the Phipps is home to administrative offices and the School of Nursing. Enter the beautifully restored marble lobby with its twin fireplaces. Straight ahead, through a set of French doors, you will find a lovely protected garden with a fountain and pool.

Francis Scott Key Medical Center 4940 Eastern Avenue 21224. (301) 550-0128. This hospital traces its origins back to 1773, when the Baltimore City and County Almshouse was established. However, the first medical patients as such were not admitted until 1823. The Almshouse moved to its present location in 1866; at that time its name was changed to Bay View Asylum, reflecting its new mission of caring for the mentally ill. In 1925 the name was changed once again, to Baltimore City Hospital. Over the years that followed, the institution evolved into a combination acute and chronic care hospital, with a rambling collection of buildings.

Like many city and county hospitals, this one was chronically plagued by financial problems; by the late 1970s its future looked bleak. In the early 1980s, the various components were losing over $6 million per year. In 1984 Johns Hopkins stepped in and purchased the entire complex, renaming the hospital, turning it into a private facility, and making it a member of the Johns Hopkins family of institutions. To turn Francis Scott Key into a profitable enterprise, Hopkins revamped management, dramatically cut uncompensated care, pumped $60 million into new facilities, tore down all the older buildings, and turned most of the 130-acre campus into the Bayview Research Campus, a biotechnology park. FSKMC now has 315 acute-care beds, 233 chronic-care beds, and 24 alcohol-rehabilitation beds. Tenants on adjacent land include the Gerontology Research Center of the National Institute of Aging, the Addiction Research Center of the National Institute of Drug Abuse, and various other biotechnology research and for-profit enterprises.

Tours of FSKMC are available through the Public Relations Office.

Spring Grove Hospital Center Wade Avenue, Catonsville 21228. (301) 455-6000. This is the fourth-oldest psychiatric hospital in the country, yielding in priority only to the hospital in Williamsburg,

Virginia (which began as a psychiatric institution) and the Institute of the Pennsylvania Hospital and the Bloomingdale Asylum (which were offshoots of earlier institutions). The hospital was originally located within the city of Baltimore, and over the years was variously known as the Public Hospital, the City Hospital, the Lunatic Asylum, and the Maryland Hospital for the Insane. Founded in 1797 for "the pauper sick and insane of the State and sea-faring persons,"the hospital was established on the grounds of what is now the Johns Hopkins Hospital.

During its first half-century, the hospital's administration and sponsorship changed several times. Initially run by the city of Baltimore, it was leased to local physicians as a profit-making enterprise from 1809 to 1834, then run by the Daughters of Charity from 1834 to 1840; thereafter it was under the full control of the state of Maryland. Although it initially accommodated both the insane and the physically ill, the hospital was restricted to the mentally ill from 1840 onward.

As an institution devoted exclusively to psychiatric problems, the hospital rapidly became overcrowded; Dorothea Dix came to Maryland to request funds from the legislature for a new facility. The Spring Grove site in Catonsville was selected in 1853, but the Civil War interrupted construction, and the buildings at the new location weren't completed until 1872. The patients were then transferred, and the old property was sold to Mr. Johns Hopkins to accommodate his new medical school and hospital. However, it wasn't until 1912 that the Hospital for the Insane was renamed the Spring Grove State Hospital. The center's current name dates from 1973.

This is one of the few hospitals in the country to have been pressed into service for the treatment of sick and injured soldiers during the War of 1812, the Civil War, and World War I.

Though the grounds here once comprised 600 acres, most of that land has been sold; the campus is now restricted to 200 acres, with some 20 buildings. The oldest patient-care buildings date to the early twentieth century, but some of the support structures date from 1872. Tours of the facility are available upon request.

④ *Old Baltimore General Dispensary* 500 West Fayette Street 21201. The inscription on the cornice (1801 BALTIMORE GENERAL DISPENSARY 1911) alludes to a past of providing health care to Baltimore's poor. When the Dispensary was founded, in 1801, Baltimore had a population of 26,000. This was the city's first charity. Funds for medical care of the poor were raised by various means, including a state lottery, benefit concerts, and fines imposed on bawdy-house operators. A second dispensary was added in 1826; by 1892, the city had fifteen dispensaries. The dispensary system in Baltimore was phased out in the mid-twentieth century as various free clinics, hospital outpatient services, and welfare organizations replaced various functions. The BGD was housed in a variety of structures, all now razed, before this simple two-story building, with its neoclassical ornamentation, was erected in 1911. The main floor featured a large dispensary room, divided into separate compartments for black and white patients; the second floor housed five rooms used for offices. In 1959 the BGD decided to sell its building, using the money thus gained to establish a foundation that would grant money to various local hospitals and clinics, allowing them to provide free medicines to the poor. Thus, the BGD continues to operate as a foundation; but its former home, after standing vacant for several years, has found new life as a Burger King outlet.

Union Memorial Hospital 201 East University Parkway 21218. (301) 554-2000. This hospital was founded in 1854 as the Union Protestant Infirmary, so named to distinguish it as the city's first non-Catholic hospital. (The city's oldest hospital, the University of Maryland Hospital, was founded in 1823 as the Baltimore Infirmary, staffed first by the Daughters of Charity and later by the Sisters of Mercy.) The UPI was taken over by government forces and used as a military hospital from 1861 to 1863. In 1920 the hospital dropped "Protestant" from its name ("in order to emphasize the nonsectarian character of the work") and added the word "Memorial" (to recognize "that the hospital has become throughout a memorial to the relatives and friends of those who have contributed so freely to its cost").

The hospital's most famous patient was admitted in 1939: Al Capone came here directly from the federal prison in Lewisburg, Pennsylvania, under the care of Dr. Joseph Moore, syphilologist. Capone was diagnosed as suffering from general paresis, with mental aberrations.

Innovations by hospital staff included the Operating Trunk, in 1899 (the first portable operating room used by the U.S. Army, developed by Omar Pancoast and John MT Finney), and the Stone Intestinal Clamp, in 1937 (developed by Harvey Stone, it helped revolutionize large-bowel surgery).

Union still operates its own nursing school, a training program that will celebrate its centennial in 1991. The hospital is currently a 353-bed facility, with the newest building dating from the late 1970s and the oldest from the 1920s. The latter still has its rooftop sunporch, visible from the street, typical of hospitals of the era, where tubercular patients were taken for healing sunshine. Contact the Community Relations Department for tours.

St. Agnes Hospital 900 Caton Avenue 21229. (301) 368-6000. This hospital was founded in 1862 by the Daughters of Charity, with the financial support of Charles M. Daugherty. At the benefactor's request, the hospital was named after Daugherty's wife Agnes. In 1898 the facility was turned into a sanatorium for hydrotherapy to treat nervous disorders and drug dependency. A fine "Water-Cure Building" was added on the 68-acre site, providing the full range of hydrotherapy, including douches, needle sprays, sitz baths, packs, and massage. A full floor was devoted to electrotherapy, including "Static, Faradic and Galvanic machines." The treatment rationale was that nervous disorders were presumed to be due to circulatory, digestive, or other organic problems that the various therapeutic techniques used here were meant to remedy.

By 1906, hydrotherapy had fallen out of vogue; St Agnes Sanitarium was once again turned into a general hospital. It quickly became a progressive establishment and, shortly thereafter, became the second hospital in the country (after Johns Hopkins) to establish a surgical residency. Tours of the sprawling modern 430-bed hospital and medical center are available through the Public Relations Department.

St Joseph Hospital 7620 York Road, Towson 21204. (301) 337-1700. This hospital traces its origins to 1864, when three Sisters from the Third Order of St Francis came to Baltimore and began to care for the sick and wounded of the Civil War. The success of their efforts led to the building of a hospital in 1872. In 1897 and 1898 the influx of wounded soldiers from the Spanish-American War so taxed the Sisters that they could no longer care for the patients themselves. Women volunteers helped with nursing duties, and the teaching of these volunteers soon evolved into the St Joseph Hospital School of Nursing. The nursing school was closed in 1988, after 87 years of operation. The hospital moved from Baltimore to its present location, in Towson, in 1965. In 1986 St Joseph established its International Center for Skeletal Dysplasia, the world's only center for the treatment of orthopedic complications of dwarfism. Tours are available through the Public Relations office.

Sinai Hospital of Baltimore 2401 West Belvedere Avenue at Greenspring 21215. (301) 578-5678. This, the fourth oldest Jewish hospital in the country, was founded in 1866. It was first known as the Hebrew Hospital and Asylum; the present name was adopted in 1926. The "asylum" was for the elderly. In the early years the aged and the sick were intermingled in rooms, a practice that persisted until after the turn of the century. Initially located in downtown Baltimore, the hospital moved to its present 29-acre landscaped site in 1959. It was here that the first automatic implantable cardio-verter-defibrillator was introduced, in 1980 by Michael Mirowski. Today, Sinai is a 516-bed hospital that occupies a sprawling complex of contemporary buildings on a hillside adjacent to Pimlico Race Course. Tours are available through the Public Relations Department.

(5) *Mercy Hospital* 301 St Paul Place 21202. (301) 332-9000. This hospital dates from 1874, when the Sisters of Mercy started providing nursing services at what had been called City Hospital. More a dispensary than an inpatient facility, City Hospital had provided clinic facilities for the Washington University School of Medicine. In 1878 Washington University merged with the College of Physicians and Surgeons, and the Sisters took over all hospital management. When a new hospital building was needed, in 1889, John Philip Sousa provided the musical entertainment for the fundraising rally. The institution remained City Hospital until 1909, when it was renamed Mercy Hospital. The last remnants of the old hospital buildings were razed in 1980, and this is now a thoroughly modern and imposing downtown medical complex. No tours are available.

(6) *Maryland General Hospital* 827 Linden Avenue 21201. (301) 225-8390. In 1881 a group of physicians established the Baltimore Medical College, as a "Christian school for the coeducation of both sexes." As the school prospered the need for a hospital soon became apparent; the Maryland General Hospital was established in 1883. By 1884, factionalism within the faculty resulted in a group's breaking away to form the Baltimore University Medical School. The MGH continued to prosper, opening an Eye, Ear, Nose, and Throat Department and a Lying-In Hospital in 1888, and a training school for nurses in 1891. Shortly after the turn of the century the Hospital negotiated a contract with the Sisters of Charity to operate and administer the facilities. The essential harmony of the situation was disrupted by the Flexner Report in 1910: although Flexner had some good things to say about the Baltimore Medical College, his conclusion was that the school was weak and he called for consolidation of Maryland's seven medical colleges. The result was that the Baltimore Medical College merged with the University of Maryland. The Hospital, suddenly without its reason for existence, was then sold to the Methodist Hospital Board.

In 1970 the hospital decided to expand its outpatient program. Instead of building new facilities for this purpose, it took over the adjacent 100-year old Richmond Market Armory, which was completely renovated and remodeled. During its century of existence the Armory had housed, at various times, a 500-stall housewives' and farmers' market, rehearsal space for the Baltimore Civic Opera Company, a drum and bugle corps, and dog obedience classes. As it stands now, the Armory (connected to the hospital by a second-story glass-enclosed pedestrian bridge) is a fine example of an adaptive modern use of an historic building. Tours are available through the Public Relations department.

(7) *Cole Pharmacy Museum* 650 West Lombard Street 21207. (301) 727-0746. This museum (located in the headquarters of the Maryland Pharmaceutical Association) is dedicated to B Olive Cole, a former dean of the University of Maryland School of Pharmacy and president of the MPA. Now that 40 percent of Maryland's pharmacists are women, the Association believes that the tribute to the "first lady of pharmacy in Maryland" is only fitting; her memorabilia are a significant portion of the collection. The museum is in two parts. On the first floor, sandwiched among offices, are two rooms, each with numerous display cases filled with elaborate antique show globes, wonderful hand-painted drug jars, various weights and measures, pill-rolling and other manufacturing devices, glass-stoppered bottles, and a huge selection of mortars and pestles. Don't fail to go downstairs, where there is an additional museum room. Though there was substantial disarray and clutter when I visited, the richness of the collection was apparent. Fine old oaken pharmacy cabinets line every wall, filled with drugs and medicaments ranging from squill compound and kava extract to three-grain quinine sulfate tablets and a bottle of Peacock's Bromide. Scattered here and there are pharmacy-related artwork, pharmaceutical glassware, various pharmacy paraphernalia, antique prescription books, and a fine collection of balances. The museum is accessible to the public during normal business hours.

(8) *William P Didusch Museum of the American Urological Association* 1120 North Charles Street 21201. (301) 727-1100. Baltimore was the home of several key figures in the development of urology, so it is not surprising that the specialty's professional association is headquartered here. Established in 1902, the American Urological Association now has 7,000 members. It is also home to a fascinating, although extraordinarily specialized, museum. The Didusch Museum is named for William P Didusch, who became staff artist for the Johns Hopkins Brady Urological Institute in 1915 and went on to become the premier medical artist of the genitourinary tract for the next 70 years.

The collection here is divided into three parts: Didusch drawings and related material, memorabilia of the great urologists, and a remarkable instrument collection. The drawings portray normal and pathological anatomy, as well as surgical techniques of urologic greats. However, it is the instrument collection, with items numbering in the thousands, that will interest most visitors. The exhibits suffer from a lack of explanatory material, but even lay people will be astounded and intrigued by the extraordinary diversity of the tools on display. There are hundreds of cystoscopes here, including one from 1890, infant models, and one made of gold. The collection includes urethroscopes, cystourethroscopes, and resectoscopes. There are lithotrites (for blindly crushing bladder stones) and lithotriptoscopes; evacuators and retractors; and every other manner of device used by urologists. Two prizes are an umbrella and a cane of nineteenth-century origin, both of which belonged to a gentleman who had prostatic enlargement in the days before prostatic surgery. He needed to be catheterized often and, because he traveled a great deal, had to carry a catheter with him for self-catheterization. The cane and the umbrella each have a hidden chamber in the tip for storing the catheter, as well as a vault in the handle for storing lubricant.

The museum is located on the third floor of the AUA headquarters, in several beautifully remodeled and furnished rooms. It can be seen by appointment only.

(9) *Emerson Bromo-Seltzer Tower* 312-318 West Lombard Street 21201. This remarkable yellow-brick, Romanesque fifteen-story tower, designed to resemble the Palazzo Vecchio in Florence, Italy, was built in 1911. It is topped with an octagonal crenellated observation post just below, which are clock faces on four sides, each face 24 feet in diameter. This is said to be the largest four-dial gravity clock in the world. Until 1936 the tower was crowned with an enormous, steel, revolving Bromo-Seltzer bottle, which was illuminated at night. The Bromo-Seltzer bottle is now gone, but the brand name is still emblazoned on the clock faces. The structure was commissioned by Isaac Emerson, an inventor and entrepreneur who devised Bromo-Seltzer as a headache remedy in 1888 and made it the foundation of the Emerson Drug Company. The formulation is named after Mt Bromo, a volcano in Java, which Emerson thought a suitably dramatic symbol for the medicine's volcanic effervescence. Emerson Drug eventually was bought out by Warner-Lambert Pharmaceutical Company; in 1967 the tower and the office building at its base were sold to the city of Baltimore. The office building was subsequently razed, but the tower remains — a testament to entrepreneurial energy and to the money to be made in headache remedies.

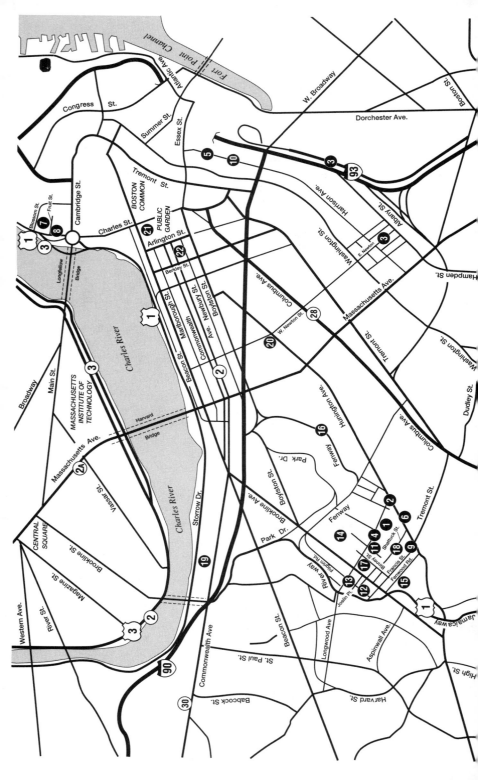

Boston and Environs

Including Cambridge, Belmont, Hull, and Everett

Map Key

(1) Harvard Medical School
(2) Massachusetts College of Pharmacy and Allied Health Sciences
(3) Boston University Medical Center
(4) Harvard School of Dental Medicine
(5) Tufts – New England Medical Center
(6) Harvard School of Public Health
(7) Massachusetts General Hospital
(8) Massachusetts Eye and Ear Infirmary
(9) Brigham and Women's Hospital
(10) Boston City Hospital
(11) Children's Hospital Medical Center
(12) New England Deaconess Hospital
(13) Joslin Diabetes Center
(14) Beth Israel Hospital
(15) Massachusetts Mental Health Center
(16) Forsyth Dental Center
(17) Dana-Farber Cancer Institute
(18) Francis A. Countway Library of Medicine, Offices of the *New England Journal of Medicine*
(19) Mugar Memorial Library
(20) First Church of Christ, Scientist
(21) Ether Monument
(22) Emmanuel Church
(23) Paul Revere House

These key numbers will be found at appropriate points in the text.

BOSTON, WITH A POPULATION of just over half a million, ranks twenty-first in size among American cities; yet some would say that as a center of medicine it is second to none. It has the country's premier private hospital (the Massachusetts General Hospital), the world's most prestigious medical journal (the *New England Journal of Medicine*), a perennially top-ranked medical school (Harvard), and numerous other prestigious and influential medical institutions.

For the traveler interested in medical history Boston is a special treat, because so many historic landmarks still exist, treasured by a city with an enormous fondness for its own past. You are welcome, for example, to visit the Ether Dome, where ether was first used as an anesthetic in 1846. You can also wander the grounds at the old New England Hospital for Women and Children, now the Dimock Community Health Center, where America's first trained nurse and first black nurse received their schooling.

The greatest concentration of medical landmarks is in the Longwood district, a compact area where you can crisscross streets and view the exteriors of all the major institutions during a pleasant hour or two's stroll. These include Harvard Medical School, Harvard School of Public Health, Harvard Dental School, the Brigham and Women's Hospital, Boston Children's, New England Deaconess, the Joslin Clinic, Beth Israel Hospital, Massachusetts Mental Health Center, Massachusetts College of Pharmacy and Allied Health Sciences, the Dana-Farber Cancer Institute, and the Countway Library.

Another area that will appeal to many is home to both the Massachusetts General Hospital (with its historic Bulfinch Building) and the Massachusetts Eye and Ear Infirmary.

Both these areas are particularly interesting and attractive, but Boston has much more to reward people with special interests, not only within the city limits but also in the communities that cluster around the city's periphery.

(1) *Harvard Medical School* Longwood Avenue at Avenue Louis Pasteur 02115. (617) 732-1590. Harvard is the nation's most famous and most prestigious school of medicine. While other medical schools may have surpassed HMS in one area or another at one time or another, Harvard's breadth of achievement and contributions over 200 years have given it a dominance attained by no other.

HMS professors have written a disproportionate number of the textbooks of choice in practically all fields of medicine. Of nationally prominent medical leaders, a hugely disproportionate number can boast of HMS affiliations at some point in their careers. The list of medical firsts by HMS faculty (when added to those at HMS-affiliated hospitals) seems unending.

Bulfinch Building, Massachusetts General Hospital *(By permission of Massachusetts General Hospital News and Archives)*

1847	Introduction of the microscope to US medical teaching by Oliver Wendell Holmes
1895	Demonstration of esophageal motility in a live being (Walter B Cannon, while still a medical student at HMS)
1914	First use of electrocardiograph in US (Paul Dudley White)
1926	Discovery of liver extract as cure for pernicious anemia, resulting in Nobel Prize for George Minot and William Murphy (in 1934)
1926	Discovery of hyperparathyroidism (Joseph Aub)
1937	Radioisotopes first used in diagnosis of disease (Saul Hertz)
1957	William Hinton (later to become the first black professor at HMS) develops the Hinton Test for the detection of syphilis

The development of the present-day HMS dates back to 1782, when medical classes were begun in nearby Cambridge in what was called the Medical Institution of Harvard College. Medical education in that era wasn't much: no academic preparation was necessary, students attended lectures for a semester or two, written exams weren't required, and newly graduated students apprenticed themselves to a practitioner for several years. Still, the school began with excellent teachers (among them John Warren and Benjamin Waterhouse), and the education was good for its time.

In 1810 HMS moved to Boston, where — because of a gift from the state — it became known as the Massachusetts Medical College of Harvard University. In 1847 it moved to a location next door to the Massachusetts General Hospital, staying there until it relocated to Copley Square in 1883. For many of those years the school was basically a proprietary operation, run for the profit of the faculty, who collected all the students' fees. Standards were notoriously lax, supervision was minimal, and testing was spotty. When Charles William Eliot became president of Harvard, in 1869, he resolved to upgrade the medical school. It was then that the modern era of Harvard's excellence began.

The present HMS location was purchased in 1906. The original plans called for brick exteriors, but the contractor substituted marble (there have been contradictory explanations given for the change), creating the awe-inspiring quadrangle (called the Quad), which consists of five neoclassical structures. The result evokes the wisdom of the ages, the dignity of scholarship, the gentility of the classics, and the wealth of Croesus. There are no more imposing medical buildings anywhere in this country.

The most impressive of the five buildings can be approached from the grassy quadrangle up a broad set of marble steps, bordered by marble walls, on top of which sit large urns placed at regular intervals. Like the other buildings here, this principal one is five stories tall; but this one is also guarded by six Ionic columns that stretch the height of the building and support a broad portico, atop which sits the Harvard crest.

Inside this building (Harvard understates its grandeur, calling it simply Building A) can be found the quite remarkable **Warren Anatomical Museum.** Though at the turn of the century the museum occupied the top three floors, competing demands for space (for both administration and teaching) and the increasing availability of other teaching tools have resulted in the gradual retrenchment of the museum so that it now occupies only a portion of the fifth-floor balcony. Still, the museum and its setting remain quite spectacular. The fifth-floor balcony surrounds a three-story, rectangular central atrium, topped by a vaulted ceiling, with all balconies protected by cast-iron railings. The museum consists of perhaps two dozen cases (most specimens are in storage) and definitely is not for the squeamish. There is an 1847 skeleton of a man with rickets, unbelievably dwarfed, with bowed upper and lower limbs. Other skeletons include those of pituitary giants and an unfortunate hunch-backed dwarf with tuberculosis of the spine. The teratology display features twins joined at the chest, others with a single body and two heads, and a siren (with legs joined together from the waist down). There are displays on bloodletting, cupping, early antisepsis, and radiology. There's a large collection of bladder stones, and another of diseased skulls. Then there is the skull of Phineas P Gage, who, in 1848, while tamping down some explosives with a pry-bar, performed the world's first known prefrontal lobotomy on himself when the resultant explosion drove the steel bar through his skull. Miraculously Gage survived, displaying only a change of temperament in which he became "fitfull (sic), vacillating, obstinate and profane." He died in San Francisco in 1861, and somehow both his skull and the steel bar found their way back to this collection. The museum was originally assembled by John Collins Warren (the founder of Massachusetts General Hospital), who donated some 1000 specimens during his lifetime and another at his death: his preserved skeleton is kept hidden in a locked wooden cabinet at one end of the balcony. The museum is accessible only to people with an HMS connection or to those who make prior special arrangements (call 732-1603 or 732-1735).

In general, HMS is not very receptive to visitors. The oft-stated rule of thumb seems to be "If you're one of us, we don't have to make special arrangements; if you're not, we don't hunger for your company." Still, this is a marvelous place for just wandering. Immediately to the left as you face Building A from the Quad is the famed Countway Library. Just behind Building A, across a dead-end traffic way, sits the Peter Bent Brigham Hospital. Near the front of the Quad are both the Harvard School of Dental Medicine and the Massachusetts College of Pharmacy. Within a few blocks are the Brigham and Women's Hospital, the Beth Israel, Children's, New England Deaconess, the Joslin Clinic, Dana-Farber, and the Massachusetts Mental Health Center. Nowhere else in the world can you find such a concentration of medical prestige and accomplishment within so few blocks.

(2) *Massachusetts College of Pharmacy and Allied Health Sciences* 179 Longwood Avenue 02115. (617) 732-2800. The Massachusetts College of Pharmacy was founded in 1823, and thus is the second oldest college of pharmacy in the country (if you accept the use of the term "college" to imply a "body of colleagues"). However, it wasn't granted a formal charter until 1852, and had no formal curriculum until 1867. The college moved to its present location in 1918, choosing to locate near Harvard Medical School in the Longwood area. The Allied Health Sciences division was added in the 1970s, but pharmacy still accounts for the vast majority of students.

The building is a neoclassical structure, with an enormous expanse of stairs leading up to an impressive portico supported by six Ionic columns. At the top of the stairs is a large entranceway protected by two huge sculpted bronze doors, which generally are kept closed (the customary entrance is on the ground level, just to the side of the central stairway). Two wings have been added to the original building, one in 1931 and the other in 1937. The interior of this impressive building has suffered somewhat from continual use, but the imposing exterior is clearly the match of any other pharmacy school in the country. There are no tours for visitors, but there is no prohibition against wandering about the school's public spaces.

(3) *Boston University Medical Center*   88 East Newton Street 02118. (617) 247-5000. BUMC traces its origins to two medical institutions, both of which have interesting stories. One was the Massachusetts Homeopathic Hospital, chartered in 1855 and formally opened, after many delays, in 1871. Homeopathy enjoyed widespread appeal in the mid-nineteenth century because it condemned such aggressive treatments as bloodletting and purging, because it stressed such good habits as sensible diets and exercise, and because its practitioners prescribed medications in such infinitesimal doses that they had no harmful side effects.

The other institution was the New England Female Medical College, founded in 1848 as the first entirely female medical college in the world. Unfortunately, of the various women's medical schools that functioned in the latter half of the nineteenth century this was one of the weakest academically, and it suffered from numerous administrative and financial problems as well. In 1873 it was absorbed by Boston University and turned into a coeducational school.

Because the medical school and the Massachusetts Homeopathic Hospital were neighbors — and some of the same people were involved in both endeavors — the two developed a close working relationship. In fact, the staff of the hospital became the faculty for the school of medicine, the result being that Boston University Medical School (BUMS) began as a homeopathic medical college. In contrast to many such institutions, however (and also in contrast to many allopathic medical schools), BUMS stressed a strong academic program from the beginning. When the Flexner report appeared, in 1910, BUMS was the only homeopathic school in the country to be credited with "progressive" scientific laboratories, and its dispensary was said to compare "favorably in equipment, organization and conduct with the best institutions of the kind in the country."

In 1917 the university assumed much more vigorous control of the medical school, and a blue-ribbon committee quickly concluded that BU's connections with homeopathy be dropped. The required courses in homeopathy were made optional, and eventually were discontinued. Changes in the hospital took a bit longer, but in 1929 the Massachusetts Homeopathic Hospital rechristened itself Massachusetts Memorial Hospital, a name that endured until 1965, when the name University Hospital was adopted.

BUMC today occupies a large campus in Boston's South End, adjacent to Boston City Hospital. BUMC's 20-odd buildings are dominated by the dramatic eight-story Atrium Pavilion, a glass-and-metal-covered spaceframe which contains most of the acute-care beds as well as many outpatient functions. Opened in 1987, the Atrium also provides the hospital's main entrance. From here, it is a short walk across East Newton Street to the lobby of the School of Medicine Building, where you will find the Bernard Appel Hall of Medicine, which consists of 12 massive stone plaques, each eight feet high, each depicting a great figure (e.g., Hippocrates, Pasteur, Curie) from the history of medicine. If you take the hallway leading to the left off the lobby, you will come to the Doris Appel American Medical History Panels. Named for the sculptress (who also created the lobby panels), these two massive stone plaques feature 27 figures who contributed to the development of medicine, especially in New England but in the rest of the country as well. On the lawn just in front of this building are some more sculptures, including an interesting bust of Hippocrates. Across the lawn is the old Talbott Building, an 1876 remnant of the old homeopathic hospital. Its interior has been remodeled; none of the old features are any longer apparent.

BUMC currently offers no public tours, but all the sites described above are easily accessible in public spaces.

④ *Harvard School of Dental Medicine* Longwood Avenue at Palace Road 02115. (617) 732-1000. Other dental schools may be older, but Harvard's was the first dental education program under the aegis of a university. The school was founded in 1867. Of the first class to graduate, in 1869, one of six members was black. Robert Tanner Freeman, the son of slaves, thus became the first black in the United States to receive a dental degree. Less than a decade later, George F Grant (who had graduated with the second class, in 1870) became the first black to serve on any dental faculty and the first black to join the faculty of Harvard University. However, while the dental school was light-years ahead of many others in its early attitudes toward blacks, it delayed another hundred years (1974) before it was prepared to graduate a woman.

Harvard Dental is, and has been for many years, the smallest dental school in the country, averaging about 20 students per graduating class. However, its biomedical research commitment is unusually strong; almost all of the faculty are deeply involved in research. The school sits side by side with the medical school, and all the professors belong to the faculty of medicine.

There are no tours, and the architecture is not particularly inviting.

(5) *Tufts–New England Medical Center* 171 Harrison Avenue 02111. (617) 956-5000. This is a mélange of a number of separate entities that appear to function smoothly as a single enterprise, but that nonetheless feel strongly about their individual identities. The key historical elements are the Boston Dispensary, Tufts Medical School, Floating Hospital for Infants and Children, and the Pratt Diagnostic Clinic.

The founding institution of the group is the **Boston Dispensary,** which in 1796 became the first organized medical-care service in New England and the third such service in the country. Boston was then a city of almost 20,000 people, suffering a serious post–Revolutionary War depression, with scarce resources, rampant infectious disease, and no hospitals. The Dispensary was supported by private contributions and the voluntary services of local physicians, and consisted primarily of a pharmacy shop from which doctors were dispatched to treat the sick in their homes. In the years that followed, the Dispensary made many pioneering contributions. In 1803 it began the nation's first mass vaccination program against smallpox. In 1873 it opened the first venereal disease clinic in the nation and the first dental clinic open to the sick and impoverished. In 1899 the Dispensary opened the country's first lung clinic, designed primarily to treat tuberculosis. By 1918 the Dispensary was operating its own Food Clinic, the first nutrition clinic in the country.

Tufts College was founded in 1852; the medical school dates from 1893. Tufts is now a university, with a downtown Boston campus that includes the School of Medicine, the School of Dental Medicine, and the School of Veterinary Medicine. The dental school began as the Boston Dental College in 1868, but was absorbed by Tufts in 1899. The Tufts School of Nutrition (the first such school in the nation) is located on the Medford (MA) campus, though the USDA Nutrition Human Research Center is on the TNEMC campus.

The **Floating Hospital** began life in 1894 as a fair-weather barge, which was towed out into Boston Harbor and anchored there during the day to provide sick infants and children under five years of age with clean air. The schedule was gradually increased from semi-weekly to daily trips, and the barge was replaced by a steam-driven ship. When the ship burned at dockside, in 1927, the Floating decided to focus its energies on building a more substantial land-based pediatric hospital adjacent to the Boston Dispensary (the Floating had already opened a small shore hospital in 1919). One of the Floating's most lasting contributions to health care was the development of the first artificial milk formula, Similac, in 1919.

The **Pratt Diagnostic Clinic** was founded in 1938 as a 100-bed, private specialty referral center associated with the Boston Dispensary, which then was still principally concerned with providing care for the indigent. The clinic was named after Joseph H Pratt, who had been named the Dispensary's physician-in-chief in 1927 and who was widely respected for his work with tuberculosis patients, advocating "outdoor sleeping boxes" for babies with TB. He also pioneered self-help classes that are now regarded as forerunners of modern group psychotherapy.

These various elements merged formally in 1965 to become the TNEMC, and the result is a vast medical complex on the edge of downtown Boston, wedged between the theater district and Chinatown. The inpatient components have almost 500 beds. The oldest structure in the group is the 1883 Boston Dispensary building, at Ash and Bennet Streets, notable for the brick relief of the Good Samaritan on its facade over the doorway. The Pratt and Farnsworth Buildings (across Bennet Street) have attractive old lobbies that usually contain historical displays. The Floating Hospital now floats only across Washington Street, but it is an attractive modern facility, which is entered via an inviting brick plaza ornamented by trees and plantings.

Medical Center tours are available from Public Relations.

(6) *Harvard School of Public Health* 665 Huntington Avenue 02115. (617) 732-1000. The three unassuming buildings situated between the Harvard School of Dental Medicine and the Brigham and Women's complex give no clue to the proud history of this school. Established in 1913, it is the oldest graduate school of public health in continued operation in this country. (Tulane's School of Public Health and Tropical Medicine was founded in the same year, but its course has been far more rocky.) Credit for the 1928 invention of the Drinker Respirator (or Iron Lung) belongs to HSPH Professor

Phillip Drinker—whose brother, Cecil Drinker, was then director of the Division of Industrial Hygiene and later went on to become Dean of HSPH (from 1935 to 1942). In 1979 Dr Arnold Spielman identified the deer tick as the vector for Lyme Disease. Above and beyond these specific achievements, HSPH has for many decades been one of the most influential public health institutions in the world, developing understanding of and standards for occupational and environmental health, infectious disease, health-care systems and policies, and health promotion and disease prevention.

HSPH has no program of tours for outsiders, but will occasionally allow visitors to join frequently scheduled tours for new employees. Call ext. 0842 for details.

McLean Hospital 115 Mill Street, Belmont 02178. (617) 855-2000. The McLean was founded as a division of the Massachusetts General Hospital, and was initially known as the Asylum to distinguish it from the rest of the General Hospital. The Asylum received its first patient in 1818, some seven years after its founding, opening its doors three years before the parent MGH formally opened. In 1826 the Asylum was officially named the McLean Asylum for the Insane (in honor of Boston merchant John McLean, who left $25,000 to the fledgling institution); in 1892, it was rechristened McLean Hospital.

From the first, the Asylum was a center for "moral treatment" of psychiatric patients, the first rule being that patients were to be treated with respect and dignity. Patients were to be distracted from their concerns through occupation and diversion. To this end, the facilities were well-stocked with such amusements as "draughts, chess, backgammon, ninepins, swinging, sawing wood, gardening, reading, writing, music," etc. In the early 1800s the McLean became the first psychiatric institution in the country to include religious worship and manual labor as routine parts of treatment.

By the late nineteenth century, the McLean was clearly one of the most prestigious institutions of its kind in the country and the only one with a physiology laboratory as a part of its research program. Dr Otto Folin, who helped devise what was for many years the standard test for sugar in the blood and who later became Harvard's first professor of biological chemistry, worked at the McLean from 1900 to 1908. In 1921 Dr Walter B Cannon, America's foremost physiologist of the time, was appointed McLean Physiologist.

The McLean was also the first mental hospital to introduce women nurses into male wards and the first to establish a school of nursing. The McLean Asylum Training School for Nurses opened in 1882, expanded to a three-year diploma program in 1906, and folded in 1968. During its 86 years of operation the school graduated some 2000 students, about 40 percent of whom were men.

The McLean was initially situated across the Charles River from the MGH; by the mid-nineteenth century, urban congestion had intruded on the originally tranquil setting, and McLean's trustees searched for a new location. Frederick Law Olmsted, who had designed Central Park in New York City and the grounds of a number of mental hospitals, was called in as a consultant. Olmsted helped to choose the present 240-acre Belmont site and to plan its principal features; in 1895 the new hospital opened its doors.

McLean still has some of the original buildings, present since the facility moved to this site, but there is little evidence of the farm and service shops that once thrived here. For many years most of the food consumed on the premises was produced on the premises; 150 cows provided the milk, vegetables and fruit were cultivated, as much as 2000 pounds of pork was butchered each week in spring and fall, and huge numbers of loaves of bread, doughnuts, and pies were baked each day. While patients contributed much of the labor at the first site, by the time McLean moved to Belmont the rather more well-to-do patients did not take kindly to the manual labor of farming; McLean had to hire employees to get the work done there and in the generator plant, the upholstery shop, the refrigeration unit, the leather shop, and the seamstress shop. However, McLean's self-sufficiency lasted until well into World War II, when wartime shortages dried up the labor supply and forced the hospital to close down the farm and most of the shops.

Today McLean has the largest research program of any private psychiatric hospital in the country. Each year it trains almost 500 students, including nurses, psychology interns, psychiatric residents, and social-work trainees. It continues to maintain its longstanding affiliations with the MGH and Harvard Medical School. In 1988 it became the first private psychiatric institution in the country to acquire an MRI scanner.

A visit to the present-day McLean provides a dramatic contrast to most research, training, and patient-care centers: here you will find a $12 million research budget tucked away in graceful old buildings, surrounded by pheasants and squirrels, and shaded by seventy species of trees (including five varieties of maple, five of birch, four of beech, and such unusual species as fringe trees and zelkova). Notable buildings are too numerous to mention individually, but all are in wonderful condition and many exhibit such architectural features as portes cochères, copper roofs, elaborate gables, and remarkable interior woodwork. Be sure to see the unusual hand-hewn spindle screen staircases in buildings such as Appleton House, Upham Building, and Bowditch House. Most of the numerous cottages scattered around the grounds were built by wealthy families to house insane relatives (usually for the rest of their lives), along with a suitable number of maids and servants. Such cottages were generally donated to the hospital upon the patient's death. McLean has the largest archives of any hospital I have visited in this country. McLean treasures its history and it has saved *everything* that has been in any way valuable to the evolution of its history. Included in this enormous treasure trove are original deeds, construction records, forms and manuals, daily nurses' reports, patients' diaries, menus from the dietary department, photos and daguerrotypes, personnel manuals, accounting books and ledgers, nursing school records, and a seemingly endless profusion of furniture, portraits, crockery, fireplace andirons, old medical instruments, and even weaving looms. It's an antique lover's and archivist's delight. The entire institution and its grounds may be toured by health professionals, with "due regard to the dignity of patients."

(7) *Massachusetts General Hospital* 32 Fruit Street 02114. (617) 726-2000. The MGH was chartered in 1811 and built in 1821. This was the country's third nonprofit general hospital, and it was by no means agreed in Boston that such a hospital was necessary. Arguments focused on whether the relief afforded by hospitals was better than various other possible treatments, and whether there were enough worthy poor in the Boston area to justify the expense (since the lazy, the debauched, and the dissolute were merely consigned to the almshouse). From the beginning the MGH did not include the insane, who instead were sent to the McLean.

Over the years, with the possible exception of Bellevue Hospital in New York, the MGH has probably been responsible for more medical breakthroughs and firsts than any other hospital. Certainly, the MGH is now the country's most prestigious hospital.

By all accounts the most dramatic event in MGH history (and, some would maintain, in all medical history anywhere) occurred on October 16, 1846. William TG Morton was an unusual and highly ambitious medical student at Harvard Medical School. Already a dentist (and a former partner of Horace Wells in Hartford), Morton was paying his way through HMS by running a dental practice, as well as operating a dental factory which manufactured false teeth. Not content with the effects of nitrous oxide anesthesia as used by Horace Wells, he learned from the chemist Charles T Jackson that ether might be a practical alternative. Morton experimented with the gas on his own dental patients and on laboratory animals, and then approached the surgeon John Collins Warren, at MGH, to arrange a demonstration. On the historic day, Morton anesthetized the patient using a glass globe inhalator of his own design and advised Warren, "Doctor, your patient is ready." Warren then removed a large tumor under the patient's jaw (the operation only took three minutes, such speed being a requisite for a surgeon in the pre-anesthesia days). When it was clear that the patient felt no pain, Warren turned to the spectators in the surgical amphitheater and intoned, "Gentlemen, this is no humbug."

In the years that followed, numerous other landmark events occurred at the MGH, among them the following:

1886   Reginald Fitz publishes the first description of appendicitis, advocating surgery as the treatment of choice
1902   Discovery of Wright's Stain, the panchromatic dye used in examining peripheral blood smears (James Wright)
1905   The first hospital-based social service department begins
1926   First description of the cause and treatment of lead poisoning
1953   Fritz Lipman shares the Nobel Prize for the discovery of coenzyme A and its metabolic role
1962   First successful reattachment of a human limb (Reginald Malt)
1981   First use of artificial skin from cowhide, shark cartilage, and plastic to replace human skin destroyed by burns
1984   First identification of the genetic marker for Huntington's disease

---

As one walks around the MGH today its long history is everywhere apparent, even though many of the 20 or so buildings on the 13.5-acre campus are quite new. The oldest structure, the vine-covered **Bulfinch Building,** is the original MGH, and is named for the famous architect Charles Bulfinch, who designed it. It's a gracious, dignified, granite structure with a facade dominated by eight huge Ionic columns, topped by an impressive portico. Atop the building is a large dome, under which sits the old surgical amphitheater (called the **Ether Dome**) in which the above mentioned event of 1846 took place. The Ether Dome's use as an operating theater was discontinued in 1867; for more than 100 years it has been used as a lecture hall. Today it is in regular use for daily grand rounds and other lectures. A large brass plaque above the front blackboard describes the historic ether demonstration. Five steeply rising tiers of seats face the front, but latecomers are forced to sit in the uppermost row, which consists of uncomfortable bicycle seats perched on iron bars. Tucked under the risers (and accessible via doors on either side) is a small museum which MGH is currently in the process of expanding. The Bulfinch Building is the only structure to be identified as a National Historic Landmark and to have one of its rooms, the Ether Dome, designated as a separate Landmark. Tours of both are given on Tuesdays and Thursdays at 2 PM, leaving from the Warren Building lobby. No reservations are necessary.

The Warren Building (1956) fronts on Charles Street and contains mostly clinical and research labs. The lobby, however, is impressive for two things: first, two fine precise models of the MGH, one showing the campus as it looked in 1830 and another showing a more contemporary version; second, the genealogy carved in marble of Boston's remarkable Warren family, which provided seven generations of Warrens to Boston medicine. Joseph Warren (1741 – 1775) was a physician who took part in the Boston Tea Party and became a general in the Continental Army. Joseph's brother John Warren (1753 – 1815) became Harvard's first professor of anatomy. John's son, John Collins Warren (1778 – 1856), was one of the founders of the MGH, one of the founders of the *New England Journal of Medicine,* and a remarkable surgeon (he did the first operation for strangulated hernia and was the surgeon who operated in the historic ether demonstration). His son, Jonathan Mason Warren (1811 – 1867), is credited with introducing plastic surgery to America, and Mason's son John Collins Warren (1842 – 1927) wrote the first complete explanation of Listerian antiseptic treatment of wounds (*NEJM,* October 7 1869).

The best-known view of the MGH is of the facade of the White Building (1939), which features an art deco column of bay windows extending the entire height of the building. The lobby and interior are not comparably impressive. However, if you walk through the White Building on its main floor and into the adjacent Bigelow Building you will find a wonderful little chapel that is well worth seeing. Designed to resemble a French provincial church, it is built entirely of stone, with the interior dominated by a beautiful rose window, mostly of Chartres blue.

A nice place to sit and have a snack is the cafeteria in the very modern, glass-enclosed Ambulatory Care Center (1982). This fronts on the broad expanse of lawn leading up to the Bulfinch Building. In the lobby of the ACC there is a beautifully restored horse-drawn MGH ambulance.

If you exit the ACC and bear left on the Bulfinch Green (close to the buildings, between the White and Bulfinch Buildings) you will see a cement well. Inside are several sturdy timbers. These are some of the original pilings from the MGH dock, which once extended out into the Charles River at this site, and where many of the hospital's patients once arrived.

Another building worth seeing is the old Resident Physician's House, about a block away from the hospital entrance, at the corner of Cambridge Street and North Grove Street. Built by the MGH in 1891 as a home for John W Pratt, the hospital's director, this fine old brick building has been moved twice. It reached its present location in 1981. Currently surrounded by a brick and cast-iron fence and in the shadow of two huge parking garages, the building is used mainly as a hospitality center for special gatherings.

Though the MGH currently has no regularly scheduled tours available (except the Bulfinch tour described above), visitors are welcome to explore the public spaces described above during daylight hours.

(8) *Massachusetts Eye and Ear Infirmary* 243 Charles Street 02114. (617) 523-7900. This institution is remarkable and impressive in

Massachusetts Eye and Ear Infirmary — new building enveloping the old *(Courtesy of the Abraham Pollen Archives and Rare Book Library of the Massachusetts Eye and Ear Infirmary)*

many respects, the most obvious of which is its architecture. The MEEI building is unique: it embodies an imaginative solution to the problem of preserving an historic building while integrating the newest of technology, in that a 16-story modern structure has been built above and around an older one.

The Infirmary's history goes back to 1824, when two young surgeons opened a one-room clinic to treat the various eye disorders that disabled many of Boston's working poor. Soon the clinic had more work than it could handle, and its facilities and scope were expanded. In 1827 Bostonians established the Massachusetts Charitable Eye and Ear Infirmary. For most of the nineteenth century, over half of the Infirmary's eye patients were afflicted with trachoma, an infectious disease now extremely rare in the United States.

The Infirmary's most famous patient was Annie Sullivan, who went on to become the renowned teacher of Helen Keller. Sullivan had been blinded by trachoma at age eight; her vision was blocked by a pannus, or coating on her cornea. First abandoned, then orphaned, then an almshouse resident, she became the second patient on whom a new surgical procedure for this disorder was attempted—and the first to have the operation succeed.

The MEEI has been a teaching institution almost from the beginning. Lectures were begun in 1830 and were formalized as a course of instruction for Tremont Medical School in 1837 (Tremont was later assimilated by Harvard Medical School). The eye service became affiliated with HMS in 1869, and the ear service developed a similar affiliation in 1888.

Over the years MEEI has played a seminal role in the development of two specialties: ophthalmology and otolaryngology. Shortly after the turn of the century it set up the first eye pathology laboratory in the country. In the early 1920s it established the country's first endowed eye research lab. Together with Harvard Medical School, it appointed the first full-time professor of otolaryngology in 1932. Other notable achievements include the following: the first diagnosis (and naming) of retrolental fibroplasia, the blindness in infants caused by exposure to too much oxygen; the discovery of the first drug to cure a viral disease (herpes simplex infection of the cornea); and the establishment of the first clinic devoted to the care and treatment of patients with detached retina.

Today MEEI sits next door to the Massachusetts General Hospital, occupying a 16-story treatment, research, and training tower that blends almost imperceptibly, on the inside, with the much smaller 1899 building, over and around which it sits. The library is particularly spacious and attractive; its collection makes it one of the most frequently consulted libraries of its kind in the world. The archives and rare book collection — containing objects dating back to the fourteenth century — are housed in an elegant wood-paneled room with glass-fronted bookcases and a huge walnut conference table, all visible from the hallway via a large glass picture window.

Tours can be arranged in advance by telephone: call 573-3163.

(9) *Brigham and Women's Hospital* 75 Francis Street 02115. (617) 732-5500. This hospital was completed in 1980, as a result of merger discussions that had taken place at least since 1958. The BWH is the culmination of four institutional histories, the longest of which belongs to the **Boston Lying-In Hospital,** founded in 1832.

Lying-In occupied a number of sites over the years, starting with a small house in Boston's South End. From the first it was a model maternity hospital, pioneering numerous obstetrical developments. It was the first American maternity hospital to use anesthesia (1847), the first to use a water-heated bassinet (1880), the first to have a mothers' milk bank (1930), and the first to perform an exchange transfusion in the treatment of erythroblastosis fetalis, or hemolytic disease of the newborn (1947).

In 1966, Lying-In merged with the **Free Hospital for Women** to form the **Boston Hospital for Women.** The Free Hospital dated from 1875 and had been an early hospital specializing in gynecology, with a Harvard Medical School affiliation dating from the turn of the century. Notable firsts stemming from this institution included the identification and description of the earliest human embryo ever discovered, composed of just 30 cells, only a few hours after fertilization (1950), the first reports on the effectiveness of oral contraceptives (1959), and the first detailed descriptions of female sex hormones and their metabolic pathways (1961). In 1973 the Boston Hospital for Women developed noninvasive fetal monitoring, which allowed physicians and nurses to detect fetal distress during pregnancy and labor. In 1980, Women's performed the first successful intrauterine decompression of a child with hydrocephalus. (The 1895 building that was home to the Free Hospital for Women still stands in Brookline, at the corner of Pond and Cumberland Avenues. The grace and charm of this orange-yellow brick building, with its profusion of arches and gables (see photo), is even more impressive when one realizes that the building was not built to entice the rich but rather to add dignity and importance to an institution designed to serve the poor. After being abandoned for many years, the Free Hospital is now an ingeniously designed col-

Free Hospital for Women, now condominiums *(By permission of Brigham and Women's Hospital Archives)*

lection of 70 apartments of diverse sizes and shapes, tucked into every part of the old building, including the boiler room.)

BWH's third component was the **Peter Bent Brigham Hospital,** which opened in 1913 as a result of a bequest by a Boston merchant, providing for the "indigent sick of Suffolk County." From the beginning the hospital has been located beside, and has had very close ties with, Harvard Medical School. It was here that the entire field of neurosurgery was developed from 1913 to 1932, due largely to the work of Harvey Cushing. While Cushing was chief surgeon here, he almost single-handedly reduced the mortality in brain surgery from almost 100 percent to less than 10 percent. Using his work in dogs and apes as a foundation, he developed an understanding of how to predict the location of tumors in the brain by observing a patient's symptoms. The Brigham also was the first American hospital to have a dietetic internship (1914), the first to assist the respirations of a polio patient with a Drinker Respirator, or iron lung (1929), the first to use and perfect the artificial kidney machine in clinical use (1947), the first to successfully repair stenotic mitral heart valves (1948), the first to use plastic bags to collect, store, and transfuse blood (1949), and the first to achieve survival of a patient after total adrenalectomy, by substituting hormonal therapy for natural function (1950). In fact, PBBH has been at the forefront of endocrinology (especially the research and treatment of adrenal disease) since Harvey Cushing identified and described the trilogy of flabby obesity, hypertension, and diabetes that came to be known as Cushing's syndrome. PBBH also achieved the first successful kidney transplant between identical twins (1954) and between nonidentical twins (1959). It was here that the lactate dehydrogenase (LDH) measurement was developed as a test for myocardial infarction, pulmonary embolism, and various types of cancer (1960), that the first artificial aortic valve was implanted (1962), and that direct electrical current was first used to restore the rhythm of an electrically disordered heart (1962).

The fourth institution involved in the merger was the **Robert B. Brigham Hospital,** a hospital for destitute incurables that was founded in 1903 by a nephew of Peter Bent Brigham. Some 22 years passed between the time these hospitals first started talking about merging and the actual accomplishment of the merger. Some of the delay was due to conflicts about how much autonomy each of the components would have to relinquish in order to achieve the union, some was due to administrative and leadership problems, and a lot was due to the tenor of the times. Once a site was selected, the consortium served notice on neighborhood residents and tenants to expect eviction within five years. This, however, was 1969, and the result was student protests, sit-ins, protests by neighborhood and taxpayer opposition groups, and the like. In the meantime, the cost of construction rose from an estimate of some $40 million to a figure almost four times that.

What eventually resulted is an interesting collection of buildings, with some components that are both attractive and innovative. The dominant structure is a 16-story hospital tower (1980), with a cloverleaf design, in which the four nearly circular patient units on each floor allow nurses in the central nursing station to visually monitor patients in every room. If you go to some of the upper floors and look down on the various lower buildings around the tower, you'll see a few anachronistic slate roofs with copper flashing—remnants of the old PBBH pavilion system that have survived various attempts at remodeling. The Ambulatory Services Building II (1987) is a real stunner, built around a vast atrium with a plaza filled with trees and walkways, and balconies that seem to float in the air. From the street it seems perfectly in scale with the three-story residential buildings opposite. A couple of blocks away, at 221 Longwood Avenue, the 1922 edition of the Boston Lying-In still stands, with some metallic fourth- and fifth-floor additions grafted onto the graceful original structure (look carefully for the bas-relief children on the facade).

Tours are sometimes available. Call for details (732-5652).

(Old) New England Hospital for Women and Children 55 Dimock
Street 02119. (617) 442-8800. The New England Hospital for
Women and Children deserves enshrinement as much as any other
medical institution in the Boston area. For many years this was one
of the few places in the country where women physicians could
gain house-officer experience, and it is a major nursing landmark.
   The New England Hospital for Women and Children was
founded in 1862 by Dr Marie Zakrzewska. Dr Zak, as she was
called, had been a midwife in Germany before emigrating to the
United States. With the help of Dr Elizabeth Blackwell she took her
medical training at the Cleveland Medical College, after which she
returned to New York to help the Blackwell sisters found the New
York Infirmary for Women. In 1862 Dr Zak came to Boston to teach
obstetrics at the short-lived New England Female Medical College
(1848 – 1873). Since the college had no hospital, Dr Zak founded
the New England Hospital for Women and Children.
   In 1872 Dr Zak was joined by Dr Susan Dimock, a Massachusetts
native who had been refused admission at Harvard Medical School
and who therefore had taken her medical degree at the University
of Zurich. Dr Dimock came to the NEHWC as its new director, and
simultaneously founded the hospital's school for nurses. Her tenure was brief, however, as she died in a boating accident in 1875.
The current Dimock Community Health Center and the street on
which it is located are named in her honor.
   The School of Nursing's first student arrived after seeing a notice
on a bookstore bulletin board, and promptly signed up for instruction as the school's lone student. A year later Dr Dimock handed
her a diploma; thus Linda Richards became the nation's first trained
nurse. Miss Richards then went to Bellevue, in New York, where
she became night superintendent of the hospital's training school,
developing a roughly-made chart for following her patients' temperatures and pulses (the forerunner of today's vital-signs charts
used in hospitals the world over). Later Richards went on to become
Superintendent of the Training School of the Massachusetts General Hospital (1874) and the founder of Boston City Hospital's
training school (1878). Her boundless energy led her to organize
and/or lead schools of nursing at numerous other hospitals, including the Brooklyn Homeopathic Hospital, the Hartford Hospital, University of Pennsylvania Hospital, the Taunton Insane Hospital, the Worcester Hospital for the Insane and the Michigan
Insane Hospital in Kalamazoo. As a result she became the most
influential person in the development of American nursing.
   Another early graduate of the NEHWC Training School for
Nurses was Mary Mahoney, who received her diploma in 1879,

becoming America's first black nursing graduate. By this time, the course of instruction had been expanded to 16 months, and the school had become larger and much better organized. There were 40 applicants for Miss Mahoney's class, of whom only 18 were accepted and only three graduated, including Miss Mahoney and two white women. By 1899 the hospital had graduated six black nurses. (*See also* Gravesite of Mary Mahoney, p 70.)

The Training School was rechristened a "School of Nursing" in the 1930s, but the institution's professional dominance gradually faded, and the school graduated its last class in 1951. The hospital closed its inpatient service in 1969; the Dimock Community Health Center, a community-based outpatient program, was opened in its stead.

The Roxbury section of Boston, in which the Center is located, is 90 percent black, and many of its residents are poor and have multiple health problems. Still, the area is on the edge of Boston's downtown, and its glorious but deteriorated older buildings are slowly being renovated, some gorgeously. Sales prices for homes are rising rapidly as the gentry moves into the area. In this environment, the eight buildings on the Dimock's nine-acre property have been coveted for possible condominium use—or, failing that, for demolition to make room for more modern and "useful" structures.

The Dimock's buildings date from 1872, when the NEHWC

New England Hospital for Women and Children, now Dimock *(Courtesy of the Society for the Preservation of New England Antiquities)*

moved to the site. A number of the structures are quite spectacular. The Zakrzewska building (see photo) — a mass of spires, bay windows, dormers, and arcade-like porches — was built in 1873, but has been abandoned for many years. It is undergoing renovation. The Sewall Building, NEHWC's old obstetric unit, still sports an old stork weather vane and a bronze stork embedded in the floor of the front porch. The old laundry building, after lying dormant for 30 years, has been thoroughly remodeled, complete with slate roof, and now houses the nation's first facility for pregnant incarcerated women. The old Carey Cottage (the smaller building in the photo), vintage 1872, houses a residential treatment facility for substance abusers.

Today the Dimock is a community health center with many busy clinics, serving a predominantly low-income and minority population. Space in some of the older buildings has been rented to a variety of other nonprofit institutions, such as day-care centers and job training programs. The grounds are overgrown with vegetation, many of the buildings show considerable evidence of deterioration, and the staff limps along with a spartan budget, but this is clearly a special place. Call the public relations office to arrange a tour.

(10) *Boston City Hospital* 818 Harrison Avenue 02118. (617) 424-5000. Boston's citizens started campaigning for a city hospital in 1849, but opposition from the Massachusetts General Hospital (which didn't want the competition) and Harvard Medical School (who feared the hospital might spawn a rival school) delayed the opening until 1864. For most of its early years, BCH's primary patient population were poor, foreign-born Irish. Bed capacity expanded rapidly from the initial 200 beds, to 600 at the turn of the century, to 2400 in the 1940s. Much of the hospital's growth in the early twentieth century was due to the influence of Mayor Curley, who took a special interest in the hospital during his lengthy and colorful tenure in the Mayor's office (the present Pediatric Building, completed in 1933, was originally known as the Mary Curley Building, in honor of the mayor's wife). By comparison to the budgets of public hospitals in other cities, Curley fairly poured money into BCH, making it one of the finest hospitals in the country — in return using BCH as a repository for patronage jobs, resulting in a dramatic overabundance of orderlies, charwomen, laborers, and the like.

From its beginnings BCH has had strong academic affiliations. In its earliest years these affiliations were dominated by Harvard Medical School, which continued its presence here for 110 years. In the middle years of the twentieth century, all three Boston medical schools (Harvard, Boston University, and Tufts) had teaching services here; but as BCH's financial problems became increasingly severe (along with those of many other city and county hospitals in the country), the hospital's functioning deteriorated dramatically, resulting in a loss of accreditation in 1970. In 1972 BCH managed to regain its accreditation, but the city then slashed its budget by 20 percent. In the ensuing turmoil, both HMS and Tufts pulled out. Since 1974 BU has had sole responsibility for student and housestaff teaching at BCH.

In some respects, BCH hit its peak of influence and national reputation during the 1920s and 1930s, when it had world-famous departments of medicine, surgery, infectious disease, and pathology. The infectious disease department here was home to Dr Maxwell Finland, who for decades was the country's most important expert in the testing and evaluation of antimicrobial agents. The Thorndike Memorial Laboratory, established in 1921 (the building still exists at BCH, but the corporate entity has moved on), was home to George Minot (who won the Nobel Prize in 1934 for his work on pernicious anemia), William Castle (who discovered the "intrinsic factor" necessary for the absorption of vitamin B_{12}), Tracy Putnam and Houston Merritt (who discovered the antiseizure properties of phenytoin, or Dilantin), as well as many others.

The BCH was originally designed on the pavilion plan, with a central administration building flanked by two wards on each side. As additional buildings were constructed, they were added railroad-car fashion in two parallel strings, extending backward on either side of the administration building, with each string connected by a seemingly endless half-submerged tunnel. The present administration building is a replacement and dates from 1931, but the two old ward buildings, BCD on the left and FGH on the right, date from 1864. Other older buildings include the Sears (1877) and the Peabody (1909). Since the hospital fell on hard times, beginning in the 1950s, significant improvements to the aging physical plant have been nonexistent, and many of the buildings are now unusable and essentially abandoned. It's an eerie experience to wander through some of these old warriors, run-down and vandalized, littered with outdated remnants of patient care, with here and there such elegant features as arched marble fireplaces that once functioned as part of the hospital's complex heating and ventilation system. Unless the local historical society is successful in its attempts to save and restore some of these buildings (money is short), most will be demolished in the next few years.

To replace the services rendered by all the older facilities, BCH has built a modern and rather plain white contemporary blockhouse (1977), which contains a 450-bed acute-care general hospital and the usual profusion of clinics.

The staff is amenable to giving tours to interested parties, though sufficient manpower is not always available. Call for details.

(11) *Children's Hospital Medical Center* 300 Longwood Avenue 02115. (617) 735-6420. Boston Children's is the nation's second-oldest children's hospital (1869), yielding only to the one in Philadelphia (1855). The hospital's list of firsts and major contibutions is substantial:

1891	First laboratory for the testing and modification of milk "certified" as being free of disease-causing bacteria
1946	First description of Rh transfusion reactions, the condition resulting from an incompatibility between the blood of the baby and the blood of the mother (by Dr Louis Diamond)
1949	First successful culture of the polio virus (by Dr John Enders and colleagues, who won the Nobel Prize in 1954 for this landmark contribution)
1954	First culture of the measles virus, leading to the development of a vaccine (again by Dr John Enders and his team)

Children's Hospital began in 1869 as a 20-bed facility in Boston's South End, and its history mirrors the nation's views of what seemed to be necessary and appropriate care of sick children. Until the turn of the century, kids under the age of two years weren't even admitted to the hospital, as it was thought impossible to alter the course of an illness in one so young. For many years parents were forbidden to visit their sick children, since the prevailing dogma held that parents only spread infection and demoralized the youngsters. Only as recently as the 1950s were parents allowed to visit their children, and during strictly limited hours (initially restricted to Sundays only). The "rooming in" policy—in which the parents actually "sleep over" in their children's hospital room — was begun only in the 1970s.

Today, the dominant and newest building at Children's is a dramatic 10-story hospital, erected in 1987, which more nearly resembles a luxury hotel than a traditional hospital. One approaches the hospital via a covered drive that leads to a circular automobile courtyard, above which the angular bulk of the hospital gradually recedes in a series of setbacks. Directly above the entrance there is a "tower of light", a 10-story spire of sun rooms and play rooms, which reflect sunlight in the daytime and radiate electric light at night. The appearance is particularly impressive after dark, though daylight makes it easier to get a feel for how the new building has been integrated into the preexisting maze of old (1930s) and newer (1956) buildings. Inside the lobby there is a glass-enclosed "Winter Garden" with serpentine benches, birch trees, rhododendrons, and azaleas.The old Hunnewell Building, at 300 Longwood Avenue, is a neoclassical hulk, its portico supported by four huge Corinthian columns (near roof level there is a bas-relief of a seminude child) topped by a huge dome.

Children's Hospital does not provide tours, but everything described here is open for public viewing.

Mt. Auburn Hospital 330 Mount Auburn Street, Cambridge 02238. Many hospitals have been founded by groups of nurses, most notably by the various orders of Catholic nursing Sisters, but this is one of the few founded by an individual nurse. Emily Parsons (1824– 1880) was 37 years old when the Civil War began. Despite such handicaps as lameness and impaired eyesight she had a passionate wish to help others less fortunate than herself, and became determined to be an Army nurse. She worked as a volunteer nurse at the Massachusetts General Hospital for a year and a half to pick up necessary skills. (This was well before the establishment of professional nursing schools.) She then became an Army nurse, first assigned to Fort Schuyler in New York, then to St Louis, and finally to a large hospital ship stationed upriver from Vicksburg, Mississippi. After completing her Army service she returned to Cambridge and at once resolved to remedy her hometown's lack of a hospital. Almost single-handedly she conceived the idea of the hospital, raised the funds, opened it, and operated it in its early years. The Parsons Building, built in 1886, is named in her honor.

At its inception the facility was called the Cambridge Hospital. The name was changed to Mt Auburn Hospital in 1947 to avoid confusion with the more recent Cambridge City Hospital.

Mt Auburn also has the distinction of being the birthplace of the only reigning monarch of American birth. On December 5, 1927, the boy who was to become King Bhumibol Adulyadej of Thailand was born here.

Mt Auburn is probably one of the most prettily situated hospitals in the country, located as it is along a pleasant stretch of the Charles River, with a lovely stretch of meadow on the opposite bank. Harvard Square is just a few minutes' walk away. Today, it is a full-service, acute-care, 305-bed hospital, with teaching affiliations involving all three Boston medical schools.

(12) *New England Deaconess Hospital* 185 Pilgrim Road 02215. (617) 732-8046. The Deaconess is the third largest hospital in Boston and

a major teaching facility for the Harvard Medical School. Its history is intimately intertwined with that of its own School of Nursing; both were founded in 1896. The impetus for the establishment of these institutions came from a group of Methodist deaconesses, and for the first several years only women who had committed themselves to service in the church were admitted to the School of Nursing. In 1899 the School was reorganized to provide a standard professional course, and other women who wished to become nurses were admitted. To this day, however, while the School is denominationally independent, its trustees and faculty strive to uphold the Christian ideals upon which it was founded. Well over 3000 students have graduated from what is now a three-year diploma program.

The first hospital was a 14-bed affair located on Massachusetts Avenue. The hospital rapidly outgrew its quarters, and in 1907 a 50-bed facility was opened on the present site. In the 1920s physician staff member Elliot P Joslin became a nationally prominent expert on the treatment of diabetes, combining research, strict treatment protocols, and careful patient education; his work helped to transform NEDH from a small local hospital to a large academic medical center with international ties. As diabetics started to live longer, the long-term complications of the disease began to appear, and NEDH strengthened its programs in treating peripheral vascular disease and eye, nerve, and kidney problems. In 1928 NEDH opened the first hospital foot clinic; it took the landmark step of bestowing staff privileges on a chiropodist (podiatrist) in 1929. Other medical firsts at NEDH include the first hospital blood bank for platelets, through a pioneering method for isolating and storing this blood component (1959); the first radiation-therapy research laboratory in the country (Shields Warren Radiation Laboratory, 1965); and the first intraoperative radiation-therapy unit installed in a standard surgical suite (1981).

The NEDH now occupies a 15-building complex in the Longwood area. Tours are not available at present.

(13) *Joslin Diabetes Center* 1 Joslin Place 02215. (617) 732-2400. This world-famous institution had its beginnings in 1898 as the private practice of Dr Elliott P Joslin (1869–1962). Basically a general internist, Joslin developed a special interest in diabetes early in his practice years. By 1916 he had published the first edition of his *Treatment of Diabetes Mellitus,* which rapidly became the standard text in the field. At about the same time Joslin released his *Diabetic Manual,* a self-help and patient education manual, which is now in its twelfth edition and is available in a number of foreign-language

editions. Joslin's approach, based on his meticulous observation of 1000 patients, emphasized precise blood-sugar control. His critics accused him of being stern, strict, and judgmental, but the patients who could follow his rigorous and demanding regimens did relatively well compared to those cared for by other physicians. When insulin was discovered, in 1922, and people with diabetes started to live more than a few years after diagnosis, Joslin's practice became a mecca for people with the disease. Joslin didn't actually invent or discover anything; instead he was a master synthesizer, public educator, and proselytizer. Gradually other physicians joined him, and services were expanded to deal with the disease's complications (e.g., eye, kidney, and vascular disease). In 1952 the group practice was formally named the Joslin Clinic. The present name was adopted in 1981.

The current center is in a five-story building that takes up a whole block. The most dramatic view of this cement, steel, and glass stucture is from the central courtyard, which can be reached most directly from a narrow pedestrian alleyway extending from Pilgrim Road. The angled and sloping facade seems to connect the building's interior with the courtyard, making the building seem open and accessible. On the ground level, near the elevators, there's a nice pictorial wall display illustrating the development of the Joslin Center. On the next level up is a fascinating wall-mounted display that traces the history of diabetes back to 1500 BC, when the disease was first described in the Papyrus Ebers. There are no formal tours available, but what I have described here is accessible to public viewing.

(14) *Beth Israel Hospital* 330 Brookline Avenue 02215. (617) 735-2000. The BI is relatively young compared to other prestigious hospitals in Boston. It was founded in 1902 as the Mt Sinai Dispensary in Boston's West End; that facility was closed in 1916, when the first BI was opened in Roxbury. Though the hospital was nonsectarian in the provision of care, the main purpose in its founding was to provide a place where Jewish patients could be served kosher food and be taken care of by people who understood their language and customs. In 1928 the hospital moved to the Brookline Avenue site; at about the same time the BI established its durable teaching affiliation with Harvard. Today, all of its chiefs-of-services and most of its staff physicians hold Harvard appointments.

Over the years the BI has achieved many distinctions. It was the first hospital anywhere to publish a patients' bill of rights (1972) and the first major medical center to implement a hospital-wide program of primary nursing care (1975). The key ingredient of this program is that each patient is assigned to one primary nurse, who is then responsible for around-the-clock nursing care plan. Any nurses who care for the patient on other shifts report to the primary nurse. This is thought to promote more consistent, more personalized care than the typical team-nursing approach—and patient satisfaction surveys seem to bear that out.

In fact, nursing has been a particularly strong feature of the BI ever since it started its own school of nursing, in 1918. Though the school folded in 1962, the BI retains its reputation as a nurse-oriented medical center. The BI has established a Nurse Scholar program, whereunder individual staff nurses are encouraged to develop their own research projects; and a Center for the Advancement of Nursing Practice, to promote professional growth and scholarly achievement.

The BI also has a strong research program, consistently ranking in the top 10 among the nation's independent hospitals in federal research monies received. The external cardiac pacemaker was developed here and was first installed here, in 1952. The BI also developed and first used the cardiac monitor (1955) and the cardiac defibrillator (1956). The Thorndike Memorial Laboratory was transferred here in 1973. The BI was the first hospital to successfully use catheter-mounted balloon valvuloplasty in the nonsurgical treatment of diseased heart valves (1986).

The BI is now a busy, modern 460-bed teaching hospital with a collection of buildings clustered around the principal hospital structure. Though the administration is not keen on giving tours, there are at least two exhibit areas accessible to the interested visitor. On the first floor of the Raab building there is an interesting collection of photographs, artifacts, and documents gathered in the Coven Gallery. On the second floor of the Stoneman Building, near the administrative offices, visitors can see a wall-mounted time line that traces BI's history from its origins to the present day. In a nearby hallway there are dozens of bronze placques, commemorating donations of time and money. Such signs of appreciation to donors are found in many Jewish-sponsored hospitals: buildings, wards, surgical and administrative suites, even elevators, are named in honor of the people who supplied the wherewithal for their creation.

Tours are available for special groups only, and only by prior arrangement (735-4431).

(15)*Massachusetts Mental Health Center* 74 Fenwood Road 02115. (617) 734-1300. This modest set of brick buildings, about a block from Brigham and Women's Hospital, houses the present-day descendant of the Boston Psychopathic Hospital, a pioneer in modern psychiatric treatment. The present facility (likely to be torn down soon and replaced by one substantially larger) doesn't look like a psychiatric hospital; indeed, in the early days it was never much more than a short-stay receiving facility, designed for acute rather than chronic care. The lobby nonetheless is an inviting place, with two black marble fireplaces, oak paneling throughout, and a floor made of four kinds of marble.

When it was founded, in 1912, the "Psycho" was one of the nation's first psychiatric teaching hospitals. As such it contributed mightily to the evolution of psychiatric thinking in this country, both because of specific developments and because of the legions of future psychiatric leaders who trained here (most prominently including Karl Menninger). An early appointee was Miss Mary Jarrett, who founded this country's first training program in psychiatric social work. In its first decade the Psycho introduced the concept of "home-visiting" to psychiatric institutions in this country. In the 1950s, the Psycho started the day-hospital movement, in which patients stayed at the hospital during the day to participate in therapeutic programs and returned to their own homes at night. Not all the Psycho's activities would be regarded as enlightened from today's perspective, however: during the 1930s seclusion and restraint were used freely, and hydrotherapy was considered an efficacious calming technique; and in the 1940s a substantial percentage of patients received electroconvulsive treatment, insulin shock, and such surgical treatments as prefrontal lobotomy.

In 1956 the institution dropped the "Psycho" label and became the Massachusetts Mental Health Center. In 1967 it assumed responsibility for a geographic catchment area characterized by a multiracial, multiethnic, largely poor population. Since then much of its patient load has been drawn from among those chronically ill individuals who were released from the state hospitals in the deinstitutionalization of the 1970s. There is still a small inpatient unit on the premises, however. There are no tours available at present.

(16)*Forsyth Dental Center* 140 The Fenway 02115. (617) 262-5200. When the Forsyth opened its doors, in 1915, dentists were still rare outside major metropolitan areas; and the dentists that did exist spent little time caring for children. The Forsyth (named for the founder, James Bennett Forsyth, who had made his money in the rubber industry) was a pioneer institution in bringing dental care to children. Parochial- and public-school children were brought here in great numbers and shown into a vast room (about 170 feet long) lined with scores of dental chairs. It all sounds very impersonal now, but when it opened it must have seemed a very grand place to the children. The walls were lined with colored tiles depicting Rip van Winkle, the Pied Piper, and other storybook characters. Great effort was expended to make the children feel welcome. As other dental institutions followed the Forsyth's lead and started offering care to children, the uniqueness of the Forsyth's postgraduate training program in children's dentistry gradually faded, and it expanded its services to include adult patients.

In its early years, however, the Forsyth (and the Eastman Dispensary in Rochester, New York) represented a major innovation that led to a half-century of free dental programs designed for schoolchildren. In the 1920s, there were as many as 500 dental-clinic programs in the public schools in various parts of the country; these programs remained popular and widespread until well into the 1960s. With the dawning of the 1970s, public-health officials began to emphasize the concept of "mainstreaming" the poor, sending them to private dental offices instead of to huge clinics, which increasingly were viewed as impersonal, ill equipped, and often demeaning. The school dentistry programs largely faded away.

The Forsyth started its School of Dental Hygiene in 1916. In 1948 it initiated a controversial educational experiment in which it tried to train dental hygienists to take over some functions normally performed by dentists, including the filling of cavities. The school came under such criticism from the dental profession that the experiment had to be dropped after only a year. In the 1960s the School of Dental Hygiene was the largest in the world, graduating over 100 students each year. The Forsyth began developing its research capacity in the 1960s, and it is now the largest private dental research facility in the world.

Few people looking at this monumental building for the first time would guess that it housed a dental clinic. The structure is made of white marble, neoclassical in design, and surrounded by a wrap-around arcade of Ionic columns. Be sure to see the bronze-relief doors, especially those on the children's side entrance that show scenes from Lewis Carroll's *Alice's Adventures in Wonderland* and Joel Chandler Harris's "Uncle Remus" stories. The abundance of tile lining the interior still includes the fanciful and colorful tiles that delighted children 75 years ago. The Forsyth welcomes visitors, but requests that they call in advance to make arrangements.

(17) *Dana-Farber Cancer Institute* 44 Binney Street 02115. (617) 732-3000. This is a relatively young institution (for Boston), but has nonetheless made substantial contributions. In 1947, the year

of its founding (as the Children's Cancer Research Foundation), its staff announced the first remissions ever achieved in acute leukemia; they had accomplished this with chemotherapy (using a compound called aminopterin). Though at that time it was the world's only major center devoted to fighting childhood cancer, the Institute expanded its mandate in 1969 to include cancer patients of all ages. The name was changed in 1983 to honor the Institute's most generous benefactor (The Charles H Dana Foundation) and the Institute's own founder and first director, Sidney Farber. Because of his work in changing acute leukemia from a uniformly fatal disease to one in which treatment is now often successful, Dr Farber is widely regarded as the father of the modern era of chemotherapy for neoplastic disease. In 1954 Dr Farber and colleagues developed a method of treating Wilms' tumors (using actinomycin D) that more than doubled the long-term survival rates, raising them from 40 percent to 90 percent.

The main building is a 17-story tower, divided about half-and-half between research and patient care. The newest building (1988), the Louis B Mayer Research Laboratories, honors the movie mogul who was once Dr Farber's patient and who established a foundation that contributed $5 million to the building's creation. The oldest building (1952) is called the Jimmy Fund Building, a name many Bostonians use to refer to the entire complex. The Jimmy Fund originated on May 22, 1948, in a "media event" choreographed by the Variety Club of Boston. A number of baseball stars from the Boston Braves paid a visit to the hospital to see a devout young Braves fan (named Jimmy) who had been stricken with cancer. The meeting was recorded in a nine-minute segment for the then nationally popular "Truth or Consequences" radio program, hosted by Ralph Edwards. Edwards concluded the joyful and emotionally charged gathering by making an appeal for funds to help Jimmy. The 1952 building was the result. Even today the Institute's primary grass-roots, fundraising organization still goes by the name "The Jimmy Fund." There are no tours available.

(18) *Francis A Countway Library of Medicine* 10 Shattuck Street 02115. (617) 732-2142. This gorgeous modern building (1965) houses one of the foremost medical libraries in the world. Actually, there are two libraries here which have been combined and function as one. The older of the two belongs to Harvard Medical School, but the larger and historically more interesting belongs to the Boston Medical Library, founded in 1875 by Oliver Wendell Holmes and a group of other distinguished Boston physicians. The latter is now the property of the Boston Medical Society.

The Countway contains virtually all the great works of medical history from 1501 onward, as well as 778 incunabula (books printed before 1501). Here is one of the world's best collections of medical Hebraica and Judaica, ranging from the fourteenth to the nineteenth century. The Countway is particularly rich in American books published between 1668 and 1820, English books published from 1475 to 1700, and European books published from the sixteenth century onward. The modern collection, both books and periodicals, contains a huge and growing number of Russian, and a rapidly increasing collection of Chinese, publications.

In design, the Countway was intended to blend with the neo-classical monumental Harvard Medical School buildings on the Quadrangle, which is adjacent. The architects therefore chose a square, vertical structure of eight stories (two below ground), set in a sunken court, the exterior covered with a buff-colored limestone. The interior is stunning, with a large central court seven stories high. On entering, you encounter a huge elliptical stairwell with double floating stairways leading downward. Everywhere there are carpets, drapes, tasteful furnishings (including comfortable chairs), and, of course, books. The fifth floor, called the History of Medicine Floor, especially impresses the visitor. The various reading rooms here are furnished with black leather reading chairs , an occasional wood burning fireplace, rare engravings on the walls, and historic memorabilia.

The library faces onto what is little more than an alley between the old Peter Bent Brigham Hospital and Building A of Harvard Medical School. This was originally intended to become a broad mall, similar to the Harvard Medical School Quadrangle, but these plans remain in limbo. The library is intended primarily for use by students and scholars associated with its sponsors, so anyone with a tie to Harvard or to the Boston Medical Society is welcome. Other physicians, as a courtesy extended by the BMS, are allowed three visits per year. Others who can qualify as bona fide medical researchers are welcome to apply for privileges. Hours are 8 AM to 11:30 PM Monday through Friday, with more restricted hours on weekends and holidays. There are currently no tours.

(19)*Mugar Memorial Library* 771 Commonwealth Avenue 02215. (617) 353-3696. The Mugar is owned by Boston University and located on its main (non-medical) campus. Within the building is a remarkable group of special collections, one of which is the History of Nursing Archives. Established in 1966 with the help of a US Public Health Service grant, this collection has grown to become the most important collection on nursing history in this country.

There is a large section devoted to Florence Nightingale, including books, manuscripts, and letters. There are histories and archival materials, relating to numerous nursing organizations, schools, and institutions, that can be found nowhere else. Dozens of nursing leaders have donated papers and memorabilia. The Library also includes a large and growing oral history collection.

The primary purpose of the Nursing Archives is to serve as a research center for scholars and students. Most of the collections are tucked away out of sight, to be brought out into the open only when a specific scholarly purpose is to be served. If you wish to visit you must make special arrangements in advance, in which you describe both your intent and your credentials. The process sounds forbidding, but the staff are pleasant and anxious to expose a wide audience to the treasures collected here — so, if you're interested, give it a try.

Once you arrive at the Mugar, you are ushered into a large, carpeted, well-appointed glass booth where you can examine things at your leisure under the watchful eyes of the staff. The treasures are brought to you one box at a time, and both you and the box are checked before you are allowed to leave.

One irony here is that an original cosponsor of the Nursing Archives was the Boston University School of Nursing, which closed for good in 1988. A number of nursing organizations that had previously used the Archives as a repository for their documents (reportedly including the American Nursing Association) became infuriated at the University for its failure to support nursing education and threatened to withdraw all past and future contributions. As of this writing, the matter has not been resolved.

Hull Life-Saving Museum 1117 Nantasket Avenue, Hull 02045. (617) 925-2570. This small but fascinating museum gives a good sense of this country's earliest system of emergency medical services. Hull is located at the tip of a small spit of land that guards the southern entrance to Boston Harbor. As the gull flies it's only a couple of miles from Boston; but by car, circling the vast harbor, the distance is closer to 20 miles. The white, red-roofed frame structure is a restored lifeboat station. The first "humane societies" for the recovery of drowning victims were established in Holland in 1767; the Massachusetts Humane Society (of which the Hull station was a part) dates back to 1786. The origin of such groups was due in part to a growing realization that people who appeared drowned were not necessarily dead and could, in some circumstances, be resuscitated. The basic principle was first to get the fluid out of the lungs and next to put air into the lungs. One of the first techniques, dating back to the 1770s, was called the inversion method and consisted of hanging the drowning victim upside down by the feet. About the same time, the barrel method came into general use, wherein the victim was draped over a barrel, which was then rolled slightly fore and aft, first increasing and then decreasing the chest pressure. In the early nineteenth century the "trotting horse method" became popular, in which the victim was draped over a horse's back, belly down, so that with each step by the horse the victim was bounced up and down. These and other early methods of what has become CPR are nicely illustrated at the Hull museum. Other displays show how lifesaving stations were organized, staffed, supplied, and operated. MHS stations were the forerunner of the United States Life Saving Service, which merged with the United States Revenue Cutter Service in 1915 to become the United States Coast Guard. The museum is open weekends, 12 to 5 PM. There is a small admission charge.

(18) *Offices of the New England Journal of Medicine* 10 Shattuck Street 02115. (617) 734-9800. The *NEJM* is the oldest continuously published medical journal in the world, and for many years it has been the most influential. With a circulation of 225,000, the *NEJM* is delivered not only to every corner of the United States but also to 140 countries around the world. Every issue is scoured by medical and science writers everywhere, because the *NEJM* has a reputation for publishing studies of landmark importance. Never mind that most non-physicians — and perhaps most physicians as well — are hard-pressed to decipher the precisely phrased language focusing on rarefied topics. What the *NEJM* prints is potentially *news!*

First published in 1812 as the *New England Journal of Medicine and Surgery and Collateral Branches of Science,* the *NEJM* was by no means America's first medical publication. That honor goes to the *Medical Repository,* which appeared in New York in 1797 and survived until 1824. Ten other medical publications preceded the *NEJM,* but none of them survived more than a few years. The Journal became the *Boston Medical and Surgical Journal* in 1828, assuming its present name only in 1928, a few years after it was purchased by the Massachusetts Medical Society.

The *Journal's* editorial offices are now located on the top (sixth) floor of the Countway Library. The business offices are located several miles away in Waltham. There are no tours and no special plaques or exhibits. In a very real sense, each issue of the *Journal* is its own monument.

(20) *First Church of Christ, Scientist* 175 Huntington Avenue 02115. (617) 450-2000. Anyone interested in the history of healing in the

United States will find much of interest here, though little of a strictly medical nature. Mary Baker Eddy's beliefs gained credence at a time when popular distrust of conventional medicine was at its greatest — and appropriately so. The profession had few standards and little scientific basis, and governmental and professional regulation was either absent or minimal. As a result numerous healing systems, some involving outright quackery and bizarre cults, developed to provide the suffering with alternatives to regular medical care.

However Mary Baker Eddy appeared to her contemporaries, both pro and con, the passage of time allows us to view her in a more balanced and understanding fashion. She was clearly a remarkable person. She succeeded, as a woman, in establishing a new Christian denomination in a religion and a society dominated by male leadership; and she succeeded as a layperson in constructing one of the few enduring systems of healing. No health professional who is sensitive to the role a person's spirit plays in many healing situations can ignore her accomplishment.

Eddy (1821–1910) led a turbulent life during her middle years and suffered from recurring bouts of nervous debility and severe, if not very well-defined, physical suffering. In 1866, while reading an account of one of Jesus' healings in the New Testament, she experienced a sudden recovery, which led to nine years of spiritual study. In 1875 she published the book *Science and Health with Key to the Scriptures*. Eddy wanted her book to provide an understanding of the "science" that underlay Jesus' works and the method that made those works repeatable. Healing, in her view, was not a technique or a miraculous intervention; it was a result of spiritual awakening and the acceptance of the ever-present healing Love which is God.

In 1879, Eddy and a small group of followers founded the Church of Christ, Scientist. The adventures and travails of the group's early years were many and often colorful, but the appeal of Eddy's message has endured. Anyone interested in learning more about Christian Science healing has a number of options in the Boston area (Eddy lived and worked in Boston for many years, and there are a number of sites dedicated to her memory), but the most fruitful choice would probably be the church headquarters in Boston's Back Bay, which includes a number of architecturally distinguished buildings (among them the Mother Church), as well as a vast plaza with lovely plantings and a huge reflecting pond. In the lobby of the high-rise administration building, there is an exhibit about Christian healing, as well as informed and interested guides available to answer questions — all available without charge. The Christian Science Center Administration Building is open Monday through Friday, from 8 AM until 4 PM and is open to visitors during this time. Other parts of the Center are open on a more restricted basis, and conducted tours are regularly available. Call for details.

Boylston Street   Anyone who spends much time in Boston will encounter this street often. It runs along one side of the Common and Public Gardens and is one of the city's main thoroughfares. Few know that the street was once known as Frogg Lane, a name that was changed in 1812 to honor Dr Zabdiel Boylston (1679–1766), who gets credit for introducing smallpox inoculation to the Colonies.

The year 1721 was a rough one for Boston. Of the city's 12,000 inhabitants, 6000 became ill with smallpox, and 900 died. The strict theologian Cotton Mather, having learned about variolation — first, from a black slave named Onesimus, who told him of the practice being employed in Africa, and later from an account in the *Transactions* of the London Royal Society, of which he was a member — attempted to persuade Boston physicians to give it a try. At first only Boylston responded. Inoculation is not the same as vaccination with cowpox, which wouldn't come into general use until Jenner's classic work some 80 years later. Boylston took pus from the sores of a man actually sick with the disease and put a small drop on a scratch on the skin of people who had not had the disease. First he tried it on his 13-year-old son and two black servants. They all got the disease, but it was exceedingly mild. Ultimately Boylston inoculated all who would let him, and they fared far better than the rest of the population. A violent controversy ensued. Some maintained that if a patient died after inoculation, the doctor ought to be hanged. (In fact, 6 did die among the 247 inoculated by Boylston and the 39 inoculated by other physicians.) Boylston was attacked on the streets; his home was bombed and set on fire. Some mobs hunted him with nooses, intending to hang him. Eventually, inoculation became accepted and even a socially advantageous experience: matrons gave "smallpox parties," where trendy guests were inoculated.

Mt Auburn Cemetery   580 Mt. Auburn Street, Cambridge 02138. (617) 547-7105. If you are the sort of person who likes to visit graves of the famous, this cemetery is for you. America's oldest garden cemetery (1831), Mt Auburn is huge both in area (170 acres) and in the number of people buried here (80,000). It is also quite beautiful, with flowering shrubs and exotic trees everywhere. The cemetery was founded by Harvard professor Dr Jacob Bigelow as an outgrowth of his concern for sanitary burial practices.

Important figures in health care who have been buried here

include Dorothea Dix, Oliver Wendell Holmes, William TG Morton, and Charles T Jackson. Mary Baker Eddy also finds rest here, in a beautiful eight-columned memorial at the edge of Halcyon Lake. To find particular graves, stop at the office, just inside the Mt Auburn Street entrance, where an excellent map is available.

Dorothea Dix (1802 – 1881) gained fame for her pioneering work in the reform of mental institutions and psychiatric care. Inspired by the social idealism of Unitarianism, she began visiting almshouses and jails and was enraged to find them filled with obviously mentally ill persons living in deplorable conditions. Many states had no public institutions for the mentally ill, and those that did often had makeshift facilities. She gave no speeches and held no indignation meetings; instead, she quietly accumulated statistics and, beginning in 1841, persuaded others to petition legislatures for constructive change, first in Massachusetts and then elsewhere. In all, she is credited with founding 40 mental hospitals in this country, in Europe, and in Japan. At the outbreak of the Civil War she took responsibility for organizing the nursing services of the Union Army, being appointed by Abraham Lincoln to be the first Superintendent of the United States Army Nurses. She lived 85 years, just long enough to see the insane asylums for whose construction she had crusaded become overcrowded, understaffed warehousing operations, sometimes only marginally better than the institutions she had sought to replace. Her grave (on Spruce Avenue) is marked by the simplest of small headstones, ivy-covered and slightly curved on the top, saying only DOROTHEA L. DIX.

Oliver Wendell Holmes (1809 – 1894) was one of the best-known men of his time, both in medicine and outside it. He practiced medicine briefly and then became an academic, first as a professor of anatomy and physiology at Dartmouth College and then, for 35 years, at Harvard Medical School. His poetry first brought him renown when he was 21, well before he became a physician, and propelled him into a lifelong friendship and association with other literary lights of his time, including Emerson, Whittier, Longfellow, Lowell, Hawthorne, Dickens, and others. He was a trenchant observer of everything about him, with a ready wit and a quick turn of phrase. He coined the terms "anaesthetic," "anaesthesia," and "Boston Brahmin." In an 1843 essay entitled "The Contagiousness of Puerperal Fever," he identified doctors and mid-wives themselves as the cause of "child-bed fever," well before Semmelweis was able to demonstrate the fact in Vienna (1847). Holmes was also a founder of the *Atlantic Monthly* (and inventor of its name), and contributed a series of essays entitled "The Autocrat of the Breakfast Table" to its early issues. Holmes is buried, along with his wife, on Lime Avenue, in a grave marked only by a simple stone carrying only their names and the dates of their lives, with no special inscription or decoration.

The contestants for the discovery of ether, however, have much more elaborate graves. William TG Morton's grave (on Spruce Avenue) is marked by a tall spire, topped with an urn from which rises a carved-stone flame. The inscription reads INVENTOR AND REVEALER OF ANESTHETIC INHALATION. Charles T Jackson's gravestone (on Mountain Avenue) declares: EMINENT AS A CHEMIST, MINERALOGIST, GEOLOGIST AND INVESTIGATOR IN ALL DEPARTMENTS OF NATURAL SCIENCE. THROUGH HIS OBSERVATIONS OF THE PECULIAR EFFECTS OF SULPHURIC ETHER ON THE NERVES OF SENSATION AND HIS BOLD DEDUCTION THEREFROM, THE BENIGN DISCOVERY OF PAINLESS SURGERY WAS MADE.

Mt Auburn Cemetery welcomes visitors from 8 AM to 7 PM, from May through September, and until 5 PM the rest of the year.

Grave of Mary Mahoney Woodlawn Cemetery, 302 Elm Street, Everett 02149. (617) 387-0800. The four-foot-tall midnight-black granite monument at 2674 Sable Path in this cemetery commemorates America's first black graduate nurse. Mary Mahoney was buried here in 1926, but for many years the grave received no

Gravestone of Mary Mahoney, America's first black trained nurse *(By permission of Emily Vaughan Wolf)*

special attention. In 1972 it was rediscovered, and in the following year the present monument was erected by Chi Eta Phi (a nursing sorority) and the American Nurses Association.

Mahoney graduated in 1879 from the New England Hospital for Women and Children's Nurses Training School, in the process becoming the nation's first black trained registered nurse. For many years Miss Mahoney performed what we would now call private duty nursing in the homes of clients. This was before the widespread acceptance of hospitals by people of means; most nursing care and even many surgical operations were routinely performed at home. Because of her highly regarded skills, Mahoney's services were sought not only in Boston but also in North Carolina, New Jersey, and Washington, DC. Later she was on the nursing staff of Boston City Hospital. In 1909 she gave the principal address at the first conference of the National Association of Colored Graduate Nurses. In 1919 the NACGN established the Mary Mahoney Award to recognize outstanding achievement. In 1951, when the NACGN merged with the ANA, the latter organization elected to continue the award. Today it is given biennially to a nurse in recognition of significant contributions to interracial relations.

Woodlawn Cemetery is one of the country's oldest non-sectarian garden-type burial sites. The grounds are open from 8 AM until sunset, and are about 10–15 minutes north of Boston by car.

(21)*Ether Monument* Boston Public Garden (near the intersection of Arlington and Marlborough streets). This monument is impressive as a manifestation of public sentiment concerning a landmark medical event. The monument itself is composed of a four-sided granite base, each side set off by a pair of rose marble pillars highlighting an alcove containing a bas-relief sculpture and an inscription. One of the inscriptions commemorates "the discovery that the inhaling of ether causes insensibility to pain, first proved to the world at the Massachusetts General Hospital in Boston, October 1846." This inscription tactfully avoids naming the individuals responsible for the event, since at the time the monument was erected (1847) several of the principals vehemently disagreed on how much credit was owed to whom. Desire for recognition was one factor in the dispute, but another was that Congress had proposed to award $100,000 to the discoverer of anesthesia. The controversy was never resolved and no satisfactory compromise could be reached, so Congress never awarded any money to anyone.

[Long, in Georgia, claimed to have been the first to use ether (1842), but refrained from writing about it until some seven years later. Wells claimed to have been the first to use anesthesia (nitrous

oxide), but he was unable to demonstrate the achievement successfully in Boston. Jackson insisted that ether was really his idea, that
he had told Morton everything. Morton, in turn, administered the
gas in the Ether Dome, jealously guarded his patent rights, and
threatened to sue any physician who used ether without his permission. The controversy brought satisfaction to no one: Wells died
in jail, Jackson in a lunatic asylum, and Morton in poverty. Long—
though he died in the relative obscurity of a rural practitioner—
was the only one to survive the tumult with his health and spirits
intact.]

   Above the base there are four more substantial fused rose granite
columns, on top of which rests a sculpture of the Good Samaritan
succoring a sufferer. The monument sits in a pool fed by streams of
water spouting from lions' heads beneath the alcoves. A huge
ginkgo tree and a burr oak provide shade.

(22)*Emmanuel Church* 15 Newbury Street 02118. (617) 536-3355.
This fine old stone church, with its marvelous Gothic interior, was
erected in 1861 and played an important role in the development of
psychotherapy in this country. In 1905, the Boston internist Dr
Joseph H Pratt began giving his tuberculosis classes here, hoping to
give poor consumptives a chance to carry out treatment of their
disease at home without the necessity of resorting to sanatoriums.
There was an instructional aspect to the classes—focusing on the
therapeutic effects of rest, fresh air, good food, and competent
medical supervision—as well as opportunities for sharing experiences and feelings. Pratt's classes are usually regarded as the beginning of modern group psychotherapy. His classes continued for 18
years. However, Pratt and his work at the Emmanuel Church are
best viewed within the context of what has come to be called the
Emmanuel Movement, the pet project of the church rector, Dr
Elwood Worcester.

   The Emmanuel Movement became a vast and enormously successful network of church outreach programs designed to assist
large numbers of unhappy people with a variety of nervous and
physical afflictions, including such habit disorders as alcoholism
and drug addiction. Wednesday Evening Health Services customarily drew 500 to 800 people for intercessory prayer and educational programs about the health of the soul and the body. In 1913
Worcester hired Courtenay Baylor as the country's first paid alcoholism therapist, and the church became one of the country's principal alcohol treatment centers, offering individual therapy, group
therapy, lectures and social hours. Today the church sustains a
variety of social and outreach programs. There are no formal tours,

but visitors are always welcome at Sunday services, and may look around the chapel when it is open and not otherwise in use.

㉓*Paul Revere House* 19 North Square 02113. (617) 523-2338. It's ironic that this multitalented man is remembered almost exclusively for his midnight ride of April 18, 1775. Revere was a fine artisan; before the Revolutionary War he specialized in gold- and silversmithing and engraving, and later he became an industrialist with busy foundry operations, eventually opening North America's first copper-rolling mill. During the years 1768–1775, Revere augmented his income by working as a dentist. In a 1770 ad in the *Boston Gazette*, Revere stated that he "still continues the business of a dentist, and flatters himself that from the experience he has had these two years (in which he has fixt [sic] some hundreds of teeth), that he can fix them as well as any surgeon-dentist who ever came from London. . ." Revere sold dentifrice, cleaned teeth, constructed and set false teeth, and repaired loose dentures. He also gets credit for the first recorded use of forensic dentistry, in a grim experience that he surely would have preferred to avoid. He had created a two-unit dental bridge for his friend Dr Joseph Warren (see "Massachusetts General Hospital," above), after whom he named his son Joseph Warren Revere. Warren was killed at the Battle of Bunker Hill and buried by the British in a mass grave. After the British evacuation, Bostonians who wished to give the distinguished Warren a proper burial were stymied until Revere was able to identify the decomposed corpse by means of the dental work he had earlier performed.

The Paul Revere House is a late seventeenth century dwelling, in which Revere lived both before and during the Revolution, located a few blocks from the popular Quincy Market. The house is now outfitted as a museum, devoted to many aspects of his life and times, including a small display on dentistry. Hours are 9:30 AM till late afternoon, the precise times varying a bit with the season. The museum is closed on Mondays and some holidays. There is a small admission charge.

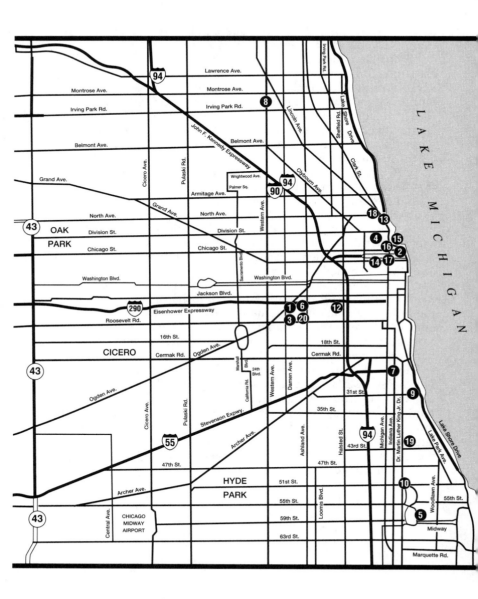

Chicago

Including Maywood and Park Ridge

Map Key ─────────────────────────────────

(1) Rush – Presbyterian – St Luke's Medical Center
(2) Northwestern University Medical Center
(3) University of Illinois Medical Center
(4) William M Scholl College of Podiatric Medicine
(5) University of Chicago Medical Center
(6) Cook County Hospital
(7) Mercy Hospital and Medical Center
(8) Martha Washington Hospital
(9) Michael Reese Hospital and Medical Center
(10) Provident Hospital
(11) (Former) Chicago Municipal Contagious Disease Hospital
(12) Hull House
(13) International Museum of Surgical Science and Hall of Fame
(14) American Medical Association
(15) American Hospital Association
(16) American Dental Association
(17) American College of Surgeons
(18) Statue of Greene Vardiman Black
(19) Daniel Hale Williams House
(20) Pasteur Park

These key numbers will be found at appropriate points in the text.

CHICAGO HAS LONG BEEN the medical epicenter of the midwest. It has four medical schools within its city limits, and not long ago had six, until two moved to the suburbs. It's home to the American Medical Association, the American Dental Association, the American Hospital Association, and a variety of other health-related organizations

75

of national importance. It has influential nursing, dental, pharmacy and podiatric schools, as well as numerous prestigious and historically important hospitals.

Two things about Chicago's history make it unique among great medical cities: the tortuousness of its politics and the interrelatedness of its various medical institutions. A rebellious faculty group from Rush Medical College, for example, begat the Chicago Medical College, which later became the Northwestern University Medical School. Rush, in turn, operated for a while as a wing of the University of Chicago, and later had the bulk of its faculty absorbed by the University of Illinois before again assuming its separate identity. Mercy Hospital, at various times in its history, has been the principal teaching hospital for six different medical schools.

While many Chicago visitors will wish to seek out sites of special interest, the easiest way to see a number of different landmarks in the course of a comfortable stroll would be to focus on either of two areas that are packed with health-related institutions.

The first of these is in the vicinity of Northwestern University Medical School. This is an attractive area, adjacent to Lake Michigan, loaded with fashionable shops and a wide range of eateries. A one- or two-hour stroll could easily include Northwestern Medical School, the William M Scholl College of Podiatric Medicine, the respective headquarters of the AMA, ADA, and AHA, the statue of G Vardiman Black, and — another mile or so away — the International Museum of Surgical Science and Hall of Fame.

The other major area is the West Side Medical Center District, a semiautonomous 365-acre tract established by the state legislature in 1941. This "Garden of Health" (as it was first called) is composed of almost 100 buildings including Rush–Presbyterian–St. Luke's, the University of Illinois Hospitals and Clinics, Cook County Hospital, and the University of Illinois College of Pharmacy, among many others. Pasteur Park is likewise located here, and Loyola University School of Medicine and the Chicago Medical School were located here before their moves to the suburbs. The entire area is readily accessible by public transportation from downtown, and can be negotiated easily on foot in an hour or two.

(1) *Rush–Presbyterian–St Luke's Medical Center* 1653 West Congress Parkway 60612. (312) 942-5580. Rush is both Chicago's oldest medical school and its youngest, depending on your perspective. The original Rush Medical College received its charter on March 2, 1837, two days before Chicago itself was incorporated as a city. The founder, Dr Daniel Brainard, named his school after Dr Benjamin Rush, in the hope that the Rush family would contribute

funds to the fledgling endeavor. Alas, these hopes were in vain; but the name remained. The school finally opened in 1843, with a curriculum consisting of two identical 16-week lecture series.

Rush has the distinction of having conferred the first doctorate of medicine bestowed on an American black by an American medical school (David Peck Jones, in 1847). Its record with women is less admirable: Rush's sole female student in the nineteenth century was Emily Blackwell, who was dismissed in 1852 after the Illinois State Medical Society censured Rush for having accepted her in the first place.

Rush faculty organized several hospitals, the first of any consequence being the Illinois General Hospital of the Lake (1850), which later became Mercy Hospital. From 1860 onward, Rush students got the bulk of their clinical training at Cook County Hospital; the two institutions rebuilt across the street from one another after the Great Fire of 1871. Still, the ever-present political turmoil at the County Hospital led Rush to search for a hospital over which it could exert substantially greater control; and in 1884 Rush faculty played a pivotal role in the founding of Presbyterian Hospital.

As the end of the century drew near, Rush increasingly felt the need for a university affiliation, a need that would remain a continuing challenge for three-quarters of a century. Rush had a nominal affiliation with Lake Forest University from 1887 to 1898, and with the University of Chicago until 1940, when, because of philosophical and practical differences, the affiliation agreement was terminated. Rush then went into mothballs: the school was closed, but the charter and the faculty were kept alive as a legal entity, with elected officers and ongoing meetings, and a bankrolled endowment of half a million dollars. Paradoxically, most of the Rush faculty became University of Illinois faculty when the U of I developed an affiliation with Presbyterian Hospital, where most of the Rush people were on the staff.

In 1959 Presbyterian merged with St Luke's Hospital (which had been founded in 1864). In 1969, after learning that the state would provide funds to both public and private medical schools to support the education of Illinois residents, Rush decided to reactivate its charter and, almost simultaneously, signed a new merger agreement that made Rush–Presbyterian–St Luke's Medical Center a legal entity. Rush Medical College reopened its doors to students in 1971; the following year it created its own university, to solve the university-affiliation problem once and forever. Rush University now offers degrees in medicine, nursing, health sciences, and various graduate science subjects. The School of Nursing initiated the "Rush Model of Nursing" when it opened, in 1973; this involves a totally integrated approach, so that Nursing faculty also staff the hospital and provide primary nursing care.

Over their century and a half of history, the Rush–Presbyterian–St Luke's components have been the sites of many landmark events:

1903	First use of roentgen rays to treat leukemia, by Nicholas Senn
1908	First description of sickle cell anemia, by James Herrick
1910	First description of coronary heart disease, by James Herrick
1915	BW Sippy becomes the first to appreciate the role of hydrochloric acid in producing ulcer pain and devises the Sippy diet (milk, cream, and frequent small meals), the mainstay of ulcer treatment for almost half a century
1923	First description of the cause of scarlet fever, by George and Gladys Dick
1962	First reattachment of a severed hand in the United States, by William Shorey
1982	First implantation of a computerized programmable morphine pump in the abdomen of a cancer patient to control pain, by Richard Penn

A visit to this medical center today reveals buildings of varying vintages, from the 1888 Jones Pavilion of Presbyterian Hospital to many strikingly modern structures. To take advantage of space limitations, the main academic building has been wrapped around the Chicago Transit Authority's "El" tracks, so that the elevated trains actually run through the heavily soundproofed building. Tours are available from the Volunteers' Office.

(2) *Northwestern University Medical Center*   303 East Chicago Avenue 60611. (312) 908-8649. This medical center began in 1859 when a group of dissident Rush faculty decided to start a new medical school. They arranged an affiliation with what was then called Lind University, becoming the Medical Department of Lind University. Their leader was Nathan Smith Davis, founder of the American Medical Association and one of medicine's visionaries in the mid-nineteenth century. Under his leadership, Lind became the first medical school in the country to inaugurate a full graded curriculum and to enforce minimum standards for premedical education. When Davis left Rush, he took with him all clinical teaching at Mercy Hospital (which he had helped to found), providing the new school with the best clinical facilities in the city.

In 1863 Lind University reorganized as Lake Forest University. Its Medical Department decided to forge an independent course, becoming a proprietary school called the Chicago Medical College. In 1870, for reasons of mutual advantage, the CMC developed a nominal affiliation with Northwestern University (which had received its charter in 1851). Though the two institutions were essentially autonomous, the medical school henceforth called itself the "Chicago Medical College, the Medical Department of Northwestern University." The medical school became fully integrated into the university in 1906.

At about this time, Northwestern adopted a second medical school. Mary Thompson graduated from CMC in 1869, but the following year women were denied admission. In 1870 Dr Thompson and a group of sympathetic physicians founded the Women's Hospital Medical College. This school functioned (though often staying only marginally afloat) until 1892, when it was absorbed by Northwestern as a segregated school providing medical education to women only. But the Women's Medical School proved a financial drain, and the university closed it in 1902. It would not admit another woman medical student until 1926.

The current medical center complex dates from 1926 and is an amalgam of the university's professional schools and numerous hospitals, the oldest of which was originally named the Chicago Homeopathic Hospital. In 1857 CHH joined with the Hahnemann Hospital (founded in 1853) to form the Hahnemann Medical College Hospital, which was renamed Chicago Memorial Hospital in 1915. Another principal component, the Passavant Hospital, was formed when the old Deaconess Hospital (1865) was renamed after its founder, Reverend William Alfred Passavant, in 1895. Passavant joined with Chicago Wesley Hospital in 1972 to form the Northwestern University Memorial Hospital. Wesley, which traces its origins to 1888, had absorbed several other hospitals along the way, including (in 1954) the Chicago Memorial Hospital.

The older buildings on the campus date from the late 1920s and are mostly high-rises faced with gray limestone, with English Gothic design and flourishes. Be sure to see the frieze that adorns the entryway at Passavant (303 East Superior Street) and the beautifully designed Wesley lobby (250 East Superior Street), which combines gloriously decorated Gothic cathedral ceilings with modern high-speed elevators encased in mirrored glass. The modern Rehabilitation Institute of Chicago (345 East Superior Street) offers a treat of a different sort: in the lobby there is a huge tapestry, the last commissioned work of Marc Chagall, completed when he was 96 years old, called *Job* and based on the Biblical passage Job 14:7: "For there is hope of a tree / If it be cut down, that it will sprout again / and the tender branch thereof will not cease."

Passavant Pavilion, Northwestern Memorial Hospital — exterior detail *(From Jim Ziv/Northwestern University Medical School)*

There are no tours of this complex available to the general public, but the public relations departments of Northwestern Memorial Hospital (908-2030) and the Rehabilitation Institute (649-6000) sometimes offer tours of their institutions.

University of Illinois – Chicago College of Pharmacy 833 South Wood Street 60612. (312) 966-7240. The Chicago College of Pharmacy dates from 1859, when 12 local druggists founded their own collegial organization. It was the sixth such organization in the country, only three had been providing regular courses of instruction (Philadelphia, 1821; New York, 1829; Baltimore, 1840). The Chicago College of Pharmacy had classes right from the beginning, and soon became a thriving operation. Like most other Chicago institutions, it suffered a major setback with the fire of 1871; but its library, furniture, and equipment were substantially restored by donations from around the world. The college was an independent entity for most of the nineteenth century; it became part of the University of Illinois in 1896. Initially it was called the School of Pharmacy. The faculty spent much of the early twentieth century struggling to attain the respect for pharmacy education that had already been accorded to medicine and dentistry. In 1932 The University of Illinois awarded the school College status. The College of Pharmacy occupied a variety of locations before moving to its present site, across from the University Hospital Clinics building, in 1954. Today, the College of Pharmacy is the oldest component of the University of Illinois. It is housed in a modern six-story brick building. There is a collection of historical displays scattered throughout a number of classrooms, but these are for student use and are not accessible to the general public. No tours are available.

(3) *University of Illinois Medical Center* 1740 Taylor Street 60612. (312) 996-7000. The University of Illinois College of Medicine traces its beginnings to 1882, when the College of Physicians and Surgeons of Chicago was formed. The College was started as a proprietary endeavor, in direct competition with the various other medical schools in the city: Rush, Northwestern, Women's Hospital Medical, Hahnemann Homeopathic, Chicago Homeopathic, and the Bennett College of Eclectic Medicine and Surgery. From the beginning, P&S, as it was called, used Cook County Hospital as its major resource for teaching.

The college had considerable financial difficulties during its first decade, but reorganized in the 1890s, put major emphasis on basic science education, and inaugurated a vigorous student recruitment drive. The enterprise prospered, and when the Flexner Report came out, in 1910, only P&S, Rush, and Northwestern, of the many Chicago medical schools, were found worth salvaging. In 1913 P&S became a part of the University of Illinois, freeing it from its dependence on student fees and consequently allowing it to raise admission standards. In the 1920s the University of Illinois College of Medicine began moving into its present home, an extensive complex of buildings, largely English collegiate Gothic in design, which for the first time included a university hospital.

UIMC underwent a major institutional crisis in the early 1950s, when Andrew C Ivy, a distinguished scientist and then vice-president in charge of all the professional schools at U of I, undertook a crusade in support of krebiozen, which he touted as a miracle cancer cure. Ivy continued his crusade despite almost total opposition from the scientific community. The controversy escalated, litigation made matters worse, and publicity was relentless. Applications from potential students plummeted, huge numbers of faculty resigned, and the College of Medicine went through three deans and several acting deans in four years.

In the 1960s the College of Medicine underwent a major reorganization stressing regionalization within the state, allowing students to take various parts of their preclinical and clinical training in Urbana, Peoria, Rockford, and Chicago, resulting in an integrated program with the largest student body of any American medical school.

Over the years, UIMC has contributed many medical firsts, including:

1914	Development of the first commercially viable incubator for infants, by Julius Hess
1948	Installation of the first betatron for medical use in the US
1953	First successful separation of Siamese twins joined at the skull

Today UIMC is one of the keystones of Chicago's mammoth West-Side Medical Center District. The U of I Hospital, with some 700 beds, is unique in that it provides an educational meeting ground for students from seven colleges of the same university: medicine, dentistry, nursing, pharmacy, public health, associated health professions, and social work. Tours are available by request and include lots of visual interest. The campus is sprinkled with statuary, including a sparkling white statue of Hippocrates (on the corner near the front of the hospital) and two WPA – vintage figures of Aesculapius and his daughter Hygeia (adjacent to the current faculty dining room). Inside the West Tower entrance, at Polk and Wolcott, the Founders' Room offers an interesting small display. Paneled in oak, the room contains a number of documents related to the founding, here, of the medical student honor society, Alpha Omega Alpha.

Loyola University Medical Center 2160 South First Street, Maywood 60153. (312) 531-3000. This medical center consists of the Strich School of Medicine, McGaw Hospital, the Loyola University School of Dentistry, and a large outpatient center.

Loyola University dates back to 1870; the medical school was formed in 1909, when the Bennett Medical School merged with Reliance Medical School and the Illinois Medical College. From 1917 onward, Loyola's medical school was located at 706 South Wolcott Avenue, near Cook County Hospital; but in 1968 it moved to the near-western suburb of Maywood. Loyola had been one of three medical schools clustered around Cook County, and the move to Maywood was motivated, at least in part, to give the school some turf of its own. An additional draw at Maywood was the Hines Veterans Administration Hospital (now a principal Loyola teaching hospital).

In the 1940s Loyola's medical school went through some major financial difficulties, which were ultimately resolved by a campaign led personally by Chicago's Archbishop, Cardinal Strich. His role was so important that in 1948 the medical school was renamed in his honor.

Loyola's School of Dentistry dates back to 1883, when Chicago's first dental school, the Chicago Dental Infirmary, was established. This pioneering institution was founded on the belief that dentistry was merely a subdivision of medicine. All applicants were required to have MD degrees, and the 20-week course of study was designed to begin immediately after a student's completion of medical school. It took only a year for the organizers to realize that they needed to broaden their applicant base if they were to have a thriving institution. So in 1884 they formed the Chicago College of Dental Surgery, which soon became the largest dental school in the world. The dental college made several geographic moves, and in 1899 became the dental school of Rush University. The school's allegiances shifted in 1905, when it became the dental department of Valparaiso University, an affiliation which lasted until 1919. It then remained independent for several years until it achieved its present union with Loyola, in 1923.

There is no provision for tours of this 63-acre campus.

④ *William M Scholl College of Podiatric Medicine* 1001 North Dearborn Street 60610. (312) 280-2940. This college was founded in 1912 as the Illinois College of Chiropody and Orthopedics. Since then it has absorbed a couple of other podiatric schools and undergone at least five name changes, assuming its present identity in 1981. Though it is one of seven podiatry colleges in the United States, Scholl has produced fully a third of the nation's podiatrists. A private, nonprofit institution, it operates the largest foot clinic in the world.

The school was founded by William Scholl, who arguably contributed more to foot health than any other person in the world. Scholl was brought up on his father's dairy farm; because he showed an early aptitude for working with leather, he became the shoemaker for his parents and 12 brothers and sisters. He was apprenticed to a local cobbler at 16 and went to work in Chicago a year later as a combination cobbler and shoe salesman. He was appalled by the condition of his customers' feet — the corns and bunions and deformities — and started searching for ways to remedy what he saw as an obviously neglected area of health care. His first step was to go to medical school, paying his way with an evening job at the shoe store. At 22 he graduated from the Illinois Medical College, by which time he had already patented his first invention, an arch support he called "the Foot Easer." Scholl was a brilliant inventor and an inspired merchandiser. He established correspondence courses for shoe salesmen, teaching them how to do their jobs better and creating in them an enduring loyalty to Scholl products, of which there grew to be more than 1000 — including everything from pads for corns and bunions to specially designed shoes. When Scholl died, in 1955, his empire comprised 10 manufacturing plants in the United States and 6 overseas, with 423 exclusive retail stores in 57 countries.

While he was building his extraordinarily successful foot-care business, Scholl was simultaneously doing whatever he could to create foot-awareness in the medical profession. He wrote many books, including the still-authoritative *The Human Foot: Anatomy, Deformities, and Treatment* (1915). After founding the college, he recruited the faculty himself and covered the school's expenses out of his own pocket for many years. Scholl, however, was viewed skeptically for decades by members of the podiatric profession, who saw him as too commercially oriented and (probably) too successful.

Though there is no connection whatsoever between the college and Scholl's commercial enterprises, the college adopted its founder's name in 1981, when the Scholl Foundation gave it a grant of $5 million. In 1971 the college moved into its present building, which for almost half a century had been a residence for young women. It's an impressive turn-of-the-century brick building, with lots of marble in the hallways and an Olympic-sized swimming pool in the basement.

On the seventh floor is the **Historical Resources Center,** which functions as museum, historical library, and archives. There's a wonderful shoe collection, including sixteenth-century Tibetan low boots, seventeenth-century high-top lace mocassins from England, eighteenth-century pom-pom slippers from Turkey, and nineteenth-century Chinese "deer-hoof" shoes for women with bound feet. There are some displays about William Scholl and the college as well. The college welcomes requests for tours, which are conducted via the Student Affairs office.

(5) *University of Chicago Medical Center* 5841 South Maryland Avenue 60637. (312) 702-6241. The University of Chicago Medical Center as it presently exists opened in 1927, but the University's involvement in medical education extends back to 1898, when it developed an affiliation with Rush. The 1927 development was a direct outgrowth of the 1910 Flexner Report; indeed, Abraham Flexner took a very active role in events. The U of C approached Rockefeller's General Education Board for "advice" about establishing a medical school modeled along the lines the GEB thought ideal (strong research orientation, full-time faculty, university hospital integrated with the school). The GEB recommended that the university invite Flexner (who by now was working for the GEB) to examine the situation and write up a report. The result was a brand-new medical school, founded with almost $8 million in Rockefeller money, having as its chief aim "the advancement of the medical sciences."

The initial quadrangular structure included the Billings Hospital (named as a result of a $1 million gift from the Billings family), a dispensary, a pathology wing, and a basic science building. In the several years that followed, other entities were either initiated or absorbed into the gradually expanding quadrangular pattern. Today the medical center includes 15 buildings with names giving tribute to various benefactors and affiliations. In 1968 the medical school was renamed the Pritzker School of Medicine in recognition of a $12 million gift.

For many years the University of Chicago has been the nation's leader in the training of medical research specialists and academicians. Its list of research contributions and medical firsts is most impressive:

1941   Charles Huggins reports that removal of the testes from patients with prostatic cancer helps slow the course of the disease

1942   First successful treatment of Hodgkin's disease with nitrogen mustard, by Leon Jacobson

1943   First transthoracic vagotomy for the relief of peptic ulcer disease symptoms, by Lester Dragstedt

1950   Discovery of primaquine as the first safe, simple cure for malaria, by Alf Alving

1961   Development of technetium 99m scanning for diagnosing thyroid cancers, by Paul Harper

1961   First use of percutaneous cordotomy to control intractable pain in cancer patients, by Paul Harper and Joseph Mullen

1986   First successful segmental liver transplant in the United States, by
_____ Peter Whitington

The center covers about 25 acres at the southwest corner of the U
of C campus. The collegiate English Gothic style of the early buildings is still much in evidence, but there are now so many additional
interconnected buildings and wings that it is impossible for visitors
to find their way through the maze-like interiors without the aid of
a map (available at the main entrance information desk). Tours are
available only to VIPs.

(6) *Cook County Hospital* 1825 West Harrison Street 60612. (312)
633-6000. Cook County Hospital is one of this country's medical
legends. Along with Bellevue in New York and Charity in New
Orleans, it is one of those places that almost never turn anyone
away, that care for the poorest and sickest people imaginable, routinely performing miracles with meager resources and in the process supplying generations of students and house officers with
some of the finest training experience in the nation.

CCH traces its origins back to 1832; it was then that the County
Board of Commissioners established a Public Alms House to care
for the destitute. The first real county hospital, however, was begun
in 1847 when the county rented Tippecanoe Hall, installed some
beds, and contracted with the Rush Medical College faculty to run
the place. The hospital moved to its present site, after occupying
several other structures, in 1876. At that time the medical staffing
was provided one-third by Rush Medical College, one-third by
Chicago Medical College, and one-third by the Board of Commissioners.

There are many ways to tell the history of this great institution,
but two themes stand out. The first is that the hospital has been
overburdened and overcrowded almost every day it has been open.
The second is that the hospital has been saddled with corruption
and graft for most of its history. The 1911 building was planned for
4000 beds, providing what one critic called "five or six miles of
sickbeds under one management, an ungovernable mass which
spells outrage and disaster," but which also provided immense
opportunities for graft and political perquisites. In the 1960s, an
estimated 900 people worked here in patronage jobs, mostly clerical
and administrative, making it almost impossible for doctors and
nurses to get anything accomplished except by doing it themselves,
usually outside of established channels. Despite the efforts of many
to change the system, the problem persisted until 1970, when a

Cook County Hospital from the air *(From James Eiberger, MD)*

"revolution" led by the house staff almost closed the hospital and ultimately succeeded in wresting control away from the political patronage system. Despite this enormous change for the better, the hospital remains almost unimaginably overburdened.

CCH currently comprises 13 buildings, the oldest being the old tuberculosis hospital, which dates from 1910. The main building, which fronts on Pasteur Park, is a massive structure of yellow-gray brick and stone, stretching an entire long block, with a facade boasting 17 Ionic columns. It was completed in 1914. Virtually all of the buildings used for patient care were constructed over 60 years ago. For the past 20 years, the county has been trying to decide whether to build an entirely new Cook County Hospital, to completely remodel and upgrade the old one, or to farm out all CCH patients to other hospitals in the community and close CCH for good.

For the present, this living historic landmark endures. Tours are available from the Volunteers Office.

(7) *Mercy Hospital and Medical Center* Stevenson Expressway at King Drive 60616. (312) 567-2000. The first Sisters of Mercy arrived in Chicago in 1846, when the city had only 17,000 inhabitants, and were soon involved with caring for the sick and impoverished. Though they first worked helping at the free dispensary of Rush Medical College, they soon attached themselves to a hospital (1850), initially called Illinois General Hospital of the Lake. The following year, responsibility for the hospital was transferred to the Sisters, and in 1852 the name was changed to the Mercy Hospital and Orphan Asylum.

Until 1859 Mercy was the principal teaching hospital for Rush Medical School; but when a group of Rush faculty splintered off to establish Chicago's second medical school, Mercy chose to affiliate with the new Medical Department of Lind University. In 1863 Mercy moved to a new location at 26th Street and Calumet Avenue and began an affiliation with the nearby Chicago Medical School. In 1869 that school was absorbed by Northwestern University, and Mercy became Northwestern's principal teaching hospital. That relationship lasted 50 years, until Loyola University established a medical school; then Mercy joined with Loyola to create a completely Catholic medical education and treatment center. The association between Loyola and Mercy was not always smooth, however, and when Loyola moved to its new suburban location Mercy chose to continue with its South-Side Chicago location and forgo any further relationship with Loyola. As a result, for most of the 1960s Mercy was without a medical school association. In 1970 Mercy began its current association with the University of Illinois School of Medicine. Thus, over almost a century and a half, Mercy has been a major teaching affiliate for six medical schools, probably more than any other private hospital in the country.

With its various teaching affiliations, Mercy has been the site of numerous medical firsts, including becoming (in 1859) the first teaching hospital to use a graded curriculum; and being the site of the first use of the arthroscope in the United States (1924, by Philip Kreuger).

Mercy is currently housed in a building that dates from 1968, though there have been several more recent additions. Tours of the 500-bed hospital and related facilities can be scheduled by calling the Public Relations Department at 567-2064.

(8) *Martha Washington Hospital* 4025 North Western Avenue 60618. (312) 583-9000. This hospital was founded during the Civil War, when the Washingtonian movement (begun in 1840) was the largest temperance movement in the United States. In 1863 a Chi-

cago temperance leader named Robert Law—concerned about drunkenness among his employees—opened the Washingtonian Home of Chicago for the cure of inebriates. For much of its first decade, the Home received 10 percent of all revenues from tavern licenses (until the measure was found unconstitutional in 1875). For a while there were separate homes for men (on Madison Avenue) and women (on Irving Park), until operations were consolidated at the present location. The roughest time for the home came with the temperance movement's biggest success: the home survived Prohibition by building a general hospital and becoming the Martha Washington Hospital. What is now the Administrative Support Building was the original hospital building and dates from 1926. Other facilities have been added to the basic 200-bed primary care hospital, and the institution now includes several buildings on its main campus, together with two alcohol and drug rehabilitation clinics, one in Chicago's Loop and one on the South Side. Tours are available by advance arrangement (ext 4352).

(9) *Michael Reese Hospital and Medical Center* Lake Shore Drive and 31st Street 60616. (312) 791-2000. The Michael Reese Hospital was founded in 1881. The hospital's eponym was a Jewish, San Francisco-based peddler-turned-millionaire who left his fortune to (among others) his Chicago-based relatives, to give to charities of their choice. Chicago's only previous Jewish hospital had burned down, after only three years' existence, in the disastrous 1871 fire, and Reese's bequest became the basis of a new one. The hospital soon grew into a thriving concern; by the turn of the century, a new wing and six new buildings had been added.

By the 1920s the area around the hospital—which once had been populated by wealthy families, including many German Jews—had begun to decline. The automobile allowed people with money to escape the city's woes and establish their own enclaves in the suburbs. As the wealthy moved out, poor people moved in, the area became increasingly crowded, health problems escalated—and by the post–World War II era, this area of Chicago's South Side had become one of the most dismal slums in the nation.

Most hospitals exposed to similar circumstances either followed their wealthy patrons to the suburbs or lost their philanthropic support and declined. Reese, however, both retained the support of the moneyed Jewish community and stayed on the South Side. It was able to do so largely because it had founded, in 1909, a hospital-based research institute—a very unusual step at that time for a private, non-university-affiliated hospital. By 1929 the institute employed a full-time director and full-time investigators. Reese soon gained a national reputation for medical research, particularly in the areas of diabetes and metabolic disease, gastroenterology, and cardiology. In 1935 Irving Stein and Michael Leventhal described one of the most common causes of infertility in women, subsequently called the Stein-Leventhal syndrome. In 1940 Franz Oppenheimer developed a technique for freeze-drying plasma, which was of enormous benefit on battlefields in World War II. Reese contributed numerous other scientific developments as well, including developing mediastinoscopy as a means of visualizing the interior of the mediastinum without need for major surgery (1970, by Edward Goldberg); and the development of the first successful intrauterine device capable of releasing small amounts of hormone to prevent pregnancy (1974, by Antonio Scommegna).

In the early post–World War II years, the rift between Michael Reese and the surrounding neighborhood grew wider. Open antagonism occasionally erupted; Reese employees, staff, and patients became fearful of traveling through hostile territory. Reese responded with an innovative plan that later was widely copied by other medical centers: they simply bought the neighborhood, leveled it, and rebuilt it according to their own desires, in the first privately financed urban redevelopment project in the country.

The mechanism involved a partnership with the Illinois Institute of Technology and a working relationship with the Chicago Housing Authority. The CHA acquired the land from 26th Street to 35th Street, exercising the right of eminent domain, declared the existing buildings substandard and unsafe, razed all the structures, and sold the land at acquisition prices to interested investors. Reese, as a result, expanded its own campus; and most of the rest of the renewal area was filled with parkland and middle-income, high-rise housing. Crime rates decreased dramatically, and Reese's paying patient population base simultaneously increased significantly.

Today Reese is a huge urban medical center comprising over two dozen buildings in a lovely 47-acre park, rimmed at a respectful distance by a row of high-rise apartment buildings. Tours are arranged usually for school groups and prospective staff, but occasionally for others as well (791-2330). Points of special interest include the still-elegant lobby of Meyer House (at East 29th and South Ellis). The lobby — with its lovely hardwoods, marble floors, huge fireplace, and beautiful bas-relief ceiling — was clearly a suitable entrance to what in 1927 was built to be one of the most luxurious private-patient pavilions in the country. About half a block behind Meyer House, in a large grassy area between the Singer Pavilion and the Levinson Building, baseball enthusiasts can find a small monument commemorating the site of the world's first softball game, which occurred here in 1887.

Children's Memorial Hospital 2300 Children's Plaza 60614. (312) 880-4009. CMH opened its doors in 1882 as the Maurice Porter Memorial Hospital, founded as a memorial to the benefactor's son, who had died at the age of 13. The birth of this children's hospital coincided with the birth of pediatrics as a specialty; prior to this era, care of children had usually been lumped together with the care of women, in hospitals and academic departments that cared for both. Cook County Hospital opened its first childrens' ward in 1885, and Michael Reese delayed until 1890. Rush started teaching pediatrics as a separate subject only in 1892, and Chicago Medical College followed in 1893. CMH now functions as a principal pediatric teaching center for Northwestern University Medical School, though it is technically an independent entity and is separated from NUMS by several miles. The current hospital dates from 1961, with a major high-rise addition dating from 1982. No tours are currently available.

(10) *Provident Hospital* 500 East 51st Street 60615. When it closed its doors, in 1987, Provident was the oldest black-owned and -operated hospital in the country. Founded in 1891 by the famed surgeon Daniel Williams, the hospital had a dual mission: to provide care to the sick and injured without regard to creed or color, and to provide a place for the training and employment of black women who wished to be nurses. Prior to the opening of Provident, Chicago's black physicians had no place to hospitalize their own patients, and black women were not accepted for nurse's training anywhere in the city. As one example, it was 1950 before Children's Memorial accepted black women on its nursing staff and allowed them to live in the nurses' residence building. Provident's nurse's training school opened in 1891. During the hospital's early years, it was truly an integrated hospital: most of the interns and a majority of the patients were white. By 1915, however, the tide had turned, and 90 percent of patients were black. The change was wrought mostly by the migration of some 50,000 blacks into the Chicago area to provide manpower for wartime industry.

Provident had a teaching affiliation with Northwestern from 1899 to 1912, and then with the University of Chicago in 1929. The signed agreement with the latter provided for a long-term relationship, but required that Provident raise a $400,000 endowment before the University would finalize its commitment. Provident raised pledges for the stipulated amount; but the Depression intervened and the pledges went uncollected. The relationship was officially terminated in 1944.

By 1976 Provident's buildings were so badly deteriorated that they were cited for health and safety violations. The hospital inaugurated a fundraising campaign and erected a new 300-bed hospital in 1983, in the hope of attracting a middle-class clientele and their physicians. These hopes were not borne out; in 1987 the hospital, $40 million in debt, filed for bankruptcy. Provident—like most black-owned hospitals—was doomed by a combination of scientific and social progress. Of the 200 black hospitals that were in operation at the turn of the century, fewer than 10 are left. Most have been marginal financially almost from the beginning, lacking capital funds for maintaining old buildings or constructing new ones. As scientific progress required ever-more-expensive equipment and more highly-paid personnel, many such marginal operations fell by the wayside. The situation became dramatically worse with the advent of integration in the 1960s and 1970s. Middle-class blacks often chose more prestigious hospitals with fuller ranges of services, and hospitals like Provident were left with an underinsured population that drained their coffers. At the same time, black health professionals no longer needed to rely on black hospitals for training, staff privileges, or employment.

At this writing, several of Provident's buildings remain, though they are locked shut, and their future remains in doubt.

(11) *(Former) Chicago Municipal Contagious Disease Hospital* West 31st Street and South California Boulevard 60608. Chicago was one of the last major cities to build a contagious-disease hospital, and the CMCDH was the last surviving municipal contagious-disease facility when it closed in 1972.

Infectious diseases were considered the major public health hazard of the nineteenth century. Chicago was especially vulnerable, as its population ballooned from essentially zero to almost 2 million over 80 years, overwhelming the city's inadequate sanitation, sewage, water supply, and housing. In the 1880s Cook County Hospital refused to accept contagious-disease cases until it was forced to do so by the judicial system. In 1893, Chicago opened a tiny 35-bed isolation hospital, but this token facility was almost immediately overwhelmed.

Finally, in 1912, Chicago authorized a bond issue for a suitable hospital; when CMCDH opened in 1917, it was the largest and most elaborate contagious-disease hospital in the country. Only 12 years passed before the hospital started going out of date. Admissions peaked in 1929. Initially, 80 percent of the patients suffered from diphtheria. By 1930, scarlet fever had become the dominant infection; and by the 1950s, a hodgepodge of nonbacterial infections constituted the majority.

The CMCDH's fall from grace was due to a number of factors. The first was a growing public-health concensus that isolation *per se* was of little value, that a majority of disease transmission was attributable to unrecognized carriers on the one hand and to people who were incubating diseases, but hadn't yet developed diagnosable symptoms, on the other. An additional factor was antibiotics, which came into general use in the late 1940s. A third factor was immunization, which eliminated smallpox and diphtheria as public health concerns by the 1950s and polio by the 1960s.

The amazing thing is that the hospital lasted as long as it did. In 1972 it operated at a cost of $1.2 million for the year, employing 142 people to care for an average of 20 patients, all of whom could easily have been cared for elsewhere at lesser cost.

The hospital still stands today, with the words Chicago Municipal Contagious Disease Hospital embossed over the portal, one of the few remaining examples of a kind of hospital that once was very common. There are four large brown-brick buildings here, clustered together on a large campus, with the open-air galleries still running between the buildings, designed so that patients could "take the air" as they traveled from one place to another. The facility is still owned by the health department, but now the space is occupied primarily by an alcoholism treatment program, with various other public-health programs tucked here and there in the vintage, but remodeled, interior.

There are no tours, and officials don't wish to be bothered with calls, but visitors are welcome to wander in public spaces.

(12)*Hull House* Polk and Halsted Streets (University of Illinois at Chicago) 60607. (312) 413-5353. Hull House is now a museum — attractive, interesting, and well worth a visit. Still, it seems a bit out of place — the neighborhood that formed it and for which it played such an important leadership role has been bulldozed out of existence and long since replaced by a huge freeway and the University of Illinois campus.

Hull House was formed in 1889 by Jane Addams and Ellen Starr, eventually to become the most influential settlement house of its day. Hull House catered to the impoverished, underfed, and often physically ill neighborhood residents, who were immigrants — first Irish, Bohemian, and German; later Greek, Italian, and eastern-European Jewish. On the one hand, Hull House provided access to food, clothing and health care; on the other, it provided a neighborhood center where immigrants could learn English, study music and art, and have social events (Benny Goodman was the most famous alumnus of the Hull House Boys' Band). The most enduring contribution of Hull House, however, was that it helped immigrants organize to seek and find solutions to shared problems. Jane Addams was an indefatigable leader, writer, and organizer, who

had a special talent for gaining the attention of, and winning cooperation from, influential people. The streets were unimaginably
filthy, filled with garbage and the stench of clogged sewers. In
response, the neighborhood organized, and Jane Addams became a
paid city garbage inspector. The House investigated the causes of
tuberculosis and typhoid, and then worked to develop a model
tenement code and establish "fresh-air schools" and sanitary public kitchens.

Miss Addams' interests spread from her neighborhood to her
nation, and to the world. She actively supported women's suffrage;
she helped found the National Association for the Advancement of
Colored People and the American Civil Liberties Union; she sec-
onded Theodore Roosevelt's nomination at the 1912 Progressive
Party convention; she founded the Women's International League
for Peace and Freedom; and in 1931 she became the first American
woman to receive the Nobel Peace Prize.

Among the many Hull House residents who went on to greater
things was Dr Alice Hamilton. Hamilton moved into Hull House in
1898 (she had graduated from the University of Michigan Medical
School five years earlier), and was soon at work on pressing public-
health issues, fighting poor sanitation and lobbying for better garbage collection. In 1902 she investigated a neighborhood typhoid
epidemic and deduced that the vector was the common housefly.
She later became one of the country's principal pioneers in the field
of industrial toxicology, and Harvard Medical School's first woman
faculty member. (The appointment was bestowed on condition that
she never march in an academic procession, never appear at the
Harvard Club, and never ask for her allotment of Harvard-Yale
football tickets.)

The work of the old Hull House continues today in the form of
the Hull House Association, headquartered at 118 North Clinton
Street (726-1526), with its programs dispersed throughout the city.
The old Hull House still stands where it has always stood, next door
to what used to be the Residents' Dining Hall. Both buildings function as a museum, where you can see Miss Addams' sitting-room
office, displays of Hull House memorabilia, and the old parlors and
library, as well as fascinating displays about Addams and Hull
House and the neighborhood with which both were so closely
intertwined. Both buildings are open Monday through Friday, 10
AM to 4 PM with expanded weekend hours in the summer. Admission is free.

⑬ *International Museum of Surgical Science and Hall of Fame* 1524
North Lake Shore Drive 60610. (312) 642-3555. The International
College of Surgeons was founded in Geneva, Switzerland, in 1935,

and now has some 12,000 members in 111 countries. The college was intended to foster the international exchange of surgical knowledge, and its museum (a full four floors) here at the organization's headquarters reflects the College's global scope.

The collection here dates from 1954, when the college asked members of various nationalities to contribute items for a museum. The result is a remarkably uneven collection, with no sustaining or unifying theme, varying enormously from one room to the next, both in the quality of the collection and in that of the presentation. Some items have labels and explanations; some have medical significance; some were merely contributed by physicians, and lack other merit.

Still, this is a marvelous building (it's a recreation of the Petit Trianon in Paris), and there are some wonderful items here. These include huge numbers of busts, statues, and portraits of physicians famed in various parts of the world, an extraordinary number and variety of surgical instruments, and an excellent collection of early x-ray equipment. I found a large collection of transfusion devices dating back to 1819 to be particularly interesting. Other exhibits of more than passing interest include: an Albert Schweitzer Library (devoted to the multiple accomplishments of this remarkable man), and the Montague Proctologic Library (with rare books on proctology and some wonderful displays of early proctologic instruments), the Hall of the Immortals (with life-sized sculptures of various world-famous medical greats), the Hall of Murals (filled with oil paintings depicting surgical procedures), and the "annex," with its extensive displays on anesthesia, urology, and obstetrics, as well as an unusual collection of decorated human skulls.

The museum is open Tuesdays through Saturdays from 10 AM to 4 PM, and Sundays from 11 AM to 5 PM. Admission is free. The museum is set up for easy browsing, but guided tours are available by prior arrangement.

Wood Library and Museum of Anesthesiology 515 Busse Highway, Park Ridge 60068. (312) 825-5586. This is more a library than a museum, though the two collections are intermingled, under the sponsorship and in the headquarters of the American Society of Anesthesiologists. There is a fine print collection here, together with various artifacts and organizational archives, the sum total of which tells the history of a specialty. Exhibits vary over time and are likely to cover everything from gas chemistry to mesmerism. The rare-book collection is one of the finest on anesthesiology in the world. The library and museum are open to professionals and interested members of the lay public on normal working days, from 9 AM to 4:45 PM.

(14) *American Medical Association* 535 North Dearborn Street 60610. (312) 645-5000. The address noted here will change in the early 1990s, when the AMA moves into its gleaming new 30-story glass-and-aluminum tower at 515 North State Street.

This organization was founded in 1846, both to promote the interests of physicians and to advance medical knowledge and its useful application. These twin goals have sometimes been in harmony, but at other times the AMA has had to choose between them. Many of the AMA's organizational efforts in the nineteenth century were directed at curtailing the influence and power of rival healing groups: homeopaths and osteopaths, electro- and hydrotherapists, and the like. The AMA developed real political clout, however, only when it decided to clean its own house, focusing on the task of upgrading allopathic medical education.

In 1900 the United States had 160 medical schools, and for the most part they were a sorry lot. Only five required any college education for admission. Some had no libraries, no laboratories, and little actual training in patient care. In 1906 the AMA Council on Medical Education drew up a 10-point standard for medical education, and called for examination of all schools to determine their acceptability. The first inspection tour was conducted in 1906–1907 by the Council's secretary Nathan Colwell. By the time the second tour was conducted, in 1909–1910, with the Council's Colwell and the Carnegie Foundation's Abraham Flexner often traveling together, some 30 schools had already closed. The Carnegie Foundation's participation in the endeavor had actually been sought by the AMA, whose directors thought that an objective outside examiner, untainted by the "suspicion of self-serving motives," would lend greater authority to the investigation. To this day the AMA retains an important role in the accreditation of medical education programs, setting residency training requirements and standards, and surveying and accrediting continuing education programs.

The AMA achieved another major victory when it took up the battle against medication fraud, phony nostrums, and contaminated food products. The struggle spanned several decades, and the AMA's leadership was uneven; but the first Food and Drug bill was passed in 1906, with major achievements continuing into the 1920s.

Though the AMA was widely regarded as a progressive force for the general welfare in the first third of this century, its reputation suffered in the middle third as the organization resisted many developments we now take for granted: prepaid insurance, group medical practice, and governmental involvement in health-care financing.

A continuing source of prestige for the organization has been its major publication, the *Journal of the American Medical Association* or *JAMA*. Begun in 1883, *JAMA* has long been a major force in improving scientific communication as well as advancing the profession's interests.

The AMA's membership reached its peak in 1965, when it could claim 70 percent of all US physicians as members. That was the year that Medicare was passed by Congress, over the AMAs implacable and flamboyant opposition. After that, membership took a nosedive as many physicians shifted their organizational affiliations to various specialty groups. After a period of disarray, the organization is once again gaining both membership and financial strength, now counting about 50 percent of American physicians as members. The Chicago headquarters employs about 1100 people; the new building, when completed, will be quite a sight, with two pedestrian plazas and a "winter garden," a glass-enclosed, garden-filled atrium designed for year-round use. The organization's extensive library is available to all physicians, members or not, on a drop-in basis. Others — and anyone interested in a formal tour — should call in advance.

(15) *American Hospital Association* 840 North Lake Shore Drive 60611. (312) 280-6000. Founded in 1899 as the Association of American Hospital Superintendents, this organization responded to the needs of a burgeoning industry to share individual energies for the common good. During the three years prior to 1900, approximately 1000 new hospitals opened in the United States — a figure which represented a 65 percent increase over what had existed prior to 1896. What was going on inside these new hospitals was even more astounding. The potential contributions of bacteriology to clinical practice were just being fully appreciated. Surgeons were just starting to wear rubber gloves, and even smaller hospitals were beginning to experiment with techniques of antisepsis. The more advanced places had crude x-ray devices. Nursing was established as a profession, and the first regulations for the licensing of nurses were just three years away.

The AHA assumed its present name in 1906. It still represents hospitals' interests to the federal government and other national groups, and acts as a forum for various special interests within the greater health-care community. It has a substanial institutional membership, and its individual membership includes over 38,000 people, from categories as diverse as hospital attorneys, hospital engineers, directors of volunteer services, and hospital planning and marketing.

The AHA headquarters (actually two buildings) does not provide tours, but the Resource Center on the ground floor is open to the public during ordinary working hours. The library here is quite strong, as is the historical collection, which contains the nation's premier collection in the field of hospital and health service administration.

(16)*American Dental Association* 211 East Chicago Avenue 60611. (312) 440-2500. The ADA was founded at Niagara Falls, New York, in 1859. With a membership close to 150,000, it is now the oldest and largest dental organization in the world. The modern, vertically-ribbed, 23-story headquarters building dates from 1966. As high-rise office buildings go, the structure is an attractive one. There is artwork in outdoor courtyards and there are museum-type items in the library and scattered around the building, including antique instruments and dental drills. Special exhibits are usually on display in cases just inside the doors to the library. This is the largest dental library in the world, with a basic collection of some 45,000 volumes, and a journal collection that includes virtually all dental periodicals in the world. The library's nationwide lending program is particularly valuable, because most dentists — unlike physicians, who usually have access to nearby hospital libraries — do not generally have access to local professional collections. The ADA is happy to take visitors on tours, preferably at 10 AM or 3 PM, by prior arrangement.

(17)*American College of Surgeons* 55 East Erie Street 60611. (312) 664-4050. In 1905, Dr Franklin Martin started a journal called *Surgery, Gynecology & Obstetrics.* The journal sponsored a popular series of gatherings designed to teach surgical technique, and these in turn led to the founding of the American College of Surgeons in 1913. The ACS played an important role in establishing minimum acceptable standards for training of resident surgeons and then, in 1918, began the Hospital Standardization Program — which, for over three decades, was this country's most influential accreditation program for hospital quality. Eventually the demands of the hospital inspection and accreditation program outgrew the resources of the ACS; in 1953, the task was assumed by the Joint Commission for the Accreditation of Hospitals, of which the ACS is one of five founding sponsors.

Today the ACS is a professional organization with some 50,000 members. It still is involved in establishing standards for patient care (especially for trauma care); it also sponsors programs for professional continuing education, residency education, and public information. It looks after the professional and economic interests of its members, and it still publishes the journal that led to its founding, *Surgery, Gynecology & Obstetrics.*

The organization's headquarters is a handsome eight-story, rough-concrete and glass building dating from 1963. Across the street (at 40 East Erie) is the Nickerson mansion, which served as the organization's headquarters from 1919 to 1963 and is still owned by the ACS. This sumptuous former private home was completed in 1884 at a cost of $450,000, and continues to be maintained in excellent condition. Next to the Nickerson (at 50 East Erie) is the **John B. Murphy Memorial,** which was dedicated in 1926 to the memory of this famous Chicago surgeon and ACS founder. (Of Murphy's many accomplishments, the most famous in his day was the "Murphy Button," a mechanical device that laid the foundation for gastrointestinal surgery. It consisted of two hollow tubes, each of which was sutured to the end of a severed intestine; the two pieces of tubing were locked together, allowing normal intestinal function.) The Murphy Building is designed in a rather dramatic

John B Murphy Memorial, American College of Surgeons *(By permission of American College of Surgeons, June 1988)*

French Renaissance style, with twin curved stairways and a central porch, with lots of marble and decorative embellishments. The bronze doors at the entrance have sculpted panels portraying Aesculapius, Pasteur, Osler, Lister, McDowell, and Gorgas. Tours are available to members, and "sometimes" to others.

(18)*Statue of Greene Vardiman Black* Lincoln Park, near the junction of North Avenue and Astor Place. Dr Black, widely known as the father of American dentistry, was largely responsible for the standardization of cavity preparation, amalgam manufacture, and dental nomenclature. He learned dentistry by the apprentice method and hung out his shingle when he was just 21. Later he became a physician (also by the apprentice method), passing the state exam and becoming licensed at 42. He taught for many years at the Missouri Dental College, the Chicago Dental Infirmary, the Chicago College of Dental Surgery, and the University of Iowa. Eventually he became dean of the Northwestern University Dental School. Several of his books became classics, dominating the field for years, including his *Dental Anatomy* (1890) and the two-volume *Operative Dentistry* (1908). The statue, in Chicago's oldest and largest park, shows a bronze Dr Black seated in a large limestone chair and looking quite solemn. Dedicated in 1918, the monument has been at this site (just around the corner from the International College of Surgeons) since 1955.

(19)*Daniel Hale Williams House* 445 East 42d Street 60653. A private dwelling, not open to the public, this structure is a National Registered Landmark. Dr Daniel Hale Williams (1856–1931) lived here from 1905 to 1929, during which time he was known as America's most influential and well-known black physician. When Williams graduated from Chicago Medical College, in 1883, he became Chicago's fourth black physician. Dedicated to expanding training and practice opportunities for black health professionals, he launched a drive to found Provident Hospital and its Nurses Training School. It was here that Williams performed, on July 9, 1893, what is usually considered to be America's first successful repair of a laceration to the pericardium. (Williams did not know that HC Dalton had performed a similar, previously unreported operation in St Louis two years earlier.) Because of Williams' outstanding reputation, he was appointed by President Grover Cleveland as surgeon-in-chief of the Freedmen's Hospital in Washington, DC, a position he held for four years. He was also influential in getting Meharry Medical College, in Nashville, Tennessee, to found its own hospital; and, largely because of his persuasion and direction, blacks in some 30 cities throughout the country also formed hospitals. In 1913 he became a charter member of the American College of Surgeons. For many years he was its only black member. The Williams home is a modest two-story frame building, in the block just east of Martin Luther King Drive.

(20)*Pasteur Park* Wood and Harrison Streets 60612. Across from Cook County Hospital there is a large grassy area that occupies an entire city block. For years it was called Convalescent Park and was a place where CCH patients could take the air. Its name was changed to Pasteur Park in 1951.

The principal feature of the park, as well as the source of the name, is a large art deco statue dedicated to the memory of Louis Pasteur. When it was unveiled, in 1928, the large marble shaft surmounted by Pasteur's bust stood in Grant Park next to the Field Museum. The monument was relocated here in 1946, and subsequently was enhanced with an iron fence and floodlights for nighttime illumination.

Another memorial in the park, this one in the northwest section, is a small marble marker commemorating the founding of the medical school honorary fraternity, Alpha Omega Alpha. The location chosen is the original site of the College of Physicians and Surgeons (now the University of Illinois), where the third-year student William Root and six classmates formed a group to promote high standards of scholastic achievement. AΩA subsequently grew to become a national medical school honorary organization. The marker used to have an attached bronze plaque, but it has been stolen by vandals.

A third memorial is a tribute to the Illinois Training School for Nurses, which functioned on this site from 1880 to 1929. Erected in 1956, the slabs of marble are arranged so that their angle marks the original corner of the school. Initially there were two bronze plaques here, one a replica of the nurses' graduation pin and the other a tribute to the school, but these have long since both disappeared.

The fourth memorial, the Guthrie Rock, is a huge reddish-gray, 40-ton boulder inscribed with the words "To Samuel Guthrie MD 1782–1848. Commemorating his discovery of chloroform. Erected by the Chicago Medical Society." Sam Guthrie, a New Yorker, described the process for preparing "chloric ether" in 1832; it was first used as a surgical anesthetic by Simpson, in Edinburgh, in 1847. The rock was presented to the city in 1904, but no one seemed to want it; not until 1957 did the boulder reach its fifth, and presumably permanent, resting place here. Like the other monuments in the park, it once bore a bronze plaque that is now missing.

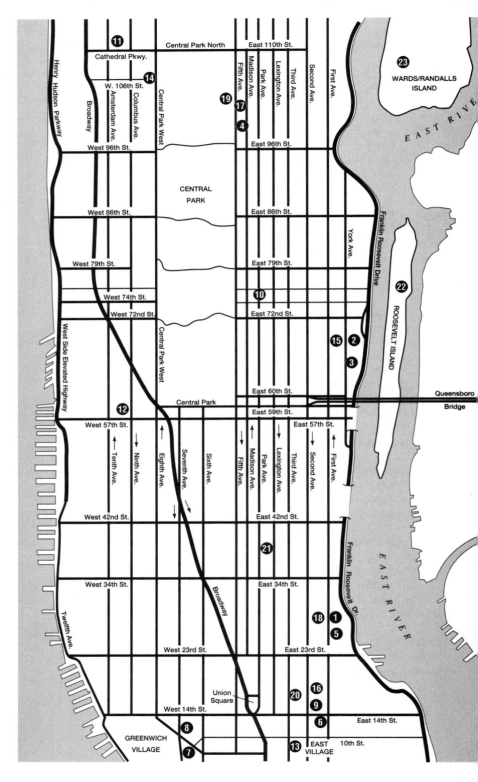

New York City

These key numbers will be found at appropriate points in the text.

NEW YORK CITY IS the biggest, richest, busiest medical community in the world. It has more doctors, more hospitals, and more medical schools than any other city anywhere. The "Big Apple" probably has more people employed in the health-care professions than in any other single industry, yet it has done almost nothing to foster health-related tourism. The city has museums of holography, broadcasting, and even Tibetan art—but its medical history has been negligently preserved. Amazingly, New York City lacks a sense of theater about its medical heritage. It has restored authors' cottages, old seamen's homes, former arsenals, farm houses, and Revolutionary War–era churches; yet you will search in vain for any doctor's office, operating theater, apothecary, or hospital that has received similar loving attention.

To appreciate New York's medical riches, you must put aside expectations nurtured by other cities. But do not be put off: New York is not like other cities, and its health-care institutions, more than any of its other industries, reveal much about its essential character.

New York is the place where health-care personnel spend inordinate amounts of time waiting for elevators, riding elevators, and cursing elevators. The city has almost 50,000 hospital beds, for the most part vertically stacked, and those are still not enough. While many of the nation's hospitals suffer from a bed surplus, New York—especially in its hospitals that cater to the poor—has the opposite problem: the beds are insufficient. Huge numbers of patients wait for beds, hospital beds spill out into the hallways, and patients who might have been discharged in other locales remain in the hospital because there is no place for them to go. The result is a plethora of enormous utilitarian edifices, designed to process masses of people, with a minimum of frills. Health care for the millions is an expensive proposition; there aren't a lot of dollars left over for appearances, despite the enormous wealth of some of the city's inhabitants.

The stark contrast between the devastating poverty of the city's poorest inhabitants and the stunning wealth of its richest creates another phenomenon that will seem foreign to many visitors: most of New York's medical institutions must be protected from those they were designed to serve. Access to most hospitals is limited. Visitors must check in with guards at the front gate, and people without valid business are turned away. Those leaving hospitals are examined almost as closely as those entering: yearly hospital losses from theft run to several thousand dollars per bed. The result is a large police presence in most hospitals. While many use "rent-a-cops," the NYC Health and Hospitals Corporation has its own police force, 1000 strong, serving only the municipal-owned hospitals.

There is an enormous amount to be seen and experienced here, both in a historical sense and in terms of contemporary importance to the health professions. Most sites can be visited by any tourist, and most are near places that would also interest nonmedical tourists. A simple way to get a good overview of Manhattan and its principal medical landmarks is to take the inexpensively priced, three-hour Circle Line boat tour (phone 563-3200 for sailing schedules). You can see many of the major medical centers (NYU – Bellevue, Columbia, Cornell, Rockefeller University) and get close-up looks at Roosevelt and Ward's islands.

If you want to see as much as possible in a brief period of time and would like strolling around a relatively compact area, try one or more of the following walks:

· The Miracle Mile — includes New York Hospital – Cornell, Rockefeller University, and Memorial Sloan-Kettering. This is a convenient clustering of some of the nation's most prestigious medical institutions.

· Stuyvesant Square — includes Beth Israel, New York Eye and Ear Infirmary, Rutherford Place, Stuyvesant Polyclinic, and the site of the New York Infirmary. This very pleasant stroll offers a diverse group of medical landmarks in an old neighborhood with lots of ethnic flavor.

· Central Park East — includes Mt Sinai, the New York Academy of Medicine, and the J Marion Sims statue. This is a fancy area, and the proximity of Central Park makes the visit particularly enjoyable.

· Roosevelt Island — (see below) If the day is pleasant, there are few more relaxed ways to take in some of New York's medical sights.

MANHATTAN

Columbia Presbyterian Medical Center 168th Street and Broadway 10032. (212) 305-3900. Columbia is the oldest medical school in New York City and the second oldest in the country. The combined Columbia Presbyterian enterprise was the first medical complex anywhere to warrant the name "medical center".

The forerunner of this medical school was chartered in 1767 as the Medical School of King's College. Though the Philadelphia Medical College awarded a baccalaureate degree in medicine (in the English tradition) in 1768, King's College was the first to award an MD in 1770. King's College shut down during the Revolutionary

War and discarded the title of the sovereign when it reopened in 1784, instead opting for the new name Columbia College. The medical school lagged behind; it reopened officially in 1792, and for the next three decades was a marginal operation.

In 1807 the Medical Society of the County of New York elected to open its own proprietary school, dubbing it the College of Physicians and Surgeons. This enterprise thrived and eventually absorbed the medical faculty of Columbia College (1813), an event which marked the end of medical education at Columbia for 78 years. For most of the nineteenth century, P & S remained a profitable place for its proprietors; it was often buffeted by the turbulence of conflicting medical personalities and did not stress its students with unduly rigorous standards.

In the 1880s, P & S attracted the generosity of the Vanderbilt family (through Vanderbilt family physician—and later P & S president—Dr James MacLane), resulting in the gift of a new school building (across the street from Roosevelt Hospital, at Tenth Avenue and 59th Street), a clinic building (the Vanderbilt Clinic), and the Sloane Hospital for Women (Emily Sloane was Cornelius Vanderbilt's daughter). P & S's handsome new facilities and new prosperity greatly interested Columbia College, which for some years had been wanting a medical school in order to elevate itself to university status. P & S was likewise interested in Columbia, in order to achieve the prestige that a university affiliation would confer. Columbia's substantial and growing endowment was also attractive, now that P & S had such a large and fine physical plant to maintain. In 1891 the two institutions were joined. (P & S, however, reserved the right to appoint its own staff and to refuse to admit women, who were excluded until 1917.)

The following years were dominated by Columbia P & S's need for adequate clinical facilities for its large student body. Before the end of the nineteenth century, clinical instruction had taken a backseat to didactic teaching in medical student education—and these minimal clinical needs had been successfully accommodated by Bellevue and New York Hospital, each of which allowed a small number of students on their wards. In 1927, however, New York Hospital concluded an agreement with Cornell University, effectively excluding P & S students; and Bellevue Hospital was dominated, first, by its own medical school, and later by NYU.

P & S, therefore, shopped around for another hospital with which it could develop an exclusive association. The obvious choice was Roosevelt Hospital, across the street, but numerous attempts to accomplish a union were torpedoed by personality conflicts between key figures. P & S also approached St Luke's, Lenox Hill

Hospital, and even Cornell, without success. In 1911, with the way being smoothed by Edward Harkness's money and behind-the-scenes negotiations, Columbia and Presbyterian decided on a joint enterprise — though it took another 17 years for the physical merger to be consummated.

Presbyterian Hospital had been founded in 1868 by the philanthropist James Lenox, and formally opened in 1872. Though the hospital was Presbyterian in name and origin, it was Mr Lenox's intention that the hospital serve "the Poor of New York without Regard to Race, Creed or Color." From the beginning Presbyterian was a forward-looking hospital. In 1876 it was the site of the first complete operation in America performed under the then brand-new Lister technique of antisepsis. (The procedure, performed by Dr Stimson, was a mid-thigh amputation accomplished under a continuing mist of carbolic spray.) Presbyterian pioneered the unit record system (1916), whereby each patient would be assigned a number under which all inpatient and outpatient records would be maintained . Prior to this, records tended to be filed consecutively by date of treatment, or by diagnosis, with inpatient and outpatient records kept separately.

The site at 168th Street and Broadway was selected in 1922; construction was completed in 1929. Thus the new medical center had the remarkable good fortune of being paid for just before the financial crash of October 1929. It was the tallest, most densely concentrated medical center in the world, and would be the role model for many others to follow. The inscription above the 168th Street entrance ("For of the Most High Cometh Healing") led local wags to comment that in the Presbyterian view, the success of the healing process seemed to depend on how high the buildings were.

In the twentieth century, Columbia Presbyterian has been one of the most influential medical centers in the country. It was here that the oxygen tent was first used (1910), that amniocentesis was first performed for predicting genetic defects in the fetus (1959), and that L-dopa was first prescribed for treating victims of Parkinson's disease (1969). It was also here (in the early 1960s) that Drs John Gorman and Vincent Freda developed RhoGAM, a "vaccine" that prevents Rh-negative mothers from developing dangerous antibodies when giving birth to Rh-positive babies.

Columbia Presbyterian was also home to the most famous woman physician of all time — arguably the physician whose name is written and spoken more often each day than that of any other in history. In the early 1950s Virginia Apgar developed a simple, yet remarkably informative and useful, scale for assessing the health of newborn infants. She was neither a pediatrician nor an obstetrician, but rather an anesthesiologist. The scale she created is based on a mnemonic using her own last name: *a*ppearance, *p*ulse, reflex *g*rasp, *a*ctivity, and *r*espirations. Every baby born in this country (and in many others) is given an Apgar rating at one minute and another at five minutes. Each Apgar score recorded or discussed is a tribute to Dr Virginia Apgar.

Today the Columbia Presbyterian Medical Center is an imposing group of 30 or so buildings on the cliffs overlooking the Hudson River. Despite the dramatic setting, the buildings in general are bulky, drab, and uninteresting. A new Presbyterian Hospital Building is scheduled to be completed in the 1990s, and advance reports suggest that it will be considerably more attractive than the present buildings. No tours are available at present.

(1) *New York University Medical Center* 550 First Avenue 10016. (212) 340-7300. Together with the adjacent Bellevue Hospital and other associated institutions, this medical center occupies a total of 70 acres, stretching from 23d Street to 34th and from the East River to both sides of First Avenue. The College of Dentistry, located on First Avenue between 24th and 25th streets, is the third oldest (founded in 1865) dental school in the country and the largest private one.

NYU's history has been intertwined with that of Bellevue Hospital since the very beginning of the school. The school was initially organized as the Medical Department of the University of New York in 1841; students and faculty soon afterward began using Bellevue for clinical instruction. In 1898, the University Medical Department combined with the Bellevue Hospital Medical College (established 1861) to form the University and Bellevue Hospital Medical College. The name was formally changed to New York University College of Medicine in 1935, and to New York University School of Medicine in 1960.

The University Hospital had its origin in 1894, when it was founded as the New York Postgraduate Hospital and Medical School. Columbia took over the hospital in a loose merger in 1929 and continued to operate it until the late 1940s, when Postgraduate seceded from Columbia and merged with NYU. The name was then changed to University Hospital, and NYU for the first time had its own hospital. The present structure dates from 1963, though there have been numerous additions since then.

One of the university's most famous components is the Howard A Rusk Institute of Rehabilitation Medicine founded in 1946 and now the largest and most complete of its kind in the world. It was in 1946 that Rusk (widely considered the father of rehabilitation medicine) founded the world's first medical-school Department of Physical Medicine and Rehabilitation, as a direct result of his experiences in developing rehabilitiation services for soldiers during World War II.

This is a huge busy medical center, with no formal arrangements for tours. Nonetheless, wandering around the campus perimeter, especially in conjunction with a tour of Bellevue, gives one a good sense of how big and imposing a university medical center in New York can be. Visitors may wish to wander into the medical school lobby, where there is a beautifully restored Bellevue Hospital horse-drawn ambulance. If you walk straight back from the front door, you will enter the medical library on its mezzanine, where there are various exhibits from the archives, including (during my visit) a large collection of microscopes and numerous portraits of individuals important in NYU's and Bellevue's history.

②️ *New York Hospital – Cornell Medical Center* 525 East 68th Street 10021. (212) 517-1401. New York Hospital is the oldest private hospital in New York City and the second oldest in the United States, yielding in priority only to Pennsylvania Hospital (1751). NYH was founded in 1771 with a royal charter from King George III, so it is ironic that the first patients cared for in NYH's small building at Worth and Duane Streets were Colonial soldiers wounded while defending the city against the British fleet in 1776. From the start some beds were devoted to psychiatric patients, but in 1821 NYH established the entirely separate Bloomingdale Asylum — which eventually was moved to White Plains. NYH moved to its present location in 1932, in a joint venture with Cornell University Medical School.

The New York Hospital was the site of a Doctors' Riot in 1788. The New York citizenry had become incensed over several episodes of grave robbing in a brief period of time, so when there was a report that four doctors at the New York Hospital had been seen dissecting a corpse, the citizens flew into a rage. A mob descended on the hospital and seized four anatomists, who later were rescued and released; but for several days all the hospital's doctors had to either hide or leave town to escape persecution. In all, five people were killed and ten were wounded before order was restored; and it was the doctors who were fined twenty-two pounds, seven shillings, and ten pence for damages to the dissection building.

Cornell University Medical School was founded in 1898, by a splinter group of faculty who had seceded from the University Medical College of New York University, together with some likewise dissident faculty from the Bellevue Hospital Medical College.

The original student body came from both of these schools, as well as from a contingent of 70 women from the Medical College of the New York Infirmary. Though Cornell professed to welcome women students, it instituted a requirement that women (and not men) take two years of training in Ithaca; the number of women students dropped rapidly to 21 in 1901, and then to ten in 1903. Originally the school was located across from Bellevue Hospital. Cornell, however, used NYH for teaching purposes from its founding, but didn't enter into a formal agreement concerning shared staff and facilities until 1927.

The complex that the two institutions now share was opened in 1932 and was widely admired from the beginning (one critic called it the "last smile of skyscraper romanticism"). Loosely modeled on the Palace of the Popes, in Avignon, France, it is a huge neo-Gothic structure composed of numerous buildings, all skillfully massed and with strong vertical lines, all held together by the repeated use of a stylized Gothic window with a pointed arch. (The construction costs for the complex were covered by a $40 million gift from Payne Whitney and a $5 million grant from the Rockefeller Foundation.) When it was opened, the medical center was widely regarded as

Gothic tower, New York Hospital – Cornell Medical Center *(Credit: Lisa Sheble)*

luxurious (perhaps unnecessarily so, in the depths of the Depression) as well as beautiful. Originally, for their meals, private patients were provided with silver-plated utensils, which were washed in a special room across from the main kitchen. There was a special shop in the powerhouse for replating the utensils when they became worn.

NYH–CUMC has contributed an enormous number of significant firsts to the development of American medicine. Some of these include:

1943 Development of the Papanicolaou ("pap") test for the detection of cervical cancer

1944 The first eye bank, for the storing of human corneas for transplant operations

1947 The first televised surgical procedure, demonstrating the potential of television as a medical teaching device

1955 Dr Vincent du Vigneaud receives the Nobel Prize for chemistry for his work resulting in the synthesis of the pituitary hormone oxytocin

Also on the NYH–CUMC campus is the **Hospital for Special Surgery,** which provides orthopedic and rheumatology services for the entire complex. Originally incorporated in 1863 as the New York Society for the Relief of the Ruptured and Crippled, the HSS is the oldest orthopedic hospital in the United States. HSS moved to its present location in 1955. In 1970 the Department of Bioengineering at HSS created the prototype for the artificial knee joint — the total condylar knee replacement — that is now the worldwide standard. In 1983, HSS developed the first computerized sytem for selection, custom design, and manufacturing of orthopedic prostheses and joint replacements.

Together, NYH–CUMC, Rockefeller University, and Memorial Sloan-Kettering make up what New Yorkers call the Miracle Mile. Over the years many observers have suggested that the institutions would function more efficiently and effectively as a single, cohesive unit; but each has chosen to go its own way.

Requests for tours are handled on a case-by-case basis. Call 517-1401 for details.

(3) *Rockefeller University* 1230 York Avenue 10021. (212) 570-8969. Rockefeller University is one of the most unique and prolific medical institutions in New York City, and probably in the world. Founded in 1901 as the Rockefeller Institute for Medical Research, it was the first American institution wholly devoted to medical

research. For the first five years it distributed research money to existing laboratories; but in 1906 the first building was completed on this 15-acre site, and the place has been going like gangbusters ever since. The money in the early years came exclusively from John D Rockefeller, Sr. Now only 30 percent comes from Rockefeller endowment funds.

Scientists here have traditionally concentrated on basic biomedical research, especially at the cellular level; the results have been spectacular. An abbreviated list of Rockefeller discoveries includes the following: The identification of blood groups, eliminating the danger of mismatches in transfusions; the first electron micrograph of a cell; the first demonstration that viruses cause cancer in animals; the first demonstration that DNA transmits hereditary information; the first chemical description of immunoglobulin, one of the body's key defenses against disease; the discovery of such cellular components as ribosomes, lysosomes, and the endoplasmic reticulum; the deciphering of the chemical structure of antibodies; and the discovery of the first effective treatment for African sleeping sickness. It's no wonder that so many Nobel Prize winners (nineteen) have been associated with Rockefeller over the years, or that five are currently working on campus.

In 1959 Rockefeller became a graduate university, chartered to grant PhD degrees. In 1965 it assumed its present name — but it may have the smallest student body of any university anywhere. It admits only about two dozen students a year, and the entire student body seldom exceeds 125. There are no formal departments and no prescribed curriculum. Rockefeller simply gathers together extraordinarily talented scientists, gives them the resources they need, and unleashes them. Patients in the 40-bed hospital are admitted primarily so that Rockefeller scientists can study their diseases; there is no charge of any kind to those accepted.

Rockefeller University is not open to the public, but a stroll along its perimeter is nonetheless fascinating. The campus extends from 62d Street to 68th Street, and from York Avenue to FDR Drive. It's a pleasing collection of low-rise and high-rise buildings, some older and some starkly modern, girded by an iron-spike fence set into brick pillars. Be sure to look through the gate at 66th and York, up the long drive to the columned, ivy-covered Founders Hall — the Institute's first permanent structure, erected in 1906. The exhibition hall here contains scientific instruments devised at Rockefeller or used by Rockefeller scientists in ground-breaking research. An example is the Carrel-Lindbergh perfusion pump, with which an animal organ was first artificially maintained outside its host body. The pump was devised by the Rockefeller Nobel laureate Alexis Carrel and the transatlantic aviator Charles Lindbergh.

Entrance, Rockefeller University *(By permission of The Rockefeller University/LR Moberg)*

(4) *Mt Sinai Medical Center* One Gustav Levy Place 10029. (212) 652-8888. The Mt Sinai Medical Center includes both the hospital complex (which has a long and colorful history) and the medical school (whose history is relatively brief). When the hospital was established, in 1852, it was known as The Jews' Hospital, and was located on 28th Street between Seventh and Eighth avenues. (It is the second-oldest Jewish-sponsored hospital in the country, after the Jewish Hospital in Cincinnati.) By the following decade the growing hospital had become substantially less sectarian; its name was changed to Mt Sinai Hospital in 1866. The present location of the complex, between Fifth and Madison Avenues, stretching from 98th Street to 102d Street, is Mt Sinai's third.

Over the years Mt Sinai has had its share of landmark events: It was here that Bernard Sachs described the disease known as amaurotic familial idiocy (later renamed Tay-Sachs disease) in 1887. In 1896, Henry Koplik described the telltale spots inside the mouth—known ever since as Koplik's spots—that are an early diagnostic sign of measles. Other research at Mt Sinai resulted in the description of Brill's disease and the Schwartzman phenomenon. Blood transfusion techniques using citrate to prevent clotting were perfected in 1915, and Crohn's disease (regional ileitis) was first described here too. Today Mt Sinai continues with one of the most vigorous research commitments in the country.

Since moving to its current location, in 1904, Mt Sinai has grown dramatically, its only backward step seeming to be the closing of its School of Nursing diploma program in 1971, after 90 years of operation. Buildings have been periodically torn down and replaced, so that the oldest building extant is Guggenheim Hall (completed in 1927), on 98th Street. The newest building (slated to be completed in 1991) is a dramatic 10-story, 625-bed hospital pavilion designed by IM Pei; it is to be composed of three towers, connected by vast atriums surmounted by two pyramidal skylights.

The Mt Sinai School of Medicine is one of the few modern schools in the country to have been established by a hospital rather than by a university. It was granted a provisional charter in 1963, and an absolute charter in 1968 (after it developed an affiliation with the City University of New York). As of last report, Mt Sinai has no formal program of tours and no permanent historical display; but that could change with the completion of the IM Pei building.

(5) *Bellevue Hospital Center* First Avenue and 27th Street 10016. (212) 561-4141. Like New York City itself, Bellevue Hospital is almost too much to comprehend. In its 250-plus years it has meant so much, and contributed so much, to so many people that its story is difficult to outline, let alone tell fully. It's a place of legends, scandals, outrages, innovations, and achievement. It's the oldest municipal hospital in the United States, and prides itself on being "the hospital that never turns anyone away." It's the subject of thousands of articles and dozens of books and plays. Gerald Green's novel *The Last Angry Man,* William Nolen's *The Making of a Surgeon,* Charles Reginald Jackson's *The Lost Weekend,* Joseph Kramm's Pulitzer Prize–winning play *The Shrike*—all of these works, and dozens more, celebrate and castigate and contemplate Bellevue. This is a hospital that has captured imaginations not only in New York City but across the country and around the world.

Bellevue traces its history to a six-bed infirmary on the second floor of the "Publick Workhouse and House of Correction of the City of New York," founded in 1736. The Almshouse Hospital (as it came to be called) was moved to Chambers Street in 1796, and then to the Belle Vue Farm in 1816. Until late in the nineteenth century, the hospital was cursed with recurrent scandals—lack of supplies and sometimes of food, crude and vicious surroundings, untrained female prisoners providing what limited nursing care there was, and frightful mortality rates. There was always more to Bellevue than the scandals suggested, always a current of talent and innovation and compassionate, dedicated care, but it wasn't until the 1870s, with the establishment of the Bellevue Nurses' Training School and the beginnings of modern scientific medical understanding and practices, that Bellevue became known worldwide as a pioneering medical institution.

Bellevue's list of firsts in the chronology of American health care is probably unmatched anywhere:

1750	First recorded instance of instruction in anatomic dissection, by Dr John Bard, using the body of an executed criminal
1808	First tying-off of a major artery (the femoral) to treat an aneurysm, by Dr David Hosack
1819	First hospital to require a qualified physician to pronounce a patient dead (subsequent to an embarrassing incident in which a patient presumed dead had proved not to be so)
1856	First use in the United States of a hypodermic syringe, introduced into this country by Dr Benjamin Fordyce Barker
1867	First hospital outpatient department, established as the "Bureau of Medical and Surgical Relief for the Out Door Poor"
1869	First hospital-based ambulance system, an instant success, subsequently widely copied around the United States
1873	First American training school for nurses based on the Florence Nightingale plan of instruction
1876	First emergency pavilion in the nation
1878	First pathology course ever given at an American medical college, presented by William Welch of the faculty of the Bellevue Medical College
1884	First US laboratory for teaching and research in the microscopic sciences, the Carnegie Laboratory (Andrew Carnegie's first public gift)
1888	First male nursing school in the US, the Mills School of Nursing
1913	First metabolism ward in the Western Hemisphere
1920	First psychiatric inpatient service for children
1939	First hospital catastrophe unit in the world
1940	First cardiopulmonary lab in the world
1956	First development of the method of cardiac catheterization, ultimately leading to the Nobel Prize for Drs Dickinson Richards and Andre Cournand

Ironically, despite its extraordinary record of service and innovation, the bulk of Bellevue's influence and reputation probably derives from its role as a training institution. Over the years it has trained tens of thousands of health professionals from all over the world, and many of them have gone on to become preeminent in their fields. The Bellevue Medical College began operations in 1861 and continued until 1898, when it joined forces with University Medical College to become the University and Bellevue Hospital Medical College. Still later it became New York University School of Medicine. Columbia College of Physicians and Surgeons provided house staff to Bellevue from 1882 onwards, and for many years Cornell was involved too, but in 1968 NYU assumed full responsibility for training and clinical services at the hospital. Bellevue's pioneering school of nursing graduated its last class in 1969, but nursing students from other institutions now rotate through the hospital.

While it is most convenient to think of Bellevue as a phenomenon unto itself, isolated from its surroundings and the community of which it is a part, it is misleading to do so. Bellevue is merely the flagship, the oldest and most visible part, of the largest municipal health system in the world: the New York Health and Hospitals Corporation. HHC operates 11 general- and four long-term – care hospitals, 5 neighborhood health centers, and more than 30 satellite ambulatory-care clinics. (Bellevue, with 1197 beds, is not even the city's largest acute-care hospital; it comes second after King's County Hospital, in Brooklyn, which has 1269 beds.) HHC handles 4.3 million outpatient visits, as well as 1.2 million emergency room visits, each year. The system employs some 43,000 personnel, including its own private police force of about 1000 officers to provide security at its various facilities.

As massive and complicated as the whole system sounds, it is nonetheless accessible to be seen. HHC's philosophy is: "All this has been paid for by the taxpayer; the public therefore deserves access." Tours are available by advance arrangement.

The central feature of Bellevue Medical Center is a 25-story high-rise tower, which was opened to inpatients in 1975. Each floor contains 1.5 acres of space, composed of 1-bed, 2-bed, and 4-bed rooms. There are no longer any wards. Bellevue has 7 separate intensive care units. Some 223 psychiatric patients are accommodated on the building's upper floors, and there are courtrooms to accommodate commitment and conservator proceedings and the like.

Most of the older buildings from Bellevue's past have been razed to accommodate the newer structures, but some relics remain. If you stand on First Avenue and face the hospital, the oldest visible building will be on your left, on the southeast corner of 29th Street and First Avenue. This is the old psychiatric hospital (called the R & S building), the only building remaining from an entire campus designed by McKim, Mead, and White in the early years of this century. As of this writing, it is being used as a shelter for homeless men; though the beauty of the interior is still apparent beneath the vandalized surfaces, you need a police escort to see it. The brick hulk tucked between the parking garage and the tower is the old administration building; the wing extending to your right (the C & D wing) is the old tuberculosis unit. A good way to get a feel for the old pavilion design is to take the formal tour of the hospital and ask to be taken into the tunnel system that used to connect all the buildings. The old brick corridors are a seemingly endless maze, lined here and there with darkened rooms, some ankle-deep in water, filled with old cribs, wheelchairs, and hospital rubble of every description. It's an eerie and fascinating trip.

The oldest Bellevue building still standing is on 26th Street, a few doors away from First Avenue. This old pressed-brick building has the name "Carnegie Laboratory" embossed over its door, and the 1884 date is clearly visible. The Carnegie was the first laboratory for teaching and research in bacteriology and pathology in the United States.

Tours of the Bellevue Hospital Center can be arranged by calling the Public Affairs office at 561-4516.

⑥ *New York Eye and Ear Infirmary*   310 East 14th Street (at Second Avenue) 10003. (212) 598-1313. New York Eye and Ear is the oldest institution of its kind in the Western Hemisphere and the third oldest hospital in New York City, dating from 1820. The current location dates from 1856. After the newer 14th Street building was added in 1968, the older (1903) 13th Street building stood partly vacant for several years. The furnishings and design seemed so old-fashioned, yet were so well preserved, that the setting was used to film the hospital scene in the movie *The Godfather*.

There's an extremely specialized small museum here that may interest some readers. Called the **Edgar B Burchell Memorial Museum,** it contains over 250,000 slides covering every known eye affliction, plus a collection of 400 temporal-bone dissections. The man after whom the museum was named prepared all the specimens. He started at Eye and Ear in 1899, at the age of 17, as a porter, was promoted to laboratory orderly, and — without any formal education — worked his way, over the years, to the post of bacteriologist and serologist. He is credited with defining the various possible positions of the seventh facial nerve via his meticulous temporal-bone dissections. As a result of his work, surgeons are much

less likely to damage the nerve during operations, and thousands of patients have been saved from needless facial paralysis as a result. Burchell received an honorary doctorate from Roanoke College in 1936, and is the only layman ever elected to Fellowship in the American Academy of Ophthalmalogy and Otolaryngology.
Call to arrange tours.

⑦ *Northern Dispensary* 165 Waverly Place 10014. (212) 242-5511. New York City guidebooks frequently mention this place because its triangular shape and fortuitous location in the middle of an intersection make it the only building in the city with one side on two streets (Christopher Street and Grove Street join here) and two sides on one street (Waverly Place forks off in two directions). Its historical significance is that it is one of the few remaining relics of a system of health care delivery that goes back to the late eighteenth century. Other dispensaries were established in Philadelphia in 1786, New York in 1791, Boston in 1796, and Baltimore in 1800; this one (founded in 1827) is the only one that still exists, and it has operated continuously since its inception.

For many years the dispensaries were the only providers of health care to the urban poor in this country; they also provided young doctors with practical postgraduate education. Essentially they were the nineteenth century's equivalent of the county hospital outpatient clinic. Bellevue, for example, opened its outpatient department in the 1860s, but Philadelphia General had no clinic until 1919 and outpatient departments at city hospitals in many other cities opened even later than that. However, the dispensaries differed from the later hospital clinics in that they were generally supported by charitable or benevolent organizations with a bias toward the working poor and against the drunkards, wastrels, and idlers who were usually seen as the natural clientele of the almshouses. The chief activity of the dispensaries was the writing and filling of prescriptions: dispensaries dispensed. Some also provided minor surgery, vaccinations, and tooth-pulling. Though the level of care given in the dispensaries was often pretty crude, it was no more so than that given in many private doctor's offices.

Most dispensaries closed in the early part of the twentieth century, when increasing specialization, improved technology, and modern surgical practices made the hospital the focal point for contemporary health care. The same developments also dried up the supply of doctors to staff the dispensaries, as young medics instead sought out house-officer positions in hospitals. Somehow the Northern Dispensary survived. Today it looks pretty much as it did in 1837, when its most famous patient, Edgar Allan Poe, was treated (free of charge) for a cold — except for the third floor, which was added in 1854. (If you look closely you can see the line of bricks where the "new" story begins.) The Dispensary still functions as a public clinic and is therefore open to visitors; but there are no provisions for tourists and there is little besides a marker, bearing the building's completion date, to indicate the building's significance. (It's also the only surviving public building of its vintage in New York.)

(8) *St Vincent's Hospital* 153 West 11th Street 10011. (212) 790-7000. This is the city's oldest and the nation's largest (813 beds) Catholic hospital. It was founded in 1849 by four Daughters of Charity, who installed 30 beds in a small brick house on East 13th Street. The hospital was moved to its present site in 1856. Over the years St Vincent's has been responsible for a number of medical firsts: The first endotracheal intubation anywhere, pioneered by Dr Joseph O'Dwyer and now the cornerstone of general anesthesia and effective cardiac resuscitation (1880); the first automotive ambulance service in the nation (1900); and the first "code blue" — St Vincent's called it "code 99" — for alerting staff about a patient's cardiac arrest (1961). The hospital has had its share of famous patients, including the survivors of the *Titanic* disaster (1912). The poet Edna St Vincent Millay owed her middle name to the fact that the life of one of her family members had been saved here; Miss Millay's parents were so grateful that they named their daughter in the hospital's honor.

The hospital now occupies much of the block bounded by Sixth and Seventh Avenues and 11th to 12th streets, as well as some peripheral buildings. The only building of any age and distinction is the Nurses' Residence building, at 158 West 12th, which sports a golden canopy over its main entrance and has a dandy bas-relief of a young nurse over another, lesser, entrance on the same street. The chapel, with its stained-glass windows, is also attractive. Call 790-7560 to arrange a tour.

Directly across Seventh Avenue from St Vincent's there used to be a plaque — now long gone — marking the site at which Georges Clemenceau lived and practiced medicine in the late 1860s, some 50 years before he became France's distinguished wartime premier.

(9) *Original Site of New York Infirmary* 15th Street and Nathan Perlman Place (on Stuyvesant Square). The history of the New York Infirmary is confusing, but interesting. The confusing part is a consequence of the manner in which corporate names are bought and

sold as hospitals consolidate and divest themselves of one another. As a result the NYI is officially located at 170 William Street, in the form of the consolidated (in 1979) NYI–Beekman Downtown Hospital. But the Stuyvesant Square location was the home of the NYI from 1875 to 1979, and if you look closely there you can still find remnants of its history.

Now for the interesting part. The New York Infirmary was built by Dr Elizabeth Blackwell, the first woman medical-school graduate in the United States. She was admitted to Geneva Medical School, in upstate New York, largely by chance and via personal connections (no precedent was established, and no other woman was allowed to graduate from the school for another 16 years) and received her MD in 1849. After a brief period of study in London and Paris, she returned to the United States to find that positions in hospitals and dispensaries simply were not open to women physicians. As a result, she opened first a small private practice and then (in 1854) the New York Dispensary for Poor Women and Children. By this time, Elizabeth's sister Emily had also graduated from medical school (she had gone to the Cleveland Medical College, after the Geneva Medical School refused to accept her), and soon joined Elizabeth. In 1857 the Blackwell sisters and a colleague, Dr Marie Zakrzewska, opened the New York Infirmary for Women and Children, the first hospital in the world run only by women. For many years it remained one of the few places where women physicians could gain practical experience. The Stuyvesant Square site was purchased in 1875.

Though by the 1860s, it was easier for women to gain a medical-school education, barriers were still substantial; in 1868 the Blackwells chartered the Medical College of the Infirmary, installing it in two old houses on Second Avenue. In 1886 a new medical-college building was erected next to the New York Infirmary, on 15th Street. The Medical College of the Infirmary maintained remarkably high standards for its time: It pioneered the three-year medical-school curriculum and offered the first course in preventive medicine (or "Hygiene") available anywhere in the country. The college continued to train women physicians until 1898, when tragedy struck: the college building with all its equipment was destroyed by fire. Cornell Medical School then suddenly opened its doors to women, and all students at the Medical College of the Infirmary moved en masse to the larger institution. The faculty of the Women's Medical College fared far less well, however; with the exception of a single minor post, no women were appointed to the teaching staff of Cornell for many years.

Despite all of this the New York Infirmary continued to grow for several decades. A new hospital was built in 1899, and an entirely new facility replaced the then-outmoded buildings in 1954. All of that is now gone; all that remains is a small plaque in the lobby of the Bernstein Pavilion of the Beth Israel Medical Center, at 15th Street and Nathan Perlman Place (the old location of the NYI), and a set of brownstones at 306–310 East 15th Street proclaiming the location of the Helen Altschul Pavilion of the New York Infirmary.

(10) *Lenox Hill Hospital* 100 East 77th Street 10021. (212) 794-4500. Until 1918 this hospital was known as the German Hospital of New York; much of its history is implicit in that name. The failure of the German revolution of 1848 resulted in an enormous outpouring of Germans onto American shores, including many German physicians. A German dispensary was organized on Canal Street, downtown, in 1857. Its offspring, the German Hospital, was completed in 1868 at the 77th Street site, on the edge of what was then a shantytown—a village of shacks whose inhabitants used the swamplands just south of the hospital for toilet facilities.

What made the German Hospital of those years so interesting was its staff. German medicine in the latter half of the nineteenth century was the most advanced in the world, especially in the areas of pathology and biological chemistry; these disciplines were, at that time, the keys to understanding the real nature of most diseases. The German-trained physicians here were among the best in this country, and their subsequent contributions reflected this advantage. Among the most famous were Max Einhorn (1860–1953), Willy Meyer (1858–1932), and Abraham Jacobi (1830–1919).

Einhorn was an early pioneer in gastroenterology. His book *Diseases of the Stomach* was one of the first gastroenterology texts to appear in English. He had the reputation of a first-rate gadgeteer, developing one of the first duodenal tubes, the "string test" for the diagnosis of bleeding from peptic ulcers, and the "golden bucket" (which was attached to a string, swallowed, and allowed to pass into the duodenum for the recovery of bile and duodenal and pancreatic juices). The Lenox Hill Einhorn Auditorium is named after him [see the bas-relief over the entrance, with the busts of three early German pioneers of gastroenterology: Adolph Kussmaul (1822–1902), Ismar Boas (1858–1938), and Carl Anton Ewald (1845–1915)].

Willy Meyer immigrated to the United States in 1884, and pioneered many surgical techniques. He introduced to this country the Trendelenburg position, in which the supine patient's head is inclined lower than the feet in order to increase the brain's blood supply during shock. He performed the first cystoscopy in this

country (1887) and was first to use the electrically lighted cysto-
scope (1896). Meyer's most dramatic innovation was the development (with his engineer brother, Julius) of the first operating room
designed to allow work under either positive or negative thoracic
pressure, resulting in intrathoracic operations at the German Hospital which were impossible elsewhere.

The greatest physician associated with the German Hospital was
Abraham Jacobi, whose contributions as a clinician, teacher, and
organizer made him a pivotal figure in the development of American medicine. He arrived in this country in 1853, after spending two
years in prison for his part in the failed German uprisings of 1848.
He was one of the organizers of the German Dispensary, as well as
of the German Hospital. It was on his initiative that the hospital
opened the first tuberculosis unit in any general hospital in the
country. Jacobi's first love, however, was pediatrics, a field that was
not a specialty until Jacobi made it one. Using the German Hospital
as a base, Jacobi expanded his activities until he was a professor at
three medical schools in New York City. He occupied the first
university chair of pediatrics in the country, was twice president of
the American Pediatric Society, and—in 1912, at the age of 82—
became the first, and to date the only, foreign-born president of the
American Medical Association.

With the onset of World War I the mood of the country changed
considerably, and anti-German sentiment became widespread. In
1917 the German Hospital's annual reports, which previously had
been bilingual, were for the first time published in English only. In
1918 the name was changed to Lenox Hill Hospital; and though it
has remained a prestigious private hospital—located, as it is, in the
middle of New York's posh Upper East Side—it has never regained
the national reputation it enjoyed under its former name. The
current buildings date from the 1960s and 1970s and are not particularly distinguished. No tours are available.

(11) *St Luke's–Roosevelt Hospital Center* Amsterdam Avenue and
114th Street 10025. (212) 523-4000. The first part of the name of
this hospital derives from the Gospel and the person of St Luke,
known to devout Christians everywhere as the "beloved physician." St Luke was the author of the parable of *The Good Samaritan*,
a story that reminds us that individual acts of compassion, kindness, and comforting can raise and sustain the spirit of mankind.

The endowment for St Luke's was begun in 1846, but it took 12
years for the Episcopal community to come up with the necessary
funds to open the hospital. The first structure was at 54th Street and
Fifth Avenue, then a rural and undeveloped part of the city. The

Exterior, St Luke's Hospital (mid-twentieth century) *(Photo courtesy of the Historic Archival Collection, The Bolling Medical Library, St Luke's–Roosevelt Hospital Center, New York. Thomas L Wood, photographer)*

move to the present site was begun in 1893, at a time when adjacent properties to the new location were building sites for the main Columbia University campus and the Cathedral of St John the Divine.

St Luke's is unusual in that it is still using its nineteenth-century hospital buildings to provide modern and technologically sophisticated treatment in an acute-care general hospital. The buildings are architecturally stunning, clearly anachronistic, and therefore probably doomed to eventual demolition. It's fun to walk into the Morningside Drive entrance, the old carriage-trade entrance, and imagine the liveried doormen assisting the elderly dowagers coming in for their checkups and rest cures. This entrance is now little-used, the brass rails are tarnished, and the fine old marble-and-hardwood lobby is cluttered with nondescript furnishings. The place has such potential! All it needs is the attention of someone with a little imagination, a sense of history, and a lot of money.

The hospital's main entrance, on 113th Street, is striking — certainly the most dramatic and impressive hospital entry in New York. One walks up the marble stairway, and suddenly the hospital chapel appears, its stunning stained-glass window providing an explosion of color. It was designed by Henry Holiday, of London, and was installed in the hospital in 1896; the central portion depicts Christ on the throne ministering to those in need, and the seven circular panels above portray "The Seven Corporal Works of Mercy": feeding the hungry, giving drink to the thirsty, clothing the naked, visiting the imprisoned, sheltering the homeless, visiting the sick, and burying the dead. Also in the chapel are five fifteenth-, seventeenth-, and eighteenth-century tapestries which, in a more subdued way, are as impressive as the window. Just to the left of the chapel, as you face it, is the doctors' cloak room, a wonderful relic, currently quite threadbare, that gives a feel for the deference accorded to physicians in the early years of this century.

As of this writing it is still possible to stroll through the marble halls of St Luke's, to savor the enormous archways and high ceilings, to see the exclusive private rooms with the maids' quarters down the hall, and to get some sense of what health care was like in one of this country's more exclusive hospitals 50 years ago.

In 1953 St Luke's merged with Women's Hospital, which had been founded in 1855 by Dr James Marion Sims (with considerable financial assistance from the Astors and other wealthy families). Women's had been the first hospital in the country to specialize in gynecology (Sims is widely regarded as the father of modern gynecology), and its success ushered in a whole generation of other specialty facilities. The first Women's Hospital was located at 53 Madison Avenue, but moved uptown to 50th Street and Park Avenue (the current site of the Waldorf-Astoria Hotel) in 1867, and then to 100th Street and Amsterdam Avenue in 1906. Currently, what is called the Women's Hospital Building is located across the street from Columbia University's main campus.

In 1979 St Luke's and Roosevelt hospitals completed the largest merger of two voluntary hospitals in the nation's history. The impetus for the merger was, of course, financial, with the hope that by combining efforts they could avoid duplication of services, increase their patient bases, and complement one another's strengths. Both were old, formerly prestigious, and wealthy hospitals that had fallen on rough times — buffeted by inflation, costly labor and technology, and an increasing burden of uninsured patients. In the 5 years before their merger, hospital closings included 85 public hospitals nationwide and 29 hospitals in the five New York City boroughs, with a substantial number in Manhattan alone.

The Roosevelt–St Luke's consortium has now embarked on an ambitious renovation and building program. What will and won't remain of the St Luke's site in the years ahead remains to be seen. At present St Luke's is a mixture of a few old, and several new, buildings. If you visit, try to arrive on a Wednesday in time for the noon services in the hospital chapel (which end at 12:30). Tours are sometimes available, by advance arrangement.

Syms Operating Theater exterior, Roosevelt Hospital *(Photo courtesy of the Archives at the Roosevelt Hospital Division of St Luke's–Roosevelt Hospital Center, New York. Ruth E Cushman, photographer)*

(12) *Roosevelt Hospital* 428 West 59th Street 10019. (212) 523-4000. Unlike most buildings and institutions that bear the Roosevelt name, this one was named after James Henry Roosevelt, a real estate and securities whiz who left a sizable portion of his estate to establish and endow Roosevelt Hospital, which opened for business in 1871. At first the hospital was formally dedicated to charity, but as the fame of its staff — particularly its surgical staff — spread, its clientele came to include many of New York's wealthiest citizens. Among other early notable achievements, Roosevelt was the place where rubber gloves were first used in an American operating room — the practice being introduced by William Halsted who was assistant attending surgeon here from 1882 to 1886, prior to becoming the first chief of surgery at Johns Hopkins. Likewise, it was here, in the early years of this century, that Roosevelt physicians developed the serial-plate method for x-ray diagnosis of gastrointestinal lesions.

Roosevelt was built on the pavilion plan, meaning a separate structure for each hospital function; so when Roosevelt added the world's most complete and elaborate operating theater, in 1892, the facility occupied its own building. Called the William J Syms building and named after the man who donated $350,000 for its construction, it was a magnificent showcase for surgical skill. Planned and directed by Dr Charles McBurney and enclosed in walls four feet thick, the lofty skylit amphitheater seated 185 observers and was surrounded by fully appointed rooms for instruments, sterilizers, supplies, and anesthesia; scrub rooms; and recovery rooms — a remarkable assemblage for the times. The entire building — walls, ceilings, even the laundry chute — was lined with marble and joined with iron fittings, to reduce the risk of infection and to allow for more efficient cleaning. The mosaic floors curved upward where they joined the walls, so that bacteria had fewer places to hide. It was here that McBurney demonstrated his famous anatomic point, where the tenderness of appendicitis is greatest, facilitating correct diagnosis. It was here, too, that McBurney performed the first McBurney incision (1893), still the favored surgical approach for appendicitis. The last operation performed in the Syms was in 1941, after which it was converted into offices. As of this writing the sparse Romanesque exterior of the Syms remains largely intact, but in the place of the gorgeous surgical amphitheater there is now only a roughly excavated cavern filled with air-conditioning ducts and bright orange I-beams. The Syms has recently achieved National Landmark status, so the exterior will remain intact, and (one hopes) the interior may be restored.

One of Roosevelt's current, more interesting projects is the Kathryn and Gilbert Miller Health Care Institute for Performing Artists. Because of Roosevelt's fortuitous location near Lincoln Center, Carnegie Hall, the Broadway theaters, and the Juilliard School — with their dancers, singers, and other performing artists, both student and professional — Roosevelt has unparalleled access to the occupational health problems that afflict such people. The institute currently operates out of modest quarters at Roosevelt, but — like the rest of the medical center — has hopes of expanding.

Current plans call for the demolition of three older buildings, including the School of Nursing Building (the school functioned from 1896 to 1973). When the planned thirteen-story hospital building is completed, at Tenth Avenue between 58th and 59th streets, four additional buildings will be torn down. Amid such turmoil, tours are doubtful. However, persons interested in seeing the Syms will find it at the corner of 59th Street and Columbus Avenue.

(13) *Stuyvesant Polyclinic* 137 Second Avenue (near East 8th Street) 10003. (212) 674-0220. This ornate pressed-brick structure

Stuyvesant Polyclinic, exterior detail *(By permission of Sr Aloysia Morelli, MSC —Administrator)*

fairly bristles with portrait busts: Celsius, Hippocrates, Aesculapius, and Galen on the porch; Harvey, Linné, Humboldt, Lavoisier, and Hufeland on the facade, beneath the cornice. The building was opened in 1884 as the German Dispensary, providing free medical care to German immigrants. It was owned for a while by the German Hospital (later to become Lenox Hill Hospital), and then by the German Polyklinik (an entirely separate charitable organization). During World War I, because of prevailing anti-German sentiment, the name was changed to Stuyvesant Polyclinic. After the war it became, again, German Dispensary — and reverted to Stuyvesant Polyclinic when anti-German feeling erupted again in World War II. By any name, it's a dramatic and interesting building. None like it are likely to be built ever again. Currently, some two dozen specialty clinics operate here on various days of the week, under the sponsorship of the nearby Cabrini Hospital. The lobby is said to have been restored to its original condition (the tilework looks old enough that the claim may be true), but the rest of the interior, of necessity, has been modernized. The management are agreeable to giving tours, so long as they are not overwhelmed by requests. Call first.

(14) *(Old) New York Cancer Hospital* 2 West 106th Street (at Central Park West) 10025. At this writing, the grand old building

that was the first hospital in the nation devoted exclusively to cancer care is a crumbling shell; but the structure has gained land-mark status, and it is likely that the building won't be bulldozed away. The story begins in 1883 when J Marion Sims, MD, then the reigning super-surgeon in the country, declared that "A cancer hospital is one of the greatest needs of the day, and it must be built. . . . The subject is too large and its interest too great to be lodged in a pavilion subsidiary to any other hospital." The French-Gothic building, of sandstone and pressed brick (completed in 1887), looks like a sixteenth-century French chateau, featuring three squat circular towers. The design (by Charles C Haight) was noteworthy for the first American use of circular wards, which were thought to provide optimum light, promote cleanliness, impede dust accumulation, and foster cheer. There was also a nifty system of ventilating each ward, even with doors and windows closed; and the circular shape afforded the nurses unobstructed views of all beds. However, financial difficulties in the 1890s led the hospital to admit non-cancer patients as well, and the name was changed in 1899 to General Memorial Hospital for Cancer and Allied Diseases. Other cancer hospitals were gradually built around the country, but Memorial Hospital, heavily funded from the beginning by the Rockefellers, has remained preeminent. (Memorial moved from 106th Street to its current location, where it has become the Memo-

New York Cancer Hospital, early drawing *(By permission of Memorial Sloan-Kettering Cancer Center)*

rial Sloan-Kettering complex in 1939.) For a while the old hospital functioned as the Towers Nursing Home, but in recent years it has been vacant and has been allowed to deteriorate. If the New York medical community were on its toes, surely someone would start a drive to turn this magnificent, historic structure into a medical museum for the city. In the meantime, tentative plans (always subject to change) are to restore the building for some yet-unspecified use, demolish the adjacent x-ray wing (constructed in the 1920s), and build a 26-story high-rise on the land thus cleared.

(15) *Memorial Sloan-Kettering Cancer Center* 1275 York Avenue (between 66th and 68th Streets) 10021. (212) 207-3628. This institution is the oldest, the largest, and probably the richest and most prestigious private cancer center in the country. Memorial Hospital, the clinical wing of the center, moved to this site from its previous location, on 106th Street (see above), in 1939. The land was donated by John D Rockefeller, Jr, and the funds were contributed by Rockefeller's General Education Board. The Sloan-Kettering Institute was founded in 1945 by the industrialists Alfred P Sloan, Jr, and Charles F Kettering, who believed that medical research — if conducted on the scale, and with the systems, that they had seen in their work at General Motors — had the potential to conquer cancer. From the early years of Sloan-Kettering, the research wing had a close affiliation with Memorial Hospital, often sharing staff, administration, and directors. Accomplishments over the years have been many. The Center was first to establish the existence of particular genes that determine resistance or susceptibility to cancer. It has been a major force in immunogenetics, some of its researchers having led in the development of specific markers for identifying and classifying different types of cancer cells. The Center was first (in 1926) to implant a radium source to treat malignancies. Today, the Center remains in the forefront of research into the molecular biology of cancer tissues, and virtually all of its 350 staff physicians are engaged in research. Lewis Thomas, the distinguished scientist-turned-popular-writer and medical observer, was president of MSKCC from 1973 until he became the Center's chancellor (1980 to 1983). MSKCC's facilities occupy over a dozen buildings in the area bounded by First and York Avenues and 66th and 68th Streets. Tours are available for groups with advance arrangements. Call 794-7972.

(16) *Beth Israel Medical Center* 10 Nathan Perlman Place 10003. (212) 420-2000. The Beth Israel was founded in 1890 as a free dispensary to care for the impoverished Eastern European Jewish

immigrants of the Lower East Side. In the hospital's early years, prejudice and discrimination played an important role in its growth. Russian, Polish, and Lithuanian Jewish doctors not only were excluded from the staffs of the various Catholic and Protestant hospitals around the city, but were not very welcome at the mostly German-Jewish Mt Sinai Hospital, uptown, which catered to a wealthier and distinctly more Americanized group. The Beth Israel moved to Stuyvesant Square in 1929, and has been gradually expanding ever since. It currently operates some 934 beds, making it one of the 100 largest medical centers in the country. Of the various buildings it occupies around the Square, by far the most interesting and attractive is the Dazian Pavilion, at 17th Street and Nathan Perlman Place. The bronze marquee over the main entrance, with its elegant Hebrew lettering, lends an air of somber dignity. Inside is a huge marble lobby, with curving staircases, decorated with busts of famous scientists and a wall-filling brass-and-marble sign calling the Beth Israel Medical Center "an enduring manifestation of Man's Humanity to Man." Tours are not currently available.

Harlem Hospital Center   506 Lenox Avenue (at 135th Street) 10037. (212) 491-1234. The history of Harlem Hospital gives a nicely condensed account of the history of blacks in American medicine — one-dimensional to be sure, but nonetheless revealing. Though the Harlem Hospital opened at its present site in 1907, its patients weren't predominantly black until the World War I years, with the advent of the great waves of black migration from the South. By 1911 the hospital was already outgrowing its physical plant; by 1915 a new wing was added, more than doubling the capacity to 390 beds. By the early 1920s, the entirely white hospital leadership was being widely criticized for fiscal incompetence and racial prejudice. In 1919 Harlem Hospital appointed its first and only black staff physician, Dr Louis Wright, as a clinical assistant in the outpatient department (the lowest job possible) — an event which created such a furor in the white power structure that the man who hired Dr Wright was, himself, tossed out. At that time Harlem was the only city hospital in the nation to have appointed a black to its medical staff, and until 1929 it was the only municipal hospital in New York City that hired black nurses. The issue of black staff at the hospital became a major issue for the Harlem community (whose members, in contrast to Southern blacks, were a voting power in the city), and the mayor's office eventually intervened. By 1929, 7 of the hospital's 64 physicians were blacks, and by the mid-1940s half of the visiting and house staff were blacks. The simple figures mask an incredible amount of factionalism, strife, morale trouble, and administrative restructuring. Along the way, in 1923, the hospital established its own training school for black nurses. (In 1917, when it began hiring black nurses, a number of white nurses quit, refusing to work alongside blacks; the hospital was compelled to start a school to create its own pool of nursing talent.) The school lasted more than 50 years, producing some 2000 nurses before it closed, in 1977.

Harlem Hospital was first opened in 1887, in a white 3-story frame building at 120th Street and the East River. Over the next 20 years, this building was added to repeatedly, and in 1907 part of the present site was occupied. Over the next 60 years the hospital underwent numerous construction programs; in 1969 it built the 18-story acute-care Martin Luther King, Jr, Pavilion.

Plagued by turmoil for most of the twentieth century, Harlem Hospital is still struggling, seemingly against the odds. In 1981 it underwent a difficult and disruptive strike of its house physicians; the strike was resolved, but most of the difficulties remain. The hospital is chronically underfunded. Harlem Hospital's catchment area ranks among the highest in the nation for poverty, crime, poor housing, and other socioeconomic problems. The hospital still serves large numbers of blacks, but its patients are increasingly Hispanic as well. The staff is now thoroughly integrated.

Hospital officials rarely have time to provide tours, but visitors are always welcome to view the public areas of the hospital. Be sure to note the huge sculptural group of a black family (by John Rhoden) on the facade of the blue-and-white King Pavilion, above the main entrance.

(17) *New York Academy of Medicine* 2 East 103d Street 10029. (212) 876-8200. The New York Academy of Medicine was founded in 1847 for the purposes of raising standards and promoting the profession of medicine in New York City. Although its organizational functions have been many over the years, the average visitor will be most interested in the academy's library, which is reputed to be the second-largest health sciences library in the world, second only to the National Library of Medicine. There are over 14 miles of closed stacks here — almost a million catalogued books, pamphlets, and illustrations. Anyone can look around the library and view the various exhibits; the staff, though cautious, are willing to let "all serious readers" look at most of the catalogued materials. The Rare Book Room and the History of Medicine Collection — containing the world's finest concentration of early medical Americana, and many early European medically-related works — can be seen by appointment only, and such appointments are not handed out lightly. The main library reading room is a classic, three stories high,

with ornate beamed ceilings hung with huge chandeliers. The library tables stretch out some 40 feet or so, with old Windsor chairs lined up along each side. Displays during a recent visit included old porcelain and glass urinals, doctor dolls from the Orient (mostly carved ivory, a couple in exotic woods, and one lush and gorgeous female figure in carved amber), old medicine chests and medicine bottles, bedpans and douche pans (of porcelain and pewter), and some infant feeders and "pap boats" (variously of handblown glass, pewter, and even one elegant little number of silver in a handwoven basket). The displays keep changing, and the academy's collection is almost limitless — even including George Washington's original dentures, made of ivory, engraved with his name, and set with human teeth, including one of Washington's own. The library is open to the public, Monday 12:30 to 5:30 and Tuesday through Friday 9 to 5. Admission is free.

(18)*Office of the Chief Medical Examiner* 520 First Avenue (at 30th Street) 10016. (212) 340-0100. Each year some 70,000 to 80,000 people die in New York City. Nearly half of those deaths are reported to the Office of the Chief Medical Examiner because they are found to have occurred "from criminal violence, by a casualty, by suicide, suddenly when in apparent health, when unattended by a physician, in [prison] facilities of the Departments of Corrections and of Juvenile Justice or in any unusual or suspicious manner." Almost 2000 turn out to be homicides. The result is a Chief Medical Examiner's office that is phenomenally busy, employing almost two dozen medical examiners and 50 field investigators, and requiring some 50,000 to 60,000 serology exams annually, 30,000 histology tissue specimens, and nearly 100,000 toxicology procedures. The scale of the task boggles the mind.

The Office of the Chief Medical Examiner was inaugurated in 1918 by an act of the State Legislature, making it the first governmental agency of its type in the country. In the same year the Office established the first toxicology laboratory; in 1938, the first serology laboratory (both at Bellevue). The department operated out of several other locations until it received its own building in 1960: the eight-story block it now occupies. The functional contemporary structure houses administrative offices and a records department, various laboratories, a mortuary and autopsy rooms, x-ray and photography facilities, a library, and a lecture hall. It also contains probably the most gruesome museum in the country, comprising some 2100 exhibits, including evidence from homicide cases and a considerable number of pathology specimens kept for teaching purposes. The entire collection is truly fascinating, and any health professional with a strong stomach can arrange to see it by calling 340-0163.

(19)*J Marion Sims Statue* Fifth Avenue and 103d Street (across the street from the New York Academy of Medicine) 10029. J Marion Sims (1813–1883) was an American original, a man of enormous charm and talent who became America's first super-surgeon and, in the process, laid the foundation for the modern specialty of gynecology. It was not by chance that Sims counted among his friends PT Barnum, the circus impresario; Sims was a gifted show-man as well as a surgeon. In 1861 he became the first American surgeon to travel in Europe to teach instead of to study. He was subsequently decorated by the governments of Italy, France, Spain, Portugal, and Belgium.

To understand Sims's achievement, one has to appreciate what "natural childbirth" meant in the mid-nineteenth century. There was little that doctors or midwives could do to help with a really difficult labor. When the child was big or the woman was small the tissues of the birth canal ripped, and the mother was often left with terrible wounds. Often such injuries would produce an opening from the bladder into the vagina—a vesicovaginal fistula—which inevitably would fail to heal and frustrate any surgeon's attempt to repair the defect. For the rest of her life, a woman with such an injury would be cursed with a continual flow of urine from her vagina. The resulting odors and hygiene problems usually con-demned such women to lives of shame and isolation, a fate made all the worse by the relative youth of the victims and the self-limiting nature of the condition—usually the sufferer lived many decades in wretched isolation.

Sims encountered many such women in his practice in rural Alabama. What the most prestigious surgeons in Europe and in America's most populous cities had failed to cure, the country doctor—operating on slave women—managed to repair. In 1852 he published his classic paper "On the Treatment of Vesico-Vaginal Fistula," followed in 1854 by "A Case of Vesico-Vaginal Fistula Resisting the Actual Cautery for More than Seven Years; Cured in Thirteen Days by the Author's Process."

Sims's success was not due merely to his surgical skill; he intro-duced an entirely new method of treatment. He placed the women on their sides (in what is now called the Sims position), employed a speculum of his own design (originally a bent spoon), inflated the vagina with air, and used a silver wire instead of the usual silk suture. After Sims's achievement became known, he left Alabama and settled in New York, organizing The Women's Hospital in 1855 (described under "St Luke's – Roosevelt Hospital Center," above). In 1876, along with numerous other honors, Sims was elected president of the American Medical Association.

Henry Street Settlement House 265 Henry Street 10002. (212) 766-9200. In the several decades following 1895, when Lillian Wald and a group of coworkers acquired this handsome three-story townhouse, the name "Henry Street Settlement House" became synonymous with three famous accomplishments. The first was the founding of the settlement house itself, where dozens of educational, organizational, and mutual-support activities were devised and implemented to help poor, and often bewildered, immigrants settle into their new country. Among the various pioneering projects that largely originated here were urban public playgrounds for children.

More directly relevant to the health professions is the Henry Street Settlement House's reputation as the birthplace of public-health nursing in general, and of the visiting-nurse program in particular. Lillian Wald (1867 – 1940) graduated from the New York Hospital Training School for Nurses in 1891, and shortly thereafter became dedicated to improving the deplorable conditions of immigrant slum-dwellers. Miss Wald, a tireless worker and inspired organizer, perceived the need for nursing in the home, and developed the nation's first system for providing exactly that. All visiting-nurse programs in this country are descendants of the Henry Street program.

Likewise, having learned that sickness was keeping a lot of children out of school, Miss Wald arranged to have Henry Street nurses provide services in a public school, and the experiment proved so successful that the New York school system eventually became home to the first public-school nursing program in the world.

The original Henry Street Settlement House still exists at its original address; behind the cast-iron railings and modest doorway it continues its work in the tradition established by Ms Wald and her coworkers. The agency operates as a nonprofit organization with numerous programs, employing several hundred workers and spending several million dollars each year. Tours of the various facilities, including three buildings on Henry Street and four others in the same neighborhood, are conducted irregularly. Call for details.

(20) *Rutherford Place* 305 Second Avenue (at 17th Street) 10003. (212) 473-9066. This marvelous eight-story brick-and-limestone building was financed by JP Morgan, who spared no expense in its design and construction. Completed in 1902, it became New York's first maternity hospital, a function hinted at by the numerous bas-relief figures of babies scattered over its facade. The New York Lying-In Hospital, as it was called, eventually moved uptown, becoming a part of New York Hospital; the building here was taken over by Manhattan General Hospital. Later still it became the property of the Beth Israel Hospital, which used it for a methadone maintenance program. Rutherford Place is now a luxury condominium development. Ask the doorman to let you see the palatial marble entrance lobby, which has been restored, with its grand staircase and the Hippocratic oath engraved in the marble. Just inside the entrance, to the right, is a reception lobby, with its original baronial fireplace and a small museum that briefly chronicles the medical history of the building.

Judson Memorial Church 55 Washington Square South 10012. (212) 477-0351. This impressive old church (and the less imposing brownstone behind it, at 237 Thompson Street) was the home of the nation's first foot clinic. Founded by the pioneering chiropodist Joseph P Solomon in 1910, the free clinic rapidly expanded its hours from two nights a week to five, serving poor people in the neighborhood. After two years these "pedicure clinics" moved to 125th Street, to be closer to the New York School of Chiropody. The foot clinics were part of a larger effort by the Baptist minister Edward Judson, who focused his missionary zeal on ameliorating the health problems of the urban poor. The church itself dates from 1892; the congregation was sponsoring well-baby and other clinics for neighborhood immigrants well before the turn of the century. The Romanesque revival church and its fanciful tower are open to visitors on weekdays from 9 to 12 and from 1 to 5. Don't miss the stained-glass windows.

Department of Health Building Worth and Centre Streets 10013. This is one of those 1930s governmental office buildings with aspirations to architectural greatness that somehow don't measure up. What makes it interesting for our purposes is that it gives a nice cameo view of the individuals who were thought to have been of greatest import to the health professions when the building was completed, in 1936. Just below the molding that rims the top of the main mass of the building (there are two smaller tiers, which recede above that) are engraved the names of 29 individuals, some known to everyone and some known only within the health professions. I doubt that anyone will be able to place every name. On the Centre Street side are Farr, Howard, Lister, Nightingale, Shattuck, Morgan, and Sims; on Leonard Street are Bard, Semmelweis, Welch, Reed, Gorgas, Smith, Dalton, and Biggs; on Lafayette Street are

Koch, Behring, Pasteur, Leeuwenhoek, Erlich, Billings, and Harvey; on Worth Street, are Moses, Jenner, Ramazinni, Hippocrates, Paracelsus, Pinel, and Lind.

(21) *The Burns Archive* 140 East 38th Street 10016. (212) 889-1938. Stanley Burns, a practicing ophthalmologist, has managed to put together a collection of over 100,000 historic and artistic medical photographs that is rivaled, in the whole world, only by the collec-· tion of the National Library of Medicine. There are huge numbers of unique photographs here (including daguerreotypes, ambrotypes, and tintypes of the 1840–1860 era), most of which depict patients with various diseases (many long since obliterated by medical progress), now-archaic medical treatments and practices, and medical professionals and institutions long gone. Burns has a large sub-collection of photographs of medical students dissecting cadavers. Some of the images are poignant, some ghoulish and disturbing, but the vast majority are fascinating. The collection is in a four-story townhouse. Dr. Burns's medical office is on the ground floor, and two floors are devoted to the archival museum. On the second floor there is a large gallery with framed photos along two walls, and museum items (medical and dental cabinets, books, and instruments and pharmacy paraphernalia) along another wall. There is also a large library room here. Dr Burns loves to show these treasures to all genuinely interested parties. The collection is open to the public, by appointment.

OTHER NEW YORK CITY ISLANDS

(22) ROOSEVELT ISLAND

Welfare Island Treatment Complex This cigar-shaped island, lying abeam from midtown Manhattan in the East River, has a fascinating history, and offers the visitor a curious mixture of the old and the new with some incongruous components mixed in. New York City bought the island from a farmer named Blackwell in 1828 and promptly built on it a penitentiary that eventually became the world's largest. The city's northern limit in those days was down on 14th Street, and Blackwell's Island seemed comfortably remote for the incarceration of undesirables. The system seemed to work so well that in 1839 the island became home also to the impecunious insane, in what was called the Municipal Pauper Lunatic Asylum. (Charles Dickens visited the place in 1842 and didn't like it at all. He said, "Everything has a lounging, listless, madhouse air about it, which is very painful.") A few years later the city added a Pauper's

Almshouse and a Hospital for Incurables. In 1854 a Smallpox Hospital was added, and in 1895 the huge Metropolitan Hospital. With the island's growing population, the need for improved (but controlled) access above and beyond the existing ferryboats became increasingly evident; so when the Queensboro bridge was built, in 1909, the engineers devised an ingenious 10-story elevator to carry trucks, ambulances, and other vehicles from the bridge's roadway to a reception building on the island.

By 1921 the island was becoming steadily more notorious on account of recurrent reports of serious overcrowding, violence, and — worst of all — evidence that the island was essentially controlled by cliques of penitentiary inmates who were also operating a heavy narcotics trade. The city's response, in a burst of wishful thinking and public-relations excess, was to rename the place Welfare Island. Conditions, however, remained essentially unchanged until a new reform-oriented administration took control in 1934 and staged a spectacular raid, which was the first step in dismantling the old system, closing the penitentiary, moving the inmates to Rikers Island, and recommitting the island to use by welfare and health-care institutions.

Recently the island (renamed, in 1973, after Franklin Delano Roosevelt) has undergone another identity change, with substantial portions of its acreage devoted to mixed-income housing and resident-oriented businesses. The population density remains low, especially by New York standards, with lots of parks mixed in — some dominated by the deteriorating ruins of abandoned hospitals — and wonderful promenades with spectacular views of midtown Manhattan. When the weather is nice, wheelchair patients from the two hospitals remaining on the island come out for a bit of sun, chatting with the apartment dwellers, meeting at a sidewalk cafe. It feels like a small town.

No one knows yet how dramatically all of this will be changed by the recent opening of the island's own subway station, linking it more directly with all of Manhattan's problems; many of the residents are clearly not enthusiastic. The most pleasant way to get to the island is still the Roosevelt Island Tramway, an aerial cable car that can be boarded at Second Avenue and East 60th Street. The fare is one subway token each way, the ride is peaceful and comfortable, and the views are inspiring. When you arrive, catch one of the free buses to the northern end of the island to begin your tour. The stroll back will be a level two miles — or you can catch a bus for portions of the trip if you wish.

The **Bird S Coler Hospital** is a city hospital for the chronically ill, with just over 1000 beds. Though constructed in 1952, Coler traces its origins to the island's old Hospital for the Incurables and calls itself the oldest long-term care hospital in the nation. The island is only about 800 feet wide at this point, and the Coler Hospital fills most of it, though the island's promenade extends along both the east and west sides. There's a particularly attractive view of the New York Hospital–Cornell Medical Center directly opposite, on Manhattan's Upper East Side. Coler itself is a functional low-rise brick structure with sun porches scattered here and there. There's a modest display in the lobby concerning the island's health-care history. The public affairs department may take you on a tour if you call in advance (688-9400, ext 477).

Just south of Coler is the **Octagon Tower,** a magnificant fenced-off ruin, all that remains of the old Municipal Lunatic Asylum. Designed by Alexander Jackson Davis, a pioneer in our nation's mid-nineteenth-century Greco-Roman revival, the tower once had a marvelous curving staircase that embraced a central rotunda where operations were performed. Metropolitan Hospital occupied the tower and adjacent buildings for many years, beginning in 1895. There are reported plans to restore the tower and make it the centerpiece of an Octagon Park.

Immediately south of the bridge is the **SS Goldwater Memorial Hospital,** a 900-bed chronic-care hospital, rehabilitation center, and skilled-nursing facility, formerly called the Chronic Disease Hospital and renamed after New York's Commissioner of Hospitals from 1934 to 1940. Dr Goldwater fiercely believed that hospitals should be designed by clinicians, not bureaucrats, and this hospital, built during his administration, reflects his priorities. He hated the increasing height of what he called the monoblock, instead opting for this long four-story building composed of a series of chevrons, each angled to give the most favorable solar orientation and view of the river. Tours are available through the public affairs office: (212)750-5980.

Just south of Goldwater is a tall fence that spans the breadth of the island, currently blocking access to what lies beyond, though there are reportedly plans to restore some of the ruins and build a park around them. The empty shells are, first, the old **City Hospital** (1858), designed to be the largest and most modern hospital in America by the noted architect James Renwick; the **Strecker Memorial Research Laboratory** (1892), which was built to provide City Hospital with such essential services as autopsy room, morgue, clinical laboratory, and animal house; and the eerie-looking old **Smallpox Hospital** (1854), just beyond the Strecker Lab, a real relic of the past. The Smallpox Hospital served the function implied by its name until 1886, and then was a nurses' home and training school for a number of years. It's a fine Gothic revival structure, and stands in mute testimony to our progress in public health. The disease got its name by comparison to the even worse killer, the "Great Pox," or syphilis. Nowadays, most American doctors have never even seen a case of smallpox, and syphilis is, for the most part, arrested in its early stages by antibiotics.

㉓ WARD'S/RANDALLS ISLANDS

Manhattan Psychiatric Center NYC 10035. (212) 369-0500. Ward's Island, now joined to Randalls Island by landfill, has served a variety of functions: potters field, refuge for sick and destitute aliens, and — from 1892 on — psychiatric hospital. Initially it was a city facility, the New York City Asylum for the Insane, which used some abandoned immigration buildings. In 1896 the state took control, and the Manhattan State Hospital (as it was then called) grew into the largest psychiatric institution in the world, peaking in 1926 at a census of more than 7000 patients. Gradually the patient population dwindled as other state facilities were built, and the institution was scheduled to be closed in the 1940s when the state's lease on the island expired. The city, however, awarded 122 acres to the state in 1946 so that the institution could continue, and kept the rest as a park. The present facility dates from the 1950s, when ground-breaking ceremonies were presided over by President Dwight D. Eisenhower. The 17-story tan structure that resulted looks like one huge ugly building when viewed end-on, but in reality is three huge ugly buildings — each named after a distinguished psychiatrist associated with Manhattan State Hospital: Adolph Meyer (once known as the dean of American psychiatry), George Kirby, and Charles Dunlap. Though once scheduled for demolition, Manhattan Psychiatric Center (as it is now known) is currently undergoing a $120-million, seven-year-long renovation designed to turn it into a state-of-the-art treatment center. Some 900 patients reside in the buildings while the work goes on; 200 to 300 others have been transferred to other state hospitals. The Kirby building currently functions as an administratively separate forensic psychiatry center. While the MPC is no one's idea of a visual delight, the rest of the island is devoted to a lovely park that provides a remarkably rural respite from nearby Manhattan. The island can be reached by footbridge from Manhattan (access where East 103d Street meets the Harlem River), by car via the Triboro Bridge, or by bus. Tours are available for mental-health professionals (369-0500, ext 3022).

NORTH BROTHER ISLAND

Old Riverside Communicable Disease Hospital Visitors to New York City who fly into La Guardia airport often wonder at the group of islands in the East River just north of the runways. The big one, Rikers Island, is home to a variety of penal institutions. Close by is North Brother Island, the 13-acre home of the now abandoned Riverside Hospital. For many years, Riverside (opened in 1903) was one of the city's principal communicable disease hospitals, with over 300 beds. It was here that "Typhoid Mary" Mallon was quarantined intermittently until her death, in 1938, at the age of 68. She was first identified as a carrier of the typhoid bacillus in 1907, but never fully comprehended the danger she posed to others. Consequently, she eluded authorities time and again by working under assumed names as a cook in various homes and restaurants around the city. She is said to have spread the disease to over 50 people and to have caused at least 3 deaths. She achieved such notoriety during the early years of the century that her nickname, "Typhoid Mary," became a term commonly used for any habitual bringer of bad fortune. Riverside Hospital, like most communicable disease hospitals in this country, closed down when the antibiotic era made it superfluous. North Brother Island is closed to the public.

BROOKLYN

SUNY Downstate Medical Center 450 Clarkson Avenue 11203. (718) 270-1000. SUNY Downstate began life in 1860 as the Long Island Hospital College of Medicine. Like most long-lived medical schools, it has gone through its share of rough times. The Flexner Report of 1910 criticized the school on the grounds that it had no full-time teachers in laboratory subjects, that it lacked a pathology museum and a library for students, that the clinical laboratories were inadequate, and that there was no laboratory teaching in physiology and pharmacology. It took another 20 years for the college to be separated from the Long Island Hospital, and *another* 20 years for the independent college to be reborn as a state institution under the sponsorship of the State University of New York.

Among the more famous medical figures associated with the college over the years were Austin Flint and Alfred Adler. Flint was a part of the college's first faculty group in 1860. Widely known as "the American Laennec," he did more than anyone else of his era to teach skills of physical diagnosis in this country and to bring the stethoscope into general use. Adler was a member of Freud's inner circle in Vienna (he coined the term "inferiority complex"). Ultimately, Adler broke with Freud when the latter refused to accept Adler's view that social needs and drives were as important as sexual needs and drives in determining human behavior. Adler became Visiting Professor of Medical Psychology at the college in 1932, and remained on the faculty until his death in 1937. In 1945 the college purchased some land on the Clarkson Avenue site, opposite Kings County Hospital, putting it in the geographic heart of Brooklyn. The centerpiece of the SUNY complex is the 354-bed University Hospital. After some years of relative stagnation in its building program, the center is currently undergoing a massive renewal. When the new $52-million health-science education building is completed in the early 1990s, the aging Basic Sciences Building and several other structures are scheduled for major renovation. Tours are not currently available.

Kings County Hospital Center New York Avenue at Winthrop Street 11203. (718) 735-3131. Though Bellevue Hospital, in Manhattan, gets all the fame, Kings County is actually the bigger hospital, with 1269 beds. Both, of course, are members of New York City's public Health and Hospitals Corporation. KCH originated in 1830, when local officials spent $3000 to purchase 200 acres for a one-room infirmary that would keep the impoverished sick well away from their better-off brethren. By 1837 the facility had outgrown its initial structure; the institution has been expanding ever since. Now KCH is the third-largest hospital in the country, providing primary care to a population well over a million, and tertiary care to even more. Though the city is planning a major rebuilding project that inevitably will alter or destroy some of the 2 dozen buildings here, much of the hospital's 41 acres currently looks much as it did in the 1930s. The main 13-story brick structure was completed in 1931 and is decorated with towers, Spanish tile roofs, and bay windows worthy of a fancy apartment house. Tours are available from the Public Relations Department (735-3114).

Long Island College Hospital Henry Street and Atlantic Avenue 11201. (718) 780-1000. This institution began its existence in 1856 as the Brooklyn German General Dispensary. In 1858, when the dispensary evolved into a hospital, Brooklyn was the third-largest city in the country, with a population of a quarter of a million. Ralph Waldo Emerson, at that time America's foremost essayist, helped to raise money for the fledgling institution by being the first speaker at a fundraising lecture program. One gets a feel for what medical practice must have been like in those years when one learns that the hospital's original staff included a cupper and a leecher. By 1860 the medical "college" part of LICH had begun operations, shortly thereafter inaugurating America's first chair of military medicine in response to the medical realities of the Civil War. In 1875 the college introduced the practice of having students perform post-mortem exams under the supervision of instructors, the first time such a program was adopted in the United States (it had been the policy for years at the University of Berlin). Though the medical school was administratively separated from the hospital in 1930, the two continued as a joint enterprise until 1950, when the Long Island College of Medicine was merged with the State University of New York to form the Downstate Medical Center. LICH remains a primary teaching affiliate for the medical school.

Part of LICH's early fame was due to its Hoagland Laboratory (founded in 1885), one of the earliest research and teaching facilities for infectious disease in the United States. Its first director was Dr George M Sternberg, America's foremost bacteriologist, who went on to even greater renown as the yellow-fever-fighting Surgeon General of the United States Army. The Hoagland building, a magnificent Romanesque Revival building with glorious art nouveau copper signs, was located at 335 Henry Street, opposite the hospital, but burned down in 1971.

LICH takes pride in having made significant contributions to the development of medical science and practice over the years. In 1952 it opened the first children's dental clinic for cerebral palsy victims. In 1964, LICH became the first place in the world to dialyze a diabetic patient with uremic kidney failure. In 1973 it became the first institution to use a dorsal column stimulator (a pacemaker for the nervous system) to improve motor function in multiple-sclerosis patients.

Today LICH is a 567-bed acute-care facility, with numerous specialty and primary-care clinics and an active teaching program. Its School of Nursing (founded in 1883) admits 100 students each year and seems to be thriving even as so many similar institutions are folding. It is currently the eighth-oldest nursing school in the country.

The hospital's facilities are difficult to describe accurately, because the current $80-million expansion program (due to be completed in the 1990s) is changing its appearance considerably. Given the turmoil, the hospital is not enthusiastic about conducting tours.

Maimonides Medical Center 4802 Tenth Avenue 11219. (718) 270-7679. Maimonides' national reputation is largely tied to a single event: Here, on December 6, 1967, the surgeon Adrian Kantrowitz performed the first human heart transplant in the United States on an 18-day-old baby. Kantrowitz was also an active participant in the development of the first cardiac pacemaker, and became widely known for having developed a pioneering intra-aortic balloon pump.

The history of this medical center begins in 1911, when a group of public-spirited women organized the New Utrecht Dispensary to serve the sick and needy. By 1916, the activities of the dispensary had grown considerably and a hospital was added, the joint enterprise eventually being renamed (1919) the Israel Hospital. The following year, Israel Hospital (by now at the present site) was combined with Zion Hospital (founded 1913) to form the United Israel Zion Hospital. In 1947, Beth Moses Hospital was also gobbled up, resulting in the Maimonides Hospital, named after the twelfth-century rabbinic authority and physician Moses Maimonides. In 1966, in recognition of the numerous other activities going on here, the "hospital" appellation was changed to "medical center."

Currently Maimonides is a 700-bed general hospital with several associated interconnected buildings, covering more than two square blocks. No tours are presently available.

Memorial to Dr Alexander JC Skene Grand Army Plaza (junction of Flatbush Avenue and Prospect Park West). Most readers will not have heard of Alexander Skene. The connection for some health professionals, if it exists at all, will be to Skene's glands, a number of tiny glands on the wall of the female urethra, which indeed are named after this pioneering surgeon and gynecologist. Skene (1837–1900) was also dean and president of the Long Island College Hospital for a number of years and was the author of numerous scientific papers. To appreciate the esteem in which he was held by Brooklynites, one must go to this monumental plaza and see the sculptural company in which Skene has been placed: There is the 80-foot-tall triumphal arch (with bas-relief portraits of Abraham Lincoln and Ulysses S Grant), a huge fountain in the center of the ellipse (with a statue of Neptune), a small marble-and-bronze tribute to John F Kennedy, and two large bronze statues of Civil War heroes. Then there is the Skene monument: a powerful bronze bust on a truncated marble obelisk, with an engraved wall of marble as a backdrop. The bust itself (by John Massey Rhind) is a character-catching beauty, depicting Skene as fiery-eyed and strong-willed, with broad shoulders that remind one of angel's wings. Grand Army Plaza is at the northern extreme of Brooklyn's Prospect Park.

THE BRONX

Albert Einstein College of Medicine (AECOM) 1300 Morris Park Avenue 10461. (212) 430-3601. AECOM, founded in 1955, was the first medical school under Jewish auspices in the United States (Mt Sinai, in Manhattan, is now the only other). At that time there was still widespread institutional anti-Semitism in the country: Jewish applicants were subject to quota systems at many medical schools, including some in New York; Jewish physicians were excluded from hospital staffs; and Jewish academicians were frequently passed over in medical-school appointments and promotions. AECOM was meant to be an exception, a first-rate school that would select students and faculty solely on the basis of ability and scholarship.

The college is, of course, named after the renowned physicist Albert Einstein and was opened just five months after his death. Though the fact that Einstein was Jewish is clearly not incidental, the use of his name here is intended to evoke the scientist's ideal "of serving humanity through scientific accomplishment combined with impassioned humanitarian concern." From the first, the institution had a strong bias in favor of research, and it remains consistently in the top ten, among the nation's 127 medical schools, with regard to federal research grants and support.

The primary College of Medicine complex (Yeshiva University is the parent institution) occupies a 16-acre site in the northeast Bronx, on a campus adjacent to the Bronx Municipal Hospital Center. Most classwork is carried out in the Furchheimer Medical Science Building, but there are also seven other buildings on campus, including the Jack Weiler College Hospital, and several buildings devoted solely to research.

Visitors are welcome on campus, but no formal tours are available.

Lincoln Medical and Mental Health Center 234 East 149th Street 10451. (212) 579-5000. Lincoln was founded in 1839 by a group of mostly wealthy whites, organized as the Society for the Relief of Worthy Aged Indigent Colored Persons. The first building was opened a few years later in Manhattan and was known as the Home of the Colored Aged. Over the next several decades, the scope of the institution was broadened to include a home for the elderly, a hospital, a nursery, and a lying-in department. As the institution grew it moved to successively larger sites. In 1882 the name was changed to The Black Home and Hospital; in 1898 the hospital moved to Concord Avenue and 14th Street in the Bronx. In the same year, the hospital's board of managers opened a private school, the Lincoln School for Nurses, one of the first nursing schools for blacks in the country (Spelman College opened a school in 1886, followed by Hampton Institute and Provident Hospital in

1891 and Tuskegee in 1892). Still, it was an extraordinary innovation in a northern city at the time, and the school remained a remarkable place until its closing in 1961. It often seems difficult now to conceive how completely blacks were excluded from educational opportunities until very recently, unless we are reminded that blacks were almost completely excluded from nursing schools — even in New York — until well into the 1940s. Truly equal access was another couple of decades away. For all of those years, the Lincoln School of Nurses remained a prize haven to blacks wishing training at a nationally accredited school. Though the school's charter was changed fairly early on to allow it to accept white students, only 1 white completed Lincoln's course of study in the school's 63 years of operation. The school closed, finally, both because of funding problems and because the circumstances that had called it forth no longer existed; there was, simply, no further need for a segregated nursing school in New York City.

The hospital changed its name from Black Home and Hospital to Lincoln Hospital and Home in 1902, and became a general hospital open to all races. In 1925 the hospital was purchased by the City of New York. The 1960s were an extraordinarily turbulent time for the hospital, with the administration pitted against various community groups in a struggle for control. In 1976 Lincoln moved into its present building, a strikingly modern, fluorescent-brick facility on nine and a half acres in the South Bronx; and in 1979 it developed a teaching affiliation with New York Medical College. Today Lincoln is a full-service medical center, catering to a heavily Spanish-speaking population. The hospital provides tours on request (call 579-5777).

Montefiore Hospital and Medical Center 111 East 210th Street 10467. (212) 920-4321. This fascinating institution began life in 1884 as the Montefiore Home for Chronic Invalids. Over the years it moved, in succession, from Manhattan's Upper East Side to Harlem to its present site in the Bronx, which was then (1913) regarded as the "green outskirts of the city." Named after Sir Moses Montefiore, a prominent Jewish philanthropist who also became London's sheriff and who was knighted by Queen Victoria, the home was originally designed to serve "ragged refugees," initially just those "belonging to the Hebrew faith," and then (after 1887) anyone, without regard to religion. Still, this remains a Jewish hospital, heavily supported by Jewish philanthropies, even though its clientele now is quite diverse and the medical center is located in the middle of an impoverished, badly deteriorated, and non-Jewish area.

Montefiore's modern renown arises largely from the 30-year

reign (1951–1980) of Martin Cherkasky, who was one of the most powerful and controversial physicians of his time. He not only changed Montefiore from a smallish chronic-disease hospital to a massive medical center; he largely invented the notion of using a hospital to implement social change and to fight evil in the neighborhood (and the world) surrounding it. Under his leadership, Montefiore became involved in providing health care to prisoners at Rikers Island, teaching poverty-level neighborhood people to become "family health workers" (as much to fight local unemployment as for health-care needs), and promoting the unionization of its own porters and maids to establish a precedent so that similar workers at other hospitals would no longer be exploited. Montefiore helped to establish local health centers for blacks and Puerto Ricans, in areas where other health personnel feared to tread, and then proceeded to appoint community people first to advisory, and then to governing, boards. Much of this was in the tumultuous sixties; Montefiore was always in the vanguard, vilified by conservatives for its radicalism and simultaneously pilloried by local activists as the only representative of the white power structure within striking distance.

Montefiore also had its problems with Albert Einstein College of Medicine. Though these two large Jewish health-care institutions were natural allies, they were also natural competitors and they were recurrently involved in strife. They were brought closer together in the late 1960s, when Blue Cross developed reimbursement schedules related to hospital size. The 800-bed Montefiore was paid $100 a day for a given service, while the much smaller AECOM Hospital was paid only $74. The result was that Montefiore made money, while the college hospital ran a deficit. The financial solution (in 1969) was to combine the two facilities into one high-reimbursement institution, basically managed by Montefiore. The union was not a peaceful one, however, and when the initial agreement expired, after 10 years, it took another 4 years for the agreement to be renewed, this time for 50 years.

Montefiore has been responsible for many medical firsts, including: the first U.S. hospital to have a fully equipped hydrotherapy unit (1889), the first cardiotachometer (invented by Ernest Boas, 1925), and the first transvenous pacemaker (Seymour Furman, 1958).

Today, Montefiore is an enormous complex of buildings, including a slim red-brick spire designed by Philip Johnson, designated the Research Institute (1966). The earliest building here dates from 1913. No tour is currently available.

Bronx Municipal Hospital Center Pelham Parkway South and East-chester Road 10461 (212) 430-8874. This huge (900-bed) acute- and general-care, and psychiatric, hospital is part of the New York City Health and Hospitals Corporation and a principal teaching site for AECOM. In the early years of this century the Bronx was a haven for working-class immigrant families who had managed to improve their lot sufficiently to escape the slums of the Lower East Side of Manhattan. There were Italians and Irish and others, but by 1930 50 percent of the million-plus population were Jews. More recently, the middle-class groups have tended to move on, to the suburbs and elsewhere (the Bronx is currently about 10 percent Jewish); and now the borough is increasingly poor, mostly non-white, and dominated by terrible slums — especially in the South Bronx. Though located in the northeast Bronx (which is predomi-nantly white and middle-class), the BMHC is the principal tertiary care facility for the entire borough, especially its poor.

The campus includes the acute-care Abraham Jacobi Hospital, the Nathan B Van Etten Hospital (specializing in a variety of chronic conditions, including chest and metabolic diseases) and a variety of residence halls and support buildings. The site encom-passes some 64 acres.

The Van Etten, which was a tuberculosis hospital when it opened in 1954, was named after a Bronx general practitioner and commu-nicable-disease specialist who went on to become president of the American Medical Association (1940). The Jacobi is named for the "dean of American pediatrics," who was so influential in New York medicine around the turn of the century. Jacobi was a tireless and passionate innovator, involved in providing service and teaching in many institutions; few New York hospitals escaped his influence. He taught at New York Medical College (1860-64), the University of New York (1865-70), and Columbia Physicians and Surgeons (1870–1902), and consulted at a long list of hospitals. The Lenox Hill Hospital established an Abraham Jacobi Pediatrics Division (1895), and Roosevelt Hospital inaugurated an Abraham Jacobi Ward for Children (1900), but the Jacobi Hospital at BMHC is the most massive of the various tributes.

Tours are available on request.

STATEN ISLAND

Bayley Seton Hospital Bay Street and Vanderbilt Avenue 10304. (718) 390-6000. This 200-bed acute-care general hospital has a lot of history tied up in both its name and its facilities. The *Bayley* in the hospital's name refers to Dr. Richard Bayley, the first health officer of the port of New York. During the Revolutionary War Bayley was Hospital Surgeon for the Colonial fleet, based in Newport, Rhode Island. Later he became Columbia University's first Professor of Anatomy and got beaten up for his efforts in the Doctors' Riots of 1788 (see "New York Hospital–Cornell University Medical Center," above). Bayley was a man of many talents: he pioneered in cataract surgery, developed local quarantine laws, and wrote an important document on yellow fever. However, none of these accomplishments alone would have warranted having the Bayley Seton named in his honor. For this achievement we must look to August 28, 1774, when Bayley's wife gave birth to the couple's second daughter, Elizabeth, who was destined to become the first American canonized by the Roman Catholic Church. At age 18 Elizabeth married William Seton, a prominent local businessman; the marriage lasted eleven years, until William's death in 1803. Shortly thereafter Elizabeth decided to leave the Episcopal church, in which she had been raised, and to become a Catholic. In the years that followed, Elizabeth (or Mother Seton, as she later became known) took her religious vows, started the first Catholic girls' school and the first Catholic orphanage in America, and pioneered an American religious order based on St Vincent de Paul's Daughters of Charity. The Bayley Seton Hospital, a Roman Catholic institution, is therefore named after the first American saint and her father.

The hospital has an interesting story as well. Some of the buildings date back to the 1830s, when the facility was first opened as the Seamen's Fund and Retreat. The US Marine Hospital moved here in 1883, when it had to move from its former home (then known as Bedloe's Island) to make way for the Statue of Liberty. The National Institutes of Health (now headquartered in Bethesda, MD) had their beginnings here in 1887, when Dr Joseph Kinyoun inaugurated his Hygienic Laboratory in a small attic room in what is now Building 7, using the tiny lab to make the first bacteriologic diagnosis of cholera in the United States (1887). This location for the Hygienic Lab made eminent sense at the time, because seamen were a continuing source of infectious disease and epidemics brought from foreign climes, especially cholera and yellow fever. The laboratory was transferred to larger quarters in Washington, DC, in 1891, but the facility here remained a dynamic place on the cutting edge of medicine for many years. In 1941, Drs Robert Hingson and James Southworth developed the use of continuous caudal anesthesia in obstetric deliveries, to the lasting gratitude of many women. In 1943 Dr James Mahoney of the Venereal Disease Research Laboratory, located here, reported the successful use of penicillin in the treatment of syphilis. This long-sought nontoxic substance revolutionized the treatment of a terribly disabling and often lethal disease.

The United States Marine Hospital Service was established in 1798 to provide care to sick and disabled seamen. The name was changed in 1902 to the United States Public and Marine Hospital Service, and again, in 1912, to United States Public Health Service. The Staten Island USPHS Hospital was decommissioned in 1981, being reborn as the Bayley Seton.

Today the most amazing thing about the facility is how many of the older buildings remain, in contrast to what has happened to medical institutions in the rest of New York City and, indeed, around the country. You can catch glimpses of Building 7 from the Bay Street driveway exit, with better views of some of the other buildings from Vanderbilt Avenue, but for the best view you need to schedule a tour in advance (390-5520).

The oldest parts of Building 7 date from the years 1834 to 1837, but there have been numerous additions and renovations over the years. Still, to the eyes of a non-architect, the basic structure remains intact. It's a huge three-story granite chunk of a building with long lateral wings fronting on Bay Street and, beyond that, the water. Kinyoun's attic room still exists, though nothing remains of the original lab. In 1987 officials created a replica of the original for the NIH Centennial; they may do so again if there is sufficient interest. Currently, the building is devoted to corporate offices and offices of some social service agencies.

The next oldest building (1842) dates from the Seamen's Retreat days, and was built as the residence of the chief physician of the Retreat. This (Building 10) is a remarkably well-preserved Greek Revival structure, also granite, which blends nicely with the main structure. The rest of the buildings date from after the turn of the century. There are lots of trees here, and the hospital's proximity to the water makes it a particularly pleasant place to visit.

Sea View Hospital & Home and Medical Museum   460 Brielle Avenue 10314. (718) 317-3000. This institution is interesting for what it has been, for what it is now, and for its medical museum—the only general medical museum open to the public not only in New York City, but in the entire state of New York. Sea View's story begins in 1829, when a Poor House was constructed to provide a refuge to the homeless in Richmond County (Staten Island). Over the years, additional land and buildings were acquired and services added until 1912, when the complex occupied 379 acres, with 63 buildings, connected by over 5 miles of paved roads. There was a pavilion for the insane, a children's hospital, a large farm colony (for alcoholics, drifters, abandoned children, and the homeless); but the jewel in the collection was the Sea View Tuberculosis Hospital, then arguably the finest in the country for "the white plague," one of the country's principal killers at the time. In the decades which followed, Sea View remained a principal treatment and research center for TB, being largely responsible for the introduction of iproniazid (under director of medicine Edward H Robitzek, MD, in the early 1950s), a powerful variant of isoniazid that produced such euphoria that it was quickly withdrawn from use. As a result of the triumph of drug therapy, in the 1950s, Sea View Tuberculosis Hospital went from a maximum patient population of 2000 (in 1941) to only a few in 1960. In 1961, the "Tuberculosis" designation was therefore discontinued, and service to the elderly was expanded. Sea View is now primarily a geriatric facility, but also is home to a variety of social service organizations. Most of the buildings date from the early years of this century, but the 304-bed skilled-nursing facility (named the Robitzek Building) was constructed in 1973. Of the 43 buildings on campus, only 8 are currently in use.

The health-care museum (named the **Stiversa A Bethel Museum,** after the woman who was for many years the director of nursing at Sea View) is located just beyond the large administration building. Material has been drawn from Sea View and other public hospitals within New York City, and assembled, in a labor of love, by Sea View staff. In light of the chronic budget crunches faced by all of New York's public hospitals, it would be unrealistic to expect anything fancy here, but the plain displays tell their story vividly. The modular units recreate a pediatric patient's room, a pharmacy, a kitchen, an x-ray unit, an operating room, an industrial shop, a tuberculosis research lab, a dental lab, and a patients' store. All are collected in a single large room in an otherwise abandoned building (the old nurses' residence). Tours are available by appointment (317-3295). Sea View can be reached by a 20-minute car or taxi ride from the Staten Island Ferry terminus.

Philadelphia

Including Essington

PHILADELPHIA HAS BEEN ONE of the world's great medical centers for 225 years. Until the Civil War, no other city in the United States even came close to Philadelphia in its number and quality of medical institutions. Much of the city's early ascendency is clearly attributable to its Quaker founders and their deep concern for human suffering, which led to the establishment of numerous institutions for the care and treatment of the sick, insane, and aged. Philadelphia is responsible for the country's first medical school, first hospital, first children's hospital, first pharmacy college, first private psychiatric hospital, and first eye hospital.

Philadelphia so dominated nineteenth-century American medicine that, for the entire century, no fewer than 25 percent of the nation's physicians came from this one city. In the mid-nineteenth century Philadelphia boasted four substantial medical schools that would survive until the present (University of Pennsylvania, Jefferson, Hahnemann, and Medical College of Pennsylvania) plus a half-dozen more that wouldn't (Medical Department of Pennsylvania College, 1840–1861; Philadelphia College of Medicine, 1847–1859; Franklin Medical College, 1847–1852; Pennsylvania Medical University, 1850–1864; American College of Medicine and the Eclectic Medical College, 1850–1872; and Philadelphia University of Medicine and Surgery, 1865–1869).

Philadelphia remains a pleasure for medical visitors because so much of historical interest is at once easily accessible by foot, open to the public, and fascinating. Clearly the place to begin any sightseeing is in the downtown historic section. Within a radius of no more than a few blocks in any direction, you can see Pennsylvania Hospital, the Hill-Physick-Keith House, Wills Eye Hospital, Jefferson University Medical Center, the Franklin Court Complex, the site of Benjamin Rush's home, the American College of Physicians, and the Pennsylvania College of Podiatric Medicine. Another easily traversed area is around the University of Pennsylvania. Here, a short walk can encompass the University of Pennsylvania complex, the Wistar Institute, Children's Hospital, the old Philadelphia General Hospital site, and the nearby Philadelphia College of Pharmacy and Science. About halfway between these two areas sits the College of Physicians, a must for any medical visitor to the city. Finally, any lover of medical museums will want to see the pharmacy and dental collections at Temple University Medical Center.

Map Key _____

(1) University of Pennsylvania Medical Center
(2) Jefferson Medical College
(3) Hahnemann University Medical Center
(4) Pennsylvania College of Podiatric Medicine
(5) Site of Philadelphia General Hospital
(6) Pennsylvania Hospital
(7) Wills Eye Hospital
(8) Children's Hospital of Philadelphia
(9) Graduate Hospital
(10) College of Physicians and Mütter Museum
(11) Hill-Physick-Keith House
(12) The Library Company
(13) Wistar Institute
(14) Benjamin Rush Home site
(15) Washington Square
(16) S Weir Mitchell Home site
(17) Franklin Court Complex
(18) American College of Physicians
(19) Joseph Leidy Statue
(20) Boericke & Tafel, Inc.

These key numbers will be found at appropriate points in the text.

(1) *University of Pennsylvania Medical Center* 3400 Spruce Street 19104. (215) 662-4000. This country's first medical school was established in 1765 by John Morgan. Morgan had begun his own medical education by apprenticing himself (at age 15) for six years to a local, successful physician. He then spent some time in London, going on to study for two years and receive his medical degree at the

University of Edinburgh. When Morgan returned to this country, he was determined to found a medical school in the Edinburgh tradition. He proposed the idea to the College of Philadelphia (later to become the University of Pennsylvania), and it was immediately accepted. Morgan was then appointed to the first chair of medicine in a chartered college in America (Professor of the Theory and Practice of Physic). The next three professors (William Shippen, Benjamin Rush, and Adam Kuhn) were all likewise Edinburgh graduates. The school's historic debt to the University of Edinburgh is symbolized even now in its seal, which is adorned with the Scottish thistle.

The first class graduated in 1768, with all graduates receiving the Bachelor of Medicine degree in the British tradition. It wasn't until 1791 that graduates were given the MD degree. The school faltered during the Revolutionary War, missing several graduations between 1774 and 1780, but has otherwise remained strong and secure. In the pre–Civil War days, when Philadelphia was a mecca for Southerners wishing to learn medicine, UP turned out fully 25 percent of the men who would go on to be the Confederate Army's surgeons.

In the early years lectures lasted for about three or four months, and students were required to attend two identical series of lectures, extending over two years. The lecture sequence was lengthened to six months in 1847, but students still had to sit through a repeat series the following year. The curriculum was strengthened in 1877 to include a third year; a fourth year (at first optional) was added the following decade.

In 1872 the school moved from its downtown location to the present site in West Philadelphia. In 1874 it constructed its own hospital, the Hospital of the University of Pennsylvania, forever after known as HUP. William Osler served as Professor of Medicine here for several years, beginning in 1884, before going to Johns Hopkins.

UP has contributed numerous pioneering developments over the years, including the first academic department of dermatology in the country (1871); the first academic department of neurology (1874); and the first use of an x-ray (then called a "skiagraph") to locate an ingested foreign body — a toy jack in a young child (1896, J William White).

Today, the UP School of Medicine and HUP occupy a vast area adjacent to the main university campus. There are no formal tours here, but this is a pleasant campus for strolling and there is much to see. The most picturesque way to approach the complex is along Hamilton Walk, beginning at 38th Street and Baltimore Avenue. As you head east, the first building on your right is the Leidy Biology Laboratories Building, engraved (just below the roofline) with the names of such eminent biologists as Schwann, Malpighi, Darwin, Linnaeus, Bernard, and many others. Next is the Goddard Laboratory Building, with its starkly modern vertical lines. Linked to the Goddard is the Alfred Newton Richards Medical Research Building, designed by Louis Kahn and probably one of the most attractive medical research buildings anywhere. If you take a right off Hamilton Walk, through a wide columned portal at the ground level of the Richards Building, you'll find a surprise: almost completely hidden, quietly peaceful and quite lovely, there is a spacious botanical garden in what seems a forested setting, complete with a large fish-filled pond.

Past the Richards, the next building is the John Morgan Building (1904). Note the Scottish thistle, which is depicted on the building. The names of the four original professors are engraved on the facade, and their portraits hang on either side of the famed Thomas Eakins painting *The Agnew Clinic,* which is on the mezzanine, directly in front of you as you enter the building. The best place to view these paintings is from the balcony facing them, where there are also detailed and interesting descriptions. Not far away, there are some displays on the history of dermatology as a specialty (in which UP played an important role) and on the evolution of scientific medicine at UP. The hallways in the Morgan also have numerous plaques, as well as portraits of distinguished alumni and faculty.

Past the Morgan, Hamilton Walk ends at the vast HUP complex.

Philadelphia College of Pharmacy and Science Woodland Avenue at 43d Street 19104. (215) 596-8800. This, the oldest pharmacy college in the Western Hemisphere, was founded in 1821 by a group of Philadelphia apothecaries, determined to improve scientific standards and to train more apprentices. Admission was originally restricted to men; the college became coeducational in 1876. Initially called the Philadelphia College of Pharmacy, the school adopted its present name in 1921, when it began granting degrees in such areas as biochemistry, medical technology, physical therapy, and toxicology.

Among the school's many accomplishments, it has served as a breeding ground for many of the key names in the development of American pharmaceutical companies. Graduates who became corporate founders or heads include John Wyeth (1854), founder of Wyeth Laboratories; William Warner (1856), founder of Warner Lambert; Henry S. Wellcome (1874) and Silas Burroughs (1877), founders of Burroughs Wellcome and Company; Eli Lilly (1907) and Josiah Lilly (1882), of Eli Lilly & Company; Gerald Rorer (1931) of Rorer, Inc; and Robert McNeil (1876) and Robert L McNeil, Jr (1938), of McNeil Laboratories.

The college has published the *American Journal of Pharmacy*, the oldest continuously published journal of its kind in America, since 1825. It is also responsible for Remington's *Pharmaceutical Sciences*, begun in 1885 and still the most widely used text and reference work in the pharmaceutical sciences. The school became the site of the nation's first geriatric pharmacy institute in 1987.

The college has occupied several other locations over the years; it moved to its present 12.5-acre tree-lined site in 1928. Composed of a dozen buildings, the campus is home to a marvelous pharmacy historical collection comprising over 8000 items dating back over five centuries. Though the exhibit in Griffith Hall is often referred to as a museum, the collection is in fact spread out in several buildings, decorating the library, various entry halls, and classrooms. There are wooden microscopes, a huge collection of apothecary jars, leech jars, mortars and pestles of every description, an enormous amount of pharmaceutical ephemera, medicine boxes and jars, various preserved animal specimens, and much more. The John England Library contains one of the largest collections of pharmaceutical books and periodicals in the world. Pending the acquisition of formally dedicated museum space, much of the collection is in storage.

The library, entryways, and hallways are accessible to the public during normal school hours. Visitors should be sure not to miss the six fine murals (totalling 100 feet in length) that decorate the ground-floor lobby in Griffith Hall, depicting important phases in the development of pharmacy. Arrange tours through the Public Relations Department.

② *Jefferson Medical College* Eleventh Street and Walnut Street 19107. (215) 928-6000. With the birth of Jefferson Medical College, in 1824, Philadelphia became a city with two medical schools, a distinction that gave it priority over such medical centers as London and Paris. Philadelphia's medical community had, for some time, been divided into two camps: those who were associated with the University of Pennsylvania medical school, and those who were on the outside looking in. Conflict developed, divisive issues multiplied, and the "out" group made several attempts to found their own medical school, always opposed by the University of Pennsylvania. Finally, a group made an end run around the University of Pennsylvania by forming an alliance with Jefferson College, in

Canonsburg, Pennsylvania, some 300 miles west of Philadelphia. A charter was then granted by the Pennsylvania legislature for a new medical college under the sponsorship of Jefferson College.

The new medical college established itself in the old Tivoli Theater downtown, a facility it rapidly outgrew. One of Jefferson's early distinctions was to allow medical students to participate, under appropriate supervision, in the diagnosis and treatment of patients. By 1825 Jefferson had established a dispensary for use by students and faculty; by 1838 the school was sufficiently solid and secure that it could apply for, and get, a charter in its own right, separate from its "mother college" at the other end of the state.

Jefferson remained one of the county's most popular and respected medical schools throughout the nineteenth century. It was particularly popular with Southern students before the Civil War; when hostilities broke out, 180 medical students precipitously left Jefferson to complete their studies at the Medical College of Virginia, in Richmond. Its most famous professor, Samuel Gross, was for many years America's premier anatomist and surgeon. (He was immortalized in a famous Thomas Eakins painting, *The Gross Clinic*, and in 1862 wrote the *Manual of Military Surgery*, which became the medical bible for both the North and the South during the rest of the Civil War.)

Jefferson remained a dominant power in medical education until the early years of the twentieth century, when its luster faded. The school underwent a rebirth in the post–World War II years, and has gradually grown into the medical complex that exists now. The medical school's official name is Jefferson Medical College of Thomas Jefferson University; the university's other components are the College of Graduate Studies, The College of Allied Health Sciences, and the Hospital. The current campus occupies 13 acres in downtown Philadelphia and includes well over a dozen buildings. The oldest, at Tenth Street and Sansom Street (Main Building), dates from 1908.

Tours of the hospital are available through the Patients' Representatives office, and of the university through its Public Relations Department. The Eakins work *The Gross Clinic* occupies a place of honor in Jefferson Alumni Hall; permission to view it may be obtained from the security officer at the guard desk just inside the door. Visitors are allowed entry Monday through Saturday, 10 AM to 4 PM, and Sunday from noon to 4 PM (except on major holidays).

(3) *Hahnemann University Medical Center* Broad Street and Vine Street 19102. (215) 448-7000. The forerunner of Hahnemann was founded in 1848 as the Homeopathic Medical College of Pennsyl-

vania. In 1869, the college merged with another institution to form the Hahnemann Medical College and Hospital.

Hahnemann was named for Christian Friedrich Samuel Hahnemann (1755–1843), the thoroughly original and talented German physician who founded homeopathy. Hahnemann was tireless in his criticism of the then-popular methods of "heroic" treatment: bleeding, blistering, purging, enemas, and massive doses of poorly understood medications of highly variable efficacy. In response, he devised a whole new therapeutic approach based on the presumptions that every powerful drug induced a particular kind of disease and that for every disease the physician should prescribe a medication capable of producing the same kind of disease — but that the medication should be prescribed only in minute doses. Thus the basic tenet of homeopathy was *similia similibus curantur,* or "like is cured by like." The secret to homeopathy's success was the minute doses, which proved to be a valuable contrast to the heroic doses prescribed by ordinary physicians. With homeopaths, in contrast to other physicians, the cure was seldom worse than the disease.

Hahnemann never came to the United States. His theories arrived in the 1840s and grew in popularity until the 1880s, when they reached their peak. As homeopathy grew more popular, opposition from other medical practitioners, and particularly organized medicine, became more vehement. Homeopathy was especially despised because, in contrast to other innovative medical disciplines and sects of the time, it tended to appeal to the urban wealthy, who had an affinity for anything European. Oliver Wendell Holmes blasted homeopathy as "a mangled mass of perverse ingenuity, of tinsel erudition, of imbecile credulity and of artful misrepresentation." Many medical societies (e.g., the Philadelphia Medical Society, in 1843) expelled all homeopaths. In 1847 the AMA adopted a code of ethics that forbade consultation with such "irregulars" as homeopaths.

This vehement opposition meant that homeopaths had to open their own medical schools. This they did, first in Philadelphia (1848), then in Cleveland (1850), New York (1860), and Chicago (1860). By the end of the century homeopathy had established 20 medical colleges, 66 general homeopathic hospitals, 74 specialty homeopathic hospitals, and numerous dispensaries. There were a plethora of national, state, and local homeopathic medical societies, and over 30 homeopathic medical journals.

In the early years, homeopaths were regular physicians who had decided to adopt homeopathic practices. Homeopathic schools — certainly, the better ones — were similar to ordinary medical schools of the period, but with the addition of coursework in homeopathy. Thus homeopathic physicians were no worse-trained than most of their allopathic counterparts; and there were often as many differences within homeopathy and allopathy, respectively, as there were between them. Indeed, toward the end of the nineteenth century, homeopathy was plagued by divisive factionalism. The Homeopathic Medical College of Philadelphia adhered rigidly to all of Hahnemann's teachings. This rigidity gave rise to a rival institution, the Hahnemann Medical College (founded in 1867 by Dr Constantine Hering, who took over the charter of the defunct Eclectic Washington Medical College, which had been founded in 1853). Dr Hering's venture was so rapidly successful that it absorbed the older Homeopathic Medical College in 1869. The school continued to be one of the best homeopathic institutions, and one of the better medical schools of any type. As science began to play an increasingly larger role in medical education and practice, Hahnemann gradually tapered the amount of homeopathy in the curriculum. The last requirement for homeopathic instruction was dropped in 1945, the last homeopathic diploma was granted in 1950, and the last homeopathic elective ceased in 1959. At the end there were no students at Hahnemann still interested in homeopathy, and no faculty members still competent to teach the subject.

The present Hahnemann University Medical Center consists of the medical school, a graduate school, a school of health sciences and humanities, and the very modern 616-bed Hahnemann University Hospital. The latter traces its history to a small hospital opened at the rear of the College in 1862. There are currently no arrangements for tours.

Medical College of Pennsylvania 3300 Henry Avenue 19129. (215) 842-4000. When it was incorporated, in 1850, as the Female Medical College of Pennsylvania, this was one of the first medical schools for women in this country. In its first years the faculty were all men; by 1890, about half were women. In 1867 the school changed its name to Woman's Medical College. Between 1850 and 1900 there were 19 medical schools for women established, but few survived for more than a few years. In the early years of this century the Woman's Medical College produced about one-third of practicing American women physicians.

For many years the college was allied with The Woman's Hospital, which had been founded in 1861 by an early graduate of the college. In 1904 the college and the hospital decided to go their separate ways, in part because of political squabbles and in part because the medical students' education was severely restricted by the hospital's policy of not admitting men patients. The college opened its own hospital in 1913.

Both the college and its associated hospitals suffered considerably at the hands of established male physicians in Philadelphia. The Philadelphia County Medical Society preached that women were "unfit for the profession due to their delicate organization and predominance of the nervous system," and refused to admit women members until 1888. The college's first graduation ceremonies were marred by a demonstration staged by 500 male medical students from other institutions, who came to protest the fact that women were receiving medical degrees. The police had to be called to maintain order. In 1860 the state medical society passed a resolution barring its members from even consulting with any of the school's faculty or graduates; and, until 1871 the society refused to recognize the college's graduates as physicians.

In 1969, subsequent to laws preventing discrimination on the basis of sex, the school began to admit men and adopted the name Medical College of Pennsylvania. A recent class was composed of about 60 percent women and 40 percent men. The current faculty is about one-third women.

The college and hospital moved to their present location in 1930. The numerous buildings on campus include a 500-bed teaching hospital and a graduate school of medical sciences. Among the attractions here is the Archives and Special Collections on Women in Medicine, the largest resource of its kind in the world.

Tours are available through the Student Affairs Office.

Temple University School of Dentistry 3223 North Broad Street 19140. (215) 221-2799. Founded as the Philadelphia Dental College in 1863, this school is now the second oldest dental college in continuous operation in America. In the early years of the school, dental education was very much an American monopoly; the school drew students from as far away as Cuba, France, Norway, Prussia, and Switzerland. The first school was located at 10th and Arch streets and was really only a storefront. By 1878, however, the school was a thriving institution. It was in that year that it opened the Hospital for Oral Surgery, the first hospital in the country devoted to oral and maxillofacial surgery.

After the turn of the century, as independent professional schools around the country began seeking university affiliations, the college merged with Temple University. In 1913 the school officially changed its name to Temple University School of Dentistry. In the first decades of the twentieth century, the school was one of the largest and most popular in the country; but the resulting overcrowding and straining of resources led to "less than satisfactory" ratings from the Dental Education Council. By 1926, however, the school was again on the right track; the failure rate of graduates on state board examinations had dropped to almost nil.

The school moved to the Broad and Allegheny location in 1947, close by other Temple health institutions. It is now in the process of completing a new $23-million clinical facility. The **Temple University Dental School Museum** is one of the four or five best in the country. The collection is enormous, and some of the items here are real gems, including the first known dental chair used in America, marvelous cabinetry, and an incredible array of machinery (e.g., a wooden x-ray machine and a primitive drum device used for nitrous-oxide anesthesia). A favorite of many visitors is a necklace of 357 human teeth, all pulled by the legendary "Painless Parker" in a single day's work. Other items include dental instruments with handles made from agate, onyx, bakelite, mother of pearl, wood, shell, buffalo horn, walrus tusk, elephant ivory, ebony, rubber, and bone. At present all of this, and much more, is tucked away in offices and scattered through hallways. The vast majority of it can be seen only by calling the Visual Education Department (221-2816), which is the collection's temporary custodian. The mu-

Oldest known dental chair in the United States (c. 1790), Temple University Dental School Museum *(By permission of the Historical Dental Museum)*

seum is expected to move into its own space (and have a full-time curator) in the early 1990s.

Philadelphia College of Osteopathic Medicine 4150–4190 City Avenue 19131. (215) 581-6000. Osteopathy, as a distinct branch of medicine, was begun in the mid-nineteenth century by Dr Andrew T Still, in Kirksville, Missouri. Now, however, DOs and MDs undergo very similar licensing procedures and perform comparable functions in most states. Osteopathic physicians specialize in all the customary medical and surgical specialties. Osteopathy, however, places much greater emphasis on the importance of the musculoskeletal system than does allopathic medicine, and graduates of osteopathic colleges are customarily skilled in "structural diagnosis" and manipulative therapy. After a long period of living in the shadow of conventional allopathic medicine, osteopathy has recently undergone something of a renaissance: in 1969 there were only five osteopathic colleges; today there are fifteen.

The Philadelphia College of Osteopathic Medicine is the largest osteopathic school in the nation. Founded in 1898 (as the Philadelphia College and Infirmary of Osteopathy) by a fiery Presbyterian minister-turned-osteopathic physician, PCOM grew rapidly with the aid of some savvy public relations: the founder went out of his way to treat newspaper editors for ailments that had not responded to conventional treatment, and his subsequent successes resulted in laudatory articles and editorials from grateful patients. The first graduating class, in 1900, included one man and one woman, and subsequent classes were as much as 40 percent women. In 1909 PCOM became the first osteopathic school to require a four-year course of study.

PCOM moved to its present site in 1957, after occupying a variety of other locations throughout the city. The complex now includes 16 acres, with a half-dozen buildings. The administrative center is in Moss House, an attractive dark-paneled baronial mansion that occupied the site long before PCOM moved here. The college operates its own 250-bed hospital, in a building that dates from 1967. PCOM also maintains some museum collections that will interest many health professionals. On the sixth floor of the Evans Building, in the Anatomy Department, is the **Angus Cathie Anatomical Collection:** case after case of normal and pathologic specimens, serial sections, and mounted preparations of all sorts. This is a first-class anatomic and pathologic collection, very nicely displayed, and open to visitors who make prior arrangements with the anatomy department.

Call the Communications Department to arrange tours.

Temple University School of Medicine Broad Street and Ontario Street 19140. (215) 221-2000. Temple is the youngest of Philadelphia's medical schools, having been founded in 1901. The school was founded by the Baptist minister Russell Conwell, who hoped to make medical education available to working people by allowing them to take all their classes after the day's work was done. In fact, Temple was one of several medical schools in the country that began as evening and weekend schools. Clinical instruction was provided at Samaritan Hospital (another institution founded by Dr Conwell, in 1892), which later became Temple University Hospital. The first graduates received their MDs in 1904; two years later the school admitted women students, becoming the first allopathic coeducational medical school in Pennsylvania. By 1907, increasing pressure on medical schools generally to bolster their curricula and intensify training programs led to the demise of the "midnight medical school" and led Temple to become a daytime venture. In 1907, Temple College became Temple University; soon other schools were added to the health-professions center, including pharmacy, dentistry and chiropody.

Since then, Temple has been the source of numerous medical discoveries and innovations:

1902 Development of bronchoscopy for the removal of foreign bodies from the throat and lungs (Chevalier Jackson)

1907 Introduction of spinal anesthesia into this country (W Wayne Babcock)

1939 Introduction of hypothermia as an adjunct to surgical procedures in certain critically ill patients (Temple Fay)

1947 Development of a stereotaxic instrument for precise neurosurgical techniques in the treatment of parkinsonism (Ernst Speigel and Henry Wycis)

1976 First blind student admitted to (and later graduated from) an American medical school (David Hartman)

1981 Implantation of artificial hearts in five brain-dead patients, leading the way for a clinically useful artificial heart (Jacob Kolff)

The School of Medicine is located on a 27-acre site that houses a large health sciences complex, including the 500-bed, entirely new Temple University Hospital. Other components include the dental school (founded 1863), pharmacy school (1901), and an allied health professions school (1965). Tours of the campus are available via the Volunteers Office.

④ *Pennsylvania College of Podiatric Medicine* Eighth Street and Race Street 19107. (215) 629-0300. Until the 1950s, podiatry was known as *chiropody*. The latter term, however, was burdened with some unfortunate problems: it was difficult to pronounce and was often confused with chiropractic, an entirely separate discipline that organized medicine tended to regard as an objectionable and unscientific cult. As a result, foot doctors changed their professional name.

This school is the Philadelphia successor to the Temple University School of Chiropody, which opened its doors in 1915 and closed in 1961. At that time, Temple University was faced with a burdensome financial deficit, which it tried to resolve, in part, by phasing out its schools of chiropody and theology. A movement then arose among podiatry alumni to establish a new school in Philadelphia, this one to be a free-standing institution. So the Pennsylvania College of Podiatric Medicine was established in 1963; it moved to its present site in 1973. The college is now the most modern center of podiatric education in the world, and one of only seven such colleges in the United States.

Visitors to the campus will be particularly interested in the **Center for the History of Foot Care and Foot Wear** and its **Shoe Museum.** This includes a fine collection of antique, unusual, ethnic, and celebrity footwear, ranging from examples of Chinese footbinding to American Indian mukluks, Egyptian burial sandals, baby shoes, clogs, wedding slippers, dance slippers, and shoes of American first ladies. About one-third of the collection is on exhibit at any one time, housed in thirteen cases located on the sixth floor of the college. The adjacent library also includes displays of podiatric surgery artifacts. The Shoe Museum may be toured by appointment with the Public Relations Department.

Pennsylvania College of Optometry 1200 West Godfrey Avenue 19141. (215) 276-6200. Founded in 1919, this is the oldest optometric college begun as a health-professional school (the Ohio State University school, in Columbus, founded in 1914, started as an outgrowth of the physics department). The Pennsylvania College of Optometry was also the first to award the doctor of optometry (OD) degree and the first to develop a four-year professional curriculum. Although it is one of fifteen such optometric institutions, PCO has graduated almost one-fifth of all optometrists practicing in the United States.

The PCO is located on a thirteen-acre campus in the residential Oak Lane section of Philadelphia. The Feinbloom Visual Rehabilitation Center here designs optical aids for people who are legally blind but nonetheless retain some residual visual potential. In 1981 it introduced the "honey bee lens," a set of six tiny telescopes that broadens a field of vision 300 percent; and in 1984 the "New Horizon Lens," which restores substantial vision to victims of retinitis pigmentosa.

Tours are available from the Admissions Office.

(5) *Site of Philadelphia General Hospital* 700 Civic Center Boulevard. When this hospital discharged its last patient, in 1977, it was the oldest public hospital in continuous service in the United States. Founded in 1731 as the Philadelphia Almshouse, it gradually assumed an increasing load of indigent ill and insane persons, so that by 1767 it was known as the "Bettering House." The almshouse moved to 170 acres in Blockley Township in 1834, and its name was changed to Philadelphia Hospital. The unofficial name, however, especially for the legions of faculty and staff who served there, remained "the Blockley." Like most city and county hospitals, it was often plagued by fiscal mismanagement, civic neglect, deteriorated facilities, and chronic shortages of labor and supplies. The patient population was heavily dominated by paupers and drunks, criminals and their victims, the feeble, and the insane. Still, Philadelphia General Hospital (as it became in 1902) was a major teaching institution for generations of medical students and house staff. Nowhere else in Philadelphia, and in few places in the entire country, could the volume and diversity of its clinical material be matched. Service on the house staff at PGH was a baptism by fire. The University of Pennsylvania began using the hospital as a teaching institution in 1770, and continued, with minor interruptions, right up to the end. In the late 1950s and early 1960s, all five of Philadelphia's allopathic schools had teaching services here.

Why did this hospital die? The reasons are many, and there is no shortage of blame cast about. In truth, PGH was caught up in currents that closed 14 public hospitals across the nation between 1970 and 1983. Medicare and medicaid made it possible for the poor to elect care at hospitals previously off-limits to them. As new knowledge and technology made hospital care more expensive, many cities became unable to support hospitals of their own. The growth of the full-time system of paid staff physicians meant that the volunteer medical staff, on which places like PGH had traditionally depended, was an endangered species.

In 1920 PGH housed 6000 patients; in the 1950s, the census hovered around 2000; in the final years, the number was about 500, many of them chronic patients with nowhere else to go. The last patient was discharged in 1977, and by 1980 the once-great hospital had been leveled and replaced by a parking lot. Today the grounds have been partially rebuilt and are occupied by the Children's Hospital, a new Veterans Administration extended-care facility, a cyclotron, a growing collection of research buildings, and a variety of construction projects. The single remnant of the old PGH is the brick, stone, and cast-iron fence, similar to those that have surrounded so many other city and county hospitals around the country.

There should be a more substantial and dignified marker. Incidentally, Civic Center Boulevard, which curves around two sides of the hospital's old perimeter, was originally known as Curie Boulevard, to honor Pierre Curie, who brought to PGH the first aliquot of radium used in America.

(6) *Pennsylvania Hospital* Eighth Street and Spruce Street 19107. (215) 829-3000. This, the Colonies' first hospital, was founded in 1751; the present building was begun in 1755. Amazingly, both the hospital and its original building have survived wars, epidemics, currency upheavals, economic crises, and technological advancement, and both continue to thrive. Though the Philadelphia General Hospital and such public hospitals as Bellevue, in New York, and Charity Hospital, in New Orleans, trace their histories back further, they were begun as poorhouses and did not assume strictly medical functions until well after Pennsylvania Hospital was founded. The idea for the hospital originated with Dr Thomas Bond, a young physician who was convinced that Philadelphia needed a hospital for the worthy poor. Bond's idea was innovative — there was no hospital anywhere in the Colonies — but the notion aroused little enthusiasm until Benjamin Franklin became Bond's principal backer. Franklin approached the Pennsylvania Assembly, nudging them with the novel suggestion that if the Assembly would contribute 2000 pounds, Franklin would raise an equal amount from private donors. Franklin was later to say, "I do not remember any of my political manoeuvers the success of which gave me at the time more pleasure; or that in afterthinking of it, I more easily excused myself for having made use of cunning." It is the first recorded matching grant and the beginning of a long line of firsts for the hospital.

Philadelphia in the 1750s was a booming metropolis of 20,000, surpassed in size in the English-speaking world only by London. Of course, social problems grew along with the population; and caring for the sick among the working poor had become a real challenge. The Pennsylvania Hospital was intended for the industrious working man or woman, of modest means, without the resources to be cared for at home. To enter the hospital, a prospective patient needed a letter of reference (vouching for his or her character) from a person of prominence in the community, ideally someone who had contributed to the hospital. Once past this hurdle, the patient appeared before two physicians and two members of the Board of Managers. With this sanction, if the patient's condition was potentially curable and noncontagious, admission was assured, regardless of whether the affliction was mental or physical. Demented persons were lodged in the basement, men patients on the first floor, women patients on the second, and staff on the third.

Care was provided by a group of six physicians, selected annually. Though they served without pay, physicians with such appointments easily secured the services of apprentices, who were allowed the privilege of following their preceptors through the wards. Students of nonhospital physicians were required to pay a fee. The hospital's salaried staff included an apothecary, a steward, a matron, cell keepers (for the insane in the basement), nurses, and maids.

During the Revolutionary War, the hospital's stringent admissions procedures were relaxed to allow for the admission of sick and injured troops of the Continental Army. On one occasion captured

Pennsylvania Hospital, Pine Street exterior *(Courtesy of Pennsylvania Hospital)*

Hessians, prisoners of war, were also admitted. When the British Army occupied the city, sick and wounded British soldiers were likewise cared for. Given the Quaker influence in the city and on the hospital's Board of Managers, the hospital accepted patients of all races: blacks and Indians were cared for from the first, commingled with whites.

The hospital's East Wing was completed in 1755. Patients who had previously been cared for on a temporary basis, in a private home, were moved in shortly thereafter. As additional funds became available and more space was needed, the rest of the original design was completed: the West Wing in 1796, and the Centre Building a few years later. The site had originally been chosen for its rural location; when construction was begun, Fifth Street was generally considered to be Philadelphia's western boundary (the site is now located in the middle of downtown Philadelphia).

From its inception, The Pennsylvania Hospital has pioneered numerous developments in patient care and medical education:

1751	First hospital in the Colonies
1752	First women's auxiliary in the Colonies
1755	First hospital pharmacy in the country
1887	First planned operation for appendicitis (Thomas G Morton)
1911	First thoracoplasty (removal of a rib) to produce collapse of a diseased lung (RG LeConte)

Today's visitor to the Pennsylvania Hospital can see a structure that looks essentially as it did when it was first constructed. When the East Wing was completed, in 1755, it was the largest edifice in the Colonies. Benjamin Franklin wrote the inscription for the cornerstone, which is still available for inspection at the southeast corner of the building.

The hospital is unique in that it not only recognizes its historic significance but makes it easy for visitors to tour and enjoy the more interesting aspects of its architecture and historic collection. Guided tours can be arranged for groups of six or more, but the hospital invites individuals to take their own walking tour of the buildings and grounds. For this, contact Marketing Services in advance, or pick up a descriptive tour brochure at their offices (second floor, Pine Building) during your visit.

The generally suggested itinerary is as follows: Start on Eighth Street, and enter through the Gate House archway and proceed toward the Gallery Pavilion. In the Elm Court you will find a guide to 12 designated markers at each of 12 historic buildings in the

Pennsylvania Hospital complex. Walk into the ground-level door-way of the Gallery Pavilion, and you'll see a large painting by Benjamin West, *Christ Healing the Sick in the Temple.* It was completed in 1817, and the Hospital made $15,000 in the early years of the nineteenth century by charging visitors admission to see it. Throughout your tour, you will see portraits by such famous artists as Thomas Sully and Thomas Eakins hanging on the walls. Walk over to the Pine Building's main floor, where the dominant feature is the colorful (and original) nineteenth-century Portuguese floor tiles. Under the staircase, there's an antique fire engine on display. It belonged to the hospital and was necessary because of the open fireplaces used for heating and the candles used for lighting.

Go up a further flight of stairs, and you will have arrived at the second floor, where you will find the Historic Medical Library. This was begun in 1762, the first institutional medical library in the Colonies. As late as 1847 it was still the country's principal medical library. The richly paneled walls are hung with paintings, and a gallery runs around four sides of the room. The library still includes numerous rare volumes, as well as rotating historic displays.

Up another flight of steps, on the third floor, you will find the entrance to the surgical amphitheater, opened in 1804, the oldest such facility in the country, now restored to its original appearance.

Surgical Amphitheater, Pine Building, Pennsylvania Hospital *(Courtesy of Pennsylvania Hospital)*

Here, Philip Syng Physick, the father of American surgery, performed numerous operations, all with available light from the skylight above. The gallery often became overcrowded when an unusual operation or a charismatic lecturer was scheduled. Walk around to the right (as you are facing the amphitheater) and down a short flight of stairs to the **Nursing Museum,** one of the few museums in the country to feature exhibits on the history of the nursing profession. The displays include nursing uniforms, pins, military paraphernalia, instructional materials, and more. An exhibit on nursing caps (some of them bronzed) is a high spot for many visitors.

Go back to the main floor and out the front door. As you face the building, the East Wing (1755) will be on your right, the West Wing (1797) on your left, and the Centre Building (1804) directly in front. The combined structure is now referred to as the Pine Building. The original cornerstone, with its Franklin inscription, is just around the corner to your right.

In front of the Pine Building's West Wing is the Physick Garden, artfully designed and filled with plants that were used as medicines in the eighteenth century. Though the idea of such a garden was proposed in 1774, financial and other constraints resulted in interminable delays. The present garden was constructed in 1976. There are over 100 species of trees, shrubs, and plants here, ranging from the great blue lobelia (used for syphilis and gonorrhea), to primrose (an antispasmodic, also used as a vermifuge and for muscle aches), to wild onion (to increase perspiration and urine flow).

(Old) Lazaretto Wanamaker Avenue at Second Street, Essington 19113. Quarantine stations — or lazarettos, as they were sometimes called — were a fact of life in America well into the nineteenth century. The term *lazaretto,* or *lazar house,* is of Biblical origin, referring to the leprous beggar Lazarus, described in the Gospel of St Luke. Lazarettos were established all over the world, over the course of many centuries, and were particularly important in seaports, where each new ship could bring exotic contagions from foreign ports. Quarantining afflicted persons was then the only means available for protecting the community.

Philadelphia's first quarantine station was located near the mouth of the Schuylkill River, in Philadelphia, but was moved to this location in 1800 when Philadelphians became concerned that diseased visitors were being housed too close to their own homes. By the end of 1800, this 10-acre site included a main building, physicians' quarters, a quarantine master's house, a custom house, and a scattering of smaller buildings. Though the installation was intended primarily to serve sick visitors arriving by ship, many locals were also hospitalized here as the occasion demanded. The facility was operated by the city of Philadelphia, with revenues raised by the state.

In 1870, disaster struck the Lazaretto. A brig loaded with timber arrived from Jamaica with a captain who had died at sea from an unknown disease. The vessel was fumigated, trash from the ship was burned, the cargo was loaded onto canal boats, and the ship's crew were put into quarantine at the Lazaretto. Soon thereafter, a woman and child on one of the canal boats died, and more people were put into quarantine. By now, it was apparent that the disease was yellow fever. While the enforced quarantine presumably helped some of the people in Philadelphia, it wreaked havoc at the Lazaretto. In a brief period of time, the dead included the Lazaretto physician, the quarantine master, and the quarantine nurse. The episode led area residents to petition for the removal of the Lazaretto. The Lazaretto was finally closed in the 1880s, when the federal government provided alternate quarantine facilities at Marcus Hook.

By the beginning of the twentieth century, the Lazaretto was being used for recreational activities by the Philadelphia Athletic Club. In 1915 it became a seaplane base and flying school. During World War I the facility was taken over by the Army Signal Corps, which called it Chambers Field and used it to train fliers. The Lazaretto served as both barracks and headquarters for the squadron. After the war the Lazaretto was abandoned for a while, becoming a seaplane base again in the late 1930s.

Today the Lazaretto is still home to the Philadelphia Seaplane Base, as well as to a congested marina. A yacht club uses the old Physicians' Building as its headquarters. Two other principal buildings remain, of which the more interesting is the old Steward's Quarters, a three-story brick Georgian structure, with a handsome cupola above the fourth-floor attic. This building is said to be substantially original, though a tin lean-to has been tacked onto one side. The center portion now houses the **Lazaretto Museum** (open Saturdays and Sundays, 1 to 4 PM). This is mostly a hodgepodge of World War I aviation memorabilia, but there are a few items having to do with the old quarantine station. The building's wings, once quarantine wards, are currently private apartments; no visitors are allowed.

Friends Hospital Roosevelt Boulevard and Adams Avenue 19124. (215) 831-4600. Founded in 1813 as "The Friends Asylum for Persons Deprived of the Use of Their Reason," this was the first private psychiatric institution in the country. Modeled after the York Retreat, a Quaker institution in England founded in 1796, this was also the first psychiatric hospital to incorporate "moral treatment" in its approach to patients. Drugs were seldom used at the York Retreat, and chains and corporal punishment were forbidden. Instead, patients were calmed with heavy meals and copious amounts to drink, and kept busy with useful amusement, together with unfailing kindness and firmness of manner.

When the asylum opened, most of the patients were transfers from other hospitals where they had been kept in chains (as was the fashion of the day), and it took them some time to become accustomed to the new regime. They also had to learn to adjust to privacy, for this was one of the few mental institutions where curious citizens were not allowed to amuse themselves by coming to gawk at the "loonies." Here each patient was given a private room with a window and engaged in conversation. Work therapy was much in vogue in the early years: women sewed and washed and busied themselves with domestic enterprise; men planted and harvested and cut wood. Until 1834, the hospital was solely for the use of members of the Society of Friends (i.e., Quakers), but after that date patients were admitted on a nonsectarian basis.

Many hospitals followed the example of Friends Hospital (and of the York Retreat before it) in providing patients with "moral treatment" — including the McLean Hospital, in Massachusetts; the Hartford Retreat, in Connecticut; and the Bloomingdale Hospital, in New York. The influence of the Friends Hospital was further extended by the men who trained here as resident physicians and later went on to become both prominent figures in psychiatry. These included Thomas Kirkbride, who trained here in 1832 and 1833 and went on to become a founding father of the American Psychiatric Association and the most influential person in asylum design in the nation's history. Dr Pliny Earle was a resident physician here from 1840 until 1844, after which he too went on to become one of the founding fathers of the American Psychiatric Association, as well as becoming superintendent at Bloomingdale. Dr Isaac Ray, the father of forensic psychiatry, was likewise here in 1873.

Today, Friends Hospital is still located on its original 100-acre campus in northeast Philadelphia. Though once out in the country, Friends is now across the busy Roosevelt Boulevard from a large Sears store. The campus is a virtual arboretum, filled with trees, shrubs, and flowers of every description, which screen out the world and make the grounds seem like a private garden. Though modern facilities have been added, the original buildings remain.

Scattergood Building, Friends Hospital *(Credit: Bruce Stromberg/Friends Hospital)*

Each spring, usually on three weekends in late April and early May, the public is invited to tour the grounds when the many azaleas are in bloom. Otherwise, the hospital and grounds are closed to the public, to ensure privacy for the patients, just as was true in 1813.

(Old) United States Naval Asylum   Gray's Ferry Avenue at Bainbridge 19146. Though there is evidence that medical care of some sort had been provided for navy personnel as early as 1771, the first dedicated facility in Philadelphia was this one, which was partially completed in 1833 and was intended for use as a final home for old and decrepit seamen. From the first, part of the building was used as a hospital, but it wasn't until 1868 that a separate structure was completed. The 1868 hospital was designed to hold 100 patients, the vast majority of whom were old men from the asylum. The hospital had the reputation of "the best planned and constructed and the worst located naval hospital on the Atlantic seaboard." The adjacent Schuylkill River was little more than an open sewer in those days, the nearby swampy land was filled with stagnant pools reeking with offensive odors (malaria was a major problem), and the water supply was so hideous that it had to be filtered and boiled before use.

The grounds include 24 acres and 4 major buildings: Biddle Hall (1827–1833), the Surgeon's Residence (1844), the Governor's Residence (1844), and the old hospital building, Laning Hall (1868). The latter remained the Philadelphia Naval Hospital until 1917, when a new complex was completed at the Philadelphia Naval Yard. The facility (known since 1889 as the United States Naval Home) then continued without the hospital until 1976, when it was closed by the Navy and put on the auction block. In 1983, some developers entered into an option-to-purchase agreement, whereby they would convert the three oldest buildings into apartments, demolish Laning Hall, and construct townhouses and a parking lot on the remaining land. As of this writing, the developers are locked in conflict with a preservation group who maintain that Laning Hall should be saved, and the matter remains tied up in court.

Though no visitors are currently allowed on the property, the buildings can be seen reasonably well from Gray's Ferry Avenue. Biddle Hall, the immense Greek Revival building, with its tall Ionic columns and broad marble staircase, remains in remarkably good condition, given the time that it has been vacant and essentially abandoned. The two much smaller Classical Revival residences sit forward and on either side of Biddle Hall, and also are reasonably well preserved. Laning Hall is the massive building in disrepair, 400 feet behind Biddle Hall.

One interesting side note is that, from 1839 until 1845, the asylum was also used as the site for instruction of midshipmen, and was thus the first US Naval Academy, the predecessor of the one at Annapolis.

(7) *Wills Eye Hospital*   Ninth Street and Walnut Street 19107. (215) 928-3000. Wills is the nation's oldest and largest hospital devoted exclusively to eye care; but when it was founded, Wills didn't limit care to eye patients. James Wills bequeathed his fortune to establish the hospital in 1834, and the terms of the bequest were that the hospital should serve the lame and the blind. At the time, both ophthalmology and orthopedics were the province of general surgeons, so the same doctors served both groups of patients. Lame patients, however, were always a minority, and the last orthopedic operation at Wills was performed in the 1870s.

Wills has been in the forefront of medical developments from the very beginning:

1834	First eye hospital in the Western Hemisphere
1839	First residency program in the nation for training ophthalmologists
1868	Invention of the iris scissors (William McClure)
1952	First implantation of an artificial intraocular lens in a cataract patient (Warren Reese and Turgut Hamdi)

The hospital began as a small one-story facility on Logan Square and evolved through several moves, coming to its present location, next to Jefferson Medical College, in 1980. Tours can be arranged with the Public Relations office.

The Institute of the Pennsylvania Hospital 111 North 49th Street 19139. (215) 471-2000. The history of this institute is inseparable from that of Pennsylvania Hospital, of which it has always been a branch. When the Pennsylvania Hospital opened, in 1751, it accepted mental patients from the first. By 1825, psychiatric patients had become so numerous that the hospital opened a separate two-story building — called the Retreat — specifically for female psychiatric patients, located on the hospital grounds. By 1836 the overcrowding was so great that the hospital managers purchased a 100-acre site west of the Schuylkill River, at the current location; by 1840 the new facility was ready to receive patients.

Known initially as the Department for the Insane (and later as the Pennsylvania Hospital for the Insane), the new institution needed someone to guide it; the person chosen was Thomas Story Kirkbride. For the next 43 years, Kirkbride not only was Superintendent and Physician-in-Chief, but also planned the hospital's buildings, lived here with his family, and used the hospital as a base to mold psychiatric institutions around the country. His identification with the institute was so great that the institute itself was popularly known as "Kirkbride's."

Kirkbride was a kind and compassionate physician, deeply committed to a life of service for his patients, but he is best known now for his achievements as an administrator and planner. In 1844 he gathered twelve other hospital superintendents together in Philadelphia and formed what has become the American Psychiatric Association. Kirkbride is also remembered for his pioneering designs of mental hospitals in the United States and throughout the world. The swept-wing plan, with the center administrative building and receding wards on either side, was the basis for several score of hospitals, some of which are still standing (and described in more detail throughout this book). Ironically, by the time Kirkbride's schema for hospitals was fully realized in his own mind, there was no room to execute the plan at his home institution.

Though the hospital site was originally chosen for its country location, it is now surrounded by the congestion of a city neighborhood that has seen better days. The original 100 acres have been reduced to 27, and many of the original buildings were razed in the 1950s because they seemed outmoded and too expensive to remodel. Still, there are many attractive older buildings here, set amid a rolling, tree-covered campus; and the early main building, now called the Kirkbride Building, remains a dominant fixture, topped by a huge dome. The dome's interior is a maze of wooden beams and rickety stairs; visitors are not routinely admitted, but it's said that the view from the tiny cupola at the top is one of the best in the city. The building's basement has a maze of underground passageways, some of which are traversed by a cog railway.

Tours are available from the Public Relations Department.

Episcopal Hospital Front Street and Lehigh Avenue 19125. (215) 427-7000. When the Episcopal community incorporated this hospital, in 1851, there were only two general hospitals in Philadelphia: the Pennsylvania Hospital, and what was later known as the Philadelphia General Hospital. Philadelphia's population was growing rapidly as the expanding shipyards, blast furnaces, railroad yards, factories, and mills provided employment for huge numbers of people; but there had been no increase in hospital beds in several decades. In 1852 the Hospital of the Protestant Episcopal Church of Philadelphia moved into an old mansion, purchased in part with a gift of $500 from the famed Swedish singer Jenny Lind. The hospital grew rapidly and in 1860 broke ground for a new building to be patterned after the then-renowned pavilion design used at the Hôpital Lariboisière in Paris. The west wing was completed in 1862, just in time to receive Civil War casualties. The east wing was completed in 1875.

Today Episcopal Hospital is a 300-bed modern hospital. The east and west wings were demolished in the late 1970s, but the chapel (built in 1860) remains. The exterior is essentially intact, and gives a flavor of the Norman architecture that characterized the other early buildings. Tours can be arranged through the Public Relations Department.

Lankenau Hospital Lancaster Avenue, west of City Line 19151. (215) 645-2000. Incorporated as the German Hospital of the City of Philadelphia in 1860, this hospital was a symbol of the vast numbers of German refugees who flocked to this country as a result of the civil unrest in Germany in 1848. The original hospital bylaws required that staff members speak German with facility. The hospital remained predominantly German until World War I. In 1917 it changed its name to Lankenau, ostensibly to honor a major benefactor who had served as president of the Board of Trustees for 32 years; but widespread anti-German sentiment aroused by the war was obviously a factor as well.

In the early years of the hospital, nursing care was provided by willing, but poorly trained and poorly paid, help. In 1884 the hospital brought over seven Lutheran deaconesses from Germany, who then provided all nursing care until the hospital began its own training school for nurses in 1899. Lankenau School of Nursing continues its tradition of turning out diploma graduates; it's one of the few hospital-based programs to have survived.

Lankenau has been a locally progressive hospital since its beginning, but the hospital's principal medical first was achieved when it moved to its present location, in 1953. In that year Lankenau opened the country's first hospital-based health museum, becoming the nation's first hospital to embrace its obligation to provide community health education. By 1970 the various health-education exhibits had become dated, and the museum was entirely remodeled and renamed the **Cyclorama of Life.** Visitors enter the Cyclorama through a historic section, which contains a three-level display, linking the histories of Lankenau, America, and world medicine. The corridor then leads into the health education area, with well-designed displays on birth, heredity, growth and development, body systems, the five senses, the brain, mental and physical health, addiction, sexual behavior, aging, and human ecology. The Cyclorama, located just inside the hospital entrance on the left, is open to the public Monday through Friday, 9 AM to 5 PM, and sometimes on weekends as well.

The 475-bed hospital is beautifully situated on a former golf course on the outskirts of Philadelphia. Tours of the entire facility are available through the Public Relations Department.

(8) *Children's Hospital of Philadelphia* 34th Street and Civic Center Boulevard. (215) 596-9100. When the Children's Hospital of Philadelphia was founded, in 1855, it was the first hospital devoted to the care of children in North America. As at most hospitals of the era, its first clientele were the poor: in this case, children whose families lacked facilities or means to cope with illness in the home. Children with infectious diseases and those under two years of age were not admitted. The hospital also had a dispensary, where advice and medicine were given free of charge six days a week in the hour before noon. There were no pediatricians at the time (the American Pediatric Society wasn't founded until 1888); all care was given by generalists, who donated their time.

Like most hospitals for children around the country, this one has depended heavily on the heartstrings of the community. Volunteers have always played major roles both in fund raising and in providing special services to patients. Fund raising has taken all forms, from concert benefits (featuring, e.g., Leonard Bernstein,

Van Cliburn, Eugene Ormandy) to substantial gifts (in 1929, Al
Capone sent a $1000 check from his cell in Holmesburg prison).
Children's has long been a source of medical innovation:

1914 First Department for the Prevention of Disease in the world
1938 Development of the first closed, transparent incubator for the care of
      the newborn, later patented as the Isolette
1965 Development of a balloon-tipped cardiac catheter for enlarging
      defective heart openings
1967 First modern pediatric intensive-care unit in the Western Hemisphere

The current Children's Hospital building is the fourth in the
institution's history. Located on the site of the old Philadelphia
General Hospital, the 9-story, 286-bed structure opened in 1974.
The open central court—which extends to the building's top—
adds a light and cheerful atmosphere. Other structures include a
research building and an ambulatory-care building. Tours are provided by the Public Relations Department.

Germantown Hospital and Medical Center One Penn Boulevard
19144. (215) 848-5244. In the Civil War era, Germantown was an
elite Philadelphia suburb. Galvanized by the passions of the times,
the community organized a "Soldiers Aid Society of Germantown"
in 1862; soon the Germantown Town Hall was offered, and accepted, as a military hospital. Known as Cuyler Army Hospital, the
Town Hall building was used for administration; and seven pavilion-style hospital wards were constructed on the adjacent grounds.
Though the Army supplied the doctors, nursing services were supplied by townspeople who did what they could. With the citizenry
so involved in health care for soldiers, it was but a short step to
providing the same services for needy locals. In 1863, the Germantown Dispensary and Hospital Association was founded. For its
first two years the dispensary operated out of a red-brick Romanesque Revival building (still standing, at 5603/5 Germantown Avenue); but after the war it moved into the old Cuyler Hospital buildings. By 1870 the Germantown Hospital and Dispensary had
constructed its own 12-bed facility. In the decades that followed,
the hospital remained remarkable for the extent of community
involvement in its operations. One manifestation of this is the teenage volunteer program, now nationally known as the "Candy-
stripers," an innovation begun at Germantown in 1957. The hospital also has the distinction of being the first in the United States to
use insulin (1930). The modern Germantown 300-bed hospital can

be toured by prior arrangement with the Public Relations Department.

Albert Einstein Medical Center York Street and Tabor Road 19141. (215) 456-7890. This is the survivor of four Jewish hospitals in Philadelphia. The first of these began as a society for visiting the sick and burying the dead, shortly after the American Revolution. Formal plans for the building of a hospital and the purchase of a site didn't actually take shape, however, until the conclusion of the Civil War, in 1865. The Philadelphia Jewish Hospital opened two years later. Its first patients were mostly peddlers and domestic servants — occupations taken by many untrained Jewish immigrants of the time. From the beginning, patients were accepted in a nonsectarian fashion, and in 1869 non-Jewish admissions exceeded Jewish admisssions. In 1873, the institution moved to its present site in North Philadelphia and changed its name to Jewish Hospital and Home for the Aged and Infirm.

In the 1890s, a second Jewish medical association was formed in South Philadelphia, this one called the Mount Sinai Hospital Association. This group was composed of recent Eastern European Jewish immigrants, who felt themselves politically and culturally distinct from the more established, more assimilated, more wealthy "uptown" Jews, who were largely of German origin. By 1903 the Mount Sinai Hospital had moved into a former factory building at 5th and Wilder streets and had begun serving the new generation of immigrants with such cultural accommodations as Cyrillic and Hebrew eye charts. A third Jewish hospital, Lebanon Hospital, opened in 1907 and remained a marginal institution until it closed, in 1920. A fourth, the Northern Liberties Hospital, opened in 1920 and continued to function until 1954.

In 1951, the three existing Jewish hospitals joined forces as the Albert Einstein Medical Center, with the old Jewish Hospital becoming the Northern Division, Mount Sinai becoming the Southern Division, and Northern Liberties the Eastern Division. The Eastern Division was closed in 1954, and the Southern Division properties were sold in 1988.

Today's Einstein is a 600-bed tertiary care teaching hospital that covers a large plot of land just off Broad Street on Philadelphia's North Side. The six granite Ionic columns so prominently displayed on its grounds have nothing to do with medical history, but rather were once a part of the facade of the old US Mint (1829–1904) at 13th and Chestnut streets. Tours of the Medical Center can be arranged through the Communications Department.

(9) *Graduate Hospital*   19th Street and Lombard Street 19146. (215) 893-2000. In the early 1880s, when the Philadelphia Polyclinic and College for Graduates in Medicine had its beginnings, it represented one kind of response to the sorry state of US medical schools in general. Two similar institutions, the New York Polyclinic and the New York Post-Graduate Medical School, were formed about the same time. Each was intended to be a clinically oriented training institution where graduate physicians could get additional training, to compensate for undergraduate medical educations in which they received MD degrees but little else of practical utility. The first Philadelphia Polyclinic was little more than a dispensary supervised by four talented teaching physicians. In 1886 some inpatient wards were added in two small leased homes; and in 1889 a full-scale hospital was established on the present site.

In the wake of the Flexner Report, many US medical schools began looking for ways to bolster their postgraduate training capabilities, in addition to strengthening their undergraduate programs. The various "graduate medical schools" scattered around the country had not fared well in Flexner's evaluation; he regarded these refresher-course "repair shops" as generally of lower quality than the better undergraduate medical schools. In 1916 the University of Pennsylvania established a medical school–based Graduate School of Medicine (the country's first), in the process absorbing the Medico-Chirurgical College and Hospital (a former medical society, turned into a medical school in 1881). The following year, this enterprise absorbed the Philadelphia Polyclinic. The new Graduate Hospital of the University of Pennsylvania then became UP's principal subspecialty training site (especially in the field of gastroenterology, under the direction of Dr Henry Bockus). When subspecialty training was absorbed by the School of Medicine, in 1964, the Graduate Hospital drifted without a clear sense of direction. In 1975, Graduate began pursuing an independent course from UP; by 1979 it had begun a vigorous expansion program. It is now the keystone of a health system that comprises 1000 beds and various healthcare facilities in eastern Pennsylvania and southern New Jersey. Tours are available through the Public Relations Department.

Old Mercy-Douglass Hospital   5000 Woodland Avenue 19143. This was the last in a series of hospitals founded by Nathan Mossell (1856–1946), a remarkable man with some remarkable experiences in the City of Brotherly Love. Mossell was the first black admitted to medical school at the University of Pennsylvania. On the first day of school, he was asked to sit behind a screen so that other students wouldn't have to look at him. He refused, sitting instead on one of the ordinary student benches. No one would sit next to him, and no one spoke to him the entire first year. Gradually, though, his fellow students warmed to him; and at commencement, in 1882, his classmates interrupted the formalities with a standing ovation for Mossell, who graduated with second honors. Dr Mossell went on to get additional postgraduate training at Guy's Hospital and St Thomas Hospital in London, and then returned to found a hospital in Philadelphia for black patients, where black physicians and nurses could likewise receive training. In 1895 he founded the Frederick Douglass Memorial Hospital and Training School for Nurses at 1512 Lombard Street. In 1907 a splinter group, who found Mossell's methods autocratic and arbitrary, broke off to form a separate hospital, which they called Mercy Hospital. The schism eventually healed; in 1948 the two groups reunited to form the Mercy-Douglass Hospital.

The 50th Street and Woodland Avenue site is where Mercy Hospital was located from 1919 onward, and where the two hospitals combined their operations in 1948. The building itself dates from 1956. In 1973, Mercy-Douglass succumbed to the pressures that have closed so many other small hospitals: the growth of technology, which made providing services so much more expensive and promoted the economics of scale, and the consequent growth of competing urban medical centers.

At present, the Mercy-Douglass building stands in a lot overgrown with weeds. The structure, a derelict, has been abandoned for almost two decades. There is no sign or plaque here to tell its story.

(10) *College of Physicians* 19 South 22d Street 19103. (215) 563-6050. The College of Physicians of Philadelphia was founded in 1787 for the "advancement of the science of medicine, and thereby, the lessening of human misery." It was a college in the old sense of the word: a collection of colleagues in pursuit of a common ideal. Benjamin Rush delivered the college's first scientific paper ("On the Means of Promoting Medical Knowledge"). Over the years, the college considered a variety of public health issues, often taking strong positions in attempts to influence legislation and public opinion. Issues that attracted the college's attention included the evils of drink (they were against them), the illumination of the streets (they were against that too), public squares with fountains (for), and the prescribing of drugs by apothecaries (against).

Over the years its membership has included most of Philadelphia's most famous physicians, including Rush, Samuel David Gross, Silas Weir Mitchell, and William Osler. The College remained an exclusively male organization for 145 years, finally admitting its first woman (a research professor of gynecology at Woman's Medical College) in 1932.

The college remains an independent professional society, not affiliated with any medical school or national organization. It moved to its present quarters in 1909, an elegant brick-and-limestone Georgian structure surrounded by a stately wrought-iron fence. The interior is equally impressive, with everything constructed to baronial proportions. The Grand Staircase leads up to the beautifully proportioned Hall of Portraits on the second floor. Here the visitor will see numerous portraits by Thomas Sully, Rembrandt Peale, Charles Willson Peale, and Gilbert Stuart.

The library here is particularly noteworthy. The huge collection (over 650,000 catalogued items) includes one of the largest medical-historical sections in the United States, comprising more than 10,000 volumes printed before 1800 and 60,000 printed before 1900. The marvelous collection includes rare editions of Hippocrates, Celsus, Vesalius, Morgagni, and Harvey, as well as medieval illuminated manuscripts and other rarities. Don't miss the library's fireplace, which was brought over from Europe in pieces and assembled here.

For most visitors the most impressive and unusual aspect of the college will be the **Mütter Museum,** arguably America's finest medical pathological and historical museum. Begun in 1856, when Dr Thomas Dent Mütter donated his vast collection of pathological specimens, the Mütter now contains over 12,000 objects that chronicle the history of American medicine from the eighteenth century to the present. The exhibit area has been recently remodeled, and the result is both pleasing to the eye and conducive to relaxed browsing. The collection includes over 100 human skulls, 100 intricate wax models of the human eye depicting various eye diseases, dozens of skeletons, and numerous specimens depicting jaws and paranasal sinuses and almost every bodily structure. The instrument collection includes Benjamin Rush's medicine chest, a Laennec stethoscope, a Helmholtz ophthalmoscope, one of Lister's carbolic-spray devices, and much more. One real crowd pleaser is the Soap Lady, a dramatically obese woman who died in the early nineteenth century and was exhumed in the 1870s. Time and the earth had turned her tissue into "adipocere," a sort of waxy soap. Other visitors marvel at the tumor removed from President Grover Cleveland's jaw, during a secret operation in 1883, or at William Osler's brain (divided, and kept in two separate specimen jars).

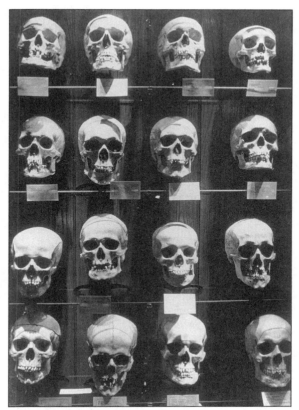

Hyrtl Skull Collection, Mütter Museum, College of Physicians *(By permission of Mütter Museum, College of Physicians of Philadelphia)*

Additional exhibits during my most recent visit included a fine series of displays on Siamese twins, one on two centuries of ophthalmology in Philadelphia, and another on "Electrotherapy: The Heat that Heals."

The College and the Mütter Museum are open to visitors Monday through Friday, 10 AM to 4 PM. Call in advance if you would like a tour, or if you wish to see any of the library's rarer volumes. Interested visitors should be sure not to miss the Herb Garden next to the building.

⑪ *Hill-Physick-Keith House* 321 South 4th Street 19106. (215) 925-7866. This house dates from 1786, when it was constructed for

Henry Hill, an importer of Madeira wine; but its medical distinction began in 1815, when it became the residence of Philip Syng Physick (1768–1837). Dubbed "The Father of American Surgery" during his lifetime, Physick had an extraordinary medical education for his time. After completing undergraduate work at the University of Pennsylvania, he underwent a three-year apprenticeship with Dr Adam Kuhn, a physician who had studied botany with Linnaeus. He attended lectures at the Medical College of Philadelphia, then went to London to study with John Hunter — probably the most celebrated anatomist and surgeon of his era. Physick received his medical degree at the University of Edinburgh, then the most demanding and honored medical school in the English-speaking world. Returning to Philadelphia, he entered into a collaborative relationship with Benjamin Rush, with Rush mainly caring for their patients' medical problems and Physick taking care of surgical aspects. As a surgeon, Physick was remarkably innovative, developing such new procedures and therapeutic devices as the stomach pump, a plastic-surgery repair for harelip, and a tonsillotome (for the removal of tonsils). In 1805 he was appointed to the first professorship of surgery in the country, at the University of Pennsylvania. Dr Sam Gross said of him, "No man that adorned the American medical profession enjoyed so universal a reputation as Physick. . . . His pupils, who idolized him, and who scattered through every nook and corner of this continent, disseminated his doctrines far and wide, and not a few of them became founders of medical schools and the great expounders of the art and science of surgery."

This house, where Physick lived until his death, in 1837, is a suitable shrine for the eminent surgeon. Beautifully restored and elegantly furnished, the four-story residence exudes Colonial-era elegance. An upstairs room has an attractive display of surgical instruments owned by Physick's son-in-law. A variety of Physick memorabilia and medical artifacts of the era are also on display. Be sure to see the lovely garden.

The house is open to the public Tuesday through Saturday, 10 AM to 4 PM, and Sunday, 1 to 4 PM, with tours scheduled at 11, 1:30, and 3:00. There is a small admission charge.

(12) *The Library Company* 1314 Locust Street 19107. (215) 546-3181. Established in 1731 by Benjamin Franklin and a group of his friends as a subscription library, The Library Company now has the largest collection of seventeenth- and eighteenth-century medical books in North America. The cornerstone of this treasure trove is the personal library of Dr Benjamin Rush, which includes some

6000 items, including books, letters, and manuscripts. Here you will find wonderful early anatomic engravings, ancient treatises on yellow fever, works on venereal disease over 400 years old, and practically any medical work printed prior to 1800. Medicine, however, is only one aspect of the collection; up until the Civil War, The Library Company was the largest public library in North America. The Library Company is an independent research library, not affiliated with any university or governmental agency. Virtually anything in its collection can be seen by interested visitors. This is a very unusual policy, which allows the interested public a rare opportunity to see extraordinary materials. Anyone can become a member of The Library Company by purchasing a share, which currently costs $20. Visitors are welcome from 9 AM to 4:45 PM.

Kendig Memorial Museum Temple University School of Pharmacy, 3307 North Broad Street 19140. (215) 221-4952. Visitors interested in pharmacy history will enjoy the Kendig Memorial Museum, located in the School of Pharmacy building, adjacent to room 410. Opened in 1957, this fine collection pays tribute to the man who was Temple's pharmacy dean from 1908 to 1950. Displays include pharmacy equipment, shelf ware, show globes, spittoons, elaborate medication containers, syringes, inhalers, mortars, and pestles, nursing bottles, and various other pharmacy paraphernalia. The entrance is decorated with two unusual gas-lit mortar-and-pestle signs. The museum is accessible to the public during normal school hours. Tours are available by advance arrangement.

(13) *Wistar Institute* 36th Street and Spruce Street 19104. (215) 898-3708. The Wistar Institute is the oldest independent biomedical research institute in the United States. Founded as the Wistar Institute of Anatomy and Biology, in 1892, the Wistar was endowed by a great-nephew of Caspar Wistar (1761 – 1818) who named the institute after his forebear. Caspar was a man of many distinctions. As a friend of Thomas Jefferson and Benjamin Franklin, he was widely known as a great conversationalist and wit. A scholarly man, he wrote the first American textbook on anatomy. He was widely regarded as the leading American physician of his day; the Wisteria vine was named in his honor.

The institute was originally built to house a museum of anatomic specimens and other "scientific objects," all part of a collection begun by Caspar to be a focus for research on anatomy and taxonomy. As time passed and anatomy's central place in medical research diminished, the museum came to play a less dominant role, and research in other areas a much greater role. The institute achieved early fame for its development of the standard laboratory animal, still used today, known as the "Wistar rat." By the middle of this century, however, the institute had lost its focus and was really little more than a museum. In the late 1950s it regained its momentum and once again became a center of important research, this time primarily in the area of virology. Since then, its achievements have been many:

1955   Development of the first line of reproducible, nonmalignant human cells for tissue culture (Leonard Hayflick and Paul Morehead)

1968   Development of the standard rabies vaccine (Hilary Koprowski, Tadeusz Wiktor, and Mario Fernandez)

1972   Development of the vaccine for rubella, or German measles (Stanley Plotkin)

Though located on the campus of the University of Pennsylvania, the Wistar is an entirely independent institution. The institute currently occupies four connected buildings, one of which is the original 1884 structure. The museum has long since been eliminated, but remnants (including some skeletons, anatomic specimens, and more) will soon be on display in an atrium which was undergoing renovation at the time of my visit. Tours are not normally available to the general public, but the atrium will probably be accessible Mondays through Fridays from 10 to 4. Call first.

National Board of Medical Examiners 3930 Chestnut Street 19104. (215) 349-6400. There were authoritative calls for standardized physician licensing examinations as early as the 1880s. The first national consortium on this issue, the National Confederation of State Medical Examining and Licensing Boards, was founded in 1891. Though this provided a convenient medium for exchange of views, the states continued to license physicians in their own idiosyncratic fashions (with ten states requiring no examination whatsoever as late as 1901). In 1902 the American Confederation of Reciprocating Examining and Licensing Boards was founded, providing the first step toward a nationally standardized licensing process. In 1913, the National Confederation and the American Confederation joined to form the Federation of State Medical Boards of the United States. Persistent difficulties with reciprocity led to the founding of the entirely separate National Board of Medical Examiners in 1915, with eight states agreeing to accept the results of its examinations. The first examination was given in 1916: of the 32 physicians who applied for the exam, 16 were accepted, 10 took the exam, and 5 passed the week-long endurance test of oral discussions, essay responses, and case discussions. In 1922 the format was altered so that candidates took an exam in basic sciences at the end of their sophomore year, an exam in clinical sciences before or immediately following graduation from an approved school, and a third exam toward the end of the first postgraduate year. By 1967 the role of the National Board had become so important that it created the Federal Licensing Examination (or FLEX), which is now accepted by all licensing jurisdictions. The National Board also administers examinations for the Foreign Medical Graduate Examination in the Medical Sciences (FMGEMS). The National Board's current home dates from 1966. There are no tours available at present.

(14) *Benjamin Rush Home Site* Third and Walnut Streets 19106. Benjamin Rush (1745 – 1813) was one of this country's most distinguished physicians and patriots. Though it is easy now to make fun of his errors, he was a remarkable innovator for his time, thoroughly dedicated to his patients and his young country, a man who courageously risked everything for the betterment of others. Rush graduated from Princeton at age fourteen, took a five-year apprenticeship with a Philadelphia physician, and then went to study in Edinburgh. Upon his return to Philadelphia, after graduation from Edinburgh, he became the first professor of chemistry at the city's new medical school. Later he was made a professor of medicine. A vigorous supporter of the Revolution, he contributed the title *Common Sense* to Tom Paine's fiery revolutionary pamphlet and later became one of five physician signers of the Declaration of Independence — the only one with a medical degree. He served at the battles of Brandywine, Trenton, and Princeton, and went on to become Surgeon General of the Continental Army. Later, in 1786, he founded the first free medical clinic for the poor in America, the Philadelphia Dispensary; and in 1787 he helped found the College of Physicians in Philadelphia. Like Benjamin Franklin, he was a founder, and later president, of America's first established organization for the abolition of slavery, the Pennsylvania Society for Promoting the Abolition of Slavery and the Relief of Free Negroes Unlawfully Held in Bondage. He likewise founded the country's first organization for rehabilitation of felons, the Philadelphia Society for Alleviating the Miseries of Public Prisons. He was deeply interested in the mentally ill and was a pioneer in the investigation of the relationship between the body and the mind. For 30 years, as both practitioner and teacher, he studied and treated the insane. In 1812 he wrote *Medical Inquiries and Observations upon the Diseases*

of the Mind, a book that remained the American authority on mental disease until the 1880s. For these and other contributions, he is generally regarded as the father of American psychiatry.

With all these accomplishments, Rush deserves to be forgiven some mistakes; but it is ironic that his errors are sometimes better remembered than his achievements. He was a leading exponent of the "heroic" school of therapy. During the disastrous yellow fever epidemic of 1793, Rush stayed in the city and ministered to the sick and dying while some 20,000 others fled. His treatment was copious bleeding and purging, and we now know he added to the carnage (4000 Philadelphians died) rather than serving to reduce it. Nonetheless, his devotion to others made him a popular hero. Rush likewise bled the insane, often removing as much as a liter per treatment. He kept madmen awake for 24 hours in a standing posture, in the belief that the resulting fatigue and debility would heal morbid excitement. He invented a "tranquilizer chair," in which madmen could be twirled about, and simultaneously bled, to the point of nausea and prostration.

The house in which Rush was born (on the northwest corner of Third and Walnut streets) was razed in 1969, amid substantial controversy. The stones and woodwork are currently in storage, and the house may yet be reconstructed upon another site. In the meantime, a small plaque in a lovely fenced garden is all that remains to memorialize this remarkable man.

(15)*Washington Square* Walnut Street between 6th Street and 7th Street 19106. As a city square, this area dates back to 1683, when it was known as Southeast Square. For many years it served as a potter's field, a burying ground for paupers. Among the 3000 bodies buried here were 2000 British and American soldiers from the Revolutionary War and numerous victims of the 1793 yellow fever epidemic.

Beyond that, the square's chief medical significance is as a home to three of the country's oldest and best known medical publishers. The most venerable of these, **Lea & Febiger** (on the southeast corner, at 6th Street and South Washington Square), built its home here in 1923. The firm itself was founded in 1785 and is the oldest publishing firm of any kind in the United States. Founded by the Irish Catholic firebrand Matthew Carey, the firm began by publishing revolutionary tracts. As the firm's leadership and name changed through progeny and marriage (though always remaining within the growing family), Carey and Lea became publishers for such American authors as Washington Irving, Edgar Allan Poe, and James Fenimore Cooper, as well as the American publishers for such British writers as Jane Austen and Charles Dickens. Though the firm published medical books from the beginning, it wasn't until after the Civil War that this became a dominant interest. The firm has been the American publisher of *Gray's Anatomy of the Human Body* since 1859 (the book is now in its 30th edition). The name Lea & Febiger was adopted in 1907, and the firm remains one of the few family-run publishing houses in the nation. The Lea and Febiger building is an Italian Renaissance design, finished in white stone. **JB Lippincott** (227 South 6th Street) traces its origins to 1792, though the name Lippincott didn't actually grace a title page until 1836. Founded primarily as a publisher of bibles, prayer books, and popular fiction, the firm began publishing medical works in the 1830s, beginning with the *Dispensatory of the United States of America*. In 1878 Lippincott published the first nursing text in America, *Handbook of Nursing*. Lippincott, now a subsidiary of Harper & Row, moved to the square in 1899. **WB Saunders Company** (now located on the third floor of the Curtis Building, facing the square across Walnut Street), the youngest of the three publishers, was founded in 1888 and moved to the square in 1912. Saunders is unique among the three in that it was founded strictly as a medical publishing venture. Walter Burns Saunders was keenly aware of the explosion in medical knowledge in the fading years of the nineteenth century, and he understood the publishing opportunity this represented. He set up shop in the shadow of Jefferson Medical College and set out to acquire authors who were leaders in their fields, promising them that the books would be published to a craftsman's standards and sold to the customer with prompt service. Saunders has published many standard medical texts over the years. Saunders' most famous title, *Dorland's Illustated Medical Dictionary* (first published in 1890, now in its 27th edition), was actually ghost-written by Saunders' editor Ryland Greene. For many years WB Saunders occupied its own building (still standing) at the corner of Locust and 7th streets.

None of these three firms provides tours or is open to the public, but it is possible, and pleasant, to sit on a bench in Washington Square, among lovely old trees and fountains, and feel medical wisdom emanating from the firms on three sides, as it has done for many years.

(16) *S Weir Mitchell Home Site* 1524 Walnut Street 19102. S Weir Mitchell (1829–1914) was a pioneering neurologist, a poet and novelist, and was generally regarded as one of the most versatile and accomplished physicians of his day. Mitchell graduated from Jefferson Medical College in 1850, after a two-year course of study.

After a year of postgraduate work in Paris, studying in part with the famous physiologist Claude Bernard, Mitchell returned to Philadelphia to begin medical practice. It wasn't until the Civil War, however, that he rose to prominence. During the War he was placed in charge of a military hospital for the treatment of nervous diseases due to injury or other aspects of army service. This was one of the first such hospitals anywhere, and subsequently Mitchell became one of America's leading neurologists. In the years that followed he published almost 250 books, papers, and reports on almost all aspects of neurology, as well as other subjects. In 1864, he wrote *Gunshot Wounds and Other Injuries of the Nerves*, a description of peripheral nerve injury syndromes that remained the classic description for half a century. In 1896, as a result of self-experimentation, Mitchell published the first complete and instructive description of mescaline intoxication.

Mitchell's greatest medical influence came about as a result of his interest in functional neurotic disorders. For patients with such problems, he devised a treatment consisting of prologed rest, seclusion, ample feeding, massage, and gentle electrical stimulation. Mitchell's "rest cure," as it was called, became so popular that it was widely used in Europe, and Mitchell received numerous honors for his work. Weir Mitchell Institutes were founded in France, and his techniques were applied also in Britain, Austria, and Italy.

However, Mitchell's greatest fame was as a novelist and poet. His literary output was inspired by, and infused with, the medical and human dramas he encountered during the Civil War. Much of this work was published in the *Atlantic Monthly*, most to enthusiastic critical acclaim. Though his literary career began after his fifty-first birthday, he published 13 novels, over 30 short stories, and several volumes of verse.

Mitchell lived at this address from 1873 until 1914. A memorial plaque on a huge high-rise building is all that is left of his presence. The bas-relief stone inscription reads, "On this spot stood the house of S. Weir Mitchell — Physician — Physiologist — Poet — Man of Letters — He taught us the use of rest for the nervous system — He created 'Hugh Wynne' — He pictured for us 'The Red City' in which he lived and laboured from 1829 until 1914."

(17) *Franklin Court Complex* Market Street between 3d Street and 4th Street 19106. (215) 597-3913. Benjamin Franklin (1706–1790), by all accounts, was one of this country's truly remarkable men; medicine and health care, generally, were among his numerous beneficiaries. Though his own family was poor and he received only two years of formal schooling, Franklin had amassed a fortune

by his forty-second birthday (in part by selling pharmaceuticals and patent medicines in his store), and he devoted the second half of his life to contributing to the general welfare and making his own life as satisfying and productive as possible.

His medical contributions include the invention of the bifocal lens for spectacles, as well as that of a flexible urethral catheter. As was true of many men of learning in his time, Franklin took a keen interest in medical matters. Most of his closest friendships were with physicians. Physicians often sought his advice on medical matters; and, though he never technically practiced medicine, he treated numerous people for various ills and wrote often on medical topics. He counseled (in his own paper, the *Pennsylvania Gazette*) that inoculation for smallpox was a safe and beneficial practice; he wrote about diet and its effect on disease; he used his pen to discuss perspiration, the common cold, sleep, deafness, blood temperature, and circulation. When Thomas Bond came up with the idea of starting the nation's first public hospital, it was Franklin whom he approached to get the job done. When the Pennsylvania Hospital was built, Franklin became its first president. Franklin likewise had a deep interest in medical education and helped young men, including Benjamin Rush, to study abroad. Though he never graduated from medical school, he was elected to membership in several medical societies. He received an honorary doctorate from the University of St Andrews (thus the title "Dr" Franklin), as well as honorary degrees from Harvard and Yale.

Philadelphia is filled with tributes to this much-loved man, but the Franklin Court Complex (where Franklin's home once stood) is probably the most convenient, satisfying, and instructive place for visitors to begin. Though the house was torn down long ago, a steel-frame outline of the structure has been built in its place, and an underground museum at the site is devoted to the life and accomplishments of this man of genius. This is an unusual and pleasing museum, a fascinating combination of eighteenth-century artifacts, flashing neon lights, and high-tech gimmicks. Here you can see an 18-minute film on Franklin, view various exhibits and demonstrations, and buy copies of publications that Franklin wrote or that were written about him. The complex is open daily from 9 AM to 5 PM.

(18) *American College of Physicians* 6th Street and Race Street 19106. (215) 351-2400. With a membership of 60,000 physicians who specialize in internal medicine, the American College of Physicians is the nation's largest specialty society. When the ACP was established, in 1915, almost all physicians were general practi-

tioners, and the few specialists were surgeons. Even the notion of "internal medicine" was a fuzzy one. Many regarded internists as glorified general practitioners who aspired to be super-diagnosticians. Others defined internists by those they couldn't treat and what they couldn't do: no children, no obstetrics, no cutting.

As the decades progressed, the place of the internist in modern medicine defined itself. The ACP has played a pivotal role in that evolution. In 1967 the ACP introduced the Medical Knowledge Self Assessment Program, or MKSAP. While self-testing was not in itself a new idea, the method and scope of MKSAP was unique, and its overwhelmingly enthusiastic reception led to its adaptation to other specialties, other languages, and other professions. Among its many other activities, the ACP publishes the *Annals of Internal Medicine,* the most widely circulated medical specialty journal in the world.

The ACP has been headquartered in Philadelphia since 1926; it moved into its new nine-story building, on Independence Mall, in 1989. Eventually the structure will include a museum area, but at present there are no provisions for public tours.

(19)*Joseph Leidy Statue* Race Street at 19th Street 19103. In front of the Academy of Natural Sciences of Philadelphia, at the edge of Logan Circle, you will find a bronze statue of Joseph Leidy appearing both relaxed and genial. Leidy (1823–1891) graduated from the University of Pennsylvania Medical College in 1844, and went on to become one of the most brilliant naturalists of his century. His *Elementary Treatise on Human Anatomy* was for many years the standard American text on the subject. He was an expert on the parasites that afflicted human beings, and his discovery of *Trichinella spiralis* led to the discovery that trichinosis could be prevented by thorough cooking of pork products. He was also a fine artist and a world-renowned paleontologist. His statue is located in front of the Academy because he was, over many years, its librarian, curator, and board chairman.

(20) *Boericke and Tafel, Inc* 1011 Arch Street 19107. (215) 922-2967. Boericke & Tafel is the nation's oldest supplier of homeopathic medicaments. It is still going strong, and in fact is growing, on account of resurgent interest in homeopathy. The firm began in 1843 as a homeopathic pharmacy operated by Dr Charles Radermacher. In 1863, the old pharmacy was bought out by Francis E Boericke, who entered into a partnership with Adolf Tafel in 1880. Under one name or another, the firm has been manufacturing

homeopathic remedies since the 1850s, and it has been at its Arch Street location since 1880. At the height of the homeopathic movement's popularity, in the late nineteenth century, B & T had branch offices in cities throughout the United States, including San Francisco, Minneapolis, and Pittsburgh. The Boericke family continued to be leaders in American homeopathy for decades; Garth Wilkinson Boericke was the last teacher of the last course in homeopathy at an American medical school (Hahnemann). Since the turn of the century B & T has been the world's largest supplier of homeopathic preparations. In 1989 it was sold to a German firm, whose management decided to move the company's American headquarters and major manufacturing operations to California — the current major market for homeopathic preparations. However, the historic Philadelphia location will continue to serve the East Coast market, and some manufacturing will continue at this site. The shop here is open during normal business hours.

Rochester, Minnesota

THIS ATTRACTIVE TOWN OF 70,000 in southern Minnesota has a name that is almost synonymous with that of its best-known institution: the Mayo Clinic. The Mayo Clinic, with its constituent parts, is by far the town's dominant employer, with a payroll of some 16,000 (the next largest employer is IBM, with a payroll about half as large). When Dr WW Mayo came to town, in 1863, Rochester's population was barely a couple of thousand. Over the years, the town and the clinic grew up together with an enormously beneficial synergy. Most of the town's attractions are tied in with, or have been funded with, Mayo money. The city park system began with land donated by the Mayos. The civic auditorium was given by the Mayos. When you check into a local hotel or motel, you will invariably be asked if you are here to go to the Clinic (you will likely be given a discount if you say yes); most hotels and motels provide shuttle-bus service to the clinic if they aren't within walking distance. Local citizens recognize how dependent their economy is on the goodwill of visitors, and they go out of their way to be helpful to outsiders. Over half a million people come to Rochester each year solely because of the Mayo Clinic. Few of the clinic's patients are locals; only half are even from Minnesota, and 80 percent are self-referred.

The most dramatic evidence of the interdependence of the town and the clinic can be found in the downtown pedestrian subway system. Begun in the early 1920s, the subway was initially designed to link the Kahler Hotel (itself an amalgam of hotel, hospital, and convalescent home) with the Mayo Clinic. Going outside in the sometimes-brutal Minnesota winter was hard enough on staff, but really daunting for patients. Gradually the subway system "metastasized," and it now links practically all of the clinic's buildings with various hotels, shops, restaurants, and parking garages. Much of it is carpeted or tiled, lined with boutiques, the walls hung with artwork. Ordinary shopping pedestrians are mixed with people in wheelchairs and on gurneys. You have to see it to believe it.

Your visit to Rochester will be more pleasant, and you will be able to see more, if you make arrangements in advance; but planning in advance is less important here than in any other Great Medical City. Mayo and its related institutions have been designed with public access in mind. This is a user-friendly place. They *want* you to look them over, and you don't have to be a physician or health professional to feel welcome. Every facility has tours or visiting hours specifically intended to encourage public use. This attitude is extraordinarily rare in complex medical centers, and it's easy, even without looking at the professional skills to be found here, to see why so many people have become so fond of Rochester and its clinic.

Mayo Clinic 2d Avenue and 2d Street SW 55901. (507) 284-2653. There is no precise date for the founding of the Mayo Clinic, because the physicians in the Mayo family practiced together for many years before they finally decided to call themselves a clinic. The patriarch of the group, Dr William Worrall Mayo, started his medical practice in Rochester in 1863, doing the sort of general practice that was typical for small-town physicians of his time. In 1883, his son "Dr Will" joined him, followed by a second son, "Dr Charlie," in 1886. For the next four years the family practiced alone, but from 1892 through 1901 four more physicians joined the group. By 1903 the group was widely recognized as an important phenomenon, in part because of their medical and surgical skill and in part because of their remarkable skill in working harmoniously together and teaching other health professionals.

In 1915 the Mayo Foundation was incorporated, and with it the Mayo Graduate School, designed to teach physicians specialized clinical skills. In the process the Mayos founded the first private group practice of medicine and helped pioneer the concept of postgraduate specialty training for physicians. Though others played important roles in those developments, the dominant personalities were clearly those of Dr Will and Dr Charlie. They were remarkable surgeons and thoroughly decent people who managed to find the best in coworkers, students, and patients. Their influence suffuses the clinic even today, despite the fact that they both died a half-century ago, in 1939.

Over the years Mayo has been the source of much medical progress. It was here (in 1905) that LB Wilson developed a technique for "frozen sections," allowing pathologists to return a diagnosis on biopsy material to the operating table in a matter of minutes. In 1921, Earl Osborne and Leonard Rowntree developed a new kind of contrast radiography in which sodium iodide is concentrated in the kidney, allowing visualization of the entire urinary tract. In 1933 Mayo established the first blood bank in the United States. In 1942, Mayo opened the first post-anesthesia care unit. In 1950, the Mayo scientists Edward Kendall and Philip Hench received the Nobel Prize for their discovery of cortisone.

In 1972 Mayo took the bold step of opening its own medical school, one distinguished by small class size (40 students per year) and extensive clinical exposure starting in the student's second year, instead of in the third as is the norm elsewhere. Though the medical school is small, the Mayo Graduate School claims to be the largest graduate medical training program in the world, with over 800 residents and fellows in training at any one time. In 1987 Mayo opened satellite operations in Scottsdale, AZ, and Jacksonville, FL.

Mayo's downtown Rochester campus is composed of some 20 buildings, plus another belonging to Rochester Methodist Hospital and a dozen belonging to St Mary's Hospital, which is about a mile away. Almost all of it is accessible by regularly scheduled tours, and much of it is open to visitors who are content to wander on their own. The huge, white, 20-story modern structure is the Mayo Building — devoted to outpatient care — which contains some 1600 examining rooms. The yellowish building with the carillon tower, across 2d Avenue SW, is the **Plummer Building** (1928), which is distinguished by ornate detailing throughout with lavish use of many kinds of marble. Be sure to see not only the gorgeous lobby but also the stunning library, which occupies both the 12th and 14th floors. On the third floor you will find the Mayo Historical Area (open to the public weekdays, 8 AM to 5 PM), which is filled with awards, plaques, photos, academic robes, and historic memorabilia related to the various Mayos.

Another building worth a peek is the **Mitchell Student Center,** which houses medical-school administrative offices and a study center. Built as the Rochester Public Library in 1940, this English Gothic building is probably the only medical-school admissions office whose portal is framed by poetry (to the left, Omar Khayyam: "A jug of wine, a loaf of bread, and thou beside me singing in the wilderness . . ." — to the right, Emily Dickinson: "There is no frigate like a book . . .").

Tours of the entire complex are given twice daily on weekdays, at 10 AM and 2 PM. The tours begin in Judd Hall, in the subway of the Mayo Building. No advance arrangements are necessary and there is no admission charge. Physicians can take advantage of a more clinically oriented tour each weekday at 2 PM. This one begins at the information desk on the 11th floor of the Mayo Building; advance reservations are preferred (284-4084).

St Mary's Hospital 1216 2d Street SW 55901. (507) 285-5123. St Mary's, with almost 1200 beds, is one of the largest private nonprofit hospitals in the world. The event that led to the founding of this hospital was a tornado that ripped through Rochester in August, 1883, killing 21 people and injuring hundreds. Medical care for this disaster was provided by Dr WW Mayo and his sons (Will finished medical school that very year; Charlie was only 18), but there were no trained nurses in the area. Instead, volunteers provided the nursing, most prominently the teaching Sisters of St Francis, who took victims into their small convent and looked after them in a local dance hall that had been turned into a temporary hospital. Afterward, the Franciscan Mother Superior suggested to Dr WW Mayo that Rochester desperately needed a hospital. Dr Mayo at first demurred, thinking the town much too small to support such an endeavor, but Mother Alfred persisted, and gradually the idea took hold. For six years the Sisters raised money for the proposed hospital, skimping on their own expenses, selling embroidery, giving music lessons, and doing whatever they could. The hospital opened in 1889: a three-story, 40- by 60-foot building. On the first day, Dr Charlie performed an operation on a man suffering from cancer, assisted by Dr Will, with the "Old Doctor" WW, giving anesthesia. Their assistants were two young Franciscan sisters, both trained as teachers, who had never before seen an operation.

For many years St Mary's was run as a traditional Catholic hospital. The administrators were nuns, and the hospital was run with the discipline, organization, and religiously inspired compassion the Sisters learned in the convent. The first administrator, Sister Joseph, led the hospital for 50 years. Other Sisters were at the helm for 10 or 20 years, or more. St Mary's is still a Catholic hospital, but the administration is secular now. Of the two most recent administrators, both were men — and as of this writing, neither had lasted more than a few years. Of the current staff of 3700, only two dozen or so are nuns.

The physician staff is drawn entirely from Mayo's, and it has a long record of accomplishment. Among other achievements, this is where the world's first intensive care unit was installed, in 1956. (Today St Mary's has seven adult ICUs and one pediatric ICU.)

This is a huge hospital, though its height is mostly six to eight stories and the apparent bulk is not overwhelming. Total space is now 1.8 million square feet, and the facility is expanding. The centralized hospital laundry processes 19,000 pounds of laundry daily, bringing it from various parts of the hospital in a vacuum tube system that transports the linens at 60 mph.

Tours are provided for visitors Tuesdays and Thursdays at 3:10 PM; they leave from the information desk in the Mary Brigh Building, which now houses the main entrance. Be sure to see the old main entrance in the Tower Building, on 2d Street. The lobby, with its four kinds of marble and the elaborate stained glass in and above the doors, is particularly impressive. There is a small historical exhibition room that can be entered from the lobby, and another off the corridor to the right. On display are such items as the common soup spoon that Dr Will used to scoop out gallstones during an operation, and a slotted operating table with a galvanized trough to collect blood. There is also a sumptuously beautiful chapel on the first floor of the Domatilla Building (services can be piped to all patient rooms via closed-circuit TV), and there are odds and ends of religious art in various places on campus.

Some of the courtyards (of which there are many) are particularly attractive. The Edith Graham Mayo courtyard memorializes Dr Charlie's wife, who was also St Mary's and Rochester's first trained nurse. In the early years of the clinic, she worked as anesthetist, office nurse, bookkeeper, and secretary for the Mayo practice. The bronze statue of her, in nursing uniform and cap, was sculpted by her granddaughter, Mayo Kooiman.

Rochester Methodist Hospital 401 West Center Street 55901. (507) 286-7890. This is Mayo's "downtown" hospital—as opposed to St Mary's, which (being 11 blocks away) is on the outskirts. (There is also another, much smaller—and non-Mayo—hospital in town, called Olmsted Community Hospital.) RMH originated in 1954, and its story illustrates a great deal about how times have changed. In 1943 the Kahler Corporation, which owned several small hospitals in town, decided to dispose of them because of "the feeling . . . that a corporation doing business for profit should not be operating hospitals." After considerable negotiation the Methodist Church agreed to purchase and sponsor the hospitals, with the Mayo Clinic providing clinical services. Since then, RMH's growth and expansion has been progressive and continual. The Colonial Hospital building (one of the original Kahler group) still stands, on 1st Avenue NW between Center Street and 1st Street NW, but the rest of the RMH buildings are post-1966. RMH is now an 800-bed hospital. Tours are operated for the public on Wednesday, at 1 PM and on Friday, at 10 AM. Reserve in advance by phone, or at the hospital information desk in the front lobby.

Mayo Medical Museum 1st Street and 3d Avenue SW 55905. (507) 284-2653. This museum was founded in the early 1930s as a concrete manifestation of the Mayo brothers' advocacy of public health education. The focus is on the human body in health and disease. Displays utilize custom-made plastic models, showing body parts in various stages of dissection, to illustrate anatomic function. For instance, there is an informative display on tonsils, how they become diseased, and how operations on them are typically accomplished. Another display focuses on orthopedic prostheses (femoral neck, elbow, shoulder, patella) and how they are inserted in operations. A number of other common health problems are likewise illustrated, including prostate and thyroid disease, backache, stroke, and lung cancer. Visitors can see and touch some classic medical machines here too, including an old Drinker-Collins Duplex Respirator (iron lung), a Mayo-Gibbon heart-lung machine, and a very early EMI head scanner. The museum also usually shows a dozen health-related films, on a staggered schedule, throughout the day. Museum hours are weekdays, 9 AM to 9 PM, Saturday, 9 to 5, and Sunday, 1 to 5 PM. There is no admission charge.

Mayowood PO Box 6411 55903. (507) 282-9447. This historic home, located on the outskirts of town, is reachable only via prior arrangement with the Olmsted County History Center, which now owns it. It was built by Dr Charles H ("Charlie") Mayo in 1911; the grounds once included 3000 acres of adjacent countryside. Now the estate is limited to 10 acres, but the 55-room house and its surroundings still impress all visitors. Three generations of Mayos lived here for varying lengths of time. Over the years the home has hosted Franklin Delano Roosevelt, Adlai Stevenson, and the King of Nepal. In 1965, Dr Charles W Mayo and his wife deeded the home, all its furnishings, and many personal belongings to the History Center. This gracious and enormous home, with furnishings from all over the world, gives dramatic evidence of how the clinic enterprise rewarded its founders. Tours are scheduled daily except Monday and Friday; a small admission fee is charged. Reservations generally need to be secured in advance. [The toll-free number outside of Minnesota is (800) 328-1461.]

Foundation House 701 4th Street SW 55901. Though not as grand as his brother's house, Mayowood, William J. Mayo's home is still worth seeing. Dr Will donated the building and its grounds to the Mayo Foundation in 1938, and now it is used primarily as a hospitality center for the Mayo Foundation — for meetings, receptions and the like. The 47-room house was completed in 1918 for a total cost of $500,000. The style is more or less English Tudor on the inside — far more formal than Mayowood — and is characterized by the lavish use of native woods, particularly mahogany, cherry, oak, and walnut. A ballroom on the third floor has been decorated with hand-carved emblems of various medical schools, but the *pièce de résistance* is a stained-glass window, installed in 1943, that depicts 2000 years of medical history. The exterior walls, including the five-story tower, have been built from Kasota stone quarried in Minnesota. Though the Foundation House is a private facility, for use by Mayo staff on Mayo business, visitors are welcome to look around the grounds. The staff, if they are not busy, may allow you to look around the entry way and adjacent areas.

Plummer House 1091 Plummer Lane 55901. (507) 281-6182. This is another of the spectacular medical mansions associated with the Mayo enterprise. It was built by, and is named for, Dr Henry Plummer. The 49-room edifice, completed in 1917, is built of native stone, with English Tudor design features. The furnishings capture the elegance so prized by the wealthy of the era. Plummer was an early associate of the Mayos and played a leading role in developing plans for an integrated group practice of medicine, which became the foundation for the modern Mayo Clinic. He was also an outstanding clinician who played an important part in clarifying the role of iodine in thyroid disease. (The Plummer Building, downtown, is named in his honor.)

The grounds of the Plummer House, including the magnificent rose gardens, are now parklands, open to the public from sunrise to sunset. Plummer House itself is owned by the city and is open for tours on Wednesdays only, from 1 to 7 PM. Call for reservations.

Mayo Brothers statue, Civic Center Plaza *(Photo used with permission of the Mayo Clinic)*

Mayo Civic Center 2d Avenue and 2d Street SE (located in a park tucked into the fork between the Zumbro River and Silver Creek). The attraction here is a splendid bronze statue of the Mayo brothers, William J ("Will") and Charles H ("Charlie"), each larger than life-size and clothed in full surgical garb. The statue, sculpted by James Earle Fraser in 1952, almost brings the brothers to life. A block away, near the corner of 1st Street and 2d Avenue SE, stands a solitary statue of their father, Dr WW Mayo, who seems lonely by comparison.

Washington, DC and Environs

Including Arlington and Alexandria, VA, and Bethesda, Glen Echo, and Rockville, MD

Map Key ————————————————————————————————

(**1**) George Washington University Medical Center
(**2**) Georgetown University Medical Center
(**3**) Howard University Medical Center
(**4**) Columbia Hospital for Women Medical Center
(**5**) National Museum of American History
(**6**) Former Veterans Administration Pension Building
(**7**) American National Red Cross Headquarters
(**8**) American Pharmaceutical Association Headquarters
(**9**) Samuel Hahnemann Memorial Statue
(**10**) Nuns of the Battlefield Monument
(**11**) National Medical Association
(**12**) United States Capitol
(**13**) Washington Monument
(**14**) National Cathedral

These key numbers will be found at appropriate points in the text.

WASHINGTON IS A BEAUTIFUL city, unmatched in the country for sculpture, monuments, museums, remarkable buildings, and important institutions entirely accessible to the public. It is also a place where health-care history blends with the history of our country so that the linkage between medicine and national events becomes apparent. Symbolically, Washington's centerpiece — the Capitol building — was designed by a physician (see "United States Capitol Building," below).

Until the Civil War, Washington was essentially a small town. Its transformation into a dynamic metropolis was a product of the political turmoil of the Civil War era, but most of its population growth was of medically-related origin. During the war Washington became a hospital center, as sick and injured troops poured into the city, along with malnourished, ill, and suddenly-freed former slaves. At times the city housed as many as 50,000 patients — this in a city whose population had been only 60,000 just before the war. Scores of buildings were appropriated for hospital use. Capitol Hill itself was called "Bloody Hill," since for two years it was covered with hundreds of tents filled with the wounded and dying. At its peak, the nation's capital housed some 85 hospitals.

Today Washington remains a major medical center, not only because of its medical schools (it has four), but because of the presence of the mammoth National Institutes of Health, the various Public Health Service institutions, major Army and Navy hospitals, and the profusion of various medical professional associations.

The health-care–oriented visitor here has many choices, some of which are easily incorporated into the usual tourist circuit. A good place to start is the Mall, with the Capitol building (and its interesting medical statuary) at one end and the Lincoln Memorial at the other (and with the beautiful American Pharmaceutical Association building just opposite). Between the two are the Smithsonian's National Museum of American History (with the largest and finest combined medical, dental, and pharmaceutical museum in the country), the Washington Monument (with its American Medical Association plaque), and — just a couple of blocks off the Mall — the headquarters of the American National Red Cross. Visitors to Arlington National Cemetery will also want to see the Nurses Memorial. A bit farther afield (but easily accessible by public transportation, and definitely worth the trip) is Bethesda, where you'll find the National Institutes of Health, the National Library of Medicine, the adjacent Bethesda Naval Hospital, and the School of Medicine of the Uniformed Services University. Museum buffs will certainly want to see the National Museum of Health and Medicine, located on the grounds of Walter Reed Army Hospital in Washington.

① *George Washington University Medical Center* 901 23d Street NW 10037. (202) 994-1000. George Washington University School of Medicine began life as the Medical Department of Columbian College in 1822. The first class, of six, graduated in 1826. Columbian College was sponsored by the Baptist Convention, but the Medical Department functioned as an independent, proprietary entity of the medical faculty. The first years of both institutions were shaky financially, and Medical Department operation was suspended for five years in the 1830s. By 1847 the Medical Department was calling itself the National Medical College, though medical degrees continued to be conferred by Columbian College.

In 1844, by Congressional action, the medical faculty (*not* the college) was given use of the Washington Infirmary, formerly both a jail and an insane asylum, "for the purposes of an infirmary, for medical instruction, and scientific purposes." During most of the decades that followed, nursing care at the infirmary was provided by the Daughters of Charity. In 1861 the Infirmary was requisitioned as a military hospital; barely six months later, it was completely destroyed by fire. Once again the Medical College was forced to suspend instruction, this time for two years. Most of the remainder of the nineteenth century was occupied by a continuing struggle to determine who would control the medical program — the medical faculty or Columbian College. Ultimately, the college — which by 1873, called itself a university — won the struggle.

For several decades after the Civil War, the Medical College was run as a night school. As Elmer Kayser put it, "Because of the tremendous increase in the size of the Civil Service, thousands of people were brought to Washington who not only filled jobs, but whose appetite for personal enrichment, further education, and professional training was whetted by the relative security of government employment, the comparative adequacy of government pay in hard cash, the brevity of the working day, the absence of entertainment in the city, and, as the University saw its opportunity, the availablility of academic and professional courses."

In 1904 Columbian University became George Washington University, and a vigorous and academically ambitious new administration phased out the night school. By the time the Flexner Report pounded the Medical School, in 1910, constructive change was already well underway. To consolidate its finances and efforts, the university, over a period of years, jettisoned its schools of pharmacy, dentistry, and nursing, and concentrated on the medical school.

The present University Hospital location, at Washington Circle, dates from 1947. The modern 501-bed institution, within walking distance of the White House and many other government offices, has a reputation for treating high government officials. In 1981 President Ronald Reagan was taken here when he was wounded in an assassination attempt. There are currently no tours available.

② *Georgetown University Medical Center* 3800 Reservoir Road NW 20007. (202) 687-5100. The School of Medicine here opened in 1851, under the Jesuit leadership of the nation's first Catholic college. The precipitating event was Congress's decision that all physicians who attended patients at the Washington Infirmary, the city's only hospital, must thenceforth be faculty members of the

Columbian Medical College. Four men who had been excluded from the Columbian College decided that the city needed a second medical school, and prevailed upon Georgetown for sponsorship. Georgetown happily complied — though, of the four, only one was a Catholic. (The others were an Episcopalian, a Methodist, and a Jew.)

Until 1895 all of Georgetown's classes were held at night. The University Hospital opened in 1893, in a 33-bed facility staffed by the Sisters of St Francis; but it proved so popular with District of Columbia patients that within 15 years 4 wings had been added, bringing the bed capacity to 266. Hospital and medical school moved to their present location in 1930. The School of Dentistry was added in 1901, and the School of Nursing in 1903.

Important developments here have included the first implantation of an artificial heart valve (1952, Charles Hufnagel); the first use of hemodialysis to treat poisoning due to salicylates, methanol, and phenytoin (1955, George Schreiner); and the first implantation of a prosthetic artery, an Orlon tube used to replace the common iliac artery (1962, Charles Hufnagel).

Today the medical center occupies over a dozen buildings clustered around the modern 535-bed Georgetown Hospital. Tours of the hospital can be arranged via the Volunteers Office.

(3) *Howard University Medical Center* 520 W Street NW 20059. (202) 636-5015. The earliest component of this medical center was born in 1862, as a hospital for blacks suddenly freed from slavery. The District of Columbia was a magnet for such people, for whom the names "Washington, DC," and "Abraham Lincoln" held an almost mystical attraction. Many were settled in a group of army barracks, at 13th and R streets, called Camp Barker. The camp was dreadfully overcrowded, some of the surrounding area was swampland, and in 1863 smallpox was epidemic. The ill-equipped hospital on the site provided little comfort. As the Civil War drew to a close, responsibility for dealing with the millions of freed and now displaced ex-slaves was lodged with the Bureau of Freedmen, Refugees and Abandoned Land. The Camp Barker hospital, now called the Freedmen's Hospital and Asylum, moved several times, ultimately lodging on the grounds of the newly established Howard University to be used as a teaching facility for Howard's medical school. It was this event that ensured that Freedmen's Hospital — alone among the more than 100 hospitals and dispensaries that would be founded for ex-slaves — would survive.

Howard University was begun by a group of white men, associated with the missionary wing of the Congregationalist Church.

The key figure in all this was the university's namesake, General OO Howard, director of the Freedmen's Bureau. The medical school opened in 1868; the first class included seven black students and one white. The early faculty was largely white, and the student body in most of the early classes, which included children of faculty, tended to be more white than black for several years.

With the demise of the Freedmen's Bureau in 1872, both Freedmen's Hospital and Howard University — separate, but related, institutions — underwent severe and continued financial hardship and uncertainty. Well into the 1880s, Freedmen's remained more asylum than hospital, providing permanent residence for dozens of elderly ex-slaves who were too infirm to send elsewhere. By the 1890s, the state of the hospital's facilities and supplies was bleak indeed. After an official investigation produced a devastating report, Congress authorized construction of a new hospital, which was finally completed in 1908. Freedmen's financial and administrative problems were by no means over, however. The hospital remained a political football. During its lengthy history, Freedmen's has been responsible to the War Department (1863–1865), the Freedmen's Bureau (1865–1872), the Department of the Interior (1872–1939), the Federal Security Agency (1939–1953), the Department of Health, Education, and Welfare (1953–1967), and more recently Howard University (from 1967 on).

When Flexner visited the District of Columbia in 1909, he found that only Howard's medical school, with its distinct mission of training the Negro physician, had an assured future. He was particularly pleased with the "new, thoroughly modern" 278-bed Freedmen's Hospital "closely identified with the medical school." In contrast, he found the medical schools at both George Washington and Georgetown to "lack adequate resources," and concluded, "Neither school is now equal to the task of training physicians of the modern type."

Both Freedmen's and the Howard University Medical School have become survivors against the odds. Of the 200 hospitals that were staffed by, and served, blacks in this country in the 1920s, only 9 remain today. Of the 8 predominately black medical schools that were operating at the turn of the century, only Howard and Meharry survive.

It's easy to forget how recently discrimination was the norm. In the late 1920s, the only large non-black hopitals in the country that accepted black physicians for house staff were Cook County, in Chicago, and Bellevue and Harlem, in New York. In 1947, 85 percent of all black physicians in the country had graduated from the only places where they could be accepted: Howard and Meharry.

As late as 1961, fewer than 7 percent of black physicians were able to get staff privileges at any Washington hospital other than Freedmen's.

In 1967, pursuant to legislation signed six years earlier by President John F Kennedy, Freedmen's Hospital was transferred to Howard University, becoming Howard University Hospital. The new 500-bed hospital building dates from 1972 and is home to some 300 residents and interns. Eighty percent of the student body here is black. Tours are available, on request, through the Public Information Department.

F Edward Hebert School of Medicine of the Uniformed Services University of the Health Sciences 4301 Jones Bridge Road, Bethesda, MD 20014. (202) 295-3049. This unique school of medicine accepted its first class in 1976 and graduated its first physicians in 1980. The university is located in four buildings on the grounds of the Bethesda Naval Hospital, but students receive their clinical and field experiences in various facilities around the nation's capital and around the world. What makes this school unique is that all the students have committed themselves to careers in the uniformed services; their education, therefore, prepares them to provide preventive and curative health care while working in "adverse physiological and psychological environments." Course work includes military studies, military preventive medicine, and combat casualties; field experiences include medical helicopter units, night operations, training with combat battalions, and airborne service. Another unique feature of the school is that all students are accepted on a tuition-free basis (in fact, all are on salary); all receive books and equipment free of charge.

Tours of these attractive modern buildings, set on the rolling landscaped hills of the Bethesda Naval Medical Center, are available every Friday at 1 PM, starting from room 1045 of Building A.

Bethesda Naval Hospital 8901 Wisconsin Avenue, Bethesda, MD 20014. (202) 295-0567. The first naval medical facility in the national capital area was established in 1802 in a building near the Washington Navy Yard. A variety of interim facilities were pressed into service over the years, until Congress appropriated funds in 1906 for the National Naval Center, at 23d and E streets. The present suburban location dates from 1942 and was selected personally by President Franklin D Roosevelt, who was particularly attracted by the small pond on the property; it inspired him to think of the biblical Pool of Bethesda, a legendary place of healing. This pond still exists and is now named Lake Eleanor, in honor of the President's wife.

The 1942 building, a high narrow tower surrounded by a low but rambling base, is modeled on a sketch by FDR, who tried to capture elements of the Nebraska State Capitol Building, in Lincoln, with which he had been much impressed. The very modern 500-bed main hospital building (and the adjacent 3-story outpatient structure) date from 1980.

The formal name of this facility is The Naval Medical Command National Capital Region. The Bethesda facility includes the hospital and outpatient clinics, an education and training branch (responsible for training all navy hospital corpsmen and dental technicians), and various research, training, and service components. The facility primarily cares for active-duty military personnel, but it also cares for dependents and retirees on a space-available basis, and — as a courtesy — for United States government officials and foreign military and embassy personnel. It is also a major training center for navy physicians.

No tours are available for the general public.

District of Columbia General Hospital 19th Street and Massachusetts Avenue SE 20003. (202) 675-5000. When this hospital was established by Congress, in 1806, its official name was the Washington Infirmary. Most people called it the Poor House, and indeed its initial role was to act as a warehouse for the poor, infirm, and disabled. In 1832 the infirmary got a new building, and its operation was turned over to the Medical Faculty of Columbian College.

By 1846 the infirmary had become known as the Washington Asylum Hospital, but it remained primarily an almshouse and workhouse. Hospital functions were added gradually. In 1922 the hospital was renamed, by act of Congress, to honor Jacob Gallinger, a senator who had sponsored legislation to improve the hospital. The new name was meant to improve the hospital's image; until then it had been seen as a dumping ground for "alcoholics, incurables and patients with obnoxious diseases." But the new Gallinger Municipal Hospital became the target of numerous charges of neglect and mismanagement, followed by numerous investigations, and the name was changed again, in 1953, to District of Columbia General Hospital. Repeated administrative reshuffling over the years, transferring organizational authority for the hospital from a board to a department to another department, only succeeded in making matters worse, and the hospital finally lost its accreditation in 1975. The result has been the establishment of an independent governing commission; and the hospital, now protected from blatant political machinations, has emerged as an attractive and modern 404-bed facility, the only public general hospital in the District.

The old Gallinger Hospital building, erected in 1922, still stands on the DCGH campus, but its future remains in doubt. The District government has proposed tearing down the older buildings and replacing them with an 800-bed prison. Meanwhile, both the old and new buildings occupy a large campus next door to Robert F Kennedy Stadium. The most modern of the two dozen or so buildings here belongs to the city jail, but the hospital itself gives a good feeling for turn-of-the-century pavilion facilities: the old single-story obstetric pavilions are along the East Service Road, the old psychiatry buildings are adjacent to the jail, and separate buildings still exist for laboratory, medical examiner, maintenance, etc. There are no tours.

St Elizabeths Hospital   2700 Martin Luther King, Jr, Avenue 20032. (202) 562-4000. Established in 1855 through the efforts of the famed mental health crusader Dorothea Dix, this hospital was first known as the Government Hospital for the Insane. During the Civil War, however, wounded soldiers sent here to recover refused to say they were in an insane asylum, instead saying they were at St Elizabeth's — the name of the tract of land upon which the hospital was located. The usage stuck, and soon everyone referred to the asylum as St Elizabeths. (The apostrophe was lost somewhere along the line.) The hospital grew dramatically over the years, by the 1930s encompassing 168 buildings spread out over an 800-acre tract. By the 1950s, it housed over 8000 patients. From its inception SEH was a prestigious institution, often an innovator in psychiatric care. The first five superintendents here served as presidents of the American Psychiatric Association. SEH was the first hospital in the country to introduce hydrotherapy, psychodrama, and poetry therapy in the treatment of the mentally ill, and the first (1963) to introduce mental-health programs for the deaf. In 1922 the hospital gained distinction by being the first in the Western Hemisphere to use the malaria treatment for syphilitic paresis. (At the time, it was the only treatment. The method involved infecting the syphilitic patient with malaria, in the hope that the resulting high fever would kill the fragile treponema.) SEH has long been a center for forensic psychiatry, providing treatment for patients in a number of highly publicized cases. The fifth patient here was a would-be assassin of President Andrew Jackson; a more recent patient in the same category was John Hinckley, Jr, who attempted to kill President Ronald Reagan in 1981. The poet Ezra Pound lived here as a patient for many years as well.

In 1987, the federal government turned SEH over to the District of Columbia. Since then the patient population has steadily declined, as has federal support. The hospital is expected to house a maximum of 1000 patients in 1991, mostly on the more modern eastern half of the campus. A Land Use Task Force has been convened to recommend uses for the older, more historic western half, where the original buildings still stand. The principal building is a typical Kirkbride structure with a central administration area and swept wings, though the construction is unusual in that the exterior is entirely of brick and features castle towers, complete with battlements and buttresses. The grounds here are quite beautiful, overlooking the Potomac and Anacostia rivers and filled with mature trees of 140 species. On the third floor of the center building you'll find the **Museum of St Elizabeths Hospital,** in the old superintendent's quarters. Appearing much as it did 125 years ago, the apartment gives a good feel for the authority and prestige accorded the superintendent. The sitting rooms contain furniture dating from the latter half of the nineteenth century, all part of the history of SEH. The guest bedroom here was for a while home to Dorothea Dix; Abraham Lincoln slept here too, when he rode up from the White House to inspect the facilities. The museum also houses a modest collection of SEH memorabilia, including Dorothea Dix's old rolltop desk. The museum is open to the public by advance arrangement (373-7719). Tours are available from the Municipal Affairs Office.

Providence Hospital 1150 Varnum Street NE 20017. (202) 269-7000. Not many hospitals can boast a charter signed by the President of the United States; Providence has one signed by Abraham Lincoln. The hospital was founded in 1861, one of 85 hospitals opened in the nation's capital during the Civil War to deal with the war's wounded. Actually, Providence was founded to serve civilians, and soon became a favorite of some members of Congress. Thaddeus Stevens, Chairman of the House Appropriations Committee, watched over the infant hospital, appropriated money for it, and kept it the only hospital in the District of Columbia to avoid being taken over by the military during the Civil War. (Providence continued to get Congressional appropriations until 1931.) The Daughters of Charity staffed the facility from opening day. Six weeks after its opening, the hospital was caring for casualties from the Battle of Bull Run.

In 1894 Providence opened the nation's first three-year nursing program, taking as its first class five girls from a nearby orphanage. A high school education wasn't a requirement for admission until 1931, and a high school diploma wasn't required until 1938. In 1943, the nursing school became the first to participate in the army's Cadet Nurse Program.

In 1896, one year after Roentgen published his initial observations on x-ray use, Providence became the first hospital to use x-rays to locate a bullet (in a patient's thigh) before removing it. Providence has moved several times during its history and has been in its present location since 1904. It's now a modern 364-bed hospital. There's a fine statue of St Vincent de Paul, founder of the Daughters of Charity and thus namesake of numerous Catholic hospitals, near the Twelfth and Varnum entrance. Tours are available via the Volunteers Office.

(4) *Columbia Hospital for Women Medical Center* 2425 L Street NW 20037. (202) 293-6500. Beginning in 1861, Washington's population exploded with people seeking refuge from the adjacent war-torn states. Thousands of women came here seeking their wounded and missing men; a significant percentage of these women were exhausted and ill from their travels and exertions, and many lacked the means to care for themselves. Women delivered babies in parks and police stations and on the steps of public buildings.

In 1866 the Secretary of War authorized funds to establish a 50-bed hospital, stipulating that 20 beds should be exclusively for the wives and widows of US soldiers. The Columbia Hospital for Women and Lying-In Asylum was established soon thereafter in a mansion at Thomas Circle. The hospital moved to its present site in 1870. As one of the earliest women's hospitals in the country, Columbia has consistently been at the forefront of medical progress in obstetrics and gynecology:

1902	First use of radium therapy in the US for gynecologic cancers
1925	First use of system of infant footprint identification
1971	Introduction of the colposcope, a device for use in the early detection of cervical cancer
1986	Establishment of REPROTOX, an on-line consultation system concerning reproductive toxicology

For its first 87 years Columbia was owned and supported by the federal government as a charitable institution. In 1953, President Eisenhower signed legislation transferring Columbia to its board of directors. Since then it has been a private, not-for-profit teaching institution. Though much modernized, and enlarged with contemporary additions, the original hospital building is well worth a look. Built of yellow brick, topped by red Spanish tile and decorated with a tall tower and sunporches jutting out at angles from the main structure, this is a fine example of turn-of-the-century hospital architecture, the sort that has been leveled by wrecking balls all over the country. In the 1960s the hospital dropped "Lying-In Asylum" from its name. Tours of the present modern 154-bed hospital are available through the Nursing Department.

Children's Hospital National Medical Center 111 Michigan Avenue NW 20010. (202) 745-5000. Founded in 1870, this is the third oldest children's hospital in the country. Children's was first established in a twelve-bed rented facility at 13th and F streets. It soon outgrew these limited quarters and moved into a new 67-bed hospital in 1879. In 1910 the hospital became the first in the nation to allow "rooming in," even taking the revolutionary step of providing space for parents to stay with their hospitalized children. The current facility, an angular mass of shimmering glass, dates from 1977; the interior is remarkable for its spacious and colorful child-oriented atrium lobby. Tours are available via the Public Affairs Office.

Walter Reed Army Medical Center 6825 16th Street NW 20307. (202) 545-6700. Walter Reed received his first MD from the University of Virginia at the age of 17, and his second from Bellevue Hospital Medical College the following year. He joined the Army Medical Corps in 1875, beginning a career that included 18 years of garrison duty. In 1893 he was promoted to major and became professor of bacteriology at the Army Medical School (now Walter Reed Army Institute of Research). In 1900, Reed was assigned the task of directing research into infectious diseases in Cuba. While there, he demonstrated conclusively that yellow fever was transmitted by the *Aedes aegypti* mosquito, thus laying the groundwork for mosquito abatement programs and the removal of yellow fever as a public health hazard in much of the world. After his death, in 1902, Congress authorized the construction of the Walter Reed General Hospital, most of which still stands on this site.

This is the largest military medical facility operated by the Department of Defense. Started in 1909 as an 80-bed hospital, it has grown to its present 1280 beds (though during World War I, over 2500 patients were housed here). Most of the early buildings, including the original hospital building, are brick Georgian structures surrounded by lawns and flower beds. The current main hospital dates from 1977; though it is huge, the strong horizontal lines of the upper building, set upon a much smaller base, make the hospital appear to float over the older structures and surrounding gardens. Patients here include Army personnel, and their dependents, heads of government, and high government officials of the United States and, as a courtesy, of many foreign nations as well.

The 133-acre grounds include, in addition to the hospital, a number of tenant activities, such as the Walter Reed Army Institute of Research, the Armed Forces Institute of Pathology, the US Army Institute of Dental Research, and the National Museum of Health and Medicine. The grounds are open to the public, but no tours are presently available.

Chestnut Lodge Hospital   500 West Montgomery Avenue, Rockville, MD 20850. (301) 424-8300. Chestnut Lodge is a small, private psychiatric hospital, founded in 1910, that specializes in the treatment of serious psychiatric disorders. The main building was once a country resort hotel for wealthy Washingtonians, and the 80 acres of grounds and the woodsy buildings still have a bucolic feel to them. The most famous person associated with Chestnut Lodge was Frieda Fromm-Reichmann, a psychiatrist renowned for her skill in working with schizophrenics. (She was immortalized as the inspiring psychiatrist in the book *I Never Promised You A Rose Garden,* written by Hannah Green, a patient of Fromm-Reichmann's.) The cottage where Fromm-Reichmann lived and worked still stands. Call for tours.

National Museum of Health and Medicine   Dahlia and 14th Streets NW, (Walter Reed Army Medical Center) 20306. (202) 576-2348. This is the granddaddy of all medical museums in this country, with the distinction of being both the oldest and the largest collection of its kind in the United States. For many years it was known as the Armed Forces Medical Museum. Begun in 1862, the museum's first function was the study of the various diseases that were bigger killers of soldiers during the Civil War than all combat-related sources combined. Walter Reed was the museum's curator for a while, and it was under the museum's auspices that he did his landmark research into yellow fever. Museum pathologists were given the solemn tasks of performing autopsies on presidents Abraham Lincoln and James Garfield after their assassinations. The museum was also responsible for the development and initial testing of early typhoid vaccines; and during World War II, it produced educational films on venereal disease that enlightened and entertained millions of soldiers. The Photographic and Medical Arts Service section was headed by Captain Frank Netter, MD, later to become America's best-known medical illustrator.

By the mid-twentieth century, the museum's functions were gradually being transformed. Collecting and displaying pathology specimens (i.e., being a repository and gallery for medical curiosities) became less important than a growing spectrum of scientific support activities. In 1944 the museum created an administrative subdivision, the Army Institute of Pathology, to be responsible for all diagnostic and investigative work. By 1946 the power had shifted, and the museum became a division of the institute. In 1950 the institute became the Armed Forces Institue of Pathology, of which the museum is still a subdivision.

The museum is currently undergoing an identity crisis. After serving the armed forces for 125 years, it is now attempting to transform itself to fit its new name. Having long served as a teaching and research center for the medical profession, the museum now wants to serve the public for health education and health promotion. Specifically, it would like to shed its "freak show" image, in which its primary attraction to the public was the opportunity to see medical curiosities. Whether it can manage the transition and still maintain its uniqueness remains to be seen. What traditionally has made this museum special has been its anatomic

Seventeenth-century monocular microscope, leather-covered and ornamented with gold stampings, National Museum of Health and Medicine *(By permission of Otis Historical Archives, National Museum of Health and Medicine, AFIP)*

collection — row upon row of cases filled with anatomic and pathologic specimens. There are over 13000 specimens here, including examples of all organs, an enormous spectrum of diseases and anatomic conditions, and over 3000 examples of dry bone pathology (including musket- and cannon-related fractures). The Billings microscope collection alone includes 2000 items, extending from the seventeenth century to the present — making it the largest of its kind in the United States, and the most comprehensive in the world.

The vast majority of this treasure trove is now in storage, as the museum revamps its image, reformulates its mission, and searches for a new home. Currently it occupies a huge barn of a room. There is still plently of hard-core pathology, not for the weak of stomach. Here you will find bone fragments from Abraham Lincoln's skull, as well as the derringer slug that killed him. A section of James Garfield's vertebral column is on display, together with a marker depicting the path of the bullet that killed him. There is a leg disarticulated at the hip, demonstrating elephantiasis, and a variety of skeletons and tissue specimens depicting various deformities and infirmities — including fetuses of every description. There are wonderful exhibits on Civil War medicine as well, including facial reconstruction à la 1861–1865, survival and recovery from traumatic wounds, and transport of the sick and wounded. During my visit there was an exhibit on AIDS, which was made unique by the museum's use of its unmatched collection to show how the armed forces (and the nation) have dealt with sexually transmitted diseases in the past.

The museum is open to the public on weekdays, 9:30 to 4:30, and weekends 11:30 to 4:30. It is open on some holidays. Special "behind-the-scenes" tours are also available, by special arrangement.

United States Public Health Service 5600 Fishers Lane, Rockville, MD 20857. (301) 443-1090. The official headquarters of the Public Health Service is downtown, but this massive collection of USPHS employees in Rockville is as good a focus as any for telling the service's story.

The PHS began as the Marine Hospital Service in 1798, when President John Adams signed a law providing for "the care and relief of sick and disabled seamen." The law required US Customs officials to assess every arriving seaman 20 cents a month to support the care of sick seamen and the building of hospitals, perhaps the first example of a prepaid health care program in this country. Since the Customs Service was an administrative arm of the Department of the Treasury, the Marine Hospital Service was likewise placed under Treasury jurisdiction. By 1807 the Secretary of the Treasury was operating hospitals in Boston, Newport, Norfolk, and Charleston, and contracting for medical services in 10 other cities. All of these enterprises operated independently, with their finances coordinated by a "Marine Hospital Clerk." By the start of the Civil War the MHS included 27 hospitals, including a facility in the Hawaiian Islands and a huge 700-bed Marine Hospital in San Francisco. In 1870 the MHS was elevated to Bureau level, for the first time with a supervising surgeon. In 1887 the service established its first research lab, at the Marine Hospital on Staten Island. The following year, a commissioned corps of physicians was established to work as a mobile force to fight disease and protect health. In 1902 the Marine Hospital Service's name was changed to Marine Hospital and Public Health Service, in recognition of its expanding functions.

The present name was adopted in 1912. From the close of World War I until the establishment of the Veterans' Bureau, in 1924, the PHS was responsible for an expanding system (ultimately 81 hospitals) for the care of sick and injured veterans. By 1930 the Commissioned Corps began to accept sanitary engineers, dentists, and pharmacists; and in 1944, enrollment expanded to include registered nurses, research scientists, and other health care specialists. In 1941, after 141 years in the Department of the Treasury, the PHS found a new home in the Federal Security Agency, the forerunner of the Department of Health, Education and Welfare. Gradually, the service's functions have expanded to include disease control, national vital statistics, hospital and health systems planning, research coordinating and funding, occupational health and safety, health promotion, and a variety of other sundry services too numerous to list. Altogether, the PHS operates the largest public health program in the world.

During this period of expansion, the PHS was losing its historical base. The American Merchant Marine was dwindling in size; the sailors who traditionally occupied most of the beds in PHS hospitals increasingly had other options for health care. In 1981 eight of the nine PHS hospitals were closed by Congress, the only one remaining being the Hansen's Disease (leprosy) Center in Carville, Louisiana. However, the PHS still funds more than 500 community and migrant health centers around the country, as well as providing care at Indian Health Service facilities.

The PHS facility here has some attractive exhibits that tell the organization's story. There is a series of 160 photos and other graphic material on the third floor, B Wing, of the Parklawn Building, lining a corridor with a string of conference rooms. The exhibit is called "Images from the History of the Public Health Service" and covers events ranging from malaria control in the Philippines to serving aboard the US Coast Guard Cutter *Bear* in 1915. There are no formal tours.

National Institutes of Health 9000 Rockville Pike, Bethesda, MD 20892. (202) 496-4000. This, the largest medical research center in the world, began as the one-room Laboratory of Hygiene in New York City in 1887. In 1891 the laboratory was moved to Washington; in 1930 it was renamed the National Institute of Health; and in 1948 the plural was added, and the NIH became the National Institutes of Health.

Currently the NIH consists of 12 research institutes and 4 divisions, the latter being composed of the 540-bed Clinical Center, the National Center for Nursing Research, the Fogarty International Center, and the National Library of Medicine. The institutes include: the National Cancer Institute (founded 1937); the National Dental Institute (founded 1948); the National Heart, Lung and Blood Institute (founded 1948 as the National Heart Institute, renamed the National Heart and Lung Institute in 1969, and given its present title in 1976); the National Institute of Diabetes and Digestive and Kidney Diseases (founded 1950 as the National Institute of Arthritis and Metabolic Diseases, in 1972 renamed the National Institute of Arthritis, Metabolism and Digestive Diseases; and given its present name in 1981); the National Institute of Neurological and Communicative Disorders and Stroke (founded 1950, established as the National Institute of Neurological Diseases and Blindness, and renamed in 1968 when the National Eye Institute was formed); the National Institute of Allergy and Infectious Diseases (founded 1948 as the National Microbiological Institute, given its present name in 1955); the National Institute of Child Health and Human Development (founded 1963); the National Institute of General Medical Sciences (founded 1963); the National Eye Institute (founded 1968); the National Institute of Environmental Health Sciences (founded 1969 and not located on the Bethesda campus, but rather on a 500-acre campus at Research Triangle Park, NC); the National Institute on Aging (founded 1974); and the National Institute of Arthritis and Musculoskeletal and Skin Diseases (founded 1985).

The NIH has been located in Bethesda since 1938; it now occupies 300 acres and over 50 buildings, employing a total of over 14,000 people. The history of the NIH, for anyone not directly involved, is a blur of legislative and administrative acts involving bureaucratic reshuffling, renaming, and reallocation of funds and priorities. The amazing thing about the NIH is that it works and works very well, though by no means perfectly. It is the center of a vast biomedical research enterprise that stretches around the globe. It funds 40 percent of all biomedical research and development in the United States. Some 80 percent of the NIH budget goes to support extramural research and training, through a competitive grant-and-contract system. Four of its intramural scientists have been recognized with Nobel Prizes, and almost 100 extramural scientists supported by NIH funds have likewise received the prize. Almost all major advances in the prevention and treatment of heart disease, cancer, dental disease, problems of premature infants, and a host of other conditions have been financed in substantial part by the NIH.

A visit to this mammoth complex would be impossibly confusing were it not for the **Visitors' Center** in Building 10C, a smoothly run operation that plays host every year to some 40,000 guests, and more — people whose interests range from the highly technical to rather basic concerns about their own health and illnesses. The displays and exhibits here outline past and present NIH discoveries and achievements as well as their implications for public health. Interested individuals should be sure to see the **DeWitt Stetten, Jr, Museum of Medical Research,** located in Building 10, arranged along the wheelchair ramp bordering the Visitor Information Center. Continuing exhibits here highlight specific research efforts at five of the oldest institutes, including sections titled *The Fluoride Story, Rocky Mountain Spotted Fever, Cell Culture, The Heart-Lung Machine,* and *Windows into the Brain.* Tours are available for individuals and groups with special interests, by advance arrangement (496-1776).

Food and Drug Administration 5600 Fishers Lane, Rockville, MD 20857. (202) 443-1544. The FDA, as a distinct organization, dates from 1931, but its history goes back much further. The United States had laws concerning the purity of food and drink mostly on a state level, as early as 1785, when Massachusetts enacted the country's first general food law. However, up until the beginning of the twentieth century, there were widespread problems with misbranded, adulterated, and spurious drugs. Physicians confronted with drugs of unknown, highly variable, or absent potency could not prescribe with any confidence.

The first national Food and Drug Act — prohibiting the misbranding and adulteration of food, drink, and drugs — was passed in 1906, and enforcement responsibilities (such as they were) were lodged with the Bureau of Chemistry, in the Department of Agriculture. In 1927 a special enforcement agency was established, first named the Food, Drug and Insecticide Administration, and then, in 1931, renamed the Food and Drug Administration. Still, the various regulations were filled with loopholes and routinely suffered judicial setbacks when challenged in court.

The act's limitations were vividly demonstrated in 1937, when one drug manufacturer decided to market an elixir of sulfanilamide. In the pre-penicillin era, sulfa was the preferred medication for the treatment of strep infections and was widely used in tablets and as a powder. When the company decided to market a liquid preparation of sulfanilamide, it tested the concoction for taste, appearance, and fragrance so that the medication would be appealing to consumers; but since it was not required to test for safety, the company chose not to do so. They were using a solvent, diethylene glycol — commonly used in automobile antifreeze — that can be lethal in small doses. Over 100 people died, giving dramatic impetus to the Food, Drug and Cosmetic Act of 1938, which, among other clauses, required predistribution clearance for safety of new drugs. The most sensational evidence of the utility of this law occurred in 1962, when Dr Frances Kelsey kept the tranquilizer thalidomide off the US market because its safety had not been demonstrated. Thalidomide was later found to be associated with the births of thousands of malformed babies in western Europe.

In 1945 the FDA urged legislation to prohibit the sale of potent drugs for self-medication. The result was a distinction between over-the-counter medications and those available only by prescription.

The FDA is now under the Department of Health and Human Services; its immediate umbrella organization is the Public Health Service. The organization's current mandate is "to protect the public from hazards to health and well-being which may be presented by any of the products it regulates," including drugs, biologics, medical devices, and radiological products. To exercise its mandate, the FDA's activities now range from tea tasting, to monitoring pollution in shellfish beds, to granting premarket approval of all new drugs. For these purposes the FDA has some 7000 employees, the largest number of whom work in the mammoth Parklawn Building at this address, as well as smaller numbers at various laboratories and offices throughout the nation. About one-third of the FDA budget is for medically-related programs, the remainder being allotted to its other responsibilities. There are no provisions for visitors here, and no displays or exhibits accessible to the public.

National Library of Medicine 8600 Rockville Pike, Building 38, National Institutes of Health Campus, Bethesda, MD 20209. (301)

496-6308. If you had to pick one place or institution most responsible for the dominance of the United States in modern medicine, this would be the most logical choice. Without the National Library of Medicine medical education, research, and patient care would be incalculably poorer, not only in the United States but throughout the world.

The collection began in 1836, when the Surgeon General of the US Army died and left a modest shelf of books and journals to his successor. Gradually other volumes accumulated, and by 1864 the collection numbered some 2100 volumes. Later in that year John Shaw Billings was placed in charge of the library, and the collection's march to greatness began. By 1868 it had tripled in size, and by 1875 it was easily the largest medical library in the country. Billings understood that the library's size was only a starting point, that knowledge within the library needed to be made accessible in order for it to be useful. In the late 1870s he began developing a complete catalog of the collection, including all journal articles listed by subject — an undertaking the likes of which had never been attempted before. In lobbying for $25,000 to support the project, Billings wrote, "The question for Congress to decide is as to whether the result would be worth the expenditure. . . . What is the value of such an index to the people of the United States as compared to an expedition to the North Pole, five miles of subsidized railroad, one company of cavalry, or a small post office building?" The first volume of the *Index-Catalogue of the Library of the Surgeon General's Office, United States Army* was published in 1880. The extraordinary value of the compilation was immediately appreciated all over the world. At about the same time Billings instituted the *Index Medicus*, a monthly supplement to the *Catalogue* that classified books and journal articles by subject and author. It was then, and is now, the most important guide to current medical literature in the world, an invaluable resource for researchers, students, teachers, and those involved in patient care.

Billings retired from the army and left the library in 1895, and various directors followed. As medical science evolved, the library's importance transcended its institutional niche. In 1956 Senators Lister Hill and John F Kennedy sponsored the National Library of Medicine Act, transferring the library to the Public Health Service. In 1962 the NLM got a new home, in Bethesda; and the collection, parts of which had been kept in locales as diverse as Ford's Theater (after President Lincoln's assassination) and Cleveland, Ohio (for 20 years, beginning during World War II), have since all been in one place.

The NLM — with more than 4 million books, journals, and technical reports, in over 70 languages — is the world's largest and most complete medical library. The historical division alone contains over half a million printed pieces, some 70,000 printed before 1801. The library's glory, thanks to Billings, is its accessibility, now substantially aided by computer technology. The MEDLARS program (Medical Literature Analysis and Retrieval System, established in 1964) makes possible individualized searches of the literature for health professionals on any topic. The MEDLINE program (the largest and most heavily used of some 25 medical data bases) makes up-to-date bibliographies on selected topics available within minutes at 3500 computer-connected sites around the country. The NLM is also the hub of a regionalized information system that includes 7 regional libraries, 135 medical school libraries, and 5000 hospital libraries.

The present NLM is located in two buildings on the NIH campus. The main library building, which contains the library's collections of printed works on some 45 miles of shelves, is low and broad and topped with a "hyperbolic paraboloid," a sort of winged skylight. The adjacent 10-story gleaming modern building, the Lister Hill Center, dates from 1980 and houses the NLM's computer facilities and numerous offices. It is here, too, that you'll find the NLM Visitors Center, the starting point for tours and a source of public information. The reading rooms are open to the public Monday through Thursday, 8:30 AM to 9 PM, and Friday and Saturday, 8:30 AM to 5 PM, with more abbreviated hours in the History of Medicine Room and during the summer. Tours are available from the lobby of Building 38A, Monday through Friday, at 1 PM.

(5) *National Museum of American History* 14th Street and Constitution Avenue NW 20560. (202) 357-2700. The Smithsonian Institution is the biggest and best museum in the world; its Medical Sciences Division is housed here, in the National Museum of American History. Its collection is enormous, encompassing over 100,000 items drawn from the fields of medicine, dentistry, pharmacy, and public health. At any given time, only 1 to 2 percent of the collection is on display.

The exhibits are located in the Hall of Medical Sciences, on the first floor. The pharmacy section contains two pharmacy-shop reconstructions, one an eighteenth-century German apothecary and the second an 1890 American drugstore. Nearby is a platform showing the development of various machines used in the pharmaceutical trade; various exhibits of pharmacy paraphernalia are in the same area. The dental collection is one of the finest in the world and includes exhibits of dental tools, chairs, and paraphernalia, as well as reconstructions of the dental offices of GV Black, Edward H

Operating room display, National Museum of American History, Smithsonian Institution *(Credit: Richard Strauss/Smithsonian Institution)*

Angle, and C Edmund Kells (who was the first to use x-rays in dentistry). The medical collection includes modern and antique surgical instruments, heart pacemakers, artificial heart valves, infant incubators, artificial limbs, various diagnostic devices, and the like. Public-health exhibits include displays on the production of vaccines and photos and artifacts related to various epidemics, including AIDS. Usually there are one or more special exhibits as well. In the past several years, these have included Pain and Its Relief, and "M*A*S*H" (featuring battlefield medicine).

Displays, however, are only one function of the Smithsonian. The museum also fosters research into our collective history; and it is our most important institution when it comes to preserving and cataloging artifacts from our past, even the vast numbers of things that will never be exhibited. The Smithsonian also regularly lends items for displays at bona fide institutions around the country.

The museum is open daily from 10 AM to 5:30 PM (longer in the summer), and admission is free.

Stabler-Leadbeater Apothecary Shop 105 – 107 South Fairfax Street, Alexandria, VA 22314. (703) 836-3713. When the Stabler-Leadbeater family closed the shop that they had operated from 1792 to 1933, they simply locked the door and walked away. Everything has remained as it was; there is much here from the nineteenth century, and even some from the eighteenth. The shop is unique in a number of ways. First, this was not only an active

Stabler-Leadbeater Apothecary shop *(By permission of Landmarks Society)*

apothecary shop for almost a 150 years; it was one frequented by some of the nation's most distinguished leaders, including George Washington, Daniel Webster, Henry Clay, John C Calhoun, Robert E Lee, and others. In fact, Lee was standing right here when Lieutenant JEB Stuart handed him orders from the War Department to suppress John Brown's raid on Harpers Ferry, in 1859. Second, this was more than just a retail drug store; it was the centerpiece of a manufacturing apothecary business that once occupied 11 buildings. The shop here is the largest and most complete repository of its kind, and anyone interested in the history of pharmacy or medicine will find it fascinating. The building itself dates from 1774 and is currently undergoing an enormously expensive and beautiful restoration. The facade is being restored to its original state; the mahogany cabinets inside will still be stocked with hundreds of handblown bottles, dozens of mortars and pestles, eyeglasses, medical instruments, pharmaceutical manufacturing equipment, and thousands of documents that will fascinate scholars.

After the restoration, the apothecary, with its wonderful furnishings and retail supplies, should remain essentially unchanged. The second-floor factory and third-floor warehouse present real challenges, however, which had not been resolved at the time of my visit. The problem is that both floors are so congested and the assembled paraphernalia so fragile that it would invite destruction to allow a steady flow of visitors up here. The second floor, for example, is lined with bins and drawers, all handhewn and all carefully labeled, still filled with Stabler-Leadbeater merchandise: hundreds of powders, gums, flowers, berries, bark, seeds, roots, leaves, etc. Here you will find such exotica as powdered dragon's blood, cuttlefish bone, and the seeds known as Job's tears. There are crates of pill boxes, labels, glassware, dyes, and correspondence. The quandary is how to allow visitors to see these treasures without destroying the feel of the place.

Plans are for the shop to be open daily, except Sunday, from 10 AM to 4:30 PM. There will probably be a small admission charge.

(6) *Former Veterans Administration Pension Building* F Street between 4th and 5th Streets NW 20001. (202) 272-2448. Veterans' benefits are as old as the country itself, but the earliest programs — with their mixture of pensions and land grants — didn't require a separate bureaucracy for their administration. The complexity built slowly, gaining substance with each new military involvement of the growing country. A National Cemetery system was added in 1862, and a National Home for Disabled Soldiers in 1865. A Veterans Bureau was created in 1921, in the wake of World War I, when the demand for medical services outgrew the limited capabilities of the National Home program. The Veterans Administration itself was created in 1930, amalgamating all veterans' benefits into a single agency.

There are currently about 27 million veterans in this country. With dependents and survivors of deceased veterans, there are over 80 million people potentially eligible for VA benefits and services. Only 40 percent of the VA budget is targeted toward medical and hospital programs; the majority consists of pension and other compensation checks and programs. The medical system alone, however, is enormous, including 172 medical centers, 10,000 buildings, 231 outpatient clinics, 117 nursing home-care units, and 27 domiciliaries. The VA employs over 12,000 physicians and more than 60,000 nursing personnel. Because of the general and growing VA partnership with this nation's medical schools, more than half of all physicians practicing today in the United States have had part of their training in a VA hospital. The VA also supports one of the world's largest programs in medical research.

The 1880 Pension Building is a monument of terra-cotta friezes and more than 15.5 million red bricks. The exterior is very loosely modeled on a sixteenth-century Roman palace. Don't fail to notice the processional frieze that encircles the building. The buff-colored terra cotta depicts an endless military procession composed of multiple military units (the medical corps are recognizable by the invalids in their midst). The interior is far more dramatic, with a huge interior courtyard, 75-foot Corinthian columns, and 4 levels of galleries facing the central space. The grandeur of the Great Hall — whose central space is tall enough to house a modern 15-story building — can be surmised by the number of presidents who have chosen this site for their inaugural balls: Taft, Cleveland, McKinley, Theodore Roosevelt, Nixon, Carter, Reagan, and more. All of this has been accessible to the public since the Pension Building became the National Building Museum, in 1980. The collection here celebrates the nation's past and present architecture and the building arts. There's also a room devoted to the history of the Pension Building itself. The museum is open weekdays, 10 to 4, and weekends, noon to 4.

Clara Barton National Historic Site 5801 Oxford Road, Glen Echo, MD 20812. (301) 492-6245. Clara Barton was one of this country's most honored women, having been decorated with the Iron Cross of Imperial Germany and the Cross of Imperial Russia, as well as with medals from Turkey, Serbia, and a variety of other nations.

She began in public service during the Civil War, volunteering to care for sick and wounded troops, first in Washington and then at the front. Bringing in hospital supplies where there had been none, she soon became known as the "Angel of the Battlefield." At the conclusion of the war she helped to locate missing prisoners of war at President Lincoln's behest. Afterward she went to Europe, became familiar with the precepts of the Red Cross (begun by the Swiss Henri Dunant), and joined Red Cross volunteers in the Franco-Prussian War. Upon her return to the United States she founded the American Red Cross, serving as its president from 1881 to 1904. Under Miss Barton's leadership, the boundaries between the organization and its charismatic (and sometimes difficult) leader were often blurred. Nowhere is that more clearly visible than here, in the building that served as Miss Barton's home for 15 years and as headquarters of the American Red Cross for 7 of those years (1897 to 1904). The building itself was once a Red Cross warehouse in Johnstown, Pennsylvania, where it was used to store supplies for victims of the Johnstown flood. The building was then dismantled, transported here, and reconstructed for Miss Barton's use.

The whole colorful story of Clara Barton and those early years of the Red Cross is told in this huge and fascinating frame building, administered by the National Park Service and located a few miles northwest of the District of Columbia. For many visitors, the furnishings (30 percent of which are original) and architecture alone will justify the visit. The house is generally open seven days a week, from 10 AM to 5 PM, but visitors should call first.

Stonestreet Medical Museum 111 West Montgomery Avenue, Rockville, MD 20850. (301) 762-1492. This one-room building was the medical office of Dr Edward Elisha Stonestreet, who practiced in Rockville from 1852 until 1903. Dr Stonestreet graduated from the University of Maryland Medical School in 1852, and then opened practice in a building constructed for him by his father. The structure was moved to this location in 1972, and since then has functioned as a museum. One corner is set up as Dr Stonestreet's office; the rest is used to display various memorabilia, including medical, dental, general surgical, and apothecary items, as well as various books and journals. Tours are available Tuesday through Saturday, noon to 4 PM, and on the first Sunday of each month, 2 to 5 PM. The small admission charge also permits access to the adjacent restored Beall-Dawson House, an early nineteenth-century home.

Heart House 9111 Old Georgetown Road, Bethesda, MD 20814. (301) 897-5400. This attractive modern building is the headquarters of the American College of Cardiology, an organization founded in 1949 to promote scholarship and collegial interchange among heart specialists. The organization now has some 17,000 members. Heart House dates from 1977 and is of interest to the general public because of a small but fascinating museum off the lobby. The collection, all supplied by the Bakken Museum in Minneapolis, MN, includes a chronology of the development of cardiology from ancient times to the present, as well as a collection of exotic technology. Included in the latter is a device thought to be the world's first heart defibrillator. Other early devices include an EKG machine (c. 1928), a spatial vector cardiograph (1947), and a phonocardiograph (1950). Just outside the entrance to Heart House there is a wonderful sculpture by Harold Kimmelman, *Man Helping Man.* The museum is open to the public during normal working hours.

Arlington National Cemetery Jefferson Davis Highway, Arlington, VA 22211. (202) 695-3250. Arlington is our nation's most famous cemetery, made sacred by the graves of John F Kennedy and many heroes whose lives span over 200 years of history. There are 200,000 veterans and their dependents buried here, on 612 acres of land. Visitors come to see the Tomb of the Unknown Soldier and the resting places of various famous people, from the prize-fighter Joe Louis to the actor Audie Murphy to Chief Justice Earl Warren. No one interested in health-care landmarks should fail to see the Nurses Memorial, near the intersection of Porter and Memorial drives, a short stroll from the Tomb of the Unknown Soldier. Erected in 1938, the memorial commemorates the nurses who served in our armed forces from the Spanish-American War through Vietnam. A stark white stone statue of a nurse stands on the hillside, overlooking the simply marked graves of hundreds of nurses. The grave of Jane Delano, Superintendent of the Army Nurse Corps from 1909 to 1912, is among them. Elsewhere in the cemetery are the graves of other medical personnel, including Walter Reed, William Gorgas, Leonard Wood, George Sternberg, and Anita Newcomb McGee (the founder of the Army Nurse Corps). Anyone wishing to find a specific grave can stop at the visitors center, just inside the main gate. Visiting hours are 8 AM to 7 PM from April to September, and 8 to 5 the rest of the year. There is a modest charge to ride in the Tourmobile, the only motorized transportation for tourists within the grounds.

(7) *American National Red Cross Headquarters* 17th Street and D Street NW 20006. (202) 737-8300. The idea for the Red Cross originated in Switzerland, where Henri Dunant proposed a neutral organization to care for the sick and wounded of armies at war. His efforts led to the forming of the International Committee of the Red Cross, and then to the Geneva (or Red Cross) Convention of 1864, which outlined principles of humanitarian treatment for war victims. Clara Barton (see "Clara Barton National Historic Site," above) worked with the International Red Cross during the Franco-Prussian War of 1870–71, and returned home resolved to found a branch in the United States. This she accomplished in 1881. The American Red Cross then originated the idea of Red Cross aid to victims of civilian disasters; it provided assistance during the 1880s to victims of fires and floods, culminating in the great Johnstown, Pennsylvania, flood of 1889. In response to a growing problem with drowning deaths in 1914, the ARC also pioneered teaching courses in swimming and water safety. Now the Red Cross's activities cover a wide range, from disaster relief to refugee support to counseling and communications support for members of the armed forces. Red Cross Blood Services collects, processes, and distributes more than half of the nation's volunteer blood supplies.

The buildings at what is informally called Red Cross Square include a number of sites worth visiting. The neoclassical Main Building, dating from 1917, commemorates the women of the

North and South who cared for the sick and wounded during the Civil War. The second-floor lobby here has a variety of paintings, sculpture, and historical displays, which visitors are welcome to inspect at their leisure. Don't miss the three stunning Tiffany windows off the second-floor lobby (you have to ask at the reception desk for permission to see these), which were commissioned to represent the theme of ministering to the sick and wounded through sacrifice. In the garden behind the Main Building are two handsome pieces of sculpture. The first depicts three people straining to help a fallen comrade, and is dedicated to Red Cross workers the world over who have given their lives to help others. The second, a statue of a woman in a quiet alcove, honors the memory of Jane Delano, founder of Red Cross Nursing and Health Services, as well as 296 other Red Cross nurses who died while serving during World War I. The marble base bears an inscription from the ninety-first psalm: "Thou shalt not be afraid for the terror by night/nor for the arrow that flieth by day/nor for the pestilence that walketh in darkness/nor for the destruction that wasteth at noonday." The grounds and the buildings are open to the public from 8:30 AM to 4:45 PM weekdays.

(8) *American Pharmaceutical Association Headquarters* 2215 Constitution Avenue NW 20037. (202) 628-4410. The Americal Pharmaceutical Association was founded in 1852, both for the promotion of pharmacy as a profession and to further the standardization of drugs and medicinal preparations. Since 1888, the year it was chartered, in Washington, the association has published the *National Formulary,* a list of standard pharmaceuticals available in the United States.

The building here was erected in 1934, paid for by contributions from 14,000 druggists throughout the land. Few buildings could be so close to—and facing—the Lincoln Memorial and survive the comparison, but this one doesn't fare too badly. Designed by John Russell Pope (who also designed the Jefferson Memorial), this is one of Washington's great monuments. It's smaller than the Lincoln Memorial and not so grand in concept, but it too is a marble shrine of classical design, with wide steps climbing gently through a terraced lawn to a formal entryway. A memorial flagstaff on the front lawn has a sculpted bronze base bearing a dedication "to all pharmacists who served in the wars of our country." On either side of the front portal are high-relief panels portraying, in neoclassical style, figures who embody the organization's ideals. Above the entrance are the words: "Dedicated to those who have contributed

Entrance, American Pharmaceutical Association Headquarters *(Photo courtesy of the American Pharmaceutical Association, Washington, DC)*

their knowledge and endeavor to the preservation of public health and to the further advancement of science in pharmacy."

The interior rotunda is one of the city's must-sees. It's a gorgeous space in its own right, beautifully proportioned and of classic Roman design, with multiple varieties of fine marble. An imposing seated statue of William Procter, Jr (1817–1874), the "Father of American Pharmacy," echoes the statue of Lincoln in the Lincoln Memorial, visible through the glass-and-brass front doors.

Anyone wishing to view the interior of this remarkable building need only enter the front door; the receptionist will be pleased to point out some of the more interesting features.

(9) *Samuel Hahnemann Memorial Statue* Massachusetts Avenue between 15th and 16th streets, NW. Tucked into a small triangle formed by Massachusetts and Rhode Island avenues and Corregidor Street, a bronze Samuel Hahnemann (1755–1843) sits looking thoughtful and, perhaps, a trifle dejected. Founder of the branch of medicine known as homeopathy, Hahnemann promoted ideas that were highly influential in this country in the latter half of the nineteenth century, resulting in the establishment of numerous homeopathic medical schools, including one in Philadelphia (no longer homeopathic) which bears his name.

This monument was erected by the American Institute of Homeopathy in 1900, at a time when homeopathy was still a national force; as a monument, it is fine indeed. Hahnemann sits beneath a beautiful mosaic half-dome, which glitters with gold leaf and bright colors. The pedestal on which he sits proclaims the first principle of homeopathy: *similia similibus curantur,* or "like is cured by like." To either side, above curving benches, are bronze bas-relief panels portraying Hahnemann as a student, hunched over thick tomes; as a cautious and precise chemist in the laboratory; as a persuasive teacher in the lecture hall; and as a compassionate physician at the bedside.

(10) *Nuns of the Battlefield Monument* Rhode Island Avenue and M Street NW. In a finger park across from the Cathedral of St Matthew, this bronze panel set in stone portrays 12 nuns wearing habits of various orders of Catholic sisters who nursed soldiers on battlefields and in hospitals during the Civil War. The inscription reads: "They comforted the dying, nursed the wounded, carried hope to the imprisoned, gave in His name a drink of water to the thirsty." In front of the simple but affecting monument sits a small bench where visitors can pause for rest and meditation. The tribute was erected in 1924 by the Ladies Auxiliary of the Ancient Order of Hibernians.

(11) *National Medical Association* 1012 10th Street NW 20001. (202) 347-1895. This national organization for black physicians, was formed in 1895 at a meeting in Atlanta. The first gathering of a dozen or so physicians was at the First Congregational Church, as there was no other public place in Atlanta that would allow such an assembly. Initially called the National Association of Colored Physicians, Dentists and Pharmacists, the organization adopted its present name in 1903. The *Journal of the National Medical Association,* founded in 1909, is the country's oldest black periodical, antedating by a year the official organ of the National Association for the Advancement of Colored People. The NMA moved to its present headquarters building in the early 1980s. Its current membership includes about 5000 physicians, many of whom belong to 1 or more of the 31 state and 58 local societies for black physicians. No tours are available.

(12) *United States Capitol* Capitol Hill 20515. (202) 224-3121. This beautiful and distinctive landmark is on most tourists' "must-see" lists in the District of Columbia; but the fact that it was designed by the physician, and amateur architect William Thornton gives it special appeal for readers of this book. Thomas Jefferson

said that the doctor's design "captivated the eyes and judgment of all." George Washington was much taken with the "grandeur, simplicity and convenience" of the building's plan. Inside the Capitol building, be sure to seek out Statuary Hall and the adjacent corridors. Beginning in 1864, each state was invited to provide not more than two statues of deceased persons whose illustrious achievements brought distinction upon their home states. Of the 92 individuals immortalized here (8 states nominated only 1 individual each), 7 have special meaning for the health professions. Crawford W Long (the marble statue was contributed by Georgia and now stands in the East Central Hall) was the first surgeon in the world to use ether anesthesia, in 1842. Ephraim McDowell (the bronze statue given by Kentucky stands in the Senate connecting corridor) was the first surgeon in the world to successfully remove an ovarian tumor. Father Damien (his bronze statue, complete with leprous lesions, was contributed by Hawaii and stands in the Hall of Columns) is often known as the Martyr of Molokai, where he spent many years of his life laboring to improve the condition of those suffering from Hansen's disease. John Gorrie (the marble statue contributed by Florida is in Statuary Hall) held the first patent on mechanical refrigeration, which he developed while trying to lower the temperatures of yellow-fever sufferers. Marcus Whitman (the bronze statue , a gift of Washington State, stands in Statuary Hall) was a pioneering physician and medical missionary in Washington Territory. Washington's second statue, located nearby, is of Mother Joseph (a nun of the Sisters of Providence) who built and administered eleven hospitals in the Northwest Territories of the United States. Florence Sabin (her bronze, seated statue was contributed by Colorado and can be found in Statuary Hall) was the first woman faculty member of The Johns Hopkins University, the first woman fellow of the Rockefeller Institute, and the first woman member of the National Academy of Sciences.

The Capitol is open daily from 9 to 4:30, with guided tours available every half-hour (the last beginning at 3:45). Call to check extended summer hours.

Charles Drew House 2505 First Street South, Arlington, VA 22210. Charles Richard Drew (1904–1950) is often regarded as America's first great black medical scientist, and he was the first black American to receive the Doctor of Science in Medicine degree. A graduate of Amherst College and McGill Medical School, he interned at Montreal General Hospital. In 1938, while a young instructor in surgery at Howard University, he received a fellowship to study at Columbia University. While there, Drew demonstrated that plasma could be kept indefinitely, thus laying the groundwork for the treatment of shock, which became the cornerstone of combat medicine during World War II. Shortly after the war's outbreak, Drew was put in charge of the first Plasma for Britain project; later he oversaw the US project for dried-plasma production. Though he is generally credited with the dramatic success of both programs, he resigned his leadership position because of blatantly racist policies adopted by the government after the start of the war: all blood was to be segregated on the basis of the race of the donor, and white soldiers were to be given only plasma from white donors. In his resignation statement, Drew asked, "In the laboratory I have found that you and I share a common blood; but will we ever, ever share a common brotherhood?" Drew then became Chairman of the Department of Surgery at Howard. He died in 1950, a year after seeing the army revoke its policy of segregating blood. The house on First Street remains essentially as it was when Drew lived here (1920– 1939): a modest two-story clapboard house sitting on brick pillars. It was named a National Historic Landmark in 1976, but it is a private dwelling. Please do not disturb the occupants.

(13) *Washington Monument* The Mall 20560. Every visitor to the District of Columbia is familiar with the Washington Monument, that stunning tribute to George Washington and his many achievements. Built at intervals between 1848 and 1885, the 555-foot spire was funded with contributions from individuals and organizations as well as federal appropriations. The interior walls are decorated with 188 carved stones presented by various individuals, states, organizations, and nations of the world. One that may interest some readers was donated by the American Medical Association. It depicts Hippocrates rejecting a bribe from Persians, at war with Greece, who are trying to win the physician's services away from the Greeks. The area containing these various "tribute stones" is currently closed to the general public because so many of the stones have been damaged by repeated touching. However, the stones may be seen on a private tour arranged in advance. (Write Mall Operations Office, 1100 Ohio Drive SW, 20242.) The monument is open seven days a week, from 9 AM to 5 PM, with extended hours in the summer.

Naval Medical Command Grounds 23d Street and D Street NW 20372. (212) 653-1297. The headquarters of the Naval Medical Command has a long and proud history. The domed building visible from the street was once the Naval Observatory, built in 1845 at the insistence of President John Quincy Adams—himself an amateur astronomer deeply concerned that the United States lagged behind Europe in astronomy. In 1893 the building was abandoned as an observatory; the following year, it became the home of the Naval Museum of Hygiene. This institution, roughly analogous to the better-known Army Institute of Pathology, had been established in 1879 for the investigation of hygiene-related matters, as well as for the gathering together of medical museum items. The museum conducted a variety of analyses — of pathologic specimens, of medicines for strength and purity, of water for drinkability, and the like.

In 1902 the navy established the United States Naval Medical School on these grounds, "for the instruction of newly appointed medical officers in professional branches peculiar to naval requirements." In 1903, Congress appropriated money for a new Naval Hospital to be constructed on Observatory Hill. Upon completion, in 1908, this hospital consisted of a pavilion-style complex of four wards, an administration building, a surgical suite, a contagious-disease building, nurses' quarters, and various support structures.

The hospital expanded considerably, to 435 beds, during World War I, leading to problems of overcrowding and the use of numerous temporary buildings. In 1942 all clinical operations were transferred to the new Naval Medical Center, in Bethesda. The old hospital, school, and museum facilities then became the home of the Bureau of Medicine and Surgery, which in 1982 was renamed the Naval Medical Command. Most of these structures still stand on Observatory Hill. In front of the 1845 Observatory building stands a bronze statue of Benjamin Rush, MD. Rush lived and worked in Philadelphia, where he was widely respected for a range of interests, knowledge, and accomplishments that rivaled that of his friend Thomas Jefferson. The granite pedestal beneath the Rush statue displays a variety of legends, including "Signer of the Declaration of Independence" and "America's First Alienist." The statue was erected in 1904 by the American Medical Association, as a gift to the US Naval Medical School and the nation.

This statue is just barely visible from the street, but anyone with a special interest can arrange tours by contacting the BUMED Historian.

⑭ *National Cathedral* Mount St Alban at Massachusetts and Wisconsin avenues 20016. (202) 537-6200. This Episcopal church has been built in the style of fourteenth-century Gothic cathedrals; it is one of the largest and finest modern examples of the genre. Among the more than 100 stained-glass windows that line and decorate the walls there are some lovely tributes to the health professions. The Florence Nightingale Window (in the East Aisle) includes six medallions depicting scenes from Miss Nightingale's life, including her service in the Crimea and the founding of St Thomas Hospital in London. The Physician's Window (in the East Clerestory) shows Christ, as Healer, flanked by Louis Pasteur and Sir Wilfred Grenfell (a British medical missionary to Labrador). The Humanitarian Window (in the North Outer Aisle of the Nave) depicts Father Damien and Albert Schweitzer, among others. In addition to the windows, a variety of people significant to the health professions occupy places of honor here. Helen Keller is buried here, as is the noted ophthalmologist William Wilmer (his body is in a vault under the chapel floor). The Cathedral is open for tours daily from 10 AM to 3:15 PM, except Sunday, when tours are scheduled at 12:30 and 2 PM.

SPECIAL ATTRACTIONS—
STATE BY STATE

ALABAMA

BIRMINGHAM

University of Alabama School of Medicine 619 South Nineteenth Street 35233. (205) 934-3884. The "Pittsburgh of the South" now finds health care to be its major industry, and pills and bandages have turned out to be as lucrative as smoke and steel ever were. One out of ten workers in Birmingham gets a paycheck from a health-care enterprise.

The medical school traces its history to 1859, when the Medical College of Alabama opened its doors in Mobile. Classes were discontinued during the Civil War, but resumed in 1868. In 1907 the college was adopted by the University of Alabama, becoming its "Medical Department." In 1919, because of financial and academic difficulties, the Medical Department ceased operations; the following year, all laboratory equipment, museum exhibits, and other school paraphernalia were shipped to Tuscaloosa, where the University of Alabama inaugurated a two-year basic-science medical program. Students who completed this program had to leave the state to get their MD's, and Alabama suffered a slow but steady drain of its physicians. To rectify this vexing problem, the legislature in 1943 decided to support a four-year school. In 1945, one was established in Birmingham. The campus now includes six health-care schools — Medicine, Dentistry, Nursing, Optometry, Public Health, and Health-Related Professions — as well as the University of Alabama Hospital and a variety of other hospitals and support structures. The complex covers more than 40 blocks.

The University of Alabama Hospital had its beginnings 1887, when the Hospital of United Charity was established. The name was changed to Hillman Hospital in 1897, to honor a benefactor. Jefferson Hospital was erected adjacent to Hillman in 1940, to provide accommodation for patients who could pay for their care. In tune with the values of the time, the 16-story, 600-bed Jefferson facility was built with separate operating rooms and wards for black and white patients, and separate cafeterias for black and white employees. Hillman and Jefferson were merged in 1944; and the two older buildings are now connected with, and a part of, the contemporary brick UAB Hospital building.

There are no tours available for the entire campus, but many visitors might enjoy a stop at the Lister Hill Library on University Boulevard at 17th Street South. On the ground floor of this building can be found the **Reynolds Historical Library** and the **Alabama Museum of the Health Sciences,** both open weekdays 8 AM to noon and 1 to 5 PM, and at other times by appointment. The Reynolds has a fine collection of rare and historic volumes and an outstanding collection of sixteenth- through eighteenth-century ivory anatomic mannequins. The mannequins are available for public viewing; but visitors wishing to see first editions of, e.g., Andreas Vesalius' *De humani corporis fabrica libri septem,* William Harvey's *De motu cordis,* or the choice medical incunabula (works printed before 1501) have to make arrangements in advance. The museum is really a series of displays, of far more modest scope and quality than the Reynolds' collection, and includes recreations of turn-of-the-century doctors' and dentists' offices as well as medical memorabilia of local and regional interest.

JACKSONVILLE

Dr Francis' Medical and Apothecary Museum 100 Gayle Avenue 36265. (205) 435-7611. This tiny building, with its imposing portico supported by four oversized Doric columns, was once the office of JC Francis, who practiced in Jacksonville for 54 years. Francis moved to the town in 1837 and built this little office shortly thereafter. The building was moved to its present location, restored, and opened as a museum in 1974. It consists of two rooms: a waiting room and an apothecary in front and an examining room in the rear. The sparse collection includes apothecary jars and medication containers of the era, surgical instruments, a few furnishings, and various books and journals that might have been used by a doctor like Francis. To see the interior of Dr Francis' office, you have to call city hall (at the number given above) to make arrangements.

MOBILE

University of South Alabama Medical Center 2451 Fillingham Street 36617. (205) 471-7000. This is a new medical center and a new medical school, but the roots of both go back many years. Mobile was the site of Alabama's first state-supported school of medicine, which opened in 1859 and operated continuously (except during the Civil War) until 1919. Thereafter, medical education (and, indeed, higher education in general) in Mobile languished until 1962, when local movers and shakers decided to build a new university from scratch; thus the University of South Alabama was born. The USA, aware of the shortage of tertiary care in South Alabama, decided to establish a new medical school. The charter class was admitted in 1973 and graduated in 1976.

The university's hospital also has a lengthy history. In 1704, when Mobile was still a French colony, two Gray Nuns established the city's first hospital and called it Hospital Royal. In the years that followed, under successive British, Spanish, and American rule, the hospital changed locations and names several times. Among its incarnations were Kings Hospital, City Hospital, and Port Hospital. In 1959, it was christened Mobile General Hospital. In 1970 the hospital was acquired by USA, and in 1975 the facility was renamed University of South Alabama Medical Center. The present location and the 400-bed, 12-story tower date from 1966.

The school's preclinical training is conducted in the handsome Basic Medical Sciences Building on the main USA campus, some five miles from the medical center. Of special interest to visitors, however, is the **Heustis Medical Museum** in the Mastin Building near the hospital, on the Medical Center campus. In the building's lobby, which is open 24 hours a day, you will find what is reputed to be the largest collection of medical memorabilia in the Southeast, including microscopes, medical and surgical instruments, and a variety of other artifacts.

Call Volunteer Services for tours of the campus.

MONTGOMERY

Alabama Pharmaceutical Association Drugstore Museum 340 Dexter Avenue 36104. (205) 262-0027. This 1930's drugstore restoration was designed to capture the feel of an era when the drugstore was a major social center in every community. Fittingly, the centerpiece here is a black-and-white marble soda fountain with gleaming silver fixtures. The refinished oak cabinets and pressed tin ceiling are all authentic, and the drugstore includes numerous apothecary jars and medicine bottles filled with herbs, nostrums, liniments, lozenges, pills, and powders. There is also a fine collection of pharmacy equipment here, including balances, mortars, pestles, and the like. The museum is in the Alabama Pharmaceutical Association headquarters, but has its own entrance from the street. It is open to the public 9 AM to 4 PM, by appointment.

MOUNT VERNON

Searcy Hospital 36560. (205) 829-9411. These hospital grounds have a remarkable amount of history tucked within their borders. Andrew Jackson made camp here during the War of 1812. In 1828, the site was made into a Federal Arsenal; its commander from 1853 to 1856 was Josiah Gorgas—the father of William Gorgas, who later became famous in the war against yellow fever. During the Civil War the arsenal was occupied by Confederate forces. In 1873 the Arsenal became a Federal Barracks, which was converted into a prison, in 1887, to incarcerate Apache Indians. From 1888–1894, Geronimo (leader of the Chiricahua Apaches) was held prisoner here, as was Natchez, son of Cochise. From 1887 until 1890, Captain Walter Reed was post surgeon; for him this was a brief stop on the way to the fame he was later to achieve in the yellow fever wars.

From 1901 to 1969, the arsenal complex functioned as a segregated state mental hospital, for black patients only. During this time, Dr George Searcy made the first diagnosis in the United States of pellagra—a disease subsequently recognized as a major cause of mental illness in the South. After the Civil Rights Act of 1964, the hospital was integrated and renamed Searcy Hospital, in honor not of Dr George Searcy but of his father James, who was superintendent here from 1892 until 1919. The hospital is now a modern psychiatric institution, with 600 beds.

The hospital complex includes buildings dating from the 1830s to the present. At least a dozen of the original brick structures remain. One structure, for example, originally an armorer's shop and later a saddler's shop, is now the dental clinic. What used to be the blacksmith's shop is now used for a rehabilitation program. The original complex, and many buildings of later vintage, are surrounded by a huge brick wall that dates from the 1830s. Varying from 12 to 16 feet high, this mile-long enclosure—in the shape of a giant horseshoe—keeps outsiders out and patients in.

Tours of this fascinating place are available through the hospital's Public Information Office.

TUSCALOOSA

Bryce Hospital 200 University Boulevard 35401. (205) 759-0448. In the 20 years before the Civil War, there was widespread belief among psychiatric leaders that insanity could be cured if patients

Main Building, Bryce Hospital *(Photograph by Kathy Fetters, Librarian, Bryce Hospital)*

could be isolated from the adverse influences of friends and family, and be protected in a therapeutic environment of kindliness, orderliness, and serenity. The architectural designs of Thomas Kirkbride became the standard to which all institutions aspired. While variations in the Kirkbride schema were eventually instituted in virtually every state in the union, in only one institution was the plan implemented in all its details: the Alabama Insane Hospital, in Tuscaloosa.

The hospital was opened for patient care in 1861, after three visits by Dorothea Dix to ensure appropriate legislative action and after construction had dragged on for nine years. The final product included a typically Kirkbridian administration building, topped by a massive dome (which housed a water tank), with wings extending laterally in a series of receding links. For a while it was the largest building under one roof in the United States.

Though the Kirkbride plan was intended to house a maximum of 250 patients, the upheaval of the Civil War and later events caused social disruptions that resulted in an enormous patient population. By the 1890s, the hospital (now called Bryce, after its first superintendent) housed 1100 patients; and by the 1930s, over 2600. By 1970, Bryce — begun as a model institution — was now a model of what a psychiatric hospital should not be. The situation became so bad that one patient filed suit, saying, in effect, "If you are going to confine me for therapeutic reasons, you must provide me with some genuine treatment." That suit resulted in the 1972 *Wyatt vs Stickney* court decision, establishing 35 criteria for hospital compliance and guaranteeing a patient's right to treatment in a humane environment. The most significant result of *Wyatt* was the deinstitutionalization of vast numbers of psychiatric patients around the entire country. Bryce now houses about 1000 patients.

The visitor to Bryce today will encounter a campus crowded with buildings, but the old Kirkbride structure remains essentially intact. The original white dome pokes up above the oaks, sycamores, and magnolias, dominating the view up the drive from the main gate. Although the hospital has undergone many renovations and additions, the 780-foot original facade still looks much as it did 130 years ago. Some of the interior spaces, especially in the monumental central pavilion, are little altered as well. Hidden behind the whitewashed brick of the original facade is a seemingly endless series of additions grafted onto the back. Bryce is currently undergoing a $35-million renovation, so the campus is in turmoil; but the Public Relations Department would be pleased to arrange tours of the older portions for interested parties.

Gorgas House University of Alabama Campus Quadrangle 35487. (205) 348-5906. The Gorgas House dates from 1829 and is the oldest building on the University of Alabama campus. It has been preserved both for its role in campus history and as a monument to the Gorgas family, various members of which lived here from 1879 until 1953. General Josiah Gorgas was a university president, his wife Amelia was university librarian (the huge library across the street bears her name), and their son William was an illustrious physician, Surgeon General of the US Armed Forces, and president of the American Medical Association. William Gorgas is credited with eradicating yellow fever from Cuba and Central and South America, ensuring — among other benefits — completion of the Panama Canal. Gorgas first proceeded on the basis of research performed by Walter Reed; after eight months of working to eradicate mosquitoes from Havana, he succeeded in wiping out yellow fever in a city that had had daily reports of the disease for over 140 years. Various family artifacts and exhibits are on display here to illustrate the story. The building is fascinating too. It was designed as a "low country raised cottage"; all of its principal rooms have been raised a story above the ground to protect the inhabitants from the damp soil below. The house is open to the public Monday through Saturday, 10 to 12 and 2 to 5, and Sunday 3 to 5.

TUSKEGEE

Tuskegee University 36088. (205-) 727-8011. Founded in 1881 by Booker T Washington as the Tuskegee Normal and Industrial Institute, this school was initially designed to prepare underprivileged blacks for teaching jobs, and later for agricultural research and other skilled jobs. The School of Nursing was an early success. Established in 1892, it survived to become the first baccalaureate nursing program in the state of Alabama (in 1948); it continues today as the School of Nursing and Allied Health.

The John A Andrew Memorial Hospital began as a facility to house sick faculty and students from the Institute; makeshift buildings were replaced by a full-fledged hospital in 1913. For many years it was a major center for postgraduate training for black physicians, who generally had few other options. Gradually the hospital grew, opening its beds to townspeople and others in surrounding communities and even neighboring states. This large patient load, which included many without insurance or other means, was ultimately the hospital's downfall. By the end of 1987 the hospital had amassed an $8-million deficit, the burden of which put Tuskegee in an intolerable position. The university reluctantly decided to close the hospital, and the Hospital Road building has since been converted into a new Center for the Natural Sciences and the Health Professions.

In 1932 the hospital responded to a personal request from the Surgeon General of the US Public Health Service and agreed to cooperate in a long-term study of advanced syphilis in 400 black males. When details of the project came to light, in 1972, and the public learned that the subjects had been systematically denied treatment for 40 years, both before and after penicillin became available as definitive therapy, the hospital and the Tuskegee Institute thoroughly dissociated themselves from the study. By 1972's standards, the facts that the research included only poor, and mostly unlettered, blacks and that the subjects were unknowingly denied available treatment for a devastating disease were inhumane and racist. In truth, it was the US Public Health Service that had conducted the experiment and that bore responsibility for its design and implementation; but the fact that the project was known as the Tuskegee Study, and widely publicized as such, was a continuing embarrassment for the institute and the John A Andrew Memorial Hospital.

Just inside the main gate to the university there is an attractive Visitors' Center and museum operated by the National Park Service. Brief walking tours of the nearby structures are led from the Visitors' Center, usually on an hourly basis. Those interested in a more intensive tour should call the Public Relations Department.

Tuskegee Veterans Administration Hospital Hospital Road 36083. (205) 727-0550. First known as the Hospital for Sick and Injured Colored War Veterans, this hospital was dedicated in 1923 with Vice President Calvin Coolidge giving the principal speech. Built on 464 acres of land, the hospital was inaugurated as the only veterans hospital for 300,000 black veterans in the South. Robert Moton, principal of the Tuskegee Institute and Booker T Washington's successor, remarked, "This hospital marks the greatest physical achievement of our government for the Negro race in America since Emancipation." The facility opened with an all-white medical and nursing staff, although "colored nursemaids" were assigned "to each white nurse, in order to save them from contact with colored patients." The staffing issue was fought bitterly by the Tuskegee Institute, the National Medical Association, and the National Association for the Advancement of Colored People; ultimately, progressive forces triumphed. By 1924 the hospital had an all-black staff. Local Ku Klux Klan members were so incensed that they paraded through the Tuskegee Institute's grounds and burned a cross on the lawn. Until 1941, this was the only hospital in the entire VA system that hired black nurses. In 1947, 24 of the 127 VA hospitals around the country still had segregated wards; 19 (all in the South) refused to admit blacks at all. Finally, in 1954, pursuant to executive order, all VA facilities were desegregated.

The hospital is now a 952-bed general medical and teaching facility, occupying 45 buildings spread out over 160 acres. The buildings here are mostly older brick structures dating from the hospital's early years. At the hospital gates, there is a large sign that states "The price of freedom is visible here." Tours are available via the Public Affairs Office.

TUSCUMBRIA

Ivy Green (Birthplace of Helen Keller) 300 West North Commons 35674. (205) 383-4066. This is a landmark that will interest anyone concerned with the blind and deaf, or fascinated by the stories of individuals who have triumphed over adversity. Built by Helen Keller's grandfather in 1820, this is the both the birthplace of that most remarkable woman and the place where she began her instruction with Annie Sullivan in 1887. The grounds here will seem familiar to anyone who has seen the film *The Miracle Worker.* There's the main house, where Helen's parents lived; the cottage where Helen lived with Sullivan; a kitchen building; a carriage house; and 10 acres of grounds. The old water pump is still here too, where Helen learned her first word as Sullivan painstakingly spelled the letters *w-a-t-e-r* into her hand. By nightfall of that first day, Helen had learned some 30 words. The various buildings are filled with Keller memorabilia: photographs, Braille books, toys, mementos, and various possessions. Ivy Green is open Monday through Saturday, 8:30 to 4:30, and Sunday, 1 to 4:30; there is a small charge for tours. As an added bonus, the play *The Miracle Worker* is presented on Friday and Saturday evenings from mid-June through July. Call for ticket information.

ALASKA

ANCHORAGE

Alaska Native Medical Center 3d Street and Gambell Street 99510. (907) 257-1252. The earliest health services for Eskimos, Aleuts, and Indians of Alaska (collectively known as Alaska Natives) were, of course, provided by tribal healers and shamans. The first contact with western medicine came after 1806, when the Russians began assigning physicians here, to take care of people working for Russian-American commercial endeavors (see below). Little of this medical care was available to Alaska Natives, however, and the situation got no better when the United States purchased the territory, in 1867.

By 1907 the Department of the Interior's Bureau of Education had begun employing some physicians and nurses to work with the natives. In 1915, the Bureau established a permanent 25-bed hospital in Juneau, followed by a variety of other health facilities built over the next 15 years. In 1931, the Bureau transferred all of its activities in Alaska to the Bureau of Indian Affairs, which expanded existing health facilities and established temporary placement of nurses in some of the larger native villages. It was during this period that the dimensions of the Alaska Natives' health problems were first fully appreciated: some 35 percent of native deaths were attributable to tuberculosis; epidemics of mumps, measles and rubella often caused devastating morbidity and mortality; dental disease was a major problem; and other conditions also contributed significantly to health impairment. Although the BIA devoted ever-increasing resources to these problems, it remained unable to attract sufficient numbers of physicians and other health personnel to make a major impact.

In 1955 responsibility for all native health services was transferred to the US Public Health Service, and a new era in Alaska Native health care began. The construction of this hospital, in Anchorage, was completed, and—most important—truly effective medications for treating tuberculosis came on the market. The ANMC, built as a tuberculosis sanatorium, developed into a tertiary-care facility—the hub of a system that includes five other hospitals and numerous widely scattered outpatient facilities. For many years, the ANMC was the largest hospital in the state and one of the few accredited by the Joint Commission for the Accreditation of Hospitals (JCAH).

Today the ANMC is a 170-bed complex with a full range of clinical services. Though most of the health-care professionals are still from the "lower 48," almost half of the work force of the Alaska Area Native Health Service are Alaska Natives or American Indians, and ever-growing numbers of Alaska Natives are entering health professions training. The ANMC staff are happy to provide visitors with tours, by advance arrangement.

SITKA

Site of Alaska's First Hospital Sitka National Historical Park, Lincoln and Baranoff Streets 99835. (907) 747-6281. Alaska had its first 20-bed hospital here in Sitka (then "New Archangel") in 1818, and a 10-bed facility shortly afterwards in Kodiak. The reason was that the Russians had a strong trade presence from the early nineteenth century; sailors and traders needed medical support to help them deal with the bitter cold, the constant threat of injury, and endemic diseases (scurvy, e.g.). Russian physicians visited the area in conjunction with service on Russian naval vessels as early as 1810. (One stayed for several months in 1814.)

By the 1830s, the New Archangel Hospital (near the present intersection of Harbor Drive and Matsoutoff Street) had expanded to 30 beds, with a smaller facility added to accommodate women patients during a smallpox epidemic. The original hospital was expanded again in the 1840s and then moved to a new location in the 1850s. During this period the hospital was staffed by several physicians, assisted by a number of *feldshers* and various native apprentices. (The Russian *feldsher* is roughly akin to our military corpsman — in the early nineteenth century trained primarily in wound management, and later trained to provide health-care services in isolated stations where no physicians were available.) In 1860 the hospital treated a total of 1400 inpatients and outpatients.

The site identified here is actually the location of Sitka's second Russian-American Company hospital. Originally built as a seminary, in about 1845, just behind the Russian Orthodox Bishop's house, the building was transferred to hospital use in 1858. The structure was used as a US Army hospital after Alaska was purchased by the United States, in 1867. Before burning down, in 1882, the building served as a boarding school for the Presbyterian Board of Home Missions. In the early 1980s, when the National Park Service was restoring the old Bishop's House for use as a museum and as an outstanding example of Russian colonial architecture, workmen came across a long-buried trash pile that contained hospital artifacts from the 1860s, including pharmaceutical bottles, syringes, flasks, cupping glasses, mortars and pestles, and other laboratory instruments. Some of these are usually on display in rotating exhibits at either the Visitors' Center (106 Metlacatla Street) or the Bishop's House (at the corner of Lincoln and Monastery Streets). Visitors are welcome seven days a week, 8 to 5, in the summers, and Monday through Friday, 8 to 5, in the winter.

ARIZONA

PHOENIX

Phoenix Indian Medical Center 4212 North 16th Street 85016. (602) 263-1200. Health services for American Indians began in the nineteenth century, when US Army physicians made efforts to curb smallpox and other forms of contagion in Indians living in or near some military posts, in part from compassion and in part from self-interest. The Bureau of Indian Affairs was transferred from the War Department to the Department of the Interior in 1849. By 1875, half the Indian agencies had physicians attached, and by 1900 the Indian Medical Service employed 83 physicians. In 1926, medical officers from the Public Health Service were detailed to the program; and in 1955 Indian health officially became the responsibility of the Public Health Service. Now the program includes 49 hospitals, 101 health centers, and numerous "health stations." The

Phoenix Indian Medical Center vies with a similar institution in Anchorage, Alaska, for the status of largest hospital in the program. The 170-bed, starkly modern institution, set on a large grassy campus, can be toured by advance arrangement with Volunteer Services.

Phoenix Baptist Hospital and Medical Center Museum 6025 North 20th Avenue 85015. (602) 249-0212. Next to this institution's gift shop, opening onto the lobby, there's a room filled with wall-to-wall display cases. The exhibits rotate, but the extensive collection includes some wonderful medical antiques, so the displays are always interesting. The collection here belongs not to the hospital, but rather to a physician staff member who has been collecting for many years. His collection got its greatest boost when he acquired three tons of "old junk" from a 130-year-old New England drugstore, so the exhibits are particularly strong on pharmaceutical artifacts and memorabilia, including rare drug jars, a Chinese opium scale, an English ceramic leech jar, sickroom supplies, and such patent-medicine rarities as digitalis tea bags. One section deals with tuberculosis and the part it played in the evolution of Arizona as a state. There are fine old surgical instruments, obstetrical forceps, and various relics of medical quackery. The hospital lobby is open 24 hours a day, seven days a week, so the museum is always accessible; but visitors are most welcome between 8 AM and 9 PM.

TOMBSTONE

OK Corral Allen Street and 3d Street 85638. John Henry ("Doc ") Holliday graduated from the Pennsylvania College of Dental Surgery in 1872. He began his dental practice in Georgia, where he had been born; but he was soon found to have tuberculosis, and he sought his health in the West. Holliday practiced dentistry in a number of towns, including Dallas, Wichita, and Dodge City, Kansas. Gambling initially was his avocation, but in time it became his principal source of income; by 1881 he had given up dentistry. In those days, gamblers needed to be able to fend for themselves on the rough-and-tumble frontier, so Holliday rigorously practiced with a six-shooter and knife until he became expert. He got into numerous fights, and is said to have killed two-dozen men in his lifetime — over cards, women, and principle. Holliday said that the only times he wasn't nervous were when he was working on teeth or fighting.

Holliday's enduring fame is tied to his longterm friendship with Wyatt Earp, one of the West's best-known lawmen. In 1881, Earp feuded with a group of outlaws that included the infamous Clanton brothers and McLowry brothers. The shootout, which became the most famous gunfight of the Old West, was fought behind a livery stable, in the open-air pens known as the OK Corral. At Earp's side, facing the outlaws' guns, were Earp's two brothers and Doc Holliday. When the shooting was over, three outlaws were dead, Earp's brothers were seriously wounded, Holliday had a flesh wound, and Wyatt was unharmed. Holliday lived another six years, to die of tuberculosis at the age of 36 in Glenwood Springs, Colorado, where he had gone in the hope that the natural sulfur fumes of the springs would help his lungs.

Tombstone's entire main street has been restored to its 1881 state; in a sense the entire town is a museum, a tribute to Doc Holliday and the Earps and the other characters of the day. However, it is at the OK Corral, where life-like figures have been placed in the positions that the gunmen held when the famous battle started, that Doc comes most alive. The Corral can be seen daily between sunrise and sunset. Call the local tourism office, at (602) 457-3548, for related tourist activities.

TUCSON

University of Arizona Health Sciences Center 1501 Campbell Avenue 85724. (602) 694-0111. This young medical center opened in 1971, in response to growing concern over Arizona's being the only state with a population greater than one million without its own medical school. Students wishing to study medicine had to leave the state to do so, and once gone they tended not to come back. The College of Medicine accepted its first students in 1967. The College of Pharmacy (founded 1947) and the College of Nursing (1957) were quickly incorporated into the new Health Sciences Center. The entire medical center, as initially constructed, did not cost the state one dollar in legislative appropriations: $3 million was raised locally, the US Public Health Service provided a $4-million grant, other federal funds accounted for $20 million more, and revenue bonds took care of the rest. During its brief history the UAHSC has been responsible for several medical firsts: In 1974, Robert Volz implanted the country's first artifical wrist; in 1974, C Donald Christian wrote the first article pinpointing the dangers of the Dalkon Shield; and in 1985, Jack Copeland performed the first successful artificial-heart implantation as a bridge to human heart implantation.

The center consists of 30 acres, with 7 buildings, including the 300-bed University Hospital. Tours are available through the Community Relations Office.

St Mary's Hospital 1601 West St Mary's Road 85745. (602) 622-5833. The first hospital in the Arizona Territory, St Mary's was founded in 1880 by the Sisters of St Joseph of Carondelet. The sisters had originally come to Tucson to establish a school (the trip from St Louis had taken them 36 days), but the area's profound need for health care turned these teachers into willing, albeit untrained, nurses. By the turn of the century, Arizona's lure as a health resort for tuberculosis sufferers drew hundreds of patients each year to St Mary's, which responded by building its own tuberculosis sanatorium. In the post–World War II years, when the Sun Belt underwent another population boom, St Mary's expanded dramatically, building a sister hospital, St Joseph's, in eastern Tucson.

St Mary's is part of a national network of Carondelet hospitals and health-care facilities operated by the Sisters of St Joseph of Carondelet. In the late 1980s, the 370-bed St Mary's — whose patient population usually is about one-third Native American — became the first non-Indian hospital in the country to establish a Department of Traditional Indian Medicine, which provides a means for Native Americans to receive traditional care from an Indian medicine man within the hospital itself. While all of the patient-care buildings here are of relatively recent vintage, the 1928 St Catherine's Chapel, restored in 1979, remains the hospital's physical link with the past. Tours are available upon request.

ARKANSAS

HOT SPRINGS

Bathhouse Row Central Avenue and Reserve Street 71902. (501) 624-3383. In 1832, Congress set aside four sections of land surrounding the hot springs here, making this the first land preserved for its resource value by the federal government. In 1877 the Secretary of the Interior appointed a superintendent to supervise the leasing of sites and the building of bathhouses, as well as the daily operation of the various commercial interests. In 1921 the reservation became the Hot Springs National Park; it operates today under the auspices of the National Park Service.

Some early visitors came here for relaxation, but from the beginning the primary magnet was the hope of therapeutic benefit. Physicians started setting up shop here in the 1850s; from then on there was a steady flow of visitors seeking relief from rheumatic disorders, skin and intestinal disorders, and venereal disease. In 1885 the single most common reason for people to seek treatment at the springs was syphilis. By 1912, the government had begun testing the competence of all physicians prescribing at the springs, and for many years it published lists of registered physicians whom it had deemed competent. In 1916 a group of local physicians set up a free clinic that was open for a couple of hours each afternoon in one building, designated the "free bathhouse." The bathhouses employed attendants who rubbed mercury into the skin of syphilitics and then, after a suitable interval, steamed the toxic element out of the patients' bodies by wrapping them in hot blankets with an outer layer of rubber. The US Public Health Service operated a major venereal disease facility here for the first several decades of the twentieth century, and physicians came from all over the country to learn about VD treatment.

At one time there were almost two dozen bathhouses here, many of them monumental in design and imaginative and wide-ranging in equipment and services. Bathhouse Row, a national landmark, consists of eight of these marvelously restored buildings, as well as

Fordyce Bathhouse, Hot Springs National Park *(By permission of the National Park Service)*

a visitors' center, together with a series of walkways and a promenade that runs behind the bathhouses. Most of the buildings date
from the second decade of the twentieth century, and the architecture is best described as international eclectic. Visitors, for a modest
charge, are still able to "take the waters," including various combi-
nations of baths, whirlpool, and massage.

The Fordyce Bathhouse Visitor Center (built in 1914 as a bathhouse and now marvelously restored, including a wonderful
stained-glass and copper marquee) has a variety of exhibits that
depict the area's history, and park rangers regularly give tours.
Groups should make arrangements several weeks in advance.

*Former Army and Navy General Hospital (now Hot Springs Rehabilita-
tion Center)* 105 Reserve Street 71902. (501) 624-4411. When this
hospital was founded in, 1882, it was the nation's first general
hospital for both army and navy personnel. It began as a simple
brick-and-slate building serving 30 patients, and eventually grew
to 59 buildings scattered over 30 acres. The years of greatest growth
were during World War II; in 1945, almost 1800 patients were being
treated here at once, the majority suffering from various arthritic
disorders. Though this was officially an army and navy facility,
most patients were army personnel, and all of the commanding
officers were from the army. After the founding of the Veterans
Bureau, the hospital regularly had a large veteran contingent in
addition to the active-duty personnel. In the 1950s, there were
repeated efforts to close the hospital as the number of active-duty
personnel diminished and the vast Veterans Administration hospital system offered other alternatives for medical care to veterans.
Finally, in 1959, the State of Arkansas took over the facility and
turned it into a vocational rehabilitation center. There are currently
some 21 acres of land with 42 buildings, including a 72-bed rehabilitation hospital and a 425-bed supervised dormitory. The principal
building remains the 11-story swept-wing brick structure that has
dominated the landscape here since 1933. Tours are available by
advance arrangement.

LITTLE ROCK

University of Arkansas for Medical Sciences 4301 West Markham
Street 72205. (501) 661-5000. The UAMS medical center is a modern campus including schools of medicine, nursing, pharmacy, and
health-related professions, as well as a graduate school. The College of Medicine started as a small proprietary school in 1879.
Though it was a for-profit enterprise, the school was nonetheless

incorporated as the Medical Department of the Arkansas Industrial University. The school soon spawned a couple of competitors: The Sulphur Rock/Gate City Medical School, and the College of Physicians and Surgeons of Little Rock. When the Flexner Report was published, in 1910, all three were found wanting. The result was a single school drawn from the wreckage of the three, henceforth known as the University of Arkansas School of Medicine. The new school, however, was poorly funded by the state legislature and poorly supported by the local medical community; it was unable to provide clinical teaching from 1919 to 1922, and lost its national accreditation in 1938. The situation changed dramatically for the better in the late 1940s and the 1950s, and the present modern campus is the result. The school made history in 1948, when it became the first previously all-white medical school in the South to admit a black (Edith Mae Irby, who graduated in 1952.) At the time, the only other medical school in the South that admitted blacks was Meharry Medical College, in Nashville, Tennessee, which was entirely black. The current campus has a dozen red-brick contemporary buildings, the University Hospital (1955) being the oldest. The modern library has a room set aside for the history of medicine; it is small but nicely done, with a particularly strong collection on Arkansas medical history. Immediately adjacent to the the campus, connected but looking out of place, is the starkly modern , cream-colored **John L McClellan Memorial Veterans Administration Hospital,** with four octagonal columnar wings, ornamented with bold geometric patterns of bright blue. (The greater Little Rock Area is unusual for a city of its size in having three VA hospitals — a testament to the Congressional clout wielded for many years by Arkansas' elected representatives.) UAMS is happy to provide tours for interested parties with advance arrangements (661-5686).

CALIFORNIA

DOWNEY

Rancho Los Amigos 7601 East Imperial Highway 90242. (213) 940-7111. Established in 1888 as the Los Angeles County Poor Farm, this is now the largest rehabilitation hospital in the world. The transformation from poor farm to hospital began about 1900, when increasing numbers of patients with various physical disorders began to come here. When an epidemic of poliomyelitis struck LA in the 1940s, accommodations were arranged for hundreds of iron-lung patients in the poor farm's hospital. So crowded did the farm become, that it was labeled a "warehouse for polio patients" and was the subject of an investigation by the National Foundation. Soon thereafter the facility was designated a "Regional Respiratory Care Center" for polio victims, and ground was broken for "the world's most modern polio facility." Designed to look more like a dude ranch than a hospital, the facility opened in 1954. In 1955 the Los Angeles County Poor Farm was renamed Rancho Los Amigos Hospital. When the Salk vaccine eradicated polio, the facility's personnel focused their talents on other incapacitating disabilities.

The 210 acres here are covered with almost 200 buildings, and Rancho Los Amigos is currently undergoing expansion. The daily census hovers around 450 inpatients, primarily with head trauma, spinal cord injuries, burns, birth defects, and strokes. The Rancho is one of seven hospitals operated by the Los Angeles County Department of Health Services. Associated with the University of Southern California's schools of Medicine, Dentistry, Social Work, Physical and Occupational Therapy, and Engineering, this is an active training center in addition to its role in providing patient care. The oldest building on campus is the 1931 Medical Building, designed to resemble the Mission San Luis Rey. Tours are available from admin-

Harriman Building, Rancho Los Amigos Medical Center *(By permission of Rancho Los Amigos)*

istration. (Incidentally, the city of Downey is named after John G Downey, a practicing pharmacist who was elected lieutenant governor of California in 1859 and was elevated to the governorship the following year.)

DUARTE

City of Hope 1500 East Duarte Road 91010. (818) 359-8111. This remarkable institution began in 1913 as two tents for tuberculosis patients, established by the National Jewish Consumptive Relief Organization. The founders were largely Los Angeles–based workingmen and women; the only land they could afford was 10 acres 20 miles from town, in the high desert at the foot of the San Gabriel mountains. In the first year a flash flood washed away the tents, and the tiny facility needed to be rebuilt: one new cottage was sponsored by the Amalgamated Clothing Workers of America, another by the International Ladies Garment Workers Union. Many furnishings were provided by the Los Angeles Junk Peddlers Protective Association and other groups.

Initially, the sponsorship was predominately local and Jewish; but (with a phenomenally imaginative and successful public relations effort) the facility captured the imagination of the public, and gradually the sponsorship has become national and nonsectarian. Almost 500 fundraising groups (called auxiliaries) all over the country compete in raising funds for this endeavor, and send delegates every other year to a national meeting in Los Angeles. These groups have included ones as diverse as the Greater Chicago Office Products Council, the Greater St Louis Labor and Management Committee, and (for a time) a prisoner group at the Federal Penitentiary at McNeil Island, WA.

The City of Hope remained a tuberculosis sanatorium until 1946, when it transformed itself into a national medical center with hospitals and clinics treating a variety of catastrophic diseases. In the late 1950s, the City of Hope also became a major research center; the institution now encompasses 55 buildings spread out over 93 acres. Patients are admitted from all over the nation (and the world) without regard to their ability to pay, so long as their conditions are consistent with the facility's research criteria. The City of Hope provides more uncompensated care than any other non–tax-supported institution in the nation.

Significant medical advances made at the City of Hope include:

1962 Discovery of the standard test for galactosemia in the newborn (Ernest Beutler)

1963   Discovery of the function of the X chromosome (Susumu Ohno)
1978   City of Hope – Genentech research team produce the first manufactured human insulin (humulin) using recombinant DNA techniques

Tours are available to the general public by advance arrangement.

LA JOLLA

The Salk Institute for Biological Sciences North Torrey Pines Road 92138. (619) 453-4100. Founded in 1960 by Jonas Salk, this is now one of the largest independent facilities for biological research in the world. At this writing, the 500-person staff includes four Nobel Laureates. (Ironically, Salk himself was never awarded the prize.) Primary research foci here include molecular and cellular biology and the neurosciences. The Institute's accomplishments are numerous, but many are so technical that they are difficult for general audiences to understand. Among the more comprehensible are the discovery that myasthenia gravis is due to an autoimmune reaction against acetylcholine receptors on muscles (1973), the preparation of monoclonal antibodies selective for human breast cancer (1985), and the determination that axons regulate myelin genes (1988). There is a Tour Office that arranges visits for interested parties.

LOMA LINDA

Loma Linda University Medical Center 11234 Anderson Street 92354. (714) 796-7311. This university medical center had its origins in 1904, when the Southern California Conference of Seventh-Day Adventists purchased a bankrupt health resort on this site with the intention of turning it into a sanatorium for members of their church. By 1906 the institution's scope had broadened, and a school was added "for the training of gospel medical missionary evangelists." The first courses were for nurses; in 1909 the school was renamed College of Medical Evangelists, and the first medical students were enrolled. When the American Medical Association inspected the institution in 1911, the administration of the CME was told that "one-horse medical schools" stood almost no chance of success, and that CME might as well fold up shop. With almost no money, no academic medical experience, and little but their faith and lots of volunteer help to bolster them, the people at CME nonetheless persevered. They raised admission and teaching standards, expanded their facilities as best they could, and in 1913 opened a clinic in Los Angeles (60 miles away) to provide students with more clinical material. The 1915 AMA inspection resulted in a "C" rating (given to unacceptable schools whose diplomas should be regarded as little more than worthless). By 1917, however, the school managed to elevate its rating to a "B," meaning that it was provisionally acceptable; and the 1922 inspection resulted in an "A" rating, placing the school among the better medical colleges in the country. In the eyes of both the AMA and the Adventist Church, the transformation was little short of miraculous. At the time of the CME's opening, in 1910, there had been five medical schools operating in southern California; by 1920 all had closed except this tiny, unendowed Adventist college.

From 1918 onward, most of the college's clinical training went on at the Ellen G White Memorial Hospital, in Los Angeles but maintaining two campuses so widely separated was a continuing drain on the college. However, as Riverside County and San Bernardino County (of which Loma Linda is a part) increased in population, the old sanatorium added hospital beds. In 1961, the College of Medical Evangelists was officially renamed the Loma Linda School of Medicine, and in 1967 a brand new Loma Linda University Medical Center was officially opened. In 1977 the complex was enriched by the opening of the nearby **Jerry L Pettis Veterans Hospital,** named for the first Seventh-Day Adventist congressman.

Loma Linda was a latecomer to medical research but its research in heart transplants among infants has garnered worldwide publicity (and controversy). In 1984, under enormous media scrutiny, the surgeon Leonard Bailey transplanted a baboon heart into twelve-day old "Baby Fae," who had been born with a hypoplastic left heart (Baby Fae died three weeks later). In 1987, Bailey performed a heart transplant on an infant three hours old (the youngest on record), using as donor a living but brain dead anencephalic infant. LLUMC has now performed two-thirds of all successful infant heart transplants worldwide, and has an 85 percent success rate.

Today LLUMC is the educational touchstone for the worldwide Seventh-Day Adventist health care system, which encompasses some 540 institutions in 68 countries. Schools here include nursing, dentistry, and public health, as well as other allied health professions, and a significant number of graduates continue to be involved in missionary work. The principal building dates from 1967, but subsequent additions have resulted in a hospital with a 630-bed capacity. Tours are available through the Community Relations office, and brochures describing a self-guided walk-through tour are usually available at the Information Desk. Visitors may make special arrangements to tour the **Alfred Shyrock Museum of Em-**

bryology, a teaching resource that focuses on specimens illustrating embryologic and fetal development. Included are uterus specimens of women who have died in pregnancy or during abortions. Also on display are full-term babies exhibiting various deformities and anomalies, some linked to various medications and toxins.

LONG BEACH

Amberry Foot Museum 2454 Atlantic Avenue 90806. (213) 426-3321. This is the podiatric office of Thomas Amberry, DPM, but it also may be the largest collection of foot-related clutter in the world. Dr Amberry has been collecting anything and everything related to feet for many years, and his free-standing office building is the repository for all that he has gathered. You may even see his "toe truck" parked out in front—a three-dimensional counterpoint to the huge "foot mural" that decorates the outside of the building. The interior is crammed—floor, walls, ceilings, shelves, furniture—with images of toes and feet: foot rugs, foot tables, foot lamps, foot planters, foot photos and paintings, ashtrays, cookie jars, bottles, and 9000 items of foot-related paraphernalia of every kind. Dr Amberry welcomes visitors, every weekday except Wednesday, during ordinary working hours.

LOS ANGELES

Los Angeles County – University of Southern California Health Sciences Campus 1200 North State Street 90033. (213) 226-6501. The history of the University of Southern California School of Medicine includes the stories of three separate schools. The first was established in 1885, in a building that had functioned as the Vaché Frères Winery. The large basement, which had been used to store wine casks, was quickly converted for storage of cadavers and anatomic specimens. The school got off to a strong start, but by 1906 it was unable to provide the expensive scientific and laboratory facilities required by twentieth-century medicine on tuition and fees alone. In 1909 it became the Los Angeles Department of the School of Medicine of the University of California, an arrangement which survived only briefly, as it meant students had to travel 500 miles, to Berkeley, for their preclinical studies.

Meanwhile, the state had chartered the College of Physicians and Surgeons of Los Angeles in 1903. The dean was a colorful physician known as Diamond Tooth Charlie (because of the diamond filling in one of his teeth) whose practice was especially devoted to "fancy women." When the old USC School of Medicine hooked up with the University of California, Diamond Tooth Charlie allied his school with USC, forming the College of Physicians and Surgeons, Medical Department of the University of Southern California. This school fared poorly; by 1920 it had no applicants at all, and was forced to suspend operations.

After an eight-year hiatus, USC opened its third medical school. In 1930, with the financial pressures of the Depression, this school had to suspend its junior year; but it soon reestablished itself as a four-year operation. USC's modern era began in the 1950s, when it built a new modern facility adjacent to Los Angeles County Hospital.

The Los Angeles County Hospital was founded in 1878, and now — at 2045 beds — is the largest teaching hospital in the country. Though it has provided teaching facilities for USC since 1885, it came under USC's exclusive control only in the 1960s, when Loma Linda moved to its new campus and the California College of Medicine moved to Irvine. The present 100-acre campus includes more than a dozen USC buildings and even more LA County structures. Tours can be arranged with the administration.

University of California, Los Angeles Medical Center 10833 LeConte Avenue 90024. (213) 825-9111. Though this is one of the more prestigious medical centers in southern California, the institutions here are of relatively recent vintage. The UCLA School of Medicine was established by the California legislature in 1946, and received its first students in 1951. The first patients were admitted here only in 1955. The Neuropsychiatric Institute and Brain Research Institute opened in 1960, and the Jules Stein Eye Institute was added in 1964. Significant accomplishments here include the first total shoulder replacement (1976) and the first stereotaxic cobalt unit in the United States (1980).

The current medical center includes — in addition to the 700-bed University Hospital and associated institutions — schools of nursing, dentistry, and public health. Tours are available from the Medical Center Volunteers (825-6001).

St Vincent Medical Center 2131 West 3d Street 90057. (213) 484-7111. When it was established, in 1856, this was one of California's first hospitals. Responding to a request from local citizens, six Daughters of Charity trekked from the East Coast to care for orphans and to teach. As part of the bargain, they also founded a small hospital to care for sick and injured individuals without means who were far from their homes — stagecoach drivers, seamen, travelers, and itinerant laborers. Originally called County

Hospital, it was renamed Los Angeles Infirmary in 1869. The hospital continued to grow; in 1918 the name was changed once again, this time to St Vincent Hospital. The present site dates from 1923, and the principal building from 1975. One interesting aspect of the hospital's current incarnation is that it has a 16-bed patient wing designed for Japanese-speaking patients, the only such facility in the mainland United States. Amenities include a Japanese-language orientation video and a diet that includes miso soup, shaved dried fish, shredded seaweed, and tofu. Tours are available from the Volunteer Office.

Cedars-Sinai Medical Center 8700 Beverly Boulevard 90048. (213) 855-5000. Though the roots of this institution go back to 1902, its present incarnation as a super-hospital for the stars is of relatively recent origin. The Kaspare Cohn Hospital opened as a tuberculosis asylum in 1902 and was later transformed into the Cedars of Lebanon Hospital. The Mount Sinai Hospital began as the Los Angeles Home for the Incurables in 1921, as one response to the devastation caused by the national influenza epidemic of a few years earlier. Cedars of Lebanon joined with Mount Sinai in 1961; the current huge, modern, combined facility dates from the late 1970s.

Though Cedars is mainly known to the public as the hospital of choice for many of Hollywood's rich and famous (there's a Steven Spielberg Pediatric Research Center and a George Burns and Gracie Allen Cardiology Chair, to mention just a few names associated with the institution), this is a place that has compiled an impressive record of medical milestones over the years. Among the major achievements is the development of the Swan-Ganz catheter, to monitor the condition of cardiac patients (HJC Swan and William Ganz), in 1965.

The 1120-bed CSMC does not currently offer any tours.

White Memorial Hospital 1720 Brooklyn Avenue 90033. (213) 268-5000. The namesake of this hospital was Ellen G White (1827–1915) — a remarkable woman by any standard, and one regarded by Seventh-Day Adventists as a messenger of God. Though she received less than three years of formal schooling, she wrote knowledgeably on numerous subjects; her published output (all initially written in longhand) totaled more than 25 million words. It was her astounding accuracy as a prophetess, derived from some 2000 "visions" experienced during her lifetime, that first brought her to public attention, as she successfully predicted the shot at Fort Sumter that started the Civil War, the San Francisco earthquake of 1906, and many other events large and small. It was she whose counsel led to the founding of Loma Linda University School of Medicine and to the founding of this hospital.

The College of Medical Evangelists was established in 1910, but inspection by the AMA quickly made apparent the fact that the school had insufficient clinical facilities to win accreditation. The school was located 60 miles away in what were then the wilds of San Bernardino County, but the Adventists decided to erect a clinic in the closest population center, which was then Los Angeles. The costs of the operation threatened to bankrupt the entire denomination, but the Adventists erected first a dispensary on Boyle Avenue and, in 1918, the Ellen G White Memorial Hospital. This continued to be the primary clinical training site for the College of Medical Evangelists until the founding of the Loma Linda University Medical Center, in the early 1960s. In 1919, when the University of Southern California's School of Medicine lost its accreditation and was expelled from the Association of American Medical Colleges, many of its stranded juniors and seniors received their clinical education here.

White Memorial still plays a role in the education of Loma Linda students; but it is also increasingly a community hospital, offering bilingual services to nearby Hispanic and Asian communities. The hospital's history is nicely illustrated in a "Heritage Corner" on the main floor. Tours of the 300-bed facility are available through the Public Relations Office.

Former Ross-Loos Medical Group (now CIGNA Hospital) 1711 West Temple Street 90026. (213) 413-1313. When the Ross-Loos Medical Group was established, on April 1, 1929, it was the country's first prepaid group practice. Prepayment itself was not new (there had long been such programs in the railroads, the lumbering industry, and the merchant marine), and neither was group practice (the Mayo brothers had pioneered the concept before the turn of the century); but Ross-Loos was the first to fuse the two concepts. Dr Donald Ross and Dr HC Loos were partners in a medical practice that contracted with the Department of Water and Power in Los Angeles to provide medical care to 1500 employees and their families. The operation was so successful that soon other groups signed up, including firemen, teachers, librarians, policemen, and many others. By 1932 there were 8000 subscribers; by 1935 there were 38,000; and by 1941, there were 77,000. During World War II the group employed 265 physicians, nurses and technicians.

The group's rapid growth, coinciding with the onset of the Depression, generated considerable controversy. Physicians in general were hard-hit by the Depression, with average net annual incomes dropping from $6500 in 1929 to $2700 in 1933. In the latter year, over 30 percent of California physicians earned less than $2000, while Ross-Loos salaried physicians were paid from $4200 to $6000. The medical group had both the advantage of serving primarily civil servants, whose positions offered both professional and financial security, and the luxury of a large fund created by the normal advance payment of $2 per insured worker per month.

The local medical community saw the Ross-Loos physicians as treating a captive group of patients, who were deprived of free choice of physicians. The Ross-Loos doctors were themselves seen as captives whose salaried positions prevented them from being free agents in prescribing treatment. The whole prepaid system was likewise seen as "communistic and socialistic." In 1934, Drs Ross and Loos were tried by the Los Angeles County Medical Association on the grounds of unethical conduct, and were expelled from the organization. The event sparked a national controversy, with passionate adherents on both sides. In 1936 the Judical Council of the American Medical Association largely resolved the controversy by determining that Drs Ross and Loos had not had a fair trial and therefore should be reinstated in the county medical society.

The Ross-Loos Medical Group continued to thrive into the late 1940s; but by the 1950s, it was no longer growing. The Kaiser Foundation Health Plan, which had begun more than a decade after the Ross-Loos group, had half a million subscribers in the Los Angeles area in 1960, when Ross-Loos had only 40,000. In 1980, Roos-Loos sold much of its stock to INA Healthplan, Inc; and in the mid-1980s, the name of the Ross-Loos Medical Center was changed to CIGNA Hospital of Los Angeles. Tours of the current building (completed in 1973) are available through the CIGNA administration.

Martin Luther King, Jr/Charles R Drew Medical Center 1621 East 120th Street 90059. (213) 563-4960. This medical center was a direct outgrowth of the unrest of the 1960s, in which 265 American cities experienced racial upheaval. After the rioting in Watts in 1965, the governor of California appointed a commission to study the circumstances that had led to the catastrophe. The McCone Commission concluded that one factor was the absence of good, accessible health care within the community. The result was the 480-bed Martin Luther King, Jr, Hospital (completed in 1972), where medical care and teaching services are provided by the privately run Charles R Drew Postgraduate Medical School, under contract to Los Angeles County, which operates the hospital. Drew currently offers 14 approved residencies, ranging from anesthesia and dentistry to orthopedic surgery. In 1981 Drew expanded its program to include an undergraduate medical training program, "in response to community needs for broader career opportunities for minorities and women." Currently, Drew and UCLA offer a combined program in which medical students take their basic science training at UCLA and their clinical training at Drew. In 1986, Drew began the process of applying for accreditation as a four-year medical college. Tours of the 26-acre site are available through the Public Relations office.

Los Angeles County Medical Association Library and Museum 634 South Westlake Avenue 90057. (213) 483-4555. Spacious, comfortable, and friendly — this is as artful a presentation of medical history as you will find. The Los Angeles County Medical Association (LACMA) is the largest organization of its type in the country, and membership support of its library and museum has led to excellent collections in both areas. (Ironically, many thousands of dollars also come in each year from the almost 100 attorneys and law firms who are subscribing members of the library, in return for which they are allowed to do research both to defend and to prosecute malpractice suits.) Exhibits at the time of my visit included pre-Columbian medical artifacts, Roman surgical instruments, a small but choice collection of antique microscopes, and a large alcove devoted to the subject of medicine and music. There's also a large museum storage room where everything is pretty much in a jumble, but the staff will be happy to show you anything in which you have a special interest. A prize item is a decalcinated skull, fragilely afloat in oil of wintergreen, displayed in a lighted glass box. One of the appeals of the LACMA Museum is that it is located in a "transitional" neighborhood, inconveniently located for daytime visits from most of its members, whose offices are some distance away. The result is that the museum is almost totally deserted and the dozen employees will not only be delighted to see you, they will have time to show you around. The building is a short drive from downtown, with a parking lot next door. It's open during ordinary business hours.

OAKLAND

Kaiser Foundation Hospital 280 West MacArthur Boulevard 94611. (415) 428-5000. The Kaiser Permanente Medical Care Program is a vast enterprise, stretching across the country to 16 states and the District of Columbia. It has become our nation's largest health maintenance organization and, in these unsettled times, the most stable. Kaiser employs some 6100 physicians, 10,500 registered nurses, and 50,000 others to provide services to over 6 million members nationwide.

The Kaiser Permanente program began in 1945 as a West Coast phenomenon, with 26,000 members. The program traces its roots to the Mojave Desert, where, in 1933, founder Dr Sidney Garfield established a 12-bed hospital to care for workers building the aqueduct that would bring water from the Colorado River to parched Los Angeles. Although Garfield began his operation on a fee-for-service basis, he soon discovered that switching to a prepaid monthly fee would make medical care more affordable for the workers, that financial considerations would not become an obstacle to providing appropriate care, and that his group of doctors still would be assured of a predictable and comfortable income. At the request of Kaiser Industries, Garfield set up a similar program in 1938 for Kaiser workers (and their families) at the construction site for the Grand Coulee Dam in Washington. When World War II began, Henry Kaiser talked Garfield into organizing prepaid medical services at shipyards in northern California and in Oregon, and near a Kaiser steelmill at Fontana in southern California. At the conclusion of the war, when the shipyards closed, Garfield and his physicians decided to continue the program, with considerable encouragement and financial backing from Henry Kaiser.

This Oakland facility was Kaiser Permanente's first urban medical center. The site housed a hospital as far back as 1887, when the Oakland Homeopathic Hospital and Dispensary erected the Fabiola Hospital here. The name Fabiola was taken from the Roman matron who founded the first hospital in Western Europe, in 380 AD. Kaiser purchased the facility in 1942. Since that time, growth has been steady; now Kaiser operates 15 hospitals and 27 medical office locations in northern California alone. In the San Francisco Bay Area, 29 percent of the population are Kaiser members; the percentage exceeds 40 percent in some communities.

Kaiser's string of hospitals owes its development to a curious irony. In the early years of the program, organized medicine was so fiercely opposed to the idea of prepaid group practices that Kaiser physicians were often denied membership in local medical societies. Lacking such membership, Kaiser physicians were excluded from staff privileges at community hospitals; without such access for its physicians, Kaiser had no choice but to build its own hospitals.

Kaiser is actually not one, but three organizations, which work in concert: the Kaiser Foundation Health Plan (which acts as an insurer, selling prepaid coverage to members); the Kaiser Foundation

Hospitals (which builds and operates the medical facilities); and the Permanente Medical Group (a physician-run group practice that contracts with the other two organizations to provide medical services).

An early Kaiser innovation was the dual choice requirement. Previously, all health insurance plans had counted it a blessing if they could be exclusive providers for any given group. Kaiser, to avoid having its health plan members feel trapped in a program they didn't want, required all groups offering its plan to offer at least one other indemnity plan so that all potential members could have a choice.

The Kaiser phenomenon has been extensively studied for its national implications, especially with regard to cost control. In 1987, for example, Kaiser averaged 387 hospital days per 1000 members, whereas the comparable figure for the fee-for-service sector was 650 days. Despite such savings, numerous studies have indicated that care for Kaiser patients is as good as, if not better than, that for patients in the fee-for-service sector.

The Oakland Kaiser facility does not offer tours for the public.

ORANGE

University of California, Irvine, Medical Center 101 City Drive 92668. (714) 634-5678. The University of California, Irvine, College of Medicine is located nearby in Irvine, but the college's clinical departments and facilities are located here. The medical school originated as the Pacific Sanitarium and School of Osteopathy, in Anaheim, in 1896. The name changed several times in the next two decades, and the school ultimately merged with the Los Angeles College of Osteopathy, to form the College of Osteopathic Physicians and Surgeons, in 1914.

In 1962, after California passed a public referendum prohibiting the licensing of new DOs (doctors of osteopathy) in the state, the college was converted to an allopathic institution under its present name. This institution, as part of an understanding involving the California Medical Association and the California Osteopathic Institution, then granted some 2500 medical degrees to licensed DOs in the state, in return for a $65 processing fee and attendance at a brief seminar. Many observers predicted that osteopathy soon would be completely absorbed by allopathic medicine and that the remaining five osteopathic colleges would either die or be absorbed by conventional medical schools. After a long court battle, the California Supreme Court ruled in 1974 that the state must resume licensing DOs; a new osteopathic medical college was chartered in

Pomona, California, a few years later. (There are now 15 osteo-pathic colleges in the country.)

In 1976, UC Irvine acquired the Orange County Medical Center and renamed it the UC Irvine Medical Center. (The OCMC had its roots in a county jail medical facility, begun in 1896, and became the County Poor Farm and Hospital in 1913.) UC Irvine has tried for a number of years to establish a hospital complex on its university campus, but these efforts have so far been unsuccessful. The UCIMC is located on a 33-acre tract, the centerpiece of which is a 493-bed hospital. Tours can be arranged by calling 856-4617.

Orange County Dental Society Museum of Dentistry 295 South Flower Street 92668. (714) 634-8944. The doorway to the Dental Society here opens directly onto working offices liberally decorated with vintage dental cabinets and equipment, many of which are used as plant stands and storage spaces for office supplies. The collection, however, is so extensive that it spills out into meeting rooms, a bathroom, and hallways. A couple of large rooms are devoted solely to museum exhibits. There are re-creations of several period offices, as well as interesting displays on porcelain and vulcanite dentures, gold-foil technology, obtunders, casting devices, articulators, and much more. The most historic item is a partial plate of four incisors that was reputedly worn by George Washington. Be sure not to neglect the photos and engravings hung about the office walls. The museum is customarily open to visitors during normal working hours, but it would be wise to call first.

PALO ALTO

Stanford University Medical Center Stanford University Campus 94304. (415) 497-2300. Stanford's is the oldest medical school in the far-western United States. Chartered in San Francisco in 1858 by Dr Samuel Cooper, the school was first called the Medical Department of the University of the Pacific, since it acquired its right to grant degrees by virtue of its nominal link to the San Jose-based University of the Pacific. The medical school survived until 1864, when it ceased operations after the death of its founder. Revived in 1870 by Dr Cooper's nephew, Levi Cooper Lane, the school functioned as the Medical College of the Pacific until 1882, when it was renamed Cooper Medical College in honor of its original founder. In 1908, Stanford University adopted the school as its own; the school was moved from its San Francisco location to the Palo Alto campus in 1959.

The move to Palo Alto was accompanied by a bold new sense of direction. The school recruited a dazzling faculty, including two who were already Nobel Prize winners and others who were destined for similar honors. Since that time, the Stanford University Medical Center has been one of the nation's pacesetters in medical education and research. Accomplishments include:

1956   First use of the linear accelerator to treat cancer in the Western Hemisphere

1968   First human heart transplant in the United States

1972   First construction of a recombinant DNA molecule, using DNA from two different species

1979   Discovery of dynorphin, a brain chemical 200 times more powerful than morphine

1981   First successful heart-lung transplant in the world

1981   First successful use of monoclonal antibodies to treat cancer

Stanford Medical Center, "A Mayan palace in a eucalyptus grove"(*Credit: Stanford University Medical Center Photo*)

When the sumptuous school and hospital were constructed, in 1959, the resulting complex was called "a Mayan palace in a eucalyptus grove," and indeed it's still quite a sight to see. Stanford is the most beautiful medical school in the country, but recent additions have not enhanced its appearance—and it's unlikely that future building projects will do any better. The original buildings were designed by Edward Durell Stone and featured lavish use of pierced-stone grilles and screens and hanging gardens. The original three-story complex is actually seven buildings, but the whole is so artfully combined around landscaped inner courtyards, and interconnected by a continuous patterned grillwork, that the entire center seems to be a single integrated unit. In front of the main entrance, embraced by two of the main building's wings, lies a reflecting pool that occupies a whole block and features multiple islands and fountains.

In 1982 Stanford embarked on a major remodeling and expansion program. The addition has been grafted onto the northern end of the original building. It has many attractive features, but suffers by proximity to the original.

Visitors who are simply interested in doing some sightseeing can get a map of the facility at the information desk near the front entrance and wander through the public spaces. If you are there between 11 AM and 2 PM, have lunch in the garden patio, amidst trees and hedges, with green-and-white table umbrellas and awnings to protect you from Palo Alto's seemingly perpetual sunshine. Or you can snack in the Galleria, in a cheery atmosphere of colorful vending carts brightened by the skylights in the three-story-high ceiling. A tour is available every Thursday at 1:30 PM, but you must be over 14 years of age, and you must reserve a place in advance. Special tours can be arranged for any weekday by calling the Public Events Office (723-6389).

SACRAMENTO

University of California, Davis, Medical Center   2525 Stockton Boulevard 95817. (916) 453-3096. The University of California, Davis, School of Medicine was founded in 1963 and admitted its first students in 1968. When the school was established on the Davis campus, the administration had hopes that a VA hospital and a university research hospital could be built on the same campus. In what was thought to be a temporary measure, the school sent its students to the Sacramento Medical Center, a county facility, for clinical training. The Davis VA hospital was never built; and in

1970 voters failed to approve a major bond issue, squelching hopes for an on-campus university hospital in Davis. At about the same time, Sacramento County decided to get out of the hospital business, as a result of major changes in the state Medi-Cal Act. In 1973, ownership and operational responsibility for the Sacramento Medical Center was transferred to the university. The result is that the UCDMC is located 18 miles from the medical school buildings on the Davis campus. The UCDMC site has housed hospitals since 1871, when the Sacramento County Hospital (founded in 1852) first located here. Though the current 467-bed hospital dates from the early 1980s, some of the 57 buildings on the 90-acre Sacramento campus were erected as early as 1916. Tours are available through the Special Events Office (453-2844).

SAN DIEGO

University of California, San Diego, Medical Center 255 Dickinson Street 92103. (619) 543-6222. The UCSD Medical School was formally established in 1962, but it was 1969 before the first class was enrolled. The medical school was constructed on the main UCSD campus, close by the world-famed Scripps Institution of Oceanography; thus the medical program could take advantage of the rich basic science resources available at Scripps. Initially, the general university departments were included in the medical school faculty, and pure biologists, mathmeticians, and others helped to design the medical students' curriculum. In the early 1970s, UCSD sophomore students twice ranked first in the nation on the basic science exams conducted by the National Board of Medical Examiners. UCSD senior students, however, did less well on their clinical exams in relation to the rest of the country; the result has been a shift away from "pure science" toward a more even balance with clinical science, a policy facilitated by the construction of a 600-bed Veterans Administration Medical Center immediately adjacent to the School of Medicine.

The UCSD Medical Center is actually 12 miles from the UCSD medical school. Beginning in 1966 the university operated the San Diego County Hospital under a lease arrangement; but in 1981 the university purchased the site and turned it into the present UCSD Medical Center. The Center is also the site of the California Teratogen Register (established in 1979), the world's only data-collecting and-dispensing system concerned with substances potentially hazardous to unborn babies.

Tours are available through the Communications Department.

SAN FRANCISCO

University of California, San Francisco, Medical Center Parnassus Avenue 94143. (415) 476-2557. UCSF is one of nine campuses operated by the University of California, and the only one devoted solely to the health sciences. Within its boundaries are four schools — medicine (founded 1864), pharmacy (1872), dentistry (1881), and nursing (1939) — that consistently rank at the top of their respective professions, plus dozens of other teaching, research, and service programs.

The School of Medicine began in 1864, when Dr Hugh Toland decided to take advantage of the demise of the Cooper Medical College (see "Stanford University Medical Center," above), electing to start his own enterprise near the San Francisco City and County Hospital. Toland then gave the school to the University of California, in 1873. It moved to Parnassus Heights in 1895. When the earthquake and fire hit San Francisco in 1906, the school buildings were turned into a makeshift hospital. The first true hospital on this site was built in 1917.

UCSF, with over 9000 employees, operates one of the biggest payrolls in the area and, with a yearly budget of over half a billion dollars, is a financial power that the city is simply unable to ignore. As with the other major medical centers across the country, calling UCSF an educational complex would be misleading. This is a bigtime industrial operation.

Among UCSF's many achievements are the following:

1931	First isolation and purification of vitamin E (Herbert Evans)
1965	First doctorate in nursing science in the United States
1973	Development of the genetic engineering technique for producing recombinant DNA (by Herbert Boyer, together with Stanford's Stanley Cohen)
1976	Discovery of oncogenes, genes capable of producing cancer (JM Bishop and Harold Varmus)
1976	Development of prenatal diagnosis, allowing the detection of sickle cell anemia in fetuses (Yuet Wai Kan and Mitchell Golbus)
1979	First cloning of the gene for human growth hormone (John Baxter and Howard Goodman)
1981	First successful in-utero surgical procedure (Michael Harrison, to correct a urinary tract defect)

The campus occupies over 100 acres, sitting astride Mt Sutro, with a magnificent view (fog permitting) of the city, the ocean, and the Golden Gate. Still, the campus feels much smaller than that, and the principal buildings can all be inspected in a short stroll along Parnassus Avenue (named after the Greek mountain favored by Apollo, father of Aesculapius — the first physician).

Visitors interested in medical history will want to visit the old UC Hospital Building (533 Parnassus Avenue), and find their way to Toland Hall (room U142). If the lecture hall is not occupied, visitors are free to enter and look around. What you will see is an old-fashioned amphitheater, built like a half-drum, with curving rows of seats in tiers reaching practically to the ceiling. Around the walls on all sides are some remarkable frescoes, painted by Bernard Zakheim in 1937 and 1938, as part of the Federal Arts Project. They depict California's medical history, from earliest times to the early years of the twentieth century. Events portrayed range from California's first autopsy (performed by Sir Francis Drake's ship's surgeon in 1579) to contemporary researchers investigating Weil's disease and psittacosis.

Just west of the UC Hospital Building is the modern and very attractive School of Dentistry Building, stepping down a hillside in layers of broad terraces, covered with greenery. Much of the credit obviously goes to the architects (John Funk & Associates, 1980), but honors must be shared by UCSF's neighbors, the organized and outspoken residents of the surrounding area, who vigorously and effectively opposed the university's efforts to build yet another high-rise, high-density building.

For a visual treat (and perhaps a snack as well), visit the Milberry Union Student Center (500 Parnassus Avenue). The cafeteria offers an unusual and spectacular view of the western part of the city, with the Golden Gate Bridge beyond. The best view on the campus is from the anatomy lab (admission by special arrangement), where the cadavers offer a grisly contrast to the beauty outside.

A 90-minute tour of the campus is given every Tuesday at 1 PM, departing from the lobby of the Medical Building (513 Parnassus Avenue). No advance arrangements are required. Arrange special tours by calling the Campus Tours and Speakers Bureau (476-4394).

Former Wright Army Hospital (now Presidio Army Museum) Presidio of San Francisco 94129. (415) 561-3319. The most historic medical building in San Francisco no longer has any medical-function, but it may still interest architectural-and medical-history buffs. The Presidio's first hospital was initially built in 1856 and then rebuilt, in 1863, with materials shipped around Cape Horn. The original exterior remains essentially intact but with various additions, most notably an octagonal 3-story tower, 19 feet in diameter, built in 1897 for laboratory use. The result is a bit of an architectural hodgepodge, but still an elegant wood frame building with handsome verandas and balustrades. The hospital treated casualties of the Spanish-American War and World War I, and treated countless civilians during the 1906 earthquake and fire. It served as an outpatient clinic in the post–World War II years, and became the Presidio Army Museum in 1973. The current Presidio medical facility is the nearby Letterman Army Medical Center, whose present quarters date from 1969. The museum has a small display on medical care during the Civil War and a few photos depicting the building's evolution, but otherwise concentrates on military history. Open Tuesday through Sunday, 10 AM to 4 PM. No admission charge.

Laguna Honda Hospital 375 Laguna Honda Boulevard 94116. (415) 664-1580. This, the nation's largest municipal long-term care facility, had its beginnings in 1866 as an "ambulatory residence" for 500 homeless and unemployed men. A 24-bed hospital was added in 1868 during a smallpox epidemic. For many years, there was no clear distinction between Laguna Honda (which means "deep pond," a reference to the nearby reservoir that for many years was San Francisco's chief source of water) and the San Francisco General Hospital. Medical and surgical functions operated on a comparable basis in both institutions. Laguna Honda underwent a dramatic expansion after the 1906 earthquake and fire, when it became a center for relief and emergency housing. By 1926, the facility housed over 1500 residents. Much of the labor was performed by the patients themselves, who were paid for their efforts in either wine or whisky. In 1911–1912 the liquor budget was $4760. Today Laguna Honda functions as a skilled-nursing facility for 1000 patients, but there is also a 30-bed acute-care hospital. A measure of the ethnic diversity of the clientele is the schedule of weekly church services, which includes Spanish Catholic Mass, Ancient Tridentine Mass, and Russian Orthodox, Greek Orthodox, Lutheran Chinese, and Jewish rites. The buildings here date from 1909. Tours are available by advance arrangement with the administration.

San Francisco General Hospital 2000 Portrero Avenue 94110. (415) 821-8200. Like most other city and county hospitals in major metropolitan areas, this place is a workhorse. True, some research goes on here, and SFGH is a major teaching facility for the University of California, San Francisco, but the primary activity is the care and treatment of huge numbers of patients, many of them desperately poor and extremely sick.

The present site of SFGH has been in use since 1872, when the city constructed a wood-frame hospital here. Although the building survived the 1906 quake, it became so badly infested by bubonic plague–carrying rats that it was purposely burned down in 1908 (patients were temporarily transferred to the Ingleside Jockey Club Race Track, where they were bedded down in horses' stalls). The replacement buildings, completed in 1915, were of Italian Renaissance design, mostly red brick embellished with terra cotta ornamentation. A few of the buildings remain, as does the wrought-iron fence with its elaborate iron filigree gate facing Portrero Avenue. The combination gives a good feel for what an attractively designed turn-of-the-century county hospital could be like. The current hospital is attractive in its own way, but its massive concrete form makes a stark contrast to the rich selection of materials and the intricacy of detail in the older buildings.

The hospital's hallways are filled with people speaking Spanish, Cantonese, Vietnamese, and Tagalog; the languages suggest the cultural diversity of San Francisco, for which the hospital must provide staff and interpreters. SFGH has one of the pioneer trauma services in the country, now treating some 75,000 patients a year, 65 percent of them sufficiently critical to require admission. The hospital is also proud of its AIDS treatment program, begun in July 1983 — the nation's first inpatient program devoted to this deadly disease.

There are no tours and no amenities for visitors, but interested individuals are welcome to view the public spaces.

Former Harkness Hospital (now Mercy Terrace) 333 Baker Street (at Fell) 94117. (415) 931-2325. Though now a residential complex for senior citizens and handicapped persons, this is a reminder of what was once America's pioneering railroad health plan.

Building the railroad into the old West was hazardous work, and much of it was done in areas without towns or medical resources. The Central Pacific Railroad began providing medical services for its employees in 1867, and built its first hospital, in Sacramento, in 1870. It was the first hospital in the country devoted solely to railroad employees. The program was financed by having each employee (except the Chinese, who presumably were expected to fend for themselves) contribute 50 cents a month. Other railroads soon followed the Central Pacific's model, building hospitals of their own: the Missouri Pacific (1872), the Northern Pacific (1882), the Wabash (1890), and the Santa Fe (1891). At the peak of the railroad hospital system, some 40 railroads throughout the country operated 35 hospitals with a total of 3700 beds.

Once the Central Pacific Hospital had been built, the railroad employed doctors at intervals along its track system to look after ill and injured employees and passengers and then to send them on to the hospital in Sacramento for continued care, if necessary. In 1887, when the railroad changed its name, the hospital became the Southern Pacific Railroad Hospital. In 1898, the company moved its corporate headquarters to San Francisco, and the hospital soon followed. The result was that the new hospital (at 14th and Mission streets) was destroyed in the earthquake and fire of 1906. The patients (and the facility) were then transferred back to Sacramento. In 1921 the hospital returned to San Francisco, and the present structure was built. At first it had 300 beds; a major addition in 1931 (funded by Edward Harkness) resulted in a 50-percent expansion and the new Harkness Pavilion. Also in 1931, the Southern Pacific opened a second hospital, in Tucson, Arizona, for use primarily as a tuberculosis sanatorium. By this time, employees were being charged $1.50 a month for health coverage.

The Southern Pacific Railroad Hospital (also known as Harkness Hospital) continued in operation until 1975, when it closed down amid allegations of financial mismanagement. (In the late 1980s, despite a dramatic reduction in railroad employees nationwide — from a peak of 2 million to the current 300,000 — there were 14 other railroad medical programs still in existence.) When its medical division ceased operation, the Southern Pacific had this 450-bed hospital, the 100-bed hospital in Tucson, and 18 emergency "hospitals" at intervals along 13,000 miles of track, plus 250 doctors under contract.

There are currently no arrangements for tours here, but the recently refurbished hospital, former nurses' residence, laundry, and other buildings still remain, looking on the outside much as they did in 1931.

Chinese Hospital 835 Jackson Street 94113. (415) 982-2400. Sooner or later, everyone in San Francisco finds their way to Chinatown, but most visitors miss the Chinese Hospital. This facility, though not very distinguished architecturally (except for a vaguely Oriental cast to the roof of the adjacent clinic building), is one of the few remaining examples of an era when the United States had many ethnic hospitals in every major city. San Francisco, for example, had a German Hospital (now Franklin Hospital), a French Hospital (purchased in 1989 by Kaiser Permanente, the ethnicity long since gone), and a Maimonides Jewish Hospital (now an assimilated Mount Zion Hospital). The Chinese Hospital is therefore something of an anachronism. The present institution is an outgrowth of the

Tung Wa dispensary, founded in 1900 by the Chinese Six Companies for the care and treatment of the poor. Now the hospital is a thoroughly modern facility, with a full range of inpatient and out-patient services. What sets it apart, however, is that everything about it is bilingual, Chinese and English — from the sign out in front, to the entire staff, to every piece of written material. Tours of the Chinese Hospital are available by advance arrangement.

San Francisco Veterans Administration Medical Center 42d Avenue and Clement Street 94121. (415) 221-4810. This site was designated the City Cemetery Reservation until 1883, when it was purchased by the Army for use as a coastal defense battery. Named Fort Miley, it remained a military installation until 1930. The site was then turned over to the Veterans Administration; the Fort Miley Veterans Administration Hospital was dedicated in 1934. Four days after the Japanese attack on Pearl Harbor, in 1941, rising concerns about the hospital's vulnerability to attack led to the evacuation of 350 patients. The hospital was quickly ringed with mobile guns, and stayed vacant until after the end of the war.

The SFVAMC sits perched on the cliff that forms the San Francisco side of the Golden Gate strait, and offers an unimpeded view of the inlet to the Bay as well as of the Marin headlands on the other side. In a city known for its extraordinary views, this unique and spectacular vista has somehow escaped all the guidebooks. To reach the best vantage point, simply follow the drive around to its northernmost side. The grounds are open to the public. Or you can visit the hospital cafeteria (also open to visitors), which is nicely situated to take advantage of the view. Don't neglect the outstanding examples of governmental art-deco architecture (with Spanish-Mayan overtones) offered by the older salmon-colored buildings, which date from 1934 and were some of the earliest governmental projects designed to be earthquake-resistant. The smaller buildings at the northeast corner of the property hark back to the days when the Veterans Administration constructed homes for five key people at all of its hospital sites: the hospital director, the chief of medicine, the chief of psychiatry (where there was one), the assistant director, and the chief engineer. The practice of building quarters was halted in the 1950s by the Office of Management and Budget, but many such quarters (including some of the ones here) are still used as residences. The huge new wing that dominates the view from Clement Street was completed about 1980 and now contains almost all the patient-care facilities.

There is no formal tour program.

Haight-Ashbury Free Clinic 1698 Haight Street 94117. (415) 431-1714. The Haight-Ashbury Free Clinic opened during 1967's "Summer of Love" and was the forerunner of more than 300 free clinics scattered around the country. Everyone was treated regardless of ability to pay, supplies were donated, the staff was entirely volunteer, and the clinic's credo was "that treatment should be nonjudgmental, demystified, and delivered as humanely as possible," with a minimum of red tape. At first the clientele were largely alienated, dropped-out youth with a predominance of problems related to drug use and sexual activity, though a large number of Third World clients were added in the 1970s. Among the clinic's innovations were establishing "calm rooms" for people on "bad" acid trips and a Rock Medicine Emergency Service, to provide emergency care at rock concerts and other large gatherings. The clinic's building suffered a major fire in 1988, but it continues to function out of temporary quarters, providing health services for everyone in need with "no fee, no patronizing and no moralizing." There are no tours for the general public.

Sun Yat-Sen Statue St Mary's Square (California Street off Grant Avenue) 94108. The most revered health professional of all time, admired by over a billion Chinese as "the Father of the Revolution," is Dr Sun Yat-Sen. Dr Sun began his medical studies in Canton (at what is now called the Sun Yat-Sen College of Medicine), but after a year transferred to Hong Kong, where he became the Hong Kong Medical School's first graduate, after five years of study ending in 1892. Dr Sun was an accomplished surgeon who practiced for varying lengths of time in Canton, Macau, and perhaps even in Maui, Hawaii. He became a US citizen in 1904, claiming falsely that he had been born in Hawaii. At the time, Dr Sun was a refugee from China, where the Manchus had put a reward of half a million dollars on his head for his efforts to overthrow the dynasty; so it's not surprising that he resorted to subterfuge to protect his life. Dr Sun spent considerable time in San Francisco raising money and organizing the ultimately successful plot to overthrow the Manchus. The statue that honors his memory, a sleek 12-foot monument of stainless steel and rose granite, was sculpted by Benjamino Bufano.

Site of Headquarters of Painless Parker 15 Stockton Street 94102. San Francisco loves its characters, but somehow it has missed putting up a plaque for that remarkable tooth plumber, the terror of ethical dentistry known as Painless Parker, DDS. When he died, in 1952, Parker was running a chain of 28 dental offices out of this Stockton

Street address, employing 80 dentists and 240 dental workers. At the time, his was the largest (and one of the first) dental group practices in the world; he was both revered and despised as one of the country's all-time great pitchmen, easily a match for Buffalo Bill or PT Barnum. Born Edgar Rudolph Randolph Parker in 1872, he took his dental training in New York and Philadelphia and developed a theory that most people stayed away from dentists for four reasons: ignorance, fear of pain, procrastination, and lack of money. Parker resolved to combat all four, taking his trade to the people with cut-rate dentistry, dispensed from a wagon, ballyhooed with an educational talk mixed with a circus extravaganza, all dissolved in the feeble local anesthetic hydrocain. Gathering crowds with his trusty cornet, Parker was an overnight sensation. By 1892 he had taken his garishly painted wagon on the road, pulling the teeth of Blackfoot Indians in Alberta and Eskimos in Alaska. Soon he added a piano player and, not long after that, a circus troupe with sword swallowers, bearded ladies, Irish tenors, and belly dancers. He filed the teeth of circus tigers and implanted diamonds in the front teeth of anyone who could pay the toll. Once, near Poughkeepsie, New York, Parker pulled 357 teeth in the light of a single day. "It was a savage and barbaric scene," Parker would later say. "The woods rang with the cries of the wounded." Ethical dentists, struggling for professional respectability, hated Parker and did what they could to curtail his popularity, deprive him of his professional credentials, and derail the incredible money train that continued to move in his direction. State after state passed laws prohibiting "dental surgery in the manifestly unsterile atmosphere of the street." A 1915 law prohibiting dental trade names (like the nom de pliers "Painless Parker") resulted in Edgar Rudolph Randolph legally changing his name to Painless Parker, DDS. Some states passed laws prohibiting dental advertising and corporate dentistry, on grounds that such practices were detrimental to the doctor-patient relationship. Parker broke these and other laws so many times that his license was often revoked or suspended. Ultimately, it was the progress of scientific dentistry as a profession that did in Parker and his emulators. Tooth plumbers and medicine-show dentistry faded, but Parker kept running his extravaganza up until his last year, working full days, most of them including the pulling of a dozen teeth or more. The old flatiron building from which Parker ran his enterprises is now gone. Perhaps someday there will be a plaque.

Museum of Ophthalmology 655 Beach Street 94133. (415) 561-8500. If you are interested in unusual museums, this one is a dandy, the

American Academy of Ophthalmology, Museum Interior (Courtesy of the Ophthalmic Heritage Department, The Foundation of the American Academy of Ophthalmology, San Francisco, CA)

only one of its kind in the world. Ophthalmology is medicine's oldest specialty. Among other claims to priority, ophthalmology established the first medical specialty board in America, in 1916. This museum, founded in 1980, is part of the Department of Ophthalmic Heritage operated by the American Academy of Ophthalmology and located on the third floor of the organization's headquarters. Most of the displays are in a single room, spread out behind the Academy's receptionist, but other items are scattered throughout various offices. If you want to see the whole collection, be sure to call in advance to make arrangements. The collection has been beautifully preserved and maintained, and has been organized in as tasteful and appealing a fashion as you are likely to find anywhere. The more than 3000 artifacts date back to the fourteenth century and include spectacles, lorgnettes, monocles, and other visual aids; pharmaceuticals, nostrums, and sundries; diagnostic and surgical instruments and ophthalmologic office furniture; art, photography, memorabilia, including postage stamps and coins; and a remarkable collection of historic ophthalmologic literature. Be sure to see the case full of handblown glass eyes, all of which have been staring out at the world since 1850. Glass eyes such as these are increasingly rare. (Most eye prostheses made in the US are now plastic, cheaper than glass and less fragile. Glass eyes — which are hollow, as opposed to the solid plastic globes — are still popular in Europe, but in the US are used only by traditionalists and those allergic to plastic.) The museum is easily accessible to anyone taking in the San Francisco tourist sites. It's located across from the Cannery at the end of the Hyde Street Cable Car line. Open Monday through Friday, 8 AM to 5 PM. Tours can be arranged in advance. Admission free.

AW Ward Museum of Dentistry of the University of the Pacific School of Dentistry 2155 Webster Street 94115. (415) 929-6400. This school dates back to 1896, when it was incorporated as part of the College of Physicians and Surgeons of San Francisco. The medicine and pharmacy divisions folded in 1918, but the dental school continued to thrive. For many years it carried on a flirtation with Stanford University (whose medical school was located across the street, and which even now lacks a dental school), but ultimately decided on a marriage to the University of the Pacific, a Stockton-based institution whose 1851 charter makes it the oldest private university in the state. The attractive and modern facility houses a museum (named after a San Francisco periodontics pioneer) which contains dental artifacts spanning more than four centuries. Exhibits spill out into the adjacent hallway and student lounge. During my visit, there was an interesting exhibit on the evolution of high-speed drills, as well as a variety of dental instruments and office furniture. Museum hours are variable, but are currently limited to Thursday and Friday afternoons. Call first.

Health Sciences Library 2395 Sacramento Street 94115. (415) 563-4321. Designed in 1912 by Albert Pissis, this classic-revival building was originally intended to house Stanford University's Lane Medical Library. After Stanford transferred its medical school to Palo Alto, in 1959, the building stayed mostly vacant for 10 years. It was reopened in 1970 as a joint project of Pacific-Presbyterian Medical Center (the geographic offspring of the old San Francisco–based Stanford Medical Center) and the University of the Pacific School of Dentistry (an entirely separate institution), and was extensively and tastefully remodeled over a number of years. The result is a building that retains the most attractive ornaments and features of the original sandstone edifice, yet houses a contemporary and thoroughly functional medium-sized health sciences library. The collection is particularly strong (including historical works) in anesthesiology, cardiology, ophthalmology, and dentistry. Be sure to see the oval staircase, with its ornate cast-iron railing winding down seven stories from the top of the building to the foyer. The huge main reading room displays a series of medically oriented murals painted by the California artist Arthur F Mathews. Open weekdays, 8 AM to 9:30 PM, and Saturdays 9 AM to 5 PM.

TIBURON

Lyford's Stone Tower 2034 Paradise Drive 94920. This circular sandstone tower is a relic of an age when "hygiene" was a national obsession. It was built in 1889 by Dr Benjamin Lyford to mark the entrance to the development that he called Hygeia, after the Greek goddess of health. An associated archway and office have been torn down, but the basic layout of old Tiburon, with its 10- and 20-footpaths between adjacent properties, reflects Lyford's original plan. It stands as mute testimony to a period when pioneers like Lyford imagined utopian communities, with healthful living the dominant value. An 1895 pamphlet about the development maintained that "The one supreme possession of man . . . is health." The turn of the century was a time when hygiene captured the American mind as few things before had done. In the wake of growing understanding of bacteria and communicable-disease transmission, Americans became fervent believers in sanitation and healthful living. Flyswatters were introduced, public drinking cups and spitting were outlawed, and sanitary engineering flourished. Lyford's Hygeia was a short-lived attempt to capitalize on these enthusiasms; but his Tower remains, an enduring symbol of turn-of-the-century hygienic ideals. On the edge of the road, abutting San Francisco Bay, and always open, it's a pleasant place for contemplation or just viewing the sights.

COLORADO

COLORADO SPRINGS

Penrose Hospital 2215 North Cascade 80933. (719) 630-5000. Colorado became a mecca for consumptives in the early 1880s. At first there were no real provisions to accommodate persons with the "white plague." Sufferers seeking the healthful mountain air merely appeared and found lodging wherever they could: on ranches, in mountain cabins, in boarding houses in Colorado's cities. Among the many hopefuls who came here were dozens of physicians; in the early twentieth century, as many as a third of

Colorado's physicians had come to the state seeking relief for tuberculosis, either for themselves or for members of their families. The first tuberculosis sanatorium in Colorado was the Albert Glockner Memorial Sanatorium, founded in 1890. Patients were charged a dollar a day; the sanatorium's benefactor, Mrs Glockner, made up the difference between operating costs and patient revenues. The sanatorium soon proved to be a financial drain, however, so Mrs Glockner bequeathed it to the Sisters of Charity of Cincinnati. The Sisters turned the Glockner into a viable operation, and it gradually expanded. In 1941 Julia Penrose endowed the Penrose Cancer Hospital, in memory of her husband, and in 1947 the combined facility became known as the Glockner-Penrose Hospital. As tuberculosis ceased to be a major focus of the hospital, and as the Penrose contributions became larger, the Glockner name was dropped from the hospital's charter.

Colorado Springs had a number of sanatoriums, the most ritzy of which was the Cragmor, a place where social graces and country-club living often obscured the limitations of invalids. It was said that the two physicians who directed the Cragmor had a talent for arranging matches between their well-heeled patients, for whom the pursuit of a TB cure was sometimes less important than the pursuit of one another. After tuberculosis ceased to be a major public health problem the Cragmor was leveled; its former site is now the location the University of Colorado at Colorado Springs. Of the original sanatoriums, only the Glockner survives, in the form of the present-day Penrose. Today, Penrose Hospital is the flagship of the Penrose–St Francis Healthcare System, which includes about a dozen facilities in the area. No tours are currently available.

DENVER

University of Colorado Health Sciences Center 4200 East Ninth Avenue 80262. (303) 399-1211. The first medical school in Colorado began as the Medical Department of the University of Denver (later called the Denver Medical College) in 1881. It remained the dominant school in the state for the next two decades, and the opening of the University of Colorado Medical Department (in Boulder) two years later provided little competition. The Boulder operation was initially distinctive in that it was open to both sexes and was tuition-free. Despite these inducements the UC medical school had continual problems in attracting students, and in 1893 the school's clinical years were transferred to Denver, where the clinical resources were more ample. In 1897, however, the State Supreme Court found this move unconstitutional, and the medical school once again installed its program in Boulder. Meanwhile, the Denver Medical College and an 1887 offshoot, the Gross Medical College, decided to combine, in 1902, to form the Denver and Gross Medical College. A Denver Homeopathic Medical College, founded in 1894, managed to survive until 1904.

The Flexner Report doomed the Denver and Gross Medical College and paved the way for the University of Colorado's ascendancy. Flexner recommended that "The State alone . . . can hope to obtain the financial backing necessary to teach medicine in the proper way, regardless of income and fees, and to it a monopoly should quickly fall." Thus, in 1911, the existing schools were consolidated under the state's aegis, with the program to be continued in Denver. A new 17-acre campus was dedicated in 1925, and the predecessor of the modern UCHSC was born.

The present UCHSC includes the Medical School, the School of Nursing (established 1898), the School of Pharmacy (1911), the School of Dentistry (1973), University Hospital (1921), and a variety of other affiliated institutions. Over the years the UCHSC has developed an enviable record of medical firsts:

1962	First identification of the "battered child" syndrome
1963	First genetic counseling team
1963	First liver transplant in the world
1965	Development of the Denver Developmental Test for evaluating developmental progress in growing children
1969	First nurse practitioner program in the country
1970	First Division of Perinatal Medicine in the world classifying human chromosomes

Tours are available through the Public Relations Office (270-5571).

Denver General Hospital 777 Bannock Street 80204. (303) 893-6000. This hospital, Colorado's oldest, had its beginnings as the Arapahoe County Poor Farm in 1860. It was founded mainly to care for the steady stream of settlers who arrived sick and penniless after their exhausting trip across the prairie. This site was purchased in 1873, and the resulting facility was called the County Hospital. At the same time the city established a pest house, in what is now the southeast corner of Cheesman Park; this was eventually replaced by the Steele Hospital for Contagious Diseases, on the County Hospital grounds. In the 1880s, Denver reportedly had more typhoid fever cases than New York City. The name of the ever-enlarging complex was formally changed to Denver General Hospital in 1924.

Like most city-county hospitals, this one had its share of scandals about mismanagement and abuses. As a reform move, in the 1940s, the hospital was placed under the general direction of Dr Florence Sabin, who was manager of the Department of Health and Charity. This remarkable woman physician, then in her seventies, who had previously been Johns Hopkins Medical School's first woman professor, was such an inspired leader that she eventually was nominated to become one of two Colorado citizens honored in the Capitol Statuary Gallery in Washington, DC.

In 1974, DGH developed the first "Poisonindex" computerized information system for the diagnosis and treatment of acute and chronic poisoning. The system is now used around the world. In 1976 the hospital developed the standard treatment for acetaminophen (Tylenol) overdoses.

Tours are available.

National Jewish Center for Immunology and Respiratory Medicine 1400 Jackson Street 80206. (303) 388-4461. In 1890 Colorado was being besieged by a steady stream of consumptives from Eastern cities who had heard that the dry mountain climate would cure their disease. For some, relocation was sufficient to arrest the disorder; but for many indigents the trip to Colorado simply meant death from starvation and exposure. A small group of civic-minded Jewish citizens decided to found a hospital to cater to these mostly indigent visitors, and founded the Jewish Hospital Association of Colorado. In 1892 the cornerstone of the new hospital was laid, inscribed with these words: "As pain knows no creed, this building is for all who come. We consecrate this structure to humanity, to our suffering fellow man, regardless of creed." Unfortunately Denver's Jewish community exhausted its resources in completing the $40,000 building, and the structure remained empty for the next seven years. The project was rescued when the national Jewish men's organization, B'nai B'rith, adopted the endeavor for their fund-raising project; in 1899 the National Jewish Home for Consumptives opened its doors as the nation's first free interfaith hospital for the treatment of tuberculosis and other respiratory ailments.

In 1925, the hospital became a principal teaching facility for the University of Colorado School of Medicine and changed its name to the National Jewish Hospital at Denver. By mid-century, tuberculosis was no longer a major public health problem; National Jewish decided to focus on asthma and other chronic respiratory diseases. In 1978 it merged with the National Asthma Center (which had been opened in 1907 as a shelter for children whose parents had tuberculosis), to form the world's largest research and treatment center devoted primarily to asthma. Currently the nation's only medical center focusing entirely on respiratory and immunologic disease, National Jewish adopted its present name in 1985. One in five of the nation's pediatric allergists has trained here.

National Jewish has had a strong research emphasis from its early years and has been the source of many important medical developments: e.g., the allergy molecule, IgE, was first identified here in 1966, and the human T-cell receptor gene was first isolated here in 1984.

National Jewish is now a sprawling modern campus of a dozen buildings, stretching from Colfax to Fourteenth Avenues, from Jackson Street to Colorado Boulevard. Tours are available through the Development Office.

CONNECTICUT

FARMINGTON

University of Connecticut Medical Center Interstate 84 at Exit 39 06032. (203) 679-2000. This huge and unusual complex occupies a hilltop about 7 miles west of Hartford. Its dominant portion is a 10-story building with a single curvilinear elbow in it. The ground, both in front of and behind the elbow, is covered with some low-rise, fan-shaped structures and, beyond them, acres and acres of terraced parking lots.

Connecticut decided to build a combined hospital and medical and dental school complex in the 1960s for the usual reasons that states undertake such an expensive endeavor. Connecticut already had one superb medical school (Yale), but it was private, very expensive, and enrolled 90 percent of its students from out of state. The only dental schools in New England were in Boston (at Harvard and Tufts). Connecticut was thus a net importer of physicians and dentists, and local young men and women who wished to enter these health professions either needed extraordinary financial resources or had to get in line for the small number of spots available to Connecticut residents at out-of-state publicly supported schools. The fact that the WK Kellogg Foundation ponied up more than a million dollars in seed money helped to turn the tide. The first students began classes in temporary quarters in 1968, with phased occupancy of the health center beginning in 1972.

What makes this center unusual is the close interplay between the medical and dental divisions, in some ways a Hartford-area legacy of Horace Wells, whose discovery of nitrous oxide anesthesia united the two professions over a century ago. In the Medical Center, the result of such interdisciplinary cooperation is superb programs in such areas as craniofacial disorders, chemosensory problems related to taste and smell, and oral pathology.

There is a small but very nice dental museum on campus in the hallway directly below the main patients' entrance lobby. A dozen or so display cases have been gathered together that showcase old instruments and the like. There is also a wonderful Victorian velvet dental chair. Requests for tours are welcome. Call (203) 679-1123.

HARTFORD

Institute of Living 400 Washington Street 06106. (203) 241-8000. This beautiful collection of buildings, set on a serene and gorgeously landscaped 35-acre campus, houses one of the country's oldest and most influential psychiatric facilities. The Hartford Retreat was modeled after England's York Retreat (opened in

The Institute of Living, Burlingame Center for Research and Education *(Courtesy of The Institute of Living Archives)*

1796), whose principles were simple: elimination of all abuse of the mentally ill, and the substitution of abuse with a regimen designed to rebuild the confidence and self-esteem of the patients. They were to be kept busy at agreeable tasks such as gardening, hobbies, household duties, games, music, and the like, with the principal therapeutic remedies being a wholesome diet, and warm baths and tonics, including wine and foaming tankards of beer. As elementary as all this sounds today, it marked a radical departure from the beatings and physical abuse which were routinely visited upon the mentally ill in the eighteenth century. More importantly, it worked. Tuke refused to call his institution an "asylum," thinking the word carried too many negative connotations. He instead opted for the name Retreat.

The Hartford Retreat's first superintendent built the hospital into a model institution, and physicians came to the Retreat from all over the country to learn how to set up similar institutions. The Retreat's most famous patient arrived in 1901. Clifford Beers was a remarkable man who was also a manic-depressive, a "certified looney" hospitalized for three years in his twenties and again at the conclusion of his life. He was an Horatio Alger of psychiatry, who overcame a bleak prognosis to become a phenomenally successful fund raiser and an innovator who originated the mental hygiene movement of the 1920s and 1930s, a movement which captured the imagination and hopes of a whole generation of medical leaders, educators, and philanthropists. His book about his experiences as a psychiatric patient, *The Mind That Found Itself*, originally printed in 1908 and never out of print since, remains the classic patient's account of mental illness. Beers was twice admitted to the Retreat, the first time undergoing considerable unpleasantness, including what he describes as inappropriate restraint. The second time he chose the Retreat over three other hospitals he had also been in, and his experience was a positive one.

Over the years, the leaders of the Retreat gradually came to feel that the hospital's name no longer captured the spirit of the evolving institution. The word "retreat" seemed to imply escape, a sojourn from real life, and even defeat. In 1943, the name was changed to Institute of Living. Though located on the edge of downtown Hartford and in a congested area, the campus itself is remarkably peaceful. The grounds were designed and originally landscaped in the 1860s by Frederick Law Olmsted, of Central Park fame. The result is a botanist's dream and now includes some of the oldest trees in the country as well as the state's largest pecan, ailanthus, sweet gum, honey locust, bur oak, English oak, and ginkgo trees.

The architectural style of the Institute is varied, ranging from contemporary to early nineteenth century. The original stucco Center Building, with its distinctive gothic spires, was built in 1823, though the wings on either side were added later. The Terry Building was originally built as a residence for the hospital superintendent in 1846. The Tudor brick-and-beam buildings date from the 1940s, when Dr. Burlingame was the Retreat's superintendent, and reflect his architectural preference. The tall brick building with the gold dome and the gold-embossed caduceus emblems just below it on four sides dates from 1942 and is named for Burlingame.

Tours of this attractive and inviting campus are available to health professionals only, by advance arrangement [call (203) 241-6909].

Horace Wells, DDS, Statue Bushnell Park (between the Capitol Grounds, Trinity, Ford, and Asylum Streets). In the United States, there are generally three schools of thought about where the greatest credit for the discovery of anesthesia belongs: the Boston view, the Georgia view, and the Connecticut view. This statue is a concrete expression of local sentiments. The inscription reads HORACE WELLS THE DISCOVERER OF ANAESTHESIA DECEMBER 1844.

On December 10, Wells attended a demonstration at the Union Hall based on the entertaining qualities of laughing gas, or nitrous oxide. One of those who inhaled the gas badly scraped his leg while under the influence, but had no awareness of pain until the gas wore off. Wells alertly made the connection, and the next day he arranged to test the pain-killing qualities of the gas. He himself was the research subject. He asked a dentist with whom he shared office space to extract a molar from his mouth, and Wells felt no pain whatever. This was clearly a momentous event, and Wells tried to make the most of it. After repeating the experiment more than a dozen times with patients, he journeyed to Boston to give a demonstration at the Massachusetts General Hospital. A fellow dentist, William Morton, arranged the details. Alas, this time the gas supply was inadequate. When the patient's molar was extracted, he screamed in pain, and Wells was jeered and booed out of the room by the students and other onlookers. Boston later bestowed the credit for the discovery of anesthesia on Morton, who demonstrated the usefulness of ether on October 16, 1846.

Wells subsequently went on to Paris, where his demonstrations were dramatically successful (Wells was given an honorary Doctor of Medicine degree); but he never really got over his experience in Boston and the fact that public recognition for the development of anesthesia went to others. Wells became quite despondent, abandoned his family, and went to New York. There he was arrested for allegedly throwing sulfuric acid on some women, and he committed suicide in jail in 1848 at the age of 33.

Still, Wells is credited by the American Dental Association, the American Medical Association, and the French Academy of Medicine with having discovered the clinical utility of anesthesia — so the statue here (unveiled in 1875) is an expression of much more than just a local viewpoint. Wells might also have gained some satisfaction from the knowledge that, a century and a half after his death, nitrous oxide is still in common use for anesthesia, whereas ether is of only historical interest. Bushnell Park is a beautifully landscaped 40-acre site, dotted with numerous statues and monuments, more or less bounded on three sides by the Park River. The Wells statue is in the eastern section, near the intersection of Trumbull and Jewell Streets.

Historical Museum of Medicine and Dentistry　230 Scarborough Street 06105. (203) 236-5613. This unique museum is jointly sponsored by the local medical and dental societies, and its collections are almost entirely made up of donations by members of these two groups. Still, this is not simply a museum of local interest. It showcases a huge collection that traces the development of health care technology and paraphernalia from the Revolutionary War era to the present. One publication has claimed that, after the Smithsonian in Washington, this museum contains the largest collection of medical Americana in the country. The claim may well be true.

The museum is located in the Hunt Memorial Building, which both houses the offices of the Hartford Medical Society and is where the Hartford Dental Society holds its meetings. Though the museum came into being only in 1973, it has grown so rapidly that it now occupies the entire building, including the walls and surfaces of a number of the offices, as well as hallways and stairwells. One room is a re-creation of a dental office circa 1920; another is devoted to Horace Wells; and a third focuses on floor-model medical equipment, including electrocautery and diathermy, and a collection of basal metabolism measuring units. A lot of love and attention has gone into the collection and display of these items. Hand instruments — many with handles of teak, rosewood, ivory, mother-of-pearl, and snakewood — have all been beautifully restored.

At the time I visited, the museum had an extensive display of some 40 doctor's bags, with an informative brochure describing their place in history. The doctor's bag originally served as a container for obstetrical instruments. The familiar black-handled valise came on the scene in the late nineteenth century, replacing the physician's saddlebag (also on display) as the buckboard and "tin lizzie" supplanted the horse as the doctor's primary mode of transportation. The doctor's bag started disappearing in the latter half of the twentieth century, as doctors stopped making house calls and all surgical instruments and paraphernalia were supplied by hospitals, where physicians increasingly treated their patients. Nowadays, few doctors own a "doctor's bag," and fewer still actually use them.

There are some wonderful items here that I've seen nowhere else. There are old copper and wood leg splints, large collections of laboratory bunsen burners, some foot-treadle operated dental drills, and a case of obstetrical instuments containing some dilators and forceps and (ominously) a hack saw. The museum is open weekdays from 10 AM to 4 PM, and the admission is free. Groups can make special arrangements to see the collection on weekends.

LEBANON

William Beaumont Homestead and Birthplace Village Green 06249. Until 1975, this building was located some four miles away in the Village Hill area, where it was subjected to recurring vandalism. In that year, members of the Beaumont Homestead Preservation Trust arranged to have it dismantled board by board and stone by stone and relocated on the Lebanon village green, alongside several other historic buildings, where it could be watched more closely.

William Beaumont was born in this building in 1785. He went on to study medicine by the apprentice system ("reading medicine," it was called) in Vermont and later became an army surgeon in the War of 1812. In 1822, he was stationed at Fort Mackinac, Michigan, where he had occasion to attend Alexis St. Martin for a gunshot wound to the abdomen. The wound never healed properly, leaving St. Martin with a permanent opening between his skin and the interior of his stomach. After some three years of trying to heal and repair the opening, Beaumont realized he had a golden opportunity: the first recorded chance to monitor the digestive processes of the human stomach. Beaumont seized the moment and, in the process, became America's first physiologist. His work and his meticulously recorded observations had profound impact on the development of physiology around the world. Museums honor him in Mackinac Island and in Prairie du Chien, Wisconsin. He is memorialized by the Beaumont Medical Club (a medical history organization in New Haven) and various other organizations and sites around the country.

The Beaumont Homestead was first tracked down in 1920 by one of the founders of New Haven's Beaumont Medical Club, and the Trust for its preservation was finally established in 1970. The place has been gradually restored and now includes some genuine Beaumont memorabilia, as well as a variety of period pieces chosen to illustrate how the home might have looked during his life there. One room includes a replica of an early 19th century doctor's office, though there is no evidence that Beaumont ever returned to the homestead once he became a physician.

The building is open to the public on Saturdays from 1 PM to 5 PM, from mid-May to mid-October, or by appointment through the Lebanon Historical Society [call (203) 642-6825].

LITCHFIELD

Oliver Wolcott House South Street, near intersection with Wolcott Avenue. This is a private home and not accessible to the public. Still, it is the oldest home in Litchfield, built in 1753 by one of the five physicians who signed the Declaration of Independence and, as a result, is worthy of our notice. Wolcott came from one of the most prominent families in Connecticut. He practiced medicine for a while in Goshen (about six miles north), had a distinguished military career (attaining the rank of Major General), and served his country and his state in a variety of political roles. He may well be the only person in US history to be a governor, the son of a governor, and the father of a governor. From this house on South Street, Wolcott journeyed to the Continental Congress. When the Sons of Liberty tore down a statue of George III, they transported it to this yard, where Mrs. Wolcott melted down the metal to make bullets for local troops. Likewise, when George Washington paid a visit to Litchfield, it was in this house that he slept. There is no marker on the house, but it is directly across the street from the Tapping Reeve School, America's oldest law school, which is clearly marked and has a small museum that showcases the history of the area. The Wolcott home is a pleasant stroll from the Litchfield village green.

The four other physicians who signed the Declaration of Independence (out of fifty-six signers in all) were Josiah Bartlett and Matthew Thornton of New Hampshire, Lyman Hall of Georgia (who graduated from Yale with Wolcott in 1747), and Benjamin Rush of Philadelphia.

NEW HAVEN

Yale – New Haven Medical Center 333 Cedar Street 06510. (203) 785-5824. Yale College has the distinction of having bestowed the first medical degree in America. Though lacking a medical school at the time (1729), Yale gave Daniel Turner an MD in return for a large donation. Local commentators said the initials stood for "multum donavit," which means "gave plenty". The medical school itself was chartered in 1810 as a joint creation of Yale College and the Connecticut Medical Society, and it wasn't until 1884 that the school came under the sole control of Yale.

The Yale–New Haven Hospital, though intertwined with the medical school from its earliest years, is technically a separate entity, which traces its origins to 1826, when it was chartered as the fourth voluntary general hospital in the country, preceded only by the Pennsylvania Hospital (1751), New York Hospital (1771), and the Massachusetts General Hospital (1811). The hospital's name has evolved through a number of changes over the years, assuming its present form in 1965. The facility has been the site of numerous important medical developments, including: the first clinical use of penicillin in the Western hemisphere (1942); the development of the prototype of the modern heart-lung machine (1949); the use of the world's first labor and delivery suite equipped for fetal monitoring (1960); the first use of chemotherapy in cancer treatment (1942); the first hospital to allow newborns to "room in " with their mothers (1944); and the first ICU for newborns (1960).

The hospital's school of nursing was originally founded in 1873 as the Connecticut Training School for Nurses, the country's third Nightingalian program for nurses, after those at Bellevue and the Massachusetts General Hospital, both of which were established in the same year. When it was only six years old, the Training School published the nation's first nursing handbook. This institution likewise underwent several name changes over the years, eventually becoming the Grace–New Haven School of Nursing, which closed its doors in 1975. The Yale School of Nursing began in 1923 and continues today as one of the nation's premier programs.

The YNHMC is composed of almost three-dozen buildings, for the most part filling a triangle bounded by Congress and Howard Avenues and North Frontage Road. The YNH Hospital (20 York Street) was completed in 1982 and is a bright, modern structure, characterized by lots of windows, courtyards and artwork splashed on many of the walls.

However, the most impressive building in my opinion is located half a block away at 333 Cedar Street. This location is generally referred to as the Sterling Hall of Medicine, the principal home for the school of medicine, but—as the engraved granite portico reveals—the building was also once home to the Institute of Human Relations, an interesting experiment in humanizing medical care that could provide some instructive lessons for anyone attempting a similar exercise today.

The Institute of Human Relations was the brainchild of Milton Winternitz, a charismatic and idealistic leader who became the medical school dean in 1920. Winternitz proposed a program of clinical sociology in which medical students would be trained to be social physicians, cognizant of and sensitive to the myriad behavioral, social, and cultural factors which influence how illness is expressed in any given patient. Over seven-and-a-half million dollars were raised for this endeavor (an enormous amount of money at the time), and a new building was erected immediately adjacent to the medical school, sharing the same entrance. The Institute was dedicated in 1931. This attempt at medical humanism lasted about four years, ultimately being discarded as too bold, too idealistic and diffuse, and simply impractical given the scientific and technologic imperatives of modern medicine. All that is left now is the engraved name above the entrance on the left, in theory still balancing the engraved name Sterling Hall of Medicine, which stretches across the curved portico to the right.

Sterling contains numerous medical school offices and facilities, including the Yale Medical Library, which is approached through the Cushing Rotunda. Harvey Cushing was a Yale graduate, who went on to become the nation's first full-time neurosurgeon. A brilliant and meticulous surgeon, he almost single-handedly succeeded in reducing brain surgery mortality from close to 100 percent to less than 10 percent. He was at Johns Hopkins from 1896 until 1912, when he became chief surgeon at the Peter Bent Brigham in Boston. In 1926, he received the Pulitzer Prize for his biography of Sir William Osler. He returned to Yale in 1933, and remained here until his death in 1939. Once in the two-story Cushing Rotunda, topped with a stained-glass skylight and usually decorated with rotating historical displays, you can either turn right into the general library or left into the historical library. While the general library is outstanding in its own right (it contains over 350,000 volumes), its component, the Yale Medical History Library, is unique and so special that it is worth a trip to New Haven entirely for its own sake. The History Library was dedicated in 1941 and its reading room looks the way a historical library should: a long hall with a fireplace at the far end, the plank floor establishing the proper woodsy tone, with two stories of filled wood bookcases arrayed along the walls both left and right, topped by gothic-style leaded windows and a high vaulted ceiling, the lighting both subdued yet perfect for reading. This historical collection was begun by Harvey Cushing and two friends, and has now become one of the

Yale Medical School Historical Library *(Courtesy of Harvey Cushing/John Hay Whitney Medical Library)*

four or five best history of medicine collections in the country. (Cushing's contribution is honored here by a re-creation of his Yale office, filled with memorabilia, including a couple of baseballs from Yale–Harvard and Yale–Princeton games, as well as copies of his various publications. The office, to the left as you enter the historical library, looks just as he might have left it after a busy day.) The gifts of the three original donors consist of over 25,000 volumes, and are particularly strong in anatomy, physiology, and pathology texts from the sixteenth, seventeenth, and eighteenth centuries. The collection includes over 300 incunabula (books printed before 1501), as well as large numbers of titles by Hippocrates, Galen, Vesalius, and Harvey (most of which are hidden away in closed substacks but are nonetheless sometimes available for viewing). There are also vast numbers of prints, paintings, portraits, engravings, and other museum-type items which are intermittently put on display. Outside the library proper, just before you enter the Cushing Rotunda, are two small displays well worth a few minutes' attention. One is the Streeter Weights and Measures Collection, in breadth and comprehensiveness said to be one of the finest such collections in the world. The other, also donated by Edward Clark Streeter, is an alcove filled with early pharmacy jars (some stunningly beautiful), ranging in origin from 1500 to the 1880s, as well as a fine collection of European pharmaceutical mortars and pestles.

YNHMC does not currently provide tours for the general public. However, if you have a "serious" interest in seeing the historical library, call (203) 436-2566 in advance to arrange access.

DELAWARE

WILMINGTON

Medical Center of Delaware 501 West 14th Street 19899. (302) 733-1000. With almost 1100 beds, this is one of the dozen largest medical centers in the country. The complex includes two acute-care hospitals (the Wilmington Hospital at the address above and the Christiana in suburban Stanton), as well as a 60-bed rehabilitation facility called the Eugene Du Pont Memorial Hospital. The Medical Center as a corporate enterprise dates from 1965, but it traces its origins back a full century.

The Homeopathic Hospital was the first hospital in Wilmington when it opened in 1888. By 1940, the popularity of homeopathy had long since waned, and the hospital was renamed Memorial Hospital. The allopathic hospital, called the Delaware Hospital, opened in 1890 at 14th and Washington; and a third hospital — first called Physicians and Surgeons and later General Hospital — opened in 1910.

By the mid-twentieth century, these three community hospitals were all laboring to survive, none had any educational programs to speak of and all were too small to achieve the economies of scale required by modern, competitive medical centers. When the three decided to merge, they agreed to build an entirely new facility in Stanton, which was a suburb of people who had fled the city woes of Wilmington. A coalition of consumer and civil rights advocates fought the move, which resulted in a long and costly court battle.

When the merger was finally accomplished, the new entity demolished and sold off the Memorial and General divisions, and renamed the Delaware division, calling it the Wilmington Hospital. The 800-bed new hospital, opened in 1985, sits on a 200-acre parklike campus. The rehab hospital, located just outside the Wilmington city limits at 3506 Kennett Pike, dates from 1955 and became affiliated with the Medical Center after the initial merger. Tours of the various components are available through the Public Affairs Office.

DISTRICT OF COLUMBIA
(See Great Medical Cities)

FLORIDA

APALACHICOLA

John Gorrie State Museum Sixth Street 32320. (904) 653-9347. In the early nineteenth century, Apalachicola was quite a shipping center, the third largest port on the Gulf. A young physician named John Gorrie arrived here in 1833 and quickly became involved in most aspects of the town's politics, economy, and culture. During his years here, he functioned as mayor, city treasurer, postmaster, council member, bank director, and founder of one of the local churches. His most important contribution, however, was in medicine. Yellow fever was a major source of morbidity and mortality in those days; and, in Gorrie's continued attempts to be helpful to his patients, he searched for efficient and practical means to cool the tremendously high fevers he encountered. As a result, he invented an ice-making machine, thus laying the groundwork for modern refrigeration and air-conditioning technology. He demonstrated his invention at an international exhibition in Florida in 1850 by cooling the temperature in a specially devised windowless sleeping room. He subsequently received a patent for his invention. This museum recounts the story of the "Ice Man from Apalachicola," displaying various mementos of his life and times, including a replica of his 1851 ice-making machine. The facility is open to visitors Thursdays through Mondays, 9 AM to 5 PM, except for some holidays.

GAINESVILLE

University of Florida Health Sciences Center SW Archer Road 32610. (904) 392-2621. Established in 1956, this center has expanded rapidly to become a major regional medical center. Situated on the greater University of Florida campus, the Health Sciences Center includes six colleges (of medicine, nursing, dentistry, pharmacy, veterinary medicine, and health-related professions), four hospitals, and a variety of other clinical, educational, and research-oriented facilities—and a huge (and expensive) expansion program is currently underway.

The principal hospital on campus is Shands, which began in 1958 as a state agency and converted to not-for-profit status in 1980 so that it could have more flexibility in running its own program and developing its own financial resources.

Since its inception, the center has been responsible for a number of important medical developments:

1958   The College of Health-Related Professions becomes the first of its kind in the country
1975   The Gildred Microsurgery Education Center becomes the first in the country devoted to training surgeons in microsurgical techniques
1976   Shands opens the first computerized cardiac catheterization laboratory in the nation
1988   Neurosurgeons here develop and use the LINAC (stereotactic linear accelerator) scalpel, delivering single doses of radiation to treat brain lesions

This is a big, busy, modern place occupying almost three million square feet of space, with all the principal elements (except the Veterans Administration Medical Center) interconnected. Tours are available to groups upon request through the phone number above. Shands Hospital conducts separate tours via its Volunteers Program [(904) 395-0111].

HOLLYWOOD

Hunter's Funeral Museum 6301 Taft Street 33024. (305) 989-1550. Many morticians regard themselves as health care professionals— in terms of their focus on death and bereavement, their need for knowledge of anatomy and bacteriology, and their role as receivers of the mistakes physicians make in diagnosis and treatment. This is the largest museum of mortuary science in the country, and the collection includes some remarkable items. Hearses once doubled as ambulances, and there are some fine examples of hearses here, including a 1917 Model T Ford hearse and a 1932 Henney hearse. There are various embalming instruments and supplies and morti-

cians' anatomy texts. There's a fine collection of caskets, including a
1500 pound glass model dating from 1922 and a turn-of-the-
century child's casket. Other items include a wicker body basket, a
funeral wreath woven of human hair, and a wide variety of funeral
memorabilia. The museum is next door to the Hunter Funeral
Home, and the collection has been accumulated by three generations of Hunter morticians. The museum is open to the public by
prior arrangement.

MIAMI

University of Miami - Jackson Memorial Medical Center 1611 NW
Twelfth Avenue 33136. (305) 325-7429. The Miami City Hospital
was founded in 1911 when the city assumed control of the faltering
Friendly Hospital. A new building (still standing and known for
years as the Alamo) was erected in 1917. The pink stucco and red
tile building received its greatest international attention when President Franklin Delano Roosevelt was taken here after an assassination attempt in which a misdirected bullet fatally wounded Mayor
Anton Cermak of Chicago. Renamed Jackson Memorial in 1924 (to
honor the hospital's first medical director), the city and county
hospital has gradually developed into a huge medical complex.

In the late 1940s, Florida was the only southern state without a
medical college, though the state had been home to the Tallahassee
College of Medicine and Surgery for a few years in the 1880s. The
legislature was receptive to the idea of establishing a medical
school, but the choice of location and sponsorship became a political football. Miami was the preferred location because of the unmatched clinical facilities of Jackson Memorial, and the University
of Florida was a leading contender as sponsor, though political
machinations hampered its attempts to found a school. In 1952 the
University of Miami, a private school headquartered in Coral
Gables, made an end run around the competition and opened its
own School of Medicine. The first site was in a building leased from
the adjoining Coral Gables Veterans Administration Hospital.
Shortly thereafter, the UM signed an agreement with Dade County
designating Jackson Memorial as the teaching hospital of the
School of Medicine. The University of Florida took another four
years before it convinced the legislature to open a medical school,
this time in Gainesville.

In the 1960s and early 1970s, the UM made a number of savvy
moves to create a major medical center in Miami. The basic science
program was moved from Coral Gables, the Veterans Administra-

tion was inveigled to put a huge hospital on campus, and a Public Health Trust was established to remove Jackson Memorial from direct city and county control. The result is that Jackson Memorial has become the fourth busiest hospital in the US and the largest and busiest in the southeast. Among other accomplishments, family medicine as an academic discipline was born here in 1965; and the first successful islet cell transplant in a patient with insulin-dependent diabetes was performed here in 1985 (by Daniel Mintz and Rodolfo Alejandro).

Today, UM/JMMC occupies a 67 acre campus, which includes the 1250-bed JMH, an 870-bed VA Hospital, the Bascom Palmer Eye Institute, and a dozen other entities. This is a most pleasant campus for strolling. A new pedestrian mall, which extends for five blocks, has been planted with 1600 palm, wild tamarind, and jatropha trees and some 23,000 shrubs and flowers. The park also includes seven fountains, some statuary, and attractive tile and brick work. The hospital's main entrance is guarded by the old Alamo Building, the 1917 two-story Spanish Colonial building which had served as the entire City Hospital and later served variously as an emergency pavilion, nurses' quarters, laboratories, on-call rooms, operating rooms, departmental offices, personnel offices, and chapel. Moved some 475 feet from its original location, the Alamo now serves as an information and welcome center and is home to a fine little medical museum. The museum is open weekdays, 8:30 AM to 5 AM, and tours of the medical center can be arranged through the public relations department [(305) 549-7304].

TAMPA

University of South Florida Medical Center 12901 Bruce B Downs Boulevard 33612. (813) 974-3300. This center dates from 1970. At that time, Florida was experiencing both a huge surge in population and a large influx of tourists. After deciding that the state's one private and one public medical school were not sufficient to provide adequate medical resources for the state, the legislature voted to develop a new college of medicine on Florida's populous west coast. The initial complex was completed in 1976, just after the establishment of a brand new 720-bed Veterans Administration Hospital, which, along with Tampa General Hospital, supplies clinical teaching facilities. The first medical school class graduated in 1974. The current campus also includes colleges of nursing and public health, as well as a variety of other clinical and research facilities. Tours are available from the Public Affairs Office.

GEORGIA

ATLANTA

Emory University Medical Center 1440 Clifton Road NE 30322. (404) 727-5686. The history of the medical school here goes back to 1854, when the Atlanta Medical College was chartered. In 1898, the AMC merged with the Southern Medical College (which had been formed in 1878), resulting in the Atlanta College of Physicians and Surgeons. In 1913, the ACPS merged with the similarly named but separate Atlanta School of Medicine (founded 1905), resulting in a rebirth of the old Atlanta Medical College, which two years later was absorbed by Emory University, a private institution sponsored by the United Methodist Church.

The Emory School of Dentistry had its origins in the Southern Dental College (founded 1887), which in 1917 merged with the Atlanta Dental College (begun in 1892) to form the Atlanta Southern Dental College. The school became a part of Emory University in 1944. The last DDS was graduated here in 1988, after which the school gave up its undergraduate dental program to concentrate on postgraduate training and research.

The current official name for the medical center is the Robert W Woodruff Health Sciences Center, which consists of six divisions. The five on campus are the schools of medicine, dentistry, and nursing, the Emory University Hospital, and the Yerkes Regional Primate Research Center. [The sixth division is the Crawford Long Hospital (see below).] All of these are arrayed along the Clifton Road side of the 550-acre Emory campus, a health professions corridor which also includes the American Cancer Society headquarters, the Centers for Disease Control, and the Egleston Hospital for Children.

This is a vast medical complex, massively impressive, set among forested rolling hills and embraced by Atlanta's plush Druid Hills residential area; the grounds of this imposing campus are attractive indeed. However, there are no arrangements for tours and no displays or attractions specifically designed for visitors.

Morehouse School of Medicine 720 Westview Drive, SW 30310. (404) 752-1730. This medical school was established in 1975 by Morehouse College, a century-old black liberal arts college. First begun as a two-year medical school, the charter class entered in 1978, but it was 1985 before MSM awarded its first MD degree. Now one of four predominately black medical colleges, MSM regards its mission as helping to make up for the shortage of black physicians, particularly in primary care specialties in underserved areas. MSM is adjacent to the liberal arts campus, with an all-new Medical Sciences Building. Clinical clerkships are held primarily at Grady Memorial Hospital, as well as a variety of other facilities. Tours of the MSM campus are available via prior arrangement with the President's Office.

Grady Memorial Hospital 80 Butler Street, SE 30335. (404) 588-4307. Opened in 1892 and named for the editor of the *Atlanta Constitution* who had campaigned for its construction, Grady began with 100 beds for charity patients and 10 for pay patients. Facilities were enlarged and new buildings constructed as the demand increased. In 1898, Grady added a school of nursing for white students and, in 1917, one for blacks. Residence halls for students were added later, for whites in 1922 and for blacks in 1946. Grady's most famous patient was Margaret Mitchell, author of *Gone With the Wind*, who died here in 1949 after being admitted as a trauma victim. Grady is now a huge complex of buildings, with 1000 beds, and caters primarily to Atlanta's indigent population. Patient responsibility is divided between Emory (which has upwards of 75 percent of the beds) and Morehouse (which has the remainder). The principal structure is a 21-story cream-brick monoblock, completed in 1958, with stubby wings sticking out at right angles. A $300 million renovation project is in progress. The original hospital building, Georgia Hall (at Butler Street and Coca Cola Place), will survive, however; current plans are to use it for office space. Also scheduled to endure is the Hughes Spalding Pavilion, erected in 1952 for black patients able to pay customary hospital rates. On the exterior of the main building are two sculpted panels. The one called the "Old South" depicts caring for the sick and wounded during the Battle of Atlanta, and the other (the "New South") portrays key individuals in the area's revitalization (HW Grady — for whom the hospital was named — is among them, but the central figure is the modern doctor). Tours can be arranged via the Public Relations Office.

Georgia Baptist Medical Center 300 Boulevard, NE 30312. (404) 653-4200. Founded in 1901 by Dr. Len Gaston Broughton, a Baptist minister and physician, and a group of women from the Tabernacle Baptist Church, this hospital began in a five-room rented house with three patients. In 1902, the hospital ambitiously added a nursing school and started calling itself the Tabernacle Infirmary and

Training School for Christian Nurses. Overextended, the hospital gradually developed an unmanageable debt. In 1913, the enterprise was acquired by the Georgia Baptist Convention and renamed the Georgia Baptist Hospital. In 1926, it moved to its present location. Now a thriving 523-bed tertiary care medical center, GBMC is a sprawling downtown Atlanta fixture, composed of over a dozen buildings. The nursing school continues to admit only female students, teaching nursing as a ministry of the Baptist Church, training women to help heal the sick. The school now operates the third largest diploma nursing program in the nation. The hospital has installed an Archives Alcove adjacent to the cafeteria in the basement, which offers rotating displays of historical artifacts. Tours are available upon request to the Public Relations Department.

Crawford Long Hospital 550 Peachtree Street NE 30365. (404) 892-4411. Founded in 1908 as the Davis-Fischer Sanitorium, the institution moved to its present site in 1911. When Dr. Davis (one of the founders) passed away in 1931, the hospital was renamed after the famous Georgia physician who had pioneered ether anesthesia almost 90 years earlier. In 1940, the entire hospital was deeded as a gift to Emory and is now the sixth division of Emory's Woodruff Health Sciences Center. The hospital has been the site of two medical firsts:

1939   First successful caesarean delivery of triplets in the US
1988   First Dornier gallbladder lithotripter in the US

CLH is now Atlanta's second largest hospital, with 7 major buildings and 520 beds, spread out over 4 city blocks. The original 1911 building still stands at 35 Linden Avenue, NE. CLH opened a small museum in 1981, dedicated in part to the hospital's history, but also highlighting the history of its namesake, Dr. Crawford William Long (see also Jefferson, Georgia). Exhibits include medical memorabilia, hospital artifacts, documents, surgical instruments, and historical clothing and furniture related to the Long family. The museum occupies a glass-enclosed room off the Peachtree Street lobby, and its hours are currently Monday, Tuesday, and Wednesday, 10 AM to 2 PM. Tours of the entire hospital complex are available by calling the Public Relations Department.

Centers for Disease Control 1600 Clifton Road NE 30333. (404) 639-3286. The CDC had its origins in the rather obscure Office of Malaria Control in War Areas, a program begun to protect servicemen from mosquito-borne diseases. The program was located in Atlanta because mosquito-borne diseases were a problem at southern military training camps. When World War II ended, the office was transformed into a Public Health Service entity called the Communicable Disease Center. As the CDC grew, there were a number of attempts to move it to Washington, DC, but it remains in Atlanta, the only major federal agency headquartered outside of the nation's capitol. The CDC moved to its present Clifton Road location in 1960, and it has been growing ever since. The most recent addition in 1988 was a $20 million virology laboratory.

The CDC has been credited with so many medical advances that it is impossible to list them all. Among the most impressive are

1977	First successful isolation of the organism responsible for Legionnaire's disease
1980	First linkage of toxic shock syndrome to tampon use
1981	First identification of the disease now known as AIDS or autoimmune deficiency disease

Though AIDS has occupied a large and ever-growing portion of the CDC's energies, it was ironically the decline of infectious disease as a dominant public health concern that led the CDC to change its name (but not its initials) in 1970 from the Communicable Disease Center to the Centers for Disease Control. Today, the CDC's mission has broadened considerably to include the prevention of noninfectious diseases and other preventable health problems. Paramount among its current involvements are efforts to control workplace and environmental hazards, monitor toxic waste sites and accidental chemical releases, and assist national and state efforts to prevent smoking-related disorders.

The CDC is now a sprawling presence in Atlanta's Clifton Road health-professions corridor. Over 4000 people work in the red-brick and concrete building complex near Emory University. There are no tours for the general public here, but the main lobby (open during normal working hours) has interesting displays which change periodically. In the auditorium adjacent to the lobby, there is a do-it-yourself slide show which the guard will be happy to show you how to use.

AUGUSTA

Medical College of Georgia Fifteenth Street and Laney Walker Boulevard 30912. (404) 721-0211. The Medical College of Georgia was founded in 1828. Initially called the Medical Academy of Georgia, the college began using two rooms in the city hospital for instruction, but moved to its own building in 1835 (see below). The college closed during the Civil War and nearly closed on two other occasions as well. Flexner found the school beyond hope and bluntly recommended that it be discontinued. MCG somehow survived, stayed in Augusta, and became an official part of the University of Georgia in 1911. It moved to its present location in 1912 and built its own teaching hospital in 1915. During the Depression, the State Board of Regents decided to close MCG due to inadequate finances; but with the support of alumni, local citizens, and the governor, the college revived.

Through the years, the MCG has contributed its share to the development of medical knowledge. In 1821, Milton Antony pioneered chest surgery by removing two ribs and a gangrenous portion of a lung. In 1850, Paul Eve performed the first abdominal hysterectomy, 29 years before the first such operation in Europe.

The MCG campus is now a 93-acre complex with more than 80 buildings, including relatively new schools of nursing, dentistry, and allied health. Tours are available via the Registrar's Office.

Old Medical College Building Telfair Street. This gracious Greek Revival building was constructed in 1835 as the new home for the Medical College of Georgia. It served that function admirably until 1912 (taking time out to function as a Confederate Hospital during the Civil War), when the college moved to new quarters. Since 1912, the building has been put to many uses, serving as a school house for a while, standing vacant from 1926–1931, providing a home for various civic organizations in the 1930s, and housing a USO Canteen during World War II. The building was then maintained as an activity center for the Augusta Council of Garden Clubs until 1988, when it was taken over by the Medical College of Georgia Foundation. After a million dollar restoration is completed in 1990, the building will be used for continuing education, alumni activities, and various community events. Call (404) 721-4003 regarding access.

Signers' Monument Greene Street at Button Gwinnett Plaza. This huge stone spire is dedicated to the memory of the three Georgia signers of the Declaration of Independence, one of whom was Lyman Hall, MD. Hall studied medicine by the apprentice method in Connecticut and moved to Georgia in 1760. While engaged in the practice of medicine, he became an active participant in the politics of revolution. He was Georgia's only representative to the second

Continental Congress. After the Revolution, he practiced medicine
for a while in Savannah, before being elected governor. His body is
buried in a crypt beneath this shaft.

COLUMBUS

Pemberton House 11 Seventh Street 31906. (404) 322-0756. This
place is a shrine for pharmacists and others who dream of riches
and fame — though ironically John Pemberton achieved neither
during his lifetime. Pemberton studied pharmacy at "an eclectic
school of medicine" in Macon, Georgia, and returned to Columbus
in 1853. A restless man with a hunger for experimentation, he
devised Globe of Flower Cough Syrup, Triplex Liver Pills, and
Indian Queen Hair Dye, among other formulas. Anxious to expand
his business, he moved to Atlanta in 1869, where he founded the
Pemberton Chemical Company. It was in Atlanta that he originated
a formula for a soft drink which he called Coca-Cola. By this time,
however, his health was poor and finances marginal, so he sold all
rights to his formula for $2000. When he died in 1888, the drink
was still essentially unknown. Pemberton is buried in Linwood
Cemetery in town.

The Pemberton House, where the man lived from 1855 to 1860,
stands as a memorial to this creative pharmacist. Composed of four
rooms, the house itself is filled with Pemberton family items and
period antiques. The outbuilding was the original kitchen, and it
was here that Pemberton worked at night experimenting with his
concoctions. The interior has been restyled to resemble the laboratory at one of Pemberton's Columbus businesses, the Eagle Drug
and Chemical Company. There are some fine pharmaceutical items
here, including an extremely rare old silver-plated soda dispenser,
and a lot of Coca-Cola memorabilia.

Tours are available through the Pemberton House (and three
other structures which compose the Columbus Heritage Corner)
Monday through Friday at 11 AM and 3 PM, and Saturday and
Sunday at 2 PM. There is a small admission fee. Call for information.

JEFFERSON

Crawford W Long Medical Museum College Street 30549. (404)
367-5307. The controversy about who deserves credit for the discovery of surgical anesthesia may simmer on in Hartford, Connecticut, and Boston, but the matter has been resolved to the satisfaction
of most Georgians: Crawford Long (1815–1858) is the man. Long
was remarkably well trained for a rural physician in the mid-

nineteenth century, having studied at Transylvania Medical College in Kentucky, the University of Pennsylvania, and the New York Hospital. While in the big city, he attended "laughing gas" parties with fellow students. On one occasion, when the laughing gas was depleted, Long substituted sulfuric ether and noticed that the celebrants suffered no pain when they injured themselves while under its influence. He returned to Jefferson (where he had initially been apprenticed in medicine) in 1841, and then used ether as an anesthetic on March 30, 1842, to successfully and painlessly remove a cyst from a patient's neck. This was a full four years before the famous demonstration at the Ether Dome in Boston. While Long continued to use ether for minor operations and tried to convince other doctors to use ether as well, he neither wrote up his experience nor sought fame. However, when he found that others were claiming priority and the $100,000 prize offered by Congress, he entered the fray. The controversy wasn't resolved during the

Crawford W Long Museum in Jefferson, Georgia *(Courtesy of Crawford W Long Museum Association, Jefferson, Georgia)*

lives of the contestants and the prize money was never awarded. Long, however, died a death that brought honor to the health professions: he suffered a stroke while caring for a woman in labor. His last words were "Care for the mother and child first."

The museum here is composed of three buildings, one of which dates from the 1850s and was constructed on the foundation of Long's original office. The focal point is a detailed diorama depicting the historic operation, but there are a variety of other professionally rendered displays, including Long family memorabilia and items supporting Long's priority in the discovery of anesthesia. Other exhibits illustrate the development of modern anesthesia and include perhaps two-dozen pieces of early twentieth century anesthesia equipment, e.g., a Connell's Anesthetometer, a bulky 1913 device developed to mix and measure ether vapors and other gasses in appropriate and accurate concentrations. One area will eventually contain a re-creation of a c. 1840 doctor's office and an apothecary. Just outside the museum, in the town square, is a tall spire erected in Long's honor in 1910. The museum is open Tuesday through Saturday, 10-1 and 2-5, and Sunday 2-5 only. Admission is free but donations are appreciated.

MACON

Mercer University School of Medicine 1550 College Avenue 31207. (912) 744-2600. This is a young school, founded specifically to supply primary care physicians to rural Georgia. It admits only Georgia residents. The idea for the school grew out of an awareness that rural areas in south and central Georgia were grossly underserved with regard to medical care. In response to this need, the Georgia General Assembly allocated funds to establish a community-based school, using the facilities of a private Baptist-sponsored university for preclinical teaching, and existing community hospitals for clinical teaching. The School of Medicine Building on the Mercer University campus was completed in 1981, and the charter class was admitted the following year. The first class graduated in 1986. Tours of the campus can be arranged through the Development Office.

MILLEDGEVILLE

Central State Hospital Swint Avenue and Vinson Highway 31062. (912) 453-4575. Founded in 1842 on a site two miles south of Milledgeville, which was then the state's capital, the Georgia Lunatic Asylum eventually grew to be one of the largest hospitals in the world, housing 12,305 patients in 1964. Since that zenith, the advent of psychotropic medication and various "deinstitutionalization" alternatives have served to cut the hospital population to a current average census of 1800 patients. The hospital was the site of a landmark experiment in 1909 when Dr. Joseph Goldberger was sent here by the US Public Health Service to look for cases of pellagra and to discover whether treatment might alter the course of the disease. From 1910 until 1913, 9 percent of 3796 patients were found to have the disease, and 21 percent of all patient deaths were due to pellagra. When patients were treated with niacin-rich diets, all signs of mental illness disappeared. Today, the campus remains huge, covering 1000 acres, with 38 principal patient care buildings (and over 60 others) surrounded by endless expanses of lawn dotted here and there with graceful old trees. Some of the buildings previously devoted to patient care are now used by a state prison which shares the property. On the first floor of the Yarbrough Building, there's a two-room museum which details the history of the facility and includes memorabilia from previous eras of psychiatric treatment. The museum is open by appointment only. Tours of the hospital are available through Volunteer Services.

SAVANNAH

Candler Hospital 5353 Reynolds Avenue 31405. (912) 354-9211. Until it moved into its new quarters in 1980, Candler was the second oldest general hospital in the United States (after the Pennsylvania Hospital) still operating out of the same quarters. The original structure was erected in 1819 as the Savannah Poor House and Hospital. Designed in part to care for seamen, the hospital was often called the Savannah Marine Hospital. In 1854 the hospital became the home of the Savannah Medical College and remained so for 10 years. Like most such institutions in the South, it served as a Confederate hospital during the Civil War. After the war, the hospital was reorganized and renamed the Savannah Hospital. The hospital fell on difficult times during the depression and was purchased in 1930 by the Georgia Hospital Board of the Methodist Episcopal Church. Renamed Candler Hospital (after Methodist Bishop Warren A Candler), the hospital's growth has been almost continuous since that time. In 1960, it absorbed the 100-year-old Telfair Hospital for Females. In 1963, Central of Georgia Railway Hospital was added to the Candler family and renamed Candler Central. In order to combine all three elements under one roof, the huge new campus-style Candler General Hospital was completed in 1980, attractively sited on a 60-acre parcel. Tours of the sprawling six-story facility can be arranged via the Volunteer Office. The old Candler General Hospital (the 1819 Savannah Poor House and Hospital) still stands at 516 Drayton Street, though it has been much expanded and altered. It is currently the Tidelands Mental Health, Mental Retardation and Drug Abuse Center, and it is not generally open for tours. The old Candler-Telfair building, opened in 1884, is likewise still standing at 17 East Park Avenue, remodeled and now used for private apartments.

Georgia Infirmary 1900 Abercorn 31499. (912) 234-6694. The Georgia Infirmary was established in 1832 as the first hospital in the country founded by whites solely "For the Relief and Protection of Afflicted and Aged Africans." Initially located about ten miles from Savannah, the hospital moved to its present location in 1838. When Sherman destroyed much of the city in 1864, the infirmary was entirely wiped out except for the land it owned. A new infirmary (the present building) was completed in 1871. The Infirmary was never a charity hospital, but rather a facility for paying patients. Indigents were always referred elsewhere. In 1904 the Infirmary organized a training school for "colored" nurses under white supervision, the only one in the South at the time (black schools under black supervision, however, were in operation at several sites). In 1964, pursuant to the demise of segregation, all references to Negroes were removed from the 131-year-old charter and the word "persons" was substituted instead. As blacks came to have other options, they began to patronize the hospitals from which they had previously been barred; unfortunately no whites came forward to fill the vacated beds. The result was that the Georgia Infirmary reexamined its mandate and decided to reopen in 1974 as a rehabilitation center. Today the Infirmary continues as an outpatient rehabilitation facility geared to frail elderly and disabled adults, especially stroke patients. (Savannah has the dubious distinction of having the highest incidence of strokes in the country.) The 1871 building remains in its original location, though wings have been added, the outside has been faced with bricks, and the inside has been thoroughly renovated. The Infirmary is happy to provide tours for interested individuals and groups.

WARM SPRINGS

Roosevelt Warm Springs Institute for Rehabilitation US Highway 27Alt 31830. (404) 655-2000. Though the springs here had been used for healing purposes by the Creek Indians since earliest times, the first formal resort at this site dates from 1832. It changed hands many times, sometimes being in fashion and sometimes in decline. In 1923 George Foster Peabody, a friend of Franklin Delano Roosevelt, took over the resort. Roosevelt, stricken by polio in 1921, came here for a visit as a private citizen in 1924. He was startled by the ease with which he could move his stricken legs in the warm waters, and his progress, described in newspapers of the time, prompted other polio victims to come here to "swim their way to health." Roosevelt made repeated visits here, both as a private citizen and as President. He ultimately bought the entire facility (1926), erected a "Little White House" here (1932), and died while in residence (1945).

FDR established the Georgia Warm Springs Foundation in 1927, both for therapeutic purposes and to investigate any techniques or observations which might prove to be useful elsewhere. In the years that followed, the facilities expanded to include an Infirmary, Brace Building, School for Physiotherapists, and Hospital. Gradually the resort atmosphere changed to that of a health care facility, though the golf links and many other amenities persisted. Many therapeutic innovations originated here, including arthritic hand splints, keyholders, locking devices for braces, and others. The first hand controls for automobiles were devised by the brace shop here, for President Roosevelt's car in 1938.

When the Salk and Sabin vaccines erased polio as a major public health threat in the mid-1950s, Warm Springs had to find a new sense of direction. The New York-based Foundation sold the facilities to the state of Georgia for one dollar in 1974 (the state had built a rehabilitation facility adjacent to the Foundation Hospital in 1964), and, within a few years, the facilities were reincarnated as the state-operated Roosevelt Warm Springs Institute for Rehabilitation.

This is a remarkably beautiful place to visit, filled with stately buildings (albeit showing signs of wear) and planted with lush flowers and shrubbery. There is also a modern 96-bed hospital and an extensive outpatient program. A Museum of Rehabilitation is planned for the early 1990s. Free tours of the Institute and its grounds are conducted three times daily by the Development Office.

The Little White House, intermittently the seat of government for the United States during FDR's lengthy administration, is administered separately by the Georgia Department of Natural Resources. The six-room cottage remains almost exactly as it was when FDR died here, a half-century ago. The 4000 acre state park is open every day except Thanksgiving and Christmas, 9 AM to 5 PM. Around the corner from the Warm Springs Institute, on Georgia Highway 85W, the combination historic dwelling and museum charges a small admission fee [(404) 655-3511].

HAWAII

OAHU

John A. Burns School of Medicine, University of Hawaii 1960 East-West Road, Honolulu 96822. This school began as a two-year basic science program in 1967, expanded to a four-year program in 1973, and graduated its first class of MD's in 1975. Instead of building a costly university medical center, the medical school conducts clinical teaching in local community hospitals, including Queen's and Kapiolani-Children's. The first two years are taught in the Biomedical Sciences Building on East-West Road, a highly stylized modern pagoda which is meant to reflect the multiethnic, multicultural nature of the student body and the surrounding locale. This Pan-Pacific perspective has led the school to conduct residency training programs for graduates of Japanese medical schools on Okinawa, physician assistant training programs for the scattered islands of the former Trust Territory, and physician training for selected Micronesians.

There are currently no tours available for visitors.

Queen's Medical Center 1301 Punchbowl Street Honolulu 96813. (808) 547-4780. Queen's is the first hospital in the United States personally founded by royalty, and the story of its establishment reveals much about the history of Hawaii. When Captain James Cook visited the Pacific is 1778, Hawaii had over 300,000 native inhabitants. The number had dropped to fewer than 60,000 by 1850 and 40,000 by 1896, largely as a result of infectious diseases such as smallpox and measles. There were no hospitals which were accessible to native Hawaiians, a fact which deeply distressed King Kamehameha IV and his wife Queen Emma. From 1853 until 1859, the two of them — then only in their twenties — personally solicited funds to build a hospital, collecting donations on the street, canvassing homes and offices, and organizing fairs and the like. A dispensary was opened in 1859, and construction for a hospital began in 1860.

The Queen's Medical Center has grown with Hawaii and now includes a 506-bed hospital. Visitors to the complex should be sure to note the profusion of exotic trees and shrubs. The hospital's first attending physician, Dr. William Hillebrand, was a noted naturalist and botanist; many of the trees he planted in the 1860s still decorate the grounds. Among the most beautiful are the flowering pink and white bombax trees in front of the hospital on Punchbowl Street.

The hospital has an Historical Room, located near the admitting office in Nalani I; it is open Monday through Friday, 10 AM to 4 PM. Tours are available through the Community Relations Department.

Kapiolani Medical Center for Women and Children 1319 Punahou Street, Honolulu 96826. (808) 947-8511. This institution represents the merger of two hospitals, the oldest of which is the Kapiolani Hospital. In 1874, Kalakaua became the seventh ruler of Hawaii, and he and his queen, Kapiolani, adopted as their slogan a Hawaiian phrase which meant ". . . to propagate and perpetuate the race." Kapiolani became interested in establishing a maternity home to support and protect the birth process. She went on a grand tour of institutions in America and England to learn how she should proceed. The Kapiolani Maternity Home was formally established in 1890 and dedicated to the motherhood of Hawaii. Only six babies were born in the hospital the first year, since local women remained suspicious of doctors and institutions. Initially dedicated to charity patients, the hospital started charging those who could pay in 1917 but for many years accepted "in kind" payments, including gifts of poi, fish, taro, fruits, and vegetables. Queen Kapiolani survived the overthrow of the monarchy in 1893 and continued to be a friend of the Hospital until her death in 1899.

The Maternity Home expanded its functions in 1929 to include noninfectious gynecologic problems. In 1976, Kapiolani and Children's Hospital (opened in 1909) formally joined their operations. The current medical center, with 226 beds and 108 bassinets/incubators can be toured by advance arrangement through the Learning Resource Center.

Kuakini Medical Center 347 North Kuakini Street, Honolulu 96817. (808) 536-2236. In the last decade of the nineteenth century, 70,000 Japanese immigrants came to Hawaii to work in the cane fields. Many of these were single men, alone, and vulnerable to injury and illness by virtue of the hard labor they performed for marginal wages. The Japanese Benevolent Society was established in 1892 to look after such individuals, and, in 1900, in the wake of an epidemic of bubonic plague, the 38-bed Japanese Charity Hospital was completed. By 1917, the hospital had moved to its present location, and the name was shortened to Japanese Hospital. The hospital underwent a major expansion to 100 beds in 1939 and installed a large dome on one building as a tribute to the Japanese emperor and empress, who contributed 10,000 yen to the expansion.

In those days, the hospital was run in the traditional Japanese manner. Oral and written communication was almost entirely in Japanese. Nurses either were trained in Japan or at the hospital's Japanese-style nursing school and were not required to speak English as a condition of employment. The attack on Pearl Harbor changed all that. Hospital administrators and some doctors were interned in relocation camps, the US Army took over control of the hospital, and the facility was renamed the Kuakini Hospital (after the street on which it was located). After the war, Kuakini became a community-oriented hospital, though the hospital management still tends to retain a Japanese heritage. Kuakini is now a licensed 250-bed hospital. English-speaking groups of ten or more people may tour the medical center (including the domed "Imperial Gift Memorial Building") free of charge; ironically, Japanese groups must pay a fee (to compensate paid interpreters for their time).

Tripler Army Medical Center Moanalua Ridge, Honolulu 96859. (808) 433-6661. The first army hospital in Hawaii opened in 1898 as a 30-bed facility in a remodeled dance hall in downtown Honolulu. As the military presence on the Islands increased and malaria and typhoid epidemics multiplied the numbers of sick, a larger post hospital was built at Fort Shafter. In 1920, the Fort Shafter facility was designated Tripler General Hospital, in honor of Charles Stuart Tripler, medical director of the Army of the Potomac during the Civil War and author of the first field manual for US military surgeons. At the outbreak of World War II, Tripler housed 450 beds, but Tripler's capacity escalated to 2400 beds during the war. Tripler's history of service includes 344 battle casualties of the attack on Pearl Harbor, 60,000 Korean conflict evacuees, and tens of thousands of Vietnam casualties.

The present 537-bed Tripler installation was completed in 1948, the tallest building on Oahu at the time. One out of four residents of the state of Hawaii is eligible for care here, including active duty military, retired military, family members of both groups, VA beneficiaries, and citizens of the Trust Territory of the Pacific Islands and American Samoa.

Though the hospital loooks distinctively pink to the casual visitor, the color's official designation is "rose coral." Tours are available to groups by prior arrangement with Public Affairs.

Father Damien Museum 130 Ohua Avenue, Honolulu 96815. (808) 923-2690. For any visitor to the Islands who is interested in the saga of Father Damien and leprosy and who is unable to visit Molokai, this is the second best place to learn the details of the story. The Damien Museum and Archives was established in 1977 (just after Damien was declared Venerable by the Roman Catholic Church) and relocated to its present site on the grounds of St. Augustine Church in 1986. The displays include artifacts and photographs related to the history of leprosy in Hawaii and, of course, to Father Damien. The museum is open Monday through Friday from 9 AM to 3 PM, and Saturday from 9 to 12. Admission is free, but donations are gratefully accepted.

MOLOKAI

Kalaupapa National Historical Park 96742. (808) 567-6171. Leprosy came to the Hawaiian Islands in the 1830s (perhaps brought by Chinese, perhaps by Europeans) and became common in the 1850s and 1860s. The heretofore isolated Hawaiians were easy prey to infectious diseases of many varieties, and huge numbers died from measles, smallpox, cholera, pertussis, influenza, and plague. Though leprosy was the least virulent of the lot, its effects were highly visible, since its victims survived and suffered for many years, with the stigmata of the disease apparent for everyone to see.

In 1865 King Kamehameha V signed the "Act to Prevent the Spread of Leprosy," and the first "shipment" of lepers were set ashore on this peninsula. Surrounded on three sides by rough seas and on the fourth by sheer 2000-foot cliffs, the invalids were imprisoned. The Hawaiian government built a variety of buildings and improvements (in the 1880s, more than five percent of the kingdom's budget went to support programs related to leprosy) and left the inmate-patients to run themselves. The abandoned community, dominated by disease and hopelessness, degenerated into lawlessness, and the mortality rate averaged 50 percent a year.

In 1873 Father Damien arrived for a brief visit, and quickly resolved to become resident priest. By acts of kindness, charity, hard work, and devotion, Damien gradually won the trust of people who had little previous reason to trust anyone, let alone a white outsider. Damien worked day and night building, planting crops, running fresh water lines, teaching music, constructing coffins, and bandaging the sores and caring for the spirits of his flock. His only concession to his own comfort was to take up pipe smoking so that he would not be oppressed by the omnipresent smell of decaying flesh. In doing so, Damien became a media phenomenon and achieved international reknown. As a result, he alerted the world to the plight of people afflicted with leprosy, gave hope to its victims everywhere, and taught a rapt audience once again that love can be powerful medicine.

In 1885 Damien himself was diagnosed as having leprosy. By the time of his death in 1889, Damien had spent 16 years at Molokai. While Damien was the most famous individual to devote much of his life to helping the afflicted in Hawaii, he was by no means the only one: others who trod the same path were Brother Joseph Dutton (45 years serving the lepers) and Mother Marianne Cope (35 years).

In 1905 Congress took what was then a dramatic step and appropriated $100,000 for a research hospital on Molokai devoted to studying patients with leprosy. It was the first federally funded hospital for research into a specific disease. The government built several buildings on a square mile of land, surrounded the entire complex with a fence, and then built another fence 10 feet inside the outer perimeter. Nine patients were then persuaded to become research subjects in this fortress. The nine Hawaiians soon discovered that they were in a prison within a prison, where they ate white men's food, had to abide by white men's rules, under the supervision of white men more interested in germs than people, without the inducement of effective treatment to convince them to stay. The original nine soon escaped, and the government was unable to attract another patient.

At about the same time, however, Damien's old colony was becoming a model treatment facility for the care of leprosy patients. By 1907, the colony had "two brass bands, several glee clubs, a shooting club, baseball clubs, athletic clubs, horse races, and a debating society." Buildings erected during the same era included a poi factory, stables, a full-service dispensary, and a steam laundry. Still, there were many reminders that this was not paradise: patients' letters to people outside the facility were fumigated until well into the 1960s, largely to make the outside world feel safe, even though the facility's officials recognized that the process was of no practical utility.

Sulfones were introduced as an effective therapy in 1946. Shortly thereafter leprosy was officially renamed "Hansen's disease," and Kalaupapa's historic role as a prison colony for lepers began to come to an end. In 1980 Kalaupapa was established as a national historic park. No new patients have been admitted since 1969, but those residents who chose to stay have been allowed to do so. (At this writing, almost 100 still live on Kalaupapa.) In the 1980s, $500,000 was raised to restore and preserve the church Damien built with his own hands, St Philomena.

Visitors to this historic spot will find the stunning beauty of land and sea that greeted almost 13,000 patient-prisoners over more than a century. The community still includes a cluster of homes, a hospital, a doctor's house, a variety of other buildings, a graveyard, and the church built by Father Damien in 1876. Damien's grave and a monument to his memory are still here, but his remains were dug up and returned to his hometown in Belgium in 1937. A few concrete pillars are all that remain of the old US Leprosy Investigation Station (torn down in 1922). Getting to this isolated peninsula is no simple feat. The only access is by small plane or by mule ride down a daunting three-mile trail. Arrangements require careful advance planning and are best made through a travel agency.

IDAHO

NAMPA

Swayne Medical Museum Twelfth Avenue South 83651. (208) 495-2688. This museum, dedicated to the rural general practitioner, is the creation of Dr. Samuel Swayne (who practiced medicine in the area from 1920 until the 1970s) and his widow. Now operated by Mrs. Swayne, the medical museum is one of seven buildings on a 155-acre site (other attractions include a chapel, the "Lord's Garden," a children's museum, a clock museum, and a nature trail). The medical component is the product of a lifetime of collecting by the Swaynes, together with contributions by local practitioners. There is a reconstructed doctor's office here, with items of varying vintage, including such oddities as a mechanical liver stimulator, along with more conventional artifacts such as doctors' bags, dental instruments, enema pans, and the like. This is a highly personal collection, and the tours and accompanying lectures narrated by Mrs. Swayne are likewise uniquely personal. The museum operates at Mrs. Swayne's convenience and is sometimes closed for extended periods. Call for appointments in advance. Donations accepted.

ILLINOIS

CHICAGO   (*See* Great Medical Cities)

GALESBURG

Mary Ann "Mother" Bickerdyke Monument Courthouse Square 61401. Mary Ann Ball was born in 1817 and was destined to be-

Statue of Mother Bickerdyke, Galesburg, Illinois *(Courtesy of Galesburg Public Library, Special Collections)*

come one of American nursing's most colorful characters. After graduation from Oberlin College, Miss Ball took her nurse's training at a physician's side in Cincinnati. At the age of 32, she married Robert Bickerdyke and moved to Galesburg. She was widowed shortly before the beginning of the Civil War and then supported herself and her three children by practicing "botanic medicine." When Abraham Lincoln appealed to the country for nurses to help with the nation's wounded, Bickerdyke (then 42 years of age) immediately answered the call. She became a Union Army nurse, participated in some nineteen Civil War battles, and is credited with setting up 300 hospitals. Sometimes called "a cyclone in calico," she was a tireless opponent of red tape, callousness toward the sick and wounded, and stupidity. She was partial toward enlisted men and could be a tigress in dealing with unreasonable officers. She was a marvelous hands-on nurse, and her skill at mobilizing resources, including food and medications from often recalcitrant suppliers, was nothing short of miraculous. The enlisted men loved her and called her "Mother," and, as a result, Abraham Lincoln said she was worth at least a regiment to the Union forces. General William Tecumseh Sherman told his officers that, wherever Mother Bickerdyke was involved, they were to take orders from her because she outranked him. After the war, she served the needy in a variety of ways (she worked with the Salvation Army in San Francisco for 11 years) but never again achieved the celebrity she gained during the war. She is buried in Linwood Cemetery (about a mile-and-a-half west of Courthouse Square) where a large but simple stone marks her grave. The Courthouse Square statue is a dandy, one of the finest tributes to nursing to be found anywhere. The monument includes a wounded soldier, who has been tenderly lifted to a half-sitting position by a kneeling army nurse, who is holding a drinking cup to his lips. The larger-than-life-size bronze figures, mounted on a granite pedestal, were sculpted in 1904 by Alice Ruggles Kittson, in her day one of the most famous of American women sculptors.

NORTH CHICAGO

The Chicago Medical School University of the Health Sciences, 3333 Greenbay Road 60064. (312) 578-3000. With a name like this, you would think that this school belongs in the metropolis 45 miles to the south. Indeed, the CMS was located in Chicago until 1980, when it relocated to this northern Illinois community which really is closer to Wisconsin than to Chicago. The CMS, a privately supported independent institution, was founded in 1912 as a nighttime medical college, intended to train men and women who worked during the days. In 1930, CMS moved its facilities to the Cook County Hospital area, where it — along with three other medical and various other professional schools — could take advantage of the clinical teaching opportunities. In 1967, the CMS became a part of the University of the Health Sciences, the first attempt in the country to establish a university solely established to train health professionals. In 1980, the UHS negotiated a long-term lease with the Veterans Administration and established a new UHS campus on 92 acres adjacent to the North Chicago VA Medical Center. Today, the UHS includes the Chicago Medical School, a School of Graduate and Postdoctoral Studies, and a School of Related Health Sciences. Most campus activities are housed in the $40 million Basic Science Building, though an additional $60 million worth of buildings is in the planning stage. Clinical teaching is carried out at the nearby VAMC, as well as the Great Lakes Naval Training Center, and a variety of other hospitals. Tours are not currently available.

Abbott Laboratories Abbott Park 60064. (312) 937-8521. This company was founded in 1888 by Wallace C Abbott, a physician who started manufacturing "dosimetric" medications first for his own patients and later for others. Prior to Abbott and others like him, the prevailing medications were "galenicals" or plant extracts, notoriously foul tasting and with uncertain potency. By 1900, the company was officially known as the Abbott Alkyloidal Company, and the catalog included some 349 kinds of granules and tablets. Landmark products included Halazone (1917, a water purifier), Nembutal (1930, a potent barbiturate sedative), Pentothal (1936, the famous "truth serum," and still a favored intravenous anesthetic), and Erythrocin (1952, one of the first, and now the longest-lived, of the penicillin substitutes). Today, prescription drugs account for less than a quarter of Abbott's sales, with Abbott's various erythromycin preparations being by far and away the largest sellers. Most of the company's sales now come from various diagnostic equipment and systems, intravenous solutions, related equipment, nutritional products (e.g., Abbott's Ross Laboratories makes Similac and Ensure), and consumer products.

Tours of Abbott's facilities are conducted by the Guest Relations Department and are restricted to persons 16 years of age or older. Reservations are necessary.

SPRINGFIELD

Southern Illinois University School of Medicine 801 North Rutledge 62708. (217) 785-2155. This institution was established in 1970, when Illinois decided it wanted a second state medical school. From the beginning, the school emphasized a competency-based curriculum, so that the students would not be in competition with one another and therefore presumably more likely to help one another master material. First-year students are taught basic sciences on the parent campus in Carbondale, and most of the rest of the curriculum is taught here in this facility. The school's principal clinical affiliations are with Memorial Medical Center (across the street) and St John's Hospital (see below), but a number of other hospitals also provide clinical teaching. Tours are available via the Public Affairs Office.

St John's Hospital 800 East Carpenter Street 62769. (217) 544-6464. This hospital, named after St John the Evangelist, was established in 1878 by a group of sisters who had fled Germany several years earlier, fearful of religious persecution. Members of the Hospital Sisters of the Third Order of St Francis, these women not only established Springfield's first hospital, in 1886 they established a hospital school of nursing which was to become a pioneering center for nurse-anesthetists. The same year, St John's Sister Secundina

Medrup became the world's first nurse-anesthetist, the first nurse specifically trained to specialize in the administration of anesthesia. In 1912, St John's also became the site of the second professional school for nurse-anesthetists in the country (after St Vincent's in Portland, Oregon). The current hospital is a thoroughly modern, full-service teaching hospital. Tours are available through the Volunteers Office.

The Pearson Museum of Medical Humanities 801 North Rutledge 62708 (217) 785-2128. This museum was opened in 1976, in conjunction with the new School of Medicine. The collection here focuses on these main areas: prehistoric artifacts of disease, domestic medicine from the frontier days onward, instrumentation from 1840 onward, patent medicine, and the history of pharmacy from 1880 onward. The unifying theme here is the intent to pay tribute to physicians who lived and worked in the greater Mississippi River basin. Permanent exhibits include a turn-of-the-century dental office, a nineteenth century pharmacy/drug store, and a period doctor's office. Additional major exhibits usually are changed every nine months, smaller exhibits more frequently. The exhibit area is located just off a courtyard attached to SIUMS' main instructional building. The museum is open to visitors weekdays from 8 AM to 4:45 PM.

INDIANA

EVANSVILLE

Mead Johnson Antique Pediatric Exhibit 2404 West Pennsylvania Street 47721. (812) 429-5000. In the lobby of Mead Johnson's administration building, there is a wonderful exhibit of infant feeding devices through the ages. Some are truly ancient (e.g., an infant feeding bottle dating from the Cyprus of 500 B.C.), but most of the items date from the eighteenth and nineteenth centuries. Examples include an English pewter tube-spoon (c. 1800), an American silver nipple and sucking tube (c. 1850), a nineteenth century Italian majolica feeding vessel, and an English Staffordshire pottery feeding bottle (c. 1820). No special arrangements are necessary to view the collection; you can simply walk into the lobby during normal working hours and browse as you will.

Edward Mead Johnson was one of the brothers who founded the Johnson and Johnson Company. However, because his infant son was sickly and intolerant of many foods, Mead gradually lost interest in adhesive plasters and became more interested in nutrition. In 1911 his company developed a product called Dextri-Maltose, which provided a nutritious substitute for infants who were intolerant of cane sugar. By 1924 Mead Johnson was a major producer of cod-liver oil, in the first preparation with a standardized potency. In 1934 the company had enormous success with the introduction of Pablum, the first pre-cooked cereal for infants (previously mothers were obliged to spend hours cooking raw cereal in order to make it digestible for their infants). Pablum's success was even more amazing, because the company promoted it only to doctors and not to the general public. This triumph was followed by such products as Poly-Vi-Sol and Tri-Vi-Sol (1949), Enfamil (1959), and Metrecal (1959). Mead Johnson and Company (which was acquired by Bristol-Myers in 1962) now markets a wide range of products.

INDIANAPOLIS

Indiana University Medical Center 1100 West Michigan Street 46223. (317) 274-5000. The IUMC is located on the west side of downtown Indianapolis and includes six hospitals, almost one hundred clinics, and schools of medicine, dentistry, nursing, and allied health sciences. The IU School of Medicine was founded in 1903, with the first group of students enrolled on the Bloomington campus. In 1908 the remaining proprietary schools in the state were combined with the IU program. From 1912 until 1958 Indiana sent its medical students to Bloomington for their first year and to Indianapolis for their second, third, and fourth years. In 1965 Indiana adopted a statewide plan for medical education using the Indianapolis campus as a base, relying on various campuses around the state for teaching basic sciences to first-year students and various hospitals for teaching experiences in the clinical years. At its peak, IU was the largest medical school in the country, with over 300 students in each graduating class (the number of students has tapered off in recent years).

The medical center is currently a huge complex, with over two-dozen buildings spread over 90 acres, and almost 2000 hospital beds. The most unusual and appealing building on campus is the **James Whitcomb Riley Hospital for Children.** Opened in 1924 and founded to honor the much loved Hoosier poet who so beautifully celebrated childhood, this is one of the most effectively designed children's hospitals anywhere. Each ward is geared to a specific developmental period: toddlers, pre-school, pre-teens, etc. Though there have been several major and minor additions over the years, it is the 1986 addition (by Ellerbe Associates, Inc.) that really makes the place so architecturally wonderful. The spectacular new lobby manages to include the facade of the original building within an enormous atrium, successfully linking it to the modern 1971 three-story addition, as well as the 1986 addition. The atrium is filled with natural light, fountains, shrubbery, fanciful elevators, vivid colors, and huge stuffed animals adorning various balconies and floor spaces. Kids, as you might imagine, love this place. The dignified lobby of the 1924 building is beautifully panelled in oak, with a stained glass wall opposite the entrance, and the marble floor is inlaid with brass plaques commemorating such medical greats as William Harvey, Crawford Long, and Walter Reed.

Indiana Medical History Museum Central State Hospital. 3000 West Washington Street 46222. (317) 635-7329. This marvelous museum is quite simply without peer in the entire country. What sets it apart from the competition is not its collection — more about that below — but rather the incredibly well-preserved building in which the collection is displayed. The old Pathology Building of the Central State Hospital for the Insane (now Central State Hospital) was erected in 1895. At the time it was the only separate research building on the grounds of a psychiatric hospital in the country. Though

Indiana Medical History Museum, Anatomical Museum *(Credit: Photograph in the collection of the Indiana Medical History Museum)*

not particularly distinguished on the outside, the 4000-square-foot interior, with 19 working rooms, was a state-of-the-art research building, a handsome mix of utility and charm. All the woodwork, all the cabinets and furniture, the built-in microscope cases and file cabinets, were built of white oak. Plumbing fixtures and laboratory tables were a mixture of tile and marble, with here and there copper sinks and brass appliances. The stunning fact about this building is that it is all still there, essentially in the same condition as at the turn of the century. Nothing was torn out and replaced, no woodwork was painted over, no one bothered to bring in metal desks and tables and tear out all the built-ins. This is a pristine, turn-of-the-century research building.

When it was built, the building's triple mission was research, teaching, and diagnostic testing. I've been unable to find any record of significant research conducted here, but the marvelous eight-tiered amphitheater was used for psychiatry, neurology, and pathology lectures for several early proprietary schools and later the IU School of Medicine. The diagnostic labs (histology, bacteriology, and clinical pathology) were all well used, and much of the glassware, equipment, and records remain here for visitors' inspection. The autopsy suite (still containing a wooden refrigerator, with two body trays) retains its old cast iron autopsy table. A speaking tube goes from the autopsy room to the second floor, so the secretary could transcribe the autopsy recitation without having to be present in the room.

The photography lab still contains the 1890s vintage photomicrography box camera that was originally installed, together with all glass negatives, numbered in order and carefully filed in oak cabinets. The anatomy museum contains thousands of specimens displaying various diseases of the brain. The oak-panelled amphitheater still has 147 cane-back chairs of the initial 150 listed on the original inventory.

Beyond all the furnishings and paraphernalia associated with the Pathology Building's function, the museum — with no acquisitions budget — has accumulated a remarkable collection of early medical Indiana, well over 15,000 items. The vast majority of this collection at the time of my visit, remained uncatalogued and not available for display. With only a part-time curator and no additional paid help, the museum has yet to realize its potential. Still, this is a very special place, worthy of a visit now and of future visits as the potential of the collection becomes more fully realized.

The museum is located on state hospital grounds and is approached via the hospital's front gate on Warren Street, between West Washington and Vermont. The museum, however, is a private operation and enjoys a 99-year lease on its 5-acre site. It is currently open Wednesdays 1 - 4 PM and by appointment.

Eli Lilly Archives and Company Museum 893 South Delaware Street 46206. (317) 276-2173. Located in a handsome building called the Lilly Center, these attractions provide a fine example of how a company can turn a public relations endeavor into a public service. The main floor houses the company archives, including some attractive displays, and a couple of rooms which commemorate the Lilly family. The second floor is home to six major exhibits, which provide fascinating displays on areas of Lilly's corporate interest, including antibiotics, diabetes, medical instrumentation, and beauty products (Lilly owns Elizabeth Arden, Inc.). The second floor also has a multivision theater, in which 21 projectors are combined to depict the company's history, in a lively, 10-minute sound-and-light program.

The Lilly company began in 1876, making pills, elixers, and extracts. Eli Lilly, however, scored an early coup when he became the first to mass market medicines in gelatin-coated capsules. Other major company milestones occurred in 1923, when it became the first to market insulin, in 1936, when it introduced the barbituate Seconal, and in 1957, when the painkiller Darvon hit the market. Over half the company's sales volume is now accounted for by various antibiotics.

The archives and museum are open Monday through Friday, 8 AM to 4 PM. There is no admission charge, no reservations are necessary, and the entire setup (including the theater presentation) can be toured without a guide. However, advance arrangements are necessary to see the 1934 replica of Colonel Lilly's original 1876 laboratory. This building, located a few minutes walk from the visitors' center, contains a small office and an early pharmaceutical production line on the ground floor, and a bottling and labeling operation upstairs.

Hook's Historic Drugstore and Pharmacy Museum Indiana State Fairgrounds. 1202 East 38th Street 46205. (317) 924-1503. Hook's is a major midwestern drugstore chain of some 300 stores, and its state fair attraction, established as a public relations contribution to the Indiana sesquicentennial in 1966, has become a major Indianapolis drawing card. The main feature here is the stunning white ash and black walnut cabinetry and counter which dates from 1849 and which is now filled with period pharmaceutical relics. There are hundreds of nineteenth century patent medicines on display, as well as surgical instruments, medical saddlebags, leech bottles, and a huge collection of mortars and pestles. This is probably the least painful way for a family to view the history of medicine and pharmacy anywhere in the country, because, mixed in with antique medicine and nursing bottles and the snake root, bitters, and salts, you will find something to interest every member of the family: antique gum dispensers and ice cream scoops, cola and root beer memorabilia, vintage cosmetic containers and tobacco packages, and various kinds of nostalgia-awakening nineteenth century candies. The primary drawing card for most nonmedical visitors, however, is the old-fashioned chocolate sodas which are served from a gleaming century-old soda fountain. The store and museum are open seven days a week, without charge, from 11 AM to 5 PM.

IOWA

ALGONA

Druggists' Mutual Drug Store Exhibition #1 Pharmacist Way. Highway 18 West 50511. (515) 295-2461. Druggists' Mutual is an insurance company which is the only company in the United States to limit coverage to members of the pharmaceutical profession. It provides fire and casualty insurance in 16 states, primarily in the midwest. In 1972, it opened this restored turn-of-the-century pharmacy exhibition, filling it with artifacts for the most part donated by policy holders. There's an 1890 soda fountain and back bar and lots of shelves stocked with old patent medicines, drugstore antiques, old boxes filled with crude drugs and herbs, and even an 1890 optometrist's kit. The museum is located in the Home Office Building, adjacent to the executive offices, in a handsomely outfitted room of about 400 square feet. Admission is free, and the museum is open to visitors Monday through Friday, 8 AM to 4:30 PM and by appointment.

CHEROKEE

Joseph A. Tallman Mental Health Museum Mental Health Institute. 1200 West Cedar Street 51012. (712) 225-2594. This is a medium-sized psychiatric museum that gives a good feeling for what state mental hospitals have been like over the past three-quarters of a century. The Cherokee Hospital once (in 1946) housed 1700 patients and cared for them with a trained medical staff consisting of one doctor and one registered nurse—plus, of course, a lot of attendants of varying skill and background. (The hospital now has only 264 beds and is staffed by ten employee physicians, a dozen resident physicians in training, and an additional 360 support personnel.) The main feature of the hospital in the old days was the farm, which covered much of the 1000-acre grounds. The patients, many of whom had a farming background, worked the farm as therapy and also because the labor was necessary to keep the institution functioning. The museum's collection captures the feeling of those days: exhibits include farming equipment, items from the shoemaking and shoe repairing shops, horseshoeing and broom making paraphernalia, and the like. There is also a three-room replica of the first superintendent's apartment with its opulent furniture, and rooms depicting patient and employee quarters and a typical examining room. A lot of kitchen equipment is on display too, since the hospital housed a bakery school for a while in the 1960s. The museum can be seen by appointment only.

DAVENPORT

Palmer College of Chiropractic 1000 Brady Street 52803. (319) 326-9600. Chiropractic is "the science which concerns itself with the relationship between structure, primarily the spine, and function, primarily the nervous system, of the human body as the relationship may affect the restoration and preservation of health." Chiropractors use neither drugs nor surgery but instead concentrate on "spinal adjustment" by applying force precisely to various spinal segments. Organized medicine has often maintained that chiropractic is bunk and quackery, and organized chiropractic has responded with accusations of "restraint of trade." In 1987, the chiropractors won a significant court battle when a Federal District court found the AMA guilty of restraint of trade, saying that, by calling chiropractors "unscientific cultists," the AMA had unfairly eroded the credibility of the profession. Still, that was only one decision, and the war may not be over.

Whatever the technical merits of such arguments, the fact is that chiropractic has now endured for almost 100 years, one of the few disciplines to challenge medical orthodoxy and survive. Chiropractic's thousands of practitioners treat a steady stream of mostly satisfied patients. The reason may be summed up in the words of chiropractic's founder: "I have never considered it beneath my dignity to do anything to relieve human suffering."

Chiropractic began right here in Davenport in 1895, when DD Palmer first "racked" a patient's vertebra back into position, thus apparently restoring hearing to a patient who had been almost deaf for 17 years. DD was a self-taught healer with a flamboyantly forceful personality, who showed no reticence in claiming that his treatment could cure practically anything. Many of chiropractic's problems with organized medicine can be traced directly to DD's extravagant style. Patients, however, flocked to him; and he founded the Davenport college to teach his disciples. He was followed at the college by his even more colorful and eccentric son BJ, who aggressively marketed and promoted chiropractic, an accomplishment eased considerably by BJ's early (1922) intuitive understanding of radio's potential to influence the masses. Whatever money he could scrape together, BJ invested in radio stations, and, as a result, the enormously successful Palmer Communications network often helped keep PCC afloat when times got rough. (It was on BJ's radio station WOC-Davenport that Ronald Reagan got his start as a radio announcer.) Though DD's and BJ's personalities were vital in launching their new therapeutic calling, it took a more conservative and sober-appearing man (BJ's son David) to stabilize the school, to organize it and make it economically viable for the latter half of the twentieth century.

Palmer College is the oldest and largest school of chiropractic in the world. As such, it is a monument to this uniquely American health profession. Equally, however, it is a monument to the Palmer family, whose influence permeates every corner of the campus. In addition to the three founders identified above, there is

Palmer College of Chiropractic — Friendship Court with Busts of Four Palmers *(Credit: Palmer College of Chiropractic, Davenport, Iowa, 1989)*

also BJ's wife Mabel (who herself was a chiropractor and who is regarded as "the first woman of chiropractic"), David's wife Agnes (another chiropractor, who also sculpted much of the statuary on campus), and David's daughter Vickie (who is now Chairperson of the Board of Trustees).

The campus sits at the top of the Brady Street hill and is composed of a dozen buildings and a variety of courtyards and monuments. At any given time, there are about 1600 students studying here, mostly from the US, but with lesser numbers from elsewhere around the world. The whole campus will interest many, but two of the buildings are quite special.

The first is the **Palmer Museum and Archives,** located in a mansion which was the principal residence of first BJ and then David. Built in 1874, the house is basically of Second Empire design but with the addition of a wrap-around, now enclosed porch which currently acts as a showcase for some of BJ's many acquisitions from travels around the world. BJ was an inveterate collector and, while some things are clearly schlock, others are quite beautiful and immensely valuable. There is an extensive collection of orientalia, with some unusual Golden Buddhas. Chess sets were one of BJ's fascinations, and his collection includes one owned by Czar Nicholas of Russia and another which is reputed to be one of the largest ivory sets in the world. A tour of this incredible collection gives a vivid sense of what this man must have been like.

An attraction of greater medical interest is the remarkable osteology collection in the **Library Building,** another tribute to BJ's avidity for collecting. There are hundreds of items here, including spines and skeletons of every configuration, from dramatic hunchbacks to tortuous scoliotics. There are skulls of all sizes (including one from a hydrocephalic), fetal skeletons, and bones of various extremities. The specimens are nicely displayed, and this is truly a fascinating exhibit.

No one visiting PCC can fail to notice the **Friendship Court,** fronting on Brady Street, with the oversized busts of DD, BJ, David, and Mabel (see photo).

PCC is happy to welcome visitors to the campus. Tours are available Monday through Friday at 12 noon while school is in session. No advance arrangements are necessary; visitors should merely be on the first floor of the administration building (1000 Brady Street) a few minutes before the tour is scheduled to begin.

INDEPENDENCE

Days of Yore Museum Mental Health Institute, Junction of Highways 20 and 248 50644. (319) 334-2583. The Mental Health Institute is Iowa's second oldest Asylum for the Insane (after the institution at Mt Pleasant), and it is truly a sight to see. Quite simply, they don't build hospitals like this anymore. Opened in 1873 and built along the Kirkbride model, it was designed by legislative mandate as "a facility which shall last 400 centuries, or until time shall be no more." The walls of the main (or Reynolds) building (which span 720 feet) are built from blocks of locally quarried stone, while the foundation is solid granite. (The windlass which was used to transport the massive blocks to the upper stories incredibly is still in place on the fifth floor of the main building.) Today, the average daily patient census is about 250, with an average stay of less than a month; in the 1930s and 1940s, as many as 1800 patients resided here, with an average stay of seven years. To accomodate the huge patient population, various buildings were added through the years.

The Days of Yore was opened in 1973 to act as a repository and to tell the story of a hospital and the people it served. Treatment styles have changed so dramatically over the years that it is sometimes difficult not to be judgmental in viewing treatment devices which now seem crude and even brutal, but the museum does its best not to demean the efforts of those who tried to do their best in days gone by. The museum occupies the old Ward 7, on Third Floor North, of the Reynolds Building, and is spread out over some two dozen rooms. There's a large exhibit of various restraint devices, which were the only means available to the miniscule staff for protecting patients who were homocidal, suicidal, or seriously disturbed. Straight jackets of strong webbed material were used on huge numbers of patients, some spending many years in such devices, their hands often becoming deformed and nearly useless from the ceaseless restriction. Other calming devices include hydro restraints (in which only the patient's head is exposed above the water), the Scotch douche (or needle-spray shower), and wet-sheet packs. There are half a dozen models of electroshock therapy machines, which were in use at the hospital over four decades until 1979 (in 1956 alone, some 700 patients received ECT). There's also a fascinating psychosurgery display: In the period from 1951 to 1953, some 200 transorbital lobotomies were performed here, some by the famous lobotomist Dr. Walter Freeman. The typical operation involved a "leukotome," which looked much like a knitting needle and was inserted under the patient's upper eyelids. The whole procedure took two or three minutes.

There are hundreds of other items here, each with its own story, each a part of the history of this place. The museum is open by advance arrangement only. There is no charge.

IOWA CITY

University of Iowa Health Center West Campus 52242. (319) 353-4966. With over 900 beds, the University of Iowa Hospital is the largest university-owned teaching hospital in the United States and, as the only university medical center in the state, draws patients from all over Iowa. To transport all these patients, the university has developed a unique statewide, university-owned ambulance system that logs well over a million miles annually.

The U of I Medical School began in 1870, first using the remodeled Old Mechanics Academy for a 20-bed hospital. In 1898, the enterprise moved to a newly built university hospital on the east side of the Iowa River. The hospital gradually expanded until 1914, by which time it had grown to 240 beds. In the next several years, legislative changes assigned the U of I Hospital as the principal treatment center for the state's medically indigent, allotting each of Iowa's 99 counties an annual quota of beds in the University Hospital. Demand for services increased, and, in 1928, much of the present University Hospital was completed, this time on the west side of the river. The health center complex also includes schools of pharmacy, dentistry, and nursing.

The Health Center now dominates a hillside alongside a portion of the lawn-rimmed Iowa River. The buildings (except for a VA hospital on campus) tend to top out at six stories, so one does not get a feeling of enormous bulk, especially with the plethora of mature trees surrounding and between the buildings. The dominant architectural feature is the vintage 1928 University Hospital Tower, a huge English-Gothic structure with dramatic arches and spires, that has been skillfully integrated and connected with more modern, less tall structures. Be sure to visit the sixth floor of the University Hospital Building and see the Tower, surrounded by air space and protective glass. Above four graceful stone arches are the words "General Hospital," and above them an ominous stone dragon, tail coiled and ready to pounce.

The medical center is in the midst of an ambitious building program, and some of the older buildings (such as the attractive 1919 psychiatric hospital) may not survive. Still, a number of the newer buildings are quite appealing. See, for example, the unusual completely mirrored atrium in the Colloton Pavilion, stretching seven stories high, hung with ivy throughout, the reflections made even more interesting by the use of sharp angulations in the walls.

The **John Martin Rare Book Room** contains nearly 2500 volumes devoted to the history of the health sciences. The collection is open to the public, Monday through Friday, 12:30 to 4:30, and "can be seen upon request by anyone interested in the history of medicine, or for that matter, in fine and beautiful books." Call (319) 335-9154. Some items in the collection are both enormously beautiful and enormously valuable, including volumes by Schedel (1493), Dryander (1537), Vesalius (1543), Harvey (1639), and de Graaf (1672), among many others.

There is a brand new museum in the Patient and Visitor Activities Center (eighth floor, Colloton Pavilion) which, as of this writing, has restricted itself to temporary exhibits. Permanent displays, directed toward the general public, are in the works. Hours are Monday to Friday, 8:00 AM to 5:00 PM, and weekends, 1:00 PM to 4:00 PM. Tours of the attractive village-like campus are available by calling (319) 335-8037.

KANSAS

KANSAS CITY

Kansas University Medical Center 39th Street and Rainbow Boulevard 66103. (913) 588-5000. The KU Medical Center had its beginnings in 1889 when a one-year preparatory medical course began in Lawrence. The curriculum was lengthened to two years in 1899, but students still needed to transfer elsewhere to complete their studies. In 1905, arrangements were made for students to do their clinical work at Bell Memorial Hospital in Rosedale. Still, the situation was far from ideal (the Flexner report called them "two half-schools"), and in 1924 the School of Medicine and a new Bell Memorial Hospital joined together in new buildings on the present campus.

KU has created an enviable record of achievement in the twentieth century. Some of these include:

1903   Walter Sutton demonstrates that chromosomes carry genetic material in cells
1904   Marshall Barber invents the micropipette, the first instrument capable of isolating a single bacterium. With it, he demonstrates that a single bacillus can cause the disease anthrax
1910   William Duke discovers the importance of platelets in blood clotting
1938   Earl Padgett and George Hood invent the dermatome, the first mechanical device for procuring skin graft material

Today, the campus occupies some 50 buildings on 50 acres on the Kansas–Missouri state line and includes schools of nursing, allied health, and graduate studies. One of the more notable structures is the Murphy Administration Building (the 1924 Bell Memorial Hospital Building, on Rainbow near 40th), a nicely refurbished structure whose entrance is guarded by Corinthian columns three-stories high. If you go in this entrance, through the fine old lobby with its gold leaf decoration on the ceiling, and down the corridor to the right, you will see pictures of all the medical classes dating back to 1906. Similar pictures of nursing and medical technology graduates are displayed inside the current hospital's main entrance (on Cambridge Street), a short escalator ride up from the spacious main lobby.

KU is home to one of the half-dozen finest history of medicine libraries in the country. The collection was begun by Logan Clendening (1884–1945), a KU professor, best-selling author, nationally syndicated medical columnist, and all-round character. The collection now includes well over 20,000 volumes and contains virtually every definitive text on medicine, as well as many wonderful rarities. The library has a 1620 first edition of William Harvey's *De Motu Cordis*, the very special heavy paper edition, one of only five or six in existence, valued at a quarter of a million dollars. Other rarities include near priceless editions of Vesalius, Avicenna, Pasteur—as well as fourteen of Florence Nightingale's letters. The anesthesia and pathology collections are particularly extensive.

The **Logan Clendening Library for the History of Medicine** was completely renovated in 1985, and the result is an enormously comfortable, inviting, and elegant space. The anteroom contains some displays from the Library's huge (and largely uncatalogued) museum collection. On my visit, the exhibits included a large number of men's and women's porcelain and glass urinals and bedpans, as well as an eighteenth century obstetrical chair and various pre-Columbian medical items, including fertility symbols and a trephined skull. The reading room is large but cozy, with plush carpeting, sofas, wing chairs, a marble fireplace, and extensive hardwood paneling (behind which hides part of the library collection).

The Library (located in the Robinson Building, adjacent to the Murphy Administration Building, *not* in the main Dykes Library) is open to public viewing during normal working hours, though the rarest books are usually shown only to qualified scholars [call (913) 588-7040 for information]. KUMC also welcomes tours of the entire facility. Call Public Relations.

TOPEKA

The Menninger Foundation 5800 West Sixth Street 66601. (913) 273-7500. America's only real psychiatric dynasty began almost by chance. In 1908 a rural general practitioner named CF Menninger journeyed to Rochester, Minnesota, to view the fledgling but already renowned Mayo Clinic. He was so impressed by Mayo's revolutionary group practice—and the family enterprise of the Mayo father and sons—that when he returned to Topeka, he told his own sons (then ages 15 and 9): "You boys are going to be doctors, and we're going to have a clinic like that. . . ." Somewhat to their father's surprise, the two boys, Karl and Will, became interested in psychiatry, and the result was a psychiatric clinic in the middle of a cornfield that was destined to become the largest psychiatric training program in the world.

The clinic began in 1919 in an old converted farmhouse that was permeated with a family atmosphere—a mixture of Freud and friendliness—that was unique in its day. Moreover, the Menningers were infused with optimism, convinced that "there is no patient for whom something helpful cannot be done". The clinic thrived, helped considerably by the prolific writing and public appearances of Dr. Karl and Dr. Will. In 1930, Dr. Karl's first book *The Human Mind* became a best seller, giving the American public a fresh view of the vagaries of human behavior. Other books followed, including *Man Against Himself* (1938), *Love Against Hate* (1942), and more. Soon professionals of all kinds were flocking to Topeka to learn "how the Menningers do it." A training program for nurses began in 1931, and the residency program for psychiatrists was accredited in 1933. The Topeka Institute for Psychoanalysis was founded in 1943, becoming the fourth such institute in the country, and the prime training center for psychoanalysts west of the Mississippi. In 1935 Fortune magazine called Menninger's the "best private mental hospital west of the Alleghenies."

The single most important boost to Menninger's growth, however, was World War II. Dr. Will became a brigadier general and was given control of the army's psychiatry program. After the war, the Veterans Administration, keenly aware that 30 percent of all World War II casualties were psychiatric problems, asked the Menningers to set up a massive training program for potential VA psychiatrists. Within a matter of weeks, Menninger's had 108 psychiatric resident physicians. (To put the matter in perspective, it's helpful to know that, previously, the nation's largest psychiatry training program, at Bellevue Hospital in New York, had included a grand total of fifteen residents.)

Since those days, Menninger's has remained one of the nation's premier psychiatric facilities, with a four-pronged program of treatment, training, research, and prevention. Dr. Will was the first psychiatrist to advocate yearly mental health checkups (akin to

Menninger Tower Building *(Credit: Merrick, Hedrich-Blessing)*

annual physicals), and the clinic subsequently pioneered preventive programs geared to such groups as business executives, physicians, policemen, and teachers.

In 1982 Menninger's consolidated its activities onto a single 310-acre campus, about two miles from the original farmhouse headquarters. The grounds are studded with ponds, mature trees, gazebos, and lovely gardens. Seven previously existing buildings (including a former orphanage and a former hospital) are more or less Georgian in architectural design, with red brick and white trim. The most dramatic, the Tower Building (currently in administrative use) was designed as a replica of Independence Hall in Philadelphia. The almost two dozen newer buildings tend to be one or two stories, all white painted brick, mostly with steeply pitched roofs, and they have the look of a California condominium development.

There is a small but nicely rendered psychiatric museum in the Tower Building. Most of the displays cover the Menningers and the development of the Topeka Clinic, but other exhibits include some straight jackets and an unusual display of hundreds of picture postcards featuring asylums around the world. Menninger's also maintains an extensive archives, again focusing mostly on their own people and programs, but also featuring others (Anna Freud, Clifford Beers, Dorothea Dix) as their activities brought them in contact with the Menningers. Tours of the facility, and access to the museum, are available by advance arrangement.

Heritage House 3535 SW 6th Street 66606. (913) 233-3800. For over 50 years, this white frame, two-and-a-half story farmhouse was the headquarters of the Menninger Foundation. After the Menningers purchased the building and an adjacent 20 acres in 1925, thirteen beds were installed for the first psychiatric patients. In time, as many other buildings were added for patient care, the old farmhouse became the Foundation's administrative headquarters. In 1982, when the Menninger Foundation moved to its new facilities, the property was abandoned and lay empty and prone to vandalism for five years. Now extensively renovated and transformed into a combination bed-and-breakfast and intimate restaurant, the building is a tribute to the kind of imaginative restoration that ideally will happen to more medical landmarks that have outlived their clinical usefulness but deserve a better fate than the wrecking ball. Guests can stay in Dr. Will's study, Dr. Karl's study, the Foundation Room, or any of twelve other beautifully appointed rooms. Call for room and/or dinner reservations. If the rooms are empty, the owners are happy to give visitors a tour.

State Capitol Building 10th and Jackson Streets 66606. (913) 296-3966. The domed executive and legislative headquarters for the state of Kansas has many attractive features, but, for our purposes, the visitor should peak in the governor's office on the second floor. To the right of the door is a fine marble bust of Charles Robinson, MD (1818–1894), the first governor of the state. Robinson was one of the original founders of the Kansas Medical Society (1859) and even saw a few patients during his governorship, but he is clearly better known for his political activities than for his medical ones. He was elected territorial governor in 1856, but was arrested by pro-slavery contingents for treason and usurpation of office. He was later freed and elected state governor (1859) on the Republican ticket, but did not assume office until Kansas became a state in 1861. The first elected lieutenant-governor was also a physician. Joseph Pomeroy Root served as a surgeon in the Second Kansas Cavalry and later as Medical Director of the Army of the Frontier during the Civil War. In 1870 he became Minister to Chile under President US Grant. Yet another physician in the state's first administration was Secretary of State John W Robinson. Tours of the capitol are available (for a small fee) weekdays 8 AM to 4 PM and weekends 9 AM to 3 PM.

KENTUCKY

DANVILLE

McDowell House and Apothecary Shop 125 South Second Street 40422. (606) 236-2804. This Georgian-style town house, across from what was once the town square, dates from the 1790s, and has been exquisitely restored to reflect the period of its namesake. Ephraim McDowell has the distinction of performing the world's first successful ovariotomy, or excision of an ovarian tumor. As a result, he is widely known as the father of abdominal surgery. On Christmas Day, 1809, he removed a 22 1/2 pound ovarian tumor from 47-year-old Jane Todd Crawford. The operation was performed without anesthesia or modern antisepsis and took 25 minutes. She reportedly repeated the Psalms and sang hymns during the operation to help her bear the terrible pain. Mrs. Crawford traveled the 60-mile route on horseback coming to the operation and returned home via the same mode of transportation 25 days after the operation. She not only survived the procedure, she lived until 1841 (McDowell, some seven years younger than his patient, survived only until 1830).

The McDowell House illustrates the kind of life McDowell must have led at the beginning of the nineteenth century, celebrates the event that made McDowell famous, and showcases an extensive collection of medical instruments and apothecary ware. (The McDowell apothecary is generally believed to be the first such establishment west of the Alleghenies.) The rear yard contains a monument honoring McDowell's courageous patient. Guided tours (lasting about 45 minutes) of the house, shop, and medicinal herb garden are conducted Monday – Saturday 10 – 12 AM and 1 – 4 PM, as well as Sundays 2 – 4 PM. The whole area is beautifully maintained, and the tour itself is a first-rate experience, conducted by interesting and knowledgeable guides. The McDowell is closed on major holidays and on Mondays during the winter. There is a modest charge. Call for details.

LEXINGTON

University of Kentucky Medical Center 800 Rose Street 40536. (606) 233-5000. While this medical center sometimes traces its origins back to the founding of Transylvania University in 1799 (see below), the history is discontinuous, and the UKMC is really of far more recent origin. The state of Kentucky first tried to establish a medical school in Lexington in 1868, but the effort petered out and nothing came of it. Similar attempts over the next 80 years likewise were in vain. However, by the 1950s, Kentucky became acutely aware that it needed a second medical school to add to the one already in Louisville. Mortality and morbidity tables revealed that the state had numerous unmet health needs; the ratio of doctors, dentists, and nurses to the population base was low and getting worse; and the demand for health care services was on the rise. In 1956 the University trustees authorized the establishment of a medical center with the appropriate professional schools. The medical and nursing schools were opened in 1960, the hospital and dental school in 1962, and the School of Allied Health Professions in 1967. The College of Pharmacy is the oldest unit of the medical center, dating back to 1870 when it was established as the Louisville College of Pharmacy. The College became a part of the University of Kentucky in 1947 and moved into its new building on this campus in 1986.

The current medical center is based in a very functional six- and eight-story stucture that, with its various components and extensions, encompasses some three million square feet. There is an active building program here, and some of the newer structures, particularly the Markey Cancer Center and the nearby research center, are quite attractive. Be sure to glance at the glassed-in Board of Trustees room just inside the Markey entrance. It is indeed sumptuous. The medical center is located on the main University of Kentucky campus, just off South Limestone Road. Tours are available from Public Relations.

Transylvania Museum of Nineteenth Century Medicine Old Morrison Building. 300 North Broadway 40508. (606) 233-8275. Transylvania Seminary was the first institution of higher learning west of the Alleghenies. Founded in 1780, it was rechartered as Transylvania University in 1799, seven years after Kentucky joined the Union. In its heyday, Transylvania was a prestigious and quite famous university. Henry Clay was on the faculty here, and its graduates include Jefferson Davis (later president of the Confederacy), two vice presidents, 50 US senators, 101 US representatives, 36 governors, and 34 ambassadors.

The medical school was begun in 1799 and retained considerable luster until the 1830s. As Lexington ceased to be the largest city west of the Alleghenies, and its cultural and economic dominance in the Ohio Valley were eclipsed by Cincinnati and Louisville, the quality of the school gradually declined. Still, it continued to function until 1859, when the medical school was transferred to Louisville (though medical certificates at the University of Louisville continued to be granted in Transylvania's name until 1906). The actual medical school building was located nearby at Second and Broadway but was destroyed by fire while being used as a military hospital by the Union Army.

The Old Morrison Building, a magnificently restored white Greek Revival structure, dates from 1833 and contains, on its third floor, a collection of scientific apparatuses (retorts, prisms, glassware, balances) dating back to Transylvania's medical school. Displays also include various early nineteenth century teaching devices (wax, plaster, and papier-mâché anatomic models, mostly of French origin), fetal skeletons of varying ages, and some fine old paintings of medicinal plants (digitalis, asafoetida, etc.). The Frances Carrick Thomas Library is just a short stroll from the Old Morrison and contains the original library from the medical school (at the beginning of the nineteenth century reportedly one of the finest medical libraries in the world).

Transylvania University is now a university in name only, graduating students with bachelor's degrees only, in various divisions of the arts, business, and sciences. The campus is located in downtown Lexington, and welcomes visitors. The Museum is usually kept locked, and it is generally necessary to phone for an appointment in advance. The rare book collection at the library is open afternoons from 1 to 4, but call first if you wish more than a superficial glance.

LOUISVILLE

University of Louisville School of Medicine Preston at Muhammed Ali Boulevard 40292. (502) 588-5555. This is the oldest medical school in continued existence west of the Alleghenies, with a history that now spans over 150 years. The school traces its origins to the Louisville Medical Institute (founded 1837) and the Louisville Collegiate Institute (1838), both of which merged in 1846 to form the University of Louisville. Over the years that followed, other medical schools were established in Louisville (in 1900 the city had seven medical schools, making it one of the premier medical cities in the country), all of which were eventually absorbed by U of L.

One of the medical school's earliest professors of clinical medicine and pathologic anatomy (1839) was Daniel Drake, the brilliant peripatetic physician who helped found and develop medical schools throughout the Ohio Valley. Samuel Gross was professor of surgery here from 1840 to 1854, before going on to Thomas Jefferson Medical School, where he reigned as one of the country's most famous anatomists and surgeons. Austin Flint, America's foremost teacher of physical diagnosis, also taught here from 1852 to 1856, serving as professor and chairman of the theory and practice of medicine.

In 1911 the country's first trauma facility opened here, a direct result of many injuries sustained by the boisterous men who worked on the riverboats which served the city.

For many years, the school existed as a semi-private, semi-municipal institution—though by the 1960's, the municipality's contributions had slowed to a trickle. As the costs of medical education skyrocketed, the medical school developed serious financial problems, which were largely resolved by two dramatic changes. The first was that, in 1970, the University was absorbed into the state system of higher education, and the second was a very creative and then unique means of turning the university hospital from a fiscal liability into a money machine that would support both medical education and research (see Humana Hospital University, below).

The university's current facilities belie its age: virtually all of the buildings are starkly contemporary in design. The basic design features are reinforced concrete frames, accented by tall rounded columns, and concrete surfaces that vary in texture from smooth to finely ribbed, vertical striping. The medical school, dental school and clinic, research facilities, and library are arrayed around a large landscaped plaza, along with lots of covered bridges, walkways, and a huge central metal sculpture.

The second floor of the Tower Building is lined with historical photographs, including over 50 years of graduation photos in which the newly minted physicians are all dressed in tuxedos. One lobby area has a mosaic memorializing Abraham Flexner, the author of the famous 1910 report which revolutionized medical education. Flexner was born in Louisville, taught Greek in the Louisville schools for a while and even founded his own preparatory school here. He worked with Rockefeller's General Education Board from 1913 until 1938 and was responsible for organizing the Institute for Advanced Studies at Princeton University in 1930, serving as its director until his death in 1939.

Lovers of old books will want to see the historical collections of the Kornhauser Health Sciences Library, just off the central plaza. Holdings include surviving volumes of the original medical school library — all acquired before 1850 — as well as archives of five nineteenth century Louisville medical schools and a huge collection of medical Kentuckiana. The collection may be inspected Monday through Friday, 9 – 5, by prior arrangement [call (502) 588-5778].

Old Marine Hospital 2215 Portland Avenue 40212. (502) 625-6520. Currently housing the Family Health Center of Louisville's Portland District, this eight-acre site, surrounded by a once-beautiful iron fence, dates back to pre-Civil War days and is home to the only remaining inland Marine Hospital of several created by an 1837 Congressional authorization act. In that year, President Van Buren signed a bill which provided for sites "for the use and benefit of sick seamen, boatmen, and other navigators on the western rivers and lakes." Seven sites were selected for hospitals, including three on the Ohio River — at Louisville, Paducah, and near Pittsburgh. Robert Mills, a protégé of Thomas Jefferson and designer of the Washington Monument in the nation's capitol, was architect for the Louisville building, which opened for patients in 1852.

During the Civil War, the Spanish-American War, and World War I, the hospital was used to treat soldiers, though it remained officially a hospital for rivermen. In 1933 a new hospital — four stories high and considerably larger — was erected in front of the old, and the older building was converted to apartments for the new hospital staff.

In 1947, the US Public Health Service declared both buildings surplus. The city of Louisville purchased the site and in 1953 turned the newer building into the Louisville Memorial Hospital for the Treatment of Chronic Illness. The last inpatient was discharged in 1976, and the newer building (after suitable renovation) was turned into a city- and county-owned community health center.

The Old Marine Hospital building has for many years served as the heating plant for its newer brother. The Old Hospital itself is hidden from view by the 1933 building, and one has to follow the drive around in back to see it. Now a bit deteriorated, with crumbling railings and galleries and missing architectural detail work, the OMH is still basically solid. One group has proposed turning the structure into a regional maritime museum and estimates for the renovation approximate $2.5 million.

Tours are scheduled at intervals throughout the year (call for information). The newer building is open to the public, and visitors are welcome to view the WPA murals which decorate hallways on three floors.

Humana Hospital University 530 South Jackson Street 40202. (502) 562-3000. In January 1983, an agreement was signed by Humana, Inc., the University of Louisville, and the governments of the city of Louisville, Jefferson County, and the Commonwealth of Kentucky. Essentially, Humana (an investor-owned, for-profit company) agreed to lease and operate a publicly owned university teaching hospital, assuming the responsibility and risk for local indigent care, in return for various guarantees, as well as the opportunity to make a profit. The experiment is being watched carefully by university hospitals around the country, some of whom have already adapted the Louisville model to their own circumstances.

The University of Louisville had used the City Hospital (later known as Louisville General) as its principal teaching facility for many years. By the 1970s, the hospital's facilities — many of which dated from the early years of the century — were badly outmoded and desperately in need of expansion and modernization. By 1973, the University had committed itself to building a new hospital. While construction was underway, the costs of the project (by now called University Hospital) escalated dramatically, and the medical school lacked the funds to both pay the construction costs and finance an expected first-year operating loss of some $10 million. The University clearly did not want to foot the bill, and neither did the City, the County, or the State. Still, the hospital was obviously badly needed, both for indigent care and for teaching. What to do? This is where Humana entered the picture, with its vast financial resources, its acknowledged management skills, and its strong desire to develop this medical center as a showcase project to highlight a corporation's ability to efficiently manage the nation's financially troubled teaching institutions.

The agreement is too complicated to detail here, but as of this writing all parties involved claim to be pleased with the evolution of events. This is a *very* interesting experiment, and its success would have a profound effect on teaching hospitals throughout the land.

Tours of the hospital are available by prior arrangement.

Humana Hospital–Audobon One Audobon Plaza Drive 40217. (502) 636-7225. This hospital is the most dramatic result of what Humana calls its "Centers of Excellence" concept. That is, Humana picks certain departments among its various hospitals, encourages them to undertake significant research efforts, funds the research programs, and provides the state-of-the-art technology. In return, Humana (which often does not employ the investigators, but rather simply provides them with a research base) reaps whatever publicity and prestige result.

Audobon is home to the Humana Heart Institute International, which began the world's first cardiac replacement program in 1983 and sponsored the program in which Dr. William DeVries accomplished a highly publicized permanent artificial heart implant (actually the world's second) on William Schroeder in 1984. Humana has pledged to underwrite the cost of 100 such implants, as long as it is satisfied that ethically sound scientific progress is being made. The program may be emblematic of an important shift in research sponsorship for high-visibility projects, from the government to the private sector.

Audobon is an 8-year old, 500-bed, acute care, tertiary hospital. Tours are available by prior arrangement.

Community Health Building 101 West Chestnut Street 40202. (502) 589-2001. This marvelous building once housed the old Louisville Medical College and dates from 1893. Constructed in the Romanesque revival style, it is notable for its dominant corner tower and the massiveness of its stone walls, topped with carved ornamentation and a red tile roof. In 1907, LMC combined with the Hospital College of Medicine to form the Louisville and Hospital College of Medicine. The following year, the LHCM merged with both the Kentucky School of Medicine and the ultimately dominant University of Louisville Medical Department. This building remained home to the surviving entity from 1908 to 1970, when the University of Louisville School of Medicine moved to its new medical center.

For several years, the "Old Medical School" building remained vacant, a frequent target for vandals and a notorious firetrap. In 1975 a group of dedicated preservationists succeeded in obtaining City Landmark status for the building, and the structure, which had been a candidate for demolition, received a stay of execution. In 1977, the building was purchased by a wing of the Jefferson County Medical Society, and an ambitious restoration project followed. It now houses the Jefferson County Medical Society, the local headquarters of the Visiting Nurses Association, and various other administrative offices.

The interior hallways are gorgeously tiled with multicolored flooring, the stairways are cast iron with intricate railings, and the ceiling is some 20 feet high. A few other old details still survive, but extensive remodeling has obscured others. There are small historical displays on both the first and second floors. Tours are available upon request.

The Humana Building 500 West Main Street 40201. (502) 580-3600. Humana, Inc., was founded in 1961 by two young lawyers as a small nursing home venture. By 1968 the company—which was then called Extendicare—owned and operated eight nursing homes and was doing so well that it decided to expand into the hospital business. By the late 1980s, Humana owned an impressive array of 85 medical facilities and was adept at maximizing its capital by a continuous process of acquisitions and divestitures. Corporate headquarters of Humana, now one of the world's largest for-profit hospital chains, has always been in Louisville.

The Humana Building is a 27-story multihued granite structure, completed in 1985 for a cost of $60 million, and designed by architect Michael Graves. By any standard it is an impressive landmark —and perhaps one more emblematic of late-twentieth century American medicine than any other structure in the country. This is a stunningly luxurious building, from the seven kinds of granite on the exterior to the five kinds of marble on the interior to the high-speed elevators, each intricately panelled with gorgeous hardwoods. As you approach the main entrance from Main Street, you pass through a loggia topped by a 1200 square foot triangular skylight. On either side of the main entrance, there are portions of a dramatic, six-sectioned waterfall that cascades 50 feet down granite pilasters into two large pools. Eight vertical fountains frame and punctuate the waterfall. Once through the entrance, you proceed via a richly appointed shopping arcade with a central Giacometti sculpture, into a stunning marble rotunda, from which you may access the upper floors of the building. The twenty-fifth floor opens onto a huge veranda which extends out from the facade of the building and is buttressed from below by steel bridge-like girders. The view from this airy perch extends for miles.

Tours of the Humana Building are conducted each Saturday, from 10 AM to 1:30 PM, with hour-long tours leaving on the half-hour. Advance arrangements are necessary only for large groups.

WENDOVER

Frontier Nursing Service's "The Big House" 41775. (606) 672-2317. The FNS was founded in 1925 by Mary Breckenridge, a woman born into privilege who, because of her own experience with tragedy, decided to devote her life to improving the staggering maternal/infant mortality rates in this rural corner of Appalachia. The pivotal events in her life were the death of her own prematurely born daughter shortly after birth, followed by the death of her son at age four after a surgical procedure. Breckenridge attended nursing school at St. Luke's Hospital in New York and took midwifery training in London, at the British Hospital for Mothers and Babies.

Started as a private philanthropic endeavor, funded largely by wealthy family friends, the FNS brought trained nursing care to women in labor in isolated mountain cabins throughout several counties in southeastern Kentucky. These "angels on horseback," as they were called, rode mostly donated American Saddlebreds across rugged and dangerous terrain, braving swollen rivers, poisonous snakes, and pitch-black nights. Breckenridge herself was once thrown from a horse, sustaining a broken back. Others survived copperhead bites and falls down cliffs. They were a tough breed of women, these pioneering nurses. In over 20,000 deliveries, there have been only 11 maternal deaths, the last 30 years ago.

The FNS is still a vital organization, though now they have such advantages as electricity, telephones, roads, four-wheel drive vehicles, and readily available back-up medical support. Today, most deliveries take place in the hospital, and the FNS concentrates its energies on home health visits and staffing primary care and district nursing centers where a wide range of health-care services can be provided. Still, there is a great deal that is unusual and worth seeing in the FNS' collection of facilities.

The Frontier School of Midwifery was founded by Breckenridge in 1939 to provide midwives for the FNS, and it still operates today, being responsible for some 25 percent of nurse-midwives in practice in this country. It is the oldest American school of nurse-midwifery still in existence. FNS deliveries are mostly accomplished at the Mary Breckenridge Hospital in Hyden, opened in 1975, where a staff of both midwives and physicians does the honors. The original FNS Clinic building in Hyden still exists, as does the log house in Wendover that Breckenridge built in 1925 and which was to be her home for 40 years (many of the rooms are much as Breckenridge left them, filled with her possessions and memorabilia). The School of Midwifery operates out of the old Hyden Hospital.

Hyden (about two hours drive from Lexington) is the center of FNS activities and a good starting point for a tour of FNS operations. The staff is happy to welcome outsiders, especially if you make arrangements in advance, and they will supply you with detailed directions (you'll need them!) to find other facilities. Wendover (about 3.5 miles from Hyden) offers the most picturesque building of the bunch, including the rustic and charming Big House, a guest house, and a conference center. Four other clinics (mostly dating from the 1920's) are within an hour's drive of Hyden. The FNS conducts open house in both the spring and the fall (check for dates), with the fall event (the first weekend in October) coinciding with Hyden's annual Mary Breckenridge Festival, complete with

The "Big House," at Wendover, Kentucky *(Credit: Copyright Gabrielle Beasley, Frontier Nursing Service, 1982)*

parade, street dancing, and much more. As you wander through the heavily forested hills and hollows, with the rocky substrata poking up through the thin topsoil, think what it must have been like for the nurses — without electricity, without roads, without telephones — tracking through this inhospitable country, trying to be helpful, with all the landscape pitted against them.

LOUISIANA

ALEXANDRIA

US Veterans Administration Medical Center Four miles north of Alexandria on Highway 71 71301. (318) 473-0010. The Alexandria VAMC campus dates back to 1852, when it was selected by the Louisiana legislature to be the home of the Louisiana State Seminary, the precursor to what is now Louisiana State University. In 1859 William Tecumseh Sherman was appointed superintendent of the Seminary. By the following year, with winds of war blowing through the South, the name was changed to Louisiana State Seminary and Military Academy. In 1861 Louisiana seceded from the

Union, and Sherman resigned to join the Union forces (later to become one of the North's most celebrated generals, leading the devastating "March to the Sea" from Atlanta to Savannah). Over the next four years, the buildings and grounds of the Seminary were used variously as the Taylor Hospital of the Confederacy, a Union forces headquarters, and a battleground for a minor Civil War skirmish. In the last thirty years of the nineteenth century, the Seminary buildings were abandoned, and the seminary itself moved to Baton Rouge, changing its name to LSU. In 1905 the grounds were used for a Louisiana Militia (National Guard) camp and renamed Camp Stafford. During World War I the area became Camp Beauregard, and a base hospital was erected. After the war control of the hospital was transferred to the US Public Health Service, which changed it into a tuberculosis hospital. In 1922 the USPHS gave it to the Veterans Bureau, which kept it as a TB hospital until 1929 when the land was split, resulting in the present VA hospital campus and — what is now across US Highway 71 — a national historic site encapsulating the history outlined above, under the jurisdiction of the US Forest Service.

The campus organization and internal architecture follows the universal floor plan which the VA adopted in the 1920s and 1930s. There's the usual dominant administration building, dining hall, ward arrangement, chapel, staff housing, and the like. The exterior architecture, however, is unique, because in those same 1920s and 1930s, the VA worked hard to blend functionalism with what it perceived to be the regional character surrounding each hospital. Thus, on the East coast, some 35 Georgian colonial hospitals were built, characteristically with red brick, white trim and columns, and pitched roofs sporting attic dormers. In Bay Pines, Florida, the VA hospital has a Spanish colonial feel, with severe walls set off by such theatrical detail as twisted columns and ornate leaf work. In Marion, Illinois, the "regionalism" almost becomes a parody of itself. There, the architect decided that the hospital's proximity to the Mississippi River was reason enough to recall Egypt's Nile River, resulting in a group of highly stylized Egyptian Revival buildings.

The Alexandria VA was constructed in the French château style, with red mansard roofs and ornate scrollwork around the dormer windows. Though French colonial architects never erected such buildings when Louisiana was in their hands, the result nonetheless clearly suggests the region's French heritage, and the size and number (32) of the buildings make them a very impressive sight indeed. The French heritage has been blended with Southern tradition in that the buildings are organized into quadrangles, set around large peaceful center lawns, the buildings themselves connected by breezeways added in the 1940s. The 149 acres of landscaping is worth a look in itself, with mature live oaks, ginkgo trees, and many other species set at stately intervals round the huge lawn, almost obscuring the hospital from the highway. The government has recently pumped some $40 million into the facility (new psychiatric building, new freestanding chapel, new surgery unit, extensively remodeled interiors), but the French château aura still dominates here — and the result is both unusual and attractive. Tours are available by prior arrangement.

CARVILLE

Gillis W Long Hansen's Disease Center (504) 642-4736. The Gillis W. Long Hansen's Disease Center (GWLHDC) is unique in all the world and is fascinating both for what it has been and what it has become. Hansen's disease is the modern name for leprosy, a term adopted in the hopes of freeing disease victims from the traditional stigma attached to the name "leper." The history of GWLHDC goes back to the latter years of the nineteenth century, when a New Orleans newspaper reporter did an exposé on the squalid conditions in which the city's lepers were forced to live. Louisiana was known to have an unusually large number of people suffering from leprosy, and they tended to be poorly and often cruelly treated wherever they went. A young Tulane professor, Dr. Isadore Dyer, then prevailed upon the state legislature to set up an institution for persons with the disease, and he was able to receive a small sum for that purpose. His original intent was to buy a facility close to Tulane, but the local citizenry became enraged, and Dr. Dyer was unable to purchase property anywhere in New Orleans. Ultimately, a piece of land known as Indian Camp Plantation, 85 miles up the Mississippi River, was selected, and, on November 30, 1894, five male and two female patients were taken by coal barge from the city to the plantation. No other form of transportation could be arranged.

For the next 20 years, the Louisiana Leper Home was operated by the state, with Dyer in charge, treating patients with the only remedy at his disposal, an ancient remedy from India called chaulmoogra oil. The facilities were, of course, segregated (even lepers, despised as they were, were not free of racial distinctions) — with black lepers housed in former slave cabins and whites in the old homestead building. Nursing was provided by the Daughters of Charity.

On January 3, 1921, the federal government purchased the home from the state, and the Carville facility became the National Leprosarium. Today, the GWLHDC (renamed in 1986 after the US Congressman from Louisiana) is the only hospital in the US specifically devoted to Hansen's disease, though there are a number of outpatient clinics and resource centers scattered around the country. Activities at the one facility include a mixture of treatment, rehabilitation, training, and research.

Carville was responsible for the initial use, in 1941, of sulfones in the treatment of Hansen's disease, a medication that remains a mainstay even now, though the incidence of sulfone-resistant disease is an increasing problem. Carville also helped with another research breakthrough in 1968 with the demonstration that the nine-banded armadillo could be infected with the disease, thus allowing for experiments involving *in vivo* culture of the organism and treatment with new drugs.

The facilities are extensive, covering several hundred acres on the bank of the Mississippi and occupying over 100 buildings. The administration building occupies an antebellum mansion that used to be the plantation mansion house. There is a huge modern infirmary, extensive resident quarters (including private rooms, apartments, and single bedroom cottages for married patients), schools, workshops, a 20-acre lake for fishing and boating, gardening plots, an 18-hole golf course, and much more. There's even a small bar where patients (and visitors) may purchase beer and wine from 2:00 to 5:00 in the afternoon.

The Old Plantation House, Carville, Louisiana *(Photo by Tanya A. Thomassie, Courtesy of the Gillis W Long Hansen's Disease Center)*

The GWLHDC is just outside Carville, about an hour and a half drive north of New Orleans. Guided tours are conducted twice daily on weekdays, at 10 AM and 1 PM (Don't miss the alligators in the hospital lake!). Specialized tours are available by advance arrangement.

NEW ORLEANS

Tulane University Medical Center 1415 Tulane Avenue 70112. (504) 588-5471. Tulane University School of Medicine is over 150 years old, but the path has not been easy. Along the way, Tulane lost its School of Pharmacy (1838–1934, one of the earliest founded in the country) and its School of Dentistry (1898–1934), and financial problems were the culprit.

Tulane traces its beginning to 1834, when three young doctors founded the Medical College of Louisiana, a proprietary school. Classes were held in various homes and in the local Presbyterian church, until 1843, when the State donated a piece of land, partially in exchange for the faculty's agreement to contribute their services to Charity Hospital free of charge for the next ten years. Thus began a love-hate relationship that dominated the history of both institutions until well into the twentieth century. In 1856, a rival school, the New Orleans School of Medicine, opened its doors across the street from Charity Hospital, and competed for students, faculty, and patients. The new school brought in Dr. Austin Flint, one of the country's most esteemed diagnosticians (Flint had previously been a professor at Buffalo and Louisville, and later went on to be professor of medicine at Bellevue Hospital Medical College from 1861 to 1886). However, the older school also had its glamour and achievements, and, in the late 1850s, New Orleans had two of the best medical schools in the country.

All this was altered dramatically by the Civil War (which forced both schools to close for the duration) and by Reconstruction (which doomed New Orleans and its medical schools to poverty for decades). From the time the schools reopened in 1865 until near the turn of the century, financial problems continually posed mortal threats. In fact, the New Orleans School of Medicine closed its doors in the early 1870s and was replaced from 1874 to 1877 by an ill-fated Charity Hospital Medical College, which likewise succumbed to financial problems. That left only the Medical College of Louisiana, which, though it functioned as an independent institution , had nominally come under the protective wing of the University of Louisiana in 1847. In 1884, after a substantial gift by wealthy philanthropist Paul Tulane, the University became the Tulane University of Louisiana. This, together with a couple of very large bequests to the medical college, made the university a far more dynamic concern and heightened its interest in its medical college. By 1905 the medical college was no longer a *de facto* proprietary college, it was under university control. When the Flexner Report on medical education was published in 1910, Tulane was described as "one of the very few existing Southern schools that deserve development." It lacked only an adequate endowment to insure its place among the top rank medical schools.

The next 50 years were characterized by the continual struggle to finance the high cost that modern, scientific, high-tech medicine imposes on medical colleges, together with conflicts among the university, the medical school, and Charity Hospital about where the money should come from and how control should be allocated. For a medical college of its stature, Tulane was unusual during this time (and until 1976) in that it had no university hospital of its own and was almost totally dependent on Charity Hospital patients for clinical teaching. Since both institutions were strapped for funds and resented and needed one another, the antagonism was considerable. The fact that Charity's leadership was dominated by political appointees who, for many years, were hostage to Huey Long's patronage system only added fuel to the quarrel.

Somehow the medical school survived those difficult years, and it also survived a long and turbulent battle over integration. In 1972 Tulane graduated its first black physician, Dr. Alvin J. Aubrey, Jr, putting Louisiana behind Arkansas, its immediate neighbor to the north, by twenty years.

Tulane's School of Public Health and Tropical Medicine has long been one of the university's strengths but the path to distinction has not been easy for it either. New Orleans' first chair in tropical medicine was established in 1902, and the School of Hygiene was formally established in 1913 (the same year Harvard established its School of Public Health). Five years later, however, World War I depleted the faculty, and Tulane was forced to suspend the school's operations. For the next 50 years, public health was either a department in the medical school or a subsection of the preventive medicine department. It wasn't until 1967 that Public Health and Tropical Medicine was reestablished as a school in its own right, this time funded almost entirely by federal grants. When federal money for medical research and education started drying up in the mid-1970s, Tulane went through another of its recurrent money crunches.

Today, the Tulane Medical Center is a relatively compact group of buildings flanking Tulane Avenue, near the CHNO. In addition to the intrinsic interest of the medical center, special attractions include the department of anatomy (on the third floor of the Burthe-Cottam building) which contains both the **Souchon Museum of Anatomy,** an award winning display of anatomical specimens, and the **Cummins Embryo Collection.** Both are kept in display cases lining a hallway which is a main thoroughfare in the building. Still, visitors must be escorted to see these remarkable specimens [(504) 588-5221]. Accessible without special arrangements is the **Rosenthal Memorial Ophthalmologic Museum.** Located on the third floor of the clinic building, this museum is composed of numerous display cases hanging on the walls of the eye clinic. Items in the collection include a wide variety of ophthalmic instruments and various types of spectacles.

The **Rudolph Matas Medical Library** dates to 1844. In an institution which has been chronically short of funds, the library has done uncommonly well, being the recipient of some important donations and endowments over the years, the most significant being a one million dollar bequest by Dr. Matas in 1937. Not surprisingly, the library was subsequently named after him. The collection is particularly strong in the areas of medical Americana, Confederate medicine, and women in medicine. Located on the second floor of the Hutchinson Building, the library often has interesting displays, and is open 8:00 AM to 11:00 PM Mondays through Fridays when school is in session.

Louisiana State University Medical Center 1440 Canal Street 70112. (504) 568-4806. LSU dates back to 1877, but its New Orleans School of Nursing began in 1929, the School of Medicine was founded in 1931, and the School of Dentistry in 1966. LSU lacks a university hospital of its own and so is dependent on teaching affiliations with over a dozen hospitals in New Orleans and the surrounding area, including the Hotel Dieu, Touro, and Ochsner. However, by far the most important clinical education site is Charity Hospital, which is just across the freeway from most of LSU's buildings (a few LSU structures are right on the Charity campus). Since LSU shares this crucial teaching facility with Tulane, and since LSU's tuition is only 20 to 40 percent as expensive as Tulane's (depending on whether the student is a state resident), LSU tends to think of itself as a much better educational bargain than the private school down the street. LSU occupies ten mostly new buildings in an area extending east of Charity Hospital, bounded on the other sides by Tulane Avenue, South Johnson Street, and Poydras Avenue. Currently, there are no tours available and no special displays of historical interest.

Charity Hospital 1532 Tulane Avenue 70140. (504) 568-2311. Charity Hospital in New Orleans (CHNO) was founded in 1736 and is thus over 250 years old, making it (along with Bellevue in New York) one of the oldest public hospitals in the country. The original hospital (at Chartres and Bienville Streets) was known generally as the St John's Hospital, but referred to in legal records as *L'hôpital des pauvres de la charité*. When Louisiana was ceded to Spain in 1763, Charity continued to care for the impoverished of the city, but under the name *Hospital de los Pobres de Caridad*. Over the next 50 years, the hospital was twice demolished, once by hurricane in 1779 and again by fire in 1809. The hospital as a consequence was moved a number of times, and all official records of the early years were lost. The hospital was totally rebuilt in 1784, on official decree of King Charles III of Spain, and for a while was called *Hospital St. Charles* in the King's honor. The Louisiana Purchase transferred the land to the United States in 1803. Louisiana became a state in 1812, and shortly thereafter the state assumed all responsibility for the hospital. The present site was selected in 1832, and the building erected shortly afterward stood until 1936. The present buildings date from 1939, though there have been the inevitable additions and renovations.

What a remarkable hospital! It has outlived the monarchies of Spain and France and the governments of the Louisiana Territory and the Confederacy. It has survived hurricanes, flood, fire, plague, and all-out war. Perhaps even more incredibly, it endured decades of gross mismanagement, graft, political corruption, and seemingly endless battles for money and control with — among others — its associated medical schools and the state government.

The first 150 years of Charity's life were dominated by a relentless succession of infectious diseases that made New Orleans arguably the most contagion-filled city in North America. Epidemics of malaria, cholera, typhoid, and, especially, yellow fever were regular features of life in the city, with yellow fever epidemics occurring almost annually. In the nineteenth century, once yellow fever gained a foothold and the victim became prostrate and jaundiced, with profuse bloody diarrhea and vomiting, there was virtually nothing any physician could do about it. Nonetheless, physicians tried their best. In Philadelphia, which had a terrible yellow fever epidemic in 1793, the treatment of choice was copious bleeding and purging. In Charity Hospital, the French influence led to a more moderate approach involving tepid baths and gentle laxatives, the principal advantage of which being that it did less harm than did the Philadelphia approach. Problems with contagion worsened after the Civil War. The South was both exhausted and impoverished by the war fought on its lands and was little able to implement public health measures. Though Louisiana had been the first state in the Union to institute a state board of health, its impact after the Civil War was nil. Pavements were decayed, garbage collection was nonexistent, human excreta was everywhere, swampland in and around the city swarmed with mosquitoes, and corrupt politicians had little interest in improving matters. In 1867, a major epidemic year in which 25 percent of the population was afflicted, there were 3300 yellow fever deaths in New Orleans. In 1878, 4406 died. After the cause of yellow fever was discovered at the turn of the century and effective mosquito abatement measures were instituted, yellow fever gradually disappeared from the United States, the last epidemic occurring in 1905.

It is impossible to separate CHNO's history from that of its nursing service and, in particular, from the Daughters of Charity, who have played such an important role in Louisiana health care. The sisters were given control of the nursing and housekeeping services in 1834, and they have been a fixture at CHNO ever since, always hardworking but not always universally loved. The Charity Hospital School of Nursing was inaugurated in 1892 and would have been established a decade earlier if issues of turf and territoriality between the sisters and the hospital board had been resolved in a more timely fashion. As it was, the first three directors of the School of Nursing were lay nurses, but for most of the twentieth century, the directorship has fallen to the Daughters of Charity, a highly unconventional circumstance for a state-owned school. The school's nurses' residence at 450 South Claiborne Avenue is called the **Sister Stanislaus Memorial Building**, named after a Daughter of Charity who was a dominant fixture in the hospital for almost 60 years. Currently, with 500 students, CHNO is the single most important source of RNs for Louisiana and one of only three diploma programs remaining in the state.

Charity Hospital is unique in the US in that it is a major metropolitan hospital devoted to the health care of the indigent — and yet it is operated not by the city or the county but by the state. Louisiana operates a string of nine charity hospitals, the most extensive network of any state, under the auspices of its Department of Health and Human Resources. CHNO is the oldest, the flagship, the tertiary care referral center for the entire system, and is thus known in the state as "Big Charity." Though physically located in New Orleans, over 50 percent of its inpatients and some 30 percent of its outpatients are from elsewhere in the state.

CHNO's medical "firsts" are almost all claimed by someone else, because all of the established New Orleans physicians who were associated with CHNO saw their private patients elsewhere. Thus, Charity regards Rudolph Matas as its most honored physician (as do Tulane, where he taught, and the Touro, where he saw his private patients) and claims that much of his pioneering work in arterial and chest surgery, his innovations with spinal anesthesia, and his introduction of saline infusions were accomplished here. It was here too that Michael DeBakey devised a pump for transfusing blood, where Charles Odom introduced epidural anesthesia, and where John Adriani devised saddle block anesthesia for pelvic surgery and childbirth.

Today, CHNO is the keystone in a downtown medical reservation which encompasses the Tulane Medical Center, the LSU Medical Center, the VA Hospital, the Hotel Dieu, and numerous other medically related buildings. CHNO itself is composed of several structures, the most dominant being the huge white hospital building constructed in 1939. At the time of its construction, the limestone hospital was the largest building in the South. The foundation is composed of 9700 separate pilings, each averaging 25 feet in depth, to secure the colossus in the moist New Orleans soil. The glazed tile necessary to line the hallways (almost 850,000 square feet) was the largest single tile order ever placed in the US. The building is more or less shaped like an "H," with an additional wing extending back from the crossbar. Its initial bed capacity was an astounding 3081 beds, though lately it has been running at about a third of that. The art deco ornamentation is notable, especially around the cornice (twenty stories up) and over the entryway. Just in front of the main entrance (and partly hidden by a poorly positioned flagpole) is a small monument covered with three wordy dedications: to Dr. Rudolph Matas; to the Sons of Aesculapius who died in wartime service; and to the conquering of "yellow jack" (yellow fever) in 1905. Inside the entrance lobby, be sure to see the portrait of Sister Stanislaus (with her flying nun headdress), dedicated to the Daughters of Charity for their contributions to the hospital from 1834 onward.

Despite its 250 year history, CHNO's future is by no means assured. In these tight money days, especially in Louisiana whose economy has been paralyzed by low oil prices and which has been suffering economic deprivations unparalleled since the 1930s, hospitals increasingly have to pay more and more of their own way. Given CHNO's historic role of providing for those who can afford no alternative, its ability to recoup costs from its patients is limited indeed. During the 1970s, six state-funded studies analyzed options ranging from renovation of the present building to the lease or sale of the building and all its operations. In 1989, the Governor proposed lopping 25 percent off Charity's already inadequate budget. The future bodes more of the same.

Tours are available by advance arrangement.

Lafon Nursing Home of the Holy Family 6900 Chef Menteur Highway. New Orleans 70126. (504) 246-1100. In appearance, the Lafon Home is an ordinary, albeit contemporary and attractive, sprawling two-story building on a large plot of land alongside a busy highway. However, behind the simple edifice lies a very special and extraordinarily inspiring story, which makes this institution unique and important. Established in 1842, it was this country's first home for the aged. Even more remarkably, from the beginning it has been operated by the Congregation of Sisters of the Holy Family, a community of black sisters. Dating from a time 20 years before the Civil War, this order is a testament to the exceptional ability and generosity of some dedicated women in caring for needy members of their own race, even during slavery, when the notion of a black nun was an affront to many members of the white community.

The story is too complicated to be told in full here, but the original sisters were "Free People of Color," a phenomenon made possible because of French and Spanish customs that antedated the Louisiana Purchase in 1803. Still, the fact that these black women were not slaves did not mean that they were fully free or legally equal. All arrangements for their community had to be oral; nowhere could there be formal, written acknowledgment of them as a religious order. They were not allowed to wear religious garb, and they were not listed in the Catholic Directory until well into the 1870s. They were ridiculed and laughed at, and their poverty was profound. Nonetheless, they endured—and the present-day Lafon Home is symbolic of uninterrupted service since 1842. Originally known as the St. Bernard Home of the Holy Family (the present site is the Home's third location), Lafon owes its name to a large bequest by Thommy Lafon, a free black man who achieved substantial wealth by investing profits from a small dry cleaning business in real estate. He died in 1893.

The sisters welcome visitors, though it would be wise to call first. The religious order has grown substantially over the years and now includes communities in nine states, Central America, and Africa. The Motherhouse is across the highway from the Lafon Home.

Touro Infirmary 1401 Foucher Street 70115. (504) 897-7011. This institution is the third oldest Jewish-sponsored hospital in the country, yielding only to Jewish Hospital in Cincinnati and Mt Sinai Hospital in New York City as far as longevity is concerned. It was founded in 1853 by Judah Touro, who bought a plantation-style mansion on the corner of Gaienne and New Levee Streets and organized it as "a charitable institution for the relief of the indigent sick." He recruited Dr Joseph Bensadon to be house surgeon for the 24-bed infirmary, a post in which he continued until he was appointed surgeon general of the Confederate Army in 1861. During the war, in order to prevent the hospital from being used by the Union Army, the Touro was converted into a home for the Jewish aged. When Judah Touro died in 1854, he directed that the hospital be renamed "The Hebrew Hospital of New Orleans," a directive that his executors (three Jews and two non-Jews) ignored in favor of retaining the name of the hospital's principal benefactor. In 1875, the hospital joined with the Gentleman's Hebrew Benevolent Association, calling the joint venture the Touro Infirmary and Hebrew Benevolent Society, a name which survived until 1911. The Touro moved to its present site (at the time a cow pasture) in 1882.

Over the years, the Touro has been associated with many firsts: Dr Abraham Levin was a pioneering gastroenterologist who invented the nasogastric tube (still called the Levin tube), the first stomach tube designed to go through the patient's nose instead of his mouth en route to the stomach. The Touro was the first hospital in the world to have a well-baby clinic, an innovation introduced by Dr LR DeBuys in 1921.

The hospital may be the only existing one in the country to be celebrated in a jazz tune. Famed cornetist Muggsy Spanier wrote "Relaxin' at the Touro" in 1938 while recovering from a series of abdominal operations at the hospital. The tune is a New Orleans-style blues composition which became extremely popular in the 1940s, selling more than 100,000 records. (The even more popular hospital lament, the "St. James Infirmary" dating from the 1890s, was derived from an English folk tune and refers to a London establishment.)

Visitors should be sure to see the three-dimensional Heritage Walk, which celebrates the Touro's first 100 years. There is also a fine art deco, limestone mural on Prytania Street, created in 1935 by artist Enrique Alferez. Tours are available on request [(504) 897-8423].

Hotel Dieu 2021 Perdido Street 70161. (504) 588-3000. To look at this hospital building, no one would guess that it is among the older hospitals in the country. This, of course, is because the building itself is relatively new (1972), and the hospital is on its third site. The New Orleans Hotel Dieu was opened (as the *Maison de Santé*) on the eve of the Civil War in 1859, by the Daughters of Charity of St. Vincent de Paul, patterned after the seventeenth century original Hôtel Dieu in Paris. Hotel Dieu was the only private hospital in New Orleans to remain open during the Civil War, and it played a pivotal role in caring for yellow fever victims in the epidemic of 1878. In 1913 it became the first private hospital in the country to install central air conditioning for its surgical suite (the system pumped a mixture of brine and ammonia). The 460-bed hospital can be toured by advance arrangement via the public relations office [(504) 588-3484].

Ochsner Medical Institutions 1512 Jefferson Highway 70121. (508) 838-4000. The Ochsner is one of a small number of well-established, highly prestigious, regionally dominant multispecialty clinics. Others in the same category include the Mayo and Cleveland clinics. Still, the Ochsner is unique, both in terms of its relatively short history and in terms of the particular exuberance it brings to its activities.

The Ochsner was founded in 1942 by Alton Ochsner and four colleagues, all restless Tulane professors in search of a new venture. Alton Ochsner was the most accomplished of the bunch, an enormously able surgeon, who was also professor and chairman of surgery at Tulane. Ochsner felt confined by the limitations of Charity Hospital, which was Tulane's only major teaching facility at the time. After repeated attempts to build a university hospital broke down, Ochsner looked for a suitable vehicle for his enormous energy and drive. He had been the first physician to link cigarette smoking and cancer, in a now-classic 1937 paper. His patients were soon to become such famous and/or influential people as Juan Peron, president and dictator of Argentina, Tomas Duque, president of Panama, golf celebrity Ben Hogan, cinema star Gary Cooper, and Texas mogul Clint Murchison. The Ochsner Clinic unleashed Alton Ochsner's enormous drive and became a social phenomenon as well as a medical enterprise.

The clinic was also enormously fortunate in the timing of its inauguration. World War II broke out three weeks before the clinic opened, siphoning off 25 percent of the physicians of New Orleans into the armed services, leaving Alton Ochsner and his post-draft-age cofounders with an oversupply of patients from Day One. It was not the sort of good fortune which endeared the Ochsner enterprise to the rest of the local medical establishment. Over the intervening years, the clinic has encountered some rough patches, though remarkably few given the turbulent currents which have buffetted most similar institutions. The clinic started as a small facility in some frame buildings left over from an old army hospital and moved to its present location in 1954.

The current Ochsner Medical Center boasts that it attracts more people to New Orleans each year than either the Mardi Gras or the Sugar Bowl. About half its patients come from out of town; ten percent come from Central and South America.

The Ochsner campus today is vibrant and optimistic, especially in contrast to the surrounding depressed Louisiana economy. Ochsner owes its accomplishments to a heady mixture of medical professional talent, shrewd business judgment, and vigorous marketing and publicizing. Ochsner opened an on-campus fitness center in 1976 (well before the crowd), a weight control clinic in 1979, and a sports division in 1981. In 1987 Ochsner began a "Men's Health Services Program" (the first of its kind in the country), followed by an aggressive marketing drive — and the program was an instant success. Likewise, Ochsner now has an OB/Gym program, a unique and highly marketable exercise program for expectant mothers.

Ochsner is clearly a place on the cutting edge of medical care innovation. It also probably has won more advertising, marketing, and public relations awards than any similar institution in the country.

Ochsner welcomes requests for tours [call (508) 838-3800], but a lot can be appreciated even without a guide. If you stand near the Jefferson Highway, looking toward the main entrance, the clinic building will be in front of you, the Ochsner Foundation Hospital will be to your right, and the Brent House Hotel will be to your left. The latter is a 300-room hotel for Ochsner patients, their families and guests, which features a six-story patio-atrium filled with fountains, trees, and flowering plants. It's definitely worth a look. Standing just in front of the hospital building is a slightly-larger-than-life–size statue of Alton Ochsner, set in a grassy area with trees, fountains, and flags nearby. In contrast to most such institutional monuments, this one shows the founder with a smile on his face. When you tour the Ochsner, you'll know why.

Historical Pharmacy Museum (La Pharmacie Française) 514 Chartres Street. New Orleans 70130. (504) 586-4392. In 1816 there were only two apothecaries licensed in the entire United States, both in New Orleans: F Grandchamp and LJ Dufilho. Whether both gentlemen actually had to pass an examination for their licenses is doubt-

Historical Pharmacy Museum, New Orleans, constructed 1823 *(Credit: New Orleans Pharmacy Museum, New Orleans, LA)*

ful, but there is no question that Louisiana was the first state to institute a system of certifying professional competence among pharmacists. The plaque to the right of the museum's doorway acknowledges this landmark in history as well as Louis Joseph Dufilho, who built his pharmacy here in 1823. The museum itself, one of the finest of its kind in the country, is located in the heart of the French Quarter and is easily accessible to New Orleans visitors. The ground floor showcases a preserved nineteenth century apothecary shop with gorgeous rosewood wall cabinets, handsome glass display cases, and an ornate 1855 Italian black and rose marble soda fountain. There is lots to see here, including numerous pharmacy jars, show globes, and examples of various proprietary and patent medicines and nostrums. Kids will love looking at the various bleeding devices, including seventeenth and eighteenth century leech jars. There's a charming old-world patio in the rear as well, a pleasant place to while away some time if the weather is decent, where Dufilho once grew medicinal herbs for use in his pharmacy practice. The second and third floors used to have other period pharmacy displays, and the top floor was formerly a recreation of the apartment inhabited by Mr. Dufilho and his family, but all the upper floors are now devoted to other non-museum uses. The museum is open Tuesday through Saturday, 10 AM to 5 PM. A small admission fee is charged.

SHREVEPORT

Louisiana State University Medical Center 1501 Kings Highway 71130. (318) 797-5000. The Shreveport medical school is one of the crop authorized in the 1960s and opened in the 1970s in response to the nation's perceived shortage of physicians. The medical center complex takes up the equivalent of a few city blocks and consists of a Comprehensive Care Teaching Facility, some basic and clinical science buildings, and the LSU Hospital. There is little to distinguish the buildings architecturally. No tours are offered. However, the LSU Hospital antedates the medical school by a hundred years and has quite a colorful past. The hospital was founded in 1876 as part of the state system for the poor, when a group of log and frame buildings at Ford Street and Pierre Avenue was purchased and called the Shreveport Charity Hospital. In 1889 and again in 1904 new hospitals were erected on a site on Texas Avenue, which is now occupied by Shreveport City Hall. These building fared poorly with the passage of years, facing chronic underfunding, crowding, and damage by fire, among other travails. A 1929 report called Shreveport Charity Hospital "an eyesore, firetrap and veritable bat-roost, accepted by our people as a dumping ground for vagabonds and streetwalkers, and to which our decent indigent sick had to be sent by persuasion and sometimes almost by force." The present building on the LSU campus (at the corner of Linwood Avenue and King's Highway) was completed in 1953 and christened the Confederate Memorial Medical Center. When it became the teaching hospital for LSU in 1978, the name was again changed to LSU Hospital in Shreveport.

Shriners' Hospital for Crippled Children 3100 Samford Avenue, Shreveport 71103. (318) 222-5704. The Shrine operates a system of 19 orthopedic hospitals and 3 burn institutes, each providing comprehensive services to needy children under 18 years of age, all completely free to the children, their parents, or any third party. The story begins here in Shreveport, where the first Shriners' Hospital was opened on September 16, 1922.

For a while after the founding of the first Shrine Temple in 1872 (by Billy Florence, an actor, and William Fleming, a physician), the Shrine was a predominantly fun-loving organization, devoted to frolic, albeit with occasional public service activities. By 1920, many members felt the need for a more serious "official philanthropy" to complement their organization's elaborate rituals and festivities. After much debate and discussion, the first children's hospital was opened in Shreveport, and, by 1927, 15 additional hospitals were open and caring for children without regard to race, religion, or any relationship to a Shriner.

During the early years, polio was the great crippler of children, but by the late 1950s and early 1960s, with the conquest of that dread disease, Shriners turned their attention to burn and spinal cord injury victims. When the Shrine opened its first burn institute in Galveston in 1966, there was only one comparable burn treatment center in the country, and that was at Brooke Army Hospital. Since that time, survival rates for patients with severe burns have almost doubled, thanks in part to the Shrine's contribution.

Over the years, Shriners have spent more than a billion dollars on their hospitals, supporting treatment, research, and training for health professionals. The money comes from a variety of sources, including a $5 annual assessment of each of the almost 900,000 North American members. Additional monies come from a large endowment fund and such fund raising activities as circuses and the annual East-West Shrine College All-Star Football Game. Shriners work hard for their hospitals and the children who use them, reflecting their belief that "No man stands so tall as when he stoops to help a burned or crippled child." Shrine hospitals emphasize a family-centered approach to treatment, encouraging at least one parent to remain with the child during the hospital stay. Schooling is also provided while the child is in the hospital.

The present Shreveport facility replaced the original building in 1985 and occupies exactly the same site, a seven-acre plot adjacent to LSU Medical Center. The dramatic 100,000 square foot building cost $13 million to build and another $3.5 million to equip and includes 45 patient beds and a large area devoted to parents' sleeping rooms. From the outside, it looks a bit like a collection of circus tents, all cream colored, with salmon and green ornamentation and peaked roofs. It's a whimsical contrast to the LSU monoblocks next door. Call in advance for tours.

MAINE

AUGUSTA

Augusta Mental Health Institute Arsenal Street 04330. (207) 289-7200. Established in 1840 as the first hospital of any type in the

The Stone Building, opened 1840, Augusta Mental Health Institute *(Credit: Peter E. Swartz, Chief of Volunteer Services)*

state of Maine, the Maine Insane Hospital was also one of the first ten mental hospitals to open in this country. The legislature appropriated the money for the land and buildings, but no money was appropriated for the operation of the hospital. Generally, this meant that the overseers of the towns where the individual patients lived were stuck with the bills. The hospital's first superintendent had only a brief stay here, but he was followed by Isaac Ray, who is known as the father of forensic psychiatry and who, while still at MIH, formed what is now known as the American Psychiatric Association. Ray spent four years here, leaving to head the Butler Hospital in Rhode Island. During the late nineteenth and early twentieth centuries, the hospital grew enormously, achieving its peak in the 1950s, with almost 2000 patients. Early in this century, the hospital expanded onto the adjacent property, which had previously been a United States Arsenal dating back to the 1820s. The name was changed to the Augusta State Hospital in 1913 and, more recently, to AMHI. The hospital is particularly interesting in that almost all of its buildings remain, from the original Kirkbride-type "swept-back wing" stone structures in front (c. 1840–1860), to the brick and wooden beam chronic wards (c. 1880) directly in back of the main administration building, to the various additions constructed at regular intervals in the twentieth century. Call the Volunteer Office [(207) 289-7217] for tours.

RANGELEY

The Wilhelm Reich Museum at Orgonon 04970. (207) 864-3443. This is the only museum in the United States which specifically memorializes any of Sigmund Freud's "inner circle." Reich graduated from the University of Vienna when he was 25 and was by then already a member of the Vienna Psychoanalytic Society. For the next decade, he devoted himself to the elaboration of the idea that orgastic potency was an essential component of mental health. He postulated that "armoring" interfered with the release of sexual energy and that this armoring had its roots in a repressive social order. Reich's work, therefore, was to revise the social order. This led to an irreparable breach with Freud, who believed that the problem was intrapsychic and the treatment therefore was psychoanalysis. Reich fled Germany in 1933, eventually arrived in the United States and, with the help of a friend, purchased a farm near Rangeley where he planned to live and study. Reich, at this time, was investigating a heretofore unknown form of energy that he called "orgone," and he named his new home Orgonon, to indicate that it would be the center for research on orgone energy. In the years that followed, he wrote and taught and developed a number of instruments, including an orgone energy accumulator and a device called a cloudbuster. In 1954, the US Food and Drug Administration filed an injunction against Reich, seeking to ban some of Reich's writings and preventing the interstate shipment of his orgone energy accumulators. Reich was furious and refused to appear in court to answer the complaint. The injunction was issued, and, later, when one of Reich's students was caught transporting an orgone energy accumulator from Maine to New York, Reich was jailed on contempt of court charges. He was found dead in his cell at the Federal Penitentiary in Lewisburg, Pennsylvania, in 1957.

What Reich called the Orgone Energy Observatory was opened as a museum in 1960. The essential feature is a massive stone house, designed by Reich himself, sitting on a wooded knoll overlooking a pond, in Maine's west-central lake and mountain district. The rooms are organized to highlight Reich's life and work, and they showcase various memorabilia and artifacts related to his theories. Reich's tomb, surmounted by a dour-looking bust of the man himself, is a short distance from the museum. Guided tours, which include a slide show, are available by appointment and according to the following schedule: July and August, Tuesday through Sunday, 1 PM to 5 PM; and September, Sundays only, 1 PM to 5 PM.

MARYLAND

BALTIMORE   (*See* **Great Medical Cities**)

BRYANTOWN

Dr. Samuel A. Mudd House Bryantown Road (off Poplar Hill Road) 20646. (301) 645-6870. Dr. Samuel Mudd gained both fame and ignominy by providing medical care for a man with a broken ankle who knocked at his door in the middle of the night. The patient was John Wilkes Booth who, just hours before, had assassinated Abraham Lincoln and then broken his own ankle when he leaped to the stage from the President's box at Ford's Theater. Fleeing south from Washington, DC, Booth and his companion stopped at the home of the 32-year-old doctor and received medical care. The assassins were captured several days later. Mudd was arrested, convicted of aiding and assisting the assassination, and sentenced to life imprisonment at Fort Jefferson, in the Dry Tortugas off the coast of Florida. Mudd was so generally reviled during this period that his name gave rise to the expression, "Your name will be Mudd."

Mudd always contended that he did not know the real identity of his patient and that he did not even know Lincoln had been assassinated the night before. Evidence brought against Mudd included the boot he cut off his patient (which had Booth's name in it) and testimony that Mudd had previously not only been seen in the company of Booth but had provided him with lodging once before. The fact that Mudd was a known Confederate sympathizer and was widely considered to have been a Confederate agent during the War didn't help any.

Mudd made several attempts to escape from prison and was finally pardoned by President Andrew Johnson for heroic work during a several-months-long yellow fever epidemic at Fort Jefferson. Thirty-eight persons had died at Fort Jefferson during the epidemic, including the post doctor and all four nurses, and Mudd stepped into the breech. After his release, Mudd returned here to his home in Charles County, just outside of Bryantown, and practiced medicine until he died in 1883.

The Mudd House sits on 10 acres and includes a museum and gift shop. It is usually open Saturdays and Sundays, from noon until 4 PM, from late March until late November. Docents in period costumes retrace Mudd's life for visitors, using original furniture and artifacts to illustrate the story. Additional tours are available by appointment [call Mrs Louise Arehart, Dr Mudd's granddaughter, at (301) 934-8464]. There is a modest admission charge.

CATONSVILLE   (*See* under Baltimore in Great Medical Cities)

CHURCHVILLE

Medical Hall West Medical Hall Road 21014. John Archer was born on this site in 1741 and built his home and office here in about 1800. What makes Archer unique is that he attended the University of Pennsylvania School of Medicine, graduating with its first class in 1768. This was the first medical school graduation in the thirteen colonies. As the graduation ceremony drew near, controversy developed about who was to have the honor of getting the first degree. Nine students were American and one was English. The predominantly British-trained faculty voted for the English student, but the Independence-minded students (in these pre-revolutionary times) threatened a boycott. The faculty ultimately backed down, instead deciding to award diplomas in alphabetical order. As a result, Archer became the first graduate in medicine in the United States.

Archer began practice here the following year. He also established a small school for physicians, training some 50 students between 1786 and 1810 (four of whom were his sons). He was also active in politics, being a member of Congress between 1802 and 1808. The current house here, called Medical Hall, actually dates from shortly after Archer's death, perhaps from 1825, and is a private dwelling. There are several small outbuildings here, of eighteenth and nineteenth century origin, as well as three archeological sites, including Archer's office and the remains of two of his homes. There is a historical marker on the highway, and some of the property is visible from the road, but there are no provisions for visitors. Please do not disturb the occupants, as this is a private residence.

EMMITSBURG

Shrine of St. Elizabeth Ann Seton St. Joseph's Provincial House. 333 South Seton Avenue 21727. (301) 447-6606. Elizabeth Seton (1774–1821) was one of those rare individuals who change the world and make it a better place. Because of her extraordinary leadership and dedication, she was selected by the Roman Catholic Church to become the first American-born female saint. The contributions of her followers to the development of American health care are incalculable.

Though Elizabeth was born an Episcopalian, personal events led her to become a Catholic after the death of her husband, William. In 1797 she helped organize the Society for the Relief of Poor Widows with Small Children, the first charitable association of women in the United States. By 1809, she had gathered a small band of religious and dedicated women about her, bringing them to Emmitsburg and founding the American branch of the Daughters of Charity. For the rest of the nineteenth century, the American Daughters of Charity could well be regarded as the most important single force in hospital development in the United States.

In 1823 the Sisters were invited to staff and administer the Baltimore Infirmary, which was eventually to become the University of Maryland Hospital. In 1828 they founded the first Catholic hospital in the United States and the first hospital west of the Mississippi, in St. Louis. They took over management of Charity Hospital in New Orleans in 1834, the Richmond (Virginia) Infirmary in 1838, and the Washington Infirmary (later George Washington University Hospital) in 1846. They established the first hospitals in Michigan (Detroit St Vincent's, in 1845) and one of the first in California (Los Angeles St Vincent's, in 1856), and dozens of others throughout the country. In 1896, the Daughters assumed responsibility for nursing care at the leprosy hospital in Carville, Louisiana, and in 1903, they did the same at the US Soldiers' Home in Washington, D.C.

To finance their various ventures, the Sisters developed remarkable innovations for their time. In 1874, to support a hospital in Saginaw, Michigan, they sold lumberjacks "hospital service tickets" for $5, good for an entire year. In Texas, they negotiated exclusive provider arrangements for employees of the railroads, and, in New Orleans, they did the same with the steamship companies.

During the Civil War, the Daughters of Charity, with their flying nun headdresses, were the single most dominant nursing presence in military hospitals and on the battlefields. Of the almost 600 Sisters from twelve different Roman Catholic orders who nursed both Union and Confederate soldiers, half were Daughters of Charity. The largest hospital of the war, Saterlee in Philadelphia, with 2400 beds, was staffed by the Daughters of Charity. Likewise, of the 300 Sisters from eight different religious communities who nursed the sick and injured in military hospitals during the Spanish-American War, 189 were Daughters of Charity.

Today, the Daughters operate a vast health-care system, with more than 13,000 beds in 43 hospitals located all across the country. Although for many years operated on a regional basis, in 1986 the

Daughters of Charity National Health System was incorporated, with national headquarters in St. Louis. Emmitsburg, however, was the early headquarters of the Daughters. During the Civil War, both Union and Confederate forces stayed here for a while, and both received nursing care during and after the Battle of Gettysburg some ten miles to the north—the bloodiest encounter of the war with a total of 46,000 casualties.

The Shrine here includes two homes in which Elizabeth Seton lived, together with a Visitor Center and museum, gift shop, and chapel (which contains her remains). There is also a Civil War memorial on the grounds. The facilities are open seven days a week (except for some holidays and the last two weeks in January), from 10 AM to 5 PM.

ROCKVILLE (*See* **under Washington, DC, in Great Medical Cities**)

MASSACHUSETTS

BOSTON (*See* **Great Medical Cities**)

FRAMINGHAM

Framingham Heart Study Clinic 98/118 Lincoln Street 01701. (508) 872-6556. It's difficult in this day and age to recognize that the words "risk factors" haven't always been a part of our health vocabulary. In fact, the words and the concept originated right here in this town of 70,000, about halfway between Boston and Worcester. The world's most famous cardiovascular epidemiology project was begun here in 1948, with some 5000 subjects. Every two years, subjects are put through an elaborate set of clinical and written tests by researchers drawn from Boston and Bethesda, plus a few from the local community. It's not by chance that Framingham has been called "the town under the microscope."

For the first dozen years, the study attracted little attention; but in 1961, the first article on cardiovascular risk factors appeared, and, since then, new developments from Framingham become front-page news. In the process, we have (1) redefined what we regard as "normal" cholesterol levels; (2) learned that the incidence of myocardial infarction can be changed by altering behavior and changing the nation's diet; (3) recognized that substantial numbers of heart attacks can be silent; and (4) found out that moderate alcohol intake can lessen the risk of heart attacks. Not all the conclusions which issued from the FHSC have been free of controversy, but Framingham is clearly deserving of at least some of the credit for the nationwide decline in cardiovascular deaths which began in the late 1960s.

Currently, the FHSC operates on an annual budget of $2 million. The program is centered in two small white frame buildings on Lincoln Street, just across from Framingham Union Hospital. The study group now includes the children of the original participants. Researchers joke that the new study should be called "son of Framingham," and local citizens say with pride that the only way to get into the study is to be born into it or to marry into it.

The headquarters buildings for this remarkable program are nothing special — in truth, they appeared run down and neglected when I visited — but nothing about their appearance can diminish the importance of what goes on here. The staff does not encourage visitors but doesn't mind sightseers so long as they don't disturb the research subjects. There are no plaques, monuments, or displays to give any hint about the study's contributions over the years.

LYNN

Lynn Historical Society 125 Green Street 01902. (617) 592-2465. There's only a small display case here which hardly does justice to its subject, but it's a starting place for a wonderful story which started and ended in Lynn. When Lydia Pinkham (1819–1883) began marketing her Vegetable Compound to women in 1875, there was no such specialty as gynecology, physicians had little accurate understanding of female physiology, and for a physician to even examine a woman's pelvic area was considered "indelicate" at best . Under the circumstances, any problems related to menstruation, ovulation, or "the change" became the province of folk medicine and proprietary treatments. Lydia Pinkham was an inveterate reader, especially partial to *The American Dispensatory* by Dr John King. She searched through King's tome for roots, herbs, and medicines which might qualify as "uterine sedatives" and then mixed up a concoction which she tried first on herself, then her neighbors and friends, and finally millions of women everywhere. The recipe called for 8 oz True Unicorn Root, 8 oz False Unicorn Root, 6 oz Life Root, 6 oz Black Cohosh, 6 oz Pleurisy Root, 12 oz Fenugreek Seed — all blended in a 40 proof alcohol solution. There was never any secret about the recipe; indeed, Pinkham took great pride in her candor and openness. The compound was vigorously promoted as "a sure cure for all Uterine Difficulties and all other complaints incident to Females," including everything from weakness and general debility to nymphomania and prolapsed uterus.

What separated the Vegetable Compound from the host of imitations which soon followed was the person of Mrs Pinkham herself. Along with her bottles of Compound, she distributed four-page facts-of-life pamphlets outlining her commonsensical views on diet, hygiene, fashion, and "feminine complaints." In 1879 her sons (who quickly became involved in the burgeoning business) decided to feature their mother's picture on the Vegetable Compound label. Amazingly, no living woman had ever been similarly featured, and the labels (with Mrs Pinkham's elderly features, her black dress, tortoise-shell comb, cameo brooch) were an instant success. By 1881, sales were $200,000 annually. Over the years, more than $40 million had been spent promoting Mrs Pinkham's visage, and the Compound was still bringing in up to $700,000 annually well into the 1970's, despite the concerted efforts of the Food and Drug Administration and medical practitioners everywhere.

When all is finally recorded about Mrs Pinkham and her Vegetable Compound, she will still be due credit for a number of pioneering steps: she was America's first successful business woman, hers was the first photograph of a woman to be used in advertising, and she wrote the first reliable facts-of-life treatise for use by women.

The Lynn Historical Society has some bottles of Vegetable Compound on display, together with some items about Mrs Pinkham herself. Occasionally, the Society mounts a special exhibit. The museum is open daily 1 PM to 4 PM, and at other hours by prior arrangement. There is a modest admission charge. Anyone wishing to see the Lydia E Pinkham Medicine Company itself will be directed to 271 Western Avenue (on Highway 107, a block up from the junction with 129). There in a pleasant residential neighborhood, you will see a large wood-frame building with some ivy-covered brick additions which have been converted into a collection of shops and offices.

NORTH OXFORD

Clara Barton Birthplace Museum 68 Clara Barton Road 01537. (508) 987-2056. Clara Barton, "the Angel of the Battlefield," was born here in 1821, eventually going on to serve as a volunteer nurse in the American Civil War. Later, she served the International Red Cross in the Franco-Prussian War, and, building on these experiences, she founded the American Red Cross in 1881 (she served as president for 23 years).

Barton's birthplace was purchased in 1921 by some members of the Unitarian-Universalist Church, to honor the church's most famous daughter on the 100th anniversary of her birth. However, it took another dozen years before anyone could find a suitable use for the property. In 1932, in the spirit of Barton's humanitarian work and with the encouragement of Dr Elliott Joslin, the land was given over to a camp for diabetic girls — a function which continues to this day.

The birthplace home itself occupies one corner of the property, has been lovingly restored by the Association of Universalist Women, and is currently maintained by the Unitarian-Universalist Women's Federation. Some of the furnishings are original and some are period pieces. The place is filled with memorabilia, including what seem to be tiny dresses (Barton weighed only 90 pounds) and a number of mementos from her colorful career. An unusual feature in the kitchen is an indoor well, complete with oaken bucket and chain, hidden by cabinetry in a corner.

Currently, the museum is open only on special occasions and by advance arrangement, though there are plans for regular visiting hours in the future. North Oxford is a tiny community near Worcester and finding the birthplace requires some care. Call for details.

Further down Route 12 South another 1.4 miles, the North Cemetery sits on the right-hand side of the road. It is here that Clara Barton is buried, her grave marked by a modest-size stone topped with an unmistakable red cross of red marble. (The grave is in the easternmost corner of the cemetery, to the right of the entrance.) Not far away is the grave of Elliott P Joslin, of Joslin Clinic fame, who also helped develop the Clara Barton Camp for Diabetic Girls.

SHREWSBURY

Worcester Foundation for Experimental Biology 222 Maple Avenue 01545 (508) 842-8921. This freestanding institute — not connected with any hospital or university — is composed of some 13 buildings on a 100-acre campus. Like most such private biomedical research centers, the vast majority of its funds comes from the federal government, either through the National Institutes of Health or the National Science Foundation. What sets Worcester apart, however, is its history. Founded in 1944 by renegade researchers Gregory Pincus and Hudson Hoagland, the place soon became like an artist colony for biological researchers, a seat-of-the-pants sort of place where everyone did his own thing. Pincus's thing, however, was reproductive biology, and it was he (along with Worcester codiscoverer Min-Chueh Chang) who was responsible for the development of the birth control pill. Most of the early research was done at the Foundation, the 1956 Puerto Rican field trials were run from the Foundation, and the final chemical formula for Enovid-10 (the world's first birth control pill) was developed here. Ironically, Pincus never bothered to apply for a patent, and thus neither he nor anyone else at the Foundation shared directly from the enormous profits that resulted from the sale of the pill.

Today, the Foundation continues its work in basic research, now concentrating on three areas: cell biology, neurobiology, and endocrine and reproductive physiology. The grounds are quite lovely, and the staff enjoys showing them to visitors with advance arrangements. The campus is located just outside Worcester, near the junction of Highways 9 and 140.

SOUTHBRIDGE

American Optical Company Museum 14 Mechanic Street 01550. (508) 765-9711. This seldom-visited museum contains the best collection of antique eye wear in the United States and is reputed to be one of the three top optical museums in the world (along with the Zeiss museum in Germany and the Pierre Marley museum in France). It has the largest and most diverse pince-nez collection anywhere, along with extensive collections of safety glasses, automobile driving goggles, glass cases, lorgnettes and spectacles, and eye wear paraphernalia of all kinds. There's a dual history portrayed here: that of corrective vision, and that of American Optical as a company.

In 1833 William Beecher began his spectacle business. Some fifty years later, AO began producing its own lenses, being the first American spectacle company to free itself from a traditional dependence on European-produced lenses — a dependence that sometimes meant up to a year's wait for customers. By 1884, AO was making the best spherical lenses anywhere and soon became the world's largest producer of ophthalmic lenses.

The building in which the museum is located is a huge Romanesque Revival structure, with a dominant clock tower, built in 1902, but the industrial campus occupies some 150 acres. The museum itself occupies several rooms and spills out into the hallways. In addition to the items already mentioned, you will find early optic equipment (lensometers and optometers), lens grinding machines, monoplex plastic eyes and glass artificial eyes in various stages of production, various kinds of eye examination and refraction equipment — and the first fiber-optic laryngoscope ever produced.

The museum was opened in 1983 and has been staffed mostly by volunteers. However, Southbridge is not near any major metropolitan area, and the museum does not get enough visitors to keep it open on a regular basis. Still, the company is always pleased to open up its fine collection to interested people by advance arrangement. There is no admission charge.

WORCESTER

Clark University 950 Main Street 01610. (508) 793-7711. Clark's place in medical history stems from its colorful and energetic first president, G Stanley Hall. Hall was a controversial fellow of vast enthusiasms, some of which led him to found the *American Journal of Psychology*, as well as to become a founder and first president of the American Psychological Association. His primary enthusiasm in 1909, however, was psychoanalysis, and as a result he invited several major figures in the field to lecture at Clark's 20th anniversary celebration. CG Jung was there and so was Sandor Ferenczi, but the star attraction was clearly Sigmund Freud, who agreed to come only after Hall offered him an honorary degree. It was to be Freud's only trip to America and the only honorary degree this

Statue of Sigmund Freud in Psychology Lounge, Clark University *(Courtesy of Clark University)*

brilliant and seminal thinker was to receive during his lifetime. Freud delivered five lectures, all in German, and the record shows they were greeted with much applause.

Clark is now a well-respected private, coeducational, liberal arts university that occupies a modest-size campus in southwest Worcester. The only reminder of the 1909 lectures is in Jonas Clark Hall, the oldest building on campus. There, tucked away in the psychology department lounge (Room 320), is a bronze statue of Sigmund Freud, dedicated by his daughter Anna. The inscription reads: "Sigmund Freud, 1856–1939. Donated by the American Psychoanalytic Association in memory of Freud's lectures at Clark University introducing psychoanalysis in the United States, September 21, 1957." The statue was originally in the hallway, but frisky undergraduates repeatedly stole it as a prank (it was once missing for six months), so it is now in safer quarters. Visitors are generally welcome in the lounge during normal business hours; call (508) 793-7273 for details.

University of Massachusetts Medical Center 55 Lake Avenue North 01605. (508) 856-0011. The University of Massachusetts dates back to 1863, but this campus was founded only as recently as 1962, and the medical school didn't actually accept its first students until 1970. Getting the Medical Center was quite a coup for Worcester. Once the University decided it wanted a medical school, there was considerable competition as to where it should be built. An outside consulting firm was called in and recommended the University's main, 1100-acre campus in Amherst as first choice. Worcester challenged the decision as being biased and argued that the medical school belonged in an urban location such as Worcester. Other factions argued for a suburban Boston location, among others. After four rounds of voting by the U Mass trustees, Amherst and Worcester were tied with 11 votes each, but Worcester managed to win on the fifth ballot, 12 to 10. The result has been more than satisfactory from Worcester's point of view: the city now has a modern 350-bed teaching hospital, a medical school with 400 students, graduate schools of Biomedical Sciences and Nursing, and a vigorous research program that brings in more NIH money than is received by any of the other 11 public medical schools in the Northeast. The Center, sitting atop a hillside overlooking Lake Quinsigamond, also acts as the major tertiary referral center for central Massachusetts.

The medical center is composed principally of two large, rectangular, gray-granite–faced edifices, the school and the hospital, designed to function as a single, integrated health-sciences facility, interconnected at every level. The school building has the health sciences library as its centerpiece, with the basic science wing, the clinical science wing, and the student laboratories arrayed along three sides. The library has a small rare book collection, together with a number of interesting historical displays both at the entrance and scattered around the library itself and in the rare book room. Tours are available by calling (508) 856-2558.

Worcester State Hospital 305 Belmont Street 01604. (508) 752-4681. As you proceed up the drive from the main gate, a magnificent relic gradually comes into view. Wooden railings crumbling, windows knocked out and often boarded up, the clock face on the tower in disrepair — only the unending stone walls do not show the ravages of time. There are over two dozen buildings here, the oldest dating to 1874 and half the rest having been built before the turn of the century, all linked together into an enormous and eerily attractive, Victorian-era stone mass. The walls are so thick and solid that tearing them down is prohibitively expensive, yet the deteriorating wood interiors and the archaic plumbing, electricity, and heating, are also prohibitively costly to repair. The result is that the vast majority of these buildings have been empty many years and are likely to remain so for the foreseeable future. What would be an adaptive, economical use for these old stone structures?

WSH opened in 1833 (as the State Lunatic Hospital) and rapidly became the prototype for state mental hospitals all around the country. Much of its early success was clearly due to its first superintendent, Samuel B Woodward, who was so highly esteemed by his contemporaries that he was elected the first president (in 1844) of what today is the American Psychiatric Association. During Woodward's thirteen years of leadership, WSH had at most 120 patients, and Woodward knew every one personally and intimately, allowing for an enormously humane relationship between the superintendent and his charges. By 1850, however, there were 500 patients, and the new superintendent had to place increasing reliance on attendants, who were low-paid, inexperienced, and too often cruel and indifferent. Inevitably, the use of physical restraints replaced kindness and understanding, and WSH, like many similar institutions, became primarily a custodial hospital. By 1890, now at its present location, the patient population at WSH was 800, and in 1901 it reached 1100.

The hospital regained a taste of its former glory in 1896 when Adolf Meyer was appointed hospital pathologist and director of clinics, with the mandate to organize a research program. Meyer was eventually to become the chairman of the department of psychiatry at Johns Hopkins and to be widely regarded as the "Dean of American Psychiatry." During Meyer's five years at WSH, the hospital regained its national reputation, this time as a major research and training center. In 1925, when the patient population was 2000, Anton Boisen started the first clinical pastoral counseling training program in the country at WSH. By the late 1940s (patient population 2800), the hospital's research division had grown so large that it was probably the most important center of schizophrenia research in the US. In the 1950s, penicillin depleted the continuing supply of syphilitic patients and the newly discovered tranquilizing medications emptied still more beds. Deinstitutionalization programs of the 1960s and 1970s turned out most of the rest, and the fiscal hard times of the 1980s left few financial resources for the small number of patients and staff remaining.

WSH continues to operate as a 400-bed state psychiatric facility, but all inpatient facilities are confined to the newish (1957) Bryan Building. This is an undistinguished brick institutional block with steel-framed escape-proof windows. The stark contrast created between it and the original buildings only serves to make the older buildings more attractive.

There are no tours for visitors here but a drive around the extensive grounds reveals many interesting items. Try to imagine how this must have appeared to Freud and Jung when they visited here in 1909. As you drive up the main entrance road, the fields to the far right are part of what was the hospital farm, initially planted with alfalfa (hayed each year) and clover to feed hospital livestock, most of which were kept where U Mass is now. The rock walls that line the roads in various places were built by one of the hospital's patients, as a continuing labor over 30 years. On the service road off to the left, you can see portions of four gambrel-roofed colonial cottages, constructed at various intervals as incentives to entice physicians to come to the hospital.

The clock tower building boasts an elaborate porte cochere. There are fantastic architectural details here, including Victorian gingerbread detailing, decorative ironwork, and now greenish copper sheeting. The interior has a five-story carved oak staircase, twirling upward around a central well, the whole lighted by a skylight at the top. The old superintendent's quarters occupied the second floor, the quarters including a dining room with a table seating 40, hallways in places 20 feet wide, a library, sitting room, several bedrooms, and maids' quarters. The steward, who acted as the superintendent's executive assistant, lived on the third floor in less elaborate quarters. The patients' wards extended out on both sides from the administrative center.

As you drive around to the right, the prominent circular building (Gage Hall, 1887) was designed for patients who were morbidly depressed. The nurses occupied a pedestal stage in the center, circled with large Corinthian columns, from which they could observe the patients in beds placed around the circumference. The 28 windows were meant to capture the sun's rays and make the place more cheerful. As you drive around to the back, you'll see a set of what obviously are service buildings, including the boiler room, a huge stable, and the old laundry. Further on, opposite the relatively modern storehouse (1957), sits the morgue and the lab. Recessed and to the left, you can see the bakery and next to that the kitchen. To the right of the morgue is the hydrotherapy unit (1937), where agitated patients were placed in baths to calm them.

MICHIGAN

ANN ARBOR

University of Michigan Medical Center 1405 East Ann 48109. (313) 764-1817. In 1850, classes began at what was then known as the Medical Department of the University of Michigan. By 1866, the increasing demand for physicians occasioned by the Civil War had swollen the student body to 575, making this the largest medical school in the United States. By the latter years of the nineteenth century, Michigan was clearly one of the country's leading schools, founding the first Department of Hygiene and Physiological Chemistry (in 1888) and the first psychiatric hospital in association with a university (in 1906). For many of its early decades, the school was far stronger in its preclinical components than in patient care, in large part because Ann Arbor was a tiny village with meager numbers of patients for the students to examine.

Still, the University is credited with having the first general hospital owned and controlled by a university solely for teaching purposes, when it opened a 20-bed facility in 1869 in a home which had belonged to a professor. In 1875 an expanded structure (called the Campus Pavilion Hospital) was built solely of wood, so it could be easily burned down ten years afterwards, since the builders assumed that by then the structure would be so badly infected it could no longer be used. Various additional structures were added over the decades which followed, and the oldest medical building now dates from 1937 (seven major buildings have been added in the past decade).

In 1875, because of widespread support for homeopathy in the state and in the legislature, the University was required to establish a homeopathic medical college. This resulted in the resignation of the entire medical faculty. The professors were persuaded to return to work but the regents were then obliged to pass a resolution forbidding discourses against homeopathy on university property. Finally, in the late 1890s, the supreme court decided that the regents could not be coerced by the legislature into maintaining a school they did not want, and the homeopathic enterprise left the University of Michigan to become the Detroit Homeopathic College.

The University Hospital and the Medical Center have contributed many medical firsts, including:

1928	First physician-training program in thoracic surgery
1941	The nation's first heredity (genetics) clinic
1956	Development of the flexible gastroscopy tube (Marvin Pollard and Arthur French)
1987	First baby fathered by a spinal-cord–injured man using an electrical stimulation technique called electroejaculation

The University's College of Pharmacy was established in 1876, the first to be started in a state university. It was also the first program which placed such emphasis on academics that it required no apprenticeship for graduation. The pharmacy academic honor society, Rho Chi, was begun here in 1922.

The School of Dentistry was established in 1875, the first to be organized as a separate part of a state university. In 1894 it became the first dental school to provide any program on the graduate level; in 1922, the first to offer graduate training in orthodontics; and in 1952, the first to conduct a program designed specifically for training teachers of dentistry.

The University of Michigan Medical Center now occupies 82 acres and includes 7 hospitals with almost 900 beds. Tours are available from the Public Relations Department.

BATTLE CREEK

Battle Creek Adventist Hospital 165 North Washington Avenue 49016. (616) 964-7121. Broad principles of healthful living, including a balanced diet, natural remedies (such as fresh air, sunlight, and rest), preventive medicine, and mental and spiritual health, have been a central feature of the Seventh-Day Adventist Church since at least the 1860s. In 1866 the Church opened the Western Health Reform Institute as the first of what would grow to be 26 sanitoriums in the United States and abroad by the turn of the century. In 1877 John Harvey Kellogg, MD (1852–1943) became the Institute's Medical Superintendent and changed its name to the Battle Creek Medical and Surgical Sanitarium. (Kellogg coined the word "sanitarium," investing the traditional "sanitorium"—a place usually providing such therapy as exercise, hydrotherapy, diet, and rest—with a special emphasis on sanitary living.) Kellogg was a remarkable speaker, surgeon, inventor, author, and innovator. To further his concepts of healthful living through vegetarianism, he invented some 80 grain and nut food products, including peanut butter, flaked breakfast cereals, and granola. His brother and protégé, WK Kellogg, a 25-year employee of the Sanitarium, went on to form the Kellogg breakfast food enterprises. A patient, CW Post, adapted Kellogg's Caramel Cereal Coffee into a similar product called Postum, and another food industry giant was launched. JH Kellogg also invented such health related products as the vibrating chair, the vibrating belt, the Universal Dynamometer (for testing strength), tanning lights, and the menthol inhaler.

As a result of Kellogg's genius and the force of his personality, the Battle Creek Sanitarium became the largest institution of its kind in the world, attracting such famous guests and patients as John D Rockefeller, George Bernard Shaw, William Jennings Bryan, Thomas Edison, Ivan Pavlov, and Dale Carnegie. Patient number 100,000 at the Sanitarium was President William Howard Taft. By the 1890s, the "San" had become a spa for celebrities, where they were "catered to, entertained, massaged, babied." The medical needs of patients were not neglected (Kellogg performed more than 22,000 operations in his lifetime), but patients also enjoyed educational lectures, cooking classes, and the company of the internationally famous and wealthy clientele. In 1895 the Sanitarium even instituted its own medical school, the American Medical Missionary College, with a four-year program divided between Battle Creek and Chicago (the school closed in 1910).

The Adventist Church had intended the Institute to be a place conducive to spiritual well-being, with an emphasis on simple, natural remedies. As Kellogg's extravaganza became less denominational and spiritual and more independent, secular, and ostentatious, a schism ensued. The Sanitarium suffered a catastrophic fire in 1902, and Kellogg rebuilt the edifice in luxurious style, with over five acres of marble floors stretching through the grand Italian renaissance structure. In 1906 the Church severed its connections with the Sanitarium, which continued to function as before until

The Battle Creek Sanitarium Complex as it appeared in 1928 (these buildings are now part of the Battle Creek Federal Center) *(Courtesy of the Battle Creek Adventist Hospital)*

the Great Depression drastically limited its income without likewise cutting its debt. In 1933 the financially overextended Sanitarium went into receivership, and the building was sold to the US Government, to become the Percy Jones General Hospital. The work of the Sanitarium continued in much smaller buildings, with Kellogg having a progressively smaller role up until his death in 1943. The facility was then operated by the Michigan Sanitarium Corporation until 1974, when it once again came under the direct ownership and control of the Seventh-Day Adventist health care system and assumed its present name.

The Battle Creek Adventist Hospital is now a modern, 155-bed facility and a member of the Adventist Health System, which includes upwards of 170 hospitals, clinics, and long-term care facilities. Tours are available by advance arrangement. The old 1903 "San" is now the Federal Defense Logistics Center, across the street and a block down North Washington. The Center is not currently open to the public, but the exterior remains most impressive in its own right.

DETROIT

Wayne State University Medical Center 540 East Canfield Avenue 48201. (313) 577-1429. This school of medicine began as a proprietary enterprise, known as the Detroit Medical College, in 1868. Lacking its own facilities, the College used one of the old Civil War buildings on the grounds of Harper Hospital. A competing institution, the Michigan College of Medicine (founded in 1880) was absorbed in 1885, allowing the newly named Detroit College of Medicine to move into the building of the extinct Michigan College. By 1913 the Detroit College was suffering from major financial problems, and the College was sold to a group of alumni and renamed the Detroit College of Medicine and Surgery. The financial problems continued, and, in 1918, the College was transferred to the Detroit Board of Education. In 1933 the Detroit College of Medicine and Surgery changed its name to Wayne University College of Medicine, in honor of Revolutionary War hero General Anthony Wayne, to whom the Indians surrendered the region in 1795.

The state assumed responsibility for the University in 1956, and the College was renamed Wayne State University School of Medicine. The late 1960s witnessed the beginnings of what is now the 110-acre Detroit Medical Center. Detroit is the largest city in the country with only one medical school, and the vast collection of health care, research, and training institutions which surrounds the School of Medicine is truly remarkable. Major facilities in this complex include Harper-Grace Hospitals, Hutzel Hospital (specializing in obstetrics and gynecology, founded 1868), Children's Hospital (1887), and Detroit Receiving Hospital (1915).

Tours of individual components of the Detroit Medical Center can be arranged by contacting the individual institutions. Tours of the School of Medicine should be arranged via its Public Affairs department.

Detroit-Riverview Hospital 7733 East Jefferson 48214. (313) 499-4000. This is the corporate descendant of what was once one of the first hospitals in the Northwest Territory, which included Michigan, Ohio, Illinois, Indiana, Wisconsin, and part of Minnesota. The hospital began in 1845, when the Daughters of Charity converted a part of their school to accommodate 30 patients. In 1850 a new facility was completed, and the hospital changed its name to St. Mary's. During the Civil War, the 150-bed facility expanded to 250 beds to care for sick and wounded soldiers. About this time, Protestant groups raised a storm of protest because of the hospital's practice of baptizing terminally ill patients, so they could "die as Catholics." By 1949 St. Mary's was an inner-city hospital with a population base that had fled to the suburbs. The Daughters of Charity then sold the facility to a group of staff physicians, and it was renamed the Detroit Memorial Hospital. By the late 1970s, the aged physical plant (with portions dating from 1879) needed an extensive and costly overhaul. In 1976 Detroit Memorial Hospital merged with Alexander Blain Memorial (founded 1924) and Jennings Memorial (1930) to create a new entity. The 315-bed, modern Riverview Hospital is the result. Tours are available by advance arrangement with administration [(313) 499-4100].

Harper-Grace Hospitals 3990 John Road 48201. (313) 745-8040. Harper General Hospital was incorporated in 1863, in the midst of the Civil War, and the land was immediately leased to the federal government for use as a military hospital. When the war ended, the government returned the eleven barracks-like buildings it had constructed, and Harper Hospital opened its doors to the general public. Grace Hospital was incorporated in 1888 and spent its early years as the teaching hospital for the Detroit Homeopathic College. In 1901 Grace opened its staff to "regular practitioners" as well as homeopaths. The two hospitals merged in 1973.

Harper-Grace has contributed much to medical progress. In 1890 Harper became the first hospital in the country to adopt an eight-hour day for nurses. In 1952 Dewey Dodrill of Harper invented the first machine to allow blood to bypass the heart during surgery (the first heart-lung machine, invented in Philadelphia in 1953, made Dodrill's discovery obsolete). In 1987 Harper installed the world's first superconducting cyclotron to treat cancers with neutrons.

Harper is now a 900-bed referral facility, located at the address above in the Detroit Medical Center. Grace [18700 Meyers Road, 48235, (313) 966-3300] is a 400-bed community hospital located some distance away. Tours of both facilities are available through their own public relations departments.

Henry Ford Hospital 2799 West Grand Boulevard 48202. (313) 876-2600. When Detroit became the automobile capital of the world just after the turn of the century, its population almost doubled in the following decade. As a result, the inadequate hospital facilities were severely strained, and various civic leaders combined to form the Detroit General Hospital Association. After four years of fund raising and construction, work ground to a halt, and a group of unfinished buildings stood as mute testimony to the inability of the organizers to get the job done. Henry Ford, who was the major financial backer of the effort and who could not abide inefficiency, paid off the rest of the financial supporters and undertook to build the hospital himself. The Henry Ford Hospital opened in 1915 as a 48-bed unit, dedicated to the efficiency of the assembly line. Hernias were repaired on Mondays, appendices removed on Tuesdays, gallbladders on Wednesdays, hysterectomies were performed on Thursdays, and prostates repaired on Fridays. The hospital staff were all salaried, in order to eliminate fee-splitting abuses, and all patients were charged a flat rate for medical treatment, surgery, and hospitalization. Ford did not believe in charity and there was no free care, but needy patients were admitted with the understanding that they would be given a job at the Ford plant after they recovered, so they could work to pay off their accounts.

Today, with 1050 beds, Henry Ford is among the nation's largest combined private hospitals and group-practice clinics, providing some 9000 jobs at its various facilities in the Detroit area. Tours of HFH can be arranged through the Volunteer Services Department.

EAST LANSING

Michigan State University College of Human Medicine Life Sciences Building. MSU Campus 48824. (517) 353-9620. Michigan State University started studying the feasibility of establishing its own medical school in 1957, but the idea did not meet with widespread enthusiasm. The state's two existing medical schools were fearful that the new venture would siphon off funding, and many observers felt that East Lansing lacked adequate clinical material to support a teaching program. Nonetheless, MSU persevered. A two-year basic-science program was established, and the first students were admitted in 1966. By 1970, the program had expanded to four full years, and the first MDs were graduated in 1972. This is a community-based program: the first two years are spent on the MSU campus, and clinical education takes place in community hospitals on "clinical campuses" located in Flint, Grand Rapids, Kalamazoo, Lansing, Saginaw, and the Upper Peninsula. At present, there are no tours available of the College's facilities on the MSU campus.

ISHPEMING

Francis A Bell Memorial Hospital 101 South Fourth Street 49849. (906) 486-4431. This is one of the few survivors of a time when industrial hospitals were scattered widely across the country. Michigan, for example, had the Calumet and Hecla Consolidated Copper Company Hospital (in Calumet), the Belding Brothers Silk Company Hospital (in Belding), and this one dedicated to caring for iron ore miners and their families. The Iron Cliff Company opened a small hospital in an Ishpeming duplex in 1872. The doctor lived on one side, and the patients were cared for on the other. Married miners paid $1 a month and single miners paid 75 cents, which entitled them to all medical benefits. Any treatment or surgical procedure that couldn't be handled locally was shipped off to Chicago or Milwaukee at the mining company's expense. The company erected a formal hospital in 1887, and, by 1892, the staff included five doctors, two drug clerks, and four nurses, among others. In 1918 the company (now known as the Cleveland Cliffs Iron Company) erected a three-story, 60-bed brick facility, decorated with huge slabs of locally quarried marble. For the first time, the doctors were placed on salaries, rather than simply receiving fees for services performed. In the early 1950s, the hospital was transformed from a company hospital to a community-owned one and named in honor of a local attorney who helped implement the change. Today Bell Memorial has 115 beds and occupies a handsome modern building, which serves the community and the surrounding area. Tours are available from the Public Relations department.

KALAMAZOO

The Upjohn Company 7000 Portage Road 49001. (616) 323-4000. Until WE Upjohn developed his "friable pill" in 1884, mass-produced tablets tended to be rock-hard (due to a loss of moisture) by the time they reached the consumer. As a result, such pills passed through the gastrointestinal tract intact, their contents never getting into the body. Upjohn, a physician, combined a spray device, powdered formula, and a revolving pan to create pills which would retain moisture and disintegrate rapidly, releasing medications into the body. By 1886 Upjohn had used his invention as the basis for a business — the Upjohn Pill and Granule Co — in which he was joined by several brothers. The firm's trademark was a thumb, crushing a tablet to powder. In the early years, Upjohn's products tended to be plant extracts of one form or another. The company's first blockbuster product was Phenolax, the first mint-flavored laxative, sold first in 1908 (100,000,000 tablets were sold in 1914 alone). Soon Upjohn had a research department and a variety of other products were released: Citrocarbonate (an antacid, 1921); Cheracol (a cough syrup, 1928); Kaopectate (for diarrhea, 1936); Heparin (an anticoagulant, 1942); Orinase (an oral antidiabetic agent, 1955); Medrol (an artificial steroid, 1957); and Motrin (an anti-inflammatory agent, 1974).

Today, Upjohn is a huge operation, employing 21,000 people in over 50 nations. However, Kalamazoo remains the company's headquarters, and the Reception Center here has a small museum where you can see a movie outlining the firm's history, and from which visitors begin a one hour tour of the manufacturing plant. Tours are conducted Mondays through Fridays at 8:15 AM, 10:30 AM, and 1:15 PM. Call (616) 323-5866 for reservations.

MACKINAC ISLAND

William Beaumont Memorial Museum Mackinac Island State Park 49757. (906) 847-3761. While there are other museums dedicated to William Beaumont (e.g., in Connecticut and Wisconsin), this is the building in which the saga of Beaumont and Alexis St Martin began. On June 6, 1822, this, the retail store of John Jacob Astor's American Fur Company, was crowded with trappers. Alexis St Martin was among them and was suddenly thrust into medical history when a shotgun discharged accidentally, hitting him in the abdomen and lower chest. Beaumont, the surgeon at the nearby fort, was called immediately and did what he could: extracted shot and wadding, removed bits of clothing and shattered rib, debrided tissue and dressed the wound. No one expected St Martin to live more than a few hours, but survive he did — and, by the fifth week, the open stomach had become firmly attached to the chest wall and "showed not the least disposition to close its orifice." There was no one else to care for St Martin, so Beaumont took him into his own home, and thus began one of the great adventures in American medicine. Beaumont, an unknown surgeon on an isolated military post, conducted landmark investigations into gastric physiology. He dangled bits of food on a silk suture, dropped them into the orifice and extracted them at varying intervals. He tested beef and barley, apples and oranges, turnips and dumplings. St Martin, intemperate and given to drunken binges, loathed the experiments, and longed for his unfettered life in the forest. The strange partnership continued off and on for a dozen years and resulted in 238 published experiments, making Beaumont America's pioneer physiologist. The doctor died in 1853, and St Martin outlived him by 27 years, dying at age 83. When St Martin died, William Osler tried to obtain the body for an autopsy, so he could preserve the famous stomach. St Martin's family responded from the north woods by wire: "Don't come for autopsy. Will be killed." St Martin's family are said to have buried their kin in an unmarked grave, eight feet deep, to make sure he would never be found by medical scientists.

The small museum here tells the story of these two remarkable men and captures the flavor of Beaumont's service at this post (1820–1825). The upper floor contains dioramas depicting the accident and phases of Beaumont's life, along with period medical instruments and some of Beaumont's medical journals. The first floor contains period furniture, together with some of Beaumont's own possessions. The museum is open from mid-May to mid-October, from 9 AM to 6 PM. There is a small admission charge.

MINNESOTA

MINNEAPOLIS

University of Minnesota Medical School 420 Delaware Street SE 55455. (612)624-5100. The first University of Minnesota Medical Department was established in 1883 as a nonteaching unit. Instead it was simply an examining body which conferred the license to practice medicine and surgery in the state. When the University established a College of Medicine in 1887, this "Medical Department" became the first state board of medical examiners in the country. The University's College of Medicine (the name was changed to U of M Medical School in 1913) eventually absorbed the successors of several earlier institutions, including the St Paul School of Medical Instruction (1870), the Winona Medical School (1872), the Medical Department of Hamline University (1880), the Minnesota College Hospital (1881), the Minneapolis College of Physicians and Surgeons (1883), and the Minnesota Homeopathic Medical College (1886).

A College of Dentistry was begun at the same time as the College of Medicine, a College of Pharmacy was added five years later in 1892 and the School of Nursing in 1908. When Flexner inspected the University of Minnesota for his famous 1910 report, it was one of the few institutions in the country to meet with his approval. He declared that "Minnesota is perhaps the first state in the union that may fairly be considered to have solved the most perplexing problems connected with medical education and practice." In 1911 Minnesota became the first medical school in the United States to require an internship year.

Other firsts associated with this institution include:

1939   Development of the Minnesota Multiphasic Personality Inventory (MMPI), destined to become the most widely used psychological test in the country

1942   Ancel Keys, director of the Physiological Hygiene Laboratory, develops K Rations, for use by soldiers

1945   Owen Wangensteen develops a simple, inexpensive device for gastrointestinal suction, designed to prevent postoperative intestinal blockage

1952   World's first successful open-heart surgery, performed by C Walton Lillehei

1958   World's first implantation of an artificial heart valve in a human being, by C Walton Lillehei

1967   World's first successful pancreas transplant, by Richard Lillehei and William Kelly

1975   Henry Buchwald develops and inserts world's first implantable heparin pump, to prevent blood clots

The current medical center is a thriving complex of more than a dozen buildings overlooking the Mississippi River, adjacent to the main university campus. The University Hospital dates from 1909 (it began as a temporary facility installed in an old fraternity building) and, for many years, was known as the Minnesota General Hospital. Most patients are currently treated in a 432-bed addition erected in 1986, but some patient services are still located in the old main hospital building, now known as the Mayo Memorial Building. The relationship between the U of M and its medical neighbors in Rochester has not always been smooth, but overall the Mayos have generally been among the university's strongest supporters. In the teens and twenties of this century, the university was considerably strengthened by gifts of $2.5 million from the Mayo brothers and the Mayo Foundation to establish a postgraduate training program.

Some U of M students receive their first two preclinical years' training at a U of M campus in Duluth.

Tours of the Minneapolis complex are available by advance arrangement.

Hennepin County Medical Center 701 Park Avenue South 55415. (612) 347-2338. The Minneapolis City Hospital officially opened its doors in 1887 but traces its origins to the "Pest House" of 1873, where smallpox patients were first quarantined. Infectious diseases were a major source of business for the hospital for many years, as Mississippi River traffic brought not only commerce, but also people laden with typhus, diphtheria, and typhoid. By the turn of the century, tuberculosis and scarlet fever were major problems, and by the 1940s, polio was the major scourge. The hospital, in fact, carries the distinction of being the first health care institution anywhere to open its doors to the controversial Sister Kenny, who was to revolutionize the care of polio patients (see below).

The hospital changed its name to Minneapolis General in 1920 and again to Hennepin County Medical Center in 1976, at the time the present structure was dedicated. The latter change was the result of considerable tumult and controversy. By 1962 the hospital's physical plant was 75-years old and—to put the matter charitably—a mess. The city government's role in providing for the health care of the poor was diminishing, and the city saw itself faced with three choices: closing the hospital, building a new physical plant and then assuming the high costs of running a modern high-tech structure, or giving the hospital to the county. To oversimplify a bit, the city's generosity to the county prevailed, and in 1964 the hospital became the county's financial burden.

Today, HCMC contains a very modern 369-bed teaching hospital, with a strong regional reputation, housed in a huge complex composed of "Cytoid" modules. These latter units are intended to supply unending flexibility to future hospital construction, using building blocks of uninterrupted space, surrounded on four corners by tower supports, each of which contains all mechanical, electrical, and engineering systems.

Tours are available by special arrangement [(612) 347-2338, ext. 2271].

Abbott Northwestern Hospital 800 East 28th Street 55407. (612) 874-4000. This hospital dates from 1882 when a group of women founded the Northwestern Hospital for Women and Children. The initial ten beds in a rented home were quickly outgrown, and, to finance further growth, board members and others agreed to sponsor free beds at $250 per bed per year. Women continued to be the prime sponsors and decision makers for the hospital until 1967, when, for the first time, men were also elected to the board of directors. In 1970 Northwestern merged with Abbott, a private for-profit hospital that had been founded in 1902.

ANH's greatest claim to fame is that it is the institutional home of the Sister Kenny Institute. Elizabeth Kenny was an essentially untrained army nurse in her native Australia (where nurses are called "sister"), who discovered that polio-paralyzed muscles responded nicely to hot packs and passive movements. Her approach sounds ludicrously simple today, but in 1940 the standard treatment was immobilization with braces and splints, together with bed rest. She tried to spread the happy news that polio-paralyzed muscles could be significantly rehabilitated, but she was unable to gain a respectful hearing in Australia, Europe, and most of the United States. Part of the problem was that she was an untrained female nurse trying to make inroads in a field dominated by status-conscious male physicians, part was that she was flying in the face of established practice, and part was that — by all accounts — she was one of the most temperamental and obstreperous persons on three continents. In any event, it wasn't until she came to Minneapolis that people began to take her seriously and that physicians in particular allowed her to demonstrate her wonderfully effective techniques.

Her first clinical work was at the General, and by 1943 wealthy supporters had helped her establish the Sister Kenny Foundation, which was to be a mecca for polio victims for many years. Her work with muscle manipulation and muscle reeducation became the foundation for modern physical therapy as it is practiced around the world. Sister Kenny died in 1952, three years before the Sabin and Salk polio vaccines were discovered. The Sister Kenny Institute went through a rough time in the 1960s when the conquest of polio left it temporarily without a focus and a mail-fraud scandal in its fund-raising operation badly damaged its public image. In 1975 the Institute was officially merged with ANH.

Currently, ANH includes 923 hospital beds, in a complex which occupies six city blocks. Tours are available by advance arrangement.

The Bakken: A Library and Museum of Electricity in Life 3537 Zenith Avenue South 55416. (612) 927-6508. This fascinating institution is surely one of the finest specialty medical museums in the country. Housed in "Westwinds," a 1928 Tudor-style mansion on the shores of Lake Calhoun, it is also one of the most beautifully located. Founded in 1976 by Earl Bakken, inventor of the first wearable cardiac pacemaker and one of the founders of Medtronic, Inc., this private, nonprofit institution now has an extensive collection of rare books, manuscripts, artwork, and instruments which illustrates and documents the history of electromagnetism and its uses in biology and medicine. The scope of the collection includes magnetism, electricity, electrophysiology, and electrotherapeutics, but there are also wonderful special collections on mesmerism and animal magnetism. The instrument collection includes everything from electrostatic generators and induction coils to modern physiological instruments. You'll find 18th century Leyden jars here, a voltaic pile (1804), and a late nineteenth century precursor to the modern cardiac pacemaker. A recent special exhibit traced developments in early cardiology such as sphygmography, electrocardiography, and phonocardiography. The history of medical electricity goes back to the Romans, who, in AD 46, used electrical discharges from the Mediterranean torpedo fish to relieve arthritic pain, and the collection tries to do justice to everything of note that has

The Bakken — A Library and Museum of Electricity in Life *(Credit: The Bakken, a library and museum of electricity in life)*

happened since. The Library is open 9 to 5 for research work, and tours of the museum are available by advance appointment.

ROCHESTER   *(See* **Great Medical Cities)**

ST PAUL

St Joseph's Hospital 69 West Exchange Street 55102. (612) 338-2229. This hospital is interesting both for its remote history and for how current circumstances have shaped its present. Founded in 1852 by the Sisters of St Joseph of Carondelet, it became the first hospital in the state. In 1870 the hospital staff organized a medical school (the St Paul School of Medical Instruction, replaced in 1885 by the St Paul Medical School), which survived until 1888. During these years, St Joe's was very much in the forefront of medical care. In 1886 Dr Justus Ohage became the first person in North America to successfully perform a cholecystectomy.

By the 1980s, however, St Joseph's was undergoing the same kind of economic pressures that afflicted so many hospitals in this country. Four other hospitals in the eastern St Paul area were being similarly buffeted by competitive pressures (with bed occupancies averaging 45 percent), and they decided to merge. The new consortium, HealthEast, includes diverse sponsorship: Catholic (St Joseph's and Divine Redeemer Memorial), Baptist (Midway), and Lutheran (St John's and Bethesda). Rumor has it that HealthEast also wished to include an economically troubled Jewish hospital in Minneapolis but was unable to extend its umbrella across the river. While the diversity of denominations may seem to make for a peculiar association, the participants view the matter more pragmatically: their newfound, combined economic strength allows the members to independently pursue their religious commitments to health care. The consortium also includes several pharmacies, long-term care facilities, physical therapy clinics, mental health facilities, an ambulance company, and various other facilities.

St. Joseph's is now a full-service, acute-care, 350-bed hospital, with most of its buildings dating from the 1970s. Tours are available by advance arrangement.

St. Paul-Ramsey Medical Center 640 Jackson Street 55101. (612) 221-3456. This complex traces its history back to 1872 when the Ramsey County Board of Control authorized the purchase of a 10-room mansion for the use of the sick poor. First known simply as the Stewart Mansion (named after the physician-mayor who sold it to the county) and then as the City and County Hospital, the institution was renamed the Ancker Hospital in 1923 in honor of the man who was the hospital superintendent for 40 years. Long a major teaching facility in the area, the hospital was home to an early nurses training school, which survived from 1891 to 1976. The hospital's most enduring claim to international fame dates from the late 1920s, when Ancker physician Frederic EB Foley invented the urethral catheter which still bears his name, one with an inflatable balloon tip which retained the catheter's perforated end in the patient's bladder. St Paul-Ramsey's current location dates from 1956. The main hospital was built in 1965, with a huge $10 million addition completed in 1977. Though begun as a city-county hospital for the indigent, the facility currently regards itself as a "community hospital for everyone" and less than 6 percent of its budget comes from the county. No tours are offerred presently.

MISSISSIPPI

JACKSON

University of Mississippi Medical Center 2500 North State Street 39216. (601) 984-1000. Mississippi's only health sciences campus contains schools of medicine, dentistry, nursing, and health-related professions. The School of Medicine was founded in 1903 as a two-year program on the Oxford campus, but the present four-year program dates from 1955. The other schools are of more recent vintage. Clinical instruction for all students occurs at the 541-bed University Hospital and the state's only Children's Hospital, also on the 155-acre campus. Medical center achievements include the nation's first adrenal gland transplant in 1963. Scheduled tours are held on the second Wednesday of each month.

WHITFIELD

Mississippi State Hospital 39193. (601) 939-1221. Established in 1855 as the Mississippi State Lunatic Asylum, the original facility was in Jackson on the site where the University of Mississippi Medical Center is now located. Dorothea Dix visited Mississippi twice to help raise financing for the institution, first in 1850 when the original appropriation was stalled in the legislature and again in 1858 when the Asylum was in desperate need of enlarging. The original asylum was a Kirkbride-style facility, extending from a vast central administration building, featuring a large Grecian dome and six stately columns at the entranceway. In 1900 the name was changed to the Mississippi State Insane Hospital. In 1926 the hospital got its current name when it was relocated to its current site, a former penal farm located about 15 miles southeast of Jackson. At its height the hospital grounds included 3800 acres with 78 buildings and housed some 5000 patients. Currently, there are 28 buildings with a bed capacity of 1600, and the campus has been reduced to 350 acres. Tours are available by prior arrangement.

MISSOURI

BRIDGETON

DePaul Health Center 12303 DePaul Drive 63044. (314) 344-6000. This hospital is the direct descendant of the first hospital west of the Mississippi River, and the oldest existing Catholic hospital under single sponsorship in the United States. In 1828 St Louis was a rough and tumble city of 6000 residents. With polluted water, non-existent sewage systems, rudimentary knowledge of hygiene, and rampant infectious disease, health conditions were atrocious. The local Catholic bishop requested assistance from the Daughters of

Charity in Emmitsburg, Maryland, and four sisters traveled 1500 difficult miles by stagecoach and steamboat to be of help. Within a few weeks, the four women had opened a three-room log hospital — two rooms for patients and one combined kitchen and sleeping room for the sisters. Within four years, the "Sisters' Hospital" (as it was called) moved into a new, two-story brick building. The sisters did such a magnificent job caring for patients during the cholera epidemic of 1832 that the mayor dubbed their enterprise the "St Louis City Hospital," a role it filled until 1845, when the city built its own hospital. In 1843 the sisters built the nation's first orphan home, called St Anne's, eventually to become a Lying-In Hospital and Foundling Asylum. In 1858 they founded St Vincent's Asylum, to care for the growing number of psychiatric patients requiring care. In 1874 the Sister's Hospital moved into brand new quarters on Montgomery Street, and the name was changed to the Mullanphy Hospital, in recognition of the many contributions of the Mullanphy family over several decades. In 1927 the Mullanphy Hospital was severely damaged by a tornado, and the replacement facility (opened in 1930) was called DePaul Hospital, in honor of St Vincent de Paul. In 1969, DePaul, St Anne's Home, and St Vincent's Asylum merged into a single corporate entity — and in 1978 the combined enterprise opened its new 611-bed health center in Bridgeton.

The Italian Romanesque, 1930-vintage DePaul Hospital still stands at 2415 North Kingshighway Boulevard in St Louis, now remodeled and used as a nursing care center. The 1895 home of St Vincent's Asylum, a five-story building which resembles a medieval castle, still stands in the nearby St Louis Normandy district (at 7301 St Charles Rock Road). It has been redeveloped and now serves as low-income apartments.

Tours of the modern DePaul Health Center are available from the Volunteers Office.

COLUMBIA

University of Missouri Columbia Medical Center One Hospital Drive 65212. (314) 882-4141. This school dates its founding from 1840, when Kemper College in St Louis began its own medical department. When Kemper dissolved in 1846, the University nominally took over the medical department, under the name of the Missouri Medical College (see Washington University in St Louis, below). When the University reorganized in 1872, it relocated a medical department in Columbia, thereafter called "The Medical Department of the University of Missouri." In 1886 the Columbia Medical

Department entered into an agreement with the Missouri Medical College to share students and resources, though the union was neither an easy nor a lasting one. The two-year course of study was expanded to three years in 1891 and to four years in 1899, reflecting changing national standards and the growing scientific base of medical education. From time to time in the latter years of the nineteenth century, various attempts were made to combine University of Missouri medical training in Columbia with that in St Louis, using Columbia for basic science education, and St Louis — with its much larger patient base — for both basic science and clinical training.

When Flexner visited Missouri in 1910, the state was blessed with twelve medical schools. In the history of the state, there have been, at various times, 44 schools, a number equalled only by Illinois and exceeded only by New York (with 45 schools). Flexner, of course, found the state dramatically over-doctored, with some of the poorest medical schools in the country. The school at Columbia fared far better than most of its competition under Flexner's scrutiny, but, because of limited clinical facilities, it was reduced to a two-year program and, in this fashion, managed to survive. In 1930 Columbia tried to expand to a four-year curriculum, but the Depression intervened, funds for expansion dried up, and the six students who had entered their third year moved on to other schools. The two-year course continued until 1955, when the school finally got the four-year program it had wanted for so many years.

Today, the University of Missouri-Columbia Hospital and Clinics is a collection of institutions clustered around the 440-bed University Hospital. The front entrance, with its double arch entrance leading into a spacious concourse, is particularly dramatic. McAlester Hall (on Sixth Street near Elm), the 1902 home of the medical school, now houses the psychology department. Tours of the Medical Center are available via the Volunteers Office.

KANSAS CITY

University of Missouri Kansas City Medical Center Hospital Hill. 2411 Holmes Street 64108. (816) 276-1802. The University of Missouri-Kansas City School of Medicine accepted its first class in 1971. The buildings came later. The program here is a six-year curriculum (each school year eleven months long) leading to a medical degree, and students are accepted into the program directly from high school. First and second year work are conducted primarily at the nearby Volker liberal arts campus. The medical school building here is unusual in that it is the site of one of the largest closed-circuit television networks in the United States. Each student has an office equipped with a color television receiver for viewing live lectures and demonstrations at various associated hospitals, and the computer terminal may be used to reach into a variety of databases. Adjacent to the Medical School is the Truman Medical Center, the school's principal hospital affiliate. TMC was opened in 1976 as the modern replacement for the aging Kansas City General Hospital (with its separate "white" and "colored" divisions), whose facilities dated from 1905. The first KCGH was built in 1870. Tours are available from Administration.

Children's Mercy Hospital 24th Street and Gillham Road 64108. (816) 234-3000. As you walk inside the dramatic canopy of glass and metal which forms the entrance to Children's Mercy Hospital, you will see on your right a wonderful bronze plaque dedicated to Alice Berry Graham, DDS, and Katherine Berry Richardson, MD, FACS, LLD.

Drs Graham and Richardson were two sisters from Ohio who came to Kansas City in the mid-1890s after receiving their professional educations in Philadelphia. Katherine decided to devote her professional life to the care of sick children and promptly set about doing things in her own uniquely personal style. The hospital began as a single bed in a rented room for a patient with no place else to stay.

In 1897 the sisters formally established this hospital for "sick and crippled children, to be forever non-sectarian, non-local, and only for those who cannot pay." The simple words give no indication of the enormous struggle involved in founding and maintaining the facility. The words "non-sectarian" effectively cut the sisters off from funding by religious groups; "non-local" did the same for civic groups; and "cannot pay" meant that patients were likewise not able to add financial support. In addition, female physicians were widely scorned by their male brethren, who would neither refer patients nor give official sanction to a female doctor's enterprise. The sisters were not deterred. Whatever funds they could scrape together from their practices, they spent on their patients. They not only provided medical services, they washed linens, scrubbed floors, prepared meals, papered the walls, painted the floors, and did virtually everything necessary to make the hospital survive.

For many years, the hospital commonly persisted on a day-by-day and week-by-week financial basis, frequently being on the verge of closing, rarely with any money in the bank, but—because of absolute financial discipline—never in debt. In time, as more children came to the hospital to be cared for and as more of them recovered, the hospital's status in the community grew, and with it the financial support available. In particular, Dr Richardson's surgical skill, especially with cleft-palate deformities (for which she was one of the first women awarded fellowship in the American College of Surgeons) helped establish the hospital's reputation. Eventually, Kansas City's finest physicians, regardless of gender, were pleased to be associated with Children's Mercy.

Dr Graham died in 1913 and Dr Richardson in 1933, but the enterprise they founded survived. The present location, the hospital's fifth, was established in 1970. Children's Mercy is now a 167-bed hospital, an integral part of the University of Missouri Kansas City Medical Center on Hospital Hill. Tours are available by request from administration.

American Nursing Association 2420 Pershing Road 64108. (816) 474-5720. The first professional schools of nursing in this country were formed in 1873, and the first nursing organizations were alumni associations of the larger schools. In 1893 eighteen superintendents of various training schools met to establish the American Society of Superintendents of Training Schools for Nurses, the first truly national organization for nurses. By 1896 the same people who founded the ASSTSN moved to form a broader organization which would include rank-and-file nurses, which was then called the Nurses' Associated Alumnae of the United States and Canada. It was under the sponsorship of this latter organization that the American Journal of Nursing was begun in 1900. By 1910 the Nurses' Associated Alumnae organization included 15,000 members, each enrolled as a member of a training school alumnae association. In 1911 the name was changed to the American Nursing Association, with state associations assuming a greater role as component organizations and alumnae associations taking a lesser role.

In the 1940s the ANA struggled with the issue of providing individual memberships for black nurses excluded from obtaining memberships through their own state associations in the South. In 1951 the 171,000-member ANA absorbed the 1700-member National Association of Colored Graduate Nurses (founded in 1908). Today, the ANA has a collective membership of 190,000, but it is the principal voice of almost two million registered nurses in this country.

The ANA established its national headquarters in New York City in 1920 but moved to Kansas City in 1972, to be closer to the geographical heart of the country. Current plans are for it to move once again in 1992, this time to Washington, DC, to be closer to the political heart of the country. At this time, no tours are available.

KIRKSVILLE

Kirksville College of Osteopathic Medicine 800 West Jefferson Street
63501. (816) 626-2121. There are some 30,000 osteopathic physicians in the United States. Though the country currently has fifteen
accredited osteopathic colleges, Kirksville is the Mother School, the
place where the profession began.

The profession's founder was AT Still, a frontier doctor, typical in
that he was trained primarily by the apprentice system with a few
lectures here and there along the way. Still was distressed with the
intrusiveness and occasional brutality of orthodox medicine in his
day: the bleeding, the purging, the scarification and cupping, the
frequent use of very toxic medicines. He believed that the human
body was basically a machine and that it ought to function well if
kept in fair running order. He designed a treatment method, intended to improve circulation and correct altered mechanics, primarily by physical manipulation.

The American School of Osteopathy was chartered in Kirksville
in 1892, with a class of seventeen, including five of Still's children
and five women. His approach became immediately popular and
an infirmary was built in 1895, with an addition two years later. The
ASO Hospital opened in 1906, and by then several other schools
following the same philosophy had opened their doors around the
country. Gradually, osteopathy expanded its scope, embracing
such specialties as obstetrics, surgery, and psychiatry. The field in
general remains general-practice–oriented, with its approaches
rooted in Still's philosophy.

The Kirksville College of Osteopathic Medicine is the lineal de-
cendant of the ASO (there are now many other American schools of
osteopathy). Presently, KCOM has about 500 students in its four-
year program, with perhaps a dozen buildings occupying some 50
acres of campus. In the early 1980s, KCOM (like many other health
care institutions) encountered major financial difficulties and attempted to solve them by leasing its hospital facilities and some
clinics to National Medical Enterprises, one of the health care me-
gacorporations. The campus acute care hospital (called KCOM-
South Wing) operates 119 beds; the inpatient psychiatric facility
(Laughlin Pavilion, at 900 East La Harpe) contains 109 beds and is
located a couple of miles away.

KCOM is happy to provide campus tours by advance arrangement.

Still National Osteopathic Museum 311 South Fourth Street 63501.
(816) 626-2359. Established in 1978, this friendly little museum
celebrates the osteopathic profession and its first family, the Stills.

Displays include a considerable number of memorabilia traceable to Dr AT, as well as one that focuses on his wife Mary and the importance of her support in the evolution of osteopathy (five of their children studied with AT, and future DO's included four grandchildren, seven great grandchildren, nine great great grandchildren, and more in the making). Some films are part of the collection, including a brief clip of AT speaking and demonstrating a simple technique (1916). A museum highlight is a mounted dissection (prepared by Kirksville students in the early part of the century) of the spinal cord, complete with all portions of the peripheral nervous system. Next door to the museum are two small buildings important to the development of the profession. The first is AT's birthplace, a tiny log cabin, shipped here disassembled from Virginia in 1928 and accurately reconstructed on the spot. The second is a two-room building which was the first school in which AT taught (1892). Both are filled primarily with period pieces, though some furnishings are original. The museum and both buildings are open to the public, Monday through Friday, 9 AM to 3 PM.

Statue of AT Still Town Square Jefferson and Washington Streets. This striking statue of the founder of osteopathy was unveiled in 1917, in ceremonies attended by Still himself. He was then 89 years old, and though he was soon to die, he must have been comforted to know that already over 5000 osteopathic physicians were treating patients in various states. The statue (by a sculptor named Zolnay) captures Still in his customary clothing, wearing a slouch hat, and walking with a staff almost as tall as he. Beneath the statue, a brass plaque proclaims DOCTOR ANDREW TAYLOR STILL 1828–1917 DISCOVERER OF OSTEOPATHIC PRINCIPLES OF MEDICAL TREATMENT — FOUNDER OF THE FIRST OSTEOPATHIC COLLEGE — THE AMERICAN SCHOOL OF OSTEOPATHY — KIRKSVILLE MISSOURI 1892. Above the plaque, the words of Still read "The God I worship demonstrates all his work."

ST JOSEPH

Psychiatric Museum of St Joseph State Hospital 34th Street and Frederick Avenue 64502. (816) 232-8431 (ext 1141). Among the several psychiatric museums scattered across the country's midlands, this is the largest in size and the most ambitious in scope. The museum chronicles the evolution of psychiatric treatment from the fifteenth century to the present, as well as the history of the State Lunatic Asylum #2 (the first Missouri state psychiatric hospital was located in Fulton). Residing in what used to be "Center North 8," an open ward for men, the museum's space stretches into some two dozen rooms from its lengthy central corridor.

Statue of AT Still—Founder of Osteopathy, Town Square, Kirksville, Missouri *(Photo courtesy of the Kirksville College of Osteopathic Medicine)*

This is a *no* budget operation, nurtured with loving care by a part-time curator and lots of volunteer labor, so you won't find any priceless medical antiquities here, but imagination, creativity, and the collected debris of 120 years of hospital history have created something quite special. Dioramas show various "physical treatments," e.g., "stomping the devil" out of madmen in the fifteenth and sixteenth centuries. A variety of full-size replicas include the "Bath of Surprise" (a seventeenth century "calming" device), Benjamin Rush's "tranquilizing chair" (eighteenth century), and O'Halloran's Swing, in which patients were spun around until they were dizzied into submission (nineteenth century Ireland). The collection includes a genuine steel-slatted Utica crib. Though each of these devices seems crude and even cruel now, each item was regarded as an innovative and helpful part of enlightened treatment.

There are such remnants of the old hospital as restraint cells, a turn of the century nursing office, lobotomy and ECT equipment, straight jackets, and "unofficial tranquilizers" (meaning handmade black jacks and billy clubs). Other displays include items from the hospital dietary department, farm, weaving shop, barber shop, and industrial shop. One bizarre exhibit shows 1446 items surgically removed from the GI tract of a compulsive swallower, including nails, spoon handles, nuts, bolts, stones, pieces of glass, pins, and even a thimble. Hydrotherapy tubs, wet packs, and various patient-created arts and crafts items are also on display.

The building which houses the museum is fascinating in its own right. Originally built in 1874, and rebuilt in 1879 after a fire, this is a marvelous Victorian Gothic structure with walls two feet thick, spires, a three-story entrance porch, an imposing mansard roof, and lots of period gingerbread. The lobby boasts enormously colorful tilework, a central rotunda with a curved walnut stairway, and tin ceilings. The hospital was originally designed on the Kirkbride plan, but five of the lateral wings have been demolished. The hospital census was once over 2800 patients but now runs less than 300. The campus, its original 1700 acres now trimmed to 225, includes some 30 buildings of various ages, though none quite so interesting as the Center Building which houses the museum.

The museum is open Monday through Friday, 8:30 AM to 4 PM, as well as on weekends (April through September) 1 to 5 PM. There is no admission charge, but donations are of course appreciated.

ST LOUIS

St Louis University Medical Center 1325 South Grand Boulevard 63104. (314) 577-8000. This is either the oldest medical school in the state or the youngest in the city, depending on how you look at it. St Louis Academy opened in 1818 and was taken over by the Jesuit Fathers in 1826. By 1832 the Academy had become a University, and in 1836 it opened its own medical department. This was not a successful venture, however, and the medical department closed its operations in 1840, apparently without graduating a single physician. The medical department was reestablished in 1841 as the semiautonomous St Louis Medical College, which became entirely independent in 1855, ultimately joining with another school to form the Washington University School of Medicine.

From 1855 until 1903, St Louis University did not have a medical school. The present medical school represents the merger of two older institutions accomplished in 1902 but which didn't become a functioning part of St Louis University until 1903. The Beaumont Hospital Medical College, founded in 1886, was named in honor of William Beaumont, the distinguished investigator of gastric physiology and an early president of the St Louis Medical Society. The Marion Sims Medical College was founded in 1890 and was named in tribute to the man widely known as the father of gynecologic surgery. The Sims College got off to a strong start, and, by 1894, had been selected by the University of Idaho (which lacked a medical college) as the site at which its students should receive their medical educations. In 1901 the Beaumont College united with Sims College, to form the Marion Sims–Beaumont Medical College. Two years later, the school was absorbed by St Louis University.

In 1943 St Louis professor Edward Doisy, Sr was awarded the Nobel Prize for his successful isolation of vitamin K four years earlier. In 1929 and 1930, Doisy had been the first to isolate the sex hormones estrone and estradiol as well.

The University Hospital here originated in 1933, with the opening of Firmin Desloge Hospital, named for a major benefactor. The University took over full ownership of the hospital in 1960, but, until then, all administrative and nursing functions came under the purview of the Sisters of St Mary. Firmin Desloge Hospital (a thirteen-story French Gothic spire, topped with a peaked copper roof) now houses faculty offices and various hospital support services, and the new University Hospital (just to the west) was opened in 1988. Tours are available via Media Relations.

Washington University Medical Center 660 South Euclid Avenue 63110. (314) 362-5000. The Washington University School of Medicine began as a distinct entity in 1899, but its history encompasses two medical schools dating from the 1840s, which, together, were the first two medical schools west of the Mississippi River.

In 1840 Joseph McDowell, MD, approached the officials of Kemper College with the idea of starting a medical school. McDowell was a talented surgeon, an articulate and colorful speaker, and a vigorously anti-Jesuit dynamo who was strongly influenced by the recent unsuccessful attempt of St Louis University to start a medical department. The new medical school got off to a strong start, but, by 1846, its parent institution (Kemper College) had closed and left the medical school an orphan. With the demise of Kemper, McDowell negotiated a new affiliation, and the school was soon known as the Medical Department of the University of Missouri. The sponsorship lasted for eleven years and then became a victim of McDowell's fierce political opinions in the unrest preceding the Civil War. In 1857 the school became an independent entity under the name of the Missouri Medical College. (With all the name changes, the school was more commonly referred to as "McDowells.") In 1861 McDowell left, offering his services to the Confederacy, and the school came to a temporary halt, with the buildings being used for awhile as a Federal prison for confederate prisoners.

McDowell returned to reorganize his school in 1865. He died three years later, but his school managed to survive without him until the turn of the century, eventually merging with the St Louis Medical College.

The St Louis Medical College began in 1841, when a splinter group from the Kemper College Medical Department (who found McDowell impossible to work with) decided to revive the St Louis University Medical Department. Anti-Catholic and anti-Jesuit feelings, in part stirred up by McDowell, became so incendiary in the city that the Medical Department tried to distance itself from its parent institution. In 1855 it severed all ties and became the St Louis Medical College. In 1891 the School developed an affiliation with Washington University while retaining its own name, and, in 1899, the St Louis Medical College united with the Missouri Medical College to form the Medical School of Washington University.

In the first decade of the twentieth century, Washington University went to great lengths to transform its new medical school into a first rank institution, upgrading standards and curriculum and erecting a new building. They were absolutely stunned, then, when Flexner visited the school in 1909 and judged that it was "a little better than the worst but absolutely inadequate essentially in every respect." Given an advance preview of this report through connections with the president of the Carnegie Foundation, Washington University took the unusual step of inviting Flexner back for a second look. When Flexner returned, he showed officials why their laboratories and their clinical facilities were insufficient, and the organization of their faculty inadequate to produce a first-rate educational enterprise. In return, Washington University did such a good job of convincing Flexner of their intent to transform themselves into the kind of school of which he approved, that Flexner became one of Washington U's strongest supporters. His official report for the Carnegie Foundation called Washington U "the main factor" in the future training of physicians for the southwest and spoke of its "manifest destiny" to become a "productive scientific center." Later, when Flexner went to work for Rockefeller's General Education Board, he was a key factor in funneling substantial grants to Washington U to help it further its goals.

The school then had the distinction of being the first to be reformed according to the specific suggestions of the Flexner Report. A new basic science building and the fully affiliated Barnes Hospital were completed in 1914, and full-time professorships in medicine, surgery, and pediatrics were funded the same year (with a grant from the General Education Board). The Medical School was completely "reformed" and modernized by 1920 and was soon a prominent contributor to the development of medical progress. In 1930, in conjunction with Barnes Hospital, the medical school established the Mallinckrodt Institute of Radiology, one of the largest and most active such centers in the world. Notable contributions from the WU Medical Center include:

1923	Development of the first method for x-ray visualization of the gallbladder, using phenolphthalein, by Evarts Graham and Warren Cole
1933	First pneumonectomy, by Evarts Graham, for the treatment of a cancerous lung
1935	First electron microscope in the United States used for biologic research
1937	Development of laminography, a means of providing x-ray "cross-sections" of the body
1944	Nobel Prize awarded to Joseph Erlanger and Herbert Gasser for the first classification of nerve fibers by function
1982	First use of hyperthermia in the treatment of cancer

Today, WUSM is one of the occupants of the 59-acre WU Medical Center, along with Barnes, a School of Dentistry, Children's Hospital, Jewish Hospital, and a number of other entities. The campus includes over 50 buildings. The School regularly ranks among the

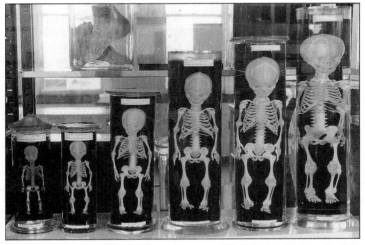

From the collection of the Anatomy Museum, Washington University School of Medicine *(Courtesy of Washington University School of Medicine)*

top ten in research support from the National Institutes of Health. Like many major medical centers, this one is currently undergoing tremendous expansion, including a new three-tower Clinical Sciences Research Building and a new $14 million library. When completed, the library will house the medical center archives and other historical displays. The School also has a marvelous **Anatomy Museum,** which is open for tours by previous arrangement.

Robert Koch Hospital 4101 Koch Road 63129. There are few places extant in this country that give as clear a notion of the historical impact of contagious diseases, especially tuberculosis, as does this collection of institutional buildings. Like most major cities of the nineteenth century, especially port cities, St Louis had repeated problems with infectious disease. A cholera epidemic in 1849, for example, resulted in a temporary quarantine of all steamboats visiting the city. This site, at the time fifteen miles south of the city center, was used from 1854 onward as a Quarantine Station for victims of yellow fever, leprosy, smallpox, and diphtheria. A terrible yellow fever outbreak in 1878 stimulated the city to establish a formal Quarantine Hospital here. As late as the 1890s, this location was so remote that it was reachable only by riverboat. By the turn of the century, when it was known as the Quarantine-Smallpox Hospital, an estimated 18,000 victims had been buried in mass or transiently marked individual graves on these grounds.

The red-brick Administration Building was built in 1907 as a center for smallpox patients, but, by the time it was completed, effective vaccination programs had essentially eliminated smallpox as a health threat to local citizens. Instead, tuberculosis was now responsible for more deaths than all other infectious diseases combined, and, in 1910, the hospital was renamed for Robert M Koch, who had originally isolated the tuberculosis bacillus, and the facilities were converted to the exclusive care of tuberculosis victims. In the decades that followed, an almost continuous building program tried to keep pace with the ever-growing need for space. In all, nineteen buildings were erected here between 1907 and 1939, including patient wards, support facilities, and housing and recreation facilities for large numbers of employees. A 105-acre farm on the northern end of the property—together with a post office, railroad stop, powerhouse, and carpentry and paint shops—made the hospital almost self-sustaining.

In the early years, treatment consisted primarily of rest, good food, fresh air, and heliotherapy (i.e., exposure to sunlight) in the many solariums. When sun lamps and quartz lights became available, they were added to the treatment regimen. When therapeutic pneumothorax (i.e., the surgical collapse of the lung) became popular as a treatment device, the hospital regularly performed almost 100 a week. By the end of World War II, new potent medications became available to treat tuberculosis, and the disease, which had killed an average of 600 St Louis citizens a year for almost half a century, lost its sting.

In the 1950s, city officials decided to turn Koch Hospital into housing for the indigent elderly. Renamed Riverside, it housed varying numbers of elderly until 1983, when funds for the project dried up, the last resident was moved out, and much of the peripheral land was sold. Since that time, the buildings have remained vacant, subject to vandalism, and the property (now 50 acres) has been up for sale. There are no formal tours here, but visitors just driving by will feel the impact of the place.

Missouri Baptist Hospital 3015 North Ballas Road 63131. (314) 432-1212. When it was founded in 1884, this was the first hospital under Baptist auspices in the United States. William Mayfield received his MD degree from St Louis Medical College (later Washington University) in 1883 and promptly set up practice in town. In contrast to most other practitioners, however, Mayfield and his wife took sick people into their home and provided them lodging and care while they recovered. In 1885 Mayfield sought denominational support for his efforts. The Baptist Ministers Alliance authorized him to establish a Baptist hospital, but "at his own risk and expense." As a result, the Mayfield home and a patient annex became the Missouri Baptist Sanitarium. Gradually the Sanitarium grew and accumulated support, and in 1892 Mayfield erected a new 81-bed facility.

From the start, the Sanitarium and its nursing school (established in 1895) were distinguished by the integration of the Christian Gospel with all care, as well as a continued emphasis on Christian service. Many nursing students and staff people have gone on to spend time as missionaries in other countries. In the late 1920s, the Sanitarium changed its name to the Missouri Baptist Hospital. Unfortunately, the hospital underwent a major expansion in 1929, just before the stock market crash, and suffered grievously during the Depression as a result. By refinancing its mortgage, cutting expenses, limiting charitable cases to 20 percent of the patient load, and aggressively seeking regional Baptist contributions of all manner of goods and services, the hospital managed to survive.

In 1965 the changing character of the neighborhood surrounding the hospital brought concerns about patient and staff safety and threatened to erode the hospital's traditional base of support among church members outside of metropolitan St Louis. As a result, the hospital moved 15 miles away to its present location. The present 500-bed hospital in west St Louis County is located on 55 acres and can be toured by prior arrangement.

Barnes Hospital 4949 Barnes Plaza 63110. (314) 362-5000. Upon his death in 1892, St Louis wholesale grocer Robert Barnes left $850,000 to construct "a modern general hospital for sick and injured persons, without distinction of creed." Though Barnes was not a Methodist, he specified that the hospital be under the auspices of the Methodist Church—and that it "be forever called and known as Barnes Hospital." The trustees of Barnes' funds were farsighted businessmen who elected not to start construction immediately. Instead, they invested the money, and, by 1912, the fund had grown to $2,000,000. They also elected to affiliate the hospital with Washington University, to the everlasting benefit of both institutions. The hospital opened in 1914 and soon began accumulating a record of accomplishment. By 1918 its surgeon-in-chief was Evarts Graham, who is widely regarded as the father of chest surgery. Other Barnes accomplishments include:

1954   Introduction of surgical "greens" to replace white linen and clothing in the operating room and thus reduce eyestrain
1969   First coronary care unit in the United States with computerized monitoring equipment
1972   Development of PET, positron emission tomography, an imaging process which helps delineate the metabolic processes of internal organs (by a team under the direction of Michel Ter-Pogossian)

Today, Barnes is a 1000-bed hospital with 40 specialized nursing divisions, a dozen intensive care units, and 56 operating rooms. It is regularly ranked among the top hospitals in the United States. Its Mallinckrodt Institute of Radiology is also generally considered a world leader in its field.

No tours are available to the general public.

Homer G Phillips Hospital 2601 Whittier Street 63103. In 1931 St Louis attorney Homer Phillips was assassinated in broad daylight as he waited for a streetcar to go to his office. His two assailants were never captured, and thus no one really knows why he was shot, but the assumption in the black community has always been that he was killed for his efforts in establishing this hospital.

In the early twentieth century, black St Louis citizens became increasingly upset and vocal about the lack of adequate health care for their people. Blacks paid taxes, yet the tax-supported City Hospital was accused of treating black patients unfairly, and black health professionals weren't permitted in municipal facilities either for training or to practice their professions. When black physicians petitioned for the opportunity to train at City Hospital, white physicians threatened to strike. In 1914 members of the black community finally persuaded city officials that they needed a hospital of their own, and the abandoned Barnes Medical College at Garrison and Lawton Avenues was purchased and turned into City Hospital #2. It opened in 1919, but by 1921 it was apparent that a 177-bed hospital could not adequately serve a black population of 70,000 people.

(The Barnes Medical College had been established in 1892 with a bequest from merchant-philantropist Robert A Barnes. Along with the medical school building, the associated Centenary Hospital was also created. In 1911 Barnes Medical College merged with the American Medical College. By 1912 the combined enterprise discontinued classes, and Centenary Hospital came under the control of the Christian Hospital and was renamed Christian-Centenary. In 1919 both the hospital and the medical college building became the site of City Hospital #2.)

In the years that followed, there was often bitter conflict about whether the city should build a larger hospital for blacks or whether an annex to City Hospital #1, staffed by whites, would suffice. The black community supported a bond issue with the understanding that a hospital run and staffed by blacks would be built, but, once the bond issue passed, city officials moved ahead with the "colored annex" to City Hospital #1. The ensuing battle, led by attorney Phillips, ultimately led to the Homer G Phillips Hospital, which was completed after Phillip's assassination and named in his honor. At the dedication, US Secretary of the Interior Harold Ickes called the 685-bed hospital the "largest and finest of its sort in the world" (meaning for the use of and staffed by blacks).

By 1944 Phillips was one of the three largest general hospitals in the country. By 1948 it provided postgraduate training for fully one-third of students graduated from the black medical schools at Howard and Meharry. Although Phillips was officially desegregated in 1955, it remained substantially black until its demise. The city began phasing out operations at the hospital in the mid-1960s, and all inpatient programs were finally closed down in 1979. After that, only outpatient clinics and an acute care facility remained.

Although largely abandoned, Homer G Phillips looks much as it did when it was completed in 1936: an administration building with four radiating six- and seven-story wards, a service building, and a nurses' residence, all brick with terra-cotta art deco ornamentation.

Grave of William Beaumont Bellefontaine Cemetery. 4947 West Florissant Avenue 63115. (314) 381-0750. William Beaumont (1785 – 1853) gained his international reputation through his studies of digestive physiology, with the help of his sometimes unwilling experimental subject, Alexis St Martin, a French-Canadian fur trapper with a gunshot wound which left the interior of his stomach forever open to, and visible from, the surface of his abdominal wall. There are museums dedicated to Beaumont's memory in Connecticut, Michigan, and Wisconsin — where he lived at various times in his life — but it was in St Louis that he retired when he left the Army in 1836. He continued in active practice here until 1853, when he slipped on some icy steps and suffered a fatal injury. Ironically, Beaumont's famous patient, St Martin, outlived his doctor by some 27 years, fathering 20 children in the process.

Beaumont's grave here, with a stone topped by a Gothic arch, is one of seven in a family plot. Each year on the anniversary of Beaumont's death (April 25), the St Louis Medical Society lays a wreath on the grave in a memorial ceremony. St Louis has additionally memorialized Beaumont by (among other tributes) naming a street, a high school, and a medical building after him. Bellefontaine Cemetery, established in 1849, encompasses some 327 tree-covered and rolling acres. Beaumont's grave is a short stroll from the office, just across Laurel Avenue from the more prominent memorial to Missouri's first senator, Thomas Hart Benton. The grounds are open daily 8 AM to 4:30 PM, and a map is available at the cemetery office (which is closed Saturday afternoon and Sunday).

E LeRoy Ryer Memorial Museum of the International Library, Archives and Museum of Optometry 243 North Lindbergh Boulevard 63141. (314) 991-4100. This fascinating, albeit highly specialized, museum is based on a collection which dates back to the 1920s. Housed in the lobby of the American Optometric Association, the various exhibits here include antique eye examination instruments, eye charts, manufacturing equipment, and various spectacles dating back as many as five centuries. One exhibit on the history of contact lenses includes a Czechoslovakian machine which is a replica of that used to make the first contact lens, as well as handmade tools and some eerie looking cosmetic scleral lenses. The museum is open to the public during normal business hours, though groups should make advance arrangements.

MONTANA

DEER LODGE

Powell County Memorial Hospital 1101 Texas Avenue 59722. (406) 846-2212. The first Deer Lodge Hospital dated from 1862, when the surgeon at the local penitentiary opened a small facility to care for sick and injured pioneers in the area. In 1873 the building which housed the first hospital was taken over by two Sisters of Charity, thus inaugurating Montana's second hospital, St Joseph's Hospital. The Sisters stocked the hospital with a small supply of quinine, mustard plasters, carbolic acid, homemade cough syrup, and some bandages and opened for business. In 1874 they moved from their tiny log cabin to a specially built two-story frame building, and felt they had finally gained a "real" hospital. By 1882 the hospital had become so popular that a new brick building was constructed, with 20 private rooms, wards that could hold 30 patients, and a separate apartment for county patients. The hospital expanded again in 1920, but no further capital improvements were added for the next 43 years. In 1963 management of the facility passed to the Lutheran Homes and Hospital Society, and it was renamed the Powell County Memorial Hospital. An entirely new building was constructed in 1965, with additions completed in 1976 and 1986. The hospital welcomes visitors, preferably with advance arrangements.

STEVENSVILLE

Father Ravalli's Pharmacy at St Mary's Mission West Fourth Street 59870. (406) 777-5734. This mission was established in 1841 by Father Pierre DeSmet and his party of Jesuit missionaries. The result was the first permanent white settlement in Montana and therefore the site of many "firsts" in the state. Father Ravalli was among the initial settlers here, and he became the first physician and surgeon in Montana, caring for the sick and injured here almost until his death in 1884. Some accounts claim there was a hospital here, though the matter remains in dispute. There is no question, however, that Ravalli operated a pharmacy here and dispensed medicines through a small window (now usually referred to as a "drive-up window" by the tour guides here). Everything has now been restored to the 1880 period, furnished with furniture mostly crafted by Father Ravalli. The pharmacy restoration includes period fixtures, show globes, patent medicines, and various pharmacy paraphernalia. Guided tours are provided from May 1 until September 30, 10 AM to 5 PM. Visitors are welcome the rest of the year by appointment. There is no charge but donations are gratefully accepted.

NEBRASKA

OMAHA

University of Nebraska Medical Center 42nd Street and Dewey Avenue 68105. (402) 559-4353. The UNMC traces its lineage to the Nebraska School of Medicine Preparatory (whose first class in 1883 contained two women and one black) and the Omaha Medical College (a proprietary school founded in 1881). The Omaha Medical College became the medical school of the University of Nebraska in 1902, but initially the first two preclinical years were taught in Lincoln and only the last two clinical years were taught in Omaha. The school has offerred a full four years at this location since 1913. Until the mid-1960s, UNMC quietly specialized in turning out doctors and nurses ready to take their places on the front lines of patient care in communities throughout the state. In 1964 Cecil Wittson became dean of the medical school and in 1969 president of the medical center. Today's campus reflects the energy, drive and creativity of the Wittson years. UNMC now occupies 50 acres with 31 buildings, containing over two million square feet of space. Included on the campus are also the schools of pharmacy (founded 1915) and nursing (1917). The dental school physically resides in Lincoln, though administratively it is part of UNMC.

The 400-bed hospital is an amalgam of the 1917 University Hospital building, with a newer (1969) extensive addition. An atrium connecting the hospital and the Wittson Basic Science Building (1969) contains a huge round stained glass window which depicts various medical school buildings from 1881 to the present. The lobby of the Wittson Building houses an attractive photo display of UNMC's development. The top three floors of this building contain UNMC's huge library, including its Rare Book Room and the History of Medicine Collection. Displays during my visit included a section focusing on medical practice in the pioneer days, as well as a large collection of obstetric forceps.

In 1938 UNMC physiologist AR McIntyre prepared the first extracts of curare from Ecuadorean tree bark, allowing standardization of dosage and facilitating the use of curare in surgical procedures and in conjunction with electroshock therapy. In 1948 neurosurgeons JJ Keegan and FD Garrett developed a chart depict-

ing the dermatome distribution in human beings, one which remains the standard today. In 1963 U of N developed the first two-way closed circuit educational television system in the US, to allow teleconferencing between its department of psychiatry and Norfolk State Mental Hospital 110 miles away.
Tours are available by advance arrangement [(402) 559-4689].

Creighton University Medical Center 28th and California Streets 68178. (402) 280-2700. Founded in 1878 and named after its principal benefactor, Edward Creighton (a banker, cattleman, and businessman, he was largely responsible for laying the transcontinental telegraph line and is the only namesake of a medical school to be inducted into the Cowboy Hall of Fame), the university early gained a reputation as a tuition-free haven for bright immigrant kids. A private Jesuit school, the University accepted not only Catholics, but also Protestant and Jewish students without discrimination. The university started charging tuition in 1924, but fees — even today — continue to be low for a private institution. The School of Medicine began in 1892, Dentistry and Pharmacy in 1905, and Nursing in 1971. Today, 25 percent of the University's 5800 students are in the health professions.

Just like other private universities, CU has gone through rocky financial times. CU is now one of only four Jesuit medical schools to survive into the 1990s. CU, with a relatively modest endowment, rectified its perilous financial situation by selling its principal teaching hospital, St Joseph's, to American Medical International in 1984, thus ridding itself of an expensive overhead problem and using the $60 million equity to give itself a reliable source of funds for the future. St Joseph's remains CU's major teaching hospital, but the relationship is now an "affiliation" with leased space rather than a matter of ownership.

The campus now occupies some 85 acres composed of 28 city blocks astride Interstate 580 on the edge of downtown Omaha. Most of the health sciences buildings date from the 1970s and 1980s, the older buildings having given way to urban renewal further downtown. The main university campus east of the interstate contains the three Criss Health Science Center buildings. In the hallway connecting Units II and III, the old stone portico from the 1892 building at 14th and Davenport Streets, emblazoned with the School of Medicine label, is on display, along with class pictures of all medical school alumni. The west campus, just across the freeway, contains the very modern St Joseph's Hospital and the Dental School. Tours are available by prior arrangement with the Public Affairs Department [(402) 280-2700, ext 2607].

WALTHILL

Susan LaFlesche Picotte Center 69067. (402) 846-5428. Susan La-Flesche Picotte (1865 – 1915) was the first Native American woman physician in the United States. A daughter of Joseph LaFlesche, the last traditional chief of the Omaha Indians, her early education was superintended first by Presbyterian missionaries and later by Quakers. In 1879 she entered the Elizabeth Institute for Young Ladies in Elizabeth, New Jersey. In 1884 Susan began college at the Hampton Normal and Agricultural Institute in Hampton, Virginia. After graduation, she was admitted to the Women's Medical College of Pennsylvania on scholarships from the Bureau of Indian Affairs and the Connecticut Indian Association. Graduating first in her class, she took her internship at Women's Medical College, and then returned to the Omaha Indian Reservation in Nebraska, where she spent the rest of her life. For years, she traveled over the rough country in all kinds of weather, first on foot and later on horseback, caring for the people who needed her. She was a forceful advocate of Indian rights, a fierce fighter for temperance, and a consistent and outspoken spokesperson for public health measures. In 1913, with the help of the Presbyterian Church and the Society of Friends, Dr Picotte built a twelve-bed hospital here in Walthill. After her death from cancer in 1915, the hospital was renamed in her honor. The hospital was closed in the 1940s, and the building was then used variously as a nursing home, a family health clinic, bakery, upholstery shop, and private residence.

In 1989 a group of local area residents began a movement to turn the old hospital into a memorial to Dr Picotte. As of this writing, the building has been purchased, and renovations are underway. Plans are to turn the three-story clapboard structure into a multipurpose center, with exhibits on Dr Picotte's life and achievements, as well as on pioneer life and traditional Indian culture. Anyone wishing to see the Picotte Center, located in northeast Nebraska, should first call for an appointment.

NEVADA

BOULDER CITY

Boulder City Hospital 901 Adams Boulevard 89005. (702) 293-4111. BCH was constructed in 1931 to care for workers who had come to the area to build the Hoover Dam. Many of the workers lived in a collection of tents and shacks called Ragtown. There was no electricity or running water, living arrangements were haphazard, and summer temperatures soared to 130 degrees. Infectious diseases and heat prostration were constant dangers, and the hazardous work led to numerous accidents. Rather than transport sick and injured workers over washboard roads to Las Vegas many miles away, the Six Companies consortium that was building the dam decided (with federal government encouragement) to build a hospital. At first the hospital was open only to employees, but it soon became clear that workers' families needed to be treated there as well. The initial facility included an eight-bed isolation ward, separated from the rest of the hospital and surrounded by an eight-foot high chain-link fence. By 1933 the hospital had expanded, the "pest house" was closed down, and workers and their families were entitled to full medical services at a cost of $1.50 per month payroll deduction.

When dam construction was completed in the late 1930s, the hospital underwent a transition to community ownership and management, resulting in a unique system of governance. Nineteen civic organizations formed a corporation, with the seven largest gaining permanent positions on the Board of Trustees and the twelve smaller rotating through six other seats. The system remains in force today for the current 35-bed modern facility. Tours are available by advance arrangement.

RENO

University of Nevada School of Medicine North Virginia Street 89557. (702) 784-6001. This school was founded in 1969, established in part with a $4 million pledge from Howard Hughes. Initially it was a two-year basic science school (with the first class enrolled in 1971), but it was converted to a four-year program in 1977, and the first MDs graduated here in 1980. The medical school campus is still devoted mostly to administration, research, and basic science space. The clinical years are spent elsewhere, at the Reno Veterans Administration Medical Center (the school's primary teaching hospital), the Washoe Medical Center, and various other hospitals, both locally and in Las Vegas. The buildings here, at the northern end of the University of Nevada-Reno campus, can be toured if prior arrangements are made with the Public Relations office [(702) 784-6001, ext 1605].

Washoe Medical Center 77 Pringle Way 89520. (702) 785-4100. When the forerunner of the hospital was founded in 1862, it was merely a few beds in a rundown printer's shop, pressed into duty to care for victims in a smallpox epidemic. It took another couple of moves for the hospital to reach its present site in 1890, which at that time was outside the city limits. The townsfolk wanted the county hospital away from town, so decent folk wouldn't have to deal with "paupers afflicted with loathsome diseases." In fact, patients in the hospital were usually referred to as inmates and they had to follow strict, prison-like rules. Today, the state's oldest hospital is the center of an extensive health network that includes almost a dozen hospitals and various other facilities in western Nevada and eastern California. WMC itself is a modern 537-bed primary and tertiary care facility, which is one of the University of Nevada's primary teaching affiliates. No tours are presently available.

NEW HAMPSHIRE

CONCORD

New Hampshire Hospital 105 Pleasant Street 03301. (603) 224-6531. When this institution opened in 1842, it was known as the New Hampshire Asylum for the Insane. It was unusual in that it was the only state mental hospital in the country which was required to be entirely self-sustaining. As a result, it charged patients $2.25 a week, raised most of the patients' food right on the grounds, made patients do all the work, and refused to admit the indigent insane. Many of the early patients were diagnosed as suffering from "religious excitement," and were required to attend religious service as an important part of their treatment. Today, the hospital occupies some 125 acres of land, includes over 35 buildings and cottages, and will soon be opening a new $30 million facility. The center portion of the present Main Building dates from 1842, and several other buildings predate the turn of the century. Tours are available to all interested parties [(603) 271-5231].

HANOVER

Dartmouth–Hitchcock Medical Center 03756. (603) 646-5000. Dartmouth Medical School was established in 1798, making it the nation's fourth oldest medical college, after the ones at the University of Pennsylvania, Columbia, and Harvard. Dartmouth was the only one of the four to be located in a small town in a rural area, and its location has been giving it problems ever since. It was tiny from the beginning and, though it had its bright moments (Oliver Wendell Holmes taught anatomy and physiology here from 1838 to 1840), the overall quality of the education was at best uneven. Flexner (in

1910) found the school unacceptable, and, in light of his report, the college trustees scaled down the program beginning in 1913 to include only two years of preclinical instruction. Even with this more limited endeavor, the school limped along for many years. In 1934, an accreditation report described the school as having "an inbred, provincial . . . unproductive and small faculty; an inbred and . . . provincial student body; (and) insufficient evidence of research." When, after another inspection, the school was put on probation in 1956, the college trustees finally decided that something had to be done. After an enormous infusion of money and talent, the program was expanded to three years in 1970 (with students transferring elsewhere for their last year) and to four years in 1980. Throughout this expansion process, there were many who contended that it made little sense to invest so much in a huge medical center stuck out in the country.

Dartmouth is currently involved in developing an entirely new $217 million, 225-acre, 1.2 million square foot medical complex about three miles away from its current aging center. Dartmouth's partners in all this are the Mary Hitchcock Memorial Hospital, the Hitchcock Clinic, and the Veterans Administration Hospital (the latter currently in White River Junction). Of these, the oldest is the Mary Hitchcock Memorial Hospital, built in 1893 by a generous benefactor whose largesse resulted in an extravagantly decorated and altogether-too-large facility. Initially built to house 36 beds, its average daily census in the first few years was barely five patients per day. A portion of this hospital still exists at 2 Maynard Street, but this will be bulldozed into the ground when the whole complex moves to nearby Lebanon on Route 120 in the early 1990s.

Current plans are to include some artifacts from the old Mary Hitchcock in the new complex, including an elegant rotunda fireplace of Siena marble, a monogram, and some columns. Amenities such as tours will all be held in abeyance until the new center is completed.

KINGSTON

Josiah Bartlett Homestead and Monument New Hampshire Route 111 opposite Village Green. In front of this white frame Colonial home, you will find a marker which reads: "Distinguished participant in founding of the republic as signer of Declaration of Independence and Articles of Confederation, and prominent in this state as Chief Justice of two courts and first holder of title of governor and innovator in medicine, he practiced in this town for 45 years". This is quite a list of accomplishments for anyone, but Josiah Bartlett (1729–1795) was a remarkably accomplished individual.

He learned medicine by the apprentice system and soon afterward set up a practice in Kingston. Medicine was not the enormously absorbing occupation it is today, certainly not for someone practicing in a tiny hamlet, and many physicians also occupied themselves with farming, the ministry, or some other occupation. In these tumultuous pre-Revolutionary times, Bartlett turned to public affairs, representing his town in the Provincial Assembly and joining the local militia. He was sent as one of three New Hampshire delegates to the Continental Congress, and when the Declaration of Independence was signed, Bartlett's signature came immediately after John Hancock's. In 1790 he was elected President of New Hampshire and was reelected twice before the state constitution was signed and Bartlett became governor. Throughout all this, Bartlett continued to practice medicine, and, in 1791, Bartlett led a group of 18 other physicians to establish the New Hampshire Medical Society, of which he became the first president. The Bartlett home still stands here in Kingston, but it is a private dwelling not accessible to the public.

NEW JERSEY

BELLEVILLE

Clara Maass Medical Center One Franklin Avenue 07109. (201) 450-2000. This institution was founded in 1868 as the Newark German Hospital. During World War I, in response to the kind of anti-German sentiment that led people to call sauerkraut "liberty cabbage" and German measles "liberty measles," the hospital was renamed Newark Memorial. In the 1940s, the hospital came under the control of the Lutheran church and was again renamed, this time Lutheran Memorial Hospital. Finally it received the name Clara Maass Memorial Hospital in 1952 and moved to its present Belleville location in 1957.

What brings this hospital national significance is its namesake, the most famous graduate of its nursing school and its onetime director of nurses, Clara Maass. Miss Maass entered the hospital's Training School for Nurses and graduated with its second class in 1895. She was briefly head nurse here in 1898 but then signed up as a contract nurse to care for soldiers in the Spanish-American War. In succession, she volunteered for duty in Florida, Georgia, Cuba, and the Philippines. When Walter Reed and William Gorgas began their famous attack on yellow fever in 1900, Maass again volunteered to care for the patients. She was clearly an adventurous, plucky, and dedicated young woman. In 1901 when investigators were trying to pin down the carrier for the disease, Maass volunteered to be bitten by the *Stegomyia* mosquito in response to the Army's request for research subjects. In fact, she was bitten on two separate occasions, the first resulting in a mild illness and the second producing an ultimately fatal case of yellow fever. She died just after her 25th birthday, the final martyr in the experiments, the person whose death proved the mosquito's role and concluded the experiments. As the *New York Times* editorialized in paying tribute to Maass at her death: "No soldier . . . placed his life in peril for better reasons than those which prompted this faithful nurse to risk hers."

In 1976 Clara Maass became the first nurse to have a United States postage stamp issued in her honor (Cuba had bestowed a similar honor on Maass in 1951). Her grave is in Newark's Fairmount Cemetery (620 Central Avenue), marked by a pink granite stone bearing a brief account of her contributions. The Maass Medical Center now includes a modern 525-bed hospital, as well as the Clara Maass School of Nursing. No tours are available.

CAMDEN

UMDNJ-School of Osteopathic Medicine   401 Haddon Avenue 08103. (609) 757-7730. This is one of the six schools which compose the UMDNJ (see Newark, below). The school was founded in 1975, after the state decided it needed a third medical school in the underserved South Jersey area. Two of the largest and most modern hospitals in the area were osteopathic facilities and a substantial number of the primary care physicians in the area likewise had osteopathic training. Thus the state decided to institute an osteopathic school, instead of an allopathic school. The institution was organized as a "school without walls" to minimize capital expenditures. SOM students share the same basic science facilities as UMDNJ-Robert Wood Johnson Medical School students and faculty, but clinical work is all pursued here in South Jersey. The Education and Research Building at this address serves as the administrative center for the school, with the primary clinical facility being the Kennedy Memorial Hospitals – University Medical Center (113 East Laurel Road, Stratford 08084). The school currently offers no tours.

LAWRENCEVILLE

Medical Society of New Jersey 2 Princess Road 08648. (609) 896-1766. The oldest state medical society in the nation was founded in 1766, when seventeen physicians met at Duff's Tavern in New Brunswick. That building has long since been gone (the spot is marked by a plaque at Albany and Peace Streets), but the medical society continues to thrive. Originally, one of the major concerns of the doctor-members was to place some controls on "quacks," especially the itinerant practitioners of indifferent training who set themselves up as "doctors of medicine." Today's medical society is composed of some 8500 active members and concerns itself — like most such organizations — with upgrading medical practice, educating the public on issues important to the society, securing benefits for its members, and improving communication on matters of interest to its members and other health professionals. During its history, the medical society has helped with the enactment of a number of landmark medical developments, including the first stringent state law to regulate the practice of medicine (1772), the first legislation calling for the examination and licensure of health officials and sanitary inspectors (1903), and the first chlorination of a public water supply (at the Boonton Reservoir of the Jersey City Water Works, 1908). The present building is a two-story brick structure which dates from 1978. There are no tours.

NEWARK

University of Medicine and Dentistry of New Jersey 30 Bergen Street 07107. (201) 456-6770. This is basically an administrative entity which oversees and coordinates the activities of all the other hyphenated UMDNJs in the state, including six health professions schools, three "core" hospitals, and a variety of related facilities. While the profusion of UMDNJs can be confusing, the story behind it is interesting and represents a unique approach to combining health care education and health care services.

There were several unsuccessful attempts to start a school of medicine in New Jersey during the eighteenth and nineteenth centuries, including three by Princeton University and two by Rutgers University, but the early twentieth century found the state without any medical schools. As a result, the state suffered from both a practitioner shortage and a lack of sophisticated medical care. Finally, in 1954, Seton Hall University (a Catholic institution) started schools of medicine and dentistry and two years later Fairleigh Dickinson University inaugurated its own dental school. In 1961 Rutgers started a medical school. All of the various institutions found that running technologically sophisticated schools was far more expensive than they had anticipated, and to varying degrees they all began foundering financially. The Seton Hall schools were the first to be acquired by the state, in the early 1960s, and were renamed the New Jersey College of Medicine and Dentistry. It fared little better under its new ownership and struggled with continuing financial problems and newfound political strife. When the Newark situation exploded in the late 1960s and 1970s (see below), the Governor tried to resolve what seemed like an impossible situation by making a single entity administratively responsible for coordinating education, research, and patient care in the health professions for the entire state. This freestanding entity was given university status in 1981, and now the UMDNJ has the unique task of integrating a statewide system of professional education and indigent patient care. The professional schools include a medical and dental school in Newark, a second medical school in Piscataway, an osteopathic medical school in Camden, and a graduate school in the biomedical sciences and an allied health professions school, both in Newark.

While New Jersey believes that medical education cannot be isolated, practically or administratively, from the needs of its most impoverished citizens, its system of integrating professional education with the care of the needy recurrently runs afoul of the medical education establishment. UMDNJ has been criticized for diffusing curriculum authority, for allowing students at one school to use the facilities of others for various portions of their training, and for placing such a heavy emphasis on service as a necessary component of education.

This is a very interesting experiment, one whose future is by no means clear.

UMDNJ – New Jersey Medical School 185 South Orange Avenue 07103. (201) 456-4538. After the state took over Seton Hall's medical school and Jersey City's political entanglements made the school's position in that city untenable, a site selection committee — after much deliberation — decided to move the school to Newark. Newark in the 1960s had some of the most desperate living conditions in the country, ranking among the nation's very worst cities in terms of unemployment, per capita income, crime, drug addiction, venereal disease, maternal mortality, and tuberculosis. It was a powder keg waiting for a spark. When the announcement was made that the college would move to Newark, necessitating the clearing of 185-acres of homes and small businesses in the city's black community, Newark erupted in sustained violence for five days, with fires and shooting. In the wake of the riots, the state government sat down with community representatives and negotiated. The result was the Newark Agreements of 1968, a contract unprecedented in medical education.

Under this contract CMDNJ (as it was then called) agreed to take primary responsibility for providing health care to Newark's most underserved population, in an endeavor that would create jobs for local residents and which would evolve with continued input from a formally constituted citizens' advisory board. Though this seemed a stunningly radical development at the time, it has since become the basis for an entire statewide system, as embodied in UMDNJ.

In 1971 the college broke ground for a $200 million campus. As the program has evolved, the medical school in Newark has developed the largest minority enrollment (about 20 percent) of any medical school in the United States outside of the traditionally black schools. University Hospital is now one of the nation's largest providers of health care to the poor, providing over half of all uncompensated care in the city. The community impact has been substantial, resulting in a 50 percent drop in infant mortality, a 60 percent reduction in tuberculosis deaths, and other equally impressive gains.

There are currently no tours available.

UMDNJ – New Jersey Dental School 110 Bergen Street 07103. (201) 456-4633. This school admitted its first students in 1956 as part of the Seton Hall College of Medicine and Dentistry. The Seton Hall complex was acquired by the state in 1965, but the Dental School did not move from Jersey City to its present address until 1976. Though the school is relatively young, it celebrates dental history with a museum that occupies a full room in the basement plus a number of cases adjacent to the school's lobby. Among the numerous items to be seen here are a portable dentist's office, packed neatly into a special suitcase; an array of patient's chairs; teeth-extracting instruments dating from the 1700s; a guard to protect dentists' fingers from biting patients; and a handmade dental cabinet (c. 1845) with a special alarm designed to alert the dentist when an unauthorized person has broken into the gold filling compartment. The museum is open to the public daily from 9 AM to 4 PM.

PISCATAWAY

UMDNJ – Robert Wood Johnson Medical School 675 Hoes Lane 08854. (201) 463-4557. This school began in 1961 as Rutgers Medical School, enrolling its first class in 1966. Until 1972 it remained a two-year school, although in 1970 it became known as the College of Medicine and Dentistry of New Jersey – Rutgers Medical School. In 1986 the college assumed its present name, in honor of General Johnson, who for many years directed the Johnson & Johnson health care enterprises. The school's primary teaching institution is the Robert Wood Johnson University Hospital in nearby New Brunswick (at One Robert Wood Johnson Plaza). Some students spend their third and fourth years in Camden with their clinical work centered around the Cooper Hospital/University Medical Center.

There are no tours.

NEW MEXICO

ALBUQUERQUE

University of New Mexico Medical Center Camino de Salud 08854. (505) 277-2413. This medical center was built around what used to be the Bernalillo County Indian Hospital, which had been founded in 1954 to serve Native Americans as well as local non-Indian indigents. The School of Medicine was founded as a two-year school and accepted its first students in 1964 but moved rapidly to expand to its present status as a four-year school. In 1968 the BCIH became the Bernalillo County Medical Center, and in 1979 it became the University of New Mexico Hospital. However, the nine member Board of Trustees still includes one representative of the All-Indian Pueblo Council. The current medical center encompasses a range of educational, research, and patient care facilities. Tours are available via the University's Department of Public Relations.

St Joseph's Hospital 400 Walter Street, NE 87102. (505) 848-8000. New Mexico had been ballyhooed in the eastern press as a health resort for tuberculars as early as 1877, but it was the completion of a railhead in Albuquerque in 1880 that allowed people to travel there with greater ease and safety. The city's commercial interests, anxious to build a population base and business opportunities, actively encouraged healthseekers — especially young, talented ones with financial independence — to come to the area and distributed a plethora of pamphlets and advertisements and sponsored lectures in eastern cities.

Though there had been several other institutions created in other parts of the state, St Joseph's Sanitorium, erected in 1902, was the first in Albuquerque, and thereby the first step in the development of a local industry. Within a year of opening its initial three-story structure, St Joseph's built an addition. In 1912 it added seventeen open air cottages, and then a dozen more in the several years following. In 1925 it underwent another major expansion. After St Joseph's, other similar institutions were created by the Presbyterians, Lutherans, Methodists, Episcopalians, blacks, and various proprietary groups. East Central Avenue was known as "San Alley" for the profusion of institutions that lined its curbs in the 1910s and 1920s. Peripheral to these were dozens of health ranches, rest homes, summer camps, and private homes that catered to those with TB. Older houses in town still show evidence of the old screen porches on the southern or eastern exposures, where the "lungers" took the air.

Of those who came, a significant number arrived too late and succumbed to their illness. In 1925, for example, TB was the primary cause of death here, with over 90 percent of the deaths being among new residents in the city. Still, large numbers of people in this "army of tuberculars" survived, and they became the single most important phenomenon in New Mexico's population growth in the first half of this century, many of them going on to make significant contributions to the state's expanding economic and cultural base. Equally important, the TB industry brought hundreds of new physicians to the state, many of whom were tuberculars themselves. Between 1906 and 1914, 737 new doctors were licensed in New Mexico, all of them trained elsewhere and all of them "chasing the cure" themselves and/or hoping to care for other unfortunates.

St Joseph's was founded by the Sisters of Charity. The Sisters first opened the Wayfarer's House in 1880 to care for the ill settlers brought in by the new railroad. In 1902 — ten years before New Mexico became a state — St Joseph's Sanitorium was opened. The sanitorium functions were phased out after World War II when TB ceased to be a major public health problem. When a brand new St Joseph's Hospital was built in 1966, it was the largest single private construction project ever undertaken in New Mexico.

Today, St Joseph's is a 300-bed modern hospital, the flagship of a multi-institution health care system. Tours of the hospital can be arranged via the Communications Department.

Presbyterian Hospital Center 1100 Central, SE 87106. (505) 841-1234. Presbyterian was established as a "sanatorium for indigent lungers" in 1908, the second after St Joseph's in Albuquerque. The first building was a five-room cottage with two large porches.

Shortly thereafter, 24 tent-cottages were added, and then a farm to feed the growing legions of lungers. In 1913 a surgery and beds were added for general hospital patients. In 1915 a twelve-room cottage was added for tubercular ministers. Patients came here from virtually every state in the Union, so the Presbyterian Sanitorium actively solicited funds from Presbyterians around the country. By 1921 it had a patient population of 110 and a waiting list of 50.

As its patient population changed, the San likewise changed its name: to the Presbyterian Hospital Center, in 1952. Now, of course, it is rare for the hospital to admit a patient with tuberculosis. The "old San" was demolished in 1967, and the current modern complex houses the largest nonfederal hospital in the state. Tours are available from the Volunteers Office.

Lovelace Medical Center 5400 Gibson Boulevard, SE 87108. (505) 262-7000. The Lovelace Clinic was founded in 1922, one of the spiritual offspring of the Mayo Clinic and one of the pioneering medical group practices in the country. Dr William R Lovelace arrived in New Mexico in 1906, seeking a cure for his tuberculosis. As his health improved, he cared for others, making "house calls" in his buckboard to the farms and ranches. He made several trips to the Mayo Clinic and, profoundly influenced by what he saw there, resolved to start a group practice in New Mexico. In 1922 he and Edgar Lasseter (another healed lunger) joined forces. By 1940 the clinic numbered some sixteen doctors (today there are 200).

The clinic's rise to national prominence began in 1947 when Lovelace's nephew and namesake, Dr W Randolph Lovelace II, joined the operation. Randy (as he was called) was a Mayo-trained surgeon whose love of flying had led him to be an early pioneer in aviation medicine. From 1942 until 1946, he was Chief of the military's Aero Medical Laboratory. He was one of the developers of the first high-altitude oxygen mask for pilots, and he became a national hero when he became the first person to test the mask, jumping from a plane at 30,000 feet, losing consciousness during fifteen minutes of descent, and rousing at 8000 feet, just in time to manage a safe (if feeble) landing. (In 1970 a crater on the moon was named in his honor.)

When Randy joined the Clinic, he brought with him many of his contacts in what was not yet called the military-industrial complex. As a result, the Clinic became an important site of research in the early space program. In 1959 the Clinic's research wing developed an extensive series of tests designed to assess the fitness of candidates for space travel and administered these tests to a group from which the Mercury astronauts, the first Americans in space, were selected. The whole process was parodied in Tom Wolfe's book (and the subsequent movie), *The Right Stuff.*

Another significant Lovelace achievement was the first experimental lung lavage procedure (1972) to treat an Atomic Energy Commission employee who accidentally inhaled radioactive materials.

The current Lovelace hospital is descended from the Bataan Memorial Methodist Hospital, established in 1952 as a tribute to the 200th Coast Artillery of the New Mexico National Guard, which fought (and suffered) in the battle on the Bataan Peninsula in the Philippines (and the famous death march which followed it) during World War II. The hospital merged with Lovelace in 1975. The 1988 additions are notable for their Southwest Indian motifs, especially in the dramatic lobby. Tours are available via the Public Information Department.

Albuquerque Veterans Administration Medical Center 2100 Ridgecrest, SE 87108. (505) 265-1711. The history of this facility dates from the 1920s, when the War Mothers Memorial Association started lobbying for a tuberculosis sanitarium exclusively for veterans. The present hospital was opened on 515 acres of essentially barren land in 1932. It was a 262-bed hospital, intended to be a "restful" place where TB patients could take advantage of the hot, dry climate. What made it unique, certainly as a veterans' hospital, was that it was designed in the pueblo-revival style, with the boxy

Albuquerque Veterans Administration Center *(Credit: Jim Janis)*

massing, wood-beam detailing, and desert setting that actually made the place look like an Indian pueblo.

The structures here have had numerous additions, some harmonizing with the pueblo design and some not; but the original buildings — with their flat roofs, archless doorways, tile-paved patios, and projecting beams — still give the impression of a pueblo. The open porches were used for the TB patients to get the fresh desert air; sometimes patients' beds were kept here 24-hours a day. By 1970 only twelve beds of the huge hospital (now of 463 beds) were used for "the white plague" patients.

The campus now occupies 83 beautifully landscaped acres, most of the rest of the original land having been annexed by Kirkland Air Force Base. The proximity of Kirkland led this hospital to become the site of the first "sharing agreement" with the Defense Department, whereby the VA and a military service jointly operated and staffed shared medical facilities, thereby reducing overlapping services and costs. In the present case the two jointly run an outpatient clinic on the VA grounds, the hospital's emergency room, a dental clinic, and such specialized activities as nuclear medicine. Tours of the facility are available via Public Affairs.

NEW YORK

ALBANY

Albany Medical College of Union University New Scotland and Holland Avenues 12208. (518) 445-3125. When the Albany Medical College was founded in 1838, Albany was still a small village. Like many other such facilities of the era, the Albany establishment was built around a single strong and charismatic physician, and the course of instruction was a series of lectures and demonstrations. The need for a large patient population for clinical instruction was not widely appreciated at the time, and small towns were therefore often preferred because the cost of living was usually much lower than in the metropolis. The Albany Medical College was built around a principal faculty of two physicians and was basically an elaboration of an earlier one doctor enterprise, "Dr. March's Practical School of Anatomy and Surgery" begun in 1832.

For a while in the 1850s, AMC had a nominal attachment to the University of Albany, which was in existence only a few years. When Union University was incorporated, AMC affiliated with it — though again the relationship was more for appearance than reality. When the Flexner Report was published in 1910, the school was found so wanting (he said that it had not "even emerged from the fee dividing stage" and that it belonged "to the past") that it is a wonder it managed to survive the subsequent furor. The final straw came in 1914 when the state of Pennsylvania refused to recognize an AMC diploma as a valid degree. Union University's board of trustees finally stepped in and issued a call for reorganization, as well as a demand for the resignation of all faculty. A new dean was installed, academic standards were upgraded, class size was reduced (the school averaged a scant 15 graduates for the next ten years), an ambitious building and fund raising program was begun, and the modern era at AMC was successfully launched , much to the surprise of many who thought it could not be done.

Today, AMC is the centerpiece of a large medical center that includes the usual collection of education, research, and treatment facilities. The AMC Hospital is the direct descendant of the Albany Hospital, which was built in conjunction with AMC in 1850. The entire complex is currently undergoing a $152 million redevelopment that will completely revamp its appearance and facilities. Call for tour information.

Throop Drugstore Museum of the Albany College of Pharmacy 106 New Scotland Avenue 12208. (518) 445-7211. Pharmacy is the newest component of Union University, dating to only 1881. It moved to the University Heights area of Albany in the 1920s, at about the same time as the medical school. Major additions were added in 1956 and 1981. The major attraction for visitors, however, is not the building but rather the unusual Throop drugstore which was installed here in the 1930s. Originally established in Schoharie, NY (about 40 miles from Albany) in 1800, the drugstore remained in the Throop family until it was moved to the college — lock, stock, and barrel. This is a complete pharmacy, from the wooden mortar and pestle to the pine fixtures to the native botanicals to the wooden safe covered with metal sheeting. There are also circulars, posters, and complete pharmacy registers available for your inspection. The drugstore is open Monday through Friday, 9 AM to 4 PM.

BUFFALO

Buffalo General Hospital 100 High Street 14203. (716) 845-5600. While Buffalo's citizens tried to establish a general public hospital as early as 1846, success didn't arrive until 1855. The first building was formally dedicated in 1858 by Millard Fillmore. In 1877 the hospital opened its Training School for Nurses, the first such institution west of New York City. (Ironically, in 1985 — as the school had just graduated five of its largest classes in history, with 100 percent of the graduates passing licensure exams — the Hospital's Board of Trustees voted not to admit any additional classes. The school was closed in 1987.)

BGH has been home to numerous innovators in American medicine, among them Lucien Howe, the ophthalmologist responsible for New York State's "Howe Law," which led to the general use of silver nitrate in infants' eyes to prevent neonatal eye infections caused by gonorrhea. More recently, BGH was the site of the world's first use of angled views in half-angled coronary angiography (1973).

BGH's principal building now is a sixteen-story tower, dedicated in 1986. The entire complex occupies some six city blocks. In the basement of Hamlin Hall (the old nurses' residence), BGH maintains its archives, which includes a large room with displays portraying the hospital's history. Tours can be arranged by calling (716) 845-5600, ext. 2041.

Children's Hospital of Buffalo 219 Bryant Street 14222. (716) 878-7000. Children's was born right at this site in 1892, though the original building has long since been replaced by many other structures. The hospital was home to the first intensive care nursery in the United States (1902), and it is one of the few children's hospitals in the country with its own maternity unit. It was here, in the early 1960s, that Robert Guthrie developed his simple, inexpensive and accurate test for phenylketonuria, which resulted in the control of this once devastating disease (the Guthrie test is now administered to every newborn in this and many other nations). Researchers here also developed Infasurf in 1986, a surfactant medication which, when given to babies born between 23 and 32 weeks gestation, helps prevent respiratory distress syndrome. Arrange tours by calling (716) 878-7000, ext. 7543.

SUNY at Buffalo Medical Center Main Street at Bailey Avenue 14214. (716) 636-2626. Though it has been a part of the state university system since 1962, the University of Buffalo was established in 1846 as a private university. Millard Fillmore, later to become the fourteenth president of the United States, was its first chancellor. Initially the University was composed solely of the medical school, but the School of Pharmacy was added in 1886 and the School of Dentistry in 1892 (the School of Nursing was delayed until 1940).

Buffalo was a pioneering and influential teaching center from the very beginning. It was here that Dr James P White introduced clinical obstetrics to the medical curriculum. Until White supervised the process in 1849, no medical student in the country had ever been allowed to perform a vaginal exam on a woman in labor. There was, of course, an enormous scandal as a result, but White was ultimately vindicated. Austin Flint, America's foremost practitioner of physical diagnosis, was likewise on the faculty for seventeen years (from 1836 to 1844 and 1845 to 1852, and again from 1856 to 1858), between stints at other institutions. The Austin Flint murmur, still learned by medical students around the world, is a diastolic murmur best heard at the cardiac apex, which sounds like mitral stenosis but is caused by aortic insufficiency. Frank Hamilton, also on the founding faculty, performed the first successful skin graft of a leg ulcer here in 1854. In 1851 John C Dalton, a renowned physiologist of the time, became the first physician in the nation to illustrate his lectures with classroom vivisection. Another Buffalo "first" was the discovery of cortisone by Frank Hartman (1930). The School of Dental Medicine was the first to create a hospital-based outpatient dental clinic and the first to establish a department of oral medicine. Lippes loop, for many years the most popular of the intrauterine devices, was designed by faculty member Jack Lippes in 1961.

Buffalo had several competing medical schools for a while (the most successful was the Niagara University School of Medicine, founded in 1883), but competition took its toll on the smaller schools, and they were all absorbed by the University of Buffalo by the turn of the century.

When visiting the campus, be sure to see the Health Sciences Library. The **Austin Flint Main Reading Room** is a gem, dating from 1935. Designed to look like a seventeenth century baronial library, it is paneled in English oak and features a huge hand-carved mantel over a large fireplace. The modern building which surrounds this room was completed in 1986 and successfully combines the classic older building with the spaciousness and functionalism of a modern structure. The elegant rare book rooms (containing some 12,000 volumes, some almost five centuries old) are lined with fine wooden shelves that were originally from the old Lockwood Library, built more than 50 years ago. The walls are decorated with sculptures, plaques, memorabilia, old instruments, and various artifacts. There are old monaural stethoscopes, antique brass microscopes, and even an unusual eighteenth century French enema syringe, made of pewter and nine inches long. Call (716) 831-3024 for information.

Roswell Park Memorial Institute 666 Elm Street 14263. (716) 845-2300. RPMI is the oldest cancer research center in the world. Founded in 1898 as the New York State Pathological Laboratory of the University of Buffalo, it is also the first example of direct governmental support for research in cancer. Other RPMI firsts include the nation's first voluntary plasmapheresis center for platelet collection (1964) and the first Adolescent Unit for the teenage cancer patient (1978). The laboratory owes its origin and early development to Buffalo surgeon Roswell Park, after whom the institution was eventually named (in 1946). He was professor of surgery at the University and chief of surgery at Buffalo General Hospital for over 30 years. From 1911 until 1946, RPMI was known as the New York State Institute for the Study of Malignant Diseases.

RPMI now occupies a campus of some 25 acres in downtown Buffalo, composed of some nineteen buildings, including a 218-bed research hospital. Tours are sometimes available by prior arrangement only.

Buffalo Psychiatric Center 400 Forest Avenue 14213. (716) 885-2261. This 100-acre campus houses a 740-bed inpatient program and a variety of other services and activities. The site dates from 1880, when it was called the Buffalo State Asylum, a name which endured for ten years until it was discarded in favor of the Buffalo State Hospital. The present name was adopted in 1974.

What makes this hospital of special interest is that most of the original buildings still stand, in the form of one incredible monster building that stretches across two-thirds of the length of the site. Designed by HH Richardson, then one of America's most noteworthy architects, this creation originally consisted of a central twin-towered administration building, with wings receding back on both sides. Richardson's use of a Romanesque Revival style, the rough dark-brown sandstone and red brick, and the enormous scale made this creation really special. Unfortunately, the three easternmost buildings were demolished in 1969, making the complex look like a huge bird with one clipped wing, but the remaining structures have now attained National Landmark status and are therefore likely to endure. However, no one quite knows what to do with them, and the wings have been vacant since 1974. From time to time someone sponsors a seminar on "adaptive reuse of historic buildings," but so far there has been no convergence of ideas and money. The central administration building has been restored, and it is from here that the rest of the facility's operations are directed. Clinical activities take place in a number of more modern buildings on campus. The grounds were landscaped by Frederick Law Olmsted, who designed both Central Park in New York City and the Buffalo park system.

Tours of the active buildings can be arranged by calling the volunteer office [(716) 885-2261, ext. 2440]. Historic tours are generally conducted on a monthly basis. Call ext. 2014 for details.

NEW YORK CITY   (*See* Great Medical Cities)

ROCHESTER

University of Rochester Medical Center 601 Elmwood Avenue 14642. (716) 275-3676. Oftentimes existing medical schools fall on hard times, and the people who run them have to try to raise money to meet deficits as well as future needs. This medical school followed an entirely different pattern. The money was ready and waiting for anyone who was willing to build a school according to a prescribed pattern and who could convince the donors that the talent and dedication existed to do the job well. In Rochester's case, the money came from John D Rockefeller's General Education Board, and the prescribed pattern was a highly academic medical school which would employ a "full-time" medical faculty. The General Education Board created or renewed a number of other schools in other parts of the country (e.g., Vanderbilt and Washington University). In New York State, it was Rochester University that got the nod. The money included $5 million from the GEB plus a "matching" grant of $4 million from George Eastman (a Rochester boy, of Eastman Kodak fame), plus smaller sums contributed by others who were pleased to provide company to Rockefeller and Eastman. On the day the institution opened in 1926, after the physical plant was paid for, Rochester University was left with an endowment of $9,014,226, making it one of the richest medical schools in the country. Many would argue that Rochester's early commitment to excellence in teaching, patient care, and research also makes it one of the best (the Medical Center is one of the top five sources for producing school faculty in this country).

The medical school's formal title is "The School of Medicine and Dentistry," but there is no dental school here in the conventional sense; that is, there is no undergraduate program in dentistry. When the school was first proposed, George Eastman (who had long been a supporter of dentistry) argued that a combined medical-dental school would help place training in dentistry on the same academic and scientific level as medicine. The result was a DDS program that demanded the same entrance requirements as the medical school and required the same preclinical course work. By the end of three years, only "one qualified candidate" had applied, and the DDS program was dropped. In its place the school instituted a postgraduate fellowship education program for dentists, designed to train academicians and to promote dental research. Though this is a small program, it has produced two university presidents, over a dozen dental school deans, and 90 percent of its graduates have become academicians. It has also been one of the principal sites where fluoride's role in preventing dental caries was elucidated.

Rochester's research contributions have been many. It was here that x-ray motion pictures (or cinefluorography) were first accomplished in 1932 and here that the first endoscopic color photographs of the stomach were taken. It was here too that medical aspects of the atomic bomb (in the Manhattan Project) were assessed. Rochester was the first in the world to offer a PhD in radiation biology (1950), and the first to point the direction toward modern day mammographic examinations of the breast (1930). Rochester scientists first isolated progesterone in 1934.

The present medical center occupies 2.62 million square feet in a single enormous building (1975), which houses the components mentioned above, plus the 741-bed **Strong Memorial Hospital** and the School of Nursing. The latter became a college in 1972, though it had existed in several forms, usually as a division in various departments, since 1925.

Tours can be arranged by contacting the Friends of Strong Memorial Hospital. The single most attractive site for visitors is the library, which represents a spectacular blending of new and old. The reading room here is the old lobby from the 1925 Strong Memorial Hospital building, preserved intact when the 1975 Strong was built and now used as the entryway for a thoroughly renovated library. The reading room is lushly lined with oak paneling, decorated with carved oak portals, surmounted with a deeply molded ceiling painted in soft shades of grey, burgundy, and blue. Historic plaques line the walls, and there is even a chunk of marble from Kos, birthplace of Aesculapius. The library also includes a fine history of medicine collection.

Rochester General Hospital 1425 Portland Avenue 14621. (716) 338-4000. This hospital was chartered in 1847 by the Rochester Female Charitable Society as an extension of their chief work, which was visiting the sick. Daily contact with the sick and needy convinced the women that adequate facilities for their care were a necessity. The ladies entered upon a vigorous fund raising program, which included two concerts by Jenny Lind and a "moral lecture" by circus impresario PT Barnum. Once founded, the hospital survived largely and handsomely on the generosity of the charitable women in town. Jams, jellies, and preserves were donated. Feathers for pillows, quilts for beds, doilies for trays — all were donated. Rooms and wards were furnished by various church groups or as memorials, and substantial donors were rewarded with free hospital service for anyone of the donor's choosing at any time.

In 1887 the hospital founded a formal volunteer organization, known as the Twigs (together these twigs formed the Hospital Tree), which has since become a model for hospital volunteer organizations across the country. In 1905 virtually every sheet used in the hospital was sewn by the Twigs, but the Twigs did far more than sew: they built fences, laid floors, painted and redecorated rooms, gave presents to patients, raised money, purchased equipment, served as aides, performed hospital public relations, and presented memorials of many kinds.

Initially called Rochester City Hospital, the name was changed in 1911 to Rochester General Hospital. (The hospital was private from the start, never a municipal hospital, and the name change was intended to avoid confusion on that score.)

The hospital opened its Training School for Nurses in 1880, the twelfth such school in the country. Student nurses were, from the first, sent out to nurse in private homes, thereby raising money for the hospital. The School's superintendent from 1896 to 1901 was Miss Sophia Palmer, who — as a sideline — founded and became the first editor of the *American Journal of Nursing* in 1900. The school graduated its last class in 1964.

RGH also operated the first and only Medical Photography School in the country from 1943 until 1959. The school closed its doors when it was no longer needed, as various professional photography schools around the country began training students in microscopic and technical photography.

Today RGH is a modern, 547-bed community and teaching hospital, which dates from 1966. Nothing remains of the previous hospital buildings (located for 102 years on West Main Street), but historically minded visitors will want to stop by the **Baker-Cederberg Museum and Archives,** which acts as a repository for items related to the hospital's history. There is a 10,000-image photo collection here, as well as an active oral history program, and a variety of exhibits that circulate through the hospital and to various hospital satellites. Call for details.

Eastman Dental Center 625 Elmwood Avenue 14620. (716) 725-4534. The Rochester Dental Dispensary was founded in 1915 as a result of a several million dollar bequest by Eastman Kodak magnate George Eastman. Eastman had been looking for a suitable beneficiary of his philanthropy and came to the conclusion that his dollars would go further in caring for the teeth of children than they would in any other available arena. His conclusion was not simply a whim. Rochester already had a long history of dental achievement. Rochester dentist John Beers deserves the credit for the invention of the first gold crown. Rochester dentists formed the first Dental Protective Association to fight litigation by those who wished to patent various dental appliances and methods. This ultimately led to the first state and national legislation prohibiting the granting of patents for methods and appliances used in the healing art.

Rochester is generally credited with establishing the first free dental clinic in the country in 1901. This operation in the City Hospital lasted a couple of years and was later replaced by two small offices in the Rochester public schools. Eastman's enterprise, however, turned these small offices into a huge assembly line where first squads of dentists and then squads of dental hygienists processed thousands of children (and later adults). In 1916 the Dispensary established the first school for dental hygienists in the US. This huge screening program incidentally revealed that large numbers of children had swollen tonsils, which at that time were thought to harbor germs and increase the likelihood of disease. In 1920 the Dispensary founded its Tonsil-Adenoid Clinic, which

The Rochester Dental Dispensary, the 1915 building of the Eastman Dental Center *(Photo courtesy of Eastman Dental Center)*

performed some 35,000 tonsillectomies until the program was suspended during WW II.

The Dispensary was much admired all over the world and widely copied. Through the benificence of Mr Eastman, similar operations were established in London (1930), Rome (1933), Brussels (1935), Stockholm (1936), and Paris (1937). In 1941 the Rochester institution was renamed the Eastman Dental Dispensary, and the current name was adopted in 1965.

Today, the EDC is housed in a distinctive modern brick structure close to URMC and functions to supply advanced training to dentists and to provide oral health care to people of all ages. The Center also maintains a large research component. The new building dates from 1978, but the old building still stands across town at 800 East Main. No tours of either are currently available.

Monroe Community Hospital 435 East Henrietta Road 14603. (716) 274-7503. This is a 600-bed geriatrics and chronic disease hospital that will probably interest most visitors primarily for its architecture. First established in 1825 as the Monroe County Poor Farm, the institution gradually grew and evolved to house orphans, the homeless, the insane, and those with various communicable diseases. The present building was begun in 1929 and sparked widespread criticism in the early depression years as being "too good looking for poor people." Indeed, the exterior is remarkably beautiful and ornate, and richly decorated with dragons, gargoyles, winged lions, various grotesques, and mythic figures. The overall style is Lombardic Romanesque, with a generous supply of pillars, arches, and turrets. The exterior of this wonderfully whimsical building was designed by Thomas Boyde, Jr, Rochester's first black architect. The hospital is pleased to arrange tours for interested parties, though the exterior can be seen without special arrangements.

SARANAC LAKE

Historic Saranac Lake (Contact Saranac Lake Area Chamber of Commerce. 30 Main Street 12983. (518) 891-1990.) This is a situation in which an entire town and a significant amount of the adjacent area is both of medical interest and worth seeing.

Saranac Lake was a tiny village when Dr Edward Livingston Trudeau moved there in 1876, hoping that the clean mountain air of the Adirondacks would help his tuberculosis. When his condition stabilized and then improved, he turned his malady into a career. In 1879 he published a paper in the *Medical Record* celebrating his community as a health resort for consumptives. In the years that followed, the initial slow trickle of patients turned into a steady flow. Trudeau built the first two-person cottage for patients (Little Red, it was called) in 1884, and from that humble beginning grew America's most famous tuberculosis sanitarium, the Adirondack Cottage Sanitarium. Later called the Trudeau Sanitarium, the doctor's enterprise eventually grew to cover an entire hillside, including more than three dozen buildings. What Trudeau offered was not simply a therapeutic method; he gave his patients a way of life: "pure air, good food, clean morals, and a cheerful frame of mind."

In 1885 the nation and Saranac Lake had only Little Red; but by 1935, the country had almost 500 sanitaria and over 400 general hospital tuberculosis facilities, and Saranac Lake had six major sanitaria, 150 private "cure cottages," and the busy Saranac Lake General Hospital. The cure cottages were devised by local citizens who decided to rent out rooms to consumptives who couldn't find space at the sanitaria. Because the "cure" was an outdoor one, each cottage had an abundance of porches, so that patients could sit outdoors and take the air. As Saranac Lake's fame spread, similar outdoor "sleeping porches" and sun porches became a fixture of middle-class house design over the entire country. By the end of the 1930s tuberculosis began to lose its sting. The incidence of new cases declined. The advent of antibiotics eased the cure of existing cases, and the Trudeau Sanitarium closed its doors in 1954. Saranac Lake's fame and economy went into a profound slump from which it has not yet fully recovered.

A tour of present-day Saranac Lake is a reminder of a time when tuberculosis caused one out of every ten deaths in America. The Trudeau Sanitarium is still largely intact, though it is now owned by the American Management Association, which uses it for offices and as a conference center. Casual visitors are not permitted. The old Trudeau Institute (established in 1894 as the nation's first tuberculosis research lab) is now a private research facility, but visitors are welcome to tour the grounds during normal business hours. The original, now-restored Little Red has been relocated here for your inspection, and you can also see a fine statue of Trudeau by Mt Rushmore sculptor Gutzon Borglum. The statue is inscribed with a maxim that some have attributed to Trudeau: TO CURE SOMETIMES, TO RELIEVE OFTEN, TO COMFORT ALWAYS. The Robert Louis Stevenson Cottage is a nice little museum which highlights Stevenson's 1887 stay here as Trudeau's patient, during which the author wrote *The Master of Ballantrae*. The Saranac Lake Free Library contains an incredible collection of local lore, often has displays related to the tuberculosis era, and has an additional archival room which is open by appointment to interested visitors [phone (518) 891-4190]. The

Statue of Edward Livingston Trudeau, sculptor Gutzon Borglum *(Photo courtesy of Trudeau Institute, Inc., Saranac Lake, NY)*

real treat here, however, is to wander the streets and observe the architecture of the numerous cure cottages and the few surviving sanitaria. Many of the old porches and balconies have been enclosed, but there are so many of them appended to houses all over town that a visitor can hardly fail to recognize the pattern. An organization called Historic Saranac Lake provides scheduled guided tours [(518) 891-0971], and the Chamber of Commerce provides booklets for self-guided tours.

STONY BROOK

SUNY at Stony Brook Medical Center Nicholls and East Loop Roads 11794. (516) 444-2700. The State University of New York at Stony Brook was itself established only as recently as 1957, and its University Hospital was opened in 1980. This then is a very new medical center, and its slightly surrealistic appearance makes it look suitable for the twenty-first century. The Health Sciences Center is composed of an enormous flat base containing various services, which serves to interconnect the other more dramatic structures. These include two large angular black towers (the University Hospital), a huge white cube which appears to be assembled from eight gambler's dice (the Medical School), and a smaller, four-dice white cube (the Basic Sciences Building). The Health Sciences campus also includes Schools of Dental Medicine, Nursing, Allied Health Professions, and Social Welfare. When combined with the adjacent Main Campus, the SUNY complex covers 1100 acres and includes 140 buildings. No tours are currently available to the general public.

SYRACUSE

SUNY at Syracuse Health Science Center 750 East Adams Street 13210. (315) 473-4416. This institution traces its origins back to 1834 when Geneva Medical College was founded, a school which will be forever famous as the place where America's first woman physician graduated. Elizabeth Blackwell had applied to, and been rejected by, a substantial number of the country's 36 medical schools when she turned to Geneva. Though family connections helped, it was ultimately the school's student body who decided the matter of her acceptance. The 1847 resolution reads in part: "Resolved . . . that the application of Elizabeth Blackwell to become a member of our class meets our entire approbation; and in extending our unanimous invitation we pledge ourselves that no conduct of ours shall cause her to regret her attendance at this institution."

Geneva Medical College survived until 1872, when a group of faculty departed to the nearby, relative metropolis of Syracuse, bringing the library and anatomical museum with them. The medical department of Syracuse University began the same year, becoming in 1875 — along with Harvard and the Chicago Medical College — one of the first three medical schools in the country to require a three-year graded curriculum for graduation. In 1896 Syracuse became the first medical school in the country to install and equip a physiology laboratory for students.

The medical college moved to its present location in 1937 when then-governor Franklin Delano Roosevelt laid the cornerstone of a new basic science building (now known as Weiskotten Hall).

In 1950 the State University of New York purchased the College of Medicine and the School of Public Health Nursing from Syracuse, setting them up as the nucleus of the Upstate Medical Center (to distinguish it from the Downstate Medical Center, which it purchased in 1948 from the Long Island College of Medicine in Brooklyn). SUNY then embarked on an ambitious development program which continues to the present day.

The present University Hospital came into being only as recently as 1965, replacing the Hospital of the Good Shepherd, which had been founded in 1872. What was once the City Pest House, and more recently the AC Silverman Communicable Disease Hospital, is now home to the College of Health Related Professions, which offers programs in such areas as extracorporeal technology, cardio-respiratory sciences, and cytotechnology. The Health Sciences Center includes several hospitals as well as numerous other research, education, and patient care facilities. No tours are currently available to the general public.

UTICA

Mohawk Valley Psychiatric Center (Utica Campus) 1400 Noyes at York 13502. (315) 797-6800. The MVPC was formed in 1985 by a consolidation of two state hospitals, but it is the Utica campus, one of the oldest and most historic psychiatric facilities in the country, which concerns us here. The institution opened in 1843 as the New York Lunatic Asylum, New York State's first hospital for the mentally ill, the largest asylum in the country at the time, and a pioneering center for the humane treatment of the impoverished insane.

A site of 130 acres was set aside for the Lunatic Asylum, and William Clark was engaged to design a suitable facility. The central building of his design—what is now called Old Main—still survives, and one has to stand on its front steps to appreciate its scale. It's thought to be the oldest Greek Revival building in the world, and it certainly must be one of the largest. Old Main is almost an eighth of a mile in length and its portico is 48 feet high, spanning 4 stories, with the crown supported by 6 massive Doric columns, each 8 feet in diameter at the base.

The first superintendent at Utica was Dr Amariah Brigham, an innovative American psychiatrist who believed that insanity was an illness, best treated by kindness, gentleness, and productive work. As a consequence, Utica became a self-sustaining community, with a farm and workshops run by the patients. All linens, towels, sheets, and patients' clothing (including shoes) were made on the grounds. The huge farm had chickens, horses, cows, a slaughterhouse, ice house, and vegetable cellars.

Brigham was active in psychiatric politics, being 1 of 13 founders of the American Association of Medical Superintendents, the forerunner of the American Psychiatric Association. Brigham also established the *American Journal of Insanity* in 1844, the first English-language publication devoted to psychiatry and the first American medical specialty journal. He paid for the journal out of his own funds, edited it, and printed it at the Lunatic Asylum. In the 1890s, the journal was purchased by the American Psychiatric Association, and in 1921 the name was changed to the *American Journal of Psychiatry.*

The Asylum was associated with some additional "firsts." While Amariah Brigham opposed all chains and manacles, he recognized that some limitation of patient movement was necessary at night to protect the other sleeping patients. He thus devised the "Utica crib," a bed with slats covered by a lid which could be fastened over a patient at night. It was a restraining device which he felt was preferable to isolation cells. Utica was also the first institution in the country to install a steam heating system (in the 1850s).

The name Lunatic Asylum was changed to the Utica State Hospital in 1890, and again to Utica Psychiatric Center in 1974. Currently the hospital houses about 800 patients, down from some 2200 in 1965.

The future of Old Main is unclear. The building is now empty, its interior deteriorated and unsafe. However, the cost of renovating it for patient use is so great (about $11 million more than an entirely new construction of comparable square footage, by a 1985 estimate) that its usefulness for patient care is doubtful. Still, the building has been designated a national historic monument, so it is unlikely to be demolished. The hope now is to keep it from deteriorating further until satisfactory plans are developed for its future. Tours of the Old Main and the entire campus are available by advance arrangement.

VALHALLA

New York Medical College Old Farm House Road 10595. (914) 993-4000. In 1860, when the New York Homeopathic Medical College was founded, there were some 300 homeopathic physicians practicing in New York City. Most were conventionally trained MDs who had chosen to follow homeopathic medical principles, especially moderation in medicinal dosage, so students at NYHMC received training in both allopathic and homeopathic medical styles. The college built Flower Hospital in 1889. In 1908 the corporate name was changed to the New York Homeopathic College and Flower Hospital. In 1936, with homeopathy having lost favor and in the wake of the College's newly developed association with the formerly homeopathic Fifth Avenue Hospital, the combined institution called itself "The New York Medical College, Flower and Fifth Avenue Hospitals." As a practical matter, most people simply called the place "Flower" from the early 1900s onward.

Before the turn of the century, the college had a teaching affiliation with the Ward's Island Homeopathic Hospital, a city hospital devoted to chronic disease patients. When that hospital was discontinued in 1894, the patients, equipment, and the teaching affiliation were transferred to Metropolitan Hospital, at that time on Blackwell's (now Roosevelt) Island. In the early years of the century, Metropolitan was New York City's largest city hospital, at almost 1200 patients. Metropolitan moved to Manhattan (First Avenue at 98th Street) in 1955 and still maintains a teaching affiliation with NYMC, the oldest continuing affiliation in the country between a private medical school and a public hospital.

In 1968 NYMC decided to move out of New York City to Westchester County, formally inaugurating its present campus in Valhalla in 1972. The facilities there include more than a dozen buildings, including the huge Westchester County Hospital and Medical Center. In addition, NYMC has teaching affiliations with some 35 hospitals in the greater New York area. The lovely, bucolic campus is about an hour's drive from New York City, and tours are available by advance arrangement.

WHITE PLAINS

New York Hospital – Cornell Medical Center, Westchester Division 21 Bloomingdale Road 10605. (914) 682-9100. The New York Hospital, the second oldest voluntary hospital in the country (see New York City), cared for psychiatric patients from its inception. However, it wasn't until 1821 that it established a separate division to care for the mentally ill. The Bloomingdale Asylum, initially located at the site of what is now the Columbia University campus, moved to White Plains in 1894 and became an integral psychiatric resource for the Cornell University Medical College in 1965.

When the Bloomingdale Asylum opened, it was patterned after the "moral treatment" pioneered by the York Retreat, and, like the English institution, it was under the direction of a lay person. Drugs were rarely given, and bloodletting and cathartics were used only in moderation. Despite (or perhaps because of) these good intentions, the institution rapidly accumulated a huge patient population, and, by 1847, the Asylum was filled with "a mass of chronic and incurable cases." Fearful of losing its wealthy clientele, the Asylum refused to accept state support in 1857, and thereafter no longer offered space to the pauper insane, who were instead sent to the newly constructed institutions at Utica and Kings County. Instead, Bloomingdale restricted its clientele to the wealthy and "indigent persons of superior respectability and personal refinement."

In 1894, simultaneous with the move to a new location and in conjunction with the general practice of removing the term "asylum" from the titles of institutions for the insane, the name was changed to "Society of the New York Hospital, Bloomingdale, White Plains." It wasn't until 1910 that the name Bloomingdale Hospital was adopted, and 1936 when the name was officially changed to New York Hospital–Westchester Division.

When initially constructed, Bloomingdale was built as a compromise between the pavilion style and the Kirkbride pattern, so that there was a central administration building with a swept wing design for the wards, but the buildings tended to be separated by corridors rather than abutting one another. These structures still exist, along with a profusion of patient cottages added in the early years of the twentieth century. The grounds, designed by Frederick Law Olmsted, remain beautifully landscaped and forested. Though the grounds are open, there are no tours here and visitors are not encouraged.

NORTH CAROLINA

BAILEY

The Country Doctor Museum 515 Vance Street 27807. (919) 235-4165. The two connected buildings here are dedicated to preserving artifacts and celebrating the life and accomplishments of the nineteenth century country doctor. It is the only museum with this express purpose in the United States. The collection is divided into three parts: pharmacy, doctor's office, and general. A pharmacy is included because early practitioners usually practiced in isolation, away from supporting professions, and needed to compound and dispense their own prescriptions. The pharmacy here is rather more elegant than you would expect to find in a simple doctor's office, with beautiful white holly and cherry wood cabinets. On display is a vast amount of glassware, containers of various construction, scales and weights, mortars, pill-making machines and molds, and various pharmacy paraphernalia. The doctor's office itself is a good reconstruction of a late nineteenth century establishment, with exhibits including monaural and binaural stethoscopes, head mirrors, speculae, a variety of scopes for various internal examinations, laboratory and diagnostic equipment, doctor's bags and saddle bags, and surgical instruments (including some of those used to amputate Stonewall Jackson's arm). The

Country Doctor Museum, Bailey, North Carolina *(Credit: Anthony of Wilson Photography)*

general collection focuses on home medical care and includes such items as sickroom supplies, enema syringes, urinals, bedpans, stomach pumps, feeding devices, obstetrical instruments (deliveries were still performed in the home), a gout stool, and a collection of herbal and botanical medicines. A shed in back protects some typical doctor's buggies, and a small medicinal herb garden completes the exhibits. This is a small museum, but a fine one of its kind, with artfully arranged exhibits. It is open to the public afternoons, Sunday through Wednesday. Call for exact times.

CHAPEL HILL

University of North Carolina at Chapel Hill Medical Center Manning Drive 27514. (919) 962-2211. The first school of medicine here was established in 1879, but the lack of clinical material in what was then a tiny village failed to sustain the enterprise, and it closed in 1885. The school was opened again in 1890 and offered only one year of instruction until 1896, when the curriculum was lengthened to two years. By the post-World War I years, there was widespread dissatisfaction that the state of North Carolina had only two-year schools (UNC/CH and Wake Forest) and that students had to leave the state to complete their educations. The establishment of Duke in 1930, however, sapped a lot of the energy that had gone into establishing a publicly supported four-year school, and it wasn't until 1954 that UNC/CH graduated its first MD. The independent North Carolina Memorial Hospital, which functions as the principal UNC teaching hospital, was constructed in 1952 as a "living memorial" to the state's war dead. Together, the Hospital and UNC have created an impressive record in a short period of time. It was here that the world's first intensive care unit was opened in 1952. Tours of the hospital are available via the Public Affairs Office.

DURHAM

Duke University Medical Center Hospital Road 27710. (919) 684-3042. As you drive into this city, the "Welcome to Durham" signs call attention to the nickname "City of Medicine." In fact, where once tobacco and textiles were king, now health care is the leading industry. One in every four working people is employed in the health industry.

The principal reason for health care's dominance here is the Duke University Medical Center and its $600 million annual budget. DUMC was founded in 1930 with a $4 million bequest from tobacco and utilities magnate James B Duke. As a result, Trinity College in Durham was renamed Duke University, and the new medical school, ensconced in a fine set of collegiate Gothic buildings, had its own brand-new university hospital. At the start, the Duke Endowment contributed a third of the each patient's daily room fee. Even today, 60 years later, the Duke Endowment still contributes some $3 million per year.

The DUMC campus occupies 160 acres at the northern end of the university campus. The original buildings still stand and remain beautiful in their classic appeal, but they are overshadowed by other modern and dramatic structures. The three-million square foot medical center is so large that one rides from the Southern Division (which includes the older buildings) to the 1980-vintage Northern Division on a commuter train that travels quietly on a quarter-inch cushion of air. The various hospital components include 1050 beds. History buffs will be particularly interested in the **Trent Collection in the History of Medicine,** which has a remarkably extensive rare book collection (especially for a school so young), as well as some choice museum pieces. Included in the latter are eighteen stunning ivory anatomical manikins dating from the 17th and 18th centuries, the second largest collection in the world (after the Wellcome Museum in London). The Trent is open Monday through Friday from 8:30 to 5:30 and is located in the Seeley G Mudd Building. Group tours of the campus can be arranged by calling Public Relations [(919) 684-4148].

GREENSBORO

Porter's (O Henry's) Drugstore Greensboro Historical Museum. 130 Summit Avenue 27401. (919) 373-2043. The Porter family of Greensboro owned or were involved in over a dozen drugstores in this town, from 1846 until the beginning of the twentieth century. The one replicated here (at about one-third original size) dates from the 1870s, about the time that William Sidney Porter clerked for his uncle Clark. William Sidney was licensed as a pharmacist in North Carolina in 1881, a credential which allowed him to serve as night pharmacist at the Ohio State Penitentiary when he was imprisoned there from 1898 to 1901 after being convicted of embezzlement. William Sidney went on to achieve fame as O Henry, perhaps the greatest short story writer the English language has known. The Porter drugstore has another claim to fame. In 1890 it was purchased by Lunsford Richardson and John Farris, who used it as a base for concocting and marketing various pharmaceutical preparations. They enjoyed sufficient success with these experiments that they established a wholesale drug company and went on to produce such well-known products as Vicks VapoRub, Vicks Medicated Cough Drops, and Vicks Inhalers. The drugstore replica is well supplied with period products, phamaceutical paraphernalia, and exhibits which tell the drugstore's story. The museum is open Tuesday to Friday 10 to 5 and Sunday 2 to 5.

GREENVILLE

East Carolina University School of Medicine Stantonsburg Road and Moye Boulevard 27858. (919) 757-2481. This was established as one of the new breed of medical schools of the 1970s, designed to bring primary care practitioners to underserved areas. The first students were admitted in 1971, serving their first year at ECU and their last three years at UNC–Chapel Hill. Money for a four-year school was appropriated in 1975, the charter class was admitted in 1977, and the first physicians graduated in 1981. The medical campus is located on a 40-acre site, adjacent to its primary teaching hospital, the 560-bed Pitt Memorial Hospital. Tours of the campus, which includes over a dozen buildings, are available on request through the Development Office [(919) 551-2238].

RALEIGH

Dorothea Dix Hospital South Boylan Avenue 27611. (919) 733-5540. Dorothea Dix, the famed promoter of state psychiatric hospitals, came to North Carolina in 1848 and spent three months combing the countryside here, investigating the circumstances of the mentally ill in some 40 of the state's counties. She then spent the late fall and winter of 1848–1849 trying to convince recalcitrant legislators that it was sensible, economical, and humane to provide an asylum for the mentally ill. Fortunately, Dix won the support of the wife of the Speaker of the House. It was also fortuitous that the woman died while the legislature was in session, and her deathbed wish to establish the asylum led her husband to deliver a forceful speech proposing the establishment of this public psychiatric hospital. The asylum opened in 1856 with a capacity of 220 beds. Demand quickly expanded, and, by the 1880s, the state had two more asylums, including one for blacks in Goldsboro. By the 1960s, this hospital had 2800 patients—though the census currently runs about 700. The hospital's original 1052 acres has gradually dwindled to 350, and the government and nearby university both covet large portions of what remains. The grounds here, around which the public is free to drive, is particularly attractive in spring, when the azaleas, dogwood, and cherry trees are in bloom. There are no tours, however.

WINSTON-SALEM

Bowman Gray School of Medicine of Wake Forest University 27103. (919) 748-2011. The School of Medicine of Wake Forest College was founded in 1902 and operated as a two-year school for many years. Flexner found the school to be a model of "intelligence and earnestness," and the president of the Carnegie Foundation said Wake Forest showed "what can be done even in an isolated college with modest means under the right spirit and when once the commercial basis is dropped." In 1941 a substantial bequest from benefactor Bowman Gray (Chairman of the Board of RJ Reynolds Tobacco Company) resulted in the school's expansion to a four-year program and a change of location from the original Wake Forest campus to its present site in Winston-Salem (the remainder of Wake Forest College joined the medical campus in Winston-Salem fifteen years later). In conjunction with its move, the School of Medicine joined with the North Carolina Baptist Hospital to establish a medical center. Baptist Hospital began as a missionary enterprise by the North Carolina State Convention in 1923 and has grown from its initial 88 beds to its present 806. The rest of the medical center is now likewise undergoing a major expansion. Among other accomplishments, the medical center was the site of the first lithotripsy of a gallstone in the common bile duct (1986). The present campus occupies 50 acres and includes about two dozen buildings. Tours are available on a limited basis only, by advance arrangement [call (919) 748-4587].

NORTH DAKOTA

BISMARCK

Saint Alexius Medical Center 311 North Ninth Street 58502. (701) 224-7000. This is the oldest hospital in what was once the Dakota Territory, a region that now roughly includes North and South Dakota. Sisters of St Benedict from St Joseph, Minnesota, arrived here in 1878 to found a girls' academy. Once here, they saw so much disease (especially typhoid fever) that they decided to devote their energies to caring for the ill, following the Rule of St Benedict "That above all else, care must be taken of the sick." The nearest hospital in those days was 450 miles away in St Paul, Minnesota. They purchased the Lanborn Hotel at Sixth and Main and opened for patients in 1885. The charge for services was a flat $1 a day and boatmen from the US Marine Service (Bismarck is on the upper reaches of the Missouri River) received a reduced rate of 90 cents. The first seven patients, however, were paupers. Other early patients included Theodore Roosevelt (who came down with pneumonia while roughing it in the Badlands) and Sitting Bull (*son* of the famous chief, transferred here from jail). Given the steady supply of people who couldn't pay their own way, the sisters resorted to fundraising by soliciting funds at area railroad camps and nearby small towns. Today, St Alexius is a modern, high-tech hospital, a regional referral and teaching center. Tours are available by calling (701) 224-7098.

Quain and Ramstad Clinic 222 North Seventh Street 58502. (701) 222-5200. Founded in 1902, the Q & R Clinic is the second oldest group practice in the country, yielding in seniority only to the Mayo Clinic. When Eric Quain and Niles Ramstad began practice here (after graduating from medical school in Minnesota, where they learned of the Mayo operation), they had to overcome political obstacles in addition to the expected medical ones. Bismarck was tightly controlled by a political boss who expected the new doctors to hire runners to get them patients and to split fees with other physicians. Both stubbornly refused and managed to survive in the community because their medical and surgical skills made them indispensable. The organization has grown over the years and now provides both primary and tertiary care, operating as a major referral center for the upper midwest and adjacent areas of Canada. Bismarck sometimes calls itself "Mayo on the Missouri." The clinic staff now includes some 60 physicians. Tours are available by calling (701) 222-5200, ext. 5413.

GRAND FORKS

University of North Dakota Medical Center 501 Columbia Road North 58201. (701) 777-2514. The School of Medicine here began in 1905 as a two-year basic science school. In 1973 the school received initial authorization to grant the doctor of medicine degree. As an interim measure, a 2 : 1 : 1 plan was adopted, whereby students took their first two years in Grand Forks, went to Mayo or the University of Minnesota for their third year, and took their final year in North Dakota, utilizing clinical facilities in community hospitals. Since 1981 all four years have been taught in North Dakota. The school administration, basic science facilities, library and some research buildings are located here, but clinical teaching is coordinated through four area campuses, using community facilities, in Bismarck, Minot, Fargo, and Grand Forks. A unique program at UND (in operation since 1973) is the Indians Into Medicine (INMED) program, whereby American Indian students from the entire United States are identified and recruited as early as junior high school, not only for medicine, but for a wide range of health careers. Tours of the campus can be arranged via the Dean's Office.

OHIO

AKRON

Archives of the History of American Psychology Bierce Library. University of Akron 44325. (216) 375-7285. Created in 1965, these archives house the world's largest single source of original documents related to the history and development of psychology. More than 550 organizations and individuals have deposited manuscripts, documents, memorabilia, and other items here. The collection includes over 5000 films concerning child development and general psychology, over 22,000 microfilmed case records, as well as thousands of photographs and psychological tests. There is also a remarkable collection of over 600 psychology instruments, mostly designed to measure or test various sensory processes. These mostly nineteenth century items range from Holmgren's wools (skeins of colored yarn designed to test color blindness) to acoumeters (to determine the intensity of the least perceptible sound) to kymographs (rotating drums which served as data recording devices). Some of these items are on display in the work room and archival office; the majority are in storage and can be seen on request. The holdings of the Archives are available only to scholars with specific research interests. Others may be admitted on a case-by-case basis. Call if you are interested.

Dr. Bob's House 855 Ardmore Avenue 44309. (216) 864-1935. Akron is where Alcoholics Anonymous got its start, and, though there are many sites in town which are important to AA's history, none is more sacred than this large yellow and white frame home at the corner of Everett. This was the home of Bob and Anne Smith and at various times provided lodging for many of AA's pioneering figures. First, in 1935, was Bill Wilson, an unemployed alcoholic stockbroker, who moved in for five months to help keep Dr Bob sober. It was Bob and Bill who worked out the principles on which AA was founded. Many of the people whose stories are chronicled in AA's *Big Book* spent time here too, usually after they underwent detoxification at the Akron City Hospital or at St Thomas Hospital.

Visitors to Dr Bob's house will find that it has the feel of a shrine, one that is internationally famous to AA members around the world. There is a small museum here that many will find interesting, together with a brief film which gives an overview of the organization's history. The house is open to visitors Monday through Friday, noon to 3 PM. Your hosts here will be happy to guide you to other spots that are relevant to AA's history, including the building where Dr Bob had his medical office, the school where the first regularly scheduled meetings of AA were held, or Mt Peace Cemetery, where Dr Bob and Anne Smith are buried.

ATHENS

Museum of Medicine Grosvenor Hall. Ohio University College of Osteopathic Medicine 45701. (614) 593-2253. Though called a museum, this is really a series of display cases scattered about the OU-COM campus (and various affiliated teaching hospitals throughout Ohio). Still, from its inception in 1980, this collection has grown rapidly to include over 1200 items, so more formal exhibits may be in the offing in the near future. The most numerous displays are located in the lobbies of Grosvenor and Irvine Halls and tend to focus on surgical equipment, old lithographs and books, antique journals, and the like. The College of Osteopathic Medicine was established in 1975 by the Ohio General Assembly to help relieve the state's shortage of primary-care physicians serving in rural areas. Members of the public are welcome to view the rotating displays.

BAINBRIDGE

Dr John Harris Dental Museum 207 Main Street (on Route 50) 45612. (614) 634-2228 (during open hours) and (614) 486-2700 (at other times). The town of Bainbridge is considered by many to be the "Cradle of Dental Education," for it was here in 1827 that Dr John Harris began the world's first dental school. True, the first full-fledged dental college was founded in Baltimore in 1840, but one of the principal founders of the Baltimore College of Dental Surgery, Chapin A Harris, learned most of his early skills right here in Bainbridge at the informal school begun by his older brother. Dr John Harris was a physician who developed an early interest in dentistry while he was a surgeon in the Ohio State Militia. When he moved to Bainbridge in 1825, he opened a practice which included medicine, surgery, and dentistry. From 1827 until 1830, he taught these subjects to interested students. In the years that followed, he traveled widely, teaching and maintaining a practice. In 1836 he applied for a charter to establish a dental college in Kentucky (marking the first ever such attempt), but his efforts went unrewarded.

Harris's years at Bainbridge were remarkable in that his students went on to such conspicuous success. His younger brother, in addition to founding the Baltimore College, also founded and became first editor of the *American Journal of Dental Science,* the first dental journal in the world. Another student, Wesley Wampler, became Abraham Lincoln's dentist. A third, Samuel T Church, invented the forceps that became the standard tool for extracting the upper third molar. A fourth, James Taylor, established the Ohio College of Dental Surgery in Cincinnati (1845), the world's second dental college.

Dr John Harris's home, where he conducted his medical and dental practices and trained his students, was purchased by the Ohio Dental Association in 1939 and was formally dedicated as a museum in 1985. The original 1820 building has been enlarged through additions over the years but that will bother few visitors. The eight rooms contain a recreation of what the original classroom and Dr Harris' office might have looked like, together with some very special displays. Along with the expected dental instruments,

Sign in Bainbridge, Ohio *(Photograph by permission of Dr Jack W Gottschalk)*

there is a fascinating collection of antique toothbrushes (silver and ivory), toothpicks and toothpick holders, most from the mid-1800s. Another display includes a large number of antique Japanese carved wooden dentures. There are several mock dental offices here, one from 1905 and another from 1924. One remarkable piece of gear is a Vulcanite Processor, dating from 1900 and used for making rubber dentures.

The museum is currently open to the public from the third week in May to the third weekend in October, on Saturdays from 10 to 4 and Sundays 1 to 4. At other times, interested people should contact the Ohio Dental Association in Columbus for information. Bainbridge is located in southwest Ohio, between Chillicothe and Cincinnati, and the museum is situated on the main thoroughfare through town.

CINCINNATI

University of Cincinnati Medical Center 234 Goodman Street 45267. (513) 558-4559. The history of this institution starts with Daniel Drake (1785–1852), one of medicine's more colorful characters of the early nineteenth century. Drake had no formal education after he was nine years old, but he had a first-rate mind, endless curiosity, and a desire to accomplish many things. He became the first diplomate physician west of the Alleghenies; he founded Cincinnati's first museum and library and the first drugstore soda fountain in the West. He brought John J Audubon to Cincinnati when Audubon was just a struggling naturalist and gave him a job. He served as professor of materia medica at Transylvania University's Medical Department (1817) and helped found the Jefferson Medical College (1830), the Miami University Medical Department (1831), and numerous other medical and educational institutions. He was editor of several medical journals in Ohio and the West, and his monumental *Systematic Treatise on the Principal Diseases of the Interior Valley of North America* (1850) is still regarded as a landmark book in public health and epidemiology.

Drake's greatest legacy, however, and the one which concerns us most here, is to medical education in Cincinnati. In 1819 he obtained a charter from the state legislature to found the Medical College of Ohio, then the tenth medical school in the country. This college became the Medical Department of the University of Cincinnati in 1896, still later becoming the University of Cincinnati College of Medicine. Shortly after founding the medical college, Drake established the Commercial Hospital and Lunatic Asylum, operating under the then revolutionary belief that any good medical school needed an associated hospital. The hospital that was constructed at Twelfth Street and Central Avenue then became the first hospital in the United States established primarily for teaching purposes and staffed exclusively by a medical school faculty. The name was simplified in 1861 when the city took it under its wing (to the Commercial Hospital of Cincinnati) and again in 1869 when it moved into a set of fancy new buildings (to Cincinnati Hospital). In 1915 the name was changed again to Cincinnati General Hospital when the facility moved to a 25-building pavilion complex spread over 27 acres at the present site adjacent to Burnet Avenue. The University of Cincinnati took control of the hospital in 1960.

At various times during the nineteenth century, Cincinnati was home to a total of seven bone fide medical colleges and seven diploma mills that essentially sold medical degrees. Among the former were three women's medical schools (Women's Medical College of Cincinnati, 1887–1895; Presbyterian Hospital Women's Medical College, 1891–1895; and Laura Memorial Women's Medical College, 1895–1903). These were ultimately absorbed by UC, as was Miami Medical College (1853–1857 and 1865–1909).

Over the years, the University of Cincinnati has been responsible for many medical firsts, including:

1959   Albert Sabin developed his oral polio vaccine and conducted initial mass testing on Cincinnati school children

1970   First emergency medicine residency in the United States
1973   Henry Heimlich devises the Heimlich maneuver to save people who
       have aspirated a solid object

The UC College of Nursing and Health began in 1889 as the independent Cincinnati Training School for Nurses, which used the Cincinnati Hospital for clinical instruction. In 1893 the school succumbed to financial pressures and the Hospital started its own training program. In 1916 the school was taken over by UC, becoming one of the first two schools in the country to award a baccalaureate degree in nursing. Though it was initially just a department in the School of Medicine, it became a college in its own right in 1942. The nursing building, Procter Hall (located at Vine Street and Melish Avenue), was opened in 1968.

The College of Pharmacy (housed in a building at the corner of Eden and Bethesda avenues) has been at its present site since 1976. The school dates from 1850, when it was incorporated as a private enterprise, making it the first educational institution in pharmacy west of the Alleghenies. The path, however, has not been smooth. The school was phased out during the Civil War due to low enrollment and financial difficulties. Reorganized in 1871, the school developed its first affiliation with UC in 1887. Nine years later, because of the financial panic of the 1890s, UC divested itself of the school. It remained an independent entity for the next 58 years, until it once again became a unit of the university in 1954. The lobby and the dean's office both contain huge display cases, each lining one wall, that contain several thousand vintage pharmaceuticals, crowded from floor to ceiling. Both areas are open to the interested public.

The current campus is a huge sprawling area, extensively landscaped and covered with dozens of buildings. The **History of Health Sciences Library and Museum** (in Room 121, Wherry Hall, adjacent to the Pharmacy Building) has a collection of over 30,000 old and rare books related to the health sciences. The collection covers the world, but it is particularly rich in regional history. The "Museum" is really a collection of exhibits in the library, which, during my visit, included displays on JS Billings (a UC grad) and medical equipment built in Cincinnati. Another impressive exhibit is a nineteenth century replica of four huge fifteenth century Italian pharmacy display cases, which house over a hundred richly colored majolica pharmaceutical jars.

Tours can be arranged via Media Relations [(513) 558-4553].

Jewish Hospital of Cincinnati 3200 Burnet Avenue 45229. (513) 569-2000. Established in 1850 to provide for sick, indigent Jews during a cholera epidemic, this is the oldest Jewish-sponsored hospital in the country (Mt Sinai in New York followed in 1852 and the Touro Infirmary in New Orleans was third in 1853). Although the hospital moved several times in its early years, it has been at the Burnet Avenue site since 1890. JH was the first general hospital to have an inpatient psychiatric service devoted to children and adolescents (1920), the first to begin taking portable, bedside x-ray films (1922), and the first to introduce physical therapy into a general hospital setting.

A hospital, of course, does not develop in isolation. Cincinnati had a huge influx of German Jews from the 1830s to the 1850s and soon became the birthplace of American Reform Judaism. Cincinnati's Plum Street Temple (still standing at Eighth and Plum) was the setting for the first ordination of rabbis in this country, and the city is likewise home to the nation's first Jewish theological college (the Hebrew Union College, 1875).

Today, JH is a nonsectarian, 664-bed teaching hospital. The principal building is an eight-story modern structure of tan brick, whose block-like exterior is ornamented by strong vertical metal inserts that house the windows. It is located adjacent to the UCMC. Tours can be arranged for individuals or groups.

Lloyd Library 917 Plum Street 45202. (513) 721-3707. The four-story, inconspicuous, 1971-vintage building at this address houses a remarkable library, that includes one of the world's largest collections of books on botany and pharmacy and similarly unique collections on mycology and eclectic medicine. The collection was begun in 1854 by the three Lloyd brothers, pharmacists all, who owned the Lloyd Brothers pharmaceutical manufacturing firm. Of the three, the most dynamic and unusual was John Uri Lloyd. As a scientist and researcher, he authored an astounding 5000 articles. He was also editor of three scientific journals, invented sixteen patented devices, and was a professor at the Eclectic Medical College and the Cincinnati College of Pharmacy. In addition to these duties — and running the family business — he found time to publish eight novels.

The library's botany and pharmacy collection includes the oldest pharmaceutical book known to exist, Mesuë's *Vulgare Della Consolatione de la Medicine Simplici Solutive*, published in Venice in 1493. The collection contains some 200,000 volumes and 120,000 pamphlets. The sets of complete serials includes rarities ranging from the *Eclectic Medical Journal* to the *Philippine Journal of Science.*

The Library is also the repository for the archives of the Eclectic Medical College of Cincinnati and its library of some 5000 volumes. The EMC trained physicians from 1833 to 1939, absorbing other schools along the way, twice shutting down for several years in lean times. "Eclectic medicine" was born as one of the many protests against the "regular," or allopathic, school of medicine. Eclectics viewed allopathics' treatment methods as being far too violent, destructive of the body's natural resistance to disease, and having more often than not a debilitating effect on the patient. Considering the bleeding, purging, and megadosing with toxic chemicals employed by most allopaths of the nineteenth century, the eclectic's criticism made a lot of sense. They in turn saw disease as an impairment of life, not simply as an entity to be purged and poisoned. The cornerstone of eclectic therapy was supportive treatment. The eclectics treated diseases "not according to their names, but according to their nature." The early eclectics relied mostly on "infusions" (primarily in the form of teas and powders); later eclectics prescribed far more widely, though they continued to rely heavily on botanical preparations. As a philosophy of medicine, eclecticism outlasted homeopathy but was unable to compete in the face of allopathic medicine's scientific advances of the mid-twentieth century.

The Lloyd Library is open to the public, weekdays from 8:30 AM to 4 PM and at other times by appointment.

Daniel Drake Gravesite Spring Grove Cemetery 4521 Spring Grove Avenue 45232. (513) 681-6680. For visitors interested in the graves of medical pioneers, this cemetery offers a particularly attractive site. Comprising of over 700 acres, it is beautifully landscaped and filled with fascinating monuments and mausoleums. Drake's grave (and that of his wife Harriet) is located in Section 77, Lot 79, a little less than a mile from the entrance gateway. It is marked by a tall limestone spire near the top of a grassy knoll. The cemetery is open from 8 AM to 5 PM.

CLEVELAND

Case Western Reserve University Medical Center 2119 Abington Road 44206. (216) 368-2000. The university of which this medical center is a part was formed in 1826 as Western Reserve University, which combined with Case Institute of Technology in 1967 to form the present corporate unit. The medical school itself dates from 1843, when it was organized as the Medical Department of WRU by four dissatisfied professors who resigned en masse from the nearby Willoughby Medical College (see OSU in Columbus, below). It developed an early reputation for a progressive approach to medical education, graduating six of the first seven women to receive degrees from recognized medical colleges in the United States. When Flexner made his famous report on American medical colleges in 1910, WRU was ranked second only to Johns Hopkins as the best medical school in the country.

In medical education circles, the WRU School of Medicine is best known for an innovative curriculum developed in 1952 that subsequently influenced medical education all over the world. This program introduced "team teaching" to medical education, pioneered the pass/fail method of grading, started students working with patients almost as soon as they arrived on campus, and provided unscheduled time for thought and personal development when such a suggestion was considered radical.

The present University Hospitals is actually a collection of several institutions, the most long-lived being Lakeside Hospital. Lakeside began during the Civil War as a refuge for political escapees from the South. First called the Home for the Friendless, it was later called the Wilson Street Dispensary and then the Cleveland City Hospital. From the first a private hospital, the trustees were dismayed when the Municipality of Cleveland erected its own public Cleveland City Hospital in 1889. The private institution soon changed its name to Lakeside Hospital. From 1898 onward, Lakeside functioned essentially as a university hospital, and, in 1931, it was administratively combined with several others under the collective name University Hospitals of Cleveland.

The CWRU School of Nursing began operations in 1898 as the Lakeside Hospital Training School for Nurses. Though initially little more than a mill to churn out cheap labor for the hospital, the school came under university control in 1922 when a half-million dollar gift from Frances Payne Bolton made the transition possible. In the past two decades, the Bolton School of Nursing has consistently ranked among the most accomplished nursing schools in the country.

The School of Dentistry has a colorful history. It was begun in 1892 as a department of the medical school, sharing the same entrance requirements, the same classes, and even a common commencement. The cordiality did not last, however. In the next decade, the dental department became an unwanted stepchild, academically and financially troubled. In 1906 the school was sold to Henry Brown, the shrewd and autocratic owner of the Cogswell Dental Supply Company, for $7500. The resulting proprietary operation, known as the Reserve Company Dental School, limped along with a dismal educational performance until the University repurchased it (under pressure from the Ohio State Dental Board) for a quarter of a million dollars in 1917.

The CWRU Medical Center is located in Cleveland's University Circle area, within easy walking distance of the Dittrick Museum, Cleveland Clinic, and the Cleveland Health Education Museum. The School of Medicine building has just undergone a thorough modernization, but the structure itself dates from 1924, when it was the largest medical school edifice in the country. The buildings of the Schools of Nursing and Dentistry, both opened in 1969, sit next to the School of Medicine and share the Health Sciences Library with it. The campus itself is remarkably attractive and compact for an urban medical center. Currently, all of the buildings, including the various hospital structures, are under eight stories, though a research building presently under construction will reach twelve stories. Part of the appeal of the medical campus results from its integration with the rest of the university on a very walkable and pleasing 128-acre site. Tours are available from Public Relations.

Cleveland Metropolitan General – Highland View Hospital 3395 Scranton Road 44109. (216) 398-6000. This institution dates back to 1837, when it was founded in a two-story house on East 14th Street and called City Hospital. Cleveland's first hospital was really little more than a poorhouse, where shelter was provided for the chronically ill, the mentally impaired, and those just down on their luck. In those days, the city population hovered around 6000. By 1855 City Hospital had moved to new quarters and was called the City Infirmary. By 1890 the population had swollen to a quarter-of-a-million, spurred onward by Cleveland's burgeoning steel industry, and the City Infirmary moved into a huge, new, pavilion-style facility. Once again called City Hospital, the institution developed its ongoing teaching affiliation with the Medical College at Western Reserve University in 1914. By the 1950s the city of Cleveland was unable to support the dramatically increased costs of medical care by itself and management of the hospital was transferred to the county. As a result, it was renamed Cleveland Metropolitan General Hospital.

Meanwhile, as the old City Hospital outgrew its function as a poorhouse, the city decided to purchase 850 acres to house the aged, infirm, insane, and other needy folk who were unable to provide for themselves. This area, known as Cooley Farms, gradually became more developed, added a tuberculosis hospital in 1913, eventually became a chronic disease and rehabilitation hospital in 1953, and thenceforth was called the Highland View Hospital. In 1978, Cleveland Metropolitan General and Highland View combined on one campus where they now share space. The complex, called "Metro" by the locals, is dominated by a strikingly modern set of twin towers, each a huge round column accented by dramatic vertical ribbing, the two connected by an equally tall wall of glass. In dramatic contrast to these modern towers, the rest of the hospital sprawls out over several square blocks, a classic turn-of-the-century-style pavilion complex of tan brick, with additions of varying vintages grafted on. The 700-bed facility is also home to the John Gannon Center for Burns and Trauma, an $18 million addition completed in 1989.

Tours are available via the Community Relations Department.

Meridia Huron Hospital 13951 Terrace Road 44112. (216) 761-3300. This hospital established one of the first schools of nursing west of the Allegheny Mountains in 1884 (see also Wisconsin Training School for Nurses). Initially called the Cleveland Training School for Nurses, the name changed in 1949 to the Huron Road Hospital School of Nursing.

Huron traces its origins back to Cleveland's first private hospital, the Cleveland Homeopathic Hospital, founded in 1856. For many of the following decades, the fate of the hospital was inextricably bound with the fortunes and misfortunes of homeopathy in Cleveland. The city's first homeopathic school, the Western College of Homeopathy, actually antedated the hospital, having been founded in 1850. Those were tumultuous years, with homeopaths quarreling with allopaths and, almost as often, among themselves. As factions and loyalties changed, so too did the institutions. The Western College of Homeopathy became the Homeopathic Hospital College of Cleveland. For a while, a group of women split off and founded the Cleveland Homeopathic College and Hospital for Women. In the 1890s, two competing colleges were named the Cleveland Medical College and the Cleveland University of Medicine and Surgery (the latter was briefly home to the first homeopathic dental school in the US).

All of these various institutions were clustered around the Huron Road Hospital and used its facilities for teaching. Though the hospital occupied some seven different locations over its lifespan, it takes its name from its 1874 address. When the Flexner Report in 1910 doomed homeopathy, the hospital adapted by appointing allopaths to the staff, and, by 1922, the hospital had severed all ties with homeopathy.

Though there is little left to indicate the history of the grounds, the current Huron Hospital was erected on John D Rockefeller's former vegetable and flower gardens. Rockefeller had long been friendly with several of Huron's physician staff (two of them played golf with Rockefeller almost daily), and he donated the land for the hospital's use. Now part of the Meridia Health System (founded 1984), a regional system currently with 15 facilities, the Meridia Huron Hospital still operates its nursing school, one of the oldest hospital-based schools in the country.

Tours are available via the Public Affairs Office.

Cleveland Clinic 9500 Euclid Avenue 44106. (216) 444-2200. The Cleveland Clinic dates from 1921, making it one of the country's oldest group-practice clinics. Of the four founders, George Crile is the most well-known. A marvelously skillful surgeon (he performed over 25,000 thyroidectomies) and a bold innovator, he is credited with administering the first blood transfusion. The Clinic opened its own hospital in 1924, five years later suffering one of the country's worst hospital disasters. In 1929 fumes from smoldering nitrocellulose x-ray films led to the deaths of 123 persons, including both Clinic employees and patients.

Most of the Clinic's history, however, has been distinguished by important contributions to the evolution of health care. In 1906 Crile reported the first successful bilateral ligation of internal jugular veins and simultaneously revealed the use of a rubber suit to support a patient's circulation during surgery, thus establishing the first known precursor of today's MAST (military anti-shock trousers) suit. It was here that the first technique for radiation dosimetry was invented (1928), that the carpal tunnel syndrome and the related Phalen test were first described (1951), that the first coronary artery catheterization was performed (1958), that coronary artery bypass surgery using the saphenous vein was begun (1967), and that the first test for lung disease due to beryllium dust was performed (1973). In 1957 Akutsu and Kolff implanted the first totally artificial heart in a dog here, and, in 1958, CC began an enterostomal therapy program and founded the first school for enterostomal therapists.

The Clinic is a major national and international referral center (some 86 percent of patients come from beyond the Cleveland metropolitan area), so it is not surprising that the Clinic campus includes a 382-room hotel. The most dramatic building, however, is the new twelve-story Clinic Building, a strikingly modern structure with horizontal lines constructed of tinted glass and pink granite, with an entrance dominated by a light-and-airy three-story atrium. The equally new (but much less dramatic) thirteen-story Hospital Wing features (on its seventh floor) special VIP suites, "suitable for heads of state." Among such patients who have come to CC for care are King Hussein of Jordan and King Jigme Wangchuk of Bhutan, the presidents of Brazil and Guinea, and members of the royal families of Nepal and Saudi Arabia. The entire complex occupies over six city blocks and, with over 9000 personnel, is Cleveland's largest employer. One particularly nice touch is the two-acre mall lined with white oaks, sweet gums, lace-bark pines, and crab-apple trees.

The Clinic is happy to arrange tours for interested individuals or groups [call (216) 444-2200, ext. 5680].

Howard Dittrick Museum of Historical Medicine 11000 Euclid Avenue 44106. (216) 368-3648. This is one of the largest and certainly one of the best medical museums in the country. The collection was officially begun in 1926 and nurtured along for many years by Dr Dittrick as a part of the parent Cleveland Medical Library Association. In 1945 the Museum was named after the man who almost single-handedly helped it survive and grow through its early years. Though the collection covers the whole pageant of medical history throughout the world, its special brilliance is in the history of medicine since 1800, especially as practiced in the Western Reserve (that region of what is now northeast Ohio, which, at the time of the American Revolution, was known as the Western Reserve of the State of Connecticut).

The collection is huge. The main gallery focuses on the local

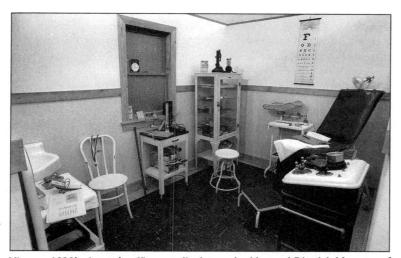

Vintage 1930's doctor's office, on display at the Howard Dittrick Museum of Historical Medicine *(Credit: Historical Division/Cleveland Health Sciences Library)*

history of medicine in the nineteenth and twentieth centuries, using regional items to portray the broad sweep of developments throughout the United States. The exhibit is divided into five areas:

1. Medicine in the early Republic, 1800–1865
2. Patent medicines, self-remedies, and pharmacy
3. Hospital Medicine, 1865–1920
4. Laboratory Medicine, 1880–1920
5. Science, Technology, and Medicine, 1885–1950.

Sample items in the collection include reflex percussion hammers (1841 ff), a huge microscope display (1750 ff), hand crank hematocrit centrifuges, a carbolic acid spray device for operating room antisepsis (1882), and one of the first American-made EKG machines manufactured by the Cambridge Instrument Company (1920). Exhibits in a separate special study area are continually changing and generally are drawn from the institution's extensive storage vaults. During my visit, these included displays of old surgical and obstetrical instruments and an intriguing depiction of the role played by the Cushing family in Cleveland medical history. (Harvey Cushing grew up in Cleveland.)

The Dittrick is located in the Allen Memorial Medical Building, which also houses an extensive archival collection and a number of rare book collections, including extensive and rare collections concerning Sigmund Freud and Charles Darwin, and books on dermatology, venereal diseases, epidemiology, and herbals. The museum is open Monday through Friday, 10 AM to 5 PM and Saturdays, noon till 5 PM. The museum is closed on major holidays, including some long weekends. Admission is free.

Cleveland Health Education Museum 8911 Euclid Avenue 44106. (216) 231-5010. This wonderful museum (across Euclid from the CC) has been serving the public since 1936 and now caters to some 100,000 visitors annually. It was the first health education museum in the western hemisphere, and it has pioneered in many fields of health education, including developing the nation's first sex education classes for elementary and secondary school students. This is a handsome, smooth, professional operation that engages the visitor with its numerous "hands-on" displays. Most of the 200 exhibits are unique, having been researched, designed, and created in-house. Kids in particular love this place, but adults will too. The Giant Tooth is a walk-in dental laboratory. Juno, the transparent talking woman, has been showing off her anatomical systems since 1950. A display on the cardiovascular system lets the visitor go through a knowledge self-assessment quiz on a computer. An exhibit on "Your Changing Senses" illustrates the ways in which our various senses alter with aging. Then too, there are constantly changing multimedia shows in the museum's several theaters, as well as numerous classes and workshops. Many classrooms are designed for specific subject material, and there is an enormous amount of creativity and sophistication at the instructor's fingertips. There are also frequent special presentations: on the day of my visit, Kaiser Permanente presented a lively bit of theater called "Professor Bodywise."

The museum is housed in a marvelous old mansion, now largely masked by a huge but handsome addition built in 1972. The museum is open Monday through Friday, 9 AM to 4:30 PM, Saturdays, 10 AM to 5 PM, and Sundays, noon to 5 PM. There is a small admission charge.

The Museum of the International Center for Artificial Organs and Transplantation 8937 Euclid Avenue 44106. (216) 421-0757. Housed in an ivy-covered, dark stone, former funeral home and surrounded by a wire mesh fence topped with three strands of barbed wire, this would not appear to be the most inviting museum in the country. Indeed, in order to find the entrance, you have to circle the block, work your way to the farthest corner of the Cleveland Health Education Museum's huge parking lot, and walk up some unmarked stairs to an inconspicuous doorway.

Once inside, however, you will be rewarded with a fascinating collection of over 2000 pieces of historical medical hardware, together with informative written panel displays that put the various items in meaningful context. The Artificial Heart Gallery contains the largest collection of such devices in the world, variously constructed of steel (1965), rubber (1966), polyurethane (1967), and ceramic (1978), from countries as diverse as Canada, France, and the USSR. The collection includes the Jarvik-7 device implanted in Dr Barney Clark, the first totally artificial heart implanted in a human being (1982). There are also a dozen or so left ventricular assist devices, together with an informative display on the evolution of the artificial heart from 1937 to the present.

Other aspects of the collection focus on pacemakers, heart valves, artificial joints, kidney transplants, tissue typing, membrane oxygenators, and plasmapheresis. The hemodialysis gallery shows the evolution of the dialysis machine and includes an early model of the Kolff-Brigham machine (c. 1948). Another item, a tribute to the profession's attempt to devise a workable and inexpensive device for home dialysis, was invented by Dr Yukihiko Nose of the CC in 1967: it's an old-fashioned Maytag washing machine, without wringer (cost, $80), fitted with four dialysis coils (cost, $50). It worked!

The International Center is closely allied with the Department of Artificial Organs at the CC but actually functions as an independent entity. The museum is currently open Saturdays and Sundays, 1 to 4 PM. There is no charge.

COLUMBUS

Ohio State University Medical Center 376 West Tenth Avenue 43210. (614) 292-5674. The OSU College of Medicine traces its origins to the Willoughby University School of Medicine, founded just outside Cleveland in 1834. When Western Reserve University was begun in 1843, the Willoughby faculty quickly decided that the small town of Cleveland would not support two medical schools and therefore decided in 1847 to move their school to Columbus, the state capitol and a thriving city of 11,000 with no medical school within 100 miles. (The old Willoughby Medical School had the distinction of appointing the first professor of psychiatry in the United States, when it made Samuel Smith professor of medical jurisprudence and insanity in 1847.) A year later, the college was renamed Starling Medical College in response to a wealthy benefactor. A faculty revolt in the 1870s resulted in the splitting off of a faction to form a separate school, the Columbus Medical College. In 1896 the factions resolved their difficulties and merged once again, only to be confronted by a new competitor, the Ohio Medical University. In 1907 the united Starling Medical College merged with Ohio Medical University to form Starling Ohio Medical College. Seven years later, SOMC merged with Ohio State University, which had just absorbed the entirely separate Cleveland-Pulte Homeopathic Medical College. OSU continued to operate both medical colleges until 1922, when the homeopathic institution was discontinued.

OSU now has a huge, thoroughly modern campus, the centerpoint of which is the 1000-bed University Hospital, which is actually composed of six linked buildings. However, one grand old relic survives from the 1920s. This is **Starling Loving Hall,** built as the university hospital and named after a prominent Columbus physician who was an 1849 graduate of the Starling Medical College. The castellated brick building is ornamented with six grotesque animal figures on its north wall, put there (according to legend) to protect patients and employees from demons and evil spirits.

There are currently no regular tours of the complex, but there is much that you can see on your own. Just outside Meiling Hall (370

West Ninth Avenue), there is a peaceful grassy area lined with comfortable benches, called Hippocrates Plaza, with a fine bronze bust, slightly larger than life-size, of the Greek Father of Medicine. If you enter Meiling Hall and walk to the lobby of the attached Graves Hall, you will find a rather large glass-enclosed display concerning early physiology at OSU. The exhibit contains a dozen or so semi-antique instruments, some quite beautiful, including microscopes, oscillographs, physiological stimulators, spirometers, colorimeters, spectroscopes, potentiometers, and the like.

The **OSU College of Dentistry** also has a nice display of a typical dental office c. 1915, encased in glass in the clinic lobby at 305 West Twelfth Ave. The collection includes an old velvet and enamel examining chair, a fine wooden instrument cabinet, a primitive electric drill, an x-ray device, and similar period furnishings. The prize, however, is an exceedingly rare, thick, pebbled-glass expectoration sink. Just behind the clinic building, you will find a large statue, sitting in the middle of a plaza, of Willoughby Dayton Miller, 1853–1907, "Dental Scientist and Educator." The OSU College of Dentistry began as a department of the medical school, first the Ohio Medical University (from 1890 to 1907) and then the Starling Medical College, before coming into its own in 1915.

Ohio College of Optometry Museum 320-338-352 West Tenth Avenue 43210. (614) 292-2647. This interesting museum consists of two parts: The first, unique in this country, is a Celebrity Eyewear Exhibit, designed to show the importance of good vision for a variety of successful people. Approximately 100 celebrities have donated previously worn eyewear, together with pictures showing them wearing their specs. Examples include actress Sophia Loren, golfer Jack Nicklaus, former President Gerald Ford, and singer Dean Martin. This collection is currently being displayed in several glass cases lining a well-traveled hallway on the main floor of the three interconnected Optometry Buildings and is available for public viewing weekdays, from 8 AM to 5 PM.

The second half of the collection is located in a formally designated museum room on the basement level of 338 West Tenth. While this room is intended to be kept open during normal business hours on weekdays, you may need to contact the receptionist at 320 West Tenth if you find it locked. The room contains a substantial collection of optometric items, varying from eyewear (lorgnettes, pince-nez, spectacles dating from the early nineteenth century, and some unusual and beautiful spectacle cases) to professional equipment of varying vintages (e.g., trial lens cases, ophthalmometers, refractors, lensometers, slit lamps, and a very unusual syntonic optometer). All interested individuals are welcome here.

The **OSU College of Optometry** is the oldest university-based program in optometry in the country. It was started in 1914 by Charles Sheard, an assistant professor of physics, as a two-year certificate course in applied optics. The following year, the program was changed to a four-year curriculum (in the College of Engineering), resulting in the first baccalaureate program for optometrists anywhere in the world. A separate School of Optometry, however, was not established until 1937, and the school didn't become a college, with its own dean, until 1967.

DAYTON

Wright State University Medical Center 3640 Colonel Glenn Highway 45435. (513) 873-3232. WSU was founded in 1964 and became an independent university only as recently as 1967. The medical school is of even more recent vintage, having been founded in 1973 and graduating its first class in 1980. The WSU Medical Center was built on the philosophy that a community-based medical school is cheaper to build and cheaper to operate than the more traditional medical megacenter and that students trained in such a place are more likely to chose a primary care career. By design, most of the basic science teaching for medical students is carried on in WSU's nonmedical campus, clinical teaching takes place mostly in nearby community hospitals, and the university itself operates only a single patient-care program, a small ambulatory care facility which emphasizes family and primary care. The medical campus, as a result, blends nicely with the rest of the nonmedical campus.

A program in which WSU takes special pride — and which has had unusual success in its brief life — is the multidisciplinary doctoral program in biomedical sciences. In 1982, a research team led by Dr Jerrold Petrofsky used a computer-controlled electrical-impulse system to renew motor activity in previously paralyzed limbs. With the help of the computer-driven system, they succeeded in getting a quadriplegic to drive a tricycle and assisted a paraplegic to walk. Because of these successes, WSU can now boast the unique **National Center for Rehabilitation Engineering.**

Tours can be arranged via Student Affairs [(513) 873-2934].

ROOTSTOWN

Northeastern Universities of Ohio College of Medicine 4209 State Route 44 (at Interstate 76) 44272. (216) 325-2511. NEUOCOM was established in 1973 in what was then little more than a bunch of fields near the relatively small village of Rootstown. How did this miniscule community snag the economic and social plum that a state-supported medical school constitutes? As one might expect, the answer only makes sense — if at all — when considered in the light of political realities. In the late 1960s and early 1970s, northeast Ohio lobbied energetically for a medical school. Though the area had nearly 25 percent of the state's population, it had only 18 percent of the medical practitioners, and the number of primary care people seemed to be going into a steep decline. In order to present the most attractive and persuasive petition possible, three universities (Kent State, Youngstown State, and Akron) combined into a consortium. When the legislature approved the petition, the consortium had to decide where to put the school. Unable to agree on Canton or Akron or Youngstown, they had to settle for a neutral location: the farmlands outside Rootstown.

NEUOCOM offers a combined BS/MD degree, obtainable in as few as six years. Students spend the first two years on one of the consortium university campuses, year three is devoted to the basic medical sciences at Rootstown, and the last three years are spent at associated community hospitals scattered throughout northeast Ohio. As a result, the buildings on the Rootstown campus are devoted primarily to classrooms, administrative offices, and research facilities. Clinical work is done elsewhere.

The college is composed of nine brick buildings, each of them one or two stories tall, joined together in a "U" shape, with a tree-filled central plaza. However, there are currently no regularly available tours.

TOLEDO

Medical College of Ohio 3000 Arlington Avenue 43699. (419) 381-4172. MCO was established in 1964 as a freestanding medical campus (meaning it is not a part of any other college or university) to include a School of Medicine, a Graduate School, a School of Allied Health, and a School of Nursing. The charter medical school class was graduated in 1972. The thoroughly modern complex (the oldest building dates from 1972) includes the usual college structures, a 318-bed Medical College Hospital, and a 25-bed Child and Adolescent Psychiatric Hospital. By the late 1980s, as medical school applications nationwide dropped from a 1974 peak of 42,000 to a low of 26,000, MCO responded with an innovative solution: it became the first medical school in modern times to advertise for applicants in college newspapers. As a result of this, as well as other achievements, MCO has been in the enviable position of having more than fourteen applicants for every opening. Tours are available via the Volunteers Office [(419) 381-3835].

St Vincent Medical Center 2213 Cherry Street 43608. (419) 321-3232. Toledo's first hospital was founded in 1855 by a group of Grey Nuns, who journeyed from Montreal to Toledo for that purpose. The Grey Nuns themselves date from 1737, when Marguerite d'Youville and three other women consecrated their lives to God and service to the poor, founding the order known more formally as the Sisters of Charity of Montreal. In 1878 the Toledo School of Medicine was established adjacent to the hospital, expanding in 1882 to become the Northwestern Ohio Medical College. In 1914 the school closed its doors in the wake of the Flexner report. With over 135 years of service, the hospital has been one of Toledo's most important patient care and teaching resources. In 1983 it became the first hospital in the country to introduce a home skeletal traction program, allowing much earlier discharge for back pain sufferers. In 1987 it achieved fame of another sort when Kaye Lani Rae Rafko, one of its oncology nurses who was also a graduate of the St Vincent School of Nursing, became Miss America. Tours are available by prior arrangement (the Chapel on the second floor is larger than many churches and is quite beautiful).

OKLAHOMA

OKLAHOMA CITY

University of Oklahoma Medical Center 800 Northeast 13th Street 73126. (405) 271-4700. The University of Oklahoma School of Medicine began in 1900, seven years before statehood, on the University's main campus in Norman. Started as a basic science program, Oklahoma's was one of seven two-year schools in the country and a good school of its kind. Flexner's 1910 report gave it an acceptable rating. Several other medical colleges were organized in Oklahoma during the same decade, all of them transient enterprises, save for the four-year program at Epworth University College of Medicine, established in Oklahoma City in 1904. Flexner gave Epworth a devastating review, placing it among the "very worst" schools in the country. Epworth then folded, selling its facilities to the University of Oklahoma, which moved its medical school to Oklahoma City and established a four-year program. The school's basic science program continued as a strong suit, but the barely adequate clinical facilities were a problem for a number of years. At first, the school rented space in the proprietary Rolater Hospital and then at the Oklahoma City General Hospital, until the first school-owned University Hospital was established in 1919. The present Oklahoma Memorial Hospital is a direct descendant of that original University Hospital. The hospital was transferred from university administration to the state's Department of Human Services in 1980 after a major financial crisis. Today the Oklahoma Teaching Hospitals function as an integrated unit, which includes Memorial, a children's hospital, a rehabilitation facility, and a child-study unit.

Tours are available from Public Relations.

St Anthony Hospital 1000 North Lee Street 73101. (405) 272-7000. Founded in 1898 by the Sisters of St Francis of Marysville, Missouri, this was the first hospital in Oklahoma Territory. Begun as a 25-bed brick structure, it has become — at its current 700 beds — the largest hospital in the state. Among its accomplishments along the way: in 1922 St Anthony's was home to the first x-ray technologist in the country, Sister Beatrice Merrigan. The present complex is all contemporary in design, and tours are available by prior arrangement.

TULSA

Oklahoma College of Osteopathic Medicine and Surgery 1111 West 17th Street 74107 (918) 582-1972. This school, one of 15 osteopathic colleges in the nation, is the country's first freestanding state-supported osteopathic medical training institution. Founded in 1972, the school graduated its first class in 1977. The state supported college is independent from the private **Oklahoma Osteopathic Hospital** [located across the Arkansas River at 744 West Ninth, (918) 599-5963] but the two work closely together. Together they form the largest osteopathic medical complex in the nation. The reason for osteopathy's strength in this area has an interesting twist to it. The profession grew enormously during World War II, largely as a result of orthodox medicine's attempts to confine it. The latter successfully lobbied to prevent DOs from gaining commissions in the military service, and, as a result, the DOs had to stay home and tend the civilian population while MDs served in the armed forces. In Tulsa, the osteopaths rapidly outgrew their tiny hospital at 14th and Peoria and, in 1944, opened Tulsa's most modern facility, the only one to have central air conditioning and centrally prepared meals. Since then, there have been no backward glances, and the Osteopathic Hospital has continued to be a community pacesetter, currently operating with 533-beds and a full range of technologically sophisticated equipment. It was the hospital's regional dominance, together with the state's keenly felt need for more general practitioners, which led to the founding of the College. The school graduates about 70 DOs a year, 78 percent of whom go into general practice. Both the College and the Hospital provide tours for interested parties.

Oral Roberts University Medical School–City of Faith Health-Care Center 8181 South Lewis Avenue 74137. (918) 493-1000. The City of Faith was born in 1977 when Oral Roberts, in mourning for a daughter killed in a plane crash, received a revelation from God showing Roberts how he could combine medicine and prayer in a unified healing effort. The hospital and its adjacent facilities opened in 1981, and together they form a most impressive complex. There are three glistening towers here, extending skyward from a broad four-story base. The tallest, 60 stories high, is an outpatient clinic building. The Hospital itself occupies a 30-story tower, and medical research and continuing education reside in the shortest, a 20-story building. In front of these towering structures, you will find the largest single bronze sculpture in the world, a 60-foot tall recreation of a pair of hands. Called *The Healing Hands,* one hand represents the hand of prayer raised to God, and the other signifies the hand of the physician, committed to mobilize all of God's healing power for every patient regardless of disease. A long causeway of water leads up to this imposing sculpture, symbolizing the River of Life, as mentioned in the Bible's Revelation.

The City of Faith is the principal teaching hospital for Oral Roberts University School of Medicine and is located just south of the ORU campus. The ORU undergraduate campus opened in 1965, and the medical school began classes in 1978. The hospital, university, and medical school are all infused with what Roberts calls "the Christian spirit," a philosophy of life and being which is intended to motivate all those who study and practice here. The City of Faith is unique in that the treatment team includes not only the physician and nurse but also the patient's prayer partner. The latter is a full-time staff member who provides ongoing spiritual care and makes rounds on patients in much the same manner as the physician.

To welcome tour groups and individual visitors, the City of Faith has installed a Visitors' Center just off the main clinic lobby. This includes two auditoriums where continuous multimedia presentations are shown daily. Hospital tours are available by prior arrangement [(918) 493-8090].

In September 1989, Oral Roberts announced that a $25 million deficit in his operations would lead him to close his 777-bed hospital in early 1990 and the medical school after summer graduation in

1990. At this time, the outcome is not clear. Roberts has survived such calamities before. Faced with an $8 million deficit in 1986, Roberts was able to raise the money through donations when he told his faithful that God would end his life if the money were not forthcoming.

OREGON

JOHN DAY

Kam Wah Chung & Company Museum Northwest Canton Street 97845. (503) 575-0028. While the original purpose of this 1860s-vintage building was to serve as a trading post, its most enduring function was as the office of "Doc" Ing Hay (1862–1952), an herbal doctor and pulsologist. Hay arrived in this country in 1883 as part of the great wave of emigration from China, fleeing overpopulation and famine and seeking jobs in the rapidly expanding western United States and Canada. The immediate John Day area in those days supported a vigorous Chinatown of 900 inhabitants, most of whom were men who worked in the local gold mining industry. The Kam Wah Chung Building was the center of the Chinese community in eastern Oregon and, as such, was stocked with everything from food and books to firecrackers and gambling equipment.

With time, the Chinese population in the area dwindled as the mines and related jobs petered out, and there were barely a dozen Chinese in the entire area at the end of Hay's life. Doc Hay had started off as a doctor for his countrymen, but, as his reputation increased and the numbers of Chinese decreased, the majority of Hay's patient population was white. His practice extended from Nevada in the south to Walla Walla in the north, from Portland in the west to Idaho in the east, but occasional clients consulted him from as far away as San Francisco and South Dakota. Doc Hay was particularly adept at treating blood poisoning, a common ailment among the hardworking, injury-prone men of the local mining, ranching, and timber industries. In those preantibiotic days, traditional physicians had little to offer patients, and Doc Hay is credited with saving many lives. Though Doc Hay was several times brought up on charges of practicing medicine without a license, no local jury could be found who would convict him.

Doc Hay threw nothing out, and the Kam Wah Chung Building has been little altered since his death. As a result, this is probably

Kam Wah Chung Museum, John Day, Oregon *(Credit: Courtesy of the Kam Wah Chung Museum)*

the largest repository of items related to traditional Chinese medicine in the western hemisphere. There are almost a thousand herbs and medicaments here, the vast majority of which were ground up finely, mixed in a brew, and administered as a broth. The building also contains Hay's patient record books, his voluminous correspondence, personal items, and memorabilia from the Chinese mining community. The museum is open (May through October) Monday through Thursday, 9 AM to 12 AM and 1 PM to 5 PM, as well as weekends from 1 PM to 5 PM. There is no phone here; the number listed above is for the City Hall. There is a small admission charge.

PORTLAND

Oregon Health Sciences University Medical Center   Sam Jackson Park Road 97201. (503) 279-8505. This university medical center traces its origins to two rival schools, the oldest being the Medical Department of Williamette University in Salem, Oregon. The Department relocated to Portland in 1878 to take advantage of the more numerous clinical opportunities in the larger city but moved back to Salem in 1895. When Flexner visited the school in 1909, he found it to be "an utterly hopeless affair, for which no word can be said." The University of Oregon Medical School opened its doors in 1887, and, in 1909, Flexner found it to be little better than its sister operation in Salem. The two schools merged in 1913, and the joint venture moved to its present site in 1919. The Multnomah County Hospital was completed on the grounds in 1923. The School of Dentistry (founded in 1898) moved to this campus in 1974. Nursing education began here in 1919, though it became a separate school only in 1960.

Significant accomplishments from this center include:

1960	First successful replacement of the mitral valve in humans using the ball-type Starr valve (Phillip Starr)
1961	First mechanical device for external chest compression during cardiopulmonary resuscitation (Charles Dotter)

Today, the Medical Center consists of 116 acres with 26 buildings. With 5000 employees, it is Portland's third largest and the state's seventh largest employer. Tours are available from the Tour Office.

National College of Naturopathic Medicine 11231 SE Market Street 97216. (503) 255-4860. Naturopathic physicians (NDs) are health care practitioners who currently can be licensed to practice in Alaska, Arizona, Connecticut, the District of Columbia, Hawaii, Oregon, and Washington, as well as five of Canada's provinces. The vast majority are in private practice and the scope of their practice includes a mixture of clinical nutrition, homeopathic medicine, botanical medicine, oriental medicine, and therapeutic manipulation. As a distinct American discipline, naturopathy dates back to the late nineteenth century, when the hydrotherapy techniques of Sebastian Kneipp were popular. A group of German-trained Kneipp practitioners decided to expand the scope of their field, incorporating all "natural" methods of healing, and called the new profession "naturopathy." The first school of naturopathy was established in New York City in 1902, and, by the late 1920s, there were more than 20 schools of naturopathy in the country, and national naturopathic conventions attracted as many as 10,000 practitioners. As the century progressed and potent new pharmaceutical agents left patients and practitioners disenchanted with "natural" remedies, naturopathy went into a decline. The National School of Naturopathic Medicine, founded in 1956, is now the oldest school of naturopathic medicine in North America, though others have been founded more recently and the profession is undergoing something of a renaissance. The National College also has the only homeopathic program accredited by the Council on Homeopathic Education. Tours of the seven-acre campus (and the extensive library on natural healing) can be arranged via Public Relations.

St Vincent Hospital and Medical Center   9205 Southwest Barnes Road 97225. (503) 297-4411. Founded in 1875, when Portland was a town of only 9000, this is the state's oldest hospital. The Sisters of Providence, who established the hospital, came here from Montreal, a journey that required several weeks of rail travel down to Omaha and then across the Great Plains. From San Francisco, the sisters took a six-day boat trip up the coast. The French-speaking nuns met with a cool reception in the predominantly Protestant Portland area, but St Vincent's first several patients were non-Catholics, and the community slowly warmed to the asset in their midst. St Vincent's established the nation's first school of nurse anesthesia in 1909, after the hospital's interns passed a resolution saying that they thought giving anesthesia was a poor use of their internship training. This school operated continuously until 1956, when it closed because of changing educational trends, the encroachment of physician anesthesiologists into areas formerly occupied by nurse anesthetists, and financial losses. St Vincent's was also the site (in 1963) of the world's first telemetry station. The hospital has outgrown several facilities along the way, and the current 40-acre campus dates from 1971. Tours are available from the Volunteers.

PENNSYLVANIA

BETHLEHEM

St Luke's Hospital   801 Ostrum Street 18015. (215) 691-4141. St Luke's is a 440-bed full-service community hospital, founded in 1872, whose teaching affiliation with Temple University School of Medicine allows it to conduct residencies in surgery, internal medicine, and obstetrics and gynecology. What makes it special from our perspective, however, is its School of Nursing. A two-year diploma program established in 1884, it is now one of the oldest diploma programs in the country.

Like most schools of nursing of the time, this one was established primarily to assure a steady supply of labor for the hospital. Still, the very conservative community bristled at the idea of young women caring for men; so the early students were permitted to care for only female patients. The first class consisted of 9 students selected from 32 applicants. The 2-year curriculum included didactic lectures (e.g., principles of nursing observation, recording of symptoms, diets of the sick, methods of managing helpless pa-

From the collection of the Historic Nursing Museum, St. Lukes Hospital, Bethlehem, Pennsylvania *(Photo courtesy of St Luke's Hospital)*

tients, etc.) and bedside training (e.g., dressing of wounds and application of leeches, poultices, fomentations, blisters, etc.).

The current hospital complex is composed of 9 buildings on a 40-acre campus. There are numerous historic murals, artifacts, and plaques lining the hallways here, most of which are accessible to casual visitors, but the Community Relations department is happy to provide tours for interested persons. The **Historic Nursing Museum,** located on the main floor of the School of Nursing Trexler Residence, occupies a large lounge and consists of a series of exhibits depicting regional nursing history, arranged around the walls. The museum is open daily when the School of Nursing is in session, and visitors are welcome by appointment.

Die Apotheke (The Moravian Apothecary Museum) 420 Main Street (rear) 18018. (215) 867-0173. Until it closed in 1951, this was the oldest continually functioning drugstore in the country. Founded in 1743, it was from the first owned and operated by members of the Unitas Fratrum, now known as the Moravian Church, a German Protestant church-centered community. Today, Die Apotheke (German for "the apothecary") is operated by the Moravian Congregation as one part of a sequence of museums and community buildings that generally are not restorations but rather are living and vital parts of continuing community life.

Die Apotheke was originally established in the Gemein Haus on Church Street, now the oldest building in Bethlehem and current home of the Moravian Museum. The Apothecary was merely one part of a dispensary, which was home to a physician who served members of the community spread out over the nearby area. In 1752 the Apothecary was moved to a building on Main Street. The early physicians, like others in the colonies, were versatile men who filled many roles, in this case serving as ordained ministers as well as surgeons, apothecaries, and administrators. It wasn't until 1839 that the Apothecary became a distinct business entity, separate from the local physician. The original Apothecary building was razed in 1862, and replaced with the present building on the same site. This 1863 building was moved 27 feet north and the facade entirely redone in 1935. The business continued under a succession of proprietors until 1951, and the old shop was turned into a museum in 1955.

The collection here is composed of artifacts from the Apothecary and the Moravian community, extending back over 250 years. Here you will find Delft-ware pharmaceutical jars, purchased in Holland in 1743 and used to store various gums, ointments, and resins. There are old blown-glass bottles, homeopathic medicine kits, mortars and pestles, pharmaceutical manufacturing equipment, and various books and labels written in German script. The original 1752 fireplace is where the early alchemists heated retorts and cooked their preparations. Be sure not to miss the herb garden (dating from 1747) just outside the door.

The Apothecary is located in a small room at the back of a commercial building, and arrangements to visit it can be made at the nearby Moravian Musuem at 66 West Church Street. The Apothecary is shown only by appointment, and there is a modest admission charge.

DANVILLE

Geisinger Medical Center North Academy Avenue 17822. (717) 271-6211. Geisinger was founded in 1915 by a coal-mining heiress in honor of her deceased husband. She hired Harold Foss, who had spent 2 years apprenticing himself to the Mayos at their famous clinic, and he set about creating an institution modeled after that of his mentors. The George F Geisinger Memorial Hospital opened 2 weeks prematurely to care for victims of a severe typhoid epidemic, and 54 typhoid patients were admitted the first week. In the years that followed, Geisinger became firmly established as one of the nation's new breed of group practice institutions, with a growing cadre of salaried, specialty-trained physicians who were not permitted to engage in fee-for-service practice.

When Geisinger opened, Danville was a mill town, population

5500 and the streets were filled with the smoke, sulfur fumes, engine sounds, and debris of a hardworking industrial town. At their height, the mills employed 2000 men, and the railroads which moved raw materials in and finished product out provided work for the rest. Now the mills and the railroads are gone, and Geisinger provides employment for 4000 people in Danville and for 2000 more in their satellites nearby. The institution changed its name to Geisinger Medical Center in the 1969s. The name now represents a system that is a mixture of affiliated hospitals, medical group practices, outreach clinics in 40 locations, a health maintenance organization, a management company, and a biomedical engineering company.

The Danville campus includes a 577-bed hospital, a School of Nursing (also established in 1915), and other associated facilities. Visitors are invited during normal business hours to view the historical displays that fill a well-marked room just off the main lobby. Additional museum articles are on display in the medical library. Tours are available via Corporate Communications.

HARRISBURG

Harrisburg State Hospital Cameron and Maclay Streets 17105. (717) 257-7600. The Pennsylvania State Lunatic Hospital and Union Hospital for the Insane was opened in 1851 on 130 acres of farmland, in response to pleas by Dorothea Dix. The hospital grew steadily and overcrowding was a recurrent problem. The original facilities, built as cheaply as possible, were no match for the increasing patient load, and, around the turn of the century, almost all the older buildings were demolished and new ones erected in their place on a campus that had grown to 760 acres.

The hospital was given its present name in 1921. Today, the hospital consists of 225 acres and 15 buildings, mostly turn-of-the-century architecture, but there also are two 1853 structures. One of these cottages, adjacent to the administration building, is called the **Dorothea Dix Library and Museum** and was actually built with funds raised personally by Miss Dix. Originally designed as a library for patient "enrichment" (one section for females and one for males), the building now contains displays about the hospital's history and about Dorothea Dix's remarkable career. The Library includes a large collection on nineteenth century mental institutions, as well as period literature on mental illness. The Museum is open to the public on the first Sunday and third Wednesday of each month, 2 PM to 4 PM, and by appointment.

HERSHEY

Pennsylvania State University Medical Center Route 322 17033. (717) 531-8521. The interest in starting a medical school here was spurred by the 1959 Surgeon General's Report which predicted a major physician shortage and projected a need for 20 to 24 additional medical schools. Penn State (founded in 1855) tried without success to pry some money out of the State Legislature, and it looked as though the venture was destined to failure, until officials of the Milton S Hershey Foundation (established by the founder of the Hershey Chocolate Company) called up and spontaneously offered a grant of $50 million to get the project underway. This, plus a $21 million grant from the US Public Health Service, resulted in a 550-acre campus that accepted its first medical students in 1967 (simultaneously inaugurating the nation's first academic department of family and community medicine) and its first patients in 1970.

The Milton S Hershey Medical Center is now central Pennsylvania's third largest employer, topped only by the state government centered 10 miles away in Harrisburg and Hershey Foods International located nearby. The principal building here (which includes both school and research functions, as well as a 350-bed hospital) is a 750-foot long, nine-story, crescent-shaped structure, with various wings projecting from its convex side. However, this is a medical center on the grow, and various large and expensive additions are underway.

LACKAWAXEN

Zane Grey Museum River Road 18435. (717) 685-7522. Before Zane Grey (1872–1939) became the world-famous author of *Riders of the Purple Sage* he was a dentist (as was his father before him), practicing in New York City. Among the many artifacts on display here, visitors will see Grey's brass shingle, embossed "Dr. Zane Grey, Dentist," as well as a pedal-driven dental drill and other professional paraphernalia.

Grey and his wife built this house in 1905 and lived in it until 1918, when he moved to California, after his novels began to find an outlet in Hollywood's growing fascination with the western. During his lifetime, Grey dominated the field of American fiction of the west (he is reputed to have made $37 million from his writing). More than 100 movies were based on Grey's stories, and his books have been translated into 20 languages. A man of many talents, Grey went to the University of Pennsylvania on a baseball scholarship, and he was a passionate fisherman who went on to achieve ten world saltwater sportfishing records, some of which still stand today. The Grey home here was for a number of years owned and operated as a museum by an old family friend. As a result, tours of this museum had a remarkably personal quality, and the rooms here were crammed with memorabilia of Grey's multifaceted life. The wall surfaces in two rooms are completely covered with newspaper articles about Grey, book jackets, photographs, prints, posters, western artwork, and the like. The National Park Service took over operation of this site in 1989 and almost certainly will be making changes, presumably clearing up some of the clutter and making the displays less vulnerable to being touched and damaged by tourists.

Visitors should call first to find the present hours of operation. Current plans are to keep the museum open daily in the summer, with more restricted hours the rest of the year. There is likely to be a small admission fee for the museum but interested people can visit Grey's grave in the small cemetery nearby without charge.

LANCASTER

Edward Hand Medical Heritage Museum 137 East Walnut Street 17602. (717) 393-9588. This museum is located in the headquarters of the Lancaster City and County Medical Society, the oldest local medical society in the country, founded in 1776. The museum has been named after Edward Hand, a physician-soldier from the Lancaster area who served in the Revolutionary War and who was ultimately promoted to the rank of major general, serving as adjutant general to General George Washington. The museum itself occupies a single room, though much of the collection is in storage. Exhibits are rotated regularly. The exhibits focus on regional medical history and, during my visit, included interesting displays on veterinary medicine, bloodletting, various suction and douching devices for multiple orifices, and a wide range of medical equipment, books, and photographs. The museum is currently open every Friday from 10 AM to noon, but interested individuals are encouraged to make an appointment to view the collection at other times as well.

Old Lancaster County Hospital 900 East King Street 17602. (717) 299-7929. Construction on this, the second oldest surviving hospital building in the United States, was begun in 1799 and completed in 1801. Until 1876 the hospital was operated as an almshouse and called the Lancaster House of the Poor and Employment. However, from the beginning the institution had a House Physician and Surgeon on retainer as well as two consulting physicians, so most people in the area feel it has a reasonable claim to being a hospital from its inception. By the end of the nineteenth century, the almshouse had evolved into The Lancaster County Home and Asylum and was used as a hospital, nursing home, and psychiatric institution. The building has not been used as a hospital for several decades and is now used by the Children and Youth Social Service Agency. It was extensively remodeled in the 1870s and again in 1983, but the exterior retains the basic integrity of the original two-and-one-half-story, 150-foot-long facade. The cave-like cells where the insane were kept under the front porch still remain, and the interior gives a rough sense of the original room layout, but no original woodwork or fixtures remain. The new County Hospital is adjacent to the historic building. This is a public building in active use. There are no tours, but visitors are welcome to look around the public spaces during ordinary working hours.

NORTHUMBERLAND

Joseph Priestly House 472 Priestly Avenue 17857. (717) 473-9474. This was the American home of the founder of modern chemistry and the discoverer of oxygen. Joseph Priestly (1733 – 1804) was an English minister who developed an interest in gases as a result of inhaling the vapors emanating from the brewery next to his home in Leeds. He "impregnated" water with what he called "fixed air," in so doing developed soda water, and thus became the father of the carbonated beverage industry. In the early 1770s, he expanded his experiments, and in short order became the first to identify a number of gases: ammonia, nitrous oxide, and hydrogen sulfide, among others. He is best known for his discovery of oxygen in 1774, which he produced by focusing the sun's rays on red mercuric oxide.

Priestly was a freethinker, a religious Dissenter, and a political radical who supported both the American and French Revolutions. As a result, he was both feared and hated in England, and mobs burned his home, laboratory, books, and manuscripts. His scientist colleagues in the Royal Society shunned him. Priestly emigrated to America, where his three sons already lived. While living here in Northumberland, Priestly continued and expanded his work. It was here that he discovered carbon monoxide. He wrote a dozen books on theology, including the last four volumes of his *General History of the Christian Church,* and he conducted Unitarian services in his home every Sunday.

The house in Northumberland was built by Priestly in 1794 for his own use and has been nicely preserved and restored. When a group of chemists met here in 1874 to commemorate the centennial of Priestley's discovery of oxygen, they simultaneously agreed to found the American Chemical Society. Furnished with period antiques, the house features a recreation of Priestley's laboratory, as well as a variety of exhibits describing his interests and accomplishments. The house is open Tuesday through Saturday, 9 to 5, and Sundays from noon to 5. The facilities are closed on some holidays. There is a small admission charge.

PHILADELPHIA   (*See* **Great Medical Cities**)

PITTSBURGH

University of Pittsburgh School of Medicine Desoto and Terrace 15261. (412) 624-2607. Although various groups endeavored to start a medical school in Pittsburgh as early as 1846, the effort was not successful until 1885, when the Western Pennsylvania Medical College was founded in conjunction with the Western Pennsylvania Hospital. The school's first graduating class included 20 men and 1 woman. In 1892 the medical college became affiliated with the Western University of Pennsylvania (later the University of Pittsburgh), but, as with many such schools, the affiliation was more nominal than real. In 1908 the affiliation became more substantial, and the school began to improve its standards and its graduates' poor performance on state board examinations. The school improved so quickly that the Flexner Report of 1910 observed that "The school has within a year undergone a complete transformation. A more thorough piece of housecleaning within so short a period is hardly credible." Flexner gave the school a very positive evaluation, with the exception of its clinical facilities, which were scattered and not under university control.

Shortly thereafter, the University began to plan for the building of its own medical center complex. New land was purchased in 1921, and the University promptly began seeking hospital affiliates to move onto the new campus. The Magee Hospital (obstetrics and gynecology) signed on in 1921, the Children's Hospital in 1924, and the Eye and Ear Hospital in 1926. The general hospital proved to be more of a problem. After being turned down by West Penn, Montefiore, Mercy, Allegheny General, and St Francis Hospitals, the University managed to entice Presbyterian Hospital to move to the campus. In 1965 the various institutions on the University campus officially combined to form the University Health Center of Pittsburgh.

Pitt's most famous medical first was the conquest of polio. Polio-myelitis was the nation's most devastating scourge of children. In 1952 more American children were killed by this disease than by any other. In that year, 57,000 children were afflicted and over 21,000 died. Pitt established a Virus Research Laboratory in 1946, installing Jonas Salk as its chief in 1947. In 1949 three researchers at Harvard succeeded in growing live polio virus in test tubes (for this achievement John Enders, Thomas Weller, and Frederick Robbins were awarded the Nobel Prize). It was Salk, however, who managed to create the first workable vaccine, performing the first successful clinical tests in 1952. Massive field testing was accomplished in 1954, and, when the vaccine was found to be safe, effective, and potent, Jonas Salk became one of the nation's true heroes. As one measure of the nation's response, five Hollywood studios wanted to make a movie about Salk, and Marlon Brando even agreed to play the title role in one of them. Another result was that Pittsburgh became the first major city in the United States to eliminate polio. By 1961 polio had been almost entirely eliminated from the United States and all other countries using the vaccine. In 1957 Pitt renamed the old Municipal Contagious Disease Hospital Salk Hall.

In 1970 Pitt overhauled its medical school curriculum, and one aspect of the overhaul was the elimination of cadaver dissection in anatomy. Instead, students learn anatomy in a **Body Parts Museum,** a fascinating collection of anatomical and pathological specimens, exclusively designed for teaching. Specimens include a female torso with 30 horizontal transections, each meticulously labeled and on display in a large wall case. There are also longitudinal transections of the body, boxes filled with limbs, and displays of fetuses, malformed parts, and diseased organs. The doors of the museum say "No Admittance"; but health professionals are usually welcome to view the collection by prior arrangement with the anatomy department curator [(412) 648-8873]. Tours of the rest of the campus are also available via the Public Relations Department.

West Penn Hospital 4800 Friendship Avenue 15224. (412) 578-5000. This hospital has a distinguished history, but it also illustrates the hazards in applying the "first" label to institutions and events. When the Western Pennsylvania Hospital was founded in 1847, it was to be the first nonmilitary hospital in western Pennsylvania, and it still calls itself the first hospital "founded" in its area. However, before the hospital finally began accepting patients in 1853, Mercy Hospital had opened in 1847 and Passavant had opened in 1849.

The impetus for the founding of the hospital came from Dorothea Dix, who, in the course of her crusade for the mentally ill, visited the area. She discovered shocking health conditions and an equally shocking lack of institutions to provide care of any sort. The result was that Pittsburghers were mobilized, and the Western Pennsylvania Hospital was organized to serve both the physically and mentally ill. In short order, however, the facilities were overrun with insane patients, and Miss Dix made another trip to the area to lobby for a separate institution for the insane. When Dixmont (eventually to become a state institution) was opened in 1862, 113 patients were transferred from West Penn, leaving only two patients in the older facility. West Penn was soon put to use caring for Civil War casualties, accommodating as many as 1500 at one time. For decades after the close of the War, West Penn served primarily as a veterans' home for the surrounding area. In the latter years of the nineteenth century, as Pittsburgh's foundries and forges, refineries and machine factories, and glassworks and railroad yards made it the industrial giant of the United States — as well as the center of industrial injuries — West Penn was the site of more major amputations than any other hospital in the country.

In 1883 the physician staff here formed the Western Pennsylvania Medical College, which was eventually to become the University of Pittsburgh School of Medicine. West Penn moved to its present location in 1911. By the 1930s, West Penn had become a center of pneumonia treatment and research, a role significantly enhanced by Pittsburgh's industrial pollution, so great that smoke almost daily blotted out the sun. As workers studied bacterial growth in cultures, a West Penn researcher became the first to develop time-lapse photography in 1937.

Today, West Penn is a 568-bed hospital. The second floor of the "S" wing now houses an **Antiquities Center,** with panels and photographs that describe the rich histories of the hospital and of the area. Additional glass cases describe the history of medicine from prehistoric times to the present. A variety of nineteenth century memorabilia are also on display. The Antiquities Center is open to the public weekdays, 8 AM to 9 PM. Tours of the hospital are available from Public Relations.

Mercy Hospital 1400 Locust Street 15219. (412) 232-8111. This, the oldest Mercy Hospital in the world, was founded by the Sisters of Mercy in 1847. The Sisters came to Pittsburgh from Dublin, Ireland, in response to a plea for help from the local Bishop. Mercy opened its own school of nursing in 1893, and the school, which is still in operation, recently graduated its 5000th student. Today, Mercy is a

500-bed teaching hospital and a part of the Eastern Mercy Health System, which includes a total of ten hospitals from Maine to Florida. The modern Pittsburgh facility can be toured by prior arrangement with Community Affairs.

North Hills Passavant Hospital 9100 Babcock Road 15237. (412) 367-6700. Established in 1849 by the Lutheran minister William Alfred Passavant, this was the first Protestant hospital in the United States. When Passavant began thinking about founding the Pittsburgh Infirmary, he journeyed to Europe to study the most advanced institutions. His travels took him to Kaiserwerth in Germany, where Florence Nightingale got her training. Theodore and Frederike Fliedner had started their hospital and school for deaconesses in Kaiserwerth in 1836, and, by Rev Fliedner's death in 1864, over 500 deaconesses were serving in institutions on four continents. Fliedner himself escorted four deaconesses here in the hospital's first year, and they provided nursing care during the Infirmary's first decades. Since the Infirmary admitted everyone in need, the small house in which the early patients were kept was regarded as a menace by its neighbors, who were fearful that cholera patients might spread their disease to those in the vicinity. After the hospital was stoned, Passavant moved the operation to the Hill District, which was then on Pittsburgh's outskirts.

The Infirmary experienced difficult financial problems in the 1880s and closed down from 1887 until 1893, when an influx of new deaconesses and a thorough overhaul restored the hospital's vitality. When the hospital's founder died in 1894, the name of this institution (and others he had founded, for example, the one in Chicago) was changed to Passavant Hospital. In 1926, to circumvent a Pennsylvania decision that barred state aid to sectarian facilities, the hospital applied for a new charter that made it a nonsectarian institution. Ironically, in the year before this legalistic maneuver took place, this Lutheran hospital's patients included 796 Jews, 544 Catholics, 440 Presbyterians, 400 Baptists, 319 Methodists, and several hundred others of various faiths, but only 213 Lutherans.

In 1964 Passavant moved from what had become an inner city location slated for urban renewal to the North Hills area. Tours of the modern North Hills Passavant Hospital are available from Public Affairs.

Shadyside Hospital 5230 Centre Avenue 15232. (412) 622-2121. When this hospital was founded in 1866, it was Pittsburgh's fourth hospital and the city's first homeopathic institution. At first called the Homeopathic Medical and Surgical Hospital and Dispensary, the enterprise grew rapidly. By 1882 the original 38-bed structure had grown to 180 beds; it expanded to 200 beds in 1910 and to 325 in 1927. In order to eliminate the suggestion of sectarianism, the homeopathic label was dropped and the present name adopted in 1938.

What makes Shadyside especially interesting, however, is its nursing school, founded in 1884, and one of the first training schools for nurses west of the Allegheny Mountains. In 1896, the Pittsburgh Training School for Nurses graduated a young woman named Mary Roberts Rinehart (1876–1958), who went on to become one of the most famous and highly paid authors of her time. In addition to writing numerous novels, plays, short stories, and essays, she was a war correspondent in World War I. In her autobiography *My Story* (1931), Miss Rinehart described her probationary period here by saying "I entered . . . a world so new and at times so terrible, that even now it hurts me to remember it . . . here was all the tragedy of the world gathered under one roof." For many years, the school of nursing here was an important source of national leadership for the nursing profession. The superintendent here from 1897 to 1906, Ida Giles, was an early president of the National League for Nursing.

Tours can be arranged by contacting the Marketing Department.

Presbyterian–University Hospital DeSoto at O'Hara Street 15213. (412) 647-2345. By the time this hospital opened its doors in 1893, it was Pittsburgh's eighth hospital. A remarkable woman, some hard work, and incredible luck transformed the tiny five-bed latecomer-of-a-hospital into the major teaching hospital in the University Medical Center.

Louise J Lyle (1842–1932) grew up in a deeply religious Presbyterian family that was also deeply committed to education. She married a Presbyterian minister during the Civil War, and, after his death in 1884, devoted herself to the temperance cause, prison work, and the Young Women's Christian Association. In 1888 she established a free dispensary for women and children in Cincinnati and led the effort to establish a women's medical college in that city. In 1890, at the age of 48, she entered the Women's Medical College in Chicago, continued her studies at the Women's Medical College in Cleveland, and completed them and received her degree from the Presbyterian Women's Medical College in Cincinnati in 1892. She was 50 years old. The following year, she moved to Pittsburgh and promptly started the Louise Lyle Hospital in a small house in the Allegheny district. By 1894 Dr Lyle had managed to wheedle and beg the Pittsburgh Presbytery into providing some support, and the facility's name was changed to the Presbyterian Hospital of Pittsburgh. With the Church's support and Dr Lyle's energetic administration, the Hospital thrived. However, in 1899, while the hospital was filled to the brim, Dr Lyle had the misfortune to place a sick woman admitted on an emergency basis in a room already occupied by a male patient. The moral sensibilities of the Presbyterian community were outraged, and Dr Lyle was forced to step down from the superintendent's role in the hospital she had founded. Dr Lyle continued in private practice, and the Presbyterian Hospital continued to grow.

Presbyterian might have remained a medium-sized sectarian hospital but for chance. In 1923 the University proposed an affiliation with Presbyterian (after being turned down by several other hospitals), and Presbyterian accepted, in the process becoming the medical school's core teaching facility. In 1986 the affiliation became more substantial, and the name of the 570-bed hospital was changed to Presbyterian–University Hospital. In 1963 Presbyterian established the world's first fellowship training program in critical care medicine. Its Stereotactic Radiosurgical Suite houses the nation's first gamma knife for treatment of brain tumors and other neurosurgical lesions. The hospital now performs more organ transplants (including heart, lung, kidney, liver, and pancreas transplants) than any other hospital in the country.

As with the rest of the medical center, a vast building program is currently underway. Tours are available via the Volunteers Office.

READING

Reading Hospital and Medical Center Sixth Avenue and Spruce Street 19603. (215) 378-6000. When the Reading Dispensary was founded in 1867, its establishment was a reflection of two circumstances. The first was that many physicians from the Reading area had just returned from service in the Civil War and had learned firsthand about the value of a hospital—an experience that was new for most. The second was that the town was undergoing an economic boom and could afford to be concerned about the care of its less well-off citizens. The board of trustees of the new dispensary read like a who's who of the local gentry, with railroad men, bankers, iron manufacturers, judges, and a brewer.

The early dispensary occupied a three-story brick building, with facilities for outpatients on the first floor, an area for inpatients on the second, and a room for the steward and his wife on the third. The Reading Dispensary and Hospital occupied a variety of more or less temporary buildings until it moved to a "permanent" structure in 1886. Further growth led to its move to the present site in 1926.

The Reading Hospital School was founded in 1889, and the 2 graduates in the first class were capped in 1891. By 1897 there were 4 graduates, and by 1942 the graduating class included over 40 nurses. By the late 1960s, this was the largest diploma nursing program in the country, with over 100 students in each class. Students worked 12-hour days until 1941, with only 2 hours off one afternoon a week and a few hours off each Sunday. The schedule was reduced to 8-hour days, 7 days a week, until 1951, when a 40-hour week was adopted. The school continues in operation today.

Much of the original 1926 hospital design, modeled after a hospital in Mannheim, Germany, remains intact. Of course, numerous buildings have been added through the years, but the original pavilion plan is clearly visible. The main hospital building, with its brick and limestone clocktower, still dominates the approach to the 38-acre campus. Tours of the hospital and School of Nursing are available through Public Relations.

RHODE ISLAND

PROVIDENCE

Brown University Medical School 97 Waterman Avenue 02912. (401) 863-3232. Brown University was founded in 1764 as Rhode Island College and, as such, is the seventh oldest college in the country. Brown's medical school is either one of the oldest or one of the youngest medical schools, depending on how you regard a 145-year lapse between classes. The medical school was first founded in 1811 (the seventh in America), but it lasted less than two decades, dying a slow death in 1827 and 1828, for reasons that still remain unclear to historians. During its years of operation, the school graduated 88 physicians and passed out a lot of honorary degrees. In the years that followed there were a number of attempts to start another medical school, none of them meeting with success. In 1899 Dr William Osler, then surely one of the country's most eminent physicians, came to Providence and tried to stir up the locals. "The existing conditions in Providence are singularly favorable for a small first-class school," he said. "Here are college laboratories of physics, chemistry and biology, and modern hospitals with 300 beds." What was lacking was the million dollars that by then was necessary to start a decent, scientifically grounded medical school — and the leadership to pry the money out of those who could give it.

It took another 75 years for conditions to change enough for a medical school to be created. In 1968 the Division of Biology and Medicine was formed as a single department of Brown University, but it was 1975 before Brown achieved accreditation as a full four-year medical school. Since then, Brown has graduated an average of 60 physicians each year—and Rhode Island changed from a state ranked 49th in the percentage of students entering medical school to its current position as 21st. Over the same interval, the state has changed from being a net importer of medical care to being a net exporter. That is, the number of non-Rhode Islanders who come into the state for medical care now exceeds the number of Rhode Islanders who leave the state to get medical care.

The principal Brown medical school building is the large Biomedical Center, located at Brown and Thayer Streets on the edge of the main University campus. That's where the majority of preclinical teaching takes place. The administration is located in the Arnold Lab building at the Waterman address listed above, and some classes are also held in the nearby Wilson Lab building. Brown does not have a university hospital; instead it uses the facilities of eight affiliated hospitals.

There are currently no tours of the medical school.

Butler Hospital 345 Blackstone Boulevard 02906. (401) 456-3700. Butler, like Brown University Medical School, is a born-again institution. In 1955, after 111 years of operation but staggering under ever increasing deficits, the hospital closed its doors. The closure caught the Providence community by surprise, since Butler tended to be regarded as a psychiatric asylum for the well-to-do, and there developed an outpouring of interest and support. Two years later, following a study by an outside consultant, Butler decided to re-open, changing its role from a long-stay refuge for the chronic patient to become a multi-purpose mental health center, with some space rented out to other agencies. When Brown's medical school opened and Butler became its major psychiatric teaching facility, Butler's previous problems in attracting high-quality medical staff largely evaporated. The result has been a dramatic turnaround for this historic hospital: it is now a thriving institution.

Butler Hospital was established in 1844 as a result of two bequests: the first of $30,000 from a prosperous merchant named Nicholas Brown, the second ($40,000) from an even more prosperous merchant named Cyrus Butler. The hospital was understandably named for the latter. Trustees were assembled, and they selected the present site of 144 acres within the city of Providence. The superintendent chosen was Isaac Ray, who served for 21 years.

Ray was one of the founders of what has come to be the American Psychiatric Association and was a remarkable man in many respects. Not only was he committed to the moral and enlightened treatment of the insane, he had—in 1838, while still a general practitioner with no appreciable experience in psychiatry or the law—authored *The Medical Jurisprudence of Insanity*, which to this day remains a classic and much quoted work. Ray is widely regarded as the Father of Forensic Psychiatry.

In the years that followed, Butler achieved both local and international acclaim for being an outstanding institution. Gradually, Butler came to be more and more a haven for the well-to-do mentally ill. Unfortunately, it is expensive to care for the rich, and Butler suffered from recurrent money problems, culminating in its 1955 closing.

A sign at Butler's front gate proclaims that the public is always welcome to tour the grounds from 0730 to sunset, provided only that "proper regard is shown" for the security and well-being of patients. The grounds are indeed lovely (there's a full-time grounds crew of six), beautifully landscaped, and manicured. Despite the fact that many buildings date from the 1840s and another eight are nineteenth century structures, the facilities are in perfect repair and are immaculate. The architectural style is English Gothic, and there are many wonderful details here, including huge wooden doors, broad and graceful archways, hand-carved wooden railings, fine tile walkways, and delicately leaded glass. More modern structures (e.g., the 1978 inpatient building) have been designed to fit esthetically and functionally with the old.

Visitors with a more scholarly bent may wish to see the Isaac Ray Archives, a treasure of psychiatric history. Included in the collection are 2000 annual reports of mental institutions in America and Great Britain, as well as Ray's personal collection of more than 1000 volumes on psychiatry, law, and medicine. Researchers are welcome by prior arrangement. Tours can be arranged similarly.

Rhode Island Hospital 593 Eddy Street 02903. (401) 277-4000. Founded in 1863 and currently operating with over 700 beds, this is the oldest and largest hospital in the state. Providence is unusual for a large, modern city in that it has no general hospital under municipal or county control; instead, it has the private Rhode Island Hospital to function as the "city hospital."

Providence was relatively slow to build a general hospital. The town of Newport built a smallpox pesthouse in 1716 (Rhode Island's first public medical institution); Providence built three pesthouses for smallpox a half century later, and a quarantine building for yellow fever victims in 1798. The latter, high on a hill overlooking the Providence River, became a Marine Hospital in 1805 when yellow fever had become less a concern, and the site was eventually conveyed to the RIH, which now occupies it. The pesthouse itself survived until 1960 (its 162nd year) used variously as a tenement, a nurses' home, a residence for hospital workers, and a hospital employment office before succumbing to the wrecking ball.

The RIH was incorporated in 1863, and the first buildings were formally dedicated in 1868. The design incorporated an elaborate ventilation system created to carry away the "foul air" that was presumed responsible for the transmission of infection. There were three intake registers for every patient bed (one at the floor, one about three feet above the bed, and another at the ceiling), each of which fed into a labyrinth of ducts that exited at the roof.

Today, the RIH is a huge complex of 26 buildings occupying 52 acres. The architecture overall is undistinguished and visually it's hard to tell that this is one of the best-endowed private hospitals in the country. The oldest building (the Southwest Pavilion, erected in 1900) is still in active use, though the metal facade that covers the brick columns and provides other ornamental detailing is gradually decaying. The entire complex is tied together by underground tunnels and, beneath them, by a sub-basement for utilities. All in all, the RIH gives a graphic picture of the manner in which many hospitals developed in the twentieth century, building new structures as new needs and enthusiasms developed and money became available, erecting them in whatever space was available or could be obtained by demolishing other structures.

Arrange tours by calling Public Relations [(401) 277-5327].

SOUTH CAROLINA

CHARLESTON

Medical University of South Carolina 171 Ashley Avenue 29425. (803) 792-2300. When the Medical College of South Carolina opened in 1824, it was the first medical school in the south. Soon after its opening the school started a free infirmary for blacks, to provide care for the patients and teaching material for the students, the latter being all white. In 1833 a group of faculty broke off from the original school and founded the Medical College of the State of South Carolina. After five years of competition, the older school collapsed and turned over all its assets to the newer institution. The school closed during the Civil War but revived promptly in 1865. For all of this time, the school was a proprietary institution, admitting essentially all interested individuals with the wherewithal to pay tuition. When Flexner examined the school in 1909, he found almost everything about the institution to be unsatisfactory — with the exception of its affiliation with Roper Hospital, which he found to be "an unusually attractive institution."

The school was faced with extinction until 1913, when it was made a state institution and therefore assured of a relatively stable financial base. The College built its own hospital in 1955. In 1969 the growing diversity of the medical complex prompted the legislature to grant it a new name: the Medical University of South Carolina, composed of the Medical College and the colleges of pharmacy (established in 1891), nursing (1919), graduate studies (1965), health-related professions (1966), and dental medicine (1967). The medical complex also includes half-a-dozen hospitals and numerous support institutions.

Tours of the campus are available through the Public Relations department. There are two places of special interest that can be visited without special arrangements. The first is the **Waring Historical Library,** which, in addition to being a library of over 7000 historical volumes, has a museum collection, parts of which are put

Waring Historical Library, Medical University of South Carolina *(Courtesy of Waring Historical Library, Medical University of South Carolina, Charleston, SC)*

on rotating display. The collection here is a magnificent jumble, with fine old books and fascinating artifacts stacked side by side on shelves, all available for visitor inspection. Prize items on display during my visit included a nineteenth century brass and porcelain croup kettle, a nineteenth century vaginal speculum made of ivory, dozens of medicine chests, and fascinating old electro-diagnostic and therapeutic equipment. The Waring occupies an 1890s brick castle at the northeast corner of the campus, and the public is welcome from 8:30 AM to 5 PM, Mondays through Fridays. The **Macauley Museum of Dental History** occupies a small building near the Waring and is accessible only by requesting admittance at the Waring. The Macauley houses what is believed to be the world's largest collection (albeit uncatalogued) of dental instruments — and there are some dandies here, including an exraordinary item crafted by Paul Revere. There are also fine exhibits of dental chairs, foot-powered drills, and x-ray equipment — as well as a fully restored c. 1880 dental office.

Old Marine Hospital Franklin Street at Poulnot Lane 29401. This building now houses the Housing Authority for the city of Charleston, which is not enthusiastic about receiving calls concerning the old hospital, so no phone number is listed. However, the marvelous building is intact and there's a story here worth telling. Like many port cities, Charleston early on tried to make some provision for sick and injured seamen. Usually poor and far from home, these unfortunates customarily became public charges. From 1749 onward, the city designated one building or another as a marine hospital for the exclusive use of sailors or other transients. A levy on ships using the port helped to pay the costs. These structures, with their rough-and-tumble inhabitants often suffering from various forms of contagion, were seldom popular with their neighbors. Finally, in 1816, Congress authorized the construction of Marine Hospitals around the country, and this lovely building is the result. Designed by noted architect Robert Mills, the Marine Hospital here was erected in 1833 for the care of "sick and disabled merchant seamen" and, incidentally, to serve as a teaching resource for both of the medical schools of the time. As constructed, there were eight wards: three for surgical cases on the first floor, and five on the second, for medical and venereal disease cases. During the Civil War, it was appropriated as a hospital to serve the needs of the Confederacy. After the war, the building was used for an Episcopal free school for black children, staffed by white southern women (the initial enrollment was 1800 students). After 1869 the building became a library, and, from 1895 until 1939, it was the home of the Jenkins Orphanage for Negroes. In 1939 it was remodeled for use by the Housing Authority. The building exists today with appearance essentially unchanged. It's probably in the best condition of any of the old surviving Marine Hospitals and gives the viewer a good feel for what similar early nineteenth century hospitals must have been like. This one has a ground level and two upper floors, with broad verandas and handsome pillars. The grounds are surrounded by a masonry fence topped with bricks. There are no tours, but the exterior and grounds are accessible to passers-by, only a few blocks walk from King Street in historic downtown Charleston.

Roper Hospital 316 Calhoun Street 29401. (803) 724-2000. Roper was founded in 1850 as the first community hospital in the Carolinas. Benefactor Thomas Roper left his money to the Medical Society of South Carolina to erect a hospital "for the permanent reception or occasional relief of all such sick . . . as need surgical and medical aid . . . without regard to complexion, religion, or nation." The hospital survived the Civil War, for a time serving as a Confederate hospital and later falling under Federal control. However, after the war, the hospital went through considerable turmoil, and it was not until 1906 that the hospital was able to construct a satisfactory new home. The present 400-bed physical plant dates mostly from the late 1960s and early 1970s, though portions were erected in the 1940s. It is still owned by the Medical Society of South Carolina. Tours are available through the Community Services office.

COLUMBIA

University of South Carolina Medical Center Garners Ferry Road 29208. (803) 733-3200. This school of medicine was made possible by the Veterans Administration, which assisted in the school's development with a grant of $25 million. The school opened in 1977, and the charter class was graduated in 1981. In 1983 the school moved to its present location, a 200,000 square-foot facility completed at federal government expense. The medical school complex is located in the 1932-vintage Columbia Veterans Administration Hospital, which became available for use when the adjacent 600-bed Dorn VA Hospital was completed in the late 1970s. All of the older VA buildings have been completely renovated, with a continuous eye for historical preservation. When first established, the Columbia VAH was one of 50 VA hospitals constructed around the country, all built to an essentially identical pavilion plan, with only the facades differing to conform to regional architectural styles. The pavilions are all connected by covered walkways. The style of the facades here is Georgian Colonial, leaning heavily toward walls decorated with raised brick and broad porticos supported by tall columns. Tours of the campus are available via the Public Relations Office [(803) 733-3210].

SOUTH DAKOTA

VERMILLION

University of South Dakota School of Medicine 414 East Clark Street 57069. (605) 677-5233. Starting in 1907 and continuing for the next 68 years, the University of South Dakota ran a two-year medical school, providing the first two years of basic science education and then sending the students elsewhere to complete their studies. In 1974, after years of deliberation, the South Dakota Legislature decided this situation was unsatisfactory and authorized a full four-year medical program. The first third-year class enrolled in 1975, and the result was a clear success for the state. In the years since the program started, the number of physicians has doubled in the state. The infant mortality rate, formerly one of the highest in the nation, is now among the lowest. The school has also helped bring over 20 new specialties into the state that previously had been unavailable, including pediatric surgery, neonatology, and infectious disease.

The main concern of this school is to provide the state with general practitioners, particularly for smaller, rural communities. The school functions by providing basic science instruction at the USD campus in Vermillion and by then farming students out for clinical instruction at hospitals throughout the state, especially those in Sioux Falls, Yankton, and Rapid City, but also in many smaller communities as well.

Tours of the Vermillion facilities can be arranged by calling the Dean's Office at (605) 339-6648.

TENNESSEE

JOHNSON CITY

East Tennessee State University Quillen-Dishner College of Medicine ETSU Campus 37614. (615) 929-6315. The medical school here had its origins in the Veterans Administration Medical Assistance and Health Training Act of 1972, which provided for the establishment of medical schools in those towns with a shortage of medical care providers which had both a Veterans Administration Hospital and a state university. Only a few cities in the entire country qualified under these criteria. (Other medical schools thus created include those at Marshall University, Wright State University, Texas A & M University, and the University of South Carolina.) The school here, named after two men instrumental in its founding, enrolled its first class in 1978 and graduated its first physicians in 1982.

Instructional facilities for the college are located on both the main university campus and on the grounds of the Mountain Home Veterans Administration facility. Clinical instruction takes place at five affiliated hospitals, chief among which is the VA. The medical library (located in Building 4 at the VA, near the ETSU campus on Dogwood Avenue) includes a historical collection of some 2000 medical texts from the early twentieth century and a small medical museum with local medical artifacts. Permission for tours should be cleared with the Dean's Office.

MEMPHIS

University of Tennessee Memphis Health Sciences Center 62 South Dunlap 38163. (901) 528-5516. In 1909 Tennessee had ten medical schools, some dating back to 1846: one in Chattanooga, two in Knoxville, three in Memphis, and four in Nashville, including Meharry and Vanderbilt. When Flexner reviewed the collection in 1910, he observed that "The State of Tennessee protects at this date more low-grade medical schools than any other Southern state." His recommendation was that the schools in Chattanooga, Knoxville, and Memphis close down operations, and that Vanderbilt — the only school in any position to do so — pick up their load. Vanderbilt decided that it had its hands full with its own operations, so the gauntlet was picked up by the University of Tennessee. In the several years following the Flexner Report, UT absorbed five of the schools and commenced operations in Memphis. The new college had its share of problems, but, over time, it thrived. In 1953 UT operated the largest medical school in the country, with 713 students, ahead of the University of Michigan with 683 and the University of Illinois with 678.

The current UT Memphis Health Science Center serves the entire state and includes colleges of nursing, dentistry, pharmacy, allied health, and graduate studies. The College of Dentistry was founded in 1878 and is the oldest in the South and the third oldest in the nation. The College of Nursing traces its origins to the Maury-

Mitchell Infirmary School of Nursing, established in 1889. The campus occupies almost three dozen buildings, the oldest of which date from the 1920s and 1930s. Tours can be arranged via the Office of University Relations [(901) 528-5516].

Baptist Memorial Hospital 899 Madison Avenue 38146. (901) 522-5252. At 2068 beds, this is the largest nongovernmental hospital in the United States. Founded in 1912 by a group of Southern Baptist leaders, the initial 150-bed facility began growing in the 1920s and hasn't stopped since. This remarkable expansion has been accomplished despite the fact that Baptist — because of its commitment to the separation of church and state — has never accepted any type of government grant. Completely self-supporting, the institution nonetheless provides $22 million in charity care annually, the largest amount of any private hospital in the South. The hospital has the most active neurosurgery service in the world (5600 admissions a year), and, because of this fact, Memphis has more neurosurgeons per capita than any city anywhere. BMH accomplishments through the years include:

1926	First physician office building in the country owned and operated by a hospital
1928	First hospital-owned-and-operated hotel for outpatients and visitors
1963	First in US to develop a radioisotope method for evaluating lipid metabolism (Carl Nurnberger and John Kersey)

BMH is now the flagship of a health-care system that includes nine other institutions in Arkansas, Mississippi, and Tennessee. BMH itself is spread out over several city blocks on the eastern end of the Memphis Medical Center, a huge complex of 45 buildings that includes almost a dozen hospitals. Tours of BMH are conducted by the hospital's Department of Religion hostesses. Call in advance to make arrangements.

St Jude Children's Research Hospital 332 North Lauderdale Street 38101. (901) 522-0300. This is a hospital that most people who watch television have heard about, though few are aware of its level of accomplishment. The hospital was founded by comedian Danny Thomas in return for guidance he received from St Jude Thaddeus, the patron saint of impossible, difficult, or hopeless causes. Thomas started raising money in the early 1950s, and the hospital finally opened its doors in 1962 as the world's first institution committed solely to conducting basic and clinical research on

Danny Thomas—ALSAC Pavilion, St Jude Children's Research Hospital
(Photo courtesy of Biomedical Communications, St Jude Hospital)

catastrophic childhood illnesses. The task of providing continuing support for the St Jude was taken up by the American Lebanese Syrian Associated Charities (ALSAC), whose sole function is raising money for St Jude. ALSAC is now the seventh largest not-for-profit fund-raising organization in the country. No patient pays a cent here, though St Jude is always happy to collect from third-party insurance payers when possible. Actually, St Jude provides primarily outpatient services, though it does have a 48-bed inpatient research facility. In cases of financial need, St Jude also supplies free transportation, meals, and lodging for patients and one parent.

    In terms of numbers of patients treated, St Jude is now the largest childhood cancer research center in the world. It admits only patients whose diseases are currently under study, and its list of accomplishments during its brief history is impressive:

1965   First immunologic diagnostic test for solid tumors in children
        (Warren Johnson)
1968   First curative treatment developed for Ewing's sarcoma, utilizing a
        combination of chemotherapy and radiotherapy
1971   Discovery of calmodulin, a protein that participates with calcium in
        regulating many cellular activities (George Chung)
1975   First demonstration of different types of acute lymphocytic leukemia
        in children (Luis Borella), paving the way for more effective treatment

St Jude is currently undergoing a $120 million expansion, so its appearance will change substantially. The principal attraction for visitors, however, will not be altered. This is the Danny Thomas ALSAC Pavilion across from the hospital entrance. Completed in 1985, this inviting building with a gold dome and Middle Eastern appearance celebrates the St Jude Hospital and its achievements and those of its founder Danny Thomas and its fund-raising wing, ALSAC. There are five large alcoves surrounding a central rotunda, each containing various exhibits. The rotunda itself is stunning, with marble and terrazzo interior, elaborately painted cupola, and beautifully drawn Arabic inscriptions. The Pavilion is open Monday through Friday, 10 AM to 4 PM, and Saturday, 11 AM to 4 PM.

NASHVILLE

Vanderbilt University Medical Center 1161 21st Avenue 37232. (615) 322-7311. This school of medicine traces its origins to 1850 when two local physicians set up a proprietary school that had a nominal affiliation with the University of Nashville. The school prospered until the Civil War, when the Union Army commandeered its facilities for an army hospital. After the War, the school limped along until the mid-1870s. At about that time, Cornelius Vanderbilt contributed a million dollars to start the university that subsequently bore his name. Vanderbilt University acquired the Medical Department of the University of Nashville, and, in 1875, one year before the rest of the University was established, Vanderbilt granted its first medical degree.

By the turn of the century, Vanderbilt had a reputation for being a progressive and scholarly school, and Flexner found it to be one of the few in the South worthy of support and encouragement.

Largely on the basis of Flexner's continued approval, Vanderbilt was singled out by Rockefeller's General Education Board and given more financial support than any other institution. As a result, Vanderbilt remained a regional and national pacesetter for the first half of the twentieth century and still continues to be a prestigious institution. Among its many accomplishments are

1925	First medical center with both the medical school and hospital under one roof
1962	First clinical research center in the country
1971	Earl Sutherland wins the Nobel Prize for the discovery of cyclic AMP, a compound crucial in regulating cellular growth and behavior

The Medical Center is located on the main Vanderbilt campus. The oldest medical structures here were constructed in the collegiate Gothic style and date from 1925, when they were built to house the medical school and hospital. The newest is a wonderfully light and airy modern ambulatory care facility, constucted in 1988 at a cost of $72 million (be sure to see the atrium courtyard, with its fountain, trees, and old-fashioned street lights). There is also a 680-bed University Hospital and a variety of other medical facilities on campus. Tours of the entire complex are available from the Volunteer Office.

Meharry Medical College 1005 Dr DB Todd Boulevard 37208. (615) 327-6111. Meharry was begun by the Methodist Church as part of its effort to assist the newly freed slave population after the Civil War. The school was founded in 1876 as the Medical Department of Central Tennessee College, eventually becoming an independent entity in 1915. The school's name is derived from the Meharry brothers, five white men who were major benefactors in the school's early years. It was one of the few medical schools in Tennessee (and, indeed, the South) to survive Flexner's scrutiny in 1910. Of the eight predominantly black medical schools operating in 1910, only Meharry and Howard survived. The College moved to its present site in 1931. The current 26-acre campus also houses the School of Dentistry (which dates from 1886), the George W Hubbard Hospital, and over a dozen other buildings.

In its early years, Meharry students labored without any bedside instruction, since they were not permitted in the City Hospital. In 1900 a black physician began a 23-bed private hospital called Mercy Hospital, and Meharry at last had facilities for clinical instruction. In 1910, the 80-bed Hubbard Hospital (named after the white physician who administered Meharry for its first 45 years) opened, and the college had its own teaching hospital.

Meharry has the distinction of having educated 40 percent of all black physicians and dentists practicing in the United States today. Two-thirds of Meharry graduates enter primary care, and three-fourths practice in medically underserved inner city and rural areas.

Tours are available through the Public Relations Office.

TEXAS

AUSTIN

Austin State Hospital 4110 Guadalupe Street 78751. (512) 452-0381. This is the oldest functioning hospital in the state and home of one of the three oldest public buildings in Texas. In 1856 the state legislature established the State Lunatic Asylum, designed more with the idea of protecting citizens and property from irrational acts than with any treatment in mind. Initially intended to hold 60 patients, the patient population soon expanded to 350 in 1882, 1400 in 1909, and 3200 (cared for by 10 doctors and 4 registered nurses) in 1949. Texas built many other state psychiatric institutions along the way, but the system as a whole limped along on a spartan budget. A 1949 US Public Health Survey found the Texas system to have the lowest standard of care in the nation. By 1957 the governor had made reform of the state hospitals a major priority.

In the years that followed, many of the buildings here were torn down, and others were constructed to take their place. A variety of modern programs have been added, and the current hospital population stands at about 500. The only old structure remaining is the original 1857 central administration building, once the centerpiece of an ambitious Kirkbride design that was never fully developed. Though new galleries were added near the turn of the century, the four-story limestone Victorian Italianate structure, still topped by its wooden dome, gives lasting evidence of the optimism with which it was originally constructed. Currently, a vigorous local effort to restore and refurbish this historic structure is underway. Tours are available from the hospital's Public Relations Office.

COLLEGE STATION

Texas A & M University College of Medicine University Drive 77843. (409) 845-3211. Students were first admitted to medical school classes here in 1977, though it was another six years before the College of Medicine had its own building. Now medical students take their first two years in the Medical Sciences Building on the Texas A&M campus, and then do their clinical work in Temple, Texas, at the 350-bed Scott & White Hospital and the 1100-bed Olin E Teague Veterans Center. Tours are available via the School Relations Office.

DALLAS

University of Texas Southwestern Medical Center 5323 Harry Hines Boulevard 75235. (214) 688-3111. The medical school here began as a proprietary enterprise called the Southwestern Medical College in 1943, with classes conducted in some ramshackle army barracks referred to ever after as "The Shacks." The school became part of the University of Texas system in 1949, but it remained in such a sorry state that the chairmen of every clinical department (save one) resigned en masse. The school, of course, was on probation but somehow managed to survive. In 1955 it moved to an entirely new facility on a 60-acre site adjoining Parkland Memorial Hospital, and the ascent to its present eminence began. The booming Texas economy and the growing role of the federal government in medical education created opportunities for an enterprising school administration, and Southwestern was alert to all of them. The medical center increased rapidly in size and scope, achieving international recognition in 1985 when Joseph Goldstein and Mike Brown won the Nobel Prize for work that uncovered the receptor-mediated endocytosis by which cells select and envelop cholesterol-laden particles from the bloodstream. This is simply the most dramatic and obvious evidence of the scientific "arrival" of which the center is immensely proud. Tours of the campus are available for groups by calling (214) 688-3404.

Parkland Memorial Hospital 5201 Harry Hines Boulevard 75235. (214) 590-8000. Parkland's beginnings stem from a small shack intended to provide medical care for paupers, established in 1872. Considered fit only for "the friendless and down-and-outers," the shack was soon replaced by a marginally more adequate building, where all patients — men, women, and children — were fed, examined, and given surgery in the same room. Finally, in 1894, a true hospital was built and named "Parkland" for the parklands in which it was situated. The hospital gradually increased in size and complexity, and, in 1943, it became the primary teaching hospital of the Southwestern Medical College. In 1954 Parkland moved to its present location.

Parkland leaped into the world's attention on November 22, 1963, when the fatally wounded President John F Kennedy and the critically injured Governor John Connally were brought here after being shot. In the next 48 hours, Parkland became the temporary seat of government for the United States and for the state of Texas, the site of the death of the 35th president, the site of the ascendency of the 36th president, and the site of the death of Kennedy's accused assassin. As terrible as all these events were, the hospital performed admirably.

Parkland is also known for having established the first pediatric burn unit in the country (1961) and the nation's first pediatric trauma intensive care unit (1984). Now a 940-bed facility, Parkland provides tours for visitors via the Community Relations Department. Something everyone wants to see is the John F Kennedy Memorial Wall in the lobby, which pays tribute to the late president and describes the role of PMH in this tragic part of the nation's history.

Baylor University Medical Center   3500 Gaston Avenue 75246. (214) 820-0111. This institution was officially chartered in 1903 as the Texas Baptist Memorial Sanitarium. The hospital was established, in large part, to provide a hospital for faculty associated with the University of Dallas Medical Department, which had been founded in 1900. At that time, the only other hospitals in Dallas were St Paul's (a private hospital whose physicians had opposed the idea of having a medical school in town), and Parkland (a public hospital, "unsuitable" for private patients and too far removed from the medical school building to be convenient for teaching). In 1903 the University of Dallas Medical Department was transferred to the control of Baylor University in Waco, a Baptist-sponsored institution, so the union of the school and the sanitarium under joint Baptist sponsorship seemed both natural and appropriate.

In the early years of the twentieth century the medical college limped along with numerous problems (Flexner called it "inferior"), and the far more vigorous and successful sanitarium tended to feel it was "carrying" its weaker sister. By the 1920s Dallas had become a boom town, and a thriving "Baylor-in-Dallas" had expanded to include the sanitarium and schools of medicine, dentistry, nursing, and pharmacy, all under the authority of the parent institution in Waco. In 1921 the sanitarium was renamed Baylor Hospital. When the Depression hit and boom turned to bust, the medical center —like many others across the country—was left with an excess of financial obligations and a dwindling income. The institution responded with what became known as the "Baylor

Plan," a "sickness benefit plan" for Dallas schoolteachers, in which each teacher contributed fifty cents a month and received in return assurance of complete medical care at Baylor Hospital. Soon the plan expanded to include local newspaper employees and others. Local insurance companies, enraged at the successful competition, filed suit, maintaining that Baylor had violated its nonprofit status and that the hospital should have to pay taxes. The bitter dispute went all the way to the Texas Legislature, where Baylor ultimately prevailed. The resultant media attention brought nationwide interest. The Baylor Plan was soon adopted in New Jersey and then in other states. In 1934 the American Hospital Association decided to set up a central office to coordinate individual plans on a nationwide basis, and the national organization was named Blue Cross. By 1940 more than 5 million persons were enrolled and, by 1985, 90 million.

Baylor's biggest challenge came in the years following 1939, when a group of local citizens decided to set up the Southwestern Medical Foundation. The Foundation raised funds for medical education and research in Dallas, with the intent of either improving what they regarded as Baylor's outmoded medical college or, failing that, setting up a competing "modern" school. The concern of some Foundation members was both economic and sectarian, centering on the strict control exerted by the firmly Baptist Baylor-in-Waco, whose tight purse strings seemed to make a modern, technically adequate teaching program impossible. As the nonsectarian Foundation accumulated more money and influence, Baylor-at-Waco found the Dallas environment to be increasingly hostile to its medical college, and, in 1943, the parent institution accepted a generous offer from Houston and moved the medical college to Houston's newly founded Texas Medical Center. Badly shaken, the Baylor University Hospital remained in Dallas, sharpened its focus on clinical service, and gradually resumed its position of prominence. In 1946 BUH organized the nation's first hospital surgical tissue committee.

The Baylor University Medical Center now includes almost 1300 beds, spread out among 5 hospitals. Administratively a part of Baylor University in Waco, the Center also includes the University's School of Nursing and College of Dentistry (the pharmacy school closed in 1931).

GALVESTON

University of Texas Medical Branch at Galveston Eighth and Mechanic Streets 77550. (409) 761-1011. The first medical school in

Texas began in 1865 and was called Galveston Medical College, an outgrowth of Soule University. Marginal from the beginning, the school folded in 1873, to be resurrected that same year as the Texas Medical College and Hospital. In 1881 the Texas Legislature authorized the founding of the University of Texas and a medical department. Unwilling to settle the controversial issue of where such institutions should be located, the Legislature left the matter up to a popular vote. The referendum determined that the University should be based in Austin and its medical branch in Galveston. Anticipating the competition from the state-supported school, the Texas Medical College shut down. In 1889 John Sealy Hospital was constructed and two years later, medical classes began. The school limped along with inadequate support for the first decade, but, ironically, the devastating Galveston hurricane of 1900 called attention to the facility's limitations and, as a result, for the first time the school received adequate financing. When Flexner examined the state's four medical schools in 1909, he found that only Galveston's graduates "deserve the right to practice among its inhabitants." The John Sealy Hospital Training School for Nurses (the predecessor of the UT School of Nursing at Galveston) opened in 1890 as the first university-affiliated school in the country.

"Old Red," The Ashbel Smith Building, University of Texas Medical Branch, Galveston, Texas (Courtesy of The University of Texas Medical Branch at Galveston)

Today the UTMB campus comprises 64 acres and over 70 buildings, including 4 schools, 7 hospitals, and numerous affiliated institutions. The campus is pleased to provide tours to groups of 5 or more, if arrangements are made in advance with the Office of Public Affairs [(409) 761-2618]. Tours are geared to special interests, but the highlight is usually **"Old Red,"** the 1891 original home of the Medical Branch. This is a brilliant Romanesque revival structure, a masterpiece of ornate red brickwork, red granite, and sandstone. Thoroughly restored in the late 1980s, this is a stunning building. Inside "Old Red," visitors can see the Hall of Medical History, consisting of twelve beautifully displayed statues (by sculptress Doris Appel) representing outstanding individuals in medical history. Also, don't miss the Grand Staircase, the pressed tin ceiling, and the Amphitheater. The Moody Medical Library, two blocks away, contains a fine history of medicine collection, with excellent collections of microscopes and medically related stamps and prints.

St Mary's Hospital 404 Eighth Street 77550. (409) 763-5301. This, the first private hospital in Texas, was founded in 1867 by three Sisters of Charity of the Incarnate Word, who came here from France. Six months later, St Mary's became a bastion for the afflicted in a yellow fever epidemic that killed 1150 in Galveston. Today, St Mary's is a 271-bed hospital, still located at its original site. Most of the original building was destroyed in the 1900 hurricane (which killed more than 6000 people in Galveston), but some elements of that structure have been incorporated into the present facility. Tours are available from Public Relations.

HOUSTON

Texas Medical Center 1155 Holcombe at Bertner 77030. (713) 790-1136. The idea of the Texas Medical Center was conceived by Houston's financial leaders, and no one has regretted the bold initiative that led to TMC's development. Though Houston has suffered grievously from an oil-based depression for many years, the TMC is booming, with over $1.5 billion in projects either planned or under way. TMC's cornerstones were the private Hermann Hospital, the Texas Cancer Hospital (initially funded in 1941), and Baylor College of Medicine (which moved here from Dallas in 1943). The TMC was incorporated in 1945, and additional elements were gradually added to the fold. TMC was catapulted into international fame by the remarkable breakthroughs in cardiac surgery, accomplished first by Michael DeBakey and later by his protégé Denton Cooley. Their successes attracted further money from and participation by the Houston community, and the TMC's growth was given a dramatic boost.

The TMC is now the world's largest concentration of health care facilities: it includes more than 40 institutions spread out over a 550-acre tract. It boasts 55,000 employees, 10,000 students, 2 medical schools, a dental school, 3 nursing schools, schools of public health and pharmacy, a high school for the health professions, 13 hospitals, a library for the entire complex, and numerous other related components. Almost all of this is accessible to visitors. The Assistance Center (at the above address) has maps and brochures to help you find your way around this vast complex and offers free tours daily.

Baylor College of Medicine   One Baylor Plaza 77030. (713) 798-4951. Founded in 1900 as the Medical Department of the University of Dallas, three years later the college developed an affiliation with Baylor University in Waco, and became known as Baylor University College of Medicine. The Flexner Report described the school as being "without resources, without ideals, without facilities" — though paradoxically Flexner thought the school might have a future if "large sums . . . were at hand." Baylor managed to survive, with a vigorous upgrading, and, by 1916, the school had earned an "A" rating. However, burdened by financial problems during the Great Depression and feeling unsupported and unappreciated by the Dallas medical community, the school reached another major crossroad. The Houston Chamber of Commerce and the MD Anderson Foundation seized the opportunity and invited the College of Medicine to come to Houston and become a cornerstone of the Texas Medical Center. In 1943, after receiving pledges for a $2 million lump sum plus $50,000 a year for 10 years as well as a gift of 20 prime acres of land, BCOM moved from Dallas to Houston. In 1969 BCOM severed its ties with Baylor University and became an independent entity, with Dr Michael DeBakey as its first president. Landmark medical events that have taken place here include:

1953	First successful carotid endarterectomy
1954	First successful resection and replacement grafts of the aorta (both thoracic and abdominal)
1956	First successful resection and graft of the ascending aorta
1964	First successful coronary artery bypass operation

The **John C. Haley Museum** (located in room M017 of the DeBakey Center for Biomedical Education and Research) offers a small anatomy collection which is open to the public during normal business hours, Monday through Friday. Tours are available through Public Affairs [(713) 798-4710].

University of Texas Health Science Center at Houston 6431 Fannin Street 77225. (713) 792-2121. The University of Texas Medical School at Houston was established in 1969, and classes were begun in 1970. The legislature requires that the school enroll 200 students per class, and that 90 percent of students in each class be residents of Texas. Though there are a number of affiliated hospitals, the primary clinical teaching site is Hermann Hospital (established 1925), which adjoins the medical school and is connected to it on a number of floors. The Health Science Center includes a Dental Branch (which traces its origins to 1905), a School of Public Health (1967), a School of Nursing (1972), as well as other components. Tours of the UTHSC-H, located in the Texas Medical Center, are conducted by Community Affairs [(713) 792-5070].

High School for Health Professions 3100 Shenandoah Street 77021. (713) 741-2410. Begun in 1972 this was the first school of its kind in the country. For its first eight years, the school's classes were conducted on the campus of Baylor College of Medicine, but since then classes have been taught in this $7.5 million building. Applicants are required to have a "serious" interest in health professions careers and to have above-average grades. Students receive training and experience in patient care, public and environmental health, dental sciences, and medical laboratories. Discipline and attendance problems are said to be nonexistent, and about 65 percent of the students go on to health professions careers. There are no provisions for tours by the general public.

Hermann Hospital 6411 Fannin Street 77030. (713) 797-4011. Hermann Hospital was established as a private community hospital in 1925 and was the first hospital in the Texas Medical Center. Now the primary teaching hospital for the University of Texas Medical School at Houston, the 900-bed institution operates the largest hospital-based air-transport system in the country. Hermann's fleet currently consists of 3 helicopters, which together have logged over 30,000 missions, as well as fixed-wing aircraft. This is a big, busy, modern facility, but the most attractive pieces of architecture may well be the original 1925 building, a series of 3 pavilions with a beautiful tiled lobby, a lush courtyard, elaborate stone detailing on the granite facade, and a profusion of elegant amenities. Tours can be arranged through Volunteer Services.

St Luke's Episcopal Hospital 6720 Bertner Street 77030. (713) 791-2011. Though opened only as recently as 1954, St Luke's has rapidly grown to its present size of 949 beds. While distinguished in many areas, it is in the area of cardiac surgery that the hospital has achieved its greatest international acclaim. Both here and at its component **Texas Heart Institute** (founded in 1962), surgeons under the leadership of surgeon-in-chief Denton Cooley have performed over 70,000 open-heart and 21,000 vascular procedures. It was here that Cooley performed the nation's first successful cardiac transplantation in 1968. The world's first implantation of a temporary artificial heart was performed at THI in 1969. Tours of St Luke's can be arranged by contacting the Public Affairs office. THI tours should be arranged by calling (713) 522-7060.

University of Texas MD Anderson Cancer Center 6723 Bertner Avenue 77030. (713) 792-2121. Established in 1941 as the State Cancer Hospital, with substantial financial support from the MD Anderson Foundation, this hospital has gone on to become (along with Memorial Sloan-Kettering in NYC) one of the two largest comprehensive cancer treatment and research facilities in the nation. MD Anderson moved to its present site in the Texas Medical Center in 1954, though there has been significant expansion since. Seventy percent of patients here are from Texas and are charged on the basis of their ability to pay. Of the remainder, the majority are from elsewhere in the United States, but one in twenty patients comes from a foreign country. Tours of the 514-bed facility are available weekdays [(713) 792-3363].

Methodist Hospital 6565 Fannin 77030. (713) 790-3311. Established in 1924 as a 90-bed community general hospital, Methodist — at over 1500 acute-care beds — is one of the largest, single-site, private hospitals in the country. In true Texas fashion, the statistics here are astounding. In a year, the hospital consumes 2.5 million medicine cups and 2.5 million syringes, 177 miles of EKG tape, and 142 miles of sutures, and more than 26,000 bed sheets and almost 15,000 patient gowns. Though Methodist was the first hospital to move to the newly developing Texas Medical Center in 1951, much of the seven-building complex is new. The entrance includes a three-lane circular drive that extends an entire block and opens onto a lobby that boasts a sculpture fountain and a lush tropical landscape that fills a two-story, sky-lighted atrium. Nearby, there's a 300-pound bronze bust of heart surgeon Michael DeBakey (who performed many of his operations here), presented by King Leopold of Belgium. Methodist is Baylor's primary private adult teaching hospital. Tours are available via Public Relations.

LUBBOCK

Texas Tech University School of Medicine 3601 Fourth Street 79430. (806) 743-3111. In the 1960s, West Texas had a physician/ population ratio half the national average, and 15 of its counties had no physicians at all. The region includes an area of 165,000 square miles — larger than all but 4 of the states in the union — and a population at the time of over 2 million — more than that of 17 states. Still, getting legislative and gubernatorial approval for a medical school here was no easy matter, and the school finally got its charter by combining it with a bill to establish the UT Medical School in Houston. The school was created in 1969 and opened in 1972 as a separate entity from, but located on the grounds of, Texas Tech University. In 1979 the encompassing entity was named the Texas Tech University Health Sciences Center, under whose umbrella Schools of Nursing (1981) and Allied Health (1983) were added. All basic science training occurs in Lubbock, but clinical training is conducted at four clinical campuses in Lubbock, Amarillo, El Paso, and Odessa. Tours of the Lubbock campus may be arranged by calling Public Relations [(806) 743-2907].

SAN ANTONIO

University of Texas Health Science Center at San Antonio 7703 Floyd Curl Drive 78284. (512) 567-7000. The medical school here was authorized by the legislature in 1959, but a heated controversy developed about whether the school should be centered in the inner city, with its needy indigent population, or out here in the Oak Hills area. After various legal maneuvers, funding difficulties, a referendum, and special legislative bills were settled, the school finally admitted its first class in 1968. The complex became a Health Sciences Center in 1972, and now includes schools of medicine, nursing, dentistry, allied health sciences, and graduate studies — as well as a Veterans Administration Hospital and a variety of other affiliated hospitals and institutions. The Medical Center Hospital is actually the oldest component, tracing its origins to the Robert B Green Hospital, founded in 1915 by the city to provide indigent health care. Burdened by financial difficulties, the hospital closed for a couple of years in the 1950s, reopening in 1955 (under county auspices) as the Bexar County Hospital. BCH has gradually shifted all its inpatient services to the Medical Center Hospital. Tours of the 100-acre campus can be arranged through the News and Information Office.

The US Army Medical Department Museum Harry Wurzbach and Stanley Roads, Fort Sam Houston 78234. (512) 221-2358. This

Combat Medic Memorial, U.S. Army Medical Museum, Ft. Sam Houston, Texas *(Courtesy of the US Army Medical Department Museum)*

museum tells the story of the Army medical department from 1775 until the present. The collection consists of both US Army medical equipment and that of various adversaries over the centuries, from Germany and Japan to China and Viet Nam. There are uniforms and medical equipment, artwork and photographs, and even a collection of restored and replica ambulances. The $2.5 million building (completed in 1989) that houses the museum has been constructed entirely with private contributions. Be sure not to miss the Combat Medic Memorial Statue, to the right of the entrance. Admission is free, and the museum's hours are Wednesday through Sunday, 10 AM to 4 PM.

The museum came to Fort Sam Houston in 1946, where it joined the Brooke Army Medical Center, the Academy of Health Sciences, and the more inclusive Health Services Command. BAMC is the lineal descendent of the Fort Sam Houston Post Surgeon's Office, begun in 1878. It is best known for having developed the burn-center concept during the Korean War, and, in fact, it was the only burn center in the United States until 1960. The Academy of Health Sciences is the largest military school for allied health professionals in the free world, and each year plays host to some 45,000 students in residence for varying lengths of time, and coordinates some 26,000 correspondence courses. The HSC is responsible for all Army health care in the United States, its territories, and the Pacific Basin, and, as such, each day administers some 5500 inpatient beds, 40,000 dental procedures, 8000 immunizations, and 567,000 laboratory procedures.

Hangar 9 — Edward H White II Memorial Museum of Flight Medicine Brooks Air Force Base 78235. (512) 536-2203. Aviation medicine began with the realization that more airplane accidents were due to human frailty than mechanical error. In 1918 the Air Service Medical Research Laboratory (later to become the School of Aviation Medicine) began its work in New York State. The School moved to Brooks in 1926 and was renamed the School of Aerospace Medicine in 1961. The museum here had its origins in 1970 when it was installed in this hangar, the only surviving World War I (1917) hangar in the United States. Dedicated to the memory of San Antonio native Edward White (the first man to walk in space), who was killed in the Apollo I spacecraft fire in 1965, the museum has 8000 square feet of space. Exhibits here cover the history of the base, the evolution of aerospace medicine, and the development of manned flight. Displays include the Barany Chair (used in 1918 to test the equilibrium of student pilots), the oldest known low-pressure chamber (built in 1918), rotational flight simulators, space cabin simulators, and exhibits concerning aeromedical evacuation, as well as early flight-nurse combat training and equipment. The museum is open weekdays, 8 AM to 4 PM, and there is no admission charge. Interested visitors can also arrange group tours of laboratory facilities of the USAF School of Aerospace Medicine by calling the Office of Public Affairs [(512) 536-3234].

UTAH

SALT LAKE CITY

University of Utah Health Sciences Center Medical Center Drive 84132. (801) 581-7201. The University of Utah inaugurated its two-year preclinical medical course in 1905. Flexner said "The spirit is excellent," but the school needed "more liberal support." When it expanded to a four-year program in 1942, it was the only four-year medical school operating between Denver and the Pacific Coast, in an area stretching from the Mexican to the Canadian borders, a land area comprising one-fourth of the United States. The medical school was hampered early on by a terrible physical facility. At the beginning, classes were taught in stables, research was carried out in a renovated army latrine, and clinical teaching was centered at the dilapidated and politically corrupt Salt Lake County General Hospital. However, the four-year school had an exceptionally strong faculty, and the institution soon achieved national prominence.

In 1945 the medical school was awarded the first extramural research grant ever by the National Institutes of Health, a $92,000 plum that was an enormous boon to the fledgling research program. Shortly thereafter, the University of Utah became the first medical school to use a VA hospital in its teaching program, an experiment that was such a success that it inspired a nationwide system. The institution's most dramatic achievement occurred in 1982, when surgeon William DeVries implanted the first permanent total artificial heart in dentist Barney Clark.

The present medical center dates from 1965, though it has been much expanded since. The new University Hospital, spectacularly sited in front of the towering Wasatch Mountains, dates from 1981. Though owned by the people of Utah, the University Hospital gets only 3 percent of its budget from legislative appropriations and the School of Medicine gets only 12 percent (the remainder comes from patient fees, research grants, and gifts).

Holy Cross Hospital 1045 East First South Street 84102. (801) 350-4111. This was the first hospital established by the Sisters of the Holy Cross in the United States. The hospital was founded in 1875 and received its support principally from area miners and railroad workers, who contributed one dollar per month in return for a guarantee of health care. The miners were largely Irish immigrants (there were 800 Catholics in Utah Territory in 1873, which made Utah the largest geographic parish in the United States), so a Catholic hospital filled an important need. The mines were primarily silver-mining operations, but lead carbonate was a major by-product. The lead dust and the fumes in the smelters predisposed the miners to lead poisoning from lead-impregnated food, air, and clothing. From the early 1870s until 1903, over 6000 patients were treated for lead poisoning, mostly by rest, clean air, and wholesome food. The lead-induced anemia, colic and peripheral nerve paralysis were seldom permanent, except in severe or repeated instances of poisoning. Just after the turn of the century, new mining practices and safety measures resulted in a dramatically lower incidence of lead-induced health problems.

Now a 300-bed acute-care hospital, Holy Cross can be toured by advance arrangements with Community Relations. Be sure to see the Chapel, completed in 1904, with its Italian marble altar.

LDS Hospital 325 Eighth Avenue 84143. (801) 321-1100. When the Mormons settled in Utah in the mid-nineteenth century, they tended to have little affection and respect for allopathic physicians, and there is no record of any allopath practicing outside of Salt Lake City until the 1870s. Caring for the sick tended to be regarded as a natural role for women, and the midwives and early healers of the area were all women. For many years the only doctors who practiced among the Mormons were Thomsonians, doctors who practiced the art of herbal medicine devised by Samuel Thomson in the early nineteenth century. Thomson's book, *New Guide to Health; or Botanic Family Physician,* was immensely popular all over the country, and, selling the book and a license to practice medicine for $20, Thomson soon became a wealthy man. However, as medicine developed a stronger scientific base and particularly as surgery became safer, with the advent of asepsis, the Mormons' views of physicians began to change. In the 1870s, Brigham Young decided to send his nephew and several other young Mormons to medical school in New York City.

The first Mormon-affiliated hospital opened in a small building in 1882, but it remained a marginal affair and closed down in 1890. In 1905 the Church opened the Dr WH Groves Latter-day Saints Hospital, named after a wealthy dentist who bequeathed funds for its establishment. The LDS Hospital remained under church sponsorship until 1975, when the Church decided to get out of the hospital business and established the nonsectarian, nonprofit Intermountain Health Care, Inc, to assume control of 15 hospitals in Utah, Idaho, and Wyoming. LDS Hospital is now a tertiary care facility that serves as a referral center for some 75 hospitals in the Intermountain area. Tours are available through Public Relations.

VERMONT

BRATTLEBORO

Brattleboro Retreat 75 Linden Street 05301. (802) 257-7785. Although the nation already had 10 hospitals for the mentally ill when this institution was founded in 1834, the Brattleboro has turned out to be one of the most durable and most interesting of the group. From the beginning, it was a private institution, but its first name, the Vermont Asylum for the Insane, and the fact that it served large numbers of state-supported patients, made it seem like a quasi-public institution. The Asylum's initial orientation was "moral treatment" — the reform orientation of the time, which led to the patients being treated with warmth and respect in a family-like setting — and the institution managed to maintain the atmosphere longer than most such psychiatric facilities. Clearly, one of its major assets has been its stunningly beautiful and bucolic setting, occupying as many as 2000 acres in Vermont's Green Mountains, bordering both the Connecticut and West rivers.

In 1837 the Asylum established its own dairy farm, both to feed the population and to provide useful occupation to the patients, making it the first psychiatric hospital in this country to have its own farm. The endeavor proved so successful that most state psychiatric institutions soon developed farms of their own. Now, over a century-and-a-half later, Brattleboro is one of the few whose farm continues to operate. In 1842 the Asylum was likewise the first to start its own patient-run newspaper. In 1878 it became the first psychiatric hospital to build a gymnasium and bowling alley for patient use, and in 1885 it became the first to inaugurate an outdoor therapeutic camping program. In the years that followed it further pioneered by building a swimming pool (1910) and a golf course (1914) — and it is probably still the only psychiatric hospital in the world to have a 70-meter ski jump on the property (1931). Clearly, this is a place where recreation is, and always has been, an important part of the treatment program.

In 1893 after the state completed the public Vermont State Asylum for the Insane at Waterbury, the private institution at Brattleboro changed its name to the Brattleboro Retreat, both to distinguish it from the public hospital and to convey an impression of restfulness. The impression of restfulness remains to this day. Situated on 1600 acres, surrounded by mountains, woods, and a wildlife refuge, this is a remarkably attractive and peaceful institution. The Retreat currently includes some 60 buildings, many of which are over 100 years old. The original Main Building is an 1838 vintage, red-brick, slate-roofed, rambling structure with multiple additions. On the west side of Linden Street, there is a 65-foot high, cylindrical, crenellated granite tower. This monument was built in 1887 by both patients and staff to commemorate Brattleboro's 50th birthday.

The administration is happy to provide tours to interested persons. Call the Marketing Division to make arrangements.

BURLINGTON

University of Vermont Medical Center Colchester and East Avenues 05405. (802) 656-2200. The Medical Department of the University of Vermont was founded in 1822, but it fared poorly and was closed in 1836 for lack of students, due largely to competition from schools at Castleton and Woodstock in Vermont, and Hanover in New Hampshire. The school reopened in 1854 and has been graduating students ever since. The Woodstock institution opened in 1827 under the name of the Clinical School of Medicine and was affiliated briefly with Waterville College and Middlebury College. It eventually closed in 1856. Since the demise of Castleton in 1862, the University of Vermont College of Medicine has been the only medical school in the state.

Since 1879 UVCM's partner in medical education and treatment has been the Mary Fletcher Hospital. In 1967, for reasons of economy of scale, the Mary Fletcher Hospital combined with Burlington's second hospital, the DeGoesbriand (est. 1922), to form the Medical Center Hospital of Vermont. Today, the Medical Center Hospital, the College of Medicine, the School of Nursing, and the School of Allied Health Sciences are all located on the 425-acre main university campus, which overlooks Burlington and Lake Champlain. Though this is a modern medical center, one early medical school structure still exists on campus. Pomeroy Hall, built in 1829 for medical instruction, is located on Main Street near its intersection with University Place.

Tours can be arranged by calling the Dean's Office [(802) 656-2150].

CASTLETON

Castleton Medical Museum Castleton State College. Seminary Street 05735. (802) 468-5611. This is the second oldest building of medical instruction surviving in the nation, yielding only to Davidge Hall in Baltimore in age. The Castleton Medical Academy dates from 1818, when it was founded to formalize the popular system of lectures that had been given for several years by local practitioners Selah Gridley and Theodore Woodward. Castleton was a thriving institution for its first decade, but it then went through a period of turmoil, troubled by rival schools, financial problems, insufficient faculty, and some grave-robbing scandals. In 1838 it suspended operation, reopening in 1840. In 1846 it received an application for enrollment by Elizabeth Blackwell. (Miss Blackwell was accepted as a student by the dean here, but she had already enrolled in Geneva

The second oldest surviving building of medical instruction in the United States, Castleton State College, Vermont *(Credit: Castleton State College photo)*

Medical College by the time she had received her acceptance from Castleton.) The school eventually became a casualty of the Civil War, closing down operations forever in 1862. During its years of operation, it awarded 1400 medical degrees. The museum building dates from 1821, when it was erected as the first building owned by the college. The two-story late-Federal period structure, with its charming cupola, has been moved twice, arriving at its present location in 1968 and finally being restored in 1988. The exhibits include a nice display on William Beaumont (who received his medical apprenticeship at St Albans, Vermont, and who joined the Medical Society of Vermont in 1812) and a growing collection of Vermont medical memorabilia. The museum is intended to be open weekdays during normal business hours (but, if it is closed, check in one of the main-floor offices in nearby Woodruff Hall).

VIRGINIA

ALEXANDRIA   *(See* **Washington, DC)**

ARLINGTON   *(See* **Washington, DC)**

CHARLOTTESVILLE

University of Virginia Medical Center Jefferson Park Avenue 22908. (804) 924-0211. This is certainly the only college of medicine in the country whose buildings were designed, curriculum developed, and faculty chosen by a president of the United States. After Thomas Jefferson retired from the presidency, he devoted considerable effort to establishing the entire state university here. No detail was so small that it escaped his attention. The curriculum was based on the Jeffersonian view that medicine should be taught from a cultural rather than a practical perspective, and thus there was no clinical instruction. The length of the teaching sessions (ten months) was unusually long for the era. Jefferson personally chose the single professor of the School of Anatomy and Medicine. Robley Dunglison was not permitted to practice medicine outside the university and thus became the first full-time professor of medicine in the country. The school opened in 1825, and the first physicians were graduated in 1828. Medical degrees have been conferred every year since, with the exception of 1862 when the Civil War intervened. The University Hospital was established in 1901 as a 25-bed facility. When Flexner visited here in 1909, he noted the "good teaching laboratories" and "enthusiastic teachers of modern training and ideals."

The first dedicated medical school building, the Anatomical Theater, was completed in 1827. Designed by Jefferson, it was unfortunately demolished in 1938 to make way for another building. However, the temporary medical school building, where Robley Dunglison lived and taught prior to the completion of the Anatomical Theater, still stands on the main university campus. Known as Pavilion 10, it was also designed by Jefferson and is now occupied as a faculty residence. The primary focus of the Health Sciences Center campus is the modern 850-bed teaching hospital, with its elegant and airy lobby. Buried deep within its various additions is the old 1901 structure, though it is all but impossible to discern. Tours of the hospital are available via the News Office.

FREDERICKSBURG

Hugh Mercer Apothecary Shop 1020 Caroline Street 22401. (703) 373-3362. Hugh Mercer practiced medicine in the Fredericksburg area for fifteen years before he joined the revolutionary effort, ultimately distinguishing himself as a war hero and dying as a brigadier general at the Battle of Princeton. The building here dates from c. 1750 (it is reputedly the oldest building to house a pharmacy in America) and is a restoration of what Mercer's combination medical office and apothecary, originally at this location, probably looked like. Visitors are treated to a tour by costumed guides, conducted in the first person in the "living history format," with events set in 1774. The assumption is that Dr Mercer is temporarily absent and our guide, an eager house servant, gives us a tour of the office and shop, telling us about Dr Mercer and his preferred remedies and therapeutic methods for various ills that might have motivated our visit. This approach brings history to life and gives us a more thorough understanding of the various medical and pharmaceutical paraphernalia on display. The shop is open daily from April 1 through October 31 from 9 AM to 5 PM, with more limited hours the rest of the year. There is a modest admission charge.

HAMPTON

Hampton Training School for Nurses Emancipation Drive at West County Road 23668. (804) 727-5252. The Hampton Normal and Agricultural Institute was founded in 1868 as a school for postemancipation blacks. In 1890 a teacher at the Hampton Institute became concerned about the health of former slaves in the area and resolved to found a nurses's training school to help remedy the problem. A program for black nursing students had been opened at Spelman College in Atlanta in 1886, and the Hampton school became the second in the country to admit blacks when it opened in May, 1891, followed the same month by Provident in Chicago and the following year by the Tuskegee Institute. Known formally as the Hampton Training School for Nurses, the School had the early advantage of an associated hospital. A small house was converted into a ten-bed, two-ward facility and christened "Dixie Hospital" — named not for the South, but rather after a horse that the school's founder had ridden when visiting the sick. In any event, the school was known ever after, informally and sometimes even officially, as the Dixie Hospital Nursing Program. Though much of the Dixie program's history was intertwined with the Hampton Institute, it was technically independent of the older and more famous institution. In 1892, when the school leased a new site on land owned by the Institute, the hospital building was transported to its new location by the students who physically lifted it and carried it by hand across fields to its new location.

Though Dixie's patients and students tended to be predominantly black, at various times both included substantial numbers of whites. Still, the program primarily served the function of training black nurses to take care of black patients. By 1900 there were a dozen such programs in the country, and by 1950 there were about

50. Many black nursing programs were not freestanding such as this one, but — especially in the South — rather were one-half of a dual program, with a relatively well-funded white training school and a significantly less well-supported black training school.

In 1913 Dixie built a new 65-bed brick structure and nurses's quarters at 503 East Queen Street. The hospital expanded and moved several times over the decades that followed, and in 1973 it was renamed Hampton General Hospital. The Dixie diploma training program for registered nurses was phased out in the 1950s, ironically being replaced in the area by a baccalaureate program begun at the Hampton Institute in 1943.

Both the 1892 Dixie Hospital building and its 1913 replacement are still standing, the former being located on Emancipation Drive, having served as a faculty residence for decades. The 1913 structure was used as a private psychiatric hospital (Bayberry) for a number of years, beginning in 1961, and is now used as an honors dormitory.

Tours of the facilities can be arranged through the Administration office at Hampton Institute.

NORFOLK

Eastern Virginia Medical School of the Medical College of Hampton Roads Colley Avenue and Olney Road 23501. (804) 446-6050. This medical school was founded in 1973, because of the community's need for convenient access to tertiary medical care. In the previous decade, the Hampton Roads area (i.e., the greater Norfolk metropolitan area) had been identified as the nation's second largest population concentration without a university-based health science center. The "Medical College of Hampton Roads" is actually an administrative umbrella for several enterprises, and the academic medical institution prefers to be known as Eastern Virginia Medical School. This is a community-based medical school, so clinical training is conducted primarily in preexisting community hospitals. The EVMS campus, with its basic science and administrative facilities, is located near the Elizabeth River at the Norfolk end of the Midtown Tunnel. Included here is the **Jones Institute of Reproductive Medicine,** which in 1981 claimed the first in vitro fertilization baby born in the United States. Tours of the campus are available via the Public Affairs office.

DePaul Medical Center 150 Kingsley Lane 23505. (804) 489-5000. The story of this hospital's founding is really the story of "The Great Pestilence," the yellow fever epidemic that raged through the Tidewater in 1855, killing 2000 people. The epidemic began when a steamer from the West Indies, ignoring orders of local health officials, discharged bilge water into the Elizabeth River, releasing swarms of mosquito larvae bearing the deadly disease. The sickness was not long in coming, and, at the epidemic's height, between 50 and 80 people died each day, and the only traffic on the streets was hearses and doctors and nurses making their rounds. Prior to 1855 the only hospitals in the Tidewater had been the Navy hospital in Portsmouth and a merchant seaman's infirmary in Norfolk. Neither was officially available to the public. As a result, eight sisters of the Daughters of Charity who taught in a local orphanage began to nurse the sick, first door-to-door, and then in a local mansion donated by a benefactress. In 1856 the Hospital of St Vincent de Paul was chartered. The hospital thrived. In 1892 it opened a training school for nurses which continues to operate today. In 1899 the hospital was totally destroyed by fire and was replaced with a magnificent structure (crowned with a copper dome), boasting Russian and Turkish baths for patients. When the hospital moved to a new location in 1944, it was during World War II, and structural steel was considered a strategic raw material. So the entire hospital (now renamed DePaul) was built by the centuries-old "keystone" method in which steel reinforcement is not necessary. Since that time, many new wings and additions have been added, and the World War II structure is barely visible. Tours of the 400-bed hospital are available from the Public Relations Department.

PORTSMOUTH

Portsmouth Naval Hospital Naval Regional Medical Center. Hospital Point 23708. (804) 398-5111. This is the oldest naval hospital in the country. The naval hospitals had their origin in the 1798 legislation that established a fund to pay for the relief of sick and disabled seamen and that ultimately led to the establishment of the US Marine Hospital Service for members of the merchant marine. Though every officer, seaman, and marine of the US Navy had twenty cents a month deducted from his pay, the Navy actually got little benefit from the fund. Therefore, in 1811, a separate Naval Hospital Fund was established, with $55,000 unexpended from the Marine Hospital Fund, and, over the next century, almost two dozen naval hospitals were built around the country.

The first of these, at Portsmouth, was built in 1830. The original building, a solid granite edifice with a portico composed of 10 Doric columns covering a horizontal expanse of 92 feet, still stands. Included in the structure were over 500,000 bricks from old Fort

Nelson, a Revolutionary War fortification that occupied the site before the present hospital. Although the outward appearance of the original structure (now called Building One) is said to be little changed, it has been extensively remodeled on the inside (the entire building was gutted in 1907), with several wings added on either side. Though the hospital was built to hold 500 patients, it never housed more than 40 until the 1855 yellow fever epidemic, which decimated the local population, and in which the Naval Hospital played an important role in treating the civilian population. The current hospital sits on a 112-acre site in downtown Portsmouth, beside the Elizabeth River. The main hospital (Building 215) is a 500-bed, fifteen-story tertiary care facility which dates from 1960. Building One houses a gynecology and maternity clinic and a small inpatient unit.

No tours are regularly available for civilians.

RICHMOND

Virginia Commonwealth University – Medical College of Virginia Medical Center Twelfth and Marshall Streets 23219. (804) 786-7327. This huge medical center traces its origins to 1837, when Hampden-Sydney College created its own medical department. The first classes were held in a local hotel, until the Egyptian Building was completed in 1845. The Medical Department of Hampden-Sydney became an independent institution, the Medical College of Virginia, in 1854. MCV's most famous faculty member was Charles E Brown-Séquard, the French physiologist who contributed importantly to our understanding of the spinal cord, who taught here from 1854 to 1855. The school got a huge boost just before the Civil War when a contingent of 300 Southern medical students, who were then studying in Philadelphia, seceded en masse, half of them enrolling in MCV. (The precipitating event was the exhibition of John Brown's body in the streets of Philadelphia following his famous raid, trial, and execution.) During the Civil War, MCV was the only medical college in the Confederacy to remain open and graduate a class each year. A second medical school (the University College of Medicine) was founded in Richmond in 1893, but it could not survive the Flexner Report, and was absorbed by MCV in 1913. The Old Dominion Hospital Training School for Nurses, which accepted white students only, was opened in 1895; its black counterpart, the St Philip School of Nursing of the Medical College of Virginia was opened in 1920.

MCV gained its own hospital in 1941. In 1968 MCV joined with the Richmond Professional Institute to form a new umbrella entity, the Virginia Commonwealth University. VCU's Health Sciences Division includes MCV as well as schools of dentistry, nursing, pharmacy, allied health professions, and basic sciences.

This is an attractive albeit highly urbanized campus, set amidst some of Richmond's most historic buildings, including homes, churches, museums, and medical buildings. Of the latter, be sure to see the **Egyptian Building** (1223 East Marshall Street), which has been used continually for medical education since it was built in 1845. When it first opened, the building contained medical lecture rooms, a dissection room, and an infirmary. Considered one of the finest examples of Egyptian Revival architecture in the country, this is a dramatic and colorful building, surrounded by a cast-iron fence with posts formed in the shape of mummy cases with toes. The walls of the structure are unusual in that they are thinner at the top than at the bottom, an architectural device that makes the building seem taller than it actually is. The building was completely restored and remodeled in 1939, and the building's interior boasts unusually strong colors, predominantly blue, red, and golden yellow, with hieroglyphics as a decorative feature.

West Hospital (1200 East Broad Street) was built in 1941 and is a fine example of a huge (eighteen stories, 600 beds) Art-Deco hospital. Be sure to note the brass bas-relief over the Broad Street entrance, depicting Hippocrates, Vesalius, Jenner, Pasteur, Galen, Harvey, Virchow, and Lister. The whole area is densely packed

Egyptian Building, Medical College of Virginia, Virginia Commonwealth University *(Credit: Special Collections and Archives, Tompkins-McCaw Library, Virginia Commonwealth University)*

with interesting structures, including many hospital buildings. There are no formal tours, but anyone wishing to stroll around the area can receive a descriptive pamphlet called *MCV Campus Tour* from the Medical College of Virginia Foundation [(804) 786-9734].

WILLIAMSBURG

Eastern State Hospital 4601 Ironbound Road 23187. (804) 253-5161. The Eastern State Hospital is the direct descendant of America's first public mental hospital, opened in 1773, a beautiful restoration of which is available for public inspection in Colonial Williamsburg. As originally proposed, the "Lunatick Hospital" was intended to be a humane asylum for "persons of insane and disordered minds," but its actual character is suggested by the fact that the first "keeper" (James Galt) had previously been employed as keeper of the Public Gaol in Williamsburg. Though the hospital had 24 rooms for patients, it was sparsely used for many years, admitting only 36 patients during its first 6 years. Patients were treated as best the hospital could, which for the day meant bleeding and purging, and controlling potential violence with chains and locked cells. In 1841 the Virginia General Assembly changed the name from The Public Hospital to the Eastern Lunatic Asylum, simultaneously appointing the first physician-superintendent, Dr John Minson Galt II, another in a long line of Galts who dominated the asylum for its first 90 years. The hospital had recurrent problems with fires, with the one in 1885 finally destroying the original building, causing the evacuation of 450 patients and the deaths of 2. Drunkenness of the attendants was said to be a contributing factor, as was the fact that the wiring in the newly installed electrical system had been run through the building in wooden tubes.

The asylum was renamed the Eastern State Hospital just after the turn of the century. By 1952 ESH housed 2048 patients. It was about this time that ESH was moved to Dunbar Farm, 3 miles west of Williamsburg, though construction at the site was not completed until the 1970s. The hospital now accommodates about 900 patients in 30 buildings on a 577-acre site. Tours are available via Volunteer Services.

The Public Hospital Colonial Williamsburg. Francis Street at Nassau Street 23187. (804) 253-0192. This is a recreation of the 1773 "lunatick asylum" that was America's first public asylum for the mentally ill. Based on 13 years of excavation, research and reconstruction, and costing some $5.5 million, this is the country's most authentic and fully achieved museum of psychiatric treatment.

Measuring 100-by-32 feet, this is an attractive two-story brick Georgian-style building, topped with a cupola and an iron weather vane.

Currently, one-half of one floor is devoted to recapturing psychiatric history (the rest of the building is devoted to endeavors entirely unrelated to medicine). The centerpiece of the exhibits here are a pair of recreated patient rooms, one representing an eighteenth century cell with straw mattress, chamber pot, and manacles, and the other representing a nineteenth century "apartment" whose plain but comfortable furniture signifies the growing belief that better conditions enhanced chances for recovery. A sound track adds an additional sense of realism. Nearby, there's an informative exhibit tracing trends in psychiatric treatment from the building's completion in 1773 until it was destroyed by fire in 1885, running the gamut from early confinement and restraint through "moral management" on to custodial care. Everything seems remarkably crude and even cruel by modern standards, but the displays stress that for the most part, the staff did the best they could with what they knew and what they had available. Objects on display include scarification devices for bleeding, a tranquilizer chair for restraining violent patients, the Utica Crib in which a prone patient could be locked for extended periods, and other artifacts depicting various aspects of psychiatric treatment through the years. Some of these are reconstructions and some are actually artifacts, charred by the 1885 fire and recovered by excavations on the site. Among the latter is a beer bottle, presumably left by drunk attendants. Another area nearby provides an audiovisual program with a brief overview of the hospital's history.

The Public Hospital is a part of Colonial Williamsburg, the nation's foremost combined reconstruction and restoration of Colonial America (it includes 173 acres and 140 buildings) and can be seen only by people holding appropriate passes. Costs vary but range about $17 to 25 for adults and $9 to 13 for children. There are no tickets that provide admission only to the hospital. Colonial Williamsburg is open every day of the year. The hours are basically 9 AM to 5 PM, but there is some seasonal variation, and visitors should check in advance.

Pasteur-Galt Apothecary Shop Colonial Williamsburg, Duke of Gloucester Street 23185. (804) 229-0192. This is a reconstruction of an apothecary shop once located on this site, named in memory of two physician-surgeon-pharmacists who lived and worked in Williamsburg. The first, William Pasteur, practiced here from 1757 until 1791, and the other, John Minson Galt, practiced from 1775 until 1808. The shop is identified by a sign that combines a mortar and pestle with the staff of Aesculapius. The front of the shop is devoted to the apothecary trade and includes a wide array of elixers, ointments, and herbal remedies, together with drug and leech jars and various other artifacts of the pharmaceutical trade. The back of the shop is intended to represent a physician's office of the time and includes a small collection of 18th century instruments, together with splints, a fracture box, medical texts of the time, and Dr Galt's diploma. An herb garden behind the shop is also open to the public. As with the Public Hospital, admission to the shop is available only to those who have general admission tickets to the Colonial Williamsburg complex.

WASHINGTON

SEATTLE

University of Washington Medical Center 1959 NE Pacific Street 98195. (206) 543-1060. While the old King County Hospital (now Harborview Medical Center) was a well-known regional teaching center for many years, the University of Washington's School of Medicine was founded only in 1945. The School began operation in some converted army barracks, finally opening its own hospital in 1959. The School took a major step forward in 1971 when it inaugurated the WAMI Program of Regionalized Education. The program set up the University of Washington as the primary medical training center for the states of Washington, Alaska, Montana, and Idaho, saving the latter three states the prohibitive cost of establishing medical schools. The cost of WAMI is supported by the participating states. The program provides for students taking their first year in their home states, the second in Seattle, and clinical experience at 17 sites spread out over the 4 states.

Among the major achievements here are:

1960   Invention of the Scribner shunt, an arteriovenous, permanently implanted shunt that makes long-term renal dialysis possible (Belding Scribner)

1961   World's first multidisciplinary pain clinic

1969   First mobile intensive care unit, equipped with life-support equipment (forerunner of today's paramedic vans)

1983   First identification of, and first simplified test for, chlamydia
        infection

The campus here includes the University Hospital and Harborview Hospital, and schools of medicine, dentistry, nursing, pharmacy, social work, public health, and community medicine. The
main Health Sciences Center is a monster building, more than a
third of a mile long, which encompasses almost three million square
feet. Tours are available through the Outreach Coordinator [(206)
543-3620].

Harborview Medical Center 325 Ninth Avenue 98104. (206)
223-3000. This hospital dates from 1869, when the commissioners
of King County set aside 160 acres as a poor farm. By 1877, the
county had awarded a one-year contract to a local physician to care
for the sick at the poor farm, and the administration of the farm was
turned over to a priest. The priest promptly requested assistance
from the Sisters of Providence in Vancouver, and they turned a
house at the farm into the first King County Hospital. Not content
with the facilities they had been given, the sisters in 1878 established the separate, church-sponsored Providence Hospital, with
whom the county then contracted to care for indigent patients.
Meanwhile, the county expanded facilities at the farm, and county
patients were looked after, both at the farm and at Providence
Hospital, by the Sisters.

In 1894 the county built a new King County Hospital on the poor
farm grounds, calling it Georgetown Hospital to distinguish it from
the older structure. The facilities here soon proved to be inadequate,
however, and the commissioners authorized the Wayside Mission
Emergency Hospital in 1899. By 1905 the county was once again
using the previously abandoned poor farm building for overflow
patients. In 1931 the county built a huge new hospital on the
present site. A contest in the local newspaper resulted in the name
Harborview Hospital, a testament to the facility's spectacular vista
of Elliott Bay, Seattle's harbor. Though used for teaching from the
start, Harborview became a University teaching hospital only in
1945 with the establishment of the University of Washington
School of Medicine. In 1967 the University was awarded a management contract for Harborview.

Harborview is now a 330-bed tertiary care hospital. Among its
other achievements, it has the largest burn center in the United
States and the third largest in the world. Like many other county-
owned facilities across the nation, this one faces a continuing financial crisis, and its future is uncertain. Tours are available from Community Relations.

VANCOUVER

St Joseph Community Hospital 600 NE 92nd Avenue 98666. (206) 256-2000. St Joseph's was the first hospital in the Northwest when it opened its doors in 1858. The Sisters of Providence who established the hospital (in response to a plea from a local group of Protestant, Jewish, and Catholic women) had come to what was then Fort Vancouver from Montreal, via a grueling 6000 mile boat voyage, crossing the Isthmus of Panama on foot. Mother Joseph, who was in charge of the group of five sisters, was one of the truly remarkable pioneers of this area. Before she died in 1902, she had established 11 hospitals, and an equal number of schools, orphanages, and other institutions for the aged and mentally ill. She is recognized by the American Institute of Architects as being the first architect of the Northwest United States. In addition, she constructed the buildings herself, raised funds, nursed the sick, and did whatever was necessary to provide care to those in need. Mother Joseph's statue is one of two placed by the State of Washington in the Statuary Gallery in the Capitol Building in Washington, DC (the other is of Marcus Whitman, see below).

The hospital grew along with the community. In 1861 St Joseph became the state's first mental institution, as the Territory of Washington paid $8 a week for each patient. In the early years, care of the sick was regarded primarily as an act of mercy, and medical contributions to patient care were pretty meager. Thus, hospital care was what the Sisters could provide. St Joseph continued to be operated by the Sisters of Providence until 1968 when the cost of rebuilding the aged physical plant, together with costly new federal and state standards, led the religious order to sell the hospital to a community group. In 1977 Vancouver Memorial Hospital and St Joseph Community Hospital merged to become the Southwest Washington Hospitals. Current plans are to consolidate all acute care at St Joseph after a $32 million renovation and expansion. Tours are available via Public Relations.

WALLA WALLA

Whitman Mission National Historic Site Route 2 99362. (509) 522-6360. The Whitman Mission, operated by the National Park Service, is a tribute to Washington's first settlers, Marcus and Narcissus Whitman. Marcus was a physician, trained at the Berkshire Medical College in Pittsfield, Massachusetts. After practicing medicine for four years in Canada, Whitman became a medical missionary, intent on carrying Christianity to the then-unsettled Northwest

Territories. After a grueling cross-country trip, he and his wife established an outpost here in 1836. The Cayuse Indians at first welcomed the Whitmans but became less and less enthusiastic about their presence as the Whitmans pressured them to reject their traditional beliefs and customs. That, together with the Indians' disillusionment when the Whitmans failed to deliver any supernatural power to the tribe and their unhappiness with the growing thousands of settlers entering the Territory, led to an all out breach. A measles epidemic in which half the tribe died but which most of the whites survived was the final straw. On November 29, 1847, the Cayuse attacked the mission, killing the Whitmans and more than a dozen others and taking fifty captives. The tragedy led to a war between the settlers and the Cayuse.

Still, the Whitmans were responsible for a number of important accomplishments in the development of the Northwest. Narcissus was the first white woman to cross the continent overland, and the family's successful trek inspired many others to follow the Oregon Trail to this area. Marcus led the first wagon train to the Columbia River area and was the first to argue in Congress that the Oregon Country should be annexed as a US Territory. The proposal was adopted only after word of the Whitman massacre arrived in the nation's capitol.

The Visitor Center here is open daily, except for some holidays, during normal business hours. The Mission includes descriptive displays in the Visitors Center, a monument (erected in 1897), several building sites, and a picnic area.

WEST VIRGINIA

HUNTINGTON

Marshall University School of Medicine 1542 Spring Valley Drive 25704. (304) 696-7300. MUSM accepted its charter class in 1978. The school was founded in response to the Veterans Administration Medical Assistance and Health Training Act, which provided for constructing medical schools in cities that had both a VA hospital and a functioning university. The program is community-based, using preexisting hospitals for clinical teaching, and devoted to preparing primary care practitioners for regional service. Since the school was established, the federal government has pumped $70 million into improving the VA Medical Center, transforming it from "a near-nursing home to a first-class center that's at least a secondary-care facility and in some specialties a tertiary-care facility." MUSM's new Medical Education Building is connected to the VA hospital via corridors on the first and second floors. Tours of the campus are available via the office of Medical Student Affairs.

MORGANTOWN

West Virginia University Medical Center Medical Center Drive 26506. (304) 293-3937. The history of medical education here dates back to at least 1878 when the University established a "Medical Department." Essentially a one-man operation, this program was succeeded in 1882 by a School of Anatomy, Physiology, and Hygiene. Both of these early efforts were used primarily as premedical training, which some established schools accepted as adequate preclinical training. A formal College of Medicine was finally created in 1902 that offered a two-year program leading to admission as a third-year student elsewhere. The school survived the Flexner Report of 1910, but only barely — and the next several decades were spent fighting to maintain accreditation and obtain resources. In 1962 the school ended its marginal existence as a two-year program, and inaugurated a four-year curriculum leading to the MD degree. In the 1980s, the University split off its University Hospital, creating a private institution, and the newly constructed 400-bed Ruby Memorial Hospital is the result. The entrance to the WVU Medical Center is distinguished by four fifteen-foot marble pylons, two sides of each being faced with bas-relief panels depicting important developments and personages in the health sciences, including dentistry and pharmacy.

The School of Pharmacy here has a rather nice museum, which attempts to capture the feel of a late-nineteenth century drugstore, using items preserved from nineteenth century pharmacies in the state. Displays occupy a large room and include lovely old apothecary cabinets, hundreds of old medicine bottles, and a variety of tools, herbs and concoctions, and furnishings. The museum is open weekdays during school hours.

The future of medical education in West Virginia, and at this school, is by no means secure. A 1989 Carnegie Foundation report suggested the state's two medical schools combine into a single unit. Money, of course, is tight, and consolidation would be consistent with a trend established in other states (most notably in New Jersey). The state remains critically short of physicians, with only 14 per 1000 persons, as compared to the nationwide average of 21 per 1000 population. Foreign-born physicians make up about one-third of the state's practitioners.

Tours are available from the Public Relations Office.

WISCONSIN

GREEN BAY

Fort Howard Hospital Museum   Heritage Hill State Park. 2640 South Webster Avenue 54301. (414) 497-4368. Opened in 1977, this 40-acre historical park is composed of 4 heritage theme areas: Pioneer, Military, Small Town, and Agricultural/Ethnic. The Fort Howard Hospital, the focal point of the Military Heritage Area, dates from 1834, when it was constructed on the west bank of the Fox River, about a mile above its junction with Green Bay. It continued as a hospital until 1852, when it was abandoned. The building subsequently belonged to several owners, serving a variety of functions, until it was finally restored and opened as a museum in 1929. In 1975 it was barged upriver to its present location, and it is currently organized and furnished as a c. 1836 military hospital. This is one of the few places where William Beaumont served that is not organized as a memorial to his achievements (Beaumont was post surgeon here from 1826 to 1828, prior to serving at Fort Crawford). The building itself is a white frame structure, with seven rooms downstairs and a bedroom and large attic space upstairs. Currently, the exhibits are rather sparse, one of the old wards being outfitted with some hospital beds and another small room set aside as a facsimile doctor's office, furnished with such paraphernalia as crutches, some medicine bottles, and a bleeding basin. The staff are actively working to upgrade the collection, however; so there may be more extensive displays in the near future. Heritage Hill is open on a variable schedule from May through mid-December, with numerous special events and organized tours in the summer and early fall. Call for details. There is a moderate admission charge.

MADISON

University of Wisconsin School of Pharmacy   Chamberlin Hall. 425 North Charter Street 53706. (608) 262-1416. Established in 1883 as the University of Wisconsin "Department of Pharmacy," this became the second pharmacy school in the country to be associated with a state university. In 1892 the school became the first in the country to establish a four-year program leading to a bachelor's degree in pharmacy. In time it also became the first to offer both masters degrees and PhDs for study in pharmacy specialties. It is the only institution in the United States to have a doctorate program in the history of pharmacy.

One of the school's outstanding resources is the depth and breadth of the library collections housed at several facilities on campus, the sum total of which makes the UW pharmaceutical library among the best in the world. In terms of pharmacopoeias alone, UW has some 500 (ranging from Amsterdam and Argentina to Yugoslavia and Zimbabwe), over 40 percent more than its closest competitor (the National Library of Medicine). Its archival, rare book, and journal collections are quite simply unmatched anywhere else in the country — and all are available for examination by interested parties.

The **Kremer Reference Files,** housed on the mezzanine level of the FB Power Pharmaceutical Library, is a unique collection that defies easy description. Housed in 100-odd, 6-drawer filing cabinets — plus a large number of bookshelves and boxes — the KRF contains a seemingly endless collection of pamphlets, photographs, tearsheets, correspondence, advertisements, articles, documents, and miscellaneous ephemera related to the history of phar-

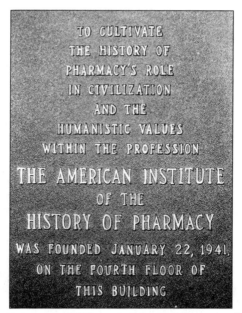

Placque at the University of Wisconsin School of Pharmacy *(Courtesy of the American Institute of the History of Pharmacy)*

macy. The catalog collection alone would keep pharmacy history buffs busy for weeks. It includes over 1000 catalogs of American schools of pharmacy (from 1885 onward) and hundreds of catalogs from pharmacy wholesalers and equipment dealers (from 1760 on). Also unique to Madison is the **American Institute for the History of Pharmacy.** Founded in 1941, the AIHP works to preserve, interpret, and make available pharmacy's heritage to anyone who is interested. The items in its collection, its journal *The History of Pharmacy,* the books and pamphlets it publishes — all capture various aspects of pharmacy's fascinating history. While the AIHP maintains no museum, there is no better place for anyone interested in the history of pharmacy to begin serious study of the subject. The AIHP encourages interested individuals to become members (current cost: $25/year), but their information services are available to everyone [call (608) 262-5378].

University of Wisconsin Medical Center 600 Highland Avenue 53792. (608) 263-6400. Since 1979 UW has operated most of its medical center functions on its 45-acre west campus, as opposed to the downtown main campus where it previously resided. The 1.5-million square foot complex accommodates a 500-bed hospital, a vast number of clinics, the School of Nursing, the clinical component of the medical school, a clinical cancer center, and numerous research labs.

Madison had a medical school briefly in the 1850s (Dr CB Chapman's Practical School of Medicine), but it wasn't until 1907 that UW actually began a medical school with a two-year basic science program. In 1924 the Wisconsin General Hospital opened on the main campus (it's still there, at 1300 University Avenue), and the following year the University of Wisconsin Medical School became a four-year institution. Basic science classes and some research continue to be located on the main campus.

Though the UW medical enterprise is comparatively young, especially in relation to many eastern schools, UWMC has nonetheless been an important contributor to medical progress. Landmark events include:

1941	Harold Rusch is the first to show which wavelengths of UV light produce cancer
1952	Charles Heidelberger discovers 5-FU (fluorouracil), one of the first generation of anticancer drugs, and still in general use
1954	Manucher Javid discovers that urea solution, injected intravenously, can lower intracranial pressure, providing an enormous boon to neurosurgery patients

1965 Harry Weisman develops a test for PKU (phenylketonuria) thus allowing early detection of the disease and prevention of brain damage

1975 Harold Temin wins Nobel Prize for demonstrating that certain viruses can cause cancer by transmitting genetic information from RNA to DNA

The six-story medical center building is composed of a seemingly endless set of interconnected diamonds. The floors are currently color-coded but the various sections are not, and you need either a map or a tour guide to find your way around. UW will happily provide the guide if you call in advance [(608) 262-6343].

MILWAUKEE

Medical College of Wisconsin 8701 Watertown Plank Road 53226. (414) 257-8296. This school is newish in name and location, but its history stretches back a hundred years. Its origins are tied to two proprietary schools, each organized on a stock basis, the Milwaukee Medical College (1894) and the Wisconsin College of Physicians and Surgeons (1893). In 1907 Marquette College, a small Jesuit liberal arts college anxious to assume university stature, took MMC under its umbrella. The affiliation had practically no meaning whatsoever, except that it allowed Marquette to call itself a university and allowed MMC to say it had a university affiliation.

This pro forma arrangement did the medical college no good when the Flexner Report came out in 1910. The report summarized both Milwaukee medical schools as follows: "The two . . . are without a redeeming feature . . . neither of the schools meets the most lenient standards in respect to laboratory outfit or teaching; and as far as the clinical facilities, they are hardly more than minimal." The end result was that, by 1913, both medical schools had died as independent entities, and Marquette University had assumed control of both medical schools, along with two dental schools and a school of pharmacy.

In the years that followed, Marquette University School of Medicine became a decent medical college, though one often troubled by finances. The university didn't subsidize the medical school at all, but instead charged the medical school for services rendered. By the late 1960s, as medical education costs escalated, the school was in big financial trouble. Because it was a Catholic medical school and the state government was forbidden (by the rule calling for separation of church and state) from subsidizing it, the medical school severed all ties with its Jesuit parent in 1967. For a while, perhaps because of nostalgia, the school retained the Marquette name. It wasn't until 1970 that a new, more regional title was adopted, and it wasn't until 1978 that the college moved to its new campus some 72 blocks west of its old building on the Marquette campus.

Today, MCW is the third largest private medical school in the nation and the kingpin of the 240-acre Milwaukee Regional Medical Center. The center is an attractive mixture of the new and the old, with some buildings dating back to before the turn of the century. Some of the oldest buildings (many now abandoned) date to when the whole site housed the county poor farm. Still, the area in suburban, southwest Milwaukee is an upbeat attractive place with lakes, fountains, and lots of green space. One notable facility on campus, among many others, is the Milwaukee County Medical Complex, composed, in part, of a huge early twentieth century structure, with wings rounded at their outermost extensions, attractive setbacks allowing sun porches, and various neoclassical design features.

The MCW had an associated College of Nursing, but its life span was brief (from the 1970s to the mid-1980s). The county, on the other hand, began its nursing school in 1883, modeled on the Bellevue Hospital system, and the school is still going strong. What began as the **Wisconsin Training School for Nurses** is now the only remaining diploma program for nurses in the state, and one of the oldest continuing schools in the country. The current name is the Milwaukee County Medical Complex School of Nursing. The Nurses' Residence (1901) is an old fashioned, high-ceilinged, multistory, stone and brick building, attractive in a turn-of-the-century sort of way, but few nursing students live there currently.

There is a fine history of medicine collection in the **Todd Wehr Library** (the most valuable item is a 1543 edition of Andreas Vesalius's *De Fabrica Corporis Humani),* which is entirely open to the public [call (414) 257-8323 to arrange a visit].

PORTAGE

Fort Winnebago Surgeons Quarters W8687 State Highway 33 East 53901. (608) 742-2949. The Surgeon's Quarters is the only remaining building of the old Fort Winnebago, which guarded the portage between the Fox and Wisconsin Rivers between 1828 and 1845. Though built earlier, the home was converted to a dwelling for the post surgeon in 1834, with the army hospital (long since demolished) nearby. The house is constructed of pine logs, plastered over on the interior, with four rooms on the main floor and a single room (plus attic spaces) up a winding stairway. The house is now furnished with period pieces, including a surgeon's operating table from the old fort hospital. There's a small but fascinating collection of medical books from the fort period, as well as surgical instruments and fort paraphernalia. The quarters are open 10 AM to 4 PM, from May 15 through October 15, and by appointment. There's a small admission charge.

PRAIRIE DU CHIEN

Fort Crawford Medical Museum & Stovall Hall of Health 717 South Beaumont Road 53821. (608) 326-6960. This town is located on the Mississippi River near the mouth of the Wisconsin River. Fort Crawford, including its post hospital, was established in the early nineteenth century, and one of the surgeons stationed here for a while was Dr William Beaumont, America's first physiologist. This medical museum and the street on which it is situated are both dedicated to Beaumont's memory. The museum is owned and operated by the State Medical Society of Wisconsin and consists of three buildings: a small administration building, a partial reconstruction of the old Fort Crawford Hospital, and the Hall of Health. Both of the latter contain numerous exhibits and each is fascinating in its own way.

The old hospital shows no evidence of having been a hospital. One room is dedicated to Beaumont and is intended to be a recreation of an 1850 physician's office. Most of the furnishings are simply period pieces, but a few items actually belonged to Beaumont, including an old family bible. There is a wonderful bas-relief, carved in wood, of Beaumont and his famed patient Alexis St Martin (who were here together from 1829 to 1831). Another room is dedicated to historic events in American medicine and contains some vividly interesting dioramas — e.g., of Dr Philip Syng Physick performing an amputation on a patient firmly restrained by some muscular attendants. There are also small displays on such infectious diseases as malaria, smallpox, and cholera. A third room traces developments in American medical practice, from early Indian medicine through doctors on horseback, horse and buggy doctors, and Model T doctors. There is also a wonderfully restored apothecary (c. 1850) and a small dentist's office (c. 1900).

Stovall Hall is pretty much an unadorned shed fixed up as an old-style museum, containing a huge number of items, with the collection seemingly determined by availability. Whatever has been bequeathed to the museum has been displayed, and there isn't much in the way of progression or cohesion to the collection. Still, there is some wonderful stuff here, including one of the largest collections of "pap" jars (used to feed infants and invalids) I've seen anywhere. There's also an informative collection of about 40 plaster sculptures that illustrate techniques used over the years for resuscitation, ranging from an American Indian method of blowing air into the rectum to the modern day Heimlich maneuver.

The museum is open seven days a week from May through October, from 10 AM to 5 PM. There is a small admission charge.

WINNEBAGO

J Farrow Museum Winnebago Mental Health Institute. Butler Avenue and Main Street 54985. (414) 235-4910. This small psychiatric museum, opened in 1973, chronicles the evolution of the Northern Hospital for the Insane (founded in 1873) through the years to its present incarnation as a 300-bed state hospital serving every Wisconsin county. WMHI occupies a secluded shoreline site, adjacent to Lake Winnebago. When the institution was in the planning stages, the architects allotted one acre per patient to provide room for exercise, sunshine, and fresh air. The museum is located in a yellow brick structure which dates back to the hospital's beginnings, for many years serving as a blacksmith shop. Displays include furniture from patient sitting rooms and the hospital superintendent's office, farming equipment, antique medical equipment, hydrotherapy tubs, restraining devices, nurses's uniforms, photographs, documents, and the like. One grisly item is a solid metal block intended for waxing floors but used by a patient in 1951 as a weapon to kill a staff member. This was the only death caused by a patient on hospital grounds. An unusual item I've seen nowhere else is a turn-of-the-century body basket, constructed of wicker and lined with metal, used for transporting deceased patients. In front of the museum is a bell that once hung in the tower of "Old Main," the old administration building, which was used to call in patients and employees working on the hospital farms. The museum is named after a nurse, Julaine Farrow, who was employed at the hospital for 36 years and was instrumental in the founding and early development of the museum. Visitors are welcome by appointment.

WYOMING

ROCK SPRINGS

Memorial Hospital of Sweetwater County 1200 College Drive 82901. (307) 362-3711. When Wyoming was granted statehood in 1890, its constitution specifically set aside land and funds for the construction and operation of a Miners' Hospital. In 1892 the people of

Wyoming voted to establish the Miners' Hospital here in Rock Springs, making this the oldest civilian hospital in the state. The hospital was officially opened in 1894 as the Wyoming General Hospital. In 1948 ownership was transferred to Sweetwater County. The present modern building dates from 1978, though it has been expanded and renovated twice since then. An important component of the present facility is the Miners' Respiratory Clinic (established under the Federal Mine Health and Safety Act of 1969), catering especially to respiratory problems and other occupational hazards of the local mining industry. When the hospital opened in 1894, bituminous coal was the principal mining resource; today, mining for soda-ash or trona (a major component in glass) is the principal activity. However, coal miners remain the major focus of the Miners' Clinic, and black lung (coal miners' pneumoconiosis) remains the principal cause of major morbidity. Tours of the hospital are available from administration.

SHERIDAN

Veterans Administration Medical Center Fort Hill Road 82801. (307) 672-3473. Originally called Fort MacKenzie, this institution was established in 1898 as a military base to protect settlers from Rocky Mountain and High Plains Indians, including Crow, Shoshone, Cheyenne, Arapaho, and Sioux. However, the Indian wars in the area were essentially over by the time the fort was established, and the closest Fort MacKenzie ever came to combat was in 1902, when two troops of the all-black (except for white officers) "Buffalo Soldiers" of the 25th Regiment were transferred here after service in the Philippines. The post was officially abandoned in 1918 and was transferred from the War Department to the Public Health Service in 1921. In 1922 it was transferred to the Veterans Bureau, becoming the Fort MacKenzie Veterans Hospital. In the post-World War II years, this was one of the largest neuropsychiatric hospitals in the Veterans Administration.

Though at one time the facility occupied over 6000 acres, the campus now includes about 300 acres. Of the 70-some buildings here, approximately two-thirds date from the first decade of the century. Constructed of red brick in a neo-classical style, these are typical of turn-of-the-century military posts. Although the current general hospital serves primarily veterans of Wyoming, Montana, and Idaho, ironically two buildings here are devoted to the Intertribal Alcohol Treatment Center, serving Indians of the tribes the original Fort MacKenzie was built to combat. Tours are available through Volunteer Services.

BIBLIOGRAPHY

WRITING ABOUT HISTORY MUST of necessity be an exercise in plagiarism: all knowledge must be drawn from the accounts of others. It has been my pleasant task to read hundreds of books and articles, thousands of public relations brochures and pamphlets, and countless communications from knowledgeable people throughout the country. Ordinarily, in an extensively researched work such as this, I would list all source material in the bibliography. However, the realist in me recognizes that a complete bibliography would either rob this book of 50 pages of medical landmark listings or result in a significantly longer and more expensive volume. As a compromise, I have listed representative references to indicate the kinds of source material I have consulted and to guide the reader who seeks more in-depth information.

As far as I have been able to determine, only three cities have had guides to their medical landmarks published. The Marion book deserves special recognition, both because it gave me the idea for *Medical Landmarks USA* and because of its exemplary quality. The Burleson and Burleson book is not, strictly speaking, a guide to Houston's medical institutions but rather only to those connected with the mammoth Texas Medical Center:

Burleson, Clyde W, and Suzy Williams Burleson: *A Guide to the Texas Medical Center*. University of Texas Press, Austin, 1987.

Marion, John Francis: *Philadelphia Medica*. SmithKline, Philadelphia, 1975.

Aesculapian Boston. Published by the Paul Dudley White Medical History Society, Boston, 1980.

Only one previous guide exists that is national in scope and that focuses on sites of health-related interest. This excellent volume concerns history of pharmacy collections and is regularly updated by the American Institute of the History of Pharmacy:

Griffenhagen, George and Ernst W Stieb: *Pharmacy Museums and Historical Collections in the United States and Canada*. American Institute of the History of Pharmacy, Madison, Wisconsin, 1988.

There are hundreds of histories of the various American health professions. They vary enormously in quality, emphasis, and detail. The following are representative, but the Flexner volume, of course, represents a medical landmark in itself, and the Ring book deserves special mention for its luxurious presentation and general appeal:

Flexner, Abraham: *Medical Education in the United States and Canada — A Report to the Carnegie Foundation for the Advancement of Teaching*. The Carnegie Foundation, New York, 1910.

Holloway, Lisabeth M: *A Fast Pace Forward — Chronicles of American Podiatry*. Pennsylvania College of Podiatric Medicine, Philadelphia, 1987.

534

Kremers, Edward, and George Urdang: *History of Pharmacy—A Guide and a Survey (2d ed)*. JB Lippincott Company, Philadelphia, 1940.

Norwood, William Frederick: *Medical Education in the United States before the Civil War*. University of Pennsylvania Press, Philadelphia, 1944.

Ring, Malvin E: *Dentistry—An Illustrated History*. Harry N Abrams, Inc, Publishers, New York City, 1985.

Starr, Paul: *The Social Transformation of American Medicine*. Basic Books, Inc, New York, 1982.

The major historical overviews often fail to do justice to the contributions of various minorities, and, to remedy this defect, studies like the following have been invaluable:

Kagan, Solomon R: *Jewish Contributions to Medicine in America from Colonial Times to the Present*. Boston Medical Publishing Company, Boston, 1939.

Morais, Herbert M: *The History of the Negro in Medicine*. Publishers Company, Inc, New York, 1967.

Morantz-Sanchez, Regina Karkell: *Sympathy and Science—Women Physicians in American Medicine*, Oxford University Press, New York, 1985.

Almost every state and region of the country has one or more histories written about the development of health professions within its borders. Of these, I particularly enjoyed the volumes written by Shikes, Quebbeman, and Fortuine.

Fortuine, Robert: *Chills and Fever—Health and Disease in the Early History of Alaska*. University of Alaska Press, Fairbanks, 1989.

Noall, Claire: *Guardians of the Hearth—Utah's Pioneer Midwives and Women Doctors*. Horizon Publishers, Utah, 1974.

Quebbeman, Frances E: *Medicine in Territorial Arizona*. Arizona Historical Foundation, Phoenix, 1966.

Shikes, Robert H: *Rocky Mountain Medicine—Doctors, Drugs, and Disease in Early Colorado*. Johnson Books, Boulder, 1986.

Spidle, Jake W, Jr: *Doctors of Medicine in New Mexico—A History of Health and Medical Practice, 1886–1986*. University of New Mexico Press, Albuquerque, 1986.

Institutional biographies of hospitals and colleges seem to be available for every institution that has passed the half-century mark and often for far younger institutions as well. Most of these are uncritical, congratulatory, self-serving enterprises, but some are fascinating for what they reveal about the individual institution and the evolution of world and community events and trends. Some of the better efforts in this category are the following:

Duffy, John: *The Tulane University Medical Center—One Hundred and Fifty Years of Medical Education*. Louisiana State University Press, Baton Rouge, 1984.

Gordon, Sarah (editor): *All Our Lives—A Centennial History of Michael Reese Hospital and Medical Center, 1881–1981*. Michael Reese Hospital and Medical Center, 1981.

Grob, Gerald N: *The State and the Mentally Ill—A History of Worcester State Hospital in Massachusetts, 1830–1920*. University of North Carolina Press, Chapel Hill, 1966.

Levenson, Dorothy: *Montefiore—The Hospital as Social Instrument, 1884–1984.* Farrar, Straus & Giroux, New York, 1984.

My most fascinating sources generally have concerned special topics, treated in depth by authors who have immersed themselves in their subjects, often discovering scandal and epic conflict in the process. Examples include:

Caldwell, Mark: *The Last Crusade—The War on Consumption, 1862–1954.* Atheneum, New York, 1988.

Dowling, Harry F: *City Hospitals—The Undercare of the Underprivileged.* Harvard University Press, Cambridge, Massachusetts, 1982.

Jones, James H: *Bad Blood—The Tuskegee Syphilis Experiment.* The Free Press, New York, 1981.

Patterson, James T: *The Dread Disease—Cancer and Modern American Culture.* Harvard University Press, Cambridge, Massachusetts, 1987.

Rosenberg, Charles E: *The Care of Strangers—The Rise of America's Hospital System.* Basic Books, 1987.

Rothstein, William G: *American Physicians in the Nineteenth Century—From Sects to Science.* The Johns Hopkins University Press, Baltimore, 1972.

History is ultimately about people, and I have often turned to individual biographies. These covered an extraordinary range, but the effort in searching them out was almost always rewarded with wonderful glimpses of exceptional individuals. Some of these are:

Barlow, Jeffrey and Christine Richardson: *China Doctor of John Day.* Thomas Binford, Publisher, Portland, Oregon, 1969.

Burton, Jean: *Lydia Pinkham Is Her Name.* Farrar, Straus, New York, 1949.

Federspiel, JF (translated by Joel Agee): *The Ballad of Typhoid Mary.* EP Dutton, NY, 1983.

Fleming, Donald: *William H. Welch and the Rise of Modern Medicine.* Little, Brown and Company, Boston, 1954.

Finally, in some locations, I have relied heavily on excellent guides, intended to acquaint the reader with tourist attractions and works of art, architecture, and the like. Among these, the WPA guides of the 1930s stand out for their comprehensiveness and insight, and the quality of their writing. Examples in this category include the following:

The Architect of the Capitol: *Art in the United States Capitol,* United States Government Printing Office, Washington, 1978.

Federal Writers' Project: *The WPA Guide to Washington, DC.* Pantheon Books, New York, 1937.

Federal Writers' Project: *New York City Guide.* Random House, New York, 1939.

Goldstone, Harmon H and Martha Dalrymple: *History Preserved—A Guide to New York City Landmarks and Historic Districts.* Simon and Schuster, New York, 1974.

Hinkel, John Vincent: *Arlington—Monument to Heroes.* Prentice-Hall, NJ, 1965.

To all of these—and to the hundreds of others that I have failed to acknowledge—I owe an enormous debt.

INDEX

INDEX

548

NOTES

NOTES

NOTES

NOTES

NOTES

NOTES

NOTES

NOTES